CONTEMPORARY'S

GED

TEST 1: WRITING SKILLS

PREPARATION FOR THE HIGH SCHOOL EQUIVALENCY EXAMINATION

Reviewers
Mary Kay Gray, GED Coordinator
Mott Adult High School
Flint, Michigan

Mary C. Kruczynski, GED Instructor
Pensacola Junior College
Pensacola, Florida

CONTEMPORARY
BOOKS

CHICAGO

Library of Congress Cataloging-in-Publication Data

GED test 1: writing skills.
     p. cm.
  ISBN 0-8092-3782-2
    1. English language—Composition and exercises—Examinations,
questions, etc.   2. General educational development tests—Study
guides. I. Title.
LB1631.G18   1994
808.042'076—dc20   93-35614
                                     CIP

Project Editor
Michael O'Neill

Contributing Writers
Susan Breemer Wickham
Judith Gallagher

Published by Jamestown Publishers,
Two Prudential Plaza, Chicago, Illinois 60601-6790
Manufactured in the United States of America
International Standard Book Number: 0-89061-3782-2
10 9 8

Editorial Director
Mark Boone

Editorial
Gerilee Hundt
Sharon Rundo
Lisa Black
Lisa Dillman

Editorial Assistant
Maggie McCann

Editorial Production Manager
Norma Underwood

Production Editor
Jean Farley Brown

Interior Design
Lucy Lesiak

Cover Design
Georgene Sainati

Photography
C. C. Cain

Art & Production
Jan Geist

Typography
Terrence Alan Stone

Cover Illustration
Mark Jasin

Contents

To the Student

If you're studying to pass the GED Tests, you're in good company. In 1992, the most recent year for which figures are available, over 790,000 people took the tests. Of this number, nearly 480,000 actually received their certificates. Why do so many people choose to take the GED Tests? Some do so to get a job or to get a better one than they already have. Others take the tests so that they can go on to college or vocational school. Still others pursue their GED diplomas to feel better about themselves or to set good examples for their children.

Americans and Canadians alike, from all walks of life, have passed their GED Tests and obtained diplomas. Some well-known graduates include country music singers Waylon Jennings and John Michael Montgomery, comedian Bill Cosby, Olympic gold medalist Mary Lou Retton, former New Jersey Governor James J. Florio, Wendy's Old-Fashioned Hamburgers founder Dave Thomas, Delaware State Senator Ruth Ann Minner, U.S. Senator Ben Nighthorse Campbell of Colorado, motion picture actor Kelly McGillis, Famous Amos Chocolate Chip Cookies creator Wally Amos, *Parade* magazine editor Walter Anderson, NBA referee Tommy Nuñez, and Triple Crown winner jockey Ron Turcotte.

This book has been designed to help you, too, succeed on the test. It will provide you with instruction in the skills you need to pass, background information on key social studies concepts, and plenty of practice with the kinds of test items you will find on the real test.

WHAT DOES GED STAND FOR?

GED stands for the Tests of General Educational Development. The GED Test is a national examination developed by the GED Testing Service of the American Council on Education. The credential received for passing the test is widely recognized by colleges, training schools, and employers as equivalent to a high school diploma.

While the GED Test measures skills and knowledge normally acquired in four years of high school, much that you have learned informally or through other types of training can help you pass the test.

The GED Test is available in English, French, and Spanish and on audiocassette, in Braille, and in large print.

WHAT SHOULD I KNOW TO PASS THE TEST?

The test consists of five examinations in the areas of writing skills, social studies, science, literature and the arts, and mathematics. The chart on the following page outlines the main content areas, the breakdown of questions, and the time allowed per test.

THE GED TESTS			
Test	*Minutes*	*Questions*	*Percentage*
1: Writing Skills Part 1: Conventions of English Part 2: The Essay	75 45	55 1 topic	Sentence Structure 35% Usage 35% Mechanics 30%
2: Social Studies	85	64	History 25% Economics 20% Political Science 20% Geography 15%* Behavioral Sciences 20%*
3: Science	95	66	Life Sciences 50% Physical Sciences 50%
4: Literature and the Arts	65	45	Popular Literature 50% Classical Literature 25% Commentary 25%
5: Mathematics	90	56	Arithmetic 50% Algebra 30% Geometry 20%

*In Canada, 20% of the test is based on Geography and 15% on Behavioral Sciences.

On all five tests, you are expected to demonstrate the ability to think about many issues. You also are tested on knowledge and skills you have acquired from life experiences, television, radio, books and newspapers, consumer products, and advertising. In addition to the above information, keep these facts in mind:

1. Three of the five tests—Literature and the Arts, Science, and Social Studies—require that you answer questions based on reading passages or interpreting cartoons, diagrams, maps, charts, and graphs in these content areas. Developing strong reading and thinking skills is the key to succeeding on these tests.

2. The Writing Skills Test requires you to be able to detect and correct errors in sentence structure, grammar, punctuation, and spelling. You also will have to write a composition of approximately 200 words on a topic familiar to most adults.

3. The Mathematics Test consists mainly of word problems to be solved. Therefore, you must be able to combine your ability to perform computations with problem-solving skills.

WHO MAY TAKE THE TESTS?

In the United States, Canada, and many territories, people who have not graduated from high school and who meet specific eligibility requirements (age, residency, etc.) may take the tests. Since eligibility requirements vary, it would be useful to contact your local GED testing center or the director of adult education in your state, province, or territory for specific information.

WHAT IS A PASSING SCORE ON THE GED TEST?

Again, this varies from area to area. To find out what you need to pass the test, contact your local GED testing center. However, you must keep two scores in mind. One score represents the minimum score you must get on each test. For example, if your state requires minimum scores of 40, you must get at least 40 points on every test. Additionally, you must meet the requirements of a minimum average score on all five tests. For example, if your state requires a minimum average score of 45, you must get a total of 225 points to pass. The two scores together, the minimum score and the minimum average score, determine whether you pass or fail the GED Test.

To understand this better, look at the scores of three people who took the test in a state that requires a minimum score of 40 and a minimum average score of 45 (225 total). Ann and Willie did not pass, but Ramon did. See if you can tell why.

	Ann	*Willie*	*Ramon*
Test 1	44	42	43
Test 2	43	43	48
Test 3	38	42	47
Test 4	50	40	52
Test 5	50	40	49
	225	207	239

Ann made the total of 225 points but fell below the minimum score on Test 3. Willie passed each test but failed to get the 225 points needed; just passing the individual tests was not enough. Ramon passed all the tests and exceeded the minimum score. Generally, to receive a GED credential, you must correctly answer half or a little more than half of the questions on each test.

MAY I RETAKE THE TEST?

You are allowed to retake some or all of the tests. Again, the regulations governing the number of times that you may retake the tests and the time you must wait before retaking them are set by your state, province, or territory. Some states require you to take a review class or to study on your own for a certain amount of time before taking the test again.

HOW CAN I BEST PREPARE FOR THE TEST?

Many libraries, community colleges, adult education centers, churches, and other institutions offer GED preparation classes. Some television stations broadcast classes to prepare people for the test. If you cannot find a GED preparation class locally, contact the director of adult education in your state, province, or territory or call the GED Hotline (800-62-MY-GED). This hotline will give you telephone numbers and addresses of adult education and testing centers in your area. The hotline is staffed 24 hours a day, seven days a week.

WHAT'S ON THE WRITING SKILLS TEST?

The GED Writing Skills Test consists of two parts: a multiple-choice test and an essay. In Part 1, there are passages followed by questions about the sentences in these passages. Some questions ask you to locate errors, while other questions ask you to restate an idea in different words. These questions check your knowledge of sentence structure, standard usage, punctuation, capitalization, and spelling. Chapter 8 of this book provides you with many more specifics about the types of questions asked and the skills tested.

Part 1 of the GED Writing Skills Test can be broken down into the following content areas:

Sentence Structure	35%
Usage	35%
Mechanics (spelling, punctuation, and capitalization)	30%

All three of the areas listed above will contain questions of the following types:

Sentence Correction	50%
Sentence Revision	35%
Construction Shift	15%

Chapter 8 of this book discusses these three types of questions and how you can best approach each kind.

In Part 2 of the GED Writing Skills Test, you will be given 45 minutes to write an essay on a topic provided for you. You will not be given a choice of topics, but you will not need any special information or knowledge to write the essay. Instead, the topic will draw on your general knowledge and ask you to explain something about a common issue or problem. In this part of the GED Writing Skills Test, an understanding of grammar and usage will not be enough to succeed. To be successful on Part 2, you should be able to plan and organize your thinking on a given issue, and you should be able to communicate these thoughts clearly on paper.

Chapters 1–5 of this book are divided into two parts corresponding to the two parts of the GED Writing Skills Test. The first part concentrates on the writing process, as you learn step by step to brainstorm your ideas, plan your essay, write paragraphs, and organize your writing. The second part focuses on sentence structure and grammar and teaches you how to avoid the pitfalls of incorrect writing.

Chapter 6 concentrates on revising and editing your writing, and Chapter 7 gives you a handy guide to capitalization and spelling, with special rules to help you remember the words that people find the most difficult.

Finally, Chapter 8 provides test-taking strategies that will help you maximize your performance on the GED Writing Skills Test.

For additional help with the GED Writing Skills Test, you may wish to consult *The GED Essay: Writing Skills to Pass the Test*, by Ellen C. Frechette. This book concentrates on the essay portion of the test and will help you learn to prewrite, draft, and revise an effective GED essay.

TEST-TAKING TIPS FOR SUCCESS

1. **Prepare physically.** Get plenty of rest and eat a well-balanced meal before the test so that you will have energy and will be able to think clearly. Last-minute cramming will probably not help as much as a relaxed and rested mind.

2. **Arrive early.** Be at the testing center at least 15 to 20 minutes before the starting time. Make sure you have time to find the room and to get situated. Keep in mind that many testing centers refuse to admit latecomers.

3. **Think positively.** Tell yourself you will do well. If you have studied and prepared for the test, you should succeed.

4. **Relax during the test.** Take half a minute several times during the test to stretch and breathe deeply, especially if you are feeling anxious or confused.

5. **Read the test directions carefully.** Be sure you understand how to answer the questions. If you have any questions about the test or about filling in the answer form, ask before the test begins.

6. **Know the time limit for each test.** The Writing Skills Test has a time limit of 120 minutes for both parts: 75 minutes for Part 1, 45 minutes for Part 2.

   Some testing centers allow extra time, while others do not. You may be able to find out the policy of your testing center before you take the test, but always work according to the official time limit. If you have extra time, go back and check your answers.

7. **Have a strategy for answering questions.** You should read through the reading passages or look over the materials once and then answer the questions that follow. Read each question two or three times to make sure you understand it. It is best to refer back to the passage or sentence in order to confirm your answer choice. Don't try to depend on your memory of what you have just read or seen. Some people like to guide their reading by skimming the questions before reading a passage. Use the method that works best for you.

8. **Don't spend a lot of time on difficult questions.** If you're not sure of an answer, go on to the next question. Answer easier questions first and then go back to the harder questions. However, when you skip a question, be sure that you have skipped the same number on your answer sheet. Although skipping difficult questions is a good strategy for making the most of your time, it is very easy to get confused and throw off your whole answer key.

   Lightly mark the margin of your answer sheet next to the numbers of the questions you did not answer so that you know what to go back to. To prevent confusion when your test is graded, be sure to erase these marks completely after you answer the questions.

9. **Answer every question on the test.** If you're not sure of an answer, take an educated guess. When you leave a question unanswered, you will always lose points, but you can possibly gain points if you make a correct guess.

   If you must guess, try to eliminate one or more answers that you are sure are not correct. Then choose from the remaining answers. Remember, you greatly increase your chances if you can eliminate one or two answers before guessing. Of course, guessing should be used only when all else has failed.

10. **Clearly fill in the circle for each answer choice.** If you erase something, erase it completely. Be sure that you give only one answer per question; otherwise, no answer will count.

11. **Practice test taking.** Use the exercises, reviews, and especially the Post-Test and Practice Test in this book to better understand your test-taking habits and weaknesses. Use them to practice different strategies such as skimming questions first or skipping hard questions until the end. Knowing your own personal test-taking style is important to your success on the GED Test.

HOW TO USE THIS BOOK

If you are a student about to prepare for the GED Tests, you are to be admired. You have decided to resume an education that had been cut short. It is never easy to get back on track after you have been derailed, but, while it may not be easy, it will not be impossible. It will require determination and a lot of hard work.

This book will guide you through the types of questions you can expect to find on the Writing Skills Test. To answer some questions successfully, you will need to focus on sentence structure, grammar, and spelling. For others, you will need to concentrate on the effective organization of sentences within a paragraph. Finally, you will need to develop your ability to organize your thoughts from paragraph to paragraph. This skill is important for success on the essay portion of the test.

Before beginning this book, you should take the Pre-Test. This will give you a preview of what the Writing Skills Test includes, but, more important, it will help you identify which skill areas you need to concentrate on most. Use the chart at the end of the Pre-Test to pinpoint the types of questions you have answered incorrectly and to determine which skills you need special work in. You may decide to concentrate on specific areas or to work through the entire book. We strongly suggest that you *do* work through the whole book to best prepare yourself for the actual test.

In this book, each chapter is divided into two sections: a "Writing Process" section and a "Conventions of English" section.

Each "Writing Process" section is indicated by the symbol .

Each "Conventions of English" section is indicated by the symbol 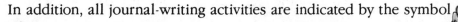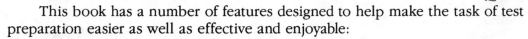 .

In addition, all journal-writing activities are indicated by the symbol .

This book has a number of features designed to help make the task of test preparation easier as well as effective and enjoyable:

- Five chapters focus specifically on developing the basic writing skills— brainstorming, prewriting, drafting, paragraph writing, and organizing an essay—and provide you with plenty of practice in applying these skills as well as work on the basics of sentence structure and clear writing.

- Essential grammar and usage rules are concise hints for reinforcing good writing habits.

- A master spelling list highlights words likely to be on the test.

- GED-type essay topics

- Journal-writing activities

- A variety of exercise types maintain interest—fill-in-the-blank, multiple-choice, and short essay questions.

- Writing activities based on thought-provoking issues provide an opportunity to practice critical thinking and writing skills for the essay portion of the GED Writing Skills Test.

- An answer key for each section explains the correct answers for the exercises; if you make a mistake, you can learn from it by reading the explanation that follows the answer and then reviewing the question to analyze the error.

After you have worked through the book and covered the entire writing process, you should take the Post-Test. The Post-Test is a simulated GED Test that presents questions in the format, at the level of difficulty, and in the percentages found on the actual test. The Post-Test will help you determine whether you are ready for the GED Writing Skills Test and, if not, what areas of the book you need to review. The Post-Test evaluation chart at the end will be especially helpful for making this decision.

We realize that practice makes perfect. Therefore, we've added a Practice Test as a final indicator of your readiness for the real GED Test. This test is just like the Post-Test in terms of its format, level of difficulty, and percentages found on the real test. After you have completed the Practice Test, you will be able to finally determine whether you are ready to take the GED Test and, if not, what areas you need to review. As with the Post-Test, an evaluation chart is included to help you judge your performance.

Contemporary Books publishes a wide range of materials to help you prepare for the tests. These books are designed for home study or classroom use. Our GED preparation books are available through schools and bookstores and directly from the publisher. For the visually impaired, a large-print version is available. For further information, call Library Reproduction Service (LRS) at (800) 255-5002.

Finally, we'd like to hear from you. If our materials have helped you to pass the test or if you feel that we can do a better job preparing you, write to us at the address on the back of the book to let us know. We hope you enjoy studying for the GED Test with our materials and wish you the greatest success.

The Editors

Writing Skills Pre-Test, Part 1

Directions: The following items are based on a paragraph that contains numbered sentences. Some of the sentences may contain errors in sentence structure, usage, or mechanics. A few sentences, however, may be correct as written. Read the paragraph and then answer the questions based on it. For each item, choose the answer that would result in the most effective writing of the sentence or sentences. The best answer must be consistent with the meaning and tone of the rest of the paragraph.

PRE-TEST ANSWER GRID

1 ① ② ③ ④ ⑤	15 ① ② ③ ④ ⑤	29 ① ② ③ ④ ⑤	43 ① ② ③ ④ ⑤
2 ① ② ③ ④ ⑤	16 ① ② ③ ④ ⑤	30 ① ② ③ ④ ⑤	44 ① ② ③ ④ ⑤
3 ① ② ③ ④ ⑤	17 ① ② ③ ④ ⑤	31 ① ② ③ ④ ⑤	45 ① ② ③ ④ ⑤
4 ① ② ③ ④ ⑤	18 ① ② ③ ④ ⑤	32 ① ② ③ ④ ⑤	46 ① ② ③ ④ ⑤
5 ① ② ③ ④ ⑤	19 ① ② ③ ④ ⑤	33 ① ② ③ ④ ⑤	47 ① ② ③ ④ ⑤
6 ① ② ③ ④ ⑤	20 ① ② ③ ④ ⑤	34 ① ② ③ ④ ⑤	48 ① ② ③ ④ ⑤
7 ① ② ③ ④ ⑤	21 ① ② ③ ④ ⑤	35 ① ② ③ ④ ⑤	49 ① ② ③ ④ ⑤
8 ① ② ③ ④ ⑤	22 ① ② ③ ④ ⑤	36 ① ② ③ ④ ⑤	50 ① ② ③ ④ ⑤
9 ① ② ③ ④ ⑤	23 ① ② ③ ④ ⑤	37 ① ② ③ ④ ⑤	51 ① ② ③ ④ ⑤
10 ① ② ③ ④ ⑤	24 ① ② ③ ④ ⑤	38 ① ② ③ ④ ⑤	52 ① ② ③ ④ ⑤
11 ① ② ③ ④ ⑤	25 ① ② ③ ④ ⑤	39 ① ② ③ ④ ⑤	53 ① ② ③ ④ ⑤
12 ① ② ③ ④ ⑤	26 ① ② ③ ④ ⑤	40 ① ② ③ ④ ⑤	54 ① ② ③ ④ ⑤
13 ① ② ③ ④ ⑤	27 ① ② ③ ④ ⑤	41 ① ② ③ ④ ⑤	55 ① ② ③ ④ ⑤
14 ① ② ③ ④ ⑤	28 ① ② ③ ④ ⑤	42 ① ② ③ ④ ⑤	

Questions 1–8 refer to the following paragraph.

(1) With new cars averaging over ten thousand dollars, buying a used car is one way to reduce transportation costs considerably. (2) However, a wise consumer shops carefully to make the best possible use of their money. (3) Before setting foot on a car lot, the type of car she wants is decided. (4) A subcompact won't accommodate a family of six. (5) A station wagon isn't necessary for a single adult. (6) With a general size and price range in mind, she searched newspaper advertisements and dealerships for likely prospects. (7) Body integrity is important. (8) She checks it by looking for signs of rust, dents, or uneven paint that might indicate a previous accident. (9) The cars interior is also important, for torn seatcovers and missing knobs indicate that it hasn't been well maintained. (10) Of course, the consumer wouldn't dream of buying a car without test-driving it to check the engine, electrical system, and how well the brakes work. (11) Finally, she takes the car to an independent mechanic for further inspection and advice before making the dealer an offer.

1. Sentence 1: **With new cars averaging over ten thousand dollars, buying a used car is one way to reduce transportation costs considerably.**

   What correction should be made to this sentence?

   (1) replace *dollars* with *dollar's*
   (2) replace *dollars, buying* with *dollars. Buying*
   (3) remove *is*
   (4) change the spelling of *considerably* to *considerabley*
   (5) no correction is necessary

2. Sentence 2: **However, a wise consumer shops carefully to make the best possible use of their money.**

   What correction should be made to this sentence?

   (1) remove the comma after *However*
   (2) change *shops* to *shop*
   (3) change the spelling of *carefully* to *carefuly*
   (4) replace *their* with *her*
   (5) no correction is necessary

3. Sentence 3: **Before setting foot on a car lot, the type of car she wants is decided.**

   Which of the following is the best way to write the underlined portion of this sentence? If you think the original is the best way, choose option (1).

   (1) the type of car she wants is decided.
   (2) deciding on the type of car she wants.
   (3) to decide on the type of car she wants.
   (4) she decides on the type of car she wants.
   (5) for her to decide on the type of car she wants.

4. Sentences 4 and 5: **A subcompact won't accommodate a family of six. A station wagon isn't necessary for a single adult.**

   The most effective combination of Sentences 4 and 5 would contain which of the following groups of words?

   (1) six, nor is a station wagon
   (2) six, nor a station wagon isn't
   (3) six although a station wagon isn't
   (4) six; despite the fact that a station wagon
   (5) six unless a station wagon

5. Sentence 6: **With a general size and price range in mind, she searched newspaper advertisements and dealerships for likely prospects.**

What correction should be made to this sentence?

(1) insert a comma after *size*
(2) change *searched* to *searches*
(3) change the spelling of *advertisements* to *advertizements*
(4) insert a comma after *dealerships*
(5) change the spelling of *prospects* to *perspects*

6. Sentences 7 and 8: **Body integrity is important. She checks it by looking for signs of rust, dents, or uneven paint that might indicate a previous accident.**

The most effective combination of Sentences 7 and 8 would include which of the following groups of words?

(1) She checks body integrity, and looking
(2) Body integrity is checked because she looks
(3) important, yet she looks
(4) important; therefore, she looks
(5) important when she looks

7. Sentence 9: **The cars interior is also important, for torn seatcovers and missing knobs indicate that it hasn't been well maintained.**

What correction should be made to this sentence?

(1) replace *cars* with *car's*
(2) remove the comma after *important*
(3) remove *for*
(4) change *indicate* to *indicates*
(5) no correction is necessary

8. Sentence 10: **Of course, the consumer wouldn't dream of buying a car without test-driving it to check the engine, electrical system, and** <u>how well the brakes work.</u>

Which of the following is the best way to write the underlined portion of this sentence? If you think the original is the best way, choose option (1).

(1) how well the brakes work.
(2) how well does it brake.
(3) if the brakes work well.
(4) test the brakes.
(5) brakes.

Questions 9–18 refer to the following paragraph.

(1) Although people may try to divide our planet into separate states and nations, nature ignores these artificial boundaries. (2) Neither water nor wind respect manmade lines, as our problems with pollution have shown. (3) Industrial wastes and sewage dumped into a river in one city contaminate the water supply of the town downstream whether or not it's citizens pledge allegiance to the same flag. (4) Oil spills occurring in the middle of the ocean, may eventually wash ashore halfway around the world. (5) Winds carrying contaminants even faster and farther than water. (6) For instance, fumes from industrial plants in the Ohio River Valley produce acid rain that damages forests and lakes in Canada. (7) Perhaps the most dramatic example of international air pollution occurred in 1986, when an accident in a nuclear plant in Ukraine releases a cloud of radioactive particles that circled the earth within a few days. (8) Hundreds of miles from the site of the plant, dairy cattle were kept inside for several days to prevent contamination of their milk, and some crops were destroyed. (9) For weeks after the accident, such imported products as vegetables grown in Italy and fish caught in scandinavian waters had to be tested for radioactivity. (10) This emphasized the need for global cooperation to maintain a livable environment.

9. Sentence 1: **Although people may try to divide our planet into separate states and nations, nature ignores these artificial boundaries.**

If you rewrote Sentence 1 beginning with

People may try to divide our planet into separate states and nations

the next word should be

(1) and
(2) so
(3) moreover
(4) therefore
(5) however

10. Sentence 2: **Neither water nor wind respect manmade lines, as our problems with pollution have shown.**

What correction should be made to this sentence?

(1) change the spelling of *Neither* to *Niether*
(2) insert a comma after *water*
(3) change *respect* to *respects*
(4) change *have* to *has*
(5) no correction is necessary

11. Sentence 3: **Industrial wastes and sewage dumped into a river in one city contaminate the water supply of the town downstream whether or not it's citizens pledge allegiance to the same flag.**

What correction should be made to this sentence?

(1) replace *river* with *River*
(2) change *contaminate* to *contaminates*
(3) replace *downstream whether* with *downstream. Whether*
(4) replace *it's* with *its*
(5) change the spelling of *citizens* to *citazens*

12. Sentence 4: **Oil spills occurring in the middle of the ocean, may eventually wash ashore halfway around the world.**

What correction should be made to this sentence?

(1) change the spelling of *occurring* to *occuring*
(2) replace *ocean* with *Ocean*
(3) remove the comma after *ocean*
(4) insert a comma after *ashore*
(5) no correction is necessary

13. Sentence 5: **Winds <u>carrying</u> contaminants even faster and farther than water.**

Which of the following is the best way to write the underlined portion of this sentence? If you think the original is the best way, choose option (1).

(1) carrying
(2) carry
(3) carried
(4) had carried
(5) that are carrying

14. Sentence 6: **For instance, fumes from industrial plants in the Ohio River Valley produce acid rain that damages forests and lakes in Canada.**

What correction should be made to this sentence?

(1) remove the comma after *instance*
(2) replace *River* with *river*
(3) change the spelling of *Valley* to *Vally*
(4) change *produce* to *produces*
(5) no correction is necessary

15. Sentence 7: **Perhaps the most dramatic example of international air pollution occurred in 1986, when an accident in a nuclear plant in Ukraine <u>releases</u> a cloud of radioactive particles that circled the earth within a few days.**

Which of the following is the best way to write the underlined portion of this sentence? If you think the original is the best way, choose option (1).

(1) releases
(2) has released
(3) is released
(4) was released
(5) released

16. Sentence 8: **Hundreds of miles from the site of the plant, dairy cattle were kept inside for several days to prevent contamination of their <u>milk, and some</u> crops were destroyed.**

Which of the following is the best way to write the underlined portion of this sentence? If you think the original is the best way, choose option (1).

(1) milk, and some
(2) milk, also some
(3) milk, in addition, some
(4) milk, some
(5) milk some

17. Sentence 9: **For weeks after the accident, such imported products as vegetables grown in Italy and fish caught in scandinavian waters had to be tested for radioactivity.**

What correction should be made to this sentence?

(1) remove the comma after *accident*
(2) change the spelling of *vegetables* to *vegtables*
(3) change *caught* to *catched*
(4) change *scandinavian* to *Scandinavian*
(5) change *had* to *have*

18. Sentence 10: **<u>This</u> emphasized the need for global cooperation to maintain a livable environment.**

Which of the following is the best way to write the underlined portion of this sentence? If you think the original is the best way, choose option (1).

(1) This
(2) This incident
(3) This more than anything else
(4) It
(5) They

Questions 19–26 refer to the following paragraph.

(1) For several decades, Americans seen dieting as an avenue to social success. (2) They firmly believe that slim equals beautiful. (3) Therefore, they have spent millions of dollars on diet books and programs. (4) In the past several years, Doctors' studies linking obesity with increased risk of heart disease and diabetes have added new members to the ranks of dieters. (5) Unfortunatly, too many of these weight-conscious people are looking for a quick, painless way to shed extra pounds. (6) They're attracted to ads promising pills and diets that melt away fat while eating all they want. (7) What they refuse to realize is that there is no miracle cure for being overweight. (8) The only solution to the problem is a permanent change in lifestyle. (9) This change includes reducing intake of sweets and fatty red meat. (10) In addition, a regular program of exercise will help keep excess weight off improve muscle tone, and provide a general feeling of attractiveness and good health. (11) This new lifestyle requires neither books nor pills, but it does demand self-discipline.

19. Sentence 1: **For several decades, Americans seen dieting as an avenue to social success.**

    What correction should be made to this sentence?

    (1) replace *Americans* with *americans*
    (2) insert *have* after *Americans*
    (3) replace *avenue* with *Avenue*
    (4) change the spelling of *success* to *sucess*
    (5) no correction is necessary

20. Sentences 2 and 3: **They firmly believe that slim equals beautiful. Therefore, they have spent millions of dollars on diet books and programs.**

    The most effective combination of Sentences 2 and 3 would contain which of the following groups of words?

    (1) If they firmly believe that slim equals beautiful, they
    (2) Firmly believing that slim equals beautiful, they have
    (3) By spending millions of dollars on diet books and programs, they firmly
    (4) Spending millions of dollars on diet books and programs because they
    (5) Slim equals beautiful so they

21. Sentence 4: **In the past several years, Doctors' studies linking obesity with increased risk of heart disease and diabetes have added new members to the ranks of dieters.**

    What correction should be made to this sentence?

    (1) change *Doctors'* to *doctors'*
    (2) change *studies* to *study's*
    (3) change the spelling of *disease* to *desese*
    (4) change *have* to *has*
    (5) insert a comma after *members*

22. Sentence 5: **Unfortunatly, too many of these weight-conscious people are looking for a quick, painless way to shed extra pounds.**

What correction should be made to this sentence?

(1) change the spelling of *Unfortunatly* to *Unfortunately*
(2) change the spelling of *too* to *to*
(3) change the spelling of *conscious* to *consious*
(4) insert a comma after *people*
(5) insert a comma after *way*

23. Sentence 6: **They're attracted to ads promising pills and diets that melt away fat while <u>eating all they want.</u>**

Which of the following is the best way to write the underlined portion of this sentence? If you think the original is the best way, choose option (1).

(1) eating all they want.
(2) eating all you want.
(3) eating all he wants.
(4) you eat all you want.
(5) the dieters eat all they want.

24. Sentences 8 and 9: **The only solution to this problem is a permanent change in lifestyle. This change includes reducing intake of sweets and fatty red meat.**

The most effective combination of Sentences 8 and 9 would include which of the following groups of words?

(1) lifestyle, and which
(2) lifestyle, and including
(3) lifestyle, or this includes
(4) lifestyle, which includes
(5) lifestyle, but this includes

25. Sentence 10: **In addition, a regular program of exercise will help keep excess weight off improve muscle tone, and provide a general feeling of attractiveness and good health.**

What correction should be made to this sentence?

(1) change the spelling of *exercise* to *exersize*
(2) insert a comma after *off*
(3) change the spelling of *muscle* to *mussel*
(4) insert a comma after *attractiveness*
(5) no correction is necessary

26. Sentence 11: **This new lifestyle requires neither books nor pills, but it does demand self-discipline.**

What correction should be made to this sentence?

(1) change *requires* to *require*
(2) insert a comma after *books*
(3) remove the comma after *pills*
(4) replace *but* with *or*
(5) no correction is necessary

Questions 27–35 refer to the following paragraph.

(1) If you're considering renting an apartment, you want to make the best selection posible. (2) Price, location, lease conditions, and size is all factors to take into account. (3) The best location depends on your lifestyle if you have children, you'll probably want to be near a good school. (4) If you don't cook, you'll want to be near a deli or restaurant and if you jog, you'll want a neighborhood without too much traffic. (5) Do you plan to commute? (6) Then you'll want to find out if there is public transportation to your job and how much it costs. (7) If you have a car, you wanted to know whether parking is available. (8) You'll want to decide how much space your furniture takes up, then find out if the new apartment is big enough to suit you. (9) One will need enough closets, kitchen cabinets, and other storage space in your apartment. (10) Be sure to note how long the lease runs (a month? a year?), how much the rent is, and are you allowed to redecorate.

27. Sentence 1: **If you're considering renting an apartment, you want to make the best selection posible.**

What correction should be made to this sentence?

(1) change *you're* to *your*
(2) insert a comma after *considering*
(3) change the spelling of *considering* to *considring*
(4) change *want* to *wanted*
(5) change the spelling of *posible* to *possible*

28. Sentence 2: **Price, location, lease conditions, and size is all factors to take into account.**

What correction should be made to this sentence?

(1) remove the comma after *Price*
(2) change the spelling of *conditions* to *condishuns*
(3) insert a comma after *size*
(4) change *is* to *are*
(5) change *to* to *two*

29. Sentence 3: **The best location depends on <u>your lifestyle if</u> you have children, you'll probably want to be near a good school.**

Which of the following is the best way to write the underlined portion of this sentence? If you think the original is the best way, choose option (1).

(1) your lifestyle if
(2) your lifestyle, if
(3) your lifestyle, but
(4) your lifestyle. If
(5) you're lifestyle if

30. Sentence 4: **If you don't cook, you'll want to be near a deli or restaurant and if you jog, you'll want a neighborhood without too much traffic.**

What correction should be made to this sentence?

(1) change the spelling of *don't* to *dont*
(2) change the spelling of *restaurant* to *restarant*
(3) insert a comma after *restaurant*
(4) change *jog* to *jogged*
(5) change *too much* to *to much*

31. Sentences 5 and 6: **Do you plan to commute? Then you'll want to find out if there is public transportation to your job and how much it costs.**

The most effective combination of Sentences 5 and 6 would contain which of the following groups of words?

(1) Since you plan to commute, you'll
(2) Even if you plan to commute, you'll
(3) If you planned to commute, you would
(4) If you plan to commute, you'll
(5) Although you plan to commute, you'll

32. Sentence 7: **If you have a car, you wanted to know whether parking is available.**

Which of the following is the best way to write the underlined portion of this sentence? If you think the original is the best way, choose option (1).

(1) you wanted
(2) you'll want
(3) you were wanting
(4) you had wanted
(5) you would have wanted

33. Sentence 8: **You'll want to decide how much space your furniture takes up, then find out if the new apartment is big enough to suit you.**

If you rewrote Sentence 8 beginning with

After you decide how much space your furniture takes up,

the next word should be

(1) it
(2) however
(3) and
(4) then
(5) so

34. Sentence 9: **One will need enough closets, kitchen cabinets, and other storage space in your apartment.**

What correction should be made to this sentence?

(1) replace *One* with *You*
(2) change *will need* to *needed*
(3) remove the comma after *closets*
(4) change the spelling of *kitchen* to *kichen*
(5) change *your* to *you're*

35. Sentence 10: **Be sure to note how long the lease runs (a month? a year?), how much the rent is, and are you allowed to redecorate.**

Which of the following is the best way to write the underlined portion of this sentence? If you think the original is the best way, choose option (1).

(1) are you allowed to redecorate.
(2) are you allowed to redecorate?
(3) can you redecorate.
(4) how much redecorating is allowed.
(5) is redecorating allowed.

Questions 36–45 refer to the following paragraph.

(1) The phrase "mans best friend" has special meaning for the owners of service and hearing dogs. (2) These dogs are similar to seeing-eye dogs. (3) The canines are specially trained to aid people with specific disabilities. (4) Service dogs may turn light switches on and off, pick up dropped items, and carrying purses in backpacks for people in wheelchairs. (5) If their owners are able to walk but need help maintaining their balance, the dogs accompanied them to provide the necessary support. (6) Hearing dogs serve as their owners' ears by alerting him to sounds such as a ringing telephone. (7) The dogs warn the owners by touch, and then they lead their masters to the source of the sound. (8) There taught to use special signals for important sounds such as fire alarms. (9) Training for both service and hearing dogs, is time-consuming and expensive; in fact, the average cost for training a single hearing dog is approximately three thousand dollars. (10) In most cases, however, recipients are not required to pay for the dogs although donations are accepted. (11) All costs are usually cover by a sponsoring community organization.

36. Sentence 1: **The phrase "mans best friend" has special meaning for the owners of service and hearing dogs.**

    What correction should be made to this sentence?

    (1) replace *mans* with *man's*
    (2) change the spelling of *friend* to *freind*
    (3) insert a comma after *meaning*
    (4) replace *owners* with *owner's*
    (5) no correction is necessary

37. Sentences 2 and 3: **These dogs are similar to seeing-eye dogs. The canines are specially trained to aid people with specific disabilities.**

    The most effective combination of Sentences 2 and 3 would contain which of the following groups of words?

    (1) Although these dogs are similar
    (2) Like seeing-eye dogs, the canines
    (3) These canines, they are like seeing-eye dogs
    (4) seeing-eye dogs, so these canines
    (5) seeing-eye dogs, which these canines are

38. Sentence 4: **Service dogs may turn light switches on and off, pick up dropped items, and <u>carrying</u> purses in backpacks for people in wheelchairs.**

    Which of the following is the best way to write the underlined portion of this sentence? If you think the original is the best way, choose option (1).

    (1) carrying
    (2) carried
    (3) carry
    (4) have carried
    (5) they have carried

39. Sentence 5: **If their owners are able to walk but need help maintaining their balance, the dogs accompanied them to provide the necessary support.**

    What correction should be made to this sentence?

    (1) insert a comma after *walk*
    (2) change the spelling of *balance* to *ballance*
    (3) insert *so* after *balance,*
    (4) change *accompanied* to *accompany*
    (5) change the spelling of *necessary* to *neccesary*

40. Sentence 6: **Hearing dogs serve as their owners' ears by alerting him to sounds such as a ringing telephone.**

What correction should be made to this sentence?

(1) change *serve* to *served*
(2) change *owners'* to *owners*
(3) replace *ears by* with *ears. By*
(4) replace *him* with *them*
(5) change the spelling of *telephone* to *telaphone*

41. Sentence 7: **The dogs warn the owners by touch, and then they lead their masters to the source of the sound.**

If you rewrote the sentence beginning with

After the dogs warn the owners by touch,

the next word should be

(1) then
(2) and
(3) they
(4) which
(5) next

42. Sentence 8: **There taught to use special signals for important sounds such as fire alarms.**

What correction should be made to this sentence?

(1) replace *There* with *They're*
(2) replace *taught* with *teach*
(3) insert a comma after *signals*
(4) replace *sounds such* with *sounds; such*
(5) no correction is necessary

43. Sentence 9: **Training for both service and hearing dogs, is time-consuming and expensive; in fact, the average cost for training a single hearing dog is approximately three thousand dollars.**

What correction should be made to this sentence?

(1) insert a comma after *service*
(2) remove the comma after *dogs*
(3) remove the comma after *fact*
(4) change the spelling of *approximately* to *aproximately*
(5) no correction is necessary

44. Sentence 10: **In most cases, however, recipients are not required to pay for the dogs although donations are accepted.**

Which of the following is the best way to write the underlined portion of this sentence? If you think the original is the best way, choose option (1).

(1) although
(2) unless
(3) as though
(4) and
(5) therefore

45. Sentence 11: **All costs are usually cover by a sponsoring community organization.**

Which of the following is the best way to write the underlined portion of this sentence? If you think the original is the best way, choose option (1).

(1) are usually cover
(2) is usually cover
(3) are usually covering
(4) is usually covered
(5) are usually covered

Questions 46–55 refer to the following paragraph.

(1) In the war between humans and cockroaches, they have been winning for centuries. (2) They can survive extremes of tempature, pressure, and altitude far better than humans, and they can live without food or water for two weeks. (3) Their diet, in addition to the foods humans consume, include cardboard, paper, glue, and toothpaste; therefore, they can almost always find something to eat. (4) Furthermore, they reproduce rapidly. (5) Every three weeks, the female german cockroach produces about forty offspring. (6) Until recently, attempts to eradicate roaches from homes and apartments meet with only limited success. (7) Insecticides were often ineffective. (8) The roaches either adapted to the chemicals or avoided the areas that had been sprayed. (9) Now however, scientists are testing a new technique. (10) Carl Djerassi, which is a professor of chemistry at Stanford University, has developed a hormone that keeps cockroaches in a permanently juvenile stage. (11) Sprayed as an insecticide, the roaches pick it up as they walk through it and ingest it during their normal grooming process. (12) The result is a break in the insects' reproductive cycle, leading to fewer and fewer unwelcome encounters with the scurrying creatures in the kitchen at midnight.

46. Sentence 1: **In the war between humans and cockroaches, they have been winning for centuries.**

    What correction should be made to this sentence?

    (1) insert a comma after *war*
    (2) remove the comma after *cockroaches*
    (3) replace *they* with *the roaches*
    (4) replace *have been* with *are*
    (5) change the spelling of *winning* to *wining*

47. Sentence 2: **They can survive extremes of tempature, pressure, and altitude far better than humans, and they can live without food or water for two weeks.**

    What correction should be made to this sentence?

    (1) replace *They* with *It*
    (2) change the spelling of *tempature* to *temperature*
    (3) remove the comma after *humans*
    (4) insert a comma after *food*
    (5) replace *weeks* with *week's*

48. Sentence 3: **Their diet, in addition to the foods humans consume, include cardboard, paper, glue, and toothpaste; therefore, they can almost always find something to eat.**

    What correction should be made to this sentence?

    (1) replace *Their* with *There*
    (2) change *include* to *includes*
    (3) remove the comma after *cardboard*
    (4) replace *therefore* with *nevertheless*
    (5) remove the comma after *therefore*

49. Sentence 5: **Every three weeks, the female german cockroach produces about forty offspring.**

    What correction should be made to this sentence?

    (1) remove the comma after *weeks*
    (2) change *german* to *German*
    (3) insert a comma after *cockroach*
    (4) change *produces* to *produced*
    (5) no correction is necessary

50. Sentence 6: **Until recently, attempts to eradicate roaches from homes and apartments meet with only limited success.**

Which of the following is the best way to write the underlined portion of this sentence? If you think the original is the best way, choose option (1).

(1) meet
(2) meets
(3) met
(4) have met
(5) had met

51. Sentences 7 and 8: **Insecticides were often ineffective. The roaches either adapted to the chemicals or avoided the areas that had been sprayed.**

The most effective combination of Sentences 7 and 8 would include which of the following groups of words?

(1) ineffective, the roaches
(2) ineffective, but the roaches
(3) ineffective; therefore, the roaches
(4) ineffective although the roaches
(5) ineffective because the roaches

52. Sentence 9: **Now however, scientists are testing a new technique.**

What correction should be made to this sentence?

(1) insert a comma after *Now*
(2) remove the comma after *however*
(3) change *scientists* to *Scientists*
(4) change *are* to *is*
(5) no correction is necessary

53. Sentence 10: **Carl Djerassi, which is a professor of chemistry at Stanford University, has developed a hormone that keeps cockroaches in a permanently juvenile stage.**

Which of the following is the best way to write the underlined portion of this sentence? If you think the original is the best way, choose option (1).

(1) which is a professor of chemistry at Stanford University,
(2) which is a Professor of chemistry at Stanford University,
(3) which is a professor of chemistry at Stanford university,
(4) who is a professor of chemistry at Stanford University,
(5) who is a Professor of chemistry at Stanford University,

54. Sentence 11: **Sprayed as an insecticide, the roaches pick it up as they walk through it and ingest it during their normal grooming process.**

Which of the following is the best way to write the underlined portion of this sentence? If you think the original is the best way, choose option (1).

(1) Sprayed as an insecticide,
(2) After being sprayed as an insecticide,
(3) When sprayed as an insecticide,
(4) When it is sprayed as an insecticide,
(5) Spraying as an insecticide,

55. Sentence 12: **The result is a break in the insects' reproductive cycle, leading to fewer and fewer unwelcome encounters with the scurrying creatures in the kitchen at midnight.**

Which of the following is the best way to write the underlined portion of this sentence? If you think the original is the best way, choose option (1).

(1) result is
(2) result, is
(3) result
(4) result being
(5) result, being

ANSWERS BEGIN ON PAGE 15.

Writing Skills Pre-Test, Part 2

Directions: This part of the test is designed to find out how well you write. In preparing your answer for this question, you should take the following steps:

1. Read all of the information accompanying the question.

2. Plan your answer carefully before you write. Use scratch paper to jot down notes and ideas you want to include.

3. Write your answer on a separate sheet of paper.

4. Revise. Read carefully what you have written and make any changes that will improve your writing.

5. Edit. Check your paragraphing, sentence structure, spelling, punctuation, capitalization, and usage and make any necessary corrections.

Take forty-five minutes to write on the following topic. When forty-five minutes have passed, stop writing.

TOPIC

We all play many roles in life. For instance, you might be a parent, a construction worker, an Italian-American, a political party member, and a student, among other things.

If you were asked to describe your role as parent, you might discuss how you feel about your children and what your relationships with them are like. You might even talk about your involvement in making the community a safe place for children.

Think of the roles that you play in your own life; then choose one role that is important to you and describe it.

POSSIBLE ANSWERS BEGIN ON PAGE 17.

Pre-Test Answer Key

PART 1

1. (5) This sentence is correct as written.

2. (4) This pronoun refers to the singular word *consumer. Her* agrees with *consumer* because *her* is singular. *Their* is plural.

3. (4) The sentence does not make clear what the phrase *Before setting foot on a car lot* is referring to. Choice (4) tells you that the phrase refers to *she*.

4. (1) The new sentence would read, "A subcompact won't accommodate a family of six, nor is a station wagon necessary for a single adult." The word *nor* connects the two original sentences in a way that makes sense.

5. (2) This passage is written in the present, but the verb *searched* puts sentence 6 in the past. Changing the verb to *searches* puts the sentence in the present.

6. (4) The new sentence would read, "Body integrity is important; therefore, she looks for signs of rust, dents, or uneven paint that might indicate a previous accident." The connecting word *therefore* tells you that the idea in the first part of the sentence causes the action in the second part.

7. (1) The possessive ending *'s* shows that *car's interior* means "interior of the car."

8. (5) The three parts of the sentence that are separated by commas should all be in parallel construction: *engine, electrical system,* and *brakes.* The phrase *how well the brakes work* is not in this form.

9. (5) The word *however* expresses the contrast between the two parts of the sentence. The rewritten sentence would read, "People may try to divide our planet into separate states and nations; however, nature ignores these artificial boundaries."

10. (3) Because the two parts of the subject, *water* and *wind,* are separated by *nor,* the verb must agree with the closer part of the subject: *wind respects. Respects* agrees with a singular subject.

11. (4) Test *it's* by replacing it with *it is . . . whether or not it is citizens . . .* makes no sense, so the contraction must be wrong. Change the contraction *it's* to the possessive pronoun *its.*

12. (3) Never separate the main parts of a sentence, the subject and predicate, with a comma.

13. (2) This word group is not a complete sentence because the verb *carrying* requires a helping verb. Choice (2) substitutes the verb *carry,* which does not require a helping verb.

14. (5) This sentence is correct as written.

15. (5) The past tense verb *occurred* and the date *1986* tell you that the event took place in the past. *Released* is the correct past tense to use instead of the present-tense *releases.*

16. (1) This sentence is correct as written.

17. (4) *Scandinavian* is a word derived from a specific region of the world, so it should always be capitalized no matter where it appears in a sentence.

18. (2) The original sentence does not make clear what the pronoun *This* refers to. Adding the word *incident* makes the subject of the sentence clear.

19. (2) The verb form *seen* is not complete without a helping verb. The correct form is *have seen.*

20. (2) This combination turns the first sentence into an introductory phrase. The new sentence reads, "Firmly believing that slim equals beautiful, they have spent millions of dollars on diet books and programs." If you test the other choices, you will find that they do not keep the meaning of the original sentences.

21. (1) In this sentence, *doctors'* is used in a general sense, not as the title or name of a specific doctor. Therefore, it should not be capitalized.

22. (1) When adding a suffix (ending) beginning with a consonant to a word ending in a silent *e,* do not drop the *e.*

23. (5) This sentence implies that the pills and diets are eating all they want; however, common sense tells you that the dieters must be the eaters. Choice (5) makes clear who is doing the eating.

24. (4) This choice both shows the relationship between the ideas in the original sentences and is worded correctly. The new sentence would read, "The only solution to this problem is a permanent change in lifestyle, which includes reducing intake of sweets and fatty red meat."

25. (2) Always separate three or more items in a series with commas: *keep excess weight off, improve muscle tone, and provide a general feeling of attractiveness and good health.*

26. (5) This sentence is correct as written.

27. (5) You may need to memorize the spelling of this tricky word.

28. (4) The subject of the sentence is compound, so a plural verb is needed: *are.*

29. (4) The original sentence contains two complete thoughts run together. Choice (4) correctly divides the two complete thoughts into separate sentences.

30. (3) Always use a comma between two complete thoughts joined by the conjunction *and.*

31. (4) The first part of the sentence is the cause, and the second part is the effect. Choice (3) also expresses this but is in the wrong tense.

32. (2) This passage is written in the future tense. Choice (2), *you'll want,* is the only choice written in the future tense.

33. (4) The new sentence has a time order relationship. Choice (4) expresses this relationship: *After . . . then.*

34. (1) The passage is written in the second person. The subject of this sentence should be second person (*You*), not third person (*One*).

35. (4) The three items in this series should all be in the same form. *How long the lease runs* and *how much the rent is* are adverbial phrases, but in the original sentence the third item starts with a verb. Choice (4) turns the third item into an adverbial phrase, *how much redecorating is allowed,* to be consistent.

36. (1) Use the ending *'s* to show possession: man has a best friend = man's best friend.

37. (2) The new sentence would read, "Like seeing-eye dogs, the canines are specially trained to aid people with specific disabilities." The word *Like* picks up the idea expressed by the word *similar* in the original sentence.

38. (3) The three items in this series should all be in the same form, starting with a verb in the present tense: *turn, pick,* and *carry.*

39. (4) The verb in the first part of the sentence is in the present tense, and both parts are happening at the same time. Therefore, the verb in the second part of the sentence should also be in the present tense.

40. (4) The pronoun refers to the word *owners',* which is plural. Therefore, the plural pronoun *them* is needed.

41. (3) The original sentences are related by time order. Starting the new sentence with *after* shows that relationship. No other time clue word (such as *then* or *next*) should be used in addition to *after.* The new sentence would read, "After the dogs warn the owners by touch, they lead their masters to the source of the sound."

42. (1) Substitute the words *They are* for *There* in the sentence. *They are taught* makes sense, so the contraction *They're* is needed.

43. (2) This comma incorrectly separates the main parts (subject and predicate) of the complete thought.

44. (1) This sentence is correct as written.

45. (5) This verb should be written in the present passive form, *are covered.* This verb form shows that the action in the sentence is performed by the sponsoring community organization.

46. (3) In the original sentence, the pronoun *they* could refer to either humans or cockroaches. Choice (3) makes the meaning clear.

47. (2) This word is hard to spell if you don't pronounce all the syllables carefully: *tem-per-a-ture.*

48. (2) Removing the interrupting phrase *in addition to the foods humans consume,* you should see that the subject of the sentence is *diet,* a singular word. *Includes* is the correct singular verb form: *diet includes.*

49. (2) The word *German* is derived from the name of a specific country, Germany, so it should always be capitalized.

50. (5) Because the action in the sentence ended before a specific time in the past, the past perfect tense is needed: *had met.*

51. (5) The new sentence would read, "Insecticides were often ineffective because the roaches either adapted to the chemicals or avoided the areas that had been sprayed." The word *because* shows that the second part of the sentence is the cause of the first part.

52. (1) When words like *however* are used as transition words, they should be set off by commas.

53. (4) The relative pronoun *who* is always used to refer to humans. The word *professor* should not be capitalized in this sentence because it is not used as a title.

54. (4) The original sentence implies that the roaches themselves are sprayed as an insecticide. Choice (4) uses the pronoun *it* to refer to *hormone* in sentence 10.

55. (1) This sentence is correct as written.

PART 2

If at all possible, give your essay to an instructor to evaluate. You'll find his or her objective opinion helpful in deciding whether you're ready for the actual GED Writing Skills Test or whether you need some study and practice.

Thinking about your own reactions during each stage of your writing will also help evaluate your readiness. How would you answer the following questions?

1. As you read the topic and planned your answer, did you find it easy to jot down ideas for your essay? Were you able to look over your notes and decide which points to include and which to discard? If this planning stage gave you trouble, pay particular attention to pages 29–31 in Chapter 2 and pages 180–184 in Chapter 5.

2. As you were writing your essay, were you able to compose paragraphs that stated a main point and supported it with plenty of logically organized details? For more work on this aspect of writing, study pages 71–77 and 121–135 in Chapters 3 and 4.

3. Were you able to write a clear introduction, body, and conclusion for your essay? Were these parts linked logically and smoothly? You'll find the structure of an essay discussed on pages 179–193 of Chapter 5.

4. Did you know how to revise your essay by adding more specific details where necessary, using words to link sentences and paragraphs, and cutting out repetitive or unnecessary sections? Suggestions and practice in revising are included on pages 233–253 of Chapter 6.

5. Did you know how to edit your writing for correct sentence structure, punctuation, usage, spelling, and capitalization? The second section of each of Chapters 2 through 6 will help you polish your editing skills.

If possible, talk to your instructor about your feelings as you wrote. Together, you'll be able to identify your current writing strengths as well as any weaknesses. Based on this combined evaluation, you can locate the sections of your textbook that you'll need to study thoroughly and the parts that you can skim lightly.

Pre-Test Evaluation Chart

On the following chart, circle the number of any item you got wrong. Next to each item you will see the pages you can review for those items that gave you the most difficulty. Pay particular attention to skill areas where you missed half or more of the questions.

Skill Area	Item Number	Review Pages
Complete sentences and fragments	13	35–40
Parts of a sentence	12, 25, 43	41–49
Nouns, pronouns	7, 11, 36, 42	50–64
Verb tense/form	5, 15, 19, 32, 39, 45, 50	79–100
Subject-verb agreement	10, 28, 48	163–168
Independent and dependent clauses	4, 6, 9, 16, 29, 30, 31, 33, 41, 44, 51	138–157
Modifiers	3, 20, 23, 37, 54	195–205
Parallel structure	8, 35, 38	205–208
Pronoun reference	2, 18, 24, 34, 40, 46, 53	209–222
Sentence and paragraph links	52	241–246
Capitalization, spelling	17, 21, 22, 27, 47, 49	255–276
No error	1, 14, 26, 55	

CHAPTER 1 PART A
Preparing for the Writing Sample

Congratulations! Opening this book means that you've made one of the most important decisions of your life: you're going to finish your high school education. You may have dropped out to get a job, to take care of a baby, or to avoid more discouragement in the classroom. But you're back now, and whatever your age, whatever your reasons for returning to school, you want to succeed this time.

One step toward your goal of earning a high school equivalency diploma is passing the GED Writing Skills Test. This test consists of two parts: Part 1 is a multiple-choice section covering sentence structure, usage, punctuation, capitalization, and spelling; and Part 2 is an essay section in which you'll be asked to write approximately two hundred words on a specified topic.

To pass the test, you'll need to know how to express yourself clearly on paper: how to make a point, support it with specific examples, organize your ideas logically, and link them smoothly. You'll also need a good command of standard written English—knowledge of the rules that good writers use to decide what makes a complete sentence, where commas belong, which words to capitalize, and when to use a particular word form.

By sharpening these writing skills, you'll accomplish far more than passing a test. You'll give yourself a gift that you can use for the rest of your life. Think about it. You may be able to go from day to day without writing a word, but when you do need to write something, you want it to be good. Do you plan to apply for a job? You may need to compose a letter of application. Put yourself in the place of an employer looking for a new worker. Which of the following statements would impress you more?

I done alot of Restrant work, so I wants to be a Manger.

After ten years as a waitress, cook, and bookkeeper in a restaurant, I feel qualified to become a manager.

As you can see, the quality of your writing reflects on you. Improving your writing will help you present yourself as a careful, thoughtful, well-educated person.

WHAT TO EXPECT ON THE GED ESSAY TEST

As part of the GED Writing Skills Test, you'll be given forty-five minutes to write an essay. The topic will require you to explain something, such as your opinion about a common issue or the causes and effects of an everyday problem. Since this essay topic will draw on your general knowledge, you won't have to know any special information in order to write on it.

Although you won't need special knowledge, you will need to know how to plan and develop your ideas in writing. In order to write an effective essay for the writing sample, you will need to be able to state the main point of your essay and back it up with supporting ideas, evidence, and examples from your own knowledge and experience. Don't worry if you're not sure right now how to go about writing an essay. You will learn a lot about it in this book—starting in this chapter.

GETTING STARTED

WRITE REGULARLY

What can you do to improve your writing skills? You can read this book, of course, but that won't be enough. Reading a car repair manual isn't the same as actually pulling an engine apart. Reading a book about basketball isn't the same as spending a half hour experimenting to find just the right angle for a bank shot. In the same way, reading a book about writing is no substitute for actual writing practice. It can provide helpful suggestions, but you'll best learn to write by writing. So read the book, but don't stop there. Do the writing assignments as well.

Don't shy away from writing practice because you think you can't do it. Nobody expects you to start your career as a pro. And don't worry about writing full essays at first. You can work up to that.

If you stop to think about it, you'll find plenty of opportunities to do some writing. You can make daily "to do" lists of things you want to accomplish or, even better, "to do" lists for someone else in your family! How about a short note to a relative or a friend who lives out of town? Don't just grumble about the defective appliance you bought; write a letter of complaint to the manufacturer. Letters to the editor or a representative in Congress are still other possibilities.

JOURNALS

One form of writing practice that both professional writers and beginners find especially useful is keeping a journal. A journal is a record of a writer's observations and ideas. It might contain writings about anything—memories, events, thoughts, anything the writer wanted to write down. Entries might range in length from a few lines to a page or more. Here are three samples of the ways in which a writer might use a journal:

May 9

Tornado season again. The sky blackened, and the warning siren sounded yesterday. Headed for the basement but couldn't stand to miss the excitement of the storm, so I periodically ran back upstairs to look outside. The wind ripped a big branch from our mulberry tree and nearly tore the metal awning from our front porch. But the twister missed us. What drives people to live on the edge of danger? I could have stayed safely underground but chose to gamble instead.

June 8

An article in today's paper said that scientists are trying to develop computers that could assess a situation and react to it much as people do. Will humans not even be needed some day?

August 4

Architectural drafting might be an interesting career for me. I've done framing and finish carpentry, and I can read blueprints well. Art used to be my favorite subject in school. Maybe I can put those skills together. But how well does it pay? Is the job market good? What training would I need?
To do—

1. Talk to an architectural drafter in a construction firm.

2. Read the *Occupational Outlook Handbook* entry on drafting.

3. Talk to a counselor at the community college.

The beauty of a journal is that you don't have to share it with anyone else unless you want to. That means you don't have to worry about spelling or sentence structure—just put your ideas down.

You can use your journal in several ways. First, it's a great writing ice-breaker—a way to develop the habit of putting your ideas on paper. Second, it's a way of discovering what you really think about a topic. The act of writing something on paper forces you to take a hazy idea and give it some form. Third, you can use the material in your journal as the basis for letters or essays you want to write later. And finally, your journal will provide interesting reading in a year or two—or more—just as a record of your thoughts.

Experiment with journal writing as you prepare for the Writing Skills Test. Get a notebook and make a habit of writing in it for ten to fifteen minutes a few times each week. Topic possibilities are endless. You can write about personal experiences, neighborhood happenings, daily routines, friends, relatives, pets, work, hobbies, news stories of interest to you, career plans, class work—whatever concerns you at the moment. You can create a family memory book. To do so, write about your children. Then read the stories to them or give them the stories to read. As an alternative, you can write short letters to people whom you usually call on the phone. Journal writing will be a regular activity in this book.

Make your first entry now on any topic that interests you. If you don't have your notebook yet, use any sheet of paper for writing. Remember, no one needs to read this but you.

FREEWRITING

In addition to keeping a journal, you may want to experiment with a second way writers get started: freewriting. This technique is especially useful to thaw writer's block—when you can't decide how to begin or how to continue a piece of writing. When freewriting, force yourself to keep your pen or pencil moving—no matter what—by writing whatever comes into your mind. If you can't think what to write next, simply write, "I can't think what to write I can't think what to write" until you get bored and something else pops into your mind. Don't let spelling or sentence structure questions of any kind slow you down. Just write. Try ten minutes of freewriting right now.

THE WRITING PROCESS

THE FIVE STEPS

By writing a journal entry and freewriting, you've discovered that you can put words on paper—ideas that make sense to you. Now, how can you write so that others understand what you mean and react the way you want them to? Most writers can't accomplish this goal in a single step, no matter how good they are. Words simply don't pour from mind to paper in a steady stream of well-organized, clearly worded sentences. Although no two writers use precisely the same process as they write, all are concerned at some point with five basic activities: (1) prewriting, (2) drafting, (3) revising, (4) editing, and (5) publishing.

PREWRITING

Prewriting is the phase in which a writer plans what to say. This is the time to consider your purpose for writing. Do you want to explain something?

Instruct? Describe? Persuade or convince? Having a purpose in mind from the beginning of the process will help as you develop your writing.

Prewriting is also the time to consider your audience. Who will read your writing? Should your tone be formal or informal? Serious or humorous? Personal or objective?

In the prewriting stage, the writer develops and organizes ideas. Although this is essentially a thinking stage, you'll find that it helps to think on paper. Identify a topic. Then jot down notes about what you may want to include. A simple list of words and phrases is often an effective planning aid. Much as in freewriting, you make a list of whatever comes to mind about your topic. To expand your list, you could look in your journal for additional ideas. Or you could do some reading, make observations, or talk to people about your topic.

Here's a sample list for a letter to a friend describing a bad day one writer had recently. Picture yourself in a similar situation, and add a few ideas of your own in the spaces at the end. What else might have gone wrong?

Rotten Day
woke up with headache and sore throat
out of breakfast cereal
car had flat—late to work
collection agency called about car payment
boss chewed me out

_____

_____

DRAFTING

In the drafting stage, the writer puts the fragments of ideas developed during the prewriting phase into sentence and paragraph form. For instance, the "rotten day" list might turn into a paragraph like the one below. Notice that there are some mistakes in grammar and spelling. Don't worry too much about these—there will be time to fix errors later. Include a sentence or two of your own based on the items you added to the prewriting list.

I still can't believe what a rotten day I had yesterday! I knew when I woke up that I was comming down with a cold. I had a headache and soar throat. When I walked into the kitchen, I discovered I was out of breakfast cereal, so all I had was a glass of milk. My car had a flat tire. Taking care of the flat meant that I was half an hour late for work. Just before lunch a collection agency called threatening to reposess my car if I didn't catch up on my payments. My boss yelled at me for being late. _____

_____

_____

REVISING

In the revising stage, the writer can add, remove, replace, and rearrange material to improve the draft. After rereading the "rotten day" paragraph, the writer decided to change the wording of a few sentences. She also added a couple of details to make the writing more lively and moved one sentence so that it fit more logically into the time sequence of the paragraph. Are there any changes you would like to make in the sentences you added? If so, rewrite them on the blank lines.

I still can't believe what a rotten day ~~I had yesterday! I know when I~~ *yesterday was! When the alarm blared at 6 A.m., a headache and soar throat announced that I* ~~woke up that I was comming down with a cold. I had a headache and~~ ~~soar throat. When I walked~~ *was comming down with a cold. Stumbling groggily, reach for the Cheerios.* into the kitchen, I ~~discovered I was out of~~ *Only to discover an empty box* ~~breakfast cereal,~~ so all I had was a glass of milk. ~~My~~ *Then my* car had a flat tire.

Taking care of the flat ~~meant that I was~~ *made me* half an hour late for work. *naturally, my boss yelled at me.* Just

before lunch a collection agency called threatening to reposess my car

if I didn't catch up on my payments. ~~My boss yelled at me for being~~

~~late.~~ _____

_____

_____

EDITING

Editing, the fourth phase of the writing process, is making corrections to eliminate errors that might distract the reader from the writer's ideas. These corrections include changes in sentence structure, word choice, spelling, punctuation, and capitalization.

Editing changes in the "rotten day" paragraph have been written in for you. Are there any corrections that you need to make in your section?

I still can't believe what a rotten day yesterday was! When the

alarm blared at 6:00 A.M., a headache and ~~soar~~ *sore* throat announced that I

was ~~comming~~ *Coming* down with a cold. Stumbling groggily into the kitchen, I

~~reach~~ *reached* for the Cheerios, ~~Only~~ *only* to discover an empty box, so all I had

was a glass of milk. Then my car had a flat tire. Taking care of the flat

made me half an hour late for work. /Naturally, my boss yelled at me.

Just before lunch a collection agency called threatening to ~~reposess~~ *repossess*

my car if I didn't catch up on my payments. _____

_____

_____

Throughout the rest of this book, you'll be studying and practicing these four phases—prewriting, drafting, revising, and editing—until they become a part of your own writing process, ready to be used on Part 2 of the GED Writing Skills Test and in any other writing situation you encounter.

PUBLISHING

Publishing, the final phase of the writing process, is sharing your work with others. An example is turning in your essay for the GED judges to read. Sending a letter, whether to a friend or to your local newspaper, is also a form of publishing. Telling your child a bedtime story that you made up is publishing. Any time you present your writing to an audience, you're publishing it.

The Multiple-Choice Section

WHAT TO EXPECT

In addition to writing an essay, you'll be taking a multiple-choice test on editing skills. This part of the test will consist of several paragraphs followed by questions about the sentences they contain. Some questions will require you to locate errors, while others will ask you to restate the same idea in different words. It's important to read the passage as a whole before you answer any of the questions, because some items will require you to think about how a sentence should fit into the paragraph.

Here's part of a typical passage followed by some sample questions. Don't worry if they seem hard now. Just read through them to get an idea of how they're constructed.

(1) Motorcycles has become a popular means of transportation in this country. (2) They are much less expensive to buy than cars, but they use much less gas. (3) Lack of safety was their one major disadvantage. (4) Riders have no surrounding structure to protect them. (5) They are more likely than passengers in cars or trucks to be badly hurt or killed in an accident.

Some questions will require you to find and correct an error in a sentence, as in Sentence 1:

1. Sentence 1: **Motorcycles has become a popular means of transportation in this country.**

   What correction should be made to this sentence?

   (1) replace *Motorcycles* with *Motorcycle's*
   (2) change *has* to *have*
   (3) change *become* to *became*
   (4) insert a comma after *transportation*
   (5) no correction is necessary

Some questions will require you to choose the most effective way of writing one section of a sentence, like this one:

To answer some questions, you'll need to think of the sentence in the context of the whole passage.

Some questions will ask you to combine two sentences or to restate a sentence in other words. In these questions, the original sentences have no errors in them. You must identify a correct way to rewrite the same ideas.

2. Sentence 2: **They are much less expensive to buy than cars, but they use much less gas.**

Which of the following is the best way to write the underlined part of this sentence? If you think the original is the best way, choose option (1).

(1) cars, but
(2) cars, so
(3) cars, and
(4) cars if
(5) cars or

3. Sentence 3: **Lack of safety was their one major disadvantage.**

Which of the following is the best way to write the underlined part of this sentence? If you think the original is the best way, choose option (1).

(1) was
(2) will be
(3) being
(4) been
(5) is

4. Sentences 4 and 5: **Riders have no surrounding structure to protect them. They are more likely than passengers in cars or trucks to be badly hurt or killed in an accident.**

The most effective combination of sentences 4 and 5 would include which of the following groups of words?

(1) Because riders have no
(2) Although riders have no
(3) Unless riders have no
(4) protect them, but they
(5) protect them, or they

Do you know what the correct answers are? Reread the passage and circle the choices that you think are right.

Answers: **1.** (2)   **2.** (3)   **3.** (5)   **4.** (1)

If you had trouble answering these questions, don't worry. This book will give you plenty of skill-building and test-taking practice to prepare you for the multiple-choice part of the test.

CHAPTER 2 PART A
Prewriting and Drafting

THINKING ON PAPER

THE PLANNING STEPS

A clean sheet of paper is lying in front of you, and you have to fill it up. Suddenly your mind may seem as blank as the paper. You may wonder how on earth a writer ever gets started. What can you do to set your pen in motion?

The answer is deceptively simple: think. When you're faced with a writing task, think about what the writing is for. Think about the information that this situation calls for and jot down some notes. (See? You will already have broken the ice: your page won't be blank anymore.) Think about a logical way to organize the information. Then begin a draft of your actual writing.

Some version of this thinking and scribbling phase forms a part of every writer's routine. With a little practice, you'll soon make it part of yours.

> Prewriting includes these three steps.
>
> **1.** Analyzing the writing situation
>
> **2.** Brainstorming ideas
>
> **3.** Organizing ideas

ANALYZING THE WRITING SITUATION

Writing seldom occurs in a vacuum. Whether the final product is a children's story, a letter to the editor, or a note to a friend, every writing task has a topic, an audience, and a purpose. To help you get started writing, you can ask yourself three questions: What am I writing about? Who is going to read my piece of writing? Why am I writing about this?

Perhaps your goal is to get a stop sign installed on the corner by the park. You might decide that a letter to the editor of your local newspaper will exert some pressure on the town council. So you write a letter about the situation to the local paper.

Perhaps you're writing to your Aunt Charlotte. She always likes a lot of family news, so you want to update her on your family's activities. What ideas might you decide to include? Your sister's broken arm (a rollerskating accident), a surprise visit from your cousins in Vermont, and your decision to study for your GED are examples.

Once you have an idea of what you're writing about and why as well as who you're writing to, you're ready to move on.

BRAINSTORMING

Now that you know what you're writing about, you can jot down ideas to include in your writing. Don't worry about wording or spelling; don't bother to write complete sentences; don't stop to decide whether a particular detail will or will not work. Just write down whatever comes to mind regarding your topic.

This random listing technique, known as **brainstorming**, is helpful for several reasons. First of all, brainstorming combats blank-paper panic. It helps you get something on the page quickly. Second, brainstorming helps you concentrate on your content. You aren't distracted by questions of phrasing, punctuation, or spelling. As a result, you're less likely to forget what you wanted to write while puzzling about how to write it.

One writer made the following list by brainstorming for five minutes on the topic "A Perfect Day." She wanted to let other members of her GED class know what a perfect day would be like for her.

A Perfect Day
sleep late
sunny day
no traffic jams
spaghetti for supper
friends compliment me
customers smile
catch up on paperwork

EXERCISE 1

Directions: Write a brainstorm list of your own ideas about *each* of the three topics below. Spend about five minutes on each topic. You will be using one of these lists as a basis for a piece of writing a little later on, so be sure to save your work.

- a perfect day (or, if you wish, a rotten day)
- a person you know well and admire
- your earliest childhood memories

ANSWERS WILL VARY.

ORGANIZING

With your brainstorm list on paper, you're ready to move to the next stage of prewriting: organizing the list. Look at the list carefully to decide which ideas you want to include in your paper; cross out anything you want to omit. Do any items now suggest additional ideas? If so, write them down.

Finally, choose a logical order for your details. You might want to put your details in time order if they are events. Or you could put them in order of their importance to you. Or you could group related details together. Keep in mind that you want your reader to be able to follow and understand your writing. Chapters 3 and 4 will present some detailed suggestions on organizing, but for now try numbering the ideas in the order you plan to write about them.

For an example of the organizing step, look again at the brainstorming list below for "A Perfect Day." Note the changes: The writer crossed out an idea and added more details. Then she numbered the ideas to show the order in which she plans to describe each item. She numbered her ideas in time order: the order they would have happened in her day. She felt that this sequence would help her readers get a good picture of what the day would be like.

A Perfect Day

~~sleep late~~

① sunny day — *blue sky; golden, scarlet leaves*

② no traffic jams — *all green lights*

⑤ spaghetti for supper

③ friends compliment me - *on how good I look at work*

④ customers smile - *and thank me for my help*

⑥ catch up on paperwork — *checkbook balances with bank statements*

EXERCISE 2

Directions: Choose one of your lists from Exercise 1 on page 30—the one that interests you most. Make any changes you wish in the list by adding new ideas or deleting ideas you don't want to use. Then number the ideas in the order you would want to write about them. You could put them in time order or in order of importance, or you could group related ideas.

Keep in mind that you'll be using this work later, so be sure to save it.

ANSWERS WILL VARY.

DRAFTING

With your organized list in hand, you're ready to begin a draft of your paper. As you write, use the list as a guide, not a dictator. If you think of something else to add or you want to change the order of your ideas, go ahead. Write your ideas as clearly as you can so others will understand you.

Look carefully at the way "A Perfect Day" has been developed from the brainstorming list. Although the framework for the draft was established in the list, a few details have been added to clarify the descriptions. In addition, the details have been grouped into two paragraphs, one for the daytime activities, the other for the evening.

A PERFECT DAY

Driving to work, I admire the golden and scarlet leaves on the trees shining against a cloudless blue sky. At 7:30 there are no traffic jams, and every light turns green as my car approaches. I reach work with fifteen minutes to spare. Everyone is in a good mood at work. I get compliments on my clothes, and several customers smile and thank me for my help.

Returning home, I remember that my cupboards are freshly stocked with food. I decide to make a delicious spaghetti dinner. Later that night I catch up on some bill paying, balance my checkbook to the penny with the bank statement, and curl up in bed with a very satisfied smile. What a perfect day it's been!

EXERCISE 3

Directions: Write a draft based on the list of ideas that you organized in Exercise 2. As you write, don't worry about making mistakes. You'll learn a lot about correcting mistakes as you move on in this book. At this point, just practice getting ideas on paper.

Be sure to save your paper when you are finished. You'll be working on it again in this chapter.

ANSWERS WILL VARY.

JOURNAL WRITING

Have you been writing in your journal regularly? Keeping a journal is a good way to get valuable writing practice. Try writing on one of the following topics in your journal, or think of your own topic.

- Saturday nights—Whom do you like to be with? Where do you like to go? What do you like to do?

- Describe a conversation that moved you—for instance, a conversation that made you laugh, cry, or feel closer to someone.

- Write about one of your dreams for your future.

- Think about your relationship with someone you know well. It might be a family member, a close friend, or someone you're dating. What do you like most about this person? What does he or she do that drives you crazy?

ANSWERS WILL VARY.

CHAPTER HIGHLIGHTS: PREWRITING AND DRAFTING

1. Prewriting involves analyzing the writing situation, brainstorming, and organizing ideas.

2. When you start writing, ask yourself what you are writing about. Why are you writing? Who will your audience be?

3. Brainstorm ideas by listing anything you can think of about your topic, without worrying about how you phrase it.

4. Organize your ideas by deciding which items to use from your brainstorming list and what order to write them in.

Sentence Basics

SENTENCES

WHAT IS A SENTENCE?

"Hungry?" "Starved!" "Want a double cheeseburger?" "With a large order of fries."

You've had many ordinary conversations like this one, in which single words and short phrases carry complete messages. Signs, too, often communicate in phrases: *No Exit. Wet Paint. One Way. Falling Rocks.* These phrases make sense because of the setting in which you see them. The words *wet paint* don't mean much on their own, but placed on a sign by a glistening park bench, they deliver a clear message.

In most written communication, however, you will find that single words or phrases are not enough to make your point clear. Without the context of a specific place, or two people face-to-face, to clarify misunderstandings, you must express your ideas in sentences so that your reader isn't left with unanswered questions.

A word group must pass three tests in order to be called a sentence. First, it must have a ***subject*** that tells whom or what the sentence is about. Whom or what is the following sentence about?

The small boy teetered on the big bicycle.

The sentence is about *the small boy*, so *the small boy* is the subject.

Second, a sentence must have a ***predicate*** that tells what the subject is or does. Everything in the sentence that is not part of the subject is part of the predicate. Underline the words in the example sentence above that tell what the subject is or does.

You should have underlined *teetered on the big bicycle*. This part of the sentence is the predicate.

Finally, a sentence must express a complete thought. That is, when you read it, you are not left with unanswered questions, such as *who did it?* or *what did she do?* The sentence *The small boy teetered on the big bicycle* expresses a complete thought. You know what happened and who was involved.

TESTS FOR A SENTENCE

1. It must have a subject that tells whom or what the sentence is about.

2. It must have a predicate that tells what the subject is or does.

3. It must express a complete thought.

A group of words that does *not* pass these three tests is called a ***fragment***. A fragment is a group of words that does not express a complete thought—it leaves a reader with unanswered questions about what the writer is trying to say. Study the examples below to see how a fragment is different from a complete sentence.

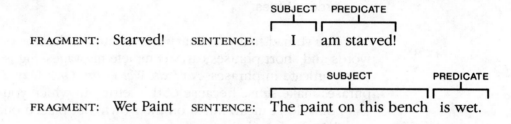

FRAGMENT: Starved!   SENTENCE: I am starved!

FRAGMENT: Wet Paint   SENTENCE: The paint on this bench is wet.

IDENTIFYING SUBJECT AND PREDICATE

By learning to identify the subject and predicate of a sentence, you'll be better able to avoid writing fragments that confuse your reader in the essay portion of the GED Test. You'll also need to be able to recognize and correct fragments for the multiple-choice section of the test.

Is the following word group a sentence or a fragment?

Sat at the kitchen table.

You're left with a question, aren't you? *Who* was sitting at the table? The word group is a fragment because the subject is missing. We can answer the question and create a complete sentence by adding a subject.

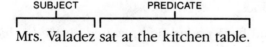

Mrs. Valadez sat at the kitchen table.

Let's take another example:

The man in the burgundy sports car.

Again, the word group raises a question: What about the man? This time the predicate is missing. We can complete the sentence by adding a statement about what the man is or what he does.

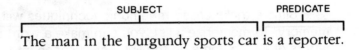

The man in the burgundy sports car is a reporter.

What question is raised by the following fragment?

At eight o'clock.

In this case a lot of information is missing. Who will do what at eight o'clock? In the space below, add some information to the phrase *at eight o'clock* to create a sentence.

———————————————————

You may have written a sentence like one of the examples below.

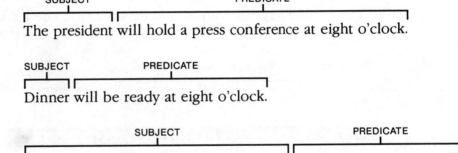

The president will hold a press conference at eight o'clock.

Dinner will be ready at eight o'clock.

A silver coach drawn by six white horses will arrive at eight o'clock.

Label the subject and predicate of your own sentence just as these examples have been marked.

CORRECTING FRAGMENTS IN A PARAGRAPH

Fragments (incomplete sentences) are fairly easy to identify and correct when they are examined alone. It's a greater challenge to find and fix them when they're within a passage.

Underline the fragments in the following paragraph.

Simple tricks called mnemonic techniques will improve your memory. To memorize a list, you can make a word using the first letters of all the items on the list. For instance, at the grocery store. The word BADGE can help you remember to buy butter, apples, dog food, grapes, and eggs. A fun technique.

You should have found two fragments: *For instance, at the grocery store* (*what happens* there?) and *A fun technique* (*what* is a fun technique?).

Now that you've identified the fragments, how can you eliminate them? The first fragment is easy to correct because it can be attached to the sentence that follows it:

For instance, at the grocery store, the word BADGE can help you remember . . .

The second fragment requires more work. You need to add words to create a subject and predicate:

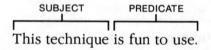

This technique is fun to use.

TWO WAYS TO CORRECT FRAGMENTS
1. Attach the fragment to the sentence before or after it.
2. Reword or add words to the fragment to make a subject and predicate.

EXERCISE 4

Directions: Study each group of words in Parts A, B, and C. If it is a sentence, punctuate it with the correct endmark. If it is a fragment, write F in the space provided.

Examples: Stacked firewood against the garage ___*F*___

You are very kind ___*!*___

Part A

1. Frantically hunted for his billfold _____

2. The teenager on the phone for hours _____

3. When will the next bus arrive _____

4. She washed the dishes _____

5. The greatest movie ever made _____

6. Pink and purple plaid _____

7. That man is choking _____

8. Caffeine is a stimulant _____

Part B

1. Do most Americans need to take vitamin pills _____ 2. Divided opinions _____

3. Some nutritional experts say that we can easily get all the vitamins we

need _____ 4. From a balanced diet _____ 5. Including several servings of bread and

cereals, fruits and vegetables, dairy products, and meat _____ 6. Others feel that

many Americans don't eat properly _____ 7. They skimp on vegetables _____

8. Substitute empty calories from junk food _____ 9. Candy, cookies, and soft

drinks _____ 10. Could both sides be correct _____

Part C

1. What mistakes are typical of beginning drivers _____ 2. One important error is

misjudging distances _____ 3. It takes practice for a driver to estimate correctly how

far his car is from the one beside him _____ 4. In the parking lot _____ 5. A related

error is misjudging braking distance _____ 6. Needs to learn how to slow down

smoothly _____ 7. For stop signs and traffic lights _____

ANSWERS ARE ON PAGE 343.

EXERCISE 5

Directions: Revise all the fragments in Exercise 4, Parts A, B, and C, to make complete sentences. In Parts B and C, rewrite the entire paragraph. You may be able to correct some fragments by attaching them to previous sentences. In other cases, you will need to add words to create a complete sentence. Remember to punctuate each sentence correctly. Does each paragraph make sense?

POSSIBLE ANSWERS ARE ON PAGE 343.

 FOCUS ON PUNCTUATION

Endmarks

Once you've written a complete sentence, be sure to punctuate it correctly. All sentences begin with a capital letter and end with an endmark. The punctuation used at the end of a sentence depends on the type of sentence.

A statement ends with a period.

> Alaska has a much harsher winter than Texas.

> Eating too much salt can lead to high blood pressure.

A question ends with a question mark.

> When will the next election be held?

> Are your taxes too high?

A command ends with a period. These sentences have *you* as the understood subject.

> Close the door quietly.

> Send in two boxtops and only fifty cents for your free magic ring.

An exclamation (a statement or instruction showing strong emotion) ends with an exclamation point.

> Call the fire department!

> Sandy's been hit by a car!

> How nice of you!

PARTS OF A SIMPLE SENTENCE

SIMPLE SUBJECTS AND VERBS

In this chapter, you'll be studying one kind of sentence, the simple sentence. You'll study other types of sentences later. A simple sentence has at least one subject and one predicate, as in the examples below. What do these three example sentences have in common?

The old man tripped over a skateboard on the sidewalk.
A well-dressed man tripped on his untied shoelaces.
The shy young man tripped over his girlfriend's doormat.

Although each sentence describes a different person and a different scene, the skeletons of the three sentences are identical. Reduced to bare-bones information, the sentences all read *man tripped*. The word *man*, from the subject part of the sentence, identifies whom the sentence is about. The word *tripped*, from the predicate, tells what the subject did. These two words are called the simple subject and the verb.

> The skeleton of a sentence is the simple subject and the verb. The **simple subject** is the key word in the subject of the sentence that tells whom or what the sentence is about, *minus* all descriptive words. The **verb** is the key word in the predicate that tells what the subject is or does, *minus* all descriptive words.

In the spaces provided, write the simple subjects and verbs of the following sentences. The first one is done for you.

<u>subject</u>   <u>predicate</u>

1. A truck loaded with cattle overturned on University Avenue.

    truck   *overturned*

2. Several confused cattle wandered through the backyards of local residents.

    _____   _____

3. The dogs in the neighborhood barked themselves hoarse.

    _____   _____

You should have written *cattle wandered* and *dogs barked*.

> **EDITING HINT:** If you're having trouble finding the simple subject and verb, locate the verb first by asking, "What's happening?" Once you've located the verb, find the subject by asking, "Who or what did it?" In sentence 1, for example, which word shows what's happening? *overturned* What overturned? *truck*

UNDERSTANDING VERBS

ACTION VERBS

As you now know, all simple sentences have a simple subject and a verb. So far, the simple sentences you have studied contain action verbs. **Action verbs** tell what kind of action the subject is performing. Examples of action verbs are *sing, run, giggle, hit*, and *buy*. In each of the following sentences, the verb is an action verb. Write the simple subject and verb in the spaces provided.

1. The lovers danced to the beat of the Purple Turtles.

_____   _____

2. My mother gave me her childhood books.

_____   _____

3. Wanda goes to work at the dog pound every day.

_____   _____

If you have any trouble finding the simple subjects and verbs, ask yourself, "What's happening?" to find the verb. Once you have found the verb, find the subject by asking, "Who or what did it?" You should have answered like this:

1. *lovers*   *danced*
2. *mother*   *gave*
3. *Wanda*   *goes*

LINKING VERBS

Although all the sample sentences you've looked at so far show action, many other sentences do not. They still contain subjects and verbs, but the verbs simply link the subjects to words that describe or rename the subjects.

Dr. Hernandez was the physician on duty last night.

The skeleton of this sentence is *Dr. Hernandez was*. The verb *was* links the subject, *Dr. Hernandez*, to the word *physician*.

Now try another example yourself. Write the subject and verb of the next sentence in the blanks.

He seemed pleased with your progress. _____   _____

He is the subject and *seemed* is the verb. The verb links *pleased* to *He*. Linking verbs are a little more difficult to spot than action verbs, so take time to learn the list in the box that follows.

COMMON LINKING VERBS

am, is, are, was, were, be, being, been,
seem, become

Then, in the spaces provided, write the simple subjects and verbs of the following sentences.

1. The boundary between the United States and Canada is the longest unguarded border in the world.

_____   _____

2. The two countries are strong allies.

_____   _____

3. Their citizens seem to have similar cultures.

_____   _____

Answers:

1. _____boundary_____   _____is_____
2. _____countries_____   _____are_____
3. _____citizens_____   _____seem_____

Use linking verbs to write three sentences about the state or province in which you live. Label the simple subject and verb in each sentence.

_____

_____

_____

⊙ FOCUS ON PUNCTUATION

Unnecessary Commas

Don't separate the subject from the verb of a simple sentence with a comma. As you write, you may recognize the boundary between subject and verb, but don't mark that boundary with a comma. If you read the sentence aloud, you'll discover that you don't pause between parts.

INCORRECT: A preschooler in torn blue overalls, was feeding mudpies to her teddy bear.

CORRECT: A preschooler in torn blue overalls was feeding mudpies to her teddy bear.

WORD ORDER

How are the sentences in column A different from those in column B?

Column A	**Column B**
You check the oil.	Check the oil.
My billfold was in my pocket.	Where was my billfold?
The money is in the billfold.	There is money in the billfold.

All the sentences in column A follow the normal pattern of word order in English: subject before verb. The sentences in column B illustrate three common exceptions to that pattern: commands, questions, and statements beginning with *Here* or *There*.

Commands

When we give commands, we frequently omit the subject of the sentence because it's understood that the subject is *you*. For example, *Sort the laundry* means *You sort the laundry*. The skeleton is *(You) Sort*.

Please lend me fifty cents.   SKELETON: (You) lend

Get out of my way.   SKELETON: (You) Get

Ilena, please tell Pedro I called.   SKELETON: (You) tell

Questions

In questions, all or part of the verb frequently appears before the subject. To write the skeleton of the sentence, put the subject first, as in the following examples.

Is he crazy?   SKELETON: he Is

Why are you so upset?   SKELETON: you are

Sometimes the verb consists of two or more words. In that case, part of the verb is placed before the subject and part is placed after it.

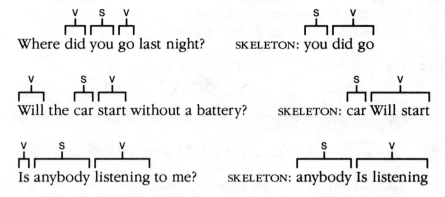

Write the skeleton of this question in the blanks:

Did you buy the groceries yet?

_____   _____

The subject is *you* and the verb is *Did buy*.

Here and *There*

When a sentence begins with *Here* or *There*, the subject follows the verb. To write the skeleton, put the subject first.

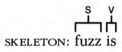

There is green fuzz on this month-old spaghetti.

SKELETON: fuzz is

Can you find the subject and verb in this sentence?

There are five people in the telephone booth.

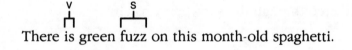

SKELETON: _____   _____

The subject is *people* and the verb is *are*.

EXERCISE 6

Directions: Write the simple subject and verb of each sentence in the spaces provided. Remember that sometimes the verb may be in two parts. Also remember that the implied subject of commands is the word *you*.

Examples: The evil empire attacked the planet Earth.

_____*empire*_____   _____*attacked*_____

When was the telephone invented?

_____*telephone*_____   _____*was invented*_____

There is a pebble in my shoe.

_____*pebble*_____   _____*is*_____

Turn left at the Laundromat.

_____*(you)*_____   _____*Turn*_____

1. This television program is boring.

_____   _____

2. The speeding truck hit a parked car.

_____   _____

3. A garter snake slithered through the strawberry patch.

_____   _____

4. Please leave immediately.

_____   _____

5. Here is today's newspaper.

_____   _____

6. Milk is an excellent source of calcium.

_____   _____

7. There were several bills in the mail.

_____   _____

8. The Statue of Liberty is a symbol of freedom.

_____   _____

ANSWERS ARE ON PAGE 344.

COMPOUNDING SIMPLE SENTENCES

WHAT IS COMPOUNDING?

> The engine sputtered. The engine died. Joan groaned. Joan got out of the car. Joan raised the hood. Her sister settled back for a long wait. Her brother settled back for a long wait.

Although the passage above is grammatically correct and consists of complete sentences, the repetition makes it deadly boring to read. What can be done to cut the wordiness and improve the quality of the writing? Let's experiment with combining ideas from some of these sentences. How might you connect the first two?

> The engine sputtered. The engine died.

Since the subject of both sentences is the same, *engine*, they can be combined by writing the subject once and connecting the simple predicates with *and*:

> The engine **sputtered and died**.

Now take the next three as a set.

> Joan groaned. Joan got out of the car. Joan raised the hood.

How can you make one sentence from the three? Again, the subject is repeated. You can write it once and connect the predicates:

> Joan **groaned, got out of the car, and raised the hood**.

The final pair of sentences have different subjects but identical predicates. What can you do to combine them?

> Her sister settled back for a long wait. Her brother settled back for a long wait.

This time connect the subjects and write the predicate once.

> **Her sister and brother** settled back for a long wait.

The simple process you've just seen is called compounding.

> *Compounding* is connecting two or more equally important sentence parts with a conjunction: *and, or, but*.

Compounding results in smoother writing, without choppy sentences or unnecessary repetition. Note how much smoother the revised passage sounds than the original:

> The engine sputtered and died. Joan groaned, got out of the car, and raised the hood. Her sister and brother settled back for a long wait.

Sometimes compounding requires changes in the wording of a sentence. What changes must be made when the sentences below are combined?

> John Lennon was a member of the Beatles. Paul McCartney was a member of the Beatles.
> John Lennon and Paul McCartney **were members** of the Beatles.

When these sentences are compounded, *was* must be changed to *were*, and *a member* must be changed to *members*. You'll learn more about these shifts in wording in Chapter 3 when you study subject-verb agreement. For the exercises in this chapter, we'll give you a clue whenever you need to change words.

◎ FOCUS ON PUNCTUATION

Compound Elements

If three or more compound elements are connected in a series, separate them with commas.

> The engine coughed, sputtered, and died.
> Kennedy, Johnson, and Nixon were all elected president during the 1960s.

If only two elements are connected, do not separate with commas.

> The engine coughed and sputtered.
> Kennedy and Johnson were both Democrats.

Never place a comma before or after the entire list of compound elements.

INCORRECT: Please send us, two dozen tulip bulbs, a trowel, and a bag of bone meal, immediately.

CORRECT: Please send us two dozen tulip bulbs, a trowel, and a bag of bone meal immediately.

EXERCISE 7

Part A

Directions: Combine the following sets of sentences by compounding. Use the conjunction given and make any other necessary changes in wording. Punctuate each sentence correctly.

Example: Jim rinsed the dirty dishes. Jim stacked the dirty dishes. *(and)*

Jim rinsed and stacked the dirty dishes.

1. Do you want scrambled eggs for breakfast? Do you want oatmeal for breakfast? Do you want grits for breakfast? *(or)*

2. Torrid romances are featured in soap operas. Fatal illnesses are featured in soap operas. *(and)*

3. Sam Abramowitz is studying to become a lawyer. Donna Tatum is studying to become a lawyer. *(and; is ⟶ are; a lawyer ⟶ lawyers)*

4. The batter swung blindly. The batter connected. The batter sprinted for first base. *(and)*

5. The food at Bob's Greasy Spoon is filling. The food at Bob's Greasy Spoon is tasteless. *(but)*

6. He printed his name at the top of the application form. He began to list his qualifications. *(and)*

Part B

Directions: Use compounding to answer the following questions. Make sure you write complete sentences.

Example: What three things might you buy with a million dollars?

I would buy a new house, a yacht, and a grand piano.

1. What are three things you enjoy doing on weekends?

2. What are two of your favorite television programs?

3. If you could visit any three countries in the world, where would you go?

4. Name two people who live near you.

5. What five subjects are covered on the GED Tests?

ANSWERS ARE ON PAGE 344.

NOUNS

WHAT ARE NOUNS?

Read the following paragraph, looking carefully at the words in bold type.

> **Denver, Colorado,** has much to offer **tourists. Attractions** like the **United States Mint,** the **State Capitol,** and excellent art and science **museums** can keep a **visitor** occupied for **days** in the **city** itself. In addition, **Denver's location** near the **foothills** of the **Rocky Mountains** offers **recreation** in a **skier's, hiker's,** and **photographer's paradise.** The **beauty** of this **area** is hard to forget.

What do the words in bold type in the paragraph above have in common? They are all nouns.

> *Nouns* are words that label people, places, things, or ideas.

PEOPLE: *tourists, visitor, skier's, hiker's, photographer's*
PLACES: *Denver, Colorado, United States Mint, State Capitol, museums, city, foothills, Rocky Mountains, paradise, location*
THINGS: *attractions, days, area*
IDEAS: *recreation, beauty*

Ideas, such as *courage, attraction, anger, unity,* and *freedom,* are sometimes hard to recognize as nouns.

Now read the next paragraph, noticing the words in bold type.

> **Misha** walked into the **office,** which was lit only by **streetlights** shining through the **windows.** This was his last **delivery.** As soon as he dropped off this **package,** he was going to go **home** and recover from a very long **day.** Suddenly **Misha's plans** were changed. He tripped over a **mound**—a **mound** that moaned. Just then his **hand** found the light **switch,** and he looked down to see a **man** sprawled on the **floor.** There was **blood** all over the **man's face.** He was breathing, but just barely. **Misha** was full of **fear,** but he tried to summon his **bravery.** He ran for the **phone** and called an **ambulance.** It was going to be a long **night** too.

PEOPLE:	*Misha, Misha's, man, man's, Misha*
PLACES:	*office, home, floor*
THINGS:	*streetlights, windows, delivery, package, day, plans, mound, mound, hand, switch, blood, face, phone, ambulance, night*
IDEAS:	*fear, bravery*

WHY STUDY NOUNS?

You've already seen one way in which knowledge of nouns is related to writing: nouns are used as the simple subjects of sentences. In Chapter 6 you'll be learning when to capitalize nouns. In this chapter, you will practice identifying nouns and then study these words for three purposes: to review the spelling of plurals, to learn how to show ownership with possessive nouns, and to introduce pronouns.

EXERCISE 8

Directions: Underline all the nouns in each sentence.

Example: Jim accidentally washed his red sweater with his white shirts.

1. Three plates, two mugs, a saucepan, and an empty vase were sitting in the sink.

2. His powerful left hook ended five consecutive fights before the fourth round.

3. The earthquake reduced large sections of Mexico City to rubble and killed thousands of people.

4. The boundary between the United States and Canada is the longest unfortified frontier in the world.

5. After watching an old western, that man swaggers like John Wayne.

6. Which team won the World Series five years ago?

7. Our society rarely honors the wisdom and courage of older Americans.

8. That chilly stare warned Suwardy that their marriage was in deep trouble.

9. Ace Manufacturing Company has announced plans to hire twenty new employees next month.

10. Parenthood requires infinite patience and hope.

11. The green vase was filled with roses and daisies.

12. There have been so many changes in countries around the world that mapmakers can barely keep up with them.

13. Monica felt frustration and anger when George was late for work again.

ANSWERS ARE ON PAGE 344.

PLURALS

Nouns have both singular (meaning *one*) and plural (meaning *more than one*) forms. When you write nouns, sometimes you want to tell your reader that you mean more than one of something. When you mean more than one of a noun, you use the plural form. Study the passage below, especially the nouns in bold type.

1   Most major **cities** in this country are battling pollution. **Cars**,
2 **trucks**, and **buses** emit **fumes** that foul the air. **Smokestacks** on
3 **factories** also contribute to the smog. On some bad **days**, **babies**
4 and **people** with respiratory **problems** are forced to stay inside
5 their **homes**.

6   But gray **skies** are only one part of the pollution problem.
7 Another is water contamination. Sewage, industrial **wastes**, and
8 agricultural **pesticides** are threatening our **rivers**, killing **fish**, and
9 endangering the **lives** of the **men**, **women**, and **children** who use
10 the **rivers** for drinking water. How can we clean up the **messes**
11 we've made?

All of the bold-type nouns in the above passage are plural; that is, they refer to more than one. How does the spelling of these plural nouns differ from the singular form? Fill in the blanks below with the correct plural form. Each plural is used in the passage above, so you can look up the correct spelling if you need to.

1. Most nouns are made plural by adding *s*.

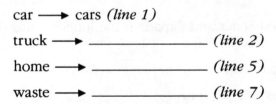

car ⟶ cars *(line 1)*

truck ⟶ _____ *(line 2)*

home ⟶ _____ *(line 5)*

waste ⟶ _____ *(line 7)*

2. Nouns ending in letters with a hissing sound (*s, sh, ch, x,* or *z*) are made plural by adding *es*. (Note that the *es* adds an extra syllable to the pronunciation of the word.)

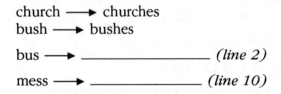

church ⟶ churches
bush ⟶ bushes

bus ⟶ _____ *(line 2)*

mess ⟶ _____ *(line 10)*

3. Nouns ending in *y* preceded by a vowel (*a, e, i, o, u*) are made plural by adding an *s.* Nouns ending in *y* preceded by a consonant (any letter except *a, e, i, o,* or *u*) are made plural by changing the *y* to *i* and adding *es.*

PRECEDED BY VOWEL:
boy ⟶ boys
turkey ⟶ turkeys

day ⟶ _____ *(line 3)*

PRECEDED BY CONSONANT:
thirty ⟶ thirties
country ⟶ countries

city ⟶ _____ *(line 1)*

sky ⟶ _____ *(line 6)*

4. Many nouns ending in *f* or *fe* are made plural by changing the *f* to *v* and adding *es.*

CHANGE:
loaf ⟶ loaves
thief ⟶ thieves
wife ⟶ wives

life ⟶ _____ *(line 9)*

NO CHANGE:
bluff ⟶ bluffs
staff ⟶ staffs
chief ⟶ chiefs

5. A few nouns do not change form when they are made plural.

deer ⟶ deer
sheep ⟶ sheep

fish ⟶ _____ *(line 8)*

6. A few nouns are made plural by changing the spelling.

foot ⟶ feet
man ⟶ men *(line 9)*

woman ⟶ _____ *(line 9)*

child ⟶ _____ *(line 9)*

person ⟶ _____ *(line 4)*

These are the most widely used rules for spelling the plural forms of nouns, but they don't cover every case. Whenever you're unsure of the correct spelling for a plural, check a dictionary. The correct plural form will be given with the definition of the singular form.

EXERCISE 9

Part A

Directions: Fill the blanks in the passage below with the correct plural forms of the nouns in parentheses. Check each one to see which of the rules on pages 52 and 53 applies to it.

Example: Most _____*nations*_____ (*nation*) couldn't survive one day without oil.

Industrialized _____ (*country*) depend on oil to fill several

_____ (*need*). For one thing, oil is used to heat many

_____ (*home*) and _____ (*business*). Without it our

_____ (*day*) and _____ (*night*) would be cold indeed.

Oil in some form is also used for fuel to power _____ (*car*),

_____ (*truck*), and machinery in _____ (*factory*).

Petroleum _____ (*product*) are even used in manufacturing synthetic

_____ (*fabric*) and plastic. Few _____ (*person*) would

argue that oil is not vital to our _____ (*life*).

Part B

Directions: The following passage contains eight errors in the spelling of plural nouns. Proofread for those errors and correct them as shown in the example.

Example: Both income and income ~~taxs~~ *taxes* have increased since 1900.

Peoples born in 1900 have witnessed incredible changes during their lifetimes.

Travelers between citys, once dependent on horse-drawn wagones, now speed down

smooth concrete highwaies in sleek motorized coachs. Instead of spending days on

the open sea, they jet thousands of miles between countries in a few hours. Lifes

that would once have been lost to bacterial diseases are now saved by antibiotics. In

fact, the average life span for both mens and womans has increased dramatically.

ANSWERS ARE ON PAGE 344.

POSSESSIVE NOUNS

In the English language, there are several ways to show ownership. The first way is to use a complete sentence:

The farmer has a tractor.

The second way is to use a phrase beginning with *of*:

the tractor of the farmer

The third way is to use a possessive noun:

the farmer's tractor

Although all three ways are grammatically correct, the first two sometimes lead to awkward sentences. Compare the three options below.

The farmer has a tractor. The tractor overturned.
The tractor of the farmer overturned.
The farmer's tractor overturned.

All three contain the same information, and all are correct. The third, the one using a possessive noun, is most economical.

◉ FOCUS ON PUNCTUATION

Apostrophes in Possessive Nouns

Possessive nouns require careful placement of the apostrophe.

1. If the possessive noun is singular, add an apostrophe + s (*'s*).

a child's toy *(A child has a toy.)*
Charles's house *(Charles has a house.)*

2. If the possessive noun is plural and the plural already ends in *s*, just add an apostrophe.

the Browns' apartment *(The Browns have an apartment.)*
the ladies' room *(The ladies have a room.)*

3. If the possessive noun is plural and the plural does not end in *s*, add an apostrophe + *s*.

the children's toys *(The children have toys.)*
three deer's hoofprints *(Three deer had hoofprints.)*

Add *'s* to all singular nouns and to plural nouns that do not end in *s*.

Add *'* to plural nouns that end in *s*.

> **EDITING HINT:** To decide if a possessive noun is singular or plural, read the whole sentence for clues.
>
> > After the *(door's, doors')* hinges were oiled, they opened more quietly.
>
> The word *they* indicates that at least two doors were oiled, so the correct punctuation is *doors'*.
>
> > The librarian repaired the *(book's, books')* binding and then put it back on the shelf.
>
> The word *it* shows that only one book was repaired, so the correct punctuation is *book's*.

EXERCISE 10

Part A

Directions: Rewrite each pair of sentences, using a possessive noun. Be sure to place the apostrophe correctly.

Example: John has a hat. The hat is green with orange stripes.

John's hat is green with orange stripes.

1. The boy has a friend. The friend moved away.

2. James has a friend. The friend moved away.

3. The boys have a friend. The friend moved away.

4. The ladies have hats. The hats are on sale.

5. The firefighters have helmets. The helmets are worn for protection.

6. Hakkim has a dog. The dog is a collie.

7. In Alaska, there are moose. Their food supply ran short last winter.

8. The players have a mascot. The mascot is a chicken.

Part B

Directions: Insert apostrophes wherever they belong in the following sentences. Remember, not all nouns ending in *s* are possessive.

1. My dogs favorite ball was out of reach behind her house.

2. In the last two seconds, the teams final chance to score appeared.

3. Chicagos skyscrapers now rival New York Citys skyline.

4. Mens coats and womens sweaters are on sale this weekend only.

5. The girls argument ended when their mothers called them for supper.

6. Lawyers and doctors fees have skyrocketed in recent years.

7. Carolines last letter arrived only yesterday.

8. The newspapers headline this morning read "Plane Crash Kills 257."

Part C

Directions: Rewrite these questions by changing the words in bold type to possessive nouns.

Example: Which stalls for **horses** have been cleaned?

Which horses' stalls have been cleaned?

1. What clothing for **men** or **women** has been on sale recently?

2. Are fees charged by **doctors** in your local clinic reasonable?

3. What do you think is the biggest problem in this **country**?

4. In your opinion, who is the greatest athlete in the **world** right now?

5. What is the major tourist attraction of your **region**?

6. What do you think is the best musical group in **America?**

7. Which of the job listings in the **newspaper** do you read?

8. In your opinion, what is the best restaurant in your **town**?

ANSWERS ARE ON PAGE 344.

PRONOUNS

WHAT IS A PRONOUN?

Imagine a language that required you to refer to a person, place, or thing by name every time. You would encounter passages like this:

> For John and Sarah, the most relaxing part of John and Sarah's vacation was spent at Leech Lake. Leech Lake is a large lake in northern Minnesota. John and Sarah stayed a week on the lake, exploring Leech Lake's reedy inlets, losing John and Sarah in the surrounding forests, and fishing from a small motorboat. John and Sarah had rented the motorboat from the owners of the cabin where John and Sarah were staying. "John would like to stay twice as long next year!" exclaimed John as John and Sarah were driving home.

Repetitious? Extremely. Boring? Definitely! Our language is saved from such dull speaking and writing by a small class of words called pronouns. Let's try the same passage with pronouns inserted in appropriate places. Each word in bold type is a pronoun.

> 1   For John and Sarah, the most relaxing part of **their** vacation
> 2   was spent at Leech Lake, **which** is a large lake in northern
> 3   Minnesota. **They** stayed a week on the lake, exploring **its** reedy
> 4   inlets, losing **themselves** in the surrounding forests, and fishing
> 5   from the small motorboat **that they** had rented from the owners of
> 6   the cabin where **they** were staying. "**I** would like to stay twice as
> 7   long next year!" exclaimed John as **they** were driving home.

> A **_pronoun_** is a word that replaces and refers to a noun. The noun that a pronoun refers to is called its **_antecedent_**.

Look at the first sentence of the passage again and draw an arrow from each pronoun in bold type to its antecedent.

> For John and Sarah, the most relaxing part of **their** vacation was spent at Leech Lake, **which** is a large lake in northern Minnesota.

Did you mark *John and Sarah* as the antecedent of *their*? *Their* replaces and refers to *John and Sarah* so that the names don't have to be repeated in the sentence. You should have marked *Leech Lake* as the antecedent of *which*. Once again, the pronoun is used so that the name *Leech Lake* doesn't have to be repeated.

EXERCISE 11

Directions: Identify the rest of the antecedents for the pronouns in the passage. Ask yourself whom or what each pronoun refers to; then write the antecedent in the right column. The first two have been done for you.

Pronoun	Antecedents
1. their *(line 1)*	*John and Sarah*
2. which *(line 2)*	*Leech Lake*
3. They *(line 3)*	
4. its *(line 3)*	
5. themselves *(line 4)*	
6. that *(line 5)*	
7. they *(line 5)*	
8. they *(line 6)*	
9. I *(line 6)*	
10. they *(line 7)*	

ANSWERS ARE ON PAGE 345.

PRONOUN FORMS

Like nouns, pronouns refer to people, places, things, and ideas. Unlike nouns, however, some pronouns, called ***personal pronouns***, change form depending on their use in a sentence. The forms are subject, object, and possessive. The way the pronoun is used in the sentence determines the form.

NOUN AS SUBJECT:	**The man** grasped my hand firmly.
PRONOUN AS SUBJECT:	**He** grasped my hand firmly.
NOUN AS OBJECT:	I thanked **the man** for helping me.
PRONOUN AS OBJECT:	I thanked **him** for helping me.
POSSESSIVE NOUN:	**The man's** voice silenced the crowd.
POSSESSIVE PRONOUN:	**His** voice silenced the crowd.

The following chart shows how personal pronouns change in form depending on their use in a sentence.

		Possessive	
Subject	*Object*	*1*	*2*
I	me	my	mine
you	you	your	yours
he	him	his	his
she	her	her	hers
it	it	its	—
we	us	our	ours
they	them	their	theirs
who	whom	whose	whose

Any pronoun from the subject list (except *who*) will fit into this sentence:

_____ felt strange.

In the sentence above, the subject pronouns act as subject of the sentence and subject of the verb *felt*.

Any pronoun from the object list (except *whom*) will fill the blank in the following sentence:

Someone finally gave _____ some food.

In the sentence above, the object pronouns fit because they are not the subject of a verb.

Possessive pronouns from column 1 (except *whose*) will fit in this sentence because they need a word following them to show what is owned:

That's _____ house.

Possessive pronouns from column 2 (except *whose*) will fit here because they can stand alone:

The house is _____.

For practice, read the sentences aloud, substituting each pronoun in turn.

SUBJECT OR OBJECT?

It's pretty easy to tell when you need to use a possessive pronoun. You use a possessive pronoun when you want to show ownership, or possession. But sometimes you may not be sure whether to use a subject pronoun or an object pronoun.

> **EDITING HINT:** If you are not sure whether to use a subject pronoun or an object pronoun, use this test:
>
> Is the pronoun the subject of the sentence—the person, place, or thing the sentence is about? If it is, you must use a subject pronoun. If it is not the subject and is not possessive, you must use an object pronoun.
>
> Sue's mother told *(she, her)* the news.
>
> Will the pronoun be the subject of a verb? No. The only verb in the sentence is *told*, and the subject of *told* is *mother*. The correct answer is the object pronoun *her*.
>
> *(He, Him)* is the killer.
>
> Will the pronoun be the subject of a verb? Yes. The only verb in the sentence is *is*, and the pronoun is the subject. The correct answer is the subject pronoun *He*.

EXERCISE 12

Directions: Replace the portion of each sentence in bold type with the correct pronoun. Check carefully to see whether you should choose a subject, object, or possessive pronoun.

Example: John, did ~~John~~ *you* watch *Frankenstein at the Beach Party* last night?

1. **Christine** is a lawyer and a power weightlifting champion.

2. The Russian leaders challenged **President Kennedy** by sending missiles to Cuba.

3. Chun insisted, "**Chun's** favorite vegetables really are rutabagas."

4. Dick assembled the scooter within an hour after buying **the scooter**.

5. **The senators** voted on an important appropriations bill yesterday.

6. What gave **the senators** the idea the voters would support **the senators'** action?

7. My friends, please give me **my friends'** trust.

8. Together, **you and I** can make our nation truly great.

9. Why do weddings make **that woman** sad?

10. Please give **my partner and me** a second chance.

ANSWERS ARE ON PAGE 345.

PRONOUNS IN COMPOUND ELEMENTS

Pronouns used in compound elements sometimes cause problems for writers. For instance, should you say "Maria gave John and **me** some pretzels" or "Maria gave John and **I** some pretzels?" You can answer that question with confidence by doing a simple test: Cross out *John and* and then decide what you would say if you used the pronoun alone.

Maria gave ~~John and~~ me some pretzels.
Maria gave ~~John and~~ I some pretzels.

Maria gave John and me some pretzels is correct. You need an object pronoun for this sentence. The only verb in the sentence is *gave*, and the subject that goes with it is *Maria*.

Try another example:

(He, Him) and *(I, me)* went to a great movie last night.
He went to a great movie. . . .
Him went to a great movie. . . .
I went to a great movie. . . .
me went to a great movie. . . .

Which choices are correct? *He and I* went to a great movie last night. These pronouns act as the subject of the sentence.

When the pronouns *I* and *me* appear in compound structures, they should be placed last. **He and I** (not *I and he*) went to that movie. The invitation was for **John and me** (not *me and John*).

EXERCISE 13

Directions: Write the correct pronoun in each blank in the sentences below.

1. Keep an eye on Young-Soo and _____ *(she, her)* until we get back.

2. Bob and _____ *(I, me)* plan to be married next month.

3. Please let your father and _____ *(I, me)* know when you plan to be home.

4. If the Kowalskis and _____ *(we, us)* will be more than fifteen minutes late, we'll call you.

5. Where did Jessica and _____ *(she, her)* go after work yesterday?

6. The flu hit _____ *(he, him)* and _____ *(I, me)* even harder than it struck Sue.

7. _____ *(They, Them)* and their cousins will hold a family reunion next month.

8. When _____ *(he, him)* and Scott passed each other at the grocery store, I thought they would at least speak.

9. The lottery winnings gave _____ *(they, them)* and their children a secure income for twenty years.

10. They met the Johnsons and _____ *(we, us)* at the union hall.

ANSWERS ARE ON PAGE 345.

◎ FOCUS ON PUNCTUATION

Possessive Pronouns and Contractions

Like possessive nouns, possessive pronouns show ownership. Unlike possessive nouns, possessive pronouns use no apostrophes. The following examples all show possession, but none contains an apostrophe.

> For two hours, our cat never took **its** eyes off the parakeet.
>
> I believe this orange sock is **yours**.
>
> The house is **theirs**, but the land it stands on is **mine**.
>
> If they ever split up, the stereo is **hers** but the amplifiers are **his**.
>
> Not every neighborhood is as noisy as **ours**.

This rule—no apostrophe in possessive pronouns—should help you decide how to choose between these pronouns and the contractions that sound just like them, such as *its* and *it's*. Don't confuse the word pairs shown in the following box.

Possessive Pronouns	*Contractions*
its	it's (it is, it has)
theirs	there's (there is, there are)
your, yours	you're (you are)
whose	who's (who is, who has)

Its eyes were black. *(possessive)*
It's been a long time. *(contraction)*

The house is **theirs**. *(possessive)*
There's nothing unusual about Ermentrude. *(contraction)*

Here is **your** house. *(possessive)*
You're getting bored, aren't you? *(contraction)*

Whose book is this? *(possessive)*
Who's been sleeping in my bed? *(contraction)*

> **EDITING HINT:** To decide whether to use a possessive pronoun or a contraction, just try substituting the two words that the contraction stands for.
>
> **Exactly what do you think** *(your, you're)* **doing?**
>
> Substitute *you are*: *Exactly what do you think* **you are** *doing?* The sentence makes sense. Therefore, choose the contraction *you're*.
>
> *(Your, You're)* car is in flames!
>
> Substitute *you are*: **You are** *car is in flames!* The sentence makes no sense. Therefore, choose the possessive pronoun *your*.

EXERCISE 14

Directions: Choose the correct word to fill each blank. Use the editing hint above to help you decide whether to choose the possessive pronoun or the contraction.

1. _____ *(Its, It's)* past time for our coffee break.

2. _____ *(Whose, Who's)* hiding behind the door?

3. _____ Although you spent *(your, you're)* childhood here,

   _____ *(your, you're)* not going to believe the changes.

4. The choice is _____ *(theirs, there's)*.

5. America gets _____ *(its, it's)* name from the explorer Amerigo Vespucci.

6. The zoning commission presented _____ *(it's, its)* report to the city council.

7. Is _____ *(your, you're)* guess really as good as mine?

8. _____ *(Whose, Who's)* name is first on the list?

9. _____ *(Whose, Who's)* been stealing the chocolate chips from these cookies?

10. _____ *(Theirs, There's)* a stranger in the room; he's neither my

    friend nor _____ *(theirs, there's)*.

ANSWERS ARE ON PAGE 345.

EDITING PRACTICE

Part A

Directions: The following passage contains ten errors. Find and correct these errors, using this checklist as your editing guide.

☐ Are all sentences complete, or are there fragments?

☐ Do sentences end with a period, a question mark, or an exclamation point?

☐ Do any unnecessary commas separate the subject from the predicate?

☐ Are commas used correctly in compound elements?

☐ Are subject and object pronouns used correctly in compound elements?

☐ Are apostrophes used correctly?

☐ Are plural nouns spelled correctly?

Janets bedroom, looks as though it's just been struck by a tornado. Blouses sweaters, socks, and jeans form a crazy quilt pattern on the floor A solid three-inch layer of old newspapers, and magazines covers her desk. Half-empty pop cans and candy bar wrapperes surround the overflowing wastebasket in the corner. Unmade bed. Peeping out from under it are the moldy remains of a large pepperoni pizza that her and her best friend shared. Two weeks ago. Never in my life have I seen a room as messy as her's!

ANSWERS ARE ON PAGE 346.

Part B

Directions: Using the checklist from Part A, proofread and correct the passage that you wrote in Exercise 3 on page 32.

ANSWERS WILL VARY.

CHAPTER HIGHLIGHTS: SENTENCE BASICS

1. A sentence has a subject and a predicate and expresses a complete thought.

2. A simple sentence contains at least one subject and one predicate and expresses only one complete thought.

3. Action verbs tell what the subject is doing. Linking verbs connect the subject to words that describe or rename it.

4. Compounding is connecting two or more equally important sentence parts with a conjunction: *and, or, but.*

5. Nouns are words that label people, places, things, or ideas. Nouns can be singular or plural. Possessive nouns show ownership.

6. A pronoun is a word that replaces and refers to a noun.

≡ GED Practice ≡
SENTENCE BASICS REVIEW

Choose the best answer to each question.

1. **Concrete blockes, old tires, branches, and leaves had been dumped in the vacant lot.**

   What correction should be made to this sentence?

   (1) change *blockes* to *blocks*
   (2) change *branches* to *branchs*
   (3) change *leaves* to *leafs*
   (4) insert a comma after *leaves*
   (5) no correction is necessary

2. **Dictionaries, encyclopedias, and reference manuals, are located behind the head librarian's desk.**

   What correction should be made to this sentence?

   (1) remove the comma after *Dictionaries*
   (2) remove the comma after *manuals*
   (3) insert a comma after *located*
   (4) change *librarian's* to *librarians*
   (5) no correction is necessary

3. **It's difficult to determine whether the accident was the drivers fault or the pedestrian's.**

   What correction should be made to this sentence?

   (1) change *It's* to *Its*
   (2) insert a comma after *determine*
   (3) change *drivers* to *driver's*
   (4) insert a comma after *fault*
   (5) change *pedestrian's* to *pedestrians*

4. **After supper last <u>night, John and me</u> drove along the lakefront.**

   Which of the following is the best way to write the underlined portion of this sentence? If you think the original is the best way, choose option (1).

   (1) night, John and me
   (2) night. John and me
   (3) night, John and I
   (4) night. John and I
   (5) night me and John

5. **There's a world of difference between Harold's sloppy work and your careful attention to detail.**

   What correction should be made to this sentence?

   (1) change *There's* to *Theirs*
   (2) insert a comma after *between*
   (3) change *Harold's* to *Harolds*
   (4) change *your* to *you're*
   (5) no correction is necessary

6. **Did you mislay <u>your glasses? Or</u> lose them entirely?**

   Which of the following is the best way to write the underlined portion of these sentences? If you think the original is the best way, choose option (1).

   (1) your glasses? Or
   (2) you're glasses? Or
   (3) your glasses, or
   (4) you're glasses, or
   (5) your glasses or

7. **You're going to be surprised both by the monster's size and by it's incredible ugliness.**

   What correction should be made to this sentence?

   (1) change *You're* to *Your*
   (2) change *monster's* to *monsters*
   (3) insert a comma after *size*
   (4) change *it's* to *its*
   (5) no correction is necessary

8. **Antique collectors may specialize in old campaign buttons, dolls kitchen utensils, or pottery.**

   What correction should be made to this sentence?

   (1) insert a comma after *in*
   (2) remove the comma after *buttons*
   (3) insert a comma after *dolls*
   (4) change *utensils* to *utensil's*
   (5) no correction is necessary

9. **<u>Toxic industrial wastes in</u> our water supply.**

   Which of the following is the best way to write the underlined portion of this sentence? If you think the original is the best way, choose option (1).

   (1) Toxic industrial wastes in
   (2) Finding toxic industrial wastes in
   (3) Toxic industrial wastes, in
   (4) Toxic industrial wastes are contaminating
   (5) Caused by toxic industrial wastes in

Questions 10–17 refer to the following paragraph.

(1) You and me may picture the typical American family as a father, a mother, and their children. (2) An increasingly inaccurate picture. (3) More and more families with children, are headed by single parents. (4) Creating some problems. (5) In most cases the single parents are women. (6) Due to welfare cuts, pay inequitys, and some women's limited job skills, many families headed by females are living in poverty. (7) Father-headed households experience their own set of problems. (8) Although men's salaries are typically higher than womens, men are often less experienced at daily homemaking tasks like cooking, cleaning, and mending. (9) Regardless of whether the single parent is a man or a woman, theirs no doubt that the children are affected. (10) For a year or more after their parents' divorce, they may experience adjustment problems, including academic difficulties, bedwetting, and fighting.

10. Sentence 1: **You and me may picture the typical American family as a father, a mother, and their children.**

What correction should be made to this sentence?

(1) change *me* to *I*
(2) insert a comma after *as*
(3) remove the comma after *father*
(4) replace *You and me* with *Me and you*
(5) no correction is necessary

11. Sentence 2: **An increasingly inaccurate picture.**

Which of the following is the best way to write the underlined portion of this sentence? If you think the original is the best way, choose option (1).

(1) An increasingly inaccurate picture.
(2) A picture increasingly inaccurate.
(3) That picture increasingly inaccurate.
(4) That picture is increasingly inaccurate.
(5) Is increasingly inaccurate.

12. Sentence 3: **More and more families with children, are headed by single parents.**

What correction should be made to this sentence?

(1) insert a comma after *More*
(2) change *families* to *families'*
(3) remove the comma after *children*
(4) change *parents* to *parents'*
(5) no correction is necessary

13. Sentence 4: **Creating some problems.**

Which of the following is the best way to write the underlined portion of this sentence? If you think the original is the best way, choose option (1).

(1) Creating some
(2) As a result creating some
(3) Is creating some
(4) A family pattern with significant and complex
(5) This new family pattern is creating some

14. Sentence 6: **Due to welfare cuts, pay inequitys, and some women's limited job skills, many families headed by females are living in poverty.**

What correction should be made to this sentence?

(1) change *inequitys* to *inequities*
(2) change *women's* to *womens*
(3) change *families* to *family's*
(4) insert a comma after *females*
(5) no correction is necessary

15. Sentence 8: **Although men's salaries are typically higher than womens, men are often less experienced at daily homemaking tasks like cooking, cleaning, and mending.**

What correction should be made to this sentence?

(1) change *men's* to *mens*
(2) change *womens* to *women's*
(3) replace *tasks like* with *tasks. Like*
(4) remove the comma after *cooking*
(5) no correction is necessary

16. Sentence 9: **Regardless of whether the single parent is a man or a woman, theirs no doubt that the children are affected.**

What correction should be made to this sentence?

(1) insert a comma after *is*
(2) change *theirs* to *there's*
(3) insert a comma after *children*
(4) insert a comma after *man*
(5) no correction is necessary

17. Sentence 10: **For a year or more after their parents' divorce, they may experience adjustment problems, including academic difficulties, bedwetting, and fighting.**

Which of the following is the best way to write the underlined portion of this sentence? If you think the original is the best way, choose option (1).

(1) problems, including academic difficulties, bedwetting, and fighting.
(2) problem's, including academic difficulties, bedwetting, and fighting.
(3) problems. Including academic difficulties, bedwetting, and fighting.
(4) problems, including, academic difficulties, bedwetting, and fighting.
(5) problems, including academic difficulties bedwetting and fighting.

ANSWERS ARE ON PAGE 346.

A paragraph is a set of related sentences that develop a central point. The first sentence is the topic sentence, which states the central point that the author wants to make in the paragraph. Supporting sentences come after the topic sentence and expand on the central point by adding relevant information.

Writing Paragraphs

In the section of Chapter 2 on planning a paragraph, you practiced organizing a list of details before writing a draft. You decided which details should be grouped and in what order they should appear. As you wrote the draft, how did you group the sentences that belonged together?

In written English, the signal for grouped ideas is the paragraph.

> A *paragraph* is a set of related sentences that develop a central point or main idea.

You show the beginning of a paragraph by indenting its first line a few spaces, giving your reader a visual signal that the group of sentences develops a central point. Look at the two sets of sentences that follow. Although both have the general shape of a paragraph—several sentences together with the first line indented—only one fits the definition of a paragraph as **a set of related sentences that develop a central point**. Can you find it?

> Motorists in the Snow Belt should always carry sand and a shovel during winter months. Driving on icy roads requires special techniques like pumping the brakes lightly to slow down and always steering into a spin. Wind-whipped snow blown across flat fields can reduce visibility tremendously. When the sun finally reemerges after the storm, ice-coated bushes and trees create a glittering wonderland.

> From November through March, if you're planning highway travel in the Snow Belt, don't leave home without a blizzard kit in the trunk. Always carry a warm blanket, hooded jacket, snow boots, ski mask, and mittens to help conserve body heat if you're stranded in a ditch for several hours. In addition, take along some easily stored foods like peanut butter, crackers, and dried fruit. With luck, a shovel for digging out of snowdrifts and a bucket of sand for traction on ice will allow you to resume your travels soon. If not, an orange plastic pennant to attach to your aerial will signal for help.

Could you find any connections among the sentences in the first group? The sentences are somewhat related: all refer to winter driving. But do they develop a central point about it? No. Each sentence discusses a different aspect of the experience. The second group, on the other hand, does qualify as a genuine paragraph. Not only do all the sentences refer to winter driving, but they also develop the central point that a traveler should carry a blizzard kit.

PARTS OF A PARAGRAPH

TOPIC SENTENCES

The first sentence of the second group is the topic sentence of the paragraph:

> From November through March, if you're planning highway travel in the Snow Belt, don't leave home without a blizzard kit in the trunk.

> A **topic sentence** clearly states the topic of the paragraph and the central point that the author is making about that topic.

All of the other sentences provide specific details to support the point. The topic sentence is the sentence, then, that unifies the entire paragraph.

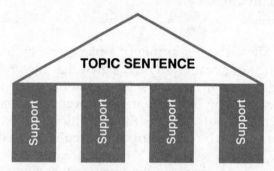

Think of a paragraph as a building. The topic sentence is the roof that covers the rest of the material in the paragraph. The supporting sentences are like columns that support the roof. It's no coincidence that the topic sentence of the paragraph on page 71 is the first sentence. Although it may appear anywhere in a paragraph, the topic sentence most frequently occurs at the beginning, so the reader can tell right away what the entire paragraph will be about.

To be effective, a topic sentence must pass two tests. First, is it a complete sentence? A fragment like *Winter driving* or *What to put in a blizzard pack* might work as a title for the paragraph. However, a topic sentence must express a complete thought. Second, does it tell the reader the central point of the paragraph? The topic sentence *From November through March, if you're planning highway travel in the Snow Belt, don't leave home without a blizzard kit in the trunk* tells the reader what the paragraph is about—what point the writer wants to make. On the other hand, the other sentences, like "In addition, take along some easily stored foods like peanut butter, crackers, and dried fruit," have a different purpose. They expand on the topic sentence, giving the reader more details and explanation.

TESTS FOR A GOOD TOPIC SENTENCE

1. Is it a complete sentence?

2. Does it tell the reader the central point of the paragraph?

EXERCISE 1

Directions: Make each group of supporting sentences below into a complete paragraph by adding a topic sentence on the blank line. Make sure your topic sentence states the central point of the paragraph and is a complete sentence.

Here are some hints to help you develop a good topic sentence:

☐ Read through the supporting sentences.

☐ Get a general idea of what the writer is discussing.

☐ Write a sentence that summarizes the writer's main point.

Example: _Will is slacking off on the job._ Every morning Will walks into the office a half hour late. He uses work time to phone his current girlfriend. Will's lunch hours and coffee breaks last twice as long as everyone else's. He often slips away from work ten to fifteen minutes before closing time.

1. _____

_____

Some of the money from the property tax increase would be used to give police officers and firefighters a cost-of-living wage increase. New books could be added to the public library. Ten more miles of city streets could be paved. A summer employment program for teenagers could be expanded.

2. _____

_____

Situps firm stomach muscles. Leg lifts tone thighs and hips. Pushups build arm strength. Running in place strengthens legs.

3. _____

_____

Sharon consistently tailgates the car in front of her. She runs red lights, narrowly missing other cars or pedestrians in the intersection. Sharon drives at least fifteen miles an hour above the posted speed limit. She challenges other drivers to race her.

4. _____

_____

For breakfast Thomas Grosso eats three fried eggs, ten slices of bacon, and half a loaf of bread. For lunch the man downs two large pizzas and a quart of cola. Midafternoon finds him snacking on a dozen chocolate chip cookies and a gallon of ice cream. Mr. Grosso's evening meal consists of five thick pork chops, a plateful of mashed potatoes, and a chocolate cake for dessert.

POSSIBLE ANSWERS ARE ON PAGE 346.

SUPPORTING SENTENCES

The following paragraph has a strong topic sentence that makes a clear point. How effective is the paragraph as a whole?

Mayor Campos cares about the people of this city. She is divorced and has two children. Her reelection campaign committee raised more than five thousand dollars in donations from private businesses. Twice a week she eats lunch with the elderly people in the group meals program to find out about their concerns.

Do you find the paragraph convincing? There's something wrong, isn't there? The topic sentence makes the point that the mayor cares about the people. But some of the other sentences don't seem to belong to the same central idea. Let's look at these supporting sentences to see what's wrong.

She is divorced and has two children.
Her reelection campaign committee raised more than five thousand dollars in donations from private businesses.

These sentences are certainly specific, but how are her personal life or campaign donations related to the point that the mayor cares about the people? These sentences are not relevant at all. Information that's not relevant to the main point of the paragraph can confuse your reader.

What about the last sentence?

Twice a week she eats lunch with the elderly people in the group meals program to find out about their concerns.

This sentence presents some solid support. It describes a specific activity of the mayor that shows she cares about elderly people in the community. Can you see that this sentence supports the writer's main point while the previous two sentences don't? Now the writer is on the right track. But is this one sentence enough to prove that the topic sentence is true? To make this into a good paragraph, the writer should add some more relevant support.

A good paragraph requires both a clear topic sentence and strong support. To test the quality of the support in a paragraph, ask these questions: Are the supporting sentences relevant? Do they actually help to prove that the topic sentence is true? Is there an adequate amount of support? One supporting sentence is rarely enough to prove a point. Usually you need at least three supporting sentences to really illustrate a point. If you aren't sure you have enough support, put yourself in the place of your reader. Will the reader understand what you have to say? Will your reader be convinced by your paragraph?

The supporting sentences in the following version of the paragraph about Mayor Campos pass these tests. What new ideas did the writer add? Do you find the revised paragraph convincing?

> Mayor Campos cares about the people of this city. Twice a week she eats lunch with the elderly people in the group meals program to find out about their concerns. When the parts plant shut down last year, she immediately set up meetings to inform the laid-off workers about government assistance programs and training opportunities for new jobs. She cares about young people, too. Under her leadership the city has opened fifty new summer jobs for teenagers, and preschool programs have been added in every community center.

TESTS FOR SUPPORTING SENTENCES

1. Are they relevant?

2. Is there an adequate amount of support to prove your point?

EXERCISE 2

Directions: Each topic sentence is followed by a list of items. Cross out the item in each list that is irrelevant to the topic sentence. Then add two more details.

Example: Junk foods are common in Americans' diets.

  a. sugary breakfast cereals
  ~~**b.** poultry and fish~~
  c. soft drinks
  d. *candy bars*
  e. *greasy french fries*

1. Many retail stores take advantage of holidays to boost sales.

  a. picnic supplies promoted before the Fourth of July
  b. Halloween candy displays in grocery stores
  c. preinventory clearance sales
  d.
  e.

2. Spelling in English is made difficult by pairs of words that sound alike but have different spellings and meanings.

  a. smart-intelligent
  b. too-to
  c. pair-pear
  d.
  e.

3. American cooking is enriched by traditional foods from many other countries.

    a. sausages—Germany
    b. chow mein—China
    c. sweet corn—Iowa
    d.
    e.

4. Television commercials are aimed specifically at the audience of the programs they sponsor.

    a. children's cartoons—breakfast foods and toys
    b. cable television—monthly fee
    c. morning game shows—denture cleansers
    d.
    e.

5. Examine a used car carefully before buying it.

    a. check number of miles on odometer
    b. may buy from used-car lot, new-car dealer, or private owner
    c. check whether tread on tires is good
    d.
    e.

POSSIBLE ANSWERS ARE ON PAGE 346.

EXERCISE 3

Directions: The following two writing assignments will allow you to combine the planning skills you learned in Chapter 2 with the paragraph-writing skills you have learned in this chapter: constructing a clear topic sentence and supporting it with specific details. Be sure to plan each paragraph before you write:

☐ Think about what you're writing about and who will be reading it. Be sure you understand the topic given before you write.

☐ Brainstorm ideas you could include in your paragraph. (You might want to reread the section on brainstorming on page 30 at this point.)

☐ Decide which ideas on your brainstormed list you will use in your paragraph, and number them in the order you plan to write them.

Paragraph 1

    Some newspapers give a "Neighbor of the Week" award based on information provided by readers. Write a one-paragraph letter to your local paper nominating someone whom you know and respect for that award. In your topic sentence, identify the person and the quality you admire. In the supporting sentences, provide specific examples of that person's actions to prove your point.

Paragraph 2

Write a one-paragraph letter to the editor of your newspaper about a problem in your community. Identify the problem in the topic sentence and use the supporting sentences to provide several examples of the problem.

Revising Your Paragraphs

You may find you want to make some changes in your paragraphs now that you have written them. First make any changes you now know you want to make. Then check your paragraphs against this checklist and make any further revisions that would improve your writing.

☐ Is there a topic sentence?

☐ Does the topic sentence state the central point of the paragraph?

☐ Do all the other sentences support the point that it makes?

Publishing Your Paragraphs

If you want, give your paragraphs to a classmate or a friend to read.

POSSIBLE ANSWERS ARE ON PAGE 346.

POSSIBLE ANSWERS ARE ON PAGE 346.

CHAPTER HIGHLIGHTS: WRITING PARAGRAPHS

1. A paragraph is a set of related sentences that develop a central point.

2. The topic sentence states the subject of the paragraph and the author's point about that subject. It must also be a complete sentence.

3. The supporting sentences provide evidence to prove or explain the topic sentence. Supporting sentences should be relevant, and they should provide enough support to prove the writer's point.

Look carefully at the verbs in bold type in this paragraph.

> Once again the Southtown Sluggers **are** in the softball finals. Last night in the semifinal round they **played** the Midcity Maulers and easily **beat** them 10–3. Next Tuesday they **will play** their archrivals, the Westside Wasters, for this year's city championship.

In Chapter 2, you learned that, to be complete, every sentence needs a verb to tell what the subject is or does. In this chapter, you'll discover that a verb does more than make a complete sentence; it also helps to show time.

> The time shown by a verb is called its *tense*.

In this chapter, we'll look at two types of verbs: regular verbs, which change tense according to a standard pattern, and irregular verbs, which change in other ways. Study the material carefully to learn how to form each verb tense correctly and, more important, *when* to use each tense.

Verbs change form in order to show tense, but they also change form depending on their subjects. You'll learn how to make sure that your subjects and verbs match each other in this chapter.

VERB TENSE

SIMPLE TENSES

How does the verb *wait* change in the following sentences to show the simple past, simple present, and simple future tenses?

> Frank **waited** all evening for his girlfriend to call.
> Frank **waits** by the phone every evening.
> Frank **will wait** by the phone tomorrow night, too.

Sometimes a single-word verb is used; at other times a verb phrase is needed, such as *will wait*, which shows future tense. In this example, *wait* is the base verb and *will* is a helping verb.

> A **_verb phrase_** is made up of a base verb and one or more helping verbs. The verb phrase can serve as the simple predicate. All verb tenses are formed by adding endings and/or helping verbs to the base verb.

Simple Present Tense

The simple present tense is used for things that are happening or are true now and for actions that are performed regularly. Also, the simple present tense is used when a statement is always true.

I **need** a cup of coffee.
The sun **rises** every morning.
Most toddlers **love** candy.

The simple present tense is formed by using the base verb or the base verb plus _s._ Study the following chart showing the simple present tense of the verb _wait._

I, you, we, they	wait
he, she, it	waits

The simple present tense of a regular verb is just the base form except when the subject is _he, she, it,_ or a singular noun. When the subject is one of these, you must add _s_ (or _es_ if the verb ends in a hissing sound).

My sister **plays** the piano.
Herman **washes** his car on Saturdays.

You'll learn more about when to use the _s_ and _es_ endings in the "Subject-Verb Agreement" section of this chapter.

Write an example sentence of your own in the present tense:

_____

Simple Past Tense

The simple past tense shows action that occurred at a specific time in the past. The simple past for any subject is formed by adding _ed_ to regular verbs.

In 1992 I **campaigned** for Bill Clinton.
Last week I **started** an accounting course.

Write an example sentence of your own in the past tense:

_____

Simple Future Tense

The future tense shows an action that will occur in the future. Form the simple future for any subject by using *will* plus the base form of the verb.

The plane **will leave** at 8:00 A.M.
I **will help** you as soon as possible.

Write an example sentence of your own in the future tense:

_____

Time Clues

How can you decide which tense to use in a sentence? Often you'll find that the correct choice comes naturally. As you proofread a sentence or paragraph, be alert for time clues provided by other words. These clues have been circled in the examples below.

Simple Present
(Now) that I'm working, I **get** up at 6:30 every morning.
(Today) most people **buy** all their groceries at a supermarket.

Simple Past
(Last year) Young Sun **entered** a poetry contest.
We **tried** to call you (yesterday.)

Future
(Next year) Andrea **will graduate** from college.
Will you please **write** (soon?)

Sometimes the clue words will be other verbs. Underline the correct verb tense in the sentence below.

Nick picked up his saxophone and *(wails, wailed)* a mournful tune.

The verb *picked* is the clue to past tense. You can tell that both actions happened in the past, so the correct choice is *wailed.*

Sela *(measures, measured)* each piece of drywall carefully before she cuts it.

The verb *cuts* is the clue to present tense. You can tell that both actions are happening in the present, so the correct choice is *measures.*

EXERCISE 4

Directions: For each sentence, underline the correct verb tense from the choices in parentheses. Circle any words that provide time clues to verb tense.

Example: I (mail, mailed, <u>will mail</u>) this letter (tomorrow.)

1. Tim *(satisfies, satisfied, will satisfy)* his hunger last night with a Reuben sandwich.

2. My daughter toddled up and *(asks, asked, will ask)* for a box of raisins.

3. Every day Jim leaves home at six o'clock and *(arrives, arrived, will arrive)* at work an hour later.

4. Tomorrow the truck drivers *(picket, picketed, will picket)* all P&Q grocery stores.

5. Light always *(travels, traveled, will travel)* at 186,000 miles per second.

6. Several times last year a lone gunman *(robs, robbed, will rob)* the convenience store on the corner.

7. Next week a new rhythm and blues group *(performs, performed, will perform)* at the club.

8. June usually *(skips, skipped, will skip)* breakfast and makes up for it at lunch.

9. Only an hour ago you *(want, wanted, will want)* to marry me.

10. Now you *(despise, despised, will despise)* the sight of me!

ANSWERS ARE ON PAGE 347.

CONTINUING TENSES

The continuing tenses are used to show continuing action—action in progress—in the past, present, or future. The present continuing tense shows action happening now:

John **is staring** at me.

The past continuing tense shows past action that continued for some time:

We **were watching** television that evening.

The future continuing tense shows ongoing action in the future:

Ann **will be staying** with her niece for a week.

As you can see from the example sentences above, the continuing tenses are formed by using helping verbs and the base form of the verb plus *ing.* The chart on page 83 shows how to form each of the continuing tenses.

CONTINUING TENSES			
Present Continuing	I	am	looking
	he, she, it	is	
	we, you, they	are	
Past Continuing	I, he, she, it	was	
	we, you, they	were	
Future Continuing	I, he, she, it, we, you, they	will be	

Now write example sentences of your own using the continuing tenses:

Present continuing: _____

Past continuing: _____

Future continuing: _____

Phrases like *right now*, *today*, and *at the moment* are clues to present continuing tense. For all three continuing tenses, keep in mind the idea of an action going on for some time.

EXERCISE 5

Directions: For each sentence, underline the correct verb tense from the choices in parentheses. Circle any words that provide time clues to verb tense.

Example: Right now you (*are working, were working, will be working*) on Exercise 5.

1. Tomorrow at this time you (*are flying, were flying, will be flying*) to Puerto Rico.

2. At present, I (*think, am thinking, was thinking*) about moving to Canada.

3. At this time last year we (*are shivering, were shivering*) in subzero temperatures.

4. We (*are visiting, were visiting, will be visiting*) our cousins in Arizona again next winter.

5. I still (*am steaming, was steaming*) over that last remark!

6. At 3:45 yesterday afternoon, I *(am returning, was returning, will be returning)* to the office from a meeting.

7. Last night Ron *(is feeling, was feeling, will be feeling)* ill.

8. At the present the rich *(are continuing, were continuing, will be continuing)* to get richer.

9. At dawn yesterday the birds *(are chirping, were chirping, will be chirping)* mercilessly.

10. Next fall Marcel *(is going, was going, will be going)* through basic training.

ANSWERS ARE ON PAGE 347.

PERFECT TENSES

The perfect tenses are used to show action completed before or continuing to a specific time. Two of the three perfect tenses are actually special forms of the past tense, and the other perfect tense is a special form of the future.

Three Types of Past Tense

You have already studied the simple past and the past continuing tenses. These tenses show actions that have been completed in the past:

She **tripped** over the cord.
Paul **was napping** in the other room.

The other two types of past tense are perfect tenses: the present perfect and the past perfect. These special past tenses show more specific time relationships.

The Present Perfect Tense

The present perfect tense shows an action that started in the past and continues into the present or has just been completed.

Sam **has worked** here since 1983.
I **have finished** my book.

As you can see from the examples above, the present perfect tense of regular verbs is formed by combining either *has* or *have* with the base form of the verb plus *ed*.

Present Perfect		
he, she, it	has	looked
I, you, we, they	have	

The Past Perfect Tense

The third type of past tense is the past perfect tense, which shows that something took place before a specific time in the past.

By 8:00 the guests had finished all the beer.

The past perfect tense of regular verbs is formed by combining *had* with the base form of the verb plus *ed.*

Past Perfect	
I, you, he, she, it, we, they	had looked

Now write example sentences of your own using the present perfect and past perfect tenses:

Present perfect: _____

Past perfect: _____

The Future Perfect Tense

You have already studied the simple future tense, which shows an action that will take place in the future:

You will take the GED Tests next week.

A different type of future tense, the future perfect tense, shows an action that will be completed by a specific time in the future.

By next year I will have finished this project.

The future perfect tense of regular verbs is formed by combining the helping verbs *will have* with the base form of the verb plus *ed.*

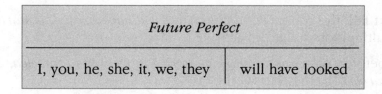

Future Perfect	
I, you, he, she, it, we, they	will have looked

Now write an example sentence of your own using the future perfect tense:

_____

Time Clues to Perfect Tenses

Time clues to perfect tenses include phrases beginning with *by.* These phrases indicate a time by which something was or will be completed.

(By 7:30 yesterday morning,) I **had finished** the book.
(By next spring,) I **will have driven** my new car 5,000 miles.

Phrases beginning with *since* and *for* often signal present perfect tense because they show an action beginning in the past and continuing in the present.

(Since yesterday afternoon,) I **have worked** without stopping.
(For the last five years,) he **has ordered** the same sandwich every day.

The words *just* and *already* may also be clues to present perfect tense. They signal an action that has recently been completed.

We **have** (just) **received** word about an earthquake in Mexico City.
Has Diane **finished** that book (already?)

EXERCISE 6

Directions: For each sentence, underline the correct verb tense from the choices in parentheses. Circle any words that provide time clues to verb tense.

Example: (Fifteen minutes from now,) you *(have finished, had finished,* <u>*will have finished*</u>*)* this exercise.

1. By six o'clock last night, we *(cleaned, have cleaned, had cleaned)* the car.

2. Raoul *(worked, has worked, will have worked)* for me since 1986.

3. Before retiring last year, Mrs. Tonini *(supervised, has supervised, had supervised)* the parts department.

4. By this time next year, you *(are passing, pass, will have passed)* all your tests.

5. I *(missed, have missed, am missing)* the bus every morning for the past week.

6. By next fall, the construction company *(will have started, is starting, starts)* on the multimillion-dollar project.

7. Long before Columbus's voyage in 1492, Viking ships *(traveled, have traveled, had traveled)* to the New World.

8. Before last week's race, I *(have, had, will have)* been running ten miles a day.

9. In the past five years, Floyd *(has failed, had failed, will have failed)* to appear on time only once.

10. In less than five minutes last night, our calm discussion *(has degenerated, had degenerated, is degenerating)* into name-calling.

ANSWERS ARE ON PAGE 347.

PASSIVE VOICE

In sentences written in the active voice, the subject does the action. In sentences written in the ***passive voice***, the subject is acted upon.

> ACTIVE: Mario programmed the computer.
> PASSIVE: The computer was programmed by Mario.

The first sentence is in the active voice because the subject (*Mario*) performs the action (*programmed*). The second sentence is in the passive voice because the subject (*computer*) receives the action (*programmed*).

Sentences written in the passive voice may be in any tense—present, past, or future.

> Economic activity **is measured** by the government.
> Last year, the economy **was harmed** by high inflation.
> Next year, inflation **will be curbed**.

As you can see, regular passive voice verbs are formed by combining a form of the verb *be* with the base verb plus *ed*. In the passive voice, the predicate is always in the form of a verb phrase.

PASSIVE VOICE			
Present	I	am	
	he, she, it	is	
	we, you, they	are	
Past	I, he, she, it	was	watched
	we, you, they	were	
Future	I, you, he, she, it, we, they	will be	

How can you easily identify sentences written in the passive voice? Many of them contain a phrase beginning with the word *by* and ending with a noun. This *by* phrase tells who performs the action of the sentence.

> Hector was nominated **by the committee**.

When the *by* phrase is not included, try mentally adding one. If you can add a *by* phrase telling who performed the action, the sentence is in the passive voice. Use this shortcut to tell whether the following sentence is in the passive voice.

Bella was picked for the volleyball team.

You can add a *by* phrase telling who performed the action of this sentence.

Bella was picked for the volleyball team [by me].

This sentence is in the passive voice.

EDITING HINT: In most cases, it is preferable to use the active voice, which is usually shorter, clearer, and more emphatic.

ACTIVE: I wrote the report.
PASSIVE: The report was written by me.

Use the passive voice when you don't want to identify who or what performed an action or when it doesn't matter who or what performed it.

Your request for a loan has been denied.
The TV was damaged during shipment.

EXERCISE 7

Directions: Rewrite each of the following passive voice sentences so that it is in the active voice.

Example: The bank was robbed by a young couple.

A young couple robbed the bank.

1. Soap operas are watched by millions of people.

_____

2. The statistics were gathered by the marketing department.

_____

3. The opposing team will be crushed by the home team!

_____

ANSWERS ARE ON PAGE 348.

SPELLING REGULAR VERB FORMS

In the Subject-Verb Agreement section of this chapter, you will review rules for adding *s* and *es* to present-tense verbs. The following rules for adding *ed* and *ing* are also useful to know, not just because they will certainly be tested on Part 2 of the GED Writing Skills Test, but also because they're used so often and have so few exceptions.

1. When adding *ed* and *ing* to most verbs, keep the normal spelling of the simple present form.

> look ⟶ looked, looking
> stagger ⟶ staggered, staggering
>
> model ⟶ _____   _____
>
> allow ⟶ _____   _____
>
> radio ⟶ _____   _____
>
> delay ⟶ _____   _____

2. When the simple present form of the verb ends in *y* preceded by a consonant, change the *y* to *i* before adding *ed*, and keep the *y* before *ing.*

> marry ⟶ married, marrying
> study ⟶ studied, studying
>
> bury ⟶ _____   _____
>
> bully ⟶ _____   _____
>
> worry ⟶ _____   _____

3. When the simple present form of the verb ends in a silent *e*, drop the *e* before adding *ed* or *ing.*

> glare ⟶ glared, glaring
> fire ⟶ fired, firing
>
> cope ⟶ _____   _____
>
> complete ⟶ _____   _____
>
> smile ⟶ _____   _____

4. When the simple present form of the verb ends in *ie*, drop the silent *e* before adding *ed*, and change the *ie* to *y* before adding *ing.*

> die ⟶ died, dying
>
> tie ⟶ _____   _____
>
> lie ⟶ _____   _____

For more information on spelling rules refer to pages 255–289.

EXERCISE 8

This exercise tests your understanding of when to use simple, continuing, perfect, and passive tenses.

Part A

Directions: Write the correct forms of the main verbs in the following sentences. Look for helping verbs that might be clues to the correct form. Be careful to spell the verbs correctly.

Example: *(type)* Last night Chantal ___*typed*___ the first chapter of her book.

1. *(play)* Last summer we _____ tennis twice a week.

2. *(hate)* Tom has always _____ to go to the dentist.

3. *(earn)* That kid is _____ extra money by selling earplugs to the parents of hard rock fans.

4. *(carry)* In the past most hardware stores _____ plumbing supplies.

5. *(hope)* Only last month Theresa _____ to become a professional mud wrestler.

6. *(study)* At the moment the class is _____ verb forms.

7. *(compare)* The two girls were _____ notes on their dates.

Part B

Directions: For each sentence, underline the correct verb tense from the choices in parentheses. Circle any words or phrases that provide clues to the correct tense. Refer to the rules and explanations on pages 79–88 as much as you need to in order to answer correctly.

1. At this moment someone in Hollywood *(films, is filmed, is filming)* a sequel to *Rocky XXIII.*

2. At ten o'clock tomorrow morning, the senator *(will announce, has announced, will be announced)* her candidacy for reelection.

3. Apparently the thieves *(are gaining, have gained, had gained)* entry by breaking a basement window sometime before 6:20.

4. Since 1980 Don *(is purchasing, purchases, has purchased)* a new car every year.

5. With a little luck and a lot of hard work, I *(will be earning, am earning, have earned)* two hundred dollars a week within six months.

6. In a fit of foul temper Yusef snarled at his goldfish and *(was drop-kicking, drop-kicked, drop-kicks)* the flower pot.

7. Two-year-olds typically *(are overusing, overused, overuse)* the word *no.*

8. The package *(will ship, is shipping, will be shipped)* to you COD within two weeks.

9. Several suspicious-looking characters *(were loitering, are loitering, loiter)* outside the apartment house last night.

10. In our neighborhood the garbage *(had picked, is pick, is picked)* up every Wednesday.

11. By next week Ramona *(will complete, will have completed, is completing)* plans for the addition to her house.

12. Passersby often *(remark, are remarking, will remark)* on the eerie lavender glow around the Munsons' garage.

ANSWERS ARE ON PAGE 348.

IRREGULAR VERB FORMS

A thief **breaks** into a basement apartment and **steals** a stereo. A passing police officer **sees** him, **goes** after him, and **catches** him. At the trial two weeks later, the jury **finds** him guilty of burglary. He **gets** a five-year sentence.

Let's use the rules you just learned to change the paragraph above from present to past tense. Here's our result:

A thief **breaked** into a basement apartment and **stealed** a stereo.

A passing police officer **seed** him, **goed** after him, and **catched** him. At

the trial two weeks later, the jury **finded** him guilty of burglary. He

getted a five-year sentence.

We've created a perfectly logical but incorrect paragraph. The source of our errors is the fact that not all English verbs shift to different tenses according to the rules for regular verbs.

Because many irregular verbs are so commonly used, you know most of these forms already. Check your skills right now by correcting the sample paragraph about the break-in. Cross out each incorrect verb and write the correct one above it.

This is how it ought to read. How well did you do?

A thief **broke** into a basement apartment and **stole** a stereo. A passing police officer **saw** him, **went** after him, and **caught** him. At the trial two weeks later, the jury **found** him guilty of burglary. He **got** a five-year sentence.

You can be sure that some questions about irregular verbs will appear on Part 1 of the GED Writing Skills Test.

PRINCIPAL PARTS OF VERBS

When you are studying irregular verbs, the three parts of each verb that you must learn are the present form, the simple past tense, and the ***past participle***, which is used in all perfect tenses and in the passive voice. Regular verbs all simply add *ed* or *d* to form the past tense and past participle. Irregular verbs do not follow this pattern for the past tense and the past participle. Study the following comparison of the principal parts of a regular and an irregular verb.

	Present Form	*Simple Past*	*Past Participle*
Regular Verb	look	looked	looked
Irregular Verb	see	saw	seen

As you may have guessed, you will need to memorize the past and past participle forms of irregular verbs you don't already know. In the following exercises, you'll practice using the most common irregular verbs.

MUST-LEARN VERBS

Some irregular verbs are used so frequently that learning them is essential to smooth writing. If your study time is limited, concentrate on these. The usual error with these verbs is confusing the simple past and past participle forms. Remember that the simple past is used alone; the past participle is used in a verb phrase with *has, have,* or *had,* or in the passive voice with a form of *be* (*am, is, are, was, were*).

INCORRECT: I **seen** you at the pool hall.
CORRECT: I **saw** you at the pool hall.
CORRECT: I **have seen** you at the pool hall.

Base	Present	Past	Past Participle
be	am, is, are	was, were	(have) been
do	do, does	did	(have) done
have	has, have	had	(have) had
go	go, goes	went	(have) gone
come	come, comes	came	(have) come
run	run, runs	ran	(have) run
see	see, sees	saw	(have) seen
bring	bring, brings	brought	(have) brought

EXERCISE 9

Directions: Underline the correct verb form to complete each sentence. If you choose the past participle, circle its helping verb. Some helping verbs may be in contractions, such as *I've* or *she's*.

Examples: I don't know where they **ve** *(went, gone)*.
She *(was, been)* a real pest on this trip.

1. I certainly hope that the werewolves have *(went, gone)*.

2. Last night we *(saw, seen)* a television program on humpback whales.

3. Have we *(ran, run)* out of brown sugar?

4. Jamal *(brung, brought)* his new girlfriend over last night.

5. I've never *(did, done)* an exercise quite like this.

6. The dog just *(came, come)* in with burrs matted in his coat.

7. We *(were, been)* expecting your call sooner.

8. Lisa has *(ran, run)* in the Boston Marathon before.

9. I've *(saw, seen)* that man somewhere before.

10. Summer has *(came, come)*.

11. Jane and Ron *(did, done)* all the housecleaning before noon last Saturday.

12. Last year we *(went, gone)* to Wyoming on vacation.

13. Has the mail carrier *(brung, brought)* the mail in yet?

14. The surgeon *(did, done)* an excellent job on the bypass.

15. Suddenly Shelby *(saw, seen)* a rhinoceros looming in the distance.

ANSWERS ARE ON PAGE 349.

I-A-U PATTERN

Some irregular verbs follow similar patterns. One common pattern is a vowel shift from *i* in present to *a* in past to *u* in past participle form.

Present	Past	Past Participle
drink, drinks	drank	(have) drunk
ring, rings	rang	(have) rung
begin, begins	began	(have) begun
shrink, shrinks	shrank	(have) shrunk
sing, sings	sang	(have) sung
sink, sinks	sank	(have) sunk
swim, swims	swam	(have) swum

EXERCISE 10

Directions: Underline the correct verb form to complete each sentence. If you choose the past participle, circle its helping verb.

Example: So far this morning, Janet (has) *(drank, drunk)* four cups of coffee.

1. We *(began, begun)* to doubt the truth of his story.

2. Has anyone ever *(swam, swum)* across the Gulf of Mexico?

3. Darrin *(sang, sung)* with a rock group for three years.

4. Gene's army uniform must have *(shrank, shrunk)* in the last ten years.

5. The oven timer just *(rang, rung)*.

6. Consuela jumped into the swimming pool and *(sank, sunk)* like a rock.

7. In the last few days, the baby has *(began, begun)* smiling and cooing.

8. I've never *(swam, swum)* in the ocean.

9. The telephone has *(rang, rung)* off the wall today.

ANSWERS ARE ON PAGE 349.

EN AND *N* VERBS

Many verbs shift to their past participle form by adding an *en* or *n* ending. Here are some of the most common:

Present	Past	Past Participle
arise(s)	arose	(have) arisen
break(s)	broke	(have) broken
speak(s)	spoke	(have) spoken
freeze(s)	froze	(have) frozen
steal(s)	stole	(have) stolen
choose(s)	chose	(have) chosen
ride(s)	rode	(have) ridden
write(s)	wrote	(have) written
eat(s)	ate	(have) eaten
take(s)	took	(have) taken
grow(s)	grew	(have) grown
know(s)	knew	(have) known
throw(s)	threw	(have) thrown
tear(s)	tore	(have) torn
wear(s)	wore	(have) worn

EXERCISE 11

Directions: Underline the correct verb to complete each sentence. If you choose the past participle, circle its helping verb.

1. The police have *(took, taken)* Tim into custody.

2. We *(choose, chose, chosen)* a new union steward at our last meeting.

3. Jack has *(stole, stolen)* everything from rubber bands to car stereos.

4. Somehow I *(knowed, knew)* the answer to that question.

5. The kid has *(grew, grown)* five inches in three months!

6. We've already *(ate, eaten)* supper.

7. I *(wrote, written)* him a letter instead of a birthday card.

8. Negotiations with management have *(broke, broken)* down completely.

9. We got up late and *(eat, ate)* a big breakfast.

10. Mr. Hiroto has just *(wrote, written)* his first letter to the editor.

ANSWERS ARE ON PAGE 349.

EXERCISE 12

Directions: The chart below lists in alphabetical order the simple present, simple past, and past participle forms of other common irregular verbs. To find the ones you need to practice, do this:

☐ Cover the second and third columns with a sheet of paper.

☐ Make a short sentence using the present-tense verb in column 1 by using *I* as the subject: I draw.

☐ Test for the past-tense form by saying, "Yesterday I _____." Yesterday I drew.

☐ Test for the past participle form by saying, "I have _____." I have drawn.

☐ Check your answers against the verbs printed in columns 2 and 3.

☐ Mark for study any that differ from your answers.

☐ Study the verbs you missed by repeating their correct forms over and over in sentence form ("Yesterday I _____; I have _____").

ANSWERS WILL VARY.

Present	*Past*	*Past Participle*
awake(s)	awoke, awaked	(have) awaked, awoken
become(s)	became	(have) become
bend(s)	bent	(have) bent
bet(s)	bet	(have) bet
bid(s) (to offer)	bid	(have) bid
bind(s)	bound	(have) bound
bite(s)	bit	(have) bitten
blow(s)	blew	(have) blown
build(s)	built	(have) built
burst(s)	burst	(have) burst
buy(s)	bought	(have) bought
cast(s)	cast	(have) cast
catch(es)	caught	(have) caught
cling(s)	clung	(have) clung
cost(s)	cost	(have) cost
creep(s)	crept	(have) crept
cut(s)	cut	(have) cut
deal(s)	dealt	(have) dealt
dig(s)	dug	(have) dug
drag(s)	dragged	(have) dragged
draw(s)	drew	(have) drawn
dream(s)	dreamed, dreamt	(have) dreamed, dreamt
drive(s)	drove	(have) driven

Present	Past	Past Participle
fall(s)	fell	(have) fallen
feed(s)	fed	(have) fed
feel(s)	felt	(have) felt
fight(s)	fought	(have) fought
find(s)	found	(have) found
flee(s)	fled	(have) fled
fly(flies)	flew	(have) flown
forget(s)	forgot	(have) forgotten
get(s)	got	(have) gotten
give(s)	gave	(have) given
hear(s)	heard	(have) heard
hide(s)	hid	(have) hidden
hold(s)	held	(have) held
hurt(s)	hurt	(have) hurt
keep(s)	kept	(have) kept
lay(s) (put or place)	laid	(have) laid
lead(s)	led	(have) led
leave(s)	left	(have) left
lend(s)	lent	(have) lent
lose(s)	lost	(have) lost
make(s)	made	(have) made
mean(s)	meant	(have) meant
meet(s)	met	(have) met
pay(s)	paid	(have) paid
put(s)	put	(have) put
read(s)	read	(have) read
rid(s)	rid	(have) rid
rise(s)	rose	(have) risen
say(s)	said	(have) said
seek(s)	sought	(have) sought
sell(s)	sold	(have) sold
send(s)	sent	(have) sent
set(s)	set	(have) set
shake(s)	shook	(have) shaken
shine(s)	shone	(have) shone
shine(s) (polish)	shined	(have) shined
shoot(s)	shot	(have) shot
sit(s)	sat	(have) sat
sleep(s)	slept	(have) slept
spend(s)	spent	(have) spent
spin(s)	spun	(have) spun
stand(s)	stood	(have) stood
strike(s)	struck	(have) struck
swear(s)	swore	(have) sworn
teach(es)	taught	(have) taught
tell(s)	told	(have) told
think(s)	thought	(have) thought
understand(s)	understood	(have) understood

THREE TROUBLESOME VERB PAIRS

Because they sound so much alike, yet have slightly different meanings, three verb pairs are tricky to use correctly: *lie-lay*, *sit-set*, and *rise-raise*.

The first verb *(lie, sit,* and *rise)* is used when the subject of the sentence is moving (or resting). It might help you to remember that the second letter of each of these verbs is *i*.

Our cat **lies** on the windowsill to catch the afternoon sun.
We sometimes **sit** on the porch swing and swat mosquitoes.
I **rise** reluctantly from bed every morning.

The second verb *(lay, set,* and *raise)* is used when the subject of the sentence moves an object.

I frequently **lay** my car keys down and forget where I put them.
The students usually **set** their books under their desks.
Dick **raises** his hand hesitantly for fear of giving a wrong answer.

The charts below summarize the forms of these three pairs of verbs.

SUBJECT IS MOVING			
Simple Present	*Present Participle*	*Simple Past*	*Past Participle*
lie(s)	lying	lay	lain
sit(s)	sitting	sat	sat
rise(s)	rising	rose	risen

SUBJECT MOVES AN OBJECT			
Simple Present	*Present Participle*	*Simple Past*	*Past Participle*
lay(s)	laying	laid	laid
set(s)	setting	set	set
raise(s)	raising	raised	raised

Notice that the same spelling is used for the simple past form of *lie* and the simple present form of *lay*. Can you see how the context of the sentence reveals the difference in meaning in the examples below? One of these sentences shows a subject moving an object. Circle the object being moved.

William **lay** in bed moaning for three days with the flu.
The Wilsons sometimes **lay** a log on the fire and eat popcorn at night.

In the first sentence, the simple past of *lie* is used. The subject, *William*, acted alone. In the second sentence, the simple present of *lay* is used. The subject, *The Wilsons*, move a *log*. You should have circled *log*.

EXERCISE 13

Directions: Underline the correct form of the verb to complete each sentence. Circle the object that is moved, if there is one.

1. The dog has been *(lying, laying)* on my bed again.

2. Don't *(sit, set)* on that chair with the broken leg.

3. A cadet *(rises, raises)* the flag at exactly 7:00 A.M.

4. She *(sat, set)* the coffee cup carefully on the table.

5. Who *(lay, laid)* this money on my desk?

6. Abe *(rose, raised)* from his seat and strode to the platform.

7. The jewelry has *(lain, laid)* in the bank vault for years.

8. Are you *(sitting, setting)* in the front row?

9. We've *(lain, laid)* our plans carefully.

10. I'd love to be *(lying, laying)* on a beach in Jamaica right now.

ANSWERS ARE ON PAGE 349.

VERB TENSE IN A PASSAGE

Time clues don't appear in every sentence. In fact, in a whole paragraph there may be only one or two sentences that contain such signals. In this situation it's particularly important to be consistent in verb tense. Don't slip unnecessarily from present to past or from past to present. Such slips are confusing; they leave the reader wondering when the action actually occurred.

Two slips in tense appear in the following paragraph, which should be written entirely in the past tense. Locate and circle these errors.

A loud growl silenced the crowd around the bar. They looked apprehensively at the entrance. Suddenly a hulking figure throws open the door and lumbered into the room. The other patrons sidled out of his path, trying to make themselves inconspicuous. Head lowered, the monstrous creature charged up to the quivering bartender and says threateningly, "One Shirley Temple on the rocks."

Did you find the two out-of-place present tense verbs? They were *throws* and *says.* Their past tense forms, *threw* and *said,* should have been used to make the paragraph consistent in tense.

Some of the questions on Part 1 of the GED Writing Skills Test will ask you to make sure that verb tense is consistent within a passage.

> **EDITING HINT:** You can check for consistent verb tense within a passage by reading the passage twice. The first time through, get a general sense of the tense of the passage as a whole. The second time, carefully check each sentence to make sure the verbs fit into the passage as a whole.

EXERCISE 14

Directions: Proofread the following paragraph for eleven errors in verb form or verb tense. Cross out the incorrect form and write the correct form above it.

Example: Joe ~~done~~ *did* a great job on the car yesterday.

Before last night, neither the Mad Dogs nor the Spartans played a good game all season. However, last night's football game begun as a defensive battle and ended as a scoring free-for-all. During the first half, both teams ran the ball. The defensive lines on both sides are strong. At the end of the first half, the score was tyed at 0–0.

In the second half, both teams openned with a new strategy. They passed the ball whenever they seen an opening. The quarterbacks done a superb job of setting up plays. The defensive lines, on the other hand, were tireing. They aren't blocking nearly as well. As a result, the final score will be 47–39. By the end of that game, the Spartans winned their first victory of the season.

ANSWERS ARE ON PAGE 349.

SUBJECT-VERB AGREEMENT

BASIC SUBJECT-VERB AGREEMENT

By learning how to choose and write the correct verb tense, you've gone halfway toward achieving proper verb form. Your final step is to learn when and how to make verbs agree with their subjects. Look at the two pairs of sentences below.

> The employees **think** the manager is an idiot.
> The employees **thinks** the manager is an idiot.
>
> The manager **wants** to open the office at 6:00 A.M.
> The manager **want** to open the office at 6:00 A.M.

Why is the first sentence in each pair correct, but not the second? The answer to this question lies in the link between subjects and present-tense verbs. In the first pair, is the subject singular or plural? *Employees* is plural, and the verb that fits with a plural subject is the plural verb *think*. Is the subject in the second pair also plural? No. *Manager* is singular. The verb *wants* fits with this singular subject.

> Choosing present-tense verbs to match singular or plural subjects is called ***subject-verb agreement***.

You can most easily learn the matching pattern for subject-verb agreement by using personal pronouns as subjects at first. Look at the pattern shown in the following example. Which pronouns require a verb with an *s* ending?

I
You
We
They
} **hate** to get up in the morning.

He
She
It
} **hates** to get up in the morning.

Which verbs end in *s*? Only those that follow the singular subjects *he, she, it*.

Some verbs require an *es* ending instead of the basic *s* ending. Study the example that follows.

I
You
We
They
} **lurch** into the kitchen.

He
She
It
} **lurches** into the kitchen.

You may recall that verbs ending in a hissing sound (*s*, *sh*, *ch*, *x*, and *z*) take an *es* ending. This rule is very similar to the rule about noun plurals that you studied on page 52. Remember that most nouns ending in *s* or *es* are plural, while verbs with these endings are generally singular.

> When personal pronouns are used as subjects, only the singular subjects *he*, *she*, and *it* are followed by verbs ending in *s* or *es*.

Does a similar subject-verb agreement rule apply in sentences using nouns as subjects? What pattern do you find in the pairs of sentences below?

The worker **belongs** to a union.
The workers **belong** to a union.

An artichoke **cooks** slowly.
Artichokes **cook** slowly.

In each pair, the subject of the first sentence is singular. The verb in each first sentence ends in *s*. The subject of the second sentence is plural in each pair. No *s* is added to the verb in the second sentence of each pair. Now you can see that nouns as subjects follow the same rule as personal pronouns.

BASIC RULES FOR SUBJECT-VERB AGREEMENT

1. The present-tense verbs of singular subjects (except *I* and *you*) end in *s* or *es*.

2. The present-tense verbs of plural subjects (and *I* and *you*) do not end in *s*.

IRREGULAR VERBS

Do the basic rules apply for irregular verbs, too? Look at the pair of sentences below.

> Jeremy **is** a member of the softball team.
> The players **are** ready for the game.

The first sentence has a singular subject, and the verb ends in *s*. The second sentence has a plural subject, and the verb does not end in *s*. In fact, the rules hold for irregular verbs as well.

Carefully study the following very common irregular verbs with different subjects. These verbs are very important because they are common helping verbs. If you learn to match these subjects and verbs correctly, you may clear up many verb problems. You'll see that although the spellings are irregular, the correct forms for *he*, *she*, and *it* all end in *s*.

Am/Is/Are	
I	am
he, she, it	is
you, we, they	are

Have/Has	
I, you, we, they	have
he, she, it	has
you, we, they	have

With only one exception, past-tense verbs do not change form when the subject changes, as in the following example.

I, you, he, she, it, we, they	loved

That exception is *was* and *were*, which follow the same pattern as *is* and *are* unless the subject is *I*.

Was/Were	
I, he, she, it	was
you, we, they	were

EDITING HINT: Don't forget subject-verb agreement when you use the words *doesn't* and *don't*.

> doesn't = does not   don't = do not

The verb *does* matches singular subjects, and the verb *do* matches plural subjects.

> He **does** the dishes.   They **do** the dishes.
> Joan **does** enjoy jazz.   The Johnsons **do** enjoy jazz.

The same pattern works with the contractions.

> He **doesn't** dry the dishes.   They **don't** dry the dishes.
> Joan **doesn't** enjoy rock.   The Johnsons **don't** enjoy rock.

If you're not sure whether to use *don't* or *doesn't*, take the contractions apart to test them.

> It *(doesn't, don't)* matter to me.

Test: *It does not matter. . . . It do not matter. . . . It* is singular, so *does* agrees with *It*. Since *It does not* is correct, choose *doesn't*.

> It **doesn't** matter to me.

EXERCISE 15

Part A

Directions: Underline the form of the verb that agrees with the subject of each sentence. First decide whether the subject is singular or plural. Then choose the verb that agrees with the subject.

Example: Al Capone *(was, were)* a famous gangland figure in the 1920s.

1. Alice *(doesn't, don't)* work here anymore.

2. We *(was, were)* just getting ready to leave.

3. The Browns' daughters *(moves, move)* to a different apartment every three months.

4. They *(lives, live)* on less than one hundred dollars a week.

5. It *(doesn't, don't)* make any sense.

6. They *(was, were)* here a few minutes ago.

7. Every other morning Jim *(jogs, jog)* to work.

8. He *(runs, run)* in good weather and bad.

9. Even thunderstorms *(doesn't, don't)* stop him.

10. I *(thinks, think)* that's remarkable.

Part B
Directions: Write a paragraph of at least five sentences describing a daily routine of yours. For subject-verb agreement practice, make *I* the subject of each sentence. Underline every verb, making sure that it agrees with the subject.

Example: Every weekday morning I <u>get</u> up at 5:30.

Part C
Directions: Rewrite the paragraph you wrote in Part B by changing the subjects from *I* to *he* or *she* and making the verbs match. Again, underline every verb.

Example: Every weekday morning he <u>gets</u> up at 5:30.

ANSWERS ARE ON PAGE 350.

PROBLEMS IN SUBJECT-VERB AGREEMENT
SOME TRICKY PATTERNS

Except for a couple of troublesome speech habits like "we was" and "it don't," you'll probably find that matching verbs to subjects isn't difficult. However, a few sentence patterns can cause problems, either because the subject is hard to find or because it's hard to decide whether the subject is singular or plural. In this section you'll have a chance to practice subject-verb agreement with four tricky patterns: compound subjects, inverted word order, interrupters between subject and verb, and indefinite pronouns as subjects.

COMPOUND SUBJECTS

The subjects of the following sentences are identical, but the verbs are not. Why? Circle the words that differ in the two sentences.

Samantha and Luigi eat out every night.
Samantha or Luigi eats out every night.

When compound subjects are used in a sentence, subject-verb agreement depends on the conjunction used to connect the two subjects. The word *and* joins two things together.

Samantha + Luigi = two people

You could logically substitute the plural pronoun *they* for the two names.

~~Samantha and Luigi~~ *They* eat out every night.

> When a compound subject is connected by *and*, the subject is plural. Therefore, the present-tense verb does not end in *s*.

CORRECT: George and his wife **bowl** every Tuesday night.
INCORRECT: George and his wife **bowls** every Tuesday night.

CORRECT: A pen, a ruler, and an eraser **are** in the top desk drawer.
INCORRECT: A pen, a ruler, and an eraser **is** in the top desk drawer.

What happens if the two subjects are linked by *or* instead of *and*? Look at this sentence.

Samantha or Luigi **eats** out every night.

Now only one person eats out, not two. In this case, the verb agrees with the subject closer to it: *Luigi eats.* The same reasoning applies to the conjunction *nor.* It makes the reader concentrate on one subject at a time.

Neither Samantha nor Luigi **eats** out every night.

> The words *or* and *nor* split a compound subject into two choices that are considered one at a time. The verb agrees with the subject closer to it.

This rule is easy to use. If you're checking subject-verb agreement when the subjects are joined by *or* or *nor*, just cover the subject farther from the verb and work with the sentence that's left.

Either Rashad or the twins *(walks, walk)* the dog hourly.

Cover the subject farther from the verb. Is the subject that's left singular or plural? *Twins* is plural. Pick the verb that agrees with the subject: Twins *walk*.

| Either Rashad or | the twins **walk** the dog hourly. |

Now it's your turn:

Either the twins or Rashad *(walks, walk)* the dog hourly.

Cover the subject farther from the verb. Is the subject that's left singular or plural?

_____

Pick the verb that agrees with the subject.

_____

| Either the twins or | Rashad **walks** the dog hourly. |

Notice that reversing the order of the singular and plural subjects requires a different verb choice.

EXERCISE 16

Directions: Underline the correct verb in each sentence below. Refer to the two rules and their explanations on pages 105–106 as much as necessary to answer correctly.

Example: James and Elizabeth *(finds, find)* raw celery disgusting.

1. Neither Juanita nor Damaris *(wants, want)* to be a hockey player forever.
2. Both the subway and the bus *(stops, stop)* near the main post office.
3. Either George or Dorothy *(checks, check)* on their elderly neighbor every evening.
4. A deadbolt lock and a burglar alarm *(provides, provide)* some security against break-ins.
5. Both sweet potatoes and carrots *(contains, contain)* large amounts of vitamin A.
6. Neither North Dakota nor Montana *(is, are)* known for mild winters.
7. Both San Francisco and Boston *(offers, offer)* many opportunities for walking tours.
8. Either a nurse or the parents *(stays, stay)* with the infant at all times.
9. Poor spelling and sloppy handwriting *(interferes, interfere)* with a writer's message.
10. Neither mountainclimbing nor downhill skiing *(appeals, appeal)* to people with a fear of heights.

ANSWERS ARE ON PAGE 350.

INVERTED WORD ORDER

You learned in Chapter 2 that subjects sometimes follow verbs in questions and in sentences beginning with *here* or *there*. Here is a common mistake you can learn to avoid:

INCORRECT: Do Jim have an extra pair of shorts?

What is the subject of this sentence? The subject is *Jim*. Does the verb in the sentence agree with the subject? Check: *Jim do have*.

You know now that a singular subject takes a verb that ends in *s*. Would you say *Jim do have* or *Jim does have*?

_____

CORRECT: **Does** Jim have an extra pair of shorts?

Circle the subjects in the sentences below.

Why are disaster films so popular?
Does the audience enjoy violence on a grand scale?
There are several explanations.

Did you circle *films*, *audience*, and *explanations*? If you had trouble finding the subjects, put the sentences back in normal word order. Rephrase questions as statements, and reverse the order of sentences beginning with *here* or *there*.

Disaster **films are** so popular.
The **audience does enjoy** violence on a grand scale.
Several **explanations are** there.

With the sentences in normal word order, you can easily make the verbs agree with their subjects.

EXERCISE 17

Part A

Directions: Circle the subject and underline the verb that agrees with it in each of the following sentences.

Example: Where *(is, __are__)* my ⟨glasses?⟩

1. There *(is, are)* three sponges playing tag in the kitchen sink.
2. Here *(is, are)* the black sock you lost in the wash last week.
3. *(Is, Are)* the car keys in your coat pocket?
4. There *(is, are)* an apple and a ham sandwich in the refrigerator for you.
5. Here *(is, are)* your hat and coat.
6. What *(is, are)* you planning to do on New Year's Eve?
7. Why *(is, are)* the Bulls and the Pistons bitter rivals?
8. *(Does, Do)* anyone over six really believe in the Tooth Fairy?
9. There *(doesn't, don't)* seem to be a doctor in the house.
10. Why *(doesn't, don't)* the government devise a fair tax system?
11. What *(has, have)* the two of you done with my gerbil?

Part B

Directions: Proofread the passage below for five errors in subject-verb agreement and correct them.

Example: ~~Does~~ most Americans want to look trim and youthful?

Is Americans becoming more interested in physical fitness? There are

many indications that they are. There have been an increase in the

popularity of swimming, biking, and brisk walking. There is many

companies that offer free use of gyms. They've found that it saves more

money on health insurance than it costs them to provide wellness

programs. Does you do anything special to keep in shape? What fitness

activities is you interested in?

ANSWERS ARE ON PAGE 350.

INTERRUPTERS
Prepositional Phrases

Some simple subjects are hard to locate because they're separated from the verb by describing phrases. If you can recognize these phrases, you'll simplify your task of making subject and verb agree. What is the simple subject of the following sentence?

The price of electricity never goes down.

If you're not sure whether the subject is *price* or *electricity*, find the verb, *goes*, and ask, "*Who* or *what* never goes down?" The answer is the simple subject: *price*. The words *of electricity* are an interrupting phrase, called a prepositional phrase, that describes *price*.

> A **prepositional phrase** is a word group that starts with a preposition and ends with a noun or pronoun. It relates to some other word in the sentence.

Here are some common prepositions to look for, with sample prepositional phrases that they might introduce. These phrases are important to recognize because they *never* contain the simple subject of a sentence.

Prepositions	*Prepositional Phrases*
of	of the three women, of December
in	in the entire universe, in a long line
for	for the little girl, for a new car
to	to the cab company, to them
from	from the president, from Mars
with	with the Doberman, with the beady eyes
on	on the third floor, on television

Other common prepositions include *above, across, at, before, between, down, into, near, through, under,* and *up.*

Use this three-step process to make subjects and verbs agree in sentences with prepositional phrase interrupters. Try the sample sentence below.

The cars on the showroom floor *(is, are)* next year's models.

1. Cross out the prepositional phrase.

The cars ~~on the showroom floor~~ *(is, are)* next year's models.

2. Circle the simple subject of the sentence. With the phrase blocked off, it's easy to see that *cars* is the subject.

3. Choose the verb that agrees with the subject.

The (cars) ~~on the showroom floor~~ **are** next year's models.

Try this three-step process with another practice sentence. First, cross out the interrupting phrase. Second, circle the simple subject. Third, underline the correct verb.

A vase of assorted wildflowers *(stands, stand)* on the kitchen table.

The correct sentence would read like this:

A (vase) ~~of assorted wildflowers~~ <u>stands</u> on the kitchen table.

Other Interrupters

Watch out for the words in the box below. Sometimes they seem to make the subject plural, but they actually introduce interrupting phrases.

as well as	along with	besides
in addition to	together with	

These phrases are usually easy to spot because they're set off by commas.

Joan Perez, **along with her three sons**, runs the photocopy shop on Clark Street.

The verb *runs* agrees with the singular subject *Joan Perez*. Subject-verb agreement isn't influenced by the interrupting phrase. Contrast this pattern to a sentence using a compound subject.

Joan Perez and her three sons run the photocopy shop on Clark Street.

In this case, the verb *run* agrees with the compound subject *Joan Perez* and *sons*. Although the two sentences have essentially the same meaning, the subject-verb agreement patterns are different.

EXERCISE 18

Directions: Circle the subject, cross out the interrupter, and underline the verb that agrees with the subject in each of the following sentences.

Example: The (dishes) ~~in the sink~~ *(is, <u>are</u>)* clean.

1. A box of butter cookies *(is, are)* sitting on the dining room table.

2. Santa Claus, with the aid of a multitude of spies, *(knows, know)* whether you've been naughty or nice.

3. Five members of the commission *(has, have)* issued a minority report.

4. Several television specials about John Kennedy *(was, were)* broadcast on the anniversary of his assassination.

5. Several members of the Central City Chamber of Commerce *(has, have)* been suspended for drug abuse.

6. The eggs in this carton *(is, are)* rotten.

7. Snow on open farmlands *(blows, blow)* mercilessly across roads and highways.

8. A charming smile, together with a healthy bank account, *(makes, make)* a bachelor eligible.

9. Ice cubes in an insulated glass *(melts, melt)* slowly even on hot summer days.

10. An unopened package of potato chips *(crunches, crunch)* like dry leaves underfoot.

11. A car loaded with five passengers *(stops, stop)* more slowly than a car with only a driver.

12. The football coach, as well as the team members, *(does, do)* calisthenics every morning.

ANSWERS ARE ON PAGE 350.

INDEFINITE PRONOUNS

Some subjects are easy to spot but difficult to label as singular or plural. What about the word *everyone*, for instance? Which is correct: *Everyone knows that you're right* or *Everyone know that you're right*? Although we could logically argue that *everyone* clearly means more than one person, the word is always considered singular. *Everyone knows that you're right* is correct.

Some **indefinite pronouns** are always considered singular in standard written English. You'll learn them easily if you concentrate on the word *one*, *thing*, or *body* at the end of each. These word parts all make you think of *one* or *single*.

> *Singular Indefinite Pronouns*
>
> | | |
> |---|---|
> | each (one) | no one |
> | either (one) | nothing |
> | neither (one) | nobody |
> | one | anyone |
> | someone | anything |
> | something | anybody |
> | somebody | everyone |
> | | everything |
> | | everybody |

Note the singular verbs in each of the sample sentences below.

Nobody **understands** him.
Does anyone **agree** with me?
Neither of the radios **works**.
Each of the survivors **gets** an equal share.

EDITING HINT: Remember to block out any interrupting phrases as you check for subject-verb agreement with indefinite pronouns. Add the word *one* after *each, either,* or *neither* to remind yourself that these words are singular.

Neither of the companies *(employs, employ)* part-time workers.
Neither *(one)* of the companies **employs** part-time workers.

Not all indefinite pronouns are singular. In fact, the indefinite pronouns in the box below are always plural.

> *Plural Indefinite Pronouns*
>
> | | | | |
> |---|---|---|---|
> | both | few | many | several |

Many are called. Few are chosen.
Both write extremely well.

Some indefinite pronouns may be either singular or plural depending on their antecedents. (Remember, the noun that a pronoun refers to is called its antecedent.)

> *Singular or Plural Indefinite Pronouns*
>
> | | | | | |
> |---|---|---|---|---|
> | some | any | none | most | all |

Study the examples below. In one sentence, *all* is plural. In the other, *all* is singular. Notice that the verb forms are different.

All of the **snow has** melted.
All of the **candy bars have** disappeared.

In the first sentence, *all* is singular because it refers to *snow*, which is singular. In the second sentence, *all* is plural because it refers to the plural noun *bars*. Is *all* singular or plural in the following example?

All of my money has been stolen.

Because it refers to the singular noun *money*, *all* is singular in this sentence.

Sometimes you may have to look in an earlier sentence for the pronoun's antecedent. Is *all* singular or plural in the pair of sentences below?

Three other girls used to live on my block. All have moved away.

Because its antecedent is *girls*, *all* is plural.

EXERCISE 19

Directions: Circle the subject, cross out any interrupters, and underline the verb that agrees with the subject in each sentence.

Example: (Each) ~~of the children~~ (<u>receives</u>, *receive*) a prize at the end of the party.

1. Everyone in the club *(wants, want)* to have a party next week.
2. None of the marbles *(belongs, belong)* to Geraldine.
3. Some of the ice from the polar caps *(melts, melt)* each summer.
4. Most of the listeners *(understands, understand)* the speaker's purpose.
5. Few of our neighbors *(likes, like)* our boa constrictor.
6. Someone in the audience *(has, have)* a question.
7. Nobody *(wishes, wish)* to argue with a rattlesnake.
8. All of the cake *(is, are)* gone.
9. All of the pieces of cake *(is, are)* gone.
10. Only one of these dogs *(bites, bite)* without provocation.
11. Anyone with an ounce of brains *(knows, know)* that the earth is round.
12. Many of my friends *(attends, attend)* night classes.

ANSWERS ARE ON PAGE 351.

EXERCISE 20

The purpose of this exercise is to test your understanding of all different patterns of subject-verb agreement. Do the exercise carefully and refer to the rules and explanations on pages 101–114 as much as necessary to answer correctly.

Directions: Underline the correct verb in each sentence below.

1. One of my pet peeves *(is, are)* people refusing to say hello when they *(enters, enter)* a room.

2. Even nonprescription drugs like aspirin *(causes, cause)* dangerous side effects in some patients.

3. Either credit cards or a personal check *(is, are)* acceptable at that store.

4. Cotton and wool *(provides, provide)* better insulation than most synthetic fibers.

5. Everybody with a lottery ticket *(hopes, hope)* to win the jackpot.

6. Why *(does, do)* the bride and groom exchange rings?

7. Some of the cookie crumbs *(has, have)* fallen onto your shirt.

8. There *(is, are)* several cars stuck on the icy streets.

ANSWERS ARE ON PAGE 351.

CHAPTER HIGHLIGHTS: USING VERBS

1. The time shown by a verb is its tense. The simple tenses are present, past, and future.

2. A verb phrase is made up of a main verb and one or more helping verbs.

3. Continuing tenses show action in progress. Perfect tenses show action completed before or continuing to a specific time.

4. Irregular verbs are not formed by the usual rules. Their tenses must be memorized.

5. Subject-verb agreement means choosing verbs that match their subjects in number (singular or plural).

6. Prepositional phrases never contain a sentence's simple subject.

7. Indefinite pronouns are generally considered singular.

GED Practice
EXERCISE 21

Choose the best answer to each question.

1. **Stan slammed the door shut, <u>throw</u> the car into reverse, and shot down the driveway.**

   Which of the following is the best way to write the underlined portion of this sentence? If you think the original is the best way, choose option (1).

   (1) throw
   (2) throws
   (3) throwed
   (4) threw
   (5) thrown

2. **One of the hottest rock groups in the country <u>was performing</u> at the Metro Stadium last night.**

   Which of the following is the best way to write the underlined portion of this sentence? If you think the original is the best way, choose option (1).

   (1) was performing
   (2) were performing
   (3) is performing
   (4) are performing
   (5) performing

3. **Ahmad is exhausted. He <u>have just ran</u> in a marathon.**

   Which of the following is the best way to write the underlined portion of this sentence? If you think the original is the best way, choose option (1).

   (1) have just ran
   (2) has just ran
   (3) had just ran
   (4) have just run
   (5) has just run

4. **Rounding the corner, Chuck stopped short and gasped at the sight. Tenants were running from the flaming building, screaming in terror, chokeing on the smoke.**

   What correction should be made to these sentences?

   (1) change *gasped* to *gasps*
   (2) change *running* to *runing*
   (3) change *screaming* to *screamming*
   (4) change *chokeing* to *choking*
   (5) no correction is necessary

5. **Neither Danita nor her seven younger brothers <u>sings</u>, "Hi-ho, hi-ho," on the way to work.**

   Which of the following is the best way to write the underlined portion of this sentence? If you think the original is the best way, choose option (1).

   (1) sings
   (2) sing
   (3) is singing
   (4) has sung
   (5) was singing

6. **Later this year, the company <u>was adding</u> a second shift to boost production.**

   Which of the following is the best way to write the underlined portion of this sentence? If you think the original is the best way, choose option (1).

   (1) was adding
   (2) has added
   (3) will add
   (4) have added
   (5) were adding

7. **Two small boys crept up to the house, rung the doorbell, then ran to the side of the house and hid behind a huge lilac bush.**

What correction should be made to this sentence?

(1) change *crept* to *creeped*
(2) change *rung* to *rang*
(3) change *ran* to *run*
(4) change *hid* to *hidden*
(5) no correction is necessary

8. **The little canary sat on its perch and sang its heart out. Meanwhile, a huge gray cat was laying below the cage, planning its attack.**

What correction should be made to these sentences?

(1) change *sat* to *set*
(2) change *sang* to *sung*
(3) change *laying* to *lying*
(4) change *planning* to *planing*
(5) no correction is necessary

ANSWERS ARE ON PAGE 352.

EDITING PRACTICE

Directions: Correct the eleven errors in the following passage. Four of these errors are related to skills that you learned in Chapter 2: sentence structure, nouns, and pronouns. The other seven errors are related to verbs. Use this checklist as your proofreading guide.

☐ Do present-tense verbs agree in number with their subjects?

☐ Is the correct verb tense used for each sentence and for the passage as a whole?

☐ Are irregular verb forms used correctly?

☐ Are regular verb forms spelled correctly?

As a child I loved having a yard full of trees. I climbed the smaller ones

and set for hours on the lower branchs. Munching apples and reading.

Often my friends and me used the trees for Wild West games. The outlaw

laid in wait behind their broad trunks, and prepared to spring out at

unsuspecting settlers. During the long summer days, our laughter mingles

with bird songs and the chatterring of squirrels.

Now I stare out of my apartment onto a barren parking lot and

remembered those days with a sigh. Is some other children haveing the time

of their lives in my old trees today?

ANSWERS ARE ON PAGE 352.

≡ GED Practice ≡
PARAGRAPH REVIEW

Questions 1–7 refer to the following paragraph.

(1) Why is dogs such popular pets worldwide? (2) They are messier than cats and less intelligent than pigs. (3) They can't be kept in cages. (4) Like hamsters and parakeets. (5) Yet not one of these other animals has been refered to as "man's best friend." (6) One reason for the popularity of dogs are their loyalty. (7) By nature following the leader of the pack just like wolves and coyotes. (8) In a dog's case, the leader of the pack had been a human being. (9) A properly trained dog obeys its master's commands.

1. Sentence 1: **Why is dogs such popular pets worldwide?**

   Which of the following is the best way to write the underlined portion of this sentence? If you think the original is the best way, choose option (1).

   (1) is dogs
   (2) was dogs
   (3) are dogs
   (4) is dogs being
   (5) has dogs been

2. Sentence 2: **They are messier than cats and less intelligent than pigs.**

   What correction should be made to this sentence?

   (1) change *are* to *is*
   (2) insert a comma after *cats*
   (3) replace *cats and* with *cats. And*
   (4) insert a comma after *and*
   (5) no correction is necessary

3. Sentences 3 and 4: **They can't be kept in cages. Like hamsters and parakeets.**

   Which of the following is the best way to write the underlined portion of these sentences? If you think the original is the best way, choose option (1).

   (1) kept in cages. Like
   (2) kept in cages like
   (3) kept in cage's like
   (4) keeped in cages. Like
   (5) keeped in cages like

4. Sentence 5: **Yet not one of these other animals has been refered to as "man's best friend."**

   What correction should be made to this sentence?

   (1) insert a comma after *animals*
   (2) change *has* to *have*
   (3) change *refered* to *referred*
   (4) change *man's* to *mans*
   (5) no correction is necessary

5. Sentence 6: **One reason for the popularity of dogs are their loyalty.**

   What correction should be made to this sentence?

   (1) change *dogs* to *dog's*
   (2) insert a comma after *dogs*
   (3) change *are* to *is*
   (4) insert a comma after *are*
   (5) no correction is necessary

6. Sentence 7: **By nature following the leader of the pack just like wolves and coyotes.**

   What correction should be made to this sentence?

   (1) replace *following* with *they follow*
   (2) replace *pack just* with *pack. Just*
   (3) change *wolves* to *wolfs*
   (4) insert a comma after *wolves*
   (5) change *coyotes* to *coyote's*

7. Sentence 8: **In a dog's case, the leader of the pack had been a human being.**

   Which of the following is the best way to write the underlined portion of this sentence? If you think the original is the best way, choose option (1).

   (1) had been
   (2) have been
   (3) was
   (4) is
   (5) are

Questions 8–14 refer to the following paragraph.

(1) Today some of the world's richest farmland was located in the American Midwest. (2) Thousands of acres of corn soybeans, and wheat cover flat plains and gently rolling hills. (3) Occasionally a grove of trees or a grain silo raises above the landscape. (4) Dairy and beef cattle graze in green fields under cottony skys. (5) Our ancestors seen a much different picture. (6) Two hundred years ago the Midwest was coverred with prairie grass and forests. (7) There were no neat farmsteads or parallel rows of grain. (8) Herds of shaggy bison roamed the plains. (9) Only the clouds were the same.

8. Sentence 1: **Today some of the world's richest farmland <u>was located</u> in the American Midwest.**

    Which of the following is the best way to write the underlined portion of this sentence? If you think the original is the best way, choose option (1).

    (1) was located
    (2) is located
    (3) is locate
    (4) will locate
    (5) had located

9. Sentence 2: **Thousands of acres of corn soybeans, and wheat cover flat plains and gently rolling hills.**

    What correction should be made to this sentence?

    (1) insert a comma after *corn*
    (2) insert a comma after *wheat*
    (3) change *cover* to *covers*
    (4) change *plains* to *plaines*
    (5) insert a comma after *plains*

10. Sentence 3: **Occasionally a grove of trees or a grain silo <u>raises</u> above the landscape.**

    Which of the following is the best way to write the underlined portion of this sentence? If you think the original is the best way, choose option (1).

    (1) raises
    (2) raise
    (3) is raising
    (4) rises
    (5) rise

11. Sentence 4: **Dairy and beef cattle graze in green fields under cottony skys.**

    What correction should be made to this sentence?

    (1) insert a comma after *dairy*
    (2) change *graze* to *grazing*
    (3) replace *fields under* with *fields. Under*
    (4) change *skys* to *skies*
    (5) no correction is necessary

12. Sentence 5: **Our ancestors <u>seen</u> a much different picture.**

    Which of the following is the best way to write the underlined portion of this sentence? If you think the original is the best way, choose option (1).

    (1) seen
    (2) saw
    (3) seed
    (4) had saw
    (5) have saw

13. Sentence 6: **Two hundred years ago the Midwest <u>was coverred</u> with prairie grass and forests.**

    Which of the following is the best way to write the underlined portion of this sentence? If you think the original is the best way, choose option (1).

    (1) was coverred
    (2) was covered
    (3) was cover
    (4) were coverred
    (5) were covered

14. Sentence 7: **There were no neat farmsteads or parallel rows of grain.**

    What correction should be made to this sentence?

    (1) change *were* to *was*
    (2) change *farmsteads* to *farmstead's*
    (3) insert a comma after *farmsteads*
    (4) change *rows* to *rowes*
    (5) no correction is necessary

ANSWERS ARE ON PAGE 352.

CHAPTER 4 PART A
Patterns of Organization

In Chapter 3 you learned that a good paragraph should have a topic sentence backed by specific, relevant supporting sentences. The paragraph below meets these standards. Do you rate it a good paragraph?

> If you drive a car, you should become familiar with this simple procedure to change a flat tire. Remove the flat and replace it with a spare tire. Place a jack under the car near the flat tire and raise the car far enough to lift the tire off the ground. Lower the car, remove the blocks, and be sure to put the tools back in the trunk. Use a lug wrench to loosen the nuts holding the tire on the axle. Block the wheels opposite the flat with bricks or large stones to keep the car from rolling. Tighten the lug nuts as much as possible.

The answer to the question is clear: this paragraph is a disaster! Although it has a main idea supported by specific details, the explanation is too disorganized to follow. To change a flat, what should you do first? second? third? After reading this paragraph, who could tell? To our definition of a good paragraph, we must add one final rule:

> A good paragraph must be well organized.

The best way to organize a paragraph will vary depending on the topic and purpose of the paragraph. In this chapter you'll study four useful patterns of organization:

- time order

- cause and effect

- comparison and contrast

- simple listing

These patterns are not just ways to organize sentences. They are also ways to organize your thinking, as you will see in the following pages.

TIME ORDER

WHEN TO USE TIME ORDER

You want to tell a beginning cook how to make great spaghetti sauce. You have to file an accident report on a fender-bender you were involved in yesterday. In a letter to a friend, you decide to describe a typical day at your new job as a salesclerk. How could you organize your information in each case?

The most logical choice is to use time order. You would place your supporting sentences in the order in which events occur.

WHEN TO USE A TIME ORDER PATTERN
1. To list steps in a process
2. To explain how something works
3. To describe a routine
4. To tell about an event

ORGANIZING DETAILS IN TIME ORDER

Paragraphs requiring time order practically organize themselves. After brainstorming a list of details, you simply need to ask yourself which happens first, second, third, and so on. Number your list accordingly. An organized list for the scrambled paragraph at the beginning of this chapter appears below as a sample.

How to Change a Flat

- (5) Remove flat and replace with spare
- (2) Put jack under car
- (3) Jack car up
- (7) Lower car
- (8) Remove blocks and replace tools
- (4) Use lug wrench to loosen nuts
- (1) Block wheels with bricks
- (6) Tighten lug nuts

The paragraph from page 121 was rewritten using this list as a guide. Note how much easier the directions are to follow now that they're sequenced in time order. Circle the words like *first* that alert the reader that the writer is moving from one step to another.

If you drive a car, you should become familiar with this simple procedure to change a flat tire. First block the wheels opposite the flat with bricks or large stones to keep the car from rolling. Then place a jack under the car near the flat tire and jack the car up enough to lift the tire off the ground. Use a lug wrench to loosen the nuts holding the tire on the axle. Remove the flat and replace it with a spare tire. Using the wrench again, tighten the lug nuts as much as possible. Finally, lower the car, remove the blocks, and put the tools back in the trunk so you'll have them for your next emergency.

You should have circled the words *first*, *then*, and *finally*. These are called **transitions**. Writers often use transitions to give readers clues to how ideas fit together. You'll study more about transitions in Chapter 6.

EXERCISE 1

Directions: Number each brainstorm list below in time order. The first few items in List 1 have been marked as an example.

1. Recent Presidents of the United States

    (a) _1_ Ford

    (b) _3_ Reagan

    (c) _2_ Carter

    (d) ___ Clinton

    (e) ___ Bush

2. How to make a cake using a mix

    (a) ___ Bake at 350 degrees about 30 minutes

    (b) ___ Blend ingredients until moist

    (c) ___ Place mix, ⅓ cup oil, and 3 eggs in mixing bowl

    (d) ___ Beat blended mixture for 2 minutes

    (e) ___ Pour into greased cake pan

    (f) ___ Cool completely before frosting

3. Steps for planning a piece of writing

    (a) ___ Brainstorm a list of details

    (b) ___ Analyze what you're writing about and why

    (c) ___ Organize the list logically

4. My disastrous morning

    (a) ___ Argument with boss

    (b) ___ Burned toast for breakfast

    (c) ___ Alarm didn't go off at 6:00

    (d) ___ Missed bus

    (e) ___ Woke up at 7:30

ANSWERS ARE ON PAGE 353.

EXERCISE 2

Directions: A friend from out of state is coming to visit you for the first time. Using some logical starting point like the edge of town or the nearest airport, railroad station, or bus depot, write a paragraph describing how to reach your home from that spot.

Prewriting and Drafting

☐ Brainstorm a list of the steps your friend would need to take.

☐ Cross out irrelevant details.

☐ Add helpful reference points like traffic lights or store names.

☐ Number the list in time order.

☐ Write a paragraph based on your list.

Revising

You may find you want to make some changes in your paragraph now that you have written it. First make any changes you now know you want to make. Then check your paragraph against this checklist and make any further revisions that would improve your writing.

☐ Is there a topic sentence? Underline it.

☐ Does the topic sentence state the central point of the paragraph?

☐ Are the supporting sentences arranged in time order?

ANSWERS WILL VARY.

CAUSE AND EFFECT

WHEN TO USE CAUSE AND EFFECT

You've missed work more than three days, and you're required to submit a written explanation of the reason for your absence. An accident on the assembly line has placed two workers in the hospital; as safety inspector, you must investigate and report on the causes. Your local school board will vote next week on closing the elementary school in your neighborhood; you decide to write the board a letter explaining how the closing would harm the community. How could you organize your writing for these projects?

Although time order might be involved in your organization, your purpose will not just be to relate a series of events in the sequence they occurred. In these cases you must tell *why* something has happened or *what will result* if a certain action is taken. That is, you'll need to trace **causes** and **effects**.

You use the cause-effect thought pattern often in everyday life. How many times have you asked questions like "Why didn't I get a raise this year? Why has Steve been so moody lately? How would my family react if I decided to take some college courses? Why didn't I get that job?"

This pattern is also used more formally by historians, scientists, and public policy makers: What were the causes of our involvement in the Vietnam War? What effect does cigarette smoking have on our lungs? What would happen if we raised federal income taxes to improve welfare programs? How has the use of computers affected our society?

WHEN TO USE A CAUSE-EFFECT PATTERN

1. To trace the reasons why an event occurred

2. To trace the results of an event

3. To predict the results of an event

WHAT TO INCLUDE

Suppose you've been asked to contribute a short article on cigarette smoking by teens to your PTA newsletter. You would like to explain why teens smoke regardless of the publicity about the dangers of smoking. What details might you use in your article?

The word *why* is the clue to the kinds of details to include. You are looking for causes of teens' smoking. On the next page is a sample brainstorming list for your article. Place a check next to the items that would *not* belong in your article.

Why Teens Smoke

_____ **1.** think they look like adults

_____ **2.** rebellion against authority

_____ **3.** increased chance of lung cancer

_____ **4.** desire to do what their friends do

_____ **5.** more girls smoking now than twenty years ago

Did you mark items 3 and 5? These are not possible causes for cigarette smoking by teens. Item 3 is an effect, not a cause, of cigarette smoking, so it doesn't belong in the paragraph. Item 5 provides information about how many girls are smoking, but it doesn't explain *why* they smoke. So now you have three good supporting ideas for your paragraph.

From these three causes, you can write a solid paragraph for your article. Here's a sample of what you might say. Underline the topic sentence and number each cause from the brainstorming list as you locate it below.

> Young teens experiment with cigarette smoking for a variety of reasons. Some kids get started because they associate smoking with adulthood. If Mom and Dad finish two packs of Marlboros a day, why shouldn't they? At the same time, smoking gives kids a chance to rebel against authority. The more their teachers and parents warn them not to smoke, the more eager they are to try it. But probably the most powerful influence on young teens is their peers. They don't want to be called "square" or "goody-goody" by their friends.

Let's look at a second example of cause-effect thinking. Suppose that you're writing a letter to a friend in which you describe how your decision to go back to school for your GED has affected the rest of your family. What kinds of details would you write about in your letter?

The key word in your topic is *affected*. You want to describe the **effects** of your decision on your family. Here's a sample brainstorming list one writer made for this topic. Place a check next to the items that would *not* belong in her letter.

_____ **1.** friends tease me, but I know they're proud of me

_____ **2.** kids take more responsibility for housework—do some of the cooking and cleaning to give me time to study

_____ **3.** kids more serious about doing their own schoolwork

_____ **4.** husband a little anxious; wonders whether I'll still look up to him if I have a diploma and he doesn't

_____ **5.** need a diploma to get a better job

You should have checked items 1 and 5. Item 1 is irrelevant since it describes the reactions of friends, not family. Item 5 deals with a reason for going back to school, not an effect. But she still has plenty of good material left for her letter.

Her finished letter might look something like the paragraph below. Underline the topic sentence. Number each of the items you just saw in the brainstorming list as you come to them in the paragraph.

> When I decided to go back to school for my GED, I had no idea how much the decision would affect Steve and the kids. Steve doesn't say too much, but he seems a little anxious when he sees me studying. Last night he asked me whether I would still respect him if I had a diploma and he didn't. The kids, on the other hand, are really proud of me. Both Jason and Rick have been taking more responsibility for the housework. They're sharing some of the cooking and cleaning jobs to give me more time to study. Best of all, they're getting more serious about their own schoolwork. Often, all three of us sit down and hit the books together.

EXERCISE 3

Directions: Each of the following topics asks you to identify either causes or effects. For each topic, brainstorm a list of ideas you could include in a paragraph about that topic. Then read over your list carefully and cross out any ideas that don't really fit. For now, you don't need to write the paragraph—just brainstorm.

Example: What are some of the causes of people's overeating?

> portions too big in restaurants
> ~~lots of people are overweight~~
> people eat too fast
> we're taught to clean our plates
> sometimes you just feel like munching

1. What are some of the effects of smoking?

2. What causes people to want to live in suburbs instead of in cities?

3. Why do people want to own cars?

4. For one reason or another, you stopped your traditional education before completing high school. What effects has leaving school had on your life?

POSSIBLE ANSWERS ARE ON PAGE 353.

EXERCISE 4

Directions: Choose *two* of the topics from Exercise 3. Write paragraphs based on your brainstorm lists for the two topics you choose.

You may find you want to make some changes in your paragraphs after you have written them. First make any changes you now know you want to make. Then check your paragraphs against the checklist below and make any further revisions that would improve your writing.

Revision Checklist

☐ Is there a topic sentence?

☐ Does the topic sentence state the cause-effect relationship you discuss in the paragraph?

☐ Do all the other sentences further develop the cause-effect relationship?

POSSIBLE ANSWERS ARE ON PAGE 353.

COMPARISON AND CONTRAST

WHEN TO USE COMPARISON-CONTRAST

You're writing a letter to the editor explaining why you favor Candidate A over Candidate B for mayor. Your company is buying a microwave for the coffee room, and your boss has asked you to investigate and report on the merits of three leading brands. You've just moved from Detroit to Denver, and you want to write a Michigan friend about your impression of the similarities and differences between the two cities. How could you organize your thinking and writing in each instance? Your task in these cases is to show how things are alike or different—in other words, to **compare** and **contrast** them.

Like the cause-and-effect pattern, comparison-contrast thinking is often used in both everyday and formal situations. Have you ever had to decide which of two apartments to rent? which job to apply for? which person to date? If so, you've probably compared and contrasted your choices before deciding. It's the same process that an economist uses to compare communism to capitalism or that an astronomer uses to see how Mercury and Jupiter differ.

WHEN TO USE A COMPARISON-CONTRAST PATTERN
1. To describe similarities or differences
2. To explain advantages and disadvantages

PLANNING A COMPARISON-CONTRAST PARAGRAPH

Writing a comparison-contrast paragraph requires careful planning to help your reader understand exactly how your subjects are alike or different. Using a chart in the planning step will help you organize your thinking.

To construct your chart, make three columns. Label the middle and right-hand columns with the names of the subjects you're comparing. Label the column on the left "Items to Discuss."

Items to Discuss	Subject A	Subject B

Let's take an example to see how the chart works. Suppose you're buying a new car. You are seriously considering two cars. You want to compare and contrast the two cars to see which would be the better car for you. What aspects of the cars will you discuss?

The price is very important, but you want to know you're getting a good car for your money. You want to get good gas mileage, and you want to buy a model with a good repair record. You decide that interior room is important because you have a family of four. These qualities are the "items to discuss." List them in the left-hand column of the chart.

Items to Discuss	Aristo	Lido
Price Gas mileage Repair record Interior room		

Now you're ready to fill in the information you've gathered about the two cars.

Items to Discuss	Aristo	Lido
Price	$9,500	$11,300
Gas mileage	25 city 32 highway	28 city 36 highway
Repair record	better than average	average
Interior room	fits 2 adults comfortably in backseat	2 kids comfortable in backseat but not two adults

Now the chart is filled in with supporting details that you can use in the paragraph. At this point you have a choice on how to organize it. You may decide to choose a **whole-to-whole pattern**; that is, write everything you have to say about one car and then go on to the other car, as in the sample paragraph below.

On the whole, I think a new Aristo is a better value than a new Lido. The Aristo costs $9,500. It gets 25 city miles per gallon and 32 highway miles per gallon. Furthermore, the repair record on this model is better than average. Another advantage of the Aristo is its roomy rear seat, which is big enough for two adults to ride in comfortably. On the other hand, the Lido is also a nice car. At $11,300, it costs more than the Aristo. It gets better gas mileage too, with 28 city and 36 highway miles per gallon. However, it has only an average repair record. In addition, the Lido has a smaller rear seat. In a few years, my kids might not fit back there! It looks like the Aristo is a better value for me.

Often, you'll find that your reader will understand your comparisons more easily if you compare your subjects *point by point*; that is, take up one discussion item at a time, as in the paragraph below.

> On the whole, I think a new Aristo is a better value than a new Lido. At $9,500, the Aristo costs less to purchase than the $11,300 Lido. The main advantage of the Lido is gas mileage. The Lido gets 28 city miles per gallon and 36 on the highway, while the Aristo gets 25 in the city and 32 on the highway. However, the Lido could cost more to operate in the long run because its repair record is not as good as the Aristo's. In addition, the Aristo has a very roomy rear seat. I'm afraid my kids would outgrow the backseat of the Lido in a couple of years. It looks like the Aristo is a better value for me.

EXERCISE 5

Directions: There are two comparison-contrast topics below. For each,

- Make a chart like the one in the example and fill it in with the details you would like to write about in your paragraph.

- Decide whether you want to write your paragraph whole to whole, like the first example on page 129, or point by point, like the second example above.

- Write your paragraph.

Part of the first chart is shown to help you get started.

1. Compare and contrast eating a meal in a restaurant with eating at home.

Items to Discuss	Eating in a Restaurant	Eating at Home
1. cost	paying someone else to do the work costs more	cooking and cleaning up yourself is cheap
2. convenience		

2. People become close friends because they have something in common: background, attitudes, or interests. Yet no two people are exactly alike. How are you and your best friend alike? How are you different? Write a paragraph comparing the two of you.

Revising Your Paragraphs

When you have finished writing your paragraphs, you may find you want to make some changes in them. First make any changes you know now you want to make. Then check your paragraphs against this checklist and make any further revisions that would improve your writing.

☐ Is there a topic sentence?

☐ Does the topic sentence state what you are comparing and contrasting?

☐ Do all the other sentences support the point that it makes?

☐ Are the sentences arranged in a logical order that will assist the reader in understanding the paragraph?

POSSIBLE ANSWERS ARE ON PAGE 353.

SIMPLE LISTING

WHEN TO USE SIMPLE LISTING

You're writing a letter to an out-of-state friend describing the tourist attractions in your area. You've been asked to write a brief summary of the fringe benefits offered by your company. In a job reference letter for a friend, you want to include a paragraph giving examples of your friend's problem-solving skills. How could you organize your writing in these situations?

For this kind of topic, no particular thought pattern imposes itself on your writing. Your supporting details can be presented in almost any order without causing confusion because they are related to one another only as specific examples of the main idea. The organization you need is *simple listing*.

You use simple listing to answer ordinary questions like "What things do you dislike about your job? What entrees are on the menu at the Royal Rib? What do you like about living near the ocean?" In more formal situations, simple listing might be used to answer such questions as "What are the arguments against the latest tax reform plan?" or "What are the different classes of mammals?"

WHEN TO USE A SIMPLE LISTING PATTERN
1. To give examples to support a main point
2. To list characteristics of an item
3. To break a large group into smaller categories

PUTTING THE LIST IN ORDER

Although no particular order is required for details when the simple listing pattern is used, you may want to establish your own order: smallest to largest, least to most unusual, least to most important. In the following sample paragraph, least-to-most-important order has been used.

> During the five years that Jacob Van Keulen worked for me, he was my most valuable employee. Mr. Van Keulen never called in sick, nor did he leave work early for any reason. On the job he produced 20 percent more parts than anyone else on the line. In fact, his time-saving suggestions resulted in a 10 percent increase in productivity for the plant as a whole.

The next paragraph is constructed in the order of smallest to largest.

> Among the animals you might run into in the woods are field mice and chipmunks. Next come rabbits and hedgehogs. Then there are foxes and raccoons, which can make as much noise as deer. In some parts of the country, you might even run into a bear in the woods.

EXERCISE 6

Directions: As part of a job application letter, you want to include a paragraph listing your qualifications for the job. Pick a job for which you feel qualified and write that paragraph. Take at least ten minutes to plan your paragraph before you write.

After you write your paragraph, take a few minutes to revise it. Make sure you have written a clear topic sentence and that your reader will be able to understand what you have written.

Publish your paragraph by reading it to a friend or a classmate.

ANSWERS WILL VARY.

READING ESSAY QUESTIONS

Part of your task on Part 2 of the GED Writing Skills Test will be to choose an appropriate pattern of organization for your essay. Often a clue word or phrase in the test question will help you pick the right pattern. For instance, in an earlier exercise, the following directions were given: *How are you and your best friend alike? How are you different? Write a paragraph comparing the two of you.* Circle the words that provided clues to the pattern of organization.

Did you find *alike, different, comparing*?

Some common terms associated with each pattern of organization are listed in the chart that follows.

Time Order	Comparison and Contrast	Simple Listing
how to	compare	list
an incident or event	contrast	kinds of
the process	similarities	types of
the procedure	alike	examples
	different	
Cause and Effect	favor	
	prefer	
reasons for	better	
causes of		
effects of		
results of		
why		

EXERCISE 7

Directions: Label the pattern of organization (time order, cause and effect, comparison/contrast, or simple listing) that each question requires and circle the terms in the question that provide a clue to the pattern.

Example: ___*time order*___ (Explain how) to change the oil in a car.

_____ **1.** Is baseball or football a more typically American game?

_____ **2.** Why are guns so common in the United States?

_____ **3.** Explain how to calm an angry toddler.

_____ **4.** What effect has the use of antibiotics had on society?

_____ **5.** Compare the advantages of living at home with your parents to living alone in an apartment.

_____ **6.** List ways that young teens might earn extra money.

_____ **7.** Give examples of some tourist attractions in your state.

_____ **8.** Trace the causes of unemployment in your city.

ANSWERS ARE ON PAGE 353.

> ### CHAPTER HIGHLIGHTS: PATTERNS OF ORGANIZATION
>
> **1.** A good paragraph must be well organized.
>
> **2.** A time order pattern is used to describe processes, routines, and events.
>
> **3.** A cause-effect pattern is used to trace reasons for an event and to trace or predict results.
>
> **4.** A comparison-contrast pattern is used to describe similarities or differences and to explain advantages or disadvantages.
>
> **5.** A simple listing pattern is used to give examples, list characteristics, and categorize.
>
> **6.** Check for clues to patterns of organization in essay test questions.

 # JOURNAL WRITING

Are you writing in your journal regularly? If so, you are getting valuable writing practice. Try writing on one or more of the following topics in your journal. Or think of your own topics. Remember, you're just writing for yourself. No one else needs to read your journal.

- What have you learned about yourself since you have been learning to write? Do you think you will continue to write even after you have completed the GED Writing Skills Test? Why or why not?

- Describe a favorite place of yours in detail. Try to cover all five senses in your description—sight, sound, smell, touch, and taste.

- Write about a trip you have been on. How did you get where you were going? What was traveling like? What did you do? Whom did you meet?

- What sport do you most enjoy playing or watching? If you swim, you might describe what it feels like to speed through the water. If you're a baseball fan, write what you like most about the game. Be as descriptive as you can.

- Your journal can be a good place to unload anger. Write about an argument you had with your parents or a friend or your boss. Put down everything you would have liked to say but didn't. Do you feel better after writing about it?

EXERCISE 8

PART A

Choose the best answer to each question.

1. Organize a paragraph in time order when you want to

    (1) list steps in a process
    (2) explain how something works
    (3) describe a routine
    (4) tell about an event
    (5) all of the above

2. Explaining why something happened or what will result from a certain action is called

    (1) time order
    (2) cause and effect
    (3) comparison and contrast
    (4) simple listing
    (5) point by point

3. Use a comparison-contrast pattern when you want to

    (1) predict results from an event
    (2) trace reasons for an event
    (3) describe how to do something
    (4) describe the order in which events occurred
    (5) describe similarities and differences

4. A simple listing pattern can be used to

    (1) compare and contrast
    (2) identify cause and effect
    (3) break a large group into smaller categories
    (4) show time order
    (5) all of the above

ANSWERS ARE ON PAGE 353.

PART B

GED Writing Topic

Directions: To help you prepare for Part 2 of the GED Writing Skills Test, a sample writing topic is included with Chapter 4 and each of the following chapters in this book. Try writing on this topic within the forty-five-minute limit that you will have on the actual test. Put all the writing skills to use that you have learned so far in paragraph construction, sentence structure, word choice, punctuation, and spelling.

Be sure to take ten minutes or so for prewriting, or planning. Read the question carefully to determine topic, purpose, audience, and probable pattern of organization. Circle any words that give clues to a particular pattern. Brainstorm a list of details. Next, write a first draft of your essay. Save the last five minutes to revise and edit it. If you want, publish your writing by showing it to a classmate or a friend.

During the past thirty years, television has become a core part of American life. Nearly every household has at least one television set. Some people say that television has benefited our society, while others see it as a cause of many problems. Explain how television has affected you. Support your explanation with specific examples.

POSSIBLE ANSWERS ARE ON PAGE 354.

Combining Ideas in Sentences

Which version of the paragraph below sounds better to you?

America has often been called the land of opportunity. My mother first came to this country at age eighteen. Her opportunities were limited indeed. She had no money for a place of her own. She boarded with her uncle and aunt. Her first year in America was spent working in a restaurant for her uncle. He was the head chef there. Mom's job was to carry heavy tubs of dirty forks, knives, and spoons into the kitchen. She was too proud to tell her parents about her real work. She wrote home, "I'm in charge of silverware!"

America has often been called the land of opportunity, but when my mother first came to this country at age eighteen, her opportunities were limited indeed. Because she had no money for a place of her own, she boarded with her uncle and aunt. Her first year in America was spent working in a restaurant for her uncle, who was the head chef there. Mom's job was to carry heavy tubs of dirty forks, knives, and spoons into the kitchen. She was too proud to tell her parents about her real work, so she wrote home, "I'm in charge of silverware!"

The first version is grammatically correct, but its sentences are all short and choppy, and the connections between them are not always clear. The second version is an improvement. The writer has combined sentences by using connecting words and punctuation, creating logical, smooth links among ideas.

Circle the connecting words that have been added in the second version. These words—*but, when, because, who,* and *so*—and others like them convert simple sentences into more complicated structures. Many of these structures are already part of your spoken English. In this section you'll learn to choose the correct wording and punctuation when you write them. As you study the next few pages, notice how often the connecting words help to reveal time order, cause-effect, comparison-contrast, and simple listing relationships.

Throughout this section, we'll be using the term *clause.*

> A ***clause*** is a group of words containing a subject and a verb.

We'll look at two kinds of clauses on the following pages: independent clauses and dependent clauses.

LINKING INDEPENDENT CLAUSES

COMPOUND SENTENCES

How might you combine each pair of sentences?

My mother hauled tubs of silverware. Her cousin poured coffee.
Their uncle hired them. He didn't pay them well.
The girls had borrowed money for their tickets to America. They had to work to repay their loans.

Although you have several possibilities, the simplest way to combine related ideas is to make a compound sentence. Here are the combined sentences:

My mother hauled tubs of silverware, **and** her cousin poured coffee.
Their uncle hired them, **but** he didn't pay them well.
The girls had borrowed money for their tickets to America, **so** they had to work to repay their loans.

> A **compound sentence** contains two or more connected independent clauses. Each clause is independent in that it could stand alone as a sentence. An **independent clause** makes a complete statement by itself.

CONJUNCTIONS

The examples above show the most common method of connecting independent clauses in a compound sentence: using a comma followed by a conjunction. Here's a list of conjunctions that link independent clauses.

Conjunctions	Use
and	adds related information
but, yet	shows an opposite or unexpected situation
or	presents a choice
nor	shows a rejection of both choices
for	links effect to cause
so	links cause to effect

Emil mowed the lawn, **and** Estella raked it.

Emil enjoyed the work, **but** Estella hated it.

Estella hated the work, **yet** she completed it.

Please be quiet, **or** I'll ask you to leave.

I won't be quiet, **nor** will I leave.

She left the dinner table, **for** she hated artichokes.

They served artichokes, **so** she left the table.

When clauses are combined with these conjunctions, the wording of both clauses is unchanged except when *nor* is used. Then the subject and verb in the second clause are reversed.

He doesn't like anchovies. He doesn't like pizza.
He doesn't like anchovies, nor **does he** like pizza.

He hasn't called. He hasn't sent a letter.
He hasn't called, **nor has he** sent a letter.

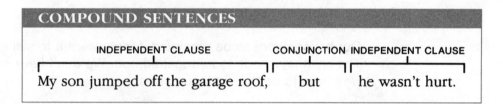

COMPOUND SENTENCES

INDEPENDENT CLAUSE	CONJUNCTION	INDEPENDENT CLAUSE
My son jumped off the garage roof,	but	he wasn't hurt.

EDITING HINT: Check to be sure the second part of any compound sentence is really an independent clause by using the tests for a complete sentence. Remember, an independent clause can stand on its own as a sentence. Here are the tests for a complete sentence or an independent clause: (1) The sentence must have a subject. (2) The sentence must have a predicate. Remember that the predicate contains the verb. (3) The sentence must express a complete thought.

The following sentence contains a very common compound sentence error. Can you find it?

Jacob went to the refrigerator, and pulled out a fish.

Test the second part of the sentence (everything that follows the conjunction) to make sure the independent clause can stand as a complete sentence: *pulled out a fish.* What is the problem? There is no subject. You could correct this problem like this:

Jacob went to the refrigerator, and **he** pulled out a fish.

Now test the second part of the sentence: *he pulled out a fish.* The clause now passes the tests for a complete sentence.

Not all clauses work well together in a compound sentence. What's wrong with the examples below?

Our house needs to be repainted, and our dog loves to eat tennis shoes.

Our house needs to be repainted, for we want it to sell more quickly, and the chimney needs to be repaired, but we don't have much money, so we'll have to do the work ourselves.

In the first sentence, the two clauses aren't logically related at all. They belong in separate sentences. A better version, with related clauses, might read like this:

Our house needs to be repainted, and the chimney needs to be repaired.

The second sentence got carried away. There are so many independent clauses strung together with conjunctions that the sentence reads as a breathless six-year-old would speak. In general, two independent clauses in a sentence are fine. Three are shaky, and four or more are bad style. Correct the problem by breaking the sentence into shorter ones:

Our house needs to be repainted, for we want it to sell more quickly. The chimney needs to be repaired, too. We don't have much money, so we'll have to do the work ourselves.

CAUTIONS ON COMPOUND SENTENCES

1. Make sure the second part of the sentence is really an independent clause.

2. Don't connect unrelated clauses.

3. Don't connect too many clauses.

EXERCISE 9

Part A

Directions: If the sentences on page 141 combine well in a compound sentence, rewrite them by placing a comma and one of the following conjunctions between them: *and, but, or, nor, for, so, yet.* (Often more than one conjunction will make sense.) Then make any necessary wording changes. If the sentences should not be combined, place an *X* in the space provided.

Examples: _____ **a.** Bob never jogs. He doesn't swim.

Bob never jogs, and he doesn't swim.

___X___ **b.** Dick despises egg salad sandwiches. He plays the banjo.

_____ **1.** Color photographs are bright at first. They begin to fade in a few years.

_____ **2.** Do you want spaghetti for supper tonight? Would you prefer pizza?

_____ **3.** Some comic strips aren't intended to be funny. Comics are printed in color for the Sunday edition.

_____ **4.** The crowd roared its approval. The cheerleaders jumped for joy.

_____ **5.** The walls of the living room are magenta. The carpet is daffodil yellow.

_____ **6.** Andrea was afraid to dive off the high board. She knew she would do a belly flop.

_____ **7.** Neither Sam nor Barbara had finished high school. They managed to put their three children through college.

_____ **8.** It was the first warm spring day. Kelly begged to go outside.

_____ **9.** Television quiz shows are exciting. Ron Matthews is the host of a local radio talk show.

_____ **10.** We might look for work in the Minneapolis area. We might move to Phoenix.

Part B

Directions: Complete each compound sentence below by using the conjunction indicated for each and adding a logical independent clause. Remember to place a comma before the conjunction.

1. *(but)* The Amadeos wanted a new car

2. *(or)* I may decide to move to Texas

3. *(yet)* He wanted to be respected

4. *(nor)* Dr. Brady didn't make house calls

5. *(for)* Tua is studying computer science

6. *(and)* Mrs. Perez painted her bathroom

7. *(so)* Frank Cataldo wants his son to do well in school

POSSIBLE ANSWERS ARE ON PAGE 354.

◎ FOCUS ON PUNCTUATION

Commas with *And*

Many beginning writers want an answer to one simple question: "Do you use a comma before *and*, or don't you?" After studying compound elements in Chapter 2 and compound sentences in this chapter, you know that there are three answers to that question.

1. Use a comma before *and* if it connects two complete thoughts (independent clauses).

John washed the dinner dishes, **and** Gina photographed the event.
The night was dark, **and** the wind whistled ominously through the trees.

2. Use a comma before *and* in a series of three or more compound elements.

Mashed potatoes, black pepper, **and** sherry are ingredients in this bread.
Stanley turned, sneered, **and** strode out of the room.

3. Don't use a comma before *and* when it connects only two compound elements.

Dimley Wedgewood **and** his sister Heloise have lived in this mansion for years.
Every afternoon Dimley drinks a cup of tea **and** retires to the den to harass the canary.

How does the above example differ from this one?

Every afternoon Dimley drinks a cup of tea, **and he** retires to the den to harass the canary.

By adding the subject *he* after the conjunction *and*, we've made a compound sentence requiring a comma.

EXERCISE 10

Directions: Some of the sentences below need to have a comma inserted before *and*. Using the three rules given on page 142, punctuate the sentences correctly.

Examples: **a.** Tam checked the oil and put some air in the tires.

b. Tam checked the oil and after that she put some air in the tires.

1. A cup of coffee and a piece of toast were all she ate that day.

2. A cup of coffee, a piece of toast and an orange were all she ate that day.

3. Tuan politely requested an application form and sat down to fill it out.

4. Tuan politely requested an application form and after that he sat down to fill it out.

5. Julio plans to become a diesel mechanic and Michael wants to play drums in a rock band.

6. Anita puts a big pot of soup on the stove every morning and dips in whenever she's hungry.

7. Automatic transmission, power steering and power brakes are standard on most models.

8. Job openings are available in restaurants, clothing stores and lawn care.

9. Maria was watching her favorite soap and Toni was studying a racing form.

10. The squirrel glanced up, froze momentarily and darted for the tree.

ANSWERS ARE ON PAGE 354.

CONNECTORS

In formal writing, a second method of connecting clauses in compound sentences is sometimes used. You might be able to spot the joining word or phrase and the punctuation used with it in the following examples.

America has often been called the land of opportunity; however, my mother's opportunities were limited indeed.
She was too proud to tell her parents about her real work; therefore, she wrote home, "I'm in charge of silverware!"

This second pattern uses a semicolon before connectors such as *however* and *therefore* and a comma after them. A list of the most common connectors used in this pattern is on page 144.

Connector	Use
moreover furthermore in addition	adds related information (like *and*)
however nevertheless	shows a contrasting or unexpected situation (like *but*)
therefore consequently	links cause to effect (like *so*)
otherwise	shows an alternative (like *or*)
for instance for example	gives specifics to illustrate a general idea
then	shows time order

Dan excels at tennis; **moreover,** he's the fastest sprinter on the track team.

The doctors had given Stacy only six months to live; **nevertheless,** she returned to work full-time.

Samuel was angry with his boss; **therefore,** he refused to work overtime.

Sit down and stop causing trouble; **otherwise,** I'll rearrange your face.

Inflation is more obvious to older people; **for instance,** I can remember buying gasoline for a quarter per gallon.

First we soaped the dog thoroughly; **then** we poured a bucket of water over her. *(Notice that no comma is needed after* then.*)*

The meaning of a connector is very important because it shows the relationship between the two ideas in a sentence. Why is the connector *moreover* used in the following example?

Tomas is a handsome man; moreover, he's very intelligent.

Moreover signals that the second clause will add related information to the first: both make positive comments about Tomas.

What relationship is signaled by the connector in the next example?

Tomas is a handsome man; consequently, women are attracted to him.

This sentence shows a cause-effect relationship. Tomas is handsome, so women like him.

Could *consequently* also be used to link the two sentences below?

Tomas is a handsome man. Elsa thinks he's ugly.

The two sentences are linked by contrast, not by cause-effect. The word *consequently* won't link them logically. What connector would logically link these two sentences? If you're not sure, look back for contrast connectors in the chart on page 144. One connector that will work is *nevertheless*:

Tomas is a handsome man; nevertheless, Elsa thinks he's ugly.

EXERCISE 11

Directions: Combine each pair of sentences below by choosing the most logical connector and rewriting them as one sentence. If you're unsure of which connector to use, check the chart on page 144 for meaning. Be sure to punctuate the sentence correctly.

Example: Tina was an independent baby. At ten months she insisted on holding her own bottle.
   a. however
   b. in addition
   (**c.**) for example
   d. then

> *Tina was an independent baby; for example, at ten months she insisted on holding her own bottle.*

1. The bus driver was frequently late to work. She lost her job.
   a. however
   b. therefore
   c. in addition
   d. for example

2. I can't stand your cooking. I despise your taste in music.
   a. moreover
   b. however
   c. therefore
   d. otherwise

3. The rear license plate was missing. The police officer didn't give Leon a ticket.
   a. furthermore
   b. however
   c. consequently
   d. for instance

4. Catch up on your child support payments by next month. We'll garnishee your wages.
   a. in addition
   b. however
   c. otherwise
   d. for example

5. Cynthia is sometimes forgetful. Once she bought three bags of groceries at the supermarket and drove home without them.
   a. furthermore
   b. otherwise
   c. therefore
   d. for instance

6. Popcorn is a tasty snack. It's more nutritious than candy.
   a. moreover
   b. nevertheless
   c. consequently
   d. for instance

7. Our ambassador spoke only English. He needed an interpreter with him at all times.
   a. furthermore
   b. however
   c. consequently
   d. otherwise

8. Eric was placed on probation for two years. He was ordered to pay back the money he stole.
   a. in addition
   b. consequently
   c. for instance
   d. however

9. She deeply distrusted his motives. She gave him her address.
   a. moreover
   b. therefore
   c. otherwise
   d. nevertheless

10. We hate hot, humid weather. We plan to stay in tropical Florida.
    a. in addition
    b. therefore
    c. however
    d. for example

ANSWERS ARE ON PAGE 355.

Part B

Directions: Complete each compound sentence below by using the connector indicated for each and adding a logical independent clause. Remember to place a semicolon before and a comma after the connector.

1. *(however)* Shan loves to stay up late

_____

_____

2. *(therefore)* I want to earn $50,000 a year

_____

_____

3. *(moreover)* Kelly bakes the best pies in town

_____

_____

4. *(otherwise)* You should cut down on your drinking

_____

_____

5. *(for example)* Theodore is the meanest kid on the block

_____

_____

POSSIBLE ANSWERS ARE ON PAGE 355.

⊙ **FOCUS ON PUNCTUATION**

Run-Ons and Comma Splices

Now that you know two correct ways to connect clauses in compound sentences, you'll find it easier to avoid the incorrect connections. In standard written English, it is incorrect to

- write a run-on sentence (run two independent clauses together with no connecting words or punctuation)

    INCORRECT: Jim says he's not feeling well he's coming to work anyway.

    CORRECT: Jim says he's not feeling well, but he's coming to work anyway.

- write a comma splice (join two independent clauses with just a comma)

    INCORRECT: Ron is a real slob, he hasn't washed his socks in two years.

    CORRECT: Ron is a real slob. He hasn't washed his socks in two years.

One problem with a run-on or comma splice is that the relationship between the two clauses is unclear. What is the relationship, or logical link, between the ideas in the comma splice below?

    INCORRECT: The car wouldn't start again today, I must need a new battery.

The link is cause to effect. If you find a run-on or comma splice like the one above while proofreading, how can you correct it?

Here are three ways to correct run-ons and comma splices:

- Connect the clauses with a comma and one of the following conjunctions: *and, but, or, nor, for, so, yet.*

    The car wouldn't start again today, so I must need a new battery.

- Connect the clauses with a semicolon, connector, and comma. (Remember, connectors are words like *however, therefore*, and *furthermore.*)

    The car wouldn't start again today; therefore, I must need a new battery.

- Place a period after the first clause to make two sentences.

    The car wouldn't start again today. I must need a new battery.

EXERCISE 12

Part A

Directions: Correct each run-on or comma splice below by using one of the three methods listed on page 148. Be sure you have used each method at least once by the time you have finished the exercise.

Example: Many teenagers don't mind lying to their parents, they can't stand having their parents lie to them.

Many teenagers don't mind lying to their parents, but they can't stand having their parents lie to them.

1. Harvey couldn't believe his eyes there was an iguana in the bathtub.

2. He tried to trap the iguana in his old guitar case, it had other ideas.

3. Harvey stared thoughtfully at the iguana, the creature stared back.

4. Suddenly Harvey slapped his forehead then he jumped up and ran away.

5. The iguana waited patiently for round two it was in no hurry to leave its porcelain palace.

6. Falling in love can be delightful, it can also be total hell.

7. Women think they have to be gorgeous men spend all their time trying to be tough.

8. Some couples manage to give up the pretenses and just love each other, those are the best relationships.

Part B

Directions: There are six run-ons and comma splices in the paragraph below. Cross out and correct them using any of the three methods you've learned. The first error has been corrected as an example.

buy, but they're

Used cars are fairly cheap to ~~buy, they're~~ not always cheap to run. We

bought a car with seventy thousand miles on the odometer it ran just fine

for three months then our troubles began. The car began to gulp two

quarts of oil a week, there was always a cloud of black smoke following us.

Then the transmission started to go we had to swear at it to get it out of

reverse. The electrical system was the last straw. We would turn the heater

on, and the lights would go off. We'd had enough, we sold our bargain to a

junk collector for ten dollars.

POSSIBLE ANSWERS ARE ON PAGE 355.

LINKING DEPENDENT CLAUSES
COMPLEX SENTENCES

You've already seen this type of sentence structure:

> My mother had no money for a place of her own, so she boarded with her uncle and aunt.

As you know, the above example is a compound sentence: two independent clauses joined by a conjunction. If we removed the conjunction *so*, each clause could stand alone as a sentence. In the sentence below, you'll find the same meaning but a different pattern used. Read each half of the sentence aloud. Could each clause stand alone?

> Because my mother had no money for a place of her own, she boarded with her uncle and aunt.

This time the first clause does not make sense by itself. It raises a question for the second clause to answer: What happened because my mother had no money? Since this first clause depends on the second to complete the thought of the sentence, it is called a dependent clause. Together the clauses make a complex sentence.

> A ***complex sentence*** contains a ***dependent clause*** connected to an independent clause.

Circle the word *because* in the second sample sentence above. Now read the first clause without that word:

> My mother had no money for a place of her own.

The clause can stand alone again, can't it? It's the word *because* that changes the clause from independent to dependent. A ***subordinating conjunction*** like *because*, *after*, or *if* makes its clause dependent and shows the logical link to the independent clause. Either clause can be placed first in the sentence:

> Lola was not at the wedding **although** the bride was her best friend.
> **Although** the bride was her best friend, Lola was not at the wedding.

To see more clearly how the conjunction provides a logical link between clauses, compare the three sentences below. Each is a complex sentence with identical clauses except for the conjunction. Circle the conjunctions. How do they change the meaning of the sentences?

> **After** Ann lost her job, she spent a week cleaning her apartment.
> **Because** Ann lost her job, she spent a week cleaning her apartment.
> **Whenever** Ann lost her job, she spent a week cleaning her apartment.

The word *After* in the first example shows a time relationship between two events: first she lost her job; then she cleaned. *Because* shows a cause-effect relationship: the reason Ann cleaned was that she had lost her job. *Whenever* shows a habitual relationship: apparently Ann regularly cleaned her apartment after losing a job. In each case just one word, the conjunction, can change the meaning of the sentence.

The following list of subordinating conjunctions is grouped by the relationships that they show. Note how many of these words are useful in expressing time order, cause-effect, and comparison-contrast.

Time	
before	Georgia becomes surly **whenever** Stan watches a football game.
after	
while	**As soon as** the water boils, we'll make
when	the poison.
whenever	
until	
as soon as	
as long as	
Reasons (Cause and Effect)	
because	We began saving our money **so that** we
since	could make a down payment on a
so that	house.
in order that	
Conditions	
if	**Unless** the snow stops soon, we'll have
unless	to spend the night here.
whether	
Contrast	
though	**Although** Julio faints at the sight of
although	blood, he wants to become a surgeon.
even though	
in spite of the fact that	I'm leaving you **despite the fact that** I
despite the fact that	care for you very much.
whereas	
Similarity	
as though	This leftover stew looks **as if** it should
as if	be thrown away.
Place	
where	**Wherever** she went, the hamster went,
wherever	too.

EDITING HINT: Pay particular attention to the conjunctions listed under "Contrast." These words have approximately the same meaning as *but*. If you're unsure whether one of them is correct to use when combining two sentences, try substituting *but*.

> EXAMPLE: Lisa felt terrible. She smiled cheerfully.
> TRY *BUT*: Lisa felt terrible, but she smiled cheerfully.

It works; the sentences do show a contrast between how Lisa felt and what she did. Therefore, we can use *despite the fact that* to combine them:

Despite the fact that Lisa felt terrible, she smiled cheerfully.

Whether you're writing on your own or taking Part 1 of the GED Writing Skills Test, it's important to choose a conjunction that clearly shows the relationship between clauses. Which subordinating conjunctions from the list might logically fit into the sentence below?

Horace became very quiet _____ he learned his fiancee was now a professional wrestler.

The words *after* and *when* make perfect sense in this sentence since the two clauses have a time relationship. Test some other choices, like *so that* and *wherever*. They make no sense at all. Be sure to read a complex sentence carefully to make sure your conjunction is logical.

What is the relationship between the two sentences below?

Lucille preferred her grasshoppers boiled. She occasionally ate them raw.

These sentences contrast with each other. Using a conjunction from the contrast category on page 151, combine them into one sentence.

_____

_____

You could have combined them like this:

Although Lucille preferred her grasshoppers boiled, she occasionally ate them raw.

Let's try one more example. What conjunction might fit into the sentence below?

Vincent's mother made him stay in the house on Saturday _____ he refused to brush his teeth.

The relationship between the clauses is cause-effect. Either *because* or *since* will link them clearly.

EXERCISE 13

Choose the best answer to each question.

1. <u>Whereas</u> **we looked in Veronica's room, there were clothes.**

   Which of the following is the best way to write the underlined portion of this sentence? If you think the original is the best way, choose option (1).

   (1) Whereas
   (2) Wherever
   (3) As long as
   (4) Since
   (5) While

2. **You look as pale <u>as if</u> you'd seen a ghost.**

   Which of the following is the best way to write the underlined portion of this sentence? If you think the original is the best way, choose option (1).

   (1) as if
   (2) as soon as
   (3) after
   (4) if
   (5) because

3. **Because you eliminate your tardiness, we'll have to fire you.**

   What correction should be made to this sentence?

   (1) change *Because* to *If*
   (2) change *Because* to *After*
   (3) change *Because* to *In order that*
   (4) change *Because* to *Unless*
   (5) no correction is necessary

4. **Sanyu sobbed loudly if everyone else in the room would feel properly sympathetic.**

   What correction should be made to this sentence?

   (1) change *if* to *despite the fact that*
   (2) change *if* to *as long as*
   (3) change *if* to *so that*
   (4) change *if* to *whenever*
   (5) no correction is necessary

5. <u>Even though</u> **Harriet's car broke down on the way to work, she still arrived ten minutes early.**

   Which of the following is the best way to write the underlined portion of this sentence? If you think the original is the best way, choose option (1).

   (1) Even though
   (2) Because
   (3) Since
   (4) As though
   (5) Before

6. <u>Unless</u> **you crack your knuckles one more time, I'll be forced to chop your fingers off.**

   Which of the following is the best way to write the underlined portion of this sentence? If you think the original is the best way, choose option (1).

   (1) Unless
   (2) Because
   (3) When
   (4) If
   (5) Although

7. **When the hour was late, the party showed no signs of winding down.**

   What correction should be made to this sentence?

   (1) change *When* to *As though*
   (2) change *When* to *Before*
   (3) change *When* to *Though*
   (4) change *When* to *If*
   (5) no correction is necessary

8. **Clementine was never popular in order that she had great clothes and piles of money.**

   What correction should be made to this sentence?

   (1) change *in order that* to *wherever*
   (2) change *in order that* to *as if*
   (3) change *in order that* to *as soon as*
   (4) change *in order that* to *despite the fact that*
   (5) no correction is necessary

9. <u>After</u> she had been in the wreck, Karen never again asked to borrow the car.

Which of the following is the best way to write the underlined portion of this sentence? If you think the original is the best way, choose option (1).

(1) After
(2) Before
(3) Whenever
(4) Whereas
(5) Although

10. <u>Until</u> she could answer his question, he fell fast asleep.

Which of the following is the best way to write the underlined portion of this sentence? If you think the original is the best way, choose option (1).

(1) Until
(2) As though
(3) After
(4) In order that
(5) Before

ANSWERS ARE ON PAGE 355.

⊙ **FOCUS ON PUNCTUATION**

Punctuating Complex Sentences

You have seen that a conjunction and the dependent clause that follows it may appear at the beginning or at the end of a complex sentence. The punctuation of the sentence is controlled by the location of the dependent clause. After studying the two pairs of sentences below, can you explain when to use a comma and when not to?

> After we scolded him, the dog retreated into his house.
> The dog retreated into his house after we scolded him.

> Because he hated to get drunk, Jeff stayed home from the New Year's Eve party.
> Jeff stayed home from the New Year's Eve party because he hated to get drunk.

In the first sentence of each pair, the dependent clause comes first and is followed by a comma. In the second sentence of each pair, the independent clause comes first, and no comma is needed before the dependent clause. Notice, too, that no comma is used *after* the conjunction in a complex sentence.

> INCORRECT: Jeff stayed home because, he hated to get drunk.
> CORRECT: Jeff stayed home because he hated to get drunk.

RULES FOR PUNCTUATING COMPLEX SENTENCES

1. When the dependent clause comes first, separate it from the independent clause with a comma.

2. When the independent clause comes first, don't use a comma.

EXERCISE 14

Directions: Place a comma where needed in the sentences below. If no comma is needed, place a *C* in the space provided.

Examples: _____ **a.** If I hear that song once more, I'll break the radio.

_**C**_ **b.** I'll break the radio if I hear that song once more.

_____ **1.** The senator was met with hostility wherever he traveled that day. _____ **2.** When he tried to speak he was pelted with rotten eggs. _____ **3.** After his constituents had booed him for the tenth time in fifteen minutes he wadded up his speech and left the platform. _____ **4.** He felt as if his political career was over. _____ **5.** Although he had done his best there was no chance for reelection. _____ **6.** Belinda arrived at the department store before the doors were unlocked. _____ **7.** While she waited for the store to open she planned her shopping strategy. _____ **8.** Although she was the only customer waiting outside she stayed close to the door. _____ **9.** All the best buys could be snatched up if anyone got into the store before her. _____ **10.** Since this clearance sale happened only once a year she was determined to take advantage of it.

ANSWERS ARE ON PAGE 356.

◉ FOCUS ON PUNCTUATION

Eliminating Dependent Clause Fragments

Remember, a written sentence should not raise unanswered questions for the reader. Does the word group below make sense by itself?

When John called last night.

The word group does have a subject, *John*, and a verb, *called*; however, it leaves you with the question "What happened when John called last night?" Therefore, it's a fragment.

> Don't mistake a dependent clause for a sentence.

Writers often overlook dependent clause fragments because within the paragraph as a whole these word groups often make sense. To find them more easily, each time you find a subordinating conjunction such as *if*, *because*, or *unless*, check to be sure that the clause following it is part of a complex sentence rather than a fragment set off by itself.

Try this technique on the passage below. Find and underline two dependent clause fragments.

Although they used to be just science fiction toys. Robots are now a reality in the business world. These computerized creatures have revolutionized the manufacturing industry. Because they can perform repetitive precision tasks with absolute accuracy, robots are replacing people on assembly lines. You can expect to see more and more in use. As companies retool for the twenty-first century.

The two fragments are *Although they used to be just science fiction toys* and *As companies retool for the twenty-first century*. Once you've found dependent clause fragments, correcting them is easy. In our sample paragraph, the first fragment can be attached to the sentence that follows it, and the second fragment can be attached to the sentence that precedes it:

Although they used to be just science fiction toys, robots are now a reality in the business world.

You can expect to see more and more in use as companies retool for the twenty-first century.

EXERCISE 15

Part A

Directions: Label each group of words in the following paragraph as a sentence *(S)* or a dependent clause fragment *(F)* in the space provided.

Examples: __F__ **a.** When you read this.   __S__ **b.** Look at each word group by itself.

_____ **1.** Riding the bus to work is an adventure in people watching.   _____ **2.** Each morning after I get on at 7:30.   _____ **3.** The same motley cast assembles.

_____ **4.** At the first stop after mine, a teenaged couple gets on.   _____ **5.** They hurry to the back of the bus.   _____ **6.** So that they can hug and kiss undisturbed.

_____ **7.** Then the sports enthusiast appears.   _____ **8.** He sits across from the driver and talks nonstop about the latest game.   _____ **9.** If the driver tries to change the subject.   _____ **10.** He simply interrupts.   _____ **11.** My favorite character is the tiny old lady with the shopping bags.   _____ **12.** Although she never says anything.

_____ **13.** She observes the other passengers with as much interest as I do.

_____ **14.** I wonder what she's thinking.   _____ **15.** As she watches our commuting companions.   _____ **16.** I'm always kind of sorry when the time comes to get off the bus.   _____ **17.** And start working.

Part B

Directions: Rewrite the paragraph in Part A to eliminate the fragments you found. As you attach these dependent clauses to independent clauses, be sure to insert commas where necessary.

ANSWERS ARE ON PAGE 356.

WORDING IN COMPLEX SENTENCES

Which of these sentences is incorrect?

Although Sam had hoped for a son, he was delighted with his daughter.

Although Sam had hoped for a son, but he was delighted with his daughter.

Sam had hoped for a son, but he was delighted with his daughter.

The first is a complex sentence linked by the subordinating conjunction *although*. The third is a compound sentence linked by the coordinating conjunction *but*. The second is an incorrect sentence because it uses linking words that have similar meanings. Don't use both in one sentence.

Use one connecting word from each of the following groups in a single sentence, but not more than one.

GROUP 1: although, but, yet, however

GROUP 2: because, so, therefore

GROUP 3: after, then

GROUP 4: when, then

EXERCISE 16

Directions: Each sentence below contains two linking words from the same group. Correct each sentence in two ways by using each of the linking words in the original sentence correctly. Be sure to punctuate each new sentence properly.

Example: Because Arturo was tired, so he fell asleep after dinner.

Because Arturo was tired, he fell asleep after dinner.

Arturo was tired, so he fell asleep after dinner.

1. After the last guest left, then we cleaned the apartment.
   a.
   b.

2. When the wind blows hard, then the windows rattle.
   a.
   b.

3. Although Rosa wants to lose weight; however, she can't resist buttered popcorn.
   a.
   b.

ANSWERS ARE ON PAGE 356.

REWRITING SENTENCES

COMBINING IDEAS IN DIFFERENT WAYS

Writers often try to combine two short sentences that each contain one idea into one longer sentence that carries all the information. Combining sentences makes writing smoother, and, as you have seen, connecting words also help make the relationship between ideas clearer.

When you are trying to combine two ideas into one sentence, usually more than one choice of sentence pattern will work to connect the ideas logically. You have learned several sentence structures and many connectors and conjunctions in this chapter. How many ways can you think of to combine the ideas in the following two sentences? It's fine to change a word or two or rearrange the order of ideas. Just make sure the meaning stays the same.

Pat had had a long hard week at work.
She was ready for a Friday night on the town.

On a piece of scratch paper, jot down three different ways you could correctly and logically combine these two sentences into one sentence.

You probably realized that the two sentences have a cause-effect relationship. Any of the following combined sentences would be correct. You might have thought of other combinations as well.

Pat had had a long hard week at work, so she was ready for a Friday night on the town.

Since Pat had had a long hard week at work, she was ready for a Friday night on the town.

Pat had had a long hard week at work; as a result, she was ready for a Friday night on the town.

EXERCISE 17

Directions: Combine each of the following pairs of sentences three different ways.

1. Leroy had had difficulty with math as a child.
   At fifty-six he mastered fractions, decimals, and percents.

2. An iguana climbed out of Harvey's bathtub.
   Harvey called the dogcatcher.

3. Bridget has lost twenty-five pounds.
   She is determined to lose fifteen pounds more.

POSSIBLE ANSWERS ARE ON PAGE 356.

REWRITING SENTENCES IN DIFFERENT WAYS

Now you have worked on finding different ways of rewriting two separate sentences to make one combined sentence. What if you wanted to rewrite a single sentence that already contained two ideas, but you didn't want to change the meaning? Sometimes you might decide that a sentence does not show the relationship between ideas as clearly as it could. Or you might decide that you had used the same sentence structure too many times, making your writing dull.

How many different ways can you think of to rewrite the following sentence? Look at the two parts of the sentence. How are the parts related? You will want to show the relationship in any new sentence you write. Try to rearrange the ideas and fit them together in new ways. You will probably have to change a few words as well as the punctuation.

Ellen sat down at the desk, and a painting fell on her head.

On a piece of scratch paper, jot down at least three ways you could correctly rewrite this sentence without changing the meaning.

You probably noticed that the two parts of the sentence are related by time order. Any of the following sentences would correctly express the same meaning as the old sentence, and other correct sentences are possible.

Ellen sat down at the desk; then a painting fell on her head.

A painting fell on Ellen's head after she sat down at the desk.

When Ellen sat down at the desk, a painting fell on her head.

In the following exercise, you'll practice rewriting sentences in different ways. Be sure to retain the meaning of the original sentence in all the rewritten sentences. Stretch your imagination and your knowledge of sentence structure to think of different ways to restate the same ideas.

EXERCISE 18

Directions: Rewrite each of the following sentences three different ways.

1. Tom did not tell Jill about losing the airline tickets, so she was angry with him.

2. Gigi was anxious to get home because she needed to feed her cats.

3. Sarah ordered lunch for the department; then she made us all watch a soap opera.

4. When Ann dialed a wrong number, she got the city morgue.

POSSIBLE ANSWERS ARE ON PAGE 357.

SENTENCE COMBINING IN GED TEST QUESTIONS

One kind of question on Part 1 of the GED Writing Skills Test will require you to change the pattern of a sentence or combine two sentences without changing the meaning. The original sentence or sentences will contain no errors at all. Your job will be to figure out what the writer is trying to say and then to choose a pattern that expresses the same idea clearly. If you can recognize which linking words in compound and complex sentences have similar meanings, you'll be able to answer many of these questions correctly. There are two types of these questions, so study the following examples carefully to get an idea of each type.

Example 1: **Although the fire was extinguished immediately, there was considerable smoke damage.**

If you rewrote the sentence beginning with

The fire was extinguished immediately,

the next word should be

(1) so
(2) then
(3) but
(4) and
(4) if

Check: **The fire was extinguished immediately, but there was considerable smoke damage**. If you do this check with the other answer choices, the sentence will not make sense. The relationship between the two ideas is a contrast.

Example 2: **Terry ran out of the house in tears. He had heard a ghost in the attic.**

The most effective combination of these sentences would include which of the following groups of words?

(1) Then he had heard a ghost in the attic, so Terry
(2) Because he had heard a ghost in the attic, Terry
(3) Terry had heard a ghost in the attic; nonetheless, he
(4) Terry had heard a ghost in the attic, but he
(5) Unless he had heard a ghost in the attic, Terry

Check: **Because he had heard a ghost in the attic, Terry ran out of the house in tears.** If you test the other answer choices this way, the combination sentence will not make sense. The relationship between the two sentences is cause and effect.

EXERCISE 19

Choose the best answer to each question.

1. **Joan put the baby to bed. Then she poured herself a cup of coffee.**

   The most effective combination of these sentences would include which of the following groups of words?

   (1) After Joan put the baby to bed, she
   (2) After Joan put the baby to bed when
   (3) Because Joan put the baby to bed when
   (4) Joan put the baby to bed when
   (5) Because Joan put the baby to bed; then

2. **Because the grocery store was closed, we couldn't buy more milk.**

   If you rewrote the sentence beginning with

   The grocery store was closed,

   the next word should be

   (1) because
   (2) for
   (3) although
   (4) and
   (5) so

3. **The vandals kicked in the door. They didn't steal anything.**

   The most effective combination of these sentences would include which of the following groups of words?

   (1) Although the vandals kicked in the door, they
   (2) Because the vandals kicked in the door, but
   (3) Although the vandals kicked in the door, and
   (4) Because the vandals kicked in the door, they
   (5) Although the vandals kicked in the door, but

4. **When the clock struck twelve, the guests decided to leave.**

   If you rewrote this sentence beginning with

   The clock struck twelve;

   the next word should be

   (1) after
   (2) for
   (3) then
   (4) until
   (5) when

5. **Although the patient is in critical condition, the doctors expect him to recover.**

   If you rewrote the sentence beginning with

   The patient is in critical condition;

   the next word should be

   (1) therefore
   (2) however
   (3) moreover
   (4) then
   (5) otherwise

ANSWERS ARE ON PAGE 357.

SEQUENCE OF TENSES

SHOWING TIME RELATIONSHIPS

You'll remember from Chapter 3 that a verb shows time by its tense. For instance, *will walk, walk, walked, have walked, had walked, are walking*, and *were walking* each indicate a different aspect of present, past, and future. To review these tenses, you may want to go back and look at pages 79–119 right now.

As you learned in the last section, a complex sentence has a dependent clause and an independent clause joined by a subordinating conjunction like *if* or *since*. A complex sentence always has two verbs, one in each clause. The tenses of these verbs must be related logically in order for the sentence to make sense.

Which of the following sentences is correct?

When George passes the last test, he received his GED.

When George passes the last test, he will receive his GED.

In the first sentence, the verb tenses are not related logically. The present tense *passes* in the dependent clause doesn't make sense with the past tense *received* in the independent clause. Has George finished, or hasn't he? In the second sentence, the verb tenses make sense. The present tense *passes* connects logically with the future tense *will receive* to show that George has not yet finished his GED Tests.

The following examples show the usual sequence of tense patterns in complex sentences. Check to make sure you understand each one by writing your own example in the space provided.

Using a dependent clause in the present tense and an independent clause in the future tense show a look into the future, with the action in the dependent clause occurring first.

PRESENT   FUTURE

If George passes his last test, he will celebrate for a week.

Your example: _____

_____

A dependent clause in the present tense and an independent clause also in the present tense show that the statement is always true.

PRESENT   PRESENT

When a student passes the last test, he is relieved.

Your example: _____

_____

A dependent clause in the past continuing tense and an independent clause in the past or past continuing tense shows two continuing actions happening at the same time.

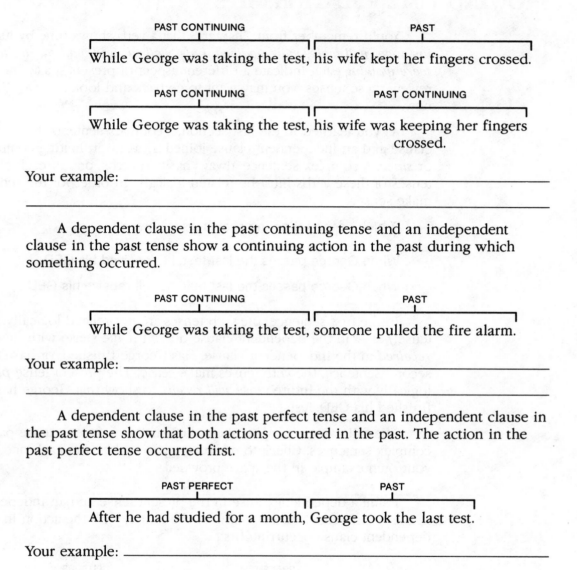

PAST CONTINUING　　　　　　　　　PAST

While George was taking the test, his wife kept her fingers crossed.

PAST CONTINUING　　　　　　　　　PAST CONTINUING

While George was taking the test, his wife was keeping her fingers crossed.

Your example: _____

_____

A dependent clause in the past continuing tense and an independent clause in the past tense show a continuing action in the past during which something occurred.

PAST CONTINUING　　　　　　　　　PAST

While George was taking the test, someone pulled the fire alarm.

Your example: _____

_____

A dependent clause in the past perfect tense and an independent clause in the past tense show that both actions occurred in the past. The action in the past perfect tense occurred first.

PAST PERFECT　　　　　　　　　PAST

After he had studied for a month, George took the last test.

Your example: _____

_____

You've already learned how to use helping verbs like *is, was, have*, and *had* to form various tenses. There are a few other helpers that you should be familiar with for proper sequence of tenses. Some are used as present or future tense verbs, others as past tense. The chart at the top of page 165 will show you how each is used.

Present or Future	*Past*
can shall will may must	could should would might had to

If the other clause is in the present tense, use a helping verb from the "present or future" column. If the other clause is in the past tense, use a verb from the "past" column.

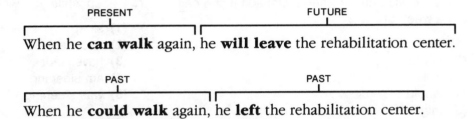

When he **can walk** again, he **will leave** the rehabilitation center.

When he **could walk** again, he **left** the rehabilitation center.

EDITING HINT: When you're trying to figure out what verb tenses to use in different clauses, you may find it helpful to isolate the subject and verb in each clause. First, read the entire sentence to understand its meaning. Then mentally read just the conjunction and the subjects and verbs from each clause:

Before we go to the movie, we will eat dinner at Maud's.

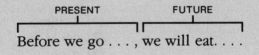

Before we go . . . , we will eat. . . .

Isolating the conjunction and the subjects and verbs may help you identify errors in sequence of tense. What is the sequence of events in the next sentence?

INCORRECT: Because Amy already read the funnies, she gave Meena the newspaper.

Because Amy read . . . , she gave. . . .

You know that when two events occurred in the past and one happened before the other, the earlier event should be in the past perfect tense. The corrected sentence should read like this:

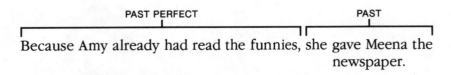

Because Amy already had read the funnies, she gave Meena the newspaper.

≡ GED Practice ≡
EXERCISE 20

Choose the best answer to each question.

1. When Sandra saw her husband's face, she <u>knows</u> something was wrong.

    (1) knows
    (2) will know
    (3) knew
    (4) had known
    (5) has known

2. Tracy will visit her brother in Canada if she <u>can</u> get a week off.

    (1) can
    (2) could
    (3) will
    (4) would
    (5) might

3. When the president holds a press conference, all the networks <u>are carrying it</u> live.

    (1) are carrying
    (2) carry
    (3) carried
    (4) have carried
    (5) had carried

4. After my dog <u>had finished</u> its supper, it stretched out on my bed.

    (1) had finished
    (2) was finishing
    (3) finishes
    (4) will finish
    (5) has finished

5. Make hay while the sun <u>will shine</u>.

    (1) will shine
    (2) shined
    (3) shines
    (4) has shined
    (5) had shined

6. After Sam <u>leaves</u> town, he missed his girlfriend.

    (1) leaves
    (2) had left
    (3) is leaving
    (4) was leaving
    (5) will leave

7. I <u>sleep</u> while you were talking.

    (1) sleep
    (2) had slept
    (3) have slept
    (4) am sleeping
    (5) was sleeping

8. Because Aidan <u>ate</u> already, Loretta dined alone.

    (1) ate
    (2) had eaten
    (3) will eat
    (4) has eaten
    (5) is eating

9. If you win the lottery, <u>would</u> you head for Hawaii?

    (1) would
    (2) could
    (3) might
    (4) did
    (5) will

10. Wherever Weird Harold <u>walked</u>, people stare.

    (1) walked
    (2) had walked
    (3) has walked
    (4) walks
    (5) will walk

ANSWERS ARE ON PAGE 357.

EXERCISE 21

Part A

Directions: Using the conjunction provided, complete each sentence logically. Write several sentences with the dependent clause at the beginning of the sentence and several with the dependent clause at the end. Be careful to punctuate each sentence correctly and to use the correct verb tense.

Example: (despite the fact that) I passed the GED Tests

Answer: I passed the GED Tests despite the fact that my hands were trembling during the Writing Skills Test.
or
Despite the fact that my hands were trembling during the Writing Skills Test, I passed the GED Tests.

1. *(if)* We move next year

2. *(because)* His parents were divorced

3. *(although)* The lake is shallow

4. *(whenever)* Hortense coughed

5. *(after)* The alien spacecraft had landed

6. *(if)* The nation will be in trouble

7. *(when)* David became furious

Part B

Directions: Write eight complex sentences of your own using the subordinating conjunctions indicated. Half of your sentences should begin with a dependent clause. Pay attention to logic and punctuation, and be sure to use verb tenses correctly.

1. although
2. because
3. whenever
4. if
5. as though
6. despite the fact that
7. before
8. until

POSSIBLE ANSWERS ARE ON PAGE 357.

CHAPTER HIGHLIGHTS: COMBINING IDEAS IN SENTENCES

1. Simple sentences can be combined in a variety of ways to show the logical connections between them and to make a paragraph sound smoother.

2. A clause is a group of words containing a subject and a verb.

3. Two independent clauses can be combined in a compound sentence connected by
   a. a comma and a conjunction like *and, but,* or *so*
   b. a semicolon, a connector like *however* or *therefore*, and a comma

4. Run-ons and comma splices occur when two independent clauses are connected improperly.

5. A dependent clause beginning with a conjunction like *when, because,* or *if* can be combined with an independent clause to form a complex sentence.

6. A dependent clause cannot stand alone as a sentence.

7. The words used to connect clauses should show the logical link between them.

EDITING PRACTICE

Part A

Directions: Find and correct the nine errors in the passage below. Four of these errors are related to skills that you learned in earlier chapters: complete sentences, compound elements, pronouns, subject-verb agreement, and verb forms. You may want to review the checklists on pages 65 and 117 to refresh your memory on what to look for. The other five errors are related to combining ideas in sentences. For these errors, use the checklist below as your proofreading guide.

☐ Are clauses linked logically by conjunctions or connectors?

☐ Are compound and complex sentences punctuated correctly?

☐ Have comma splices and run-ons been avoided?

☐ Have dependent clause fragments been avoided?

☐ Do verbs follow a logical sequence of tenses?

Do you remember when being a child meant having, red measles, German measles, mumps, and whooping cough? If you do you're probably at least thirty, for in the last few decades scientists has developed vaccines that immunize children against all of these diseases. Although many people thought they were harmless, however, they could actually be quite dangerous. If a pregnant woman catched German measles. Her child might have severe birth defects. Another serious disease was mumps it could cause sterility in adult males. Today even though the medical community has worked so hard to eliminate them, these diseases are not likely to bother you or you're children.

ANSWERS ARE ON PAGE 358.

Part B

Directions: Revise one of the paragraphs you wrote in Exercises 4, 5, and 6 in this chapter. Combine sentences where appropriate to add variety and to link ideas logically. Then apply the proofreading checklist that you used in Part A to check for errors.

ANSWERS WILL VARY.

GED Practice
EXERCISE 22

Questions 1–8 refer to the following paragraph.

(1) I'll never forget the day where my purse was stolen. (2) Because I had heard there were file clerk positions open at an insurance company, I went to put in my application. (3) When I first walked in a secretary took me to the waiting room outside the personnel office. (4) In a few minutes my name was called, and I went in for an interview. (5) Without thinking, I left my purse in the waiting room. (6) After the interview was over, then I returned to the waiting room. (7) My purse was gone. (8) At first, I kept checking the same chair in order that the purse was just temporarily invisible. (9) Then I asked the secretary if she had seen anyone take it, she said she hadn't. (10) Finally, I realized that I would have to replace everything from my lipstick to my pictures of family members. (11) Although I got the job as a file clerk, it was not my lucky day.

1. Sentence 1: **I'll never forget the day where my purse was stolen.**

   Which of the following is the best way to write the underlined portion of this sentence? If you think the original is the best way, choose option (1).

   (1) where
   (2) when
   (3) whenever
   (4) because
   (5) as though

2. Sentence 2: **Because I had heard there were file clerk positions open at an insurance company, I went to put in my application.**

   If you rewrote the sentence beginning with

   I had heard there were file clerk positions open at an insurance company,

   the next word should be

   (1) and
   (2) but
   (3) for
   (4) yet
   (5) so

3. Sentence 3: **When I first walked in a secretary took me to the waiting room outside the personnel office.**

   Which of the following is the best way to write the underlined portion of this sentence? If you think the original is the best way, choose option 1.

   (1) walked in a
   (2) walked in. A
   (3) walked in, a
   (4) walk in; a
   (5) walk in, a

4. Sentence 4: **In a few minutes my name was called, and I went in for an interview.**

   Which of the following is the best way to write the underlined portion of this sentence? If you think the original is the best way, choose option 1.

   (1) called, and
   (2) called and
   (3) called, for
   (4) called for
   (5) called. For

5. Sentence 6: **After the interview was over, then I returned to the waiting room.**

What correction should be made to this sentence?

(1) replace *After* with *While*
(2) insert a comma following *After*
(3) remove the comma after *over*
(4) remove *then*
(5) no correction is necessary

6. Sentence 8: **At first, I kept checking the same chair <u>in order that</u> the purse was just temporarily invisible.**

Which of the following is the best way to write the underlined portion of this sentence? If you think the original is the best way, choose option 1.

(1) in order that
(2) despite the fact that
(3) as if
(4) as
(5) if

7. Sentence 9: **Then I asked the secretary if she had seen anyone take it, she said she hadn't.**

What correction should be made to this sentence?

(1) insert a comma after *secretary*
(2) remove the comma after *it*
(3) replace *it, she* with *it. She*
(4) change *hadn't* to *hasn't*
(5) no correction is necessary.

8. Sentence 11: **Although I got the job as a file clerk, it was not my lucky day.**

What correction should be made to this sentence?

(1) replace *Although* with *Because*
(2) remove the comma after *clerk*
(3) replace *clerk, it* with *clerk, but it*
(4) change *was* to *is*
(5) no correction is necessary

Questions 9–15 refer to the following paragraph.

(1) Do you have an inherited tendency toward a specific disease? (2) There may be good news for you. (3) Medical researchers have found that many people can reduce their risk of developing the disease. (4) If they take proper care of themselves. (5) Men who have a history of heart disease in their families should exercise regularly; however, they should keep their cholesterol level down by eating foods that are low in animal fats. (6) People with a tendency toward diabetes should watch their diets, too, they should be especially careful not to consume too much sugar. (7) Although, these protective measures won't guarantee freedom from disease, they will dramatically increase the chances for a long and healthy life. (8) Unfortunately, there are still some diseases for which heredity is everything. (9) People who are born with a certain genetic blueprint will inevitably develop sickle-cell anemia. (10) Until a breakthrough in genetic engineering is made, their suffering continued.

9. Sentences 1 and 2: **Do you have an inherited tendency toward a specific disease? There may be good news for you.**

The most effective combination of Sentences 1 and 2 would include which of the following groups of words?

(1) If you have
(2) As if you have
(3) Unless you have
(4) Where you have
(5) Whereas you have

10. Sentences 3 and 4: **Medical researchers have found that many people can reduce their risk of developing the <u>disease. If they take</u> proper care of themselves.**

Which of the following is the best way to write the underlined portion of these sentences? If you think the original is the best way, choose option 1.

(1) disease. If they take
(2) disease. If they took
(3) disease; if they took
(4) disease, if they take
(5) disease if they take

11. Sentence 5: **Men who have a history of heart disease in their families should exercise regularly; however, they should keep their cholesterol level down by eating foods that are low in animal fats.**

What correction should be made to this sentence?

(1) replace *Men* with *If men*
(2) replace *regularly; however* with *regularly, however*
(3) replace *however* with *in addition*
(4) remove the comma after *however*
(5) no correction is necessary

12. Sentence 6: **People with a tendency toward diabetes should watch their diets, <u>too, they</u> should be especially careful not to consume too much sugar.**

Which of the following is the best way to write the underlined portion of this sentence? If you think the original is the best way, choose option (1).

(1) too, they
(2) too. They
(3) too, then they
(4) too, although they
(5) too, nor should they

13. Sentence 7: **Although, these protective measures won't guarantee freedom from disease, they will dramatically increase the chances for a long and healthy life.**

What correction should be made to this sentence?

(1) change *Although* to *As though*
(2) remove the comma after *Although*
(3) remove the comma after *disease*
(4) change *will* to *would*
(5) no correction is necessary

14. Sentences 8 and 9: **Unfortunately, there are still some diseases for which heredity is everything. People who are born with a certain genetic blueprint will inevitably develop sickle cell anemia.**

The most effective combination of Sentences 8 and 9 would include which of the following groups of words?

(1) everything, but people
(2) everything; for instance, people
(3) everything, however, people
(4) everything; however, people
(5) everything; in addition, people

15. Sentence 10: **Until a breakthrough in genetic engineering is made, their suffering continued.**

What correction should be made to this sentence?

(1) replace *Until* with *If*
(2) insert a comma after *Until*
(3) remove the comma after *made*
(4) change *continued* to *will continue*
(5) no correction is necessary

ANSWERS ARE ON PAGE 358.

GED Practice
ORGANIZATION REVIEW

Questions 1–10 refer to the following paragraph.

(1) As I sat down in the jury box, I realized that a person's reputation and freedom was in my hands. (2) I seen the defendant sitting next to the defense attorney with his arms folded. (3) He was staring at the other jurors and I as if he wanted to read our minds. (4) He whispered something to the defense attorney, then he glanced at us again. (5) We all rose when the judge entered the courtroom. (6) Officially beginning the trial at that moment. (7) Witness after witness was sworn in questioned, and cross-examined. (8) I listened carefully to the police officer who had made the arrest, the owner of the car that had been stolen, and the defendant's girlfriend. (9) The defendant was expressionless throughout the proceedings. (10) The constant drumming of his fingertips on the table in front of him revealed his nervousness. (11) The case was going badly, and he will have to testify next.

1. Sentence 1: **As I sat down in the jury box, I realized that a person's reputation and freedom was in my hands.**

   What correction should be made to this sentence?

   (1) replace *As* with *If*
   (2) replace *sat* with *set*
   (3) remove the comma after *box*
   (4) change *person's* to *persons*
   (5) change *was* to *were*

2. Sentence 2: **I seen the defendant sitting next to the defense attorney with his arms folded.**

   What correction should be made to this sentence?

   (1) change *seen* to *saw*
   (2) replace *defendant sitting* with *defendant. Sitting*
   (3) replace *attorney with* with *attorney. With*
   (4) change *arms* to *arms'*
   (5) no correction is necessary

3. Sentence 3: **He was staring at the other jurors and I as if he wanted to read our minds.**

   Which of the following is the best way to write the underlined portion of this sentence? If you think the original is the best way, choose option (1).

   (1) I as
   (2) I, as
   (3) I; as
   (4) me as
   (5) me, as

4. Sentence 4: **He whispered something to the defense attorney, then he glanced at us again.**

   Which of the following is the best way to write the underlined portion of this sentence? If you think the original is the best way, choose option (1).

   (1) attorney, then he glanced
   (2) attorney then he glanced
   (3) attorney; then he glanced
   (4) attorney. Then glanced
   (5) attorney. Then glancing

5. Sentence 5: **We all rose when the judge entered the courtroom.**

   What correction should be made to this sentence?

   (1) replace *rose* with *raised*
   (2) insert a comma after *rose*
   (3) change *entered* to *enters*
   (4) insert a comma after *entered*
   (5) no correction is necessary

6. Sentence 6: **Officially beginning the trial at that moment.**

   Which of the following is the best way to write this sentence? If you think the original is the best way, choose option (1).

   (1) Offically beginning the trial at that moment.
   (2) The trial beginning officially at that moment.
   (3) At that moment when the trial officially began.
   (4) At that moment the trial officially began.
   (5) At that moment the trial officially begun.

7. Sentence 7: **Witness after witness was sworn in questioned, and cross-examined.**

   What correction should be made to this sentence?

   (1) change *sworn* to *swore*
   (2) insert a comma after *in*
   (3) change *questioned* to *question*
   (4) remove the comma after *questioned*
   (5) no correction is necessary

8. Sentence 8: **I listened carefully to the police officer who had made the arrest, the owner of the car that had been stolen, and the defendant's girlfriend.**

   What correction should be made to this sentence?

   (1) change *had made* to *made*
   (2) change *had been* to *have been*
   (3) change *stolen* to *stole*
   (4) change *defendant's* to *defendants*
   (5) no correction is necessary

9. Sentences 9 and 10: **The defendant was expressionless throughout the proceedings. The constant drumming of his fingertips on the table in front of him revealed his nervousness.**

   The most effective combination of Sentences 9 and 10 would include which of the following groups of words?

   (1) proceedings; however, the constant
   (2) proceedings, and the constant
   (3) proceedings because the constant
   (4) proceedings; furthermore, the constant
   (5) proceedings if the constant

10. Sentence 11: **The case was going badly, and he will have to testify next.**

    Which of the following is the best way to write the underlined portion of this sentence? If you think the original is the best way, choose option (1).

    (1) will have to
    (2) will
    (3) would have to
    (4) has to
    (5) must

Questions 11–18 refer to the following paragraph.

(1) Space travel, which once was just a subject of science fiction storys, became an amazing reality in the early 1960s. (2) A whole nation pauses in 1961 as Americans gathered around their television sets to watch Alan Shepard become the first American astronaut to rocket into space. (3) When John Glenn orbited the earth a year later we looked on in awe again. (4) These astronauts became instant national heroes. (5) They received banner headlines and ticker-tape parades for being pioneers in space. (6) In the following months reporters kept their names alive by writting countless feature stories. (7) Space travel became big news again in 1986. (8) Schoolteacher Christa MacAuliffe was chosen to be the first civilian in space. (9) Then the crew, MacAuliffe, and the shuttle was destroyed in the most tragic accident in the history of space flight. (10) This accident had a profound effect on space programs for years to come.

11. Sentence 1: **Space travel, which once was just a subject of science fiction storys, became an amazing reality in the early 1960s.**

What correction should be made to this sentence?

(1) change *was* to *is*
(2) change the spelling of *storys* to *stories*
(3) change *became* to *become*
(4) change the spelling of *amazing* to *amazeing*
(5) no correction is necessary

12. Sentence 2: **A whole nation pauses in 1961 as Americans gathered around their television sets to watch Alan Shepard become the first American astronaut to rocket into space.**

What correction should be made to this sentence?

(1) change *pauses* to *paused*
(2) replace *as* with *whenever*
(3) change *Americans* to *American's*
(4) change the spelling of *gathered* to *gatherred*
(5) replace *astronaut to* with *astronaut. To*

13. Sentence 3: **When John Glenn orbited the earth a year later we looked on in awe again.**

What correction should be made to this sentence?

(1) replace *When* with *Even though*
(2) change the spelling of *orbited* to *orbitted*
(3) insert a comma after *later*
(4) change *looked* to *look*
(5) no correction is necessary

14. Sentences 4 and 5: **These astronauts became instant national heroes. They received banner headlines and ticker-tape parades for being pioneers in space.**

Which of the following is the best way to write the underlined portions of these sentences? If you think the original is the best way, choose option (1).

(1) heroes. They
(2) heroes, they
(3) heroes they
(4) heroes because they
(5) heroes, because they

15. Sentence 6: **In the following months, reporters kept their names alive by writting countless feature stories.**

What correction should be made to this sentence?

(1) change the spelling of *months* to *monthes*
(2) replace *months reporters* with *months. Reporters*
(3) replace *alive by* with *alive. By*
(4) change the spelling of *writting* to *writing*
(5) no correction is necessary

16. Sentences 7 and 8: **Space travel became big news again in 1986. Schoolteacher Christa MacAuliffe was chosen to be the first civilian in space.**

The most effective combination of Sentences 7 and 8 would contain which of the following groups of words?

(1) When schoolteacher Christa MacAuliffe
(2) If schoolteacher Christa MacAuliffe
(3) In spite of the fact that schoolteacher Christa MacAuliffe
(4) Although schoolteacher Christa MacAuliffe
(5) As if schoolteacher Christa MacAuliffe

17. Sentence 9: **Then the crew, MacAuliffe, and the shuttle was destroyed in the most tragic accident in the history of space flight.**

What correction should be made to this sentence?

(1) insert a comma after *shuttle*
(2) change *was* to *were*
(3) remove the comma after *crew*
(4) change *was* to *has been*
(5) no correction is necessary

18. Sentence 10: **This accident had a profound effect on space programs for years to come.**

Which of the following is the best way to write the underlined portion of this sentence? If you think the original is the best way, choose option (1).

(1) had
(2) was having
(3) will have
(4) had been
(5) has

ANSWERS ARE ON PAGE 358.

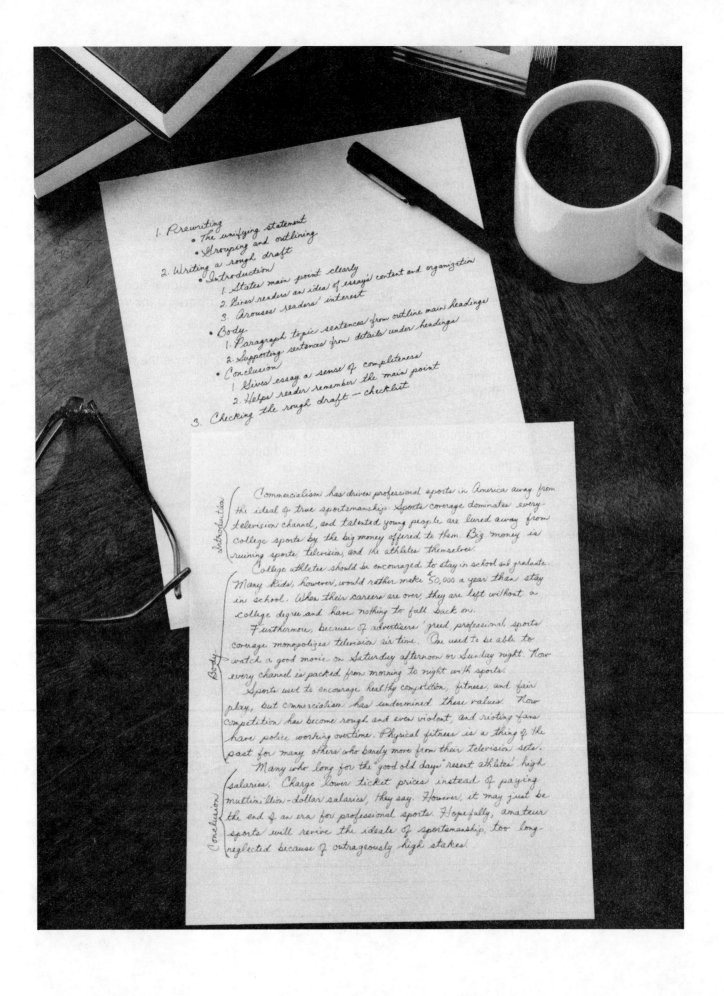

1. Prewriting
   - The unifying statement
   - Grouping and outlining
2. Writing a rough draft
   - Introduction
     1. States main point clearly
     2. Gives readers an idea of essay's content and organization
     3. Arouses readers' interest
   - Body
     1. Paragraph topic sentences from outline main headings
     2. Supporting sentences from details under headings
   - Conclusion
     1. Gives essay a sense of completeness
     2. Helps reader remember the main point
3. Checking the rough draft — checklist

Introduction

Commercialism has driven professional sports in America away from the ideal of true sportsmanship. Sports coverage dominates every television channel, and talented young people are lured away from college sports by the big money offered to them. Big money is ruining sports, television, and the athletes themselves.

Body

College athletes should be encouraged to stay in school and graduate. Many kids, however, would rather make $50,000 a year than stay in school. When their careers are over, they are left without a college degree and have nothing to fall back on.

Furthermore, because of advertisers' greed, professional sports coverage monopolizes television air time. One used to be able to watch a good movie on Saturday afternoon or Sunday night. Now every channel is packed from morning to night with sports.

Sports used to encourage healthy competition, fitness, and fair play, but commercialism has undermined these values. Now competition has become rough and even violent, and rioting fans have police working overtime. Physical fitness is a thing of the past for many others who barely move from their television sets.

Conclusion

Many who long for the "good old days" resent athletes' high salaries. Charge lower ticket prices instead of paying multimillion-dollar salaries, they say. However, it may just be the end of an era for professional sports. Hopefully, amateur sports will revive the ideals of sportsmanship, too long-neglected because of outrageously high stakes.

Writing an Essay

In Chapter 4, you wrote a paragraph describing how television has affected you. You might have had a lot to say about this topic—maybe even more ideas than you could fit easily into one paragraph. Here is the topic again:

> **During the past thirty years, television has become a core part of American life. Nearly every household has at least one television set. Some people say that television has benefited our society, while others see it as a cause of many problems. Explain how television has affected you. Support your explanation with specific examples.**

With this topic, you might want more room to answer the question than one paragraph would give you. To respond really thoroughly, with enough details to satisfy both you and your reader, you could write an essay.

> An ***essay*** is a group of related paragraphs about one topic.

Like a paragraph, an essay has a main idea that is usually stated at the beginning and followed by support. In an essay, however, the main idea usually appears in a separate ***introductory paragraph***.

The supporting ideas in an essay are organized in separate paragraphs. This section, the ***body***, is what makes the essay roomy enough to accommodate several related ideas.

Finally, because of its length, an essay needs a ***concluding paragraph*** to give the writing a sense of completeness. Study the pictures below to see how the parts of a paragraph and the parts of an essay compare.

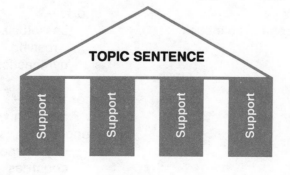

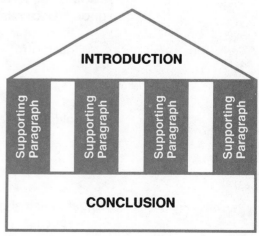

Writing a good essay requires prewriting, writing, revising, and editing. This is the same process you've been using to write paragraphs. This chapter demonstrates a careful, thorough approach to writing an essay so that you will become familiar with the structure of an essay. In Chapter 7, you'll learn strategies for approaching the GED Test essay.

PREWRITING

THE UNIFYING STATEMENT

The prewriting, or planning, phase is even more important in essay writing than in paragraph writing because of the greater length of the essay. To give some direction to your planning, try to state the main point of an essay in one simple statement. You then need to make sure that you have a clear main point with plenty of supporting details organized logically.

A *unifying statement* is a sentence that states the main point of the essay. (You may have heard it called a *thesis statement.*) The same unifying statement you use to help focus your brainstorming may not actually be used in your essay. Later, you'll consider how you might expand or revise a unifying statement into an introduction for the essay.

Many unifying statements are possible for the essay on the effects of television. This writer chose the following one:

Television has provided several benefits to me.

Like a good topic sentence, a unifying statement should pass three tests. First, it should identify the topic (television) and the main point of the essay (television has provided several benefits). Second, a unifying statement should be a complete sentence. Third, the writer should be able to support it with specific examples, reasons, or ideas in the rest of the essay.

With the unifying statement in mind, you can brainstorm a list of supporting details. Here's what the writer jotted down:

Benefits of Television

good way to relax
    tired, sit in comfortable chair,
    doze off

sports—
    basketball,
    wrestling,
    gymnastics

movies—
    old, last year, made for TV

information—
    news on wars,
Congress,
    city council, other
    countries

singer, musical groups—
    specials

documentaries—
    science, history,
    other cultures

GROUPING AND OUTLINING

Now, how can the list be organized? Since you'll be writing several paragraphs, you need to group the details for each paragraph. An **outline** is a convenient way to do this. Its main headings will become topic sentences for your paragraphs, and its subpoints will become the supporting sentences.

Looking over the brainstorm list on benefits of television, the writer found one clear statement of benefit: it's a good way to relax. The rest of the items were types of programs he watched. How could those be grouped? Sports, movies, and musical groups are all forms of entertainment. News and documentaries are both informative. He decided to try a three-part grouping: relaxation, entertainment, and information.

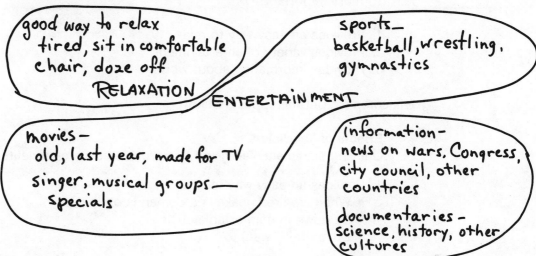

A second way of organizing the brainstorm list is called *clustering*. Look at the example below.

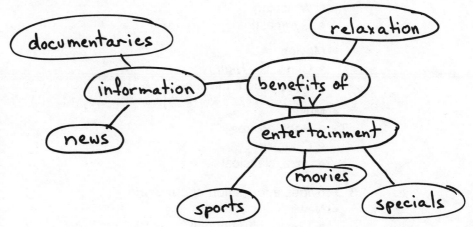

If you had been writing this essay, your grouping or clustering might have been entirely different from his. There is no one correct way to sort items; just make sure to group details in a way that makes sense to you and that will seem logical to your reader.

After the items have been grouped informally, you can make an informal outline. Each label for a group will become a heading in the outline, showing how the items under it are related to one another. When you outline, you decide on the order in which you will present the ideas in your essay. Think about how you might want to order your paragraphs. You could put ideas in order of importance, for example. Or your ideas might suggest a time sequence.

The writer made three headings for his outline and listed them in order of least to most important:

1. Provides an easy way to relax
2. Provides variety of entertainment
3. Provides information about world

His complete outline appears below:

Effects of Television
Unifying statement: Television has provided several benefits to me.

1. Provides an easy way to relax
   - When I'm tired, makes no demands on me
   - Sit down in comfortable chair
   - Doze off if I want to

2. Provides variety of entertainment
   - Sports
     - Basketball
     - Wrestling
     - Gymnastics

   - Movies
     - Classics—*High Noon*
     - More recent movies—*Dick Tracy*

   - Music
     - Rock groups
     - Country
     - Jazz, classical

3. Provides information about world
   - News
     - Local—city council
     - National—presidential press conference
     - International—war, arms race

   - Documentaries
     - Science
     - History
     - Other countries

Once you have made an outline, check it against your unifying statement. Is everything relevant to that statement? Should the statement be reworded to cover the outline, or should the outline be changed? This is the time to cross out irrelevant material and to add missing details.

HOW TO MAKE AN OUTLINE

1. Brainstorm a list of details.

2. Group related details.

3. Make a heading for each group.

4. Choose an order for the headings.

5. List the related details under each heading.

6. Check the outline against the unifying statement.

EXERCISE 1

Directions: Sort details from the following lists into logical groups, create headings to label the groups, and arrange headings and details in outline form. Use the outline skeletons provided, if you wish, or construct an outline of your own. The first one has been started for you.

1. water skiing, hockey, baseball, golf, tennis, ice skating, cross-country skiing

Outdoor Sports

1. *Summer sports*
   - *Water skiing*
   -
   -
   -

2.
   -
   -
   -

2. buses, helicopters, motorcycles, planes, cars, bicycles, trains

Transportation

1.
   -
   -
   -

2.
   -
   -

3.
   -
   -

3. argue with boss, steal office supplies, get in fights with coworkers, regularly arrive late for work, take long breaks, steal store merchandise, treat customers rudely, leave work early

How to Lose Your Job

1.
   -
   -
   -

2.
   -
   -
   -

3.
   -
   -

POSSIBLE ANSWERS ARE ON PAGE 359.

EXERCISE 2

Directions: Choose **one** of the topics below and work through the entire prewriting phase **only**, using the following steps:

- Write a preliminary unifying statement. Make sure that it is a complete sentence that states the main point of the essay. Be sure that you can support it with specific examples. (If you're not certain what your main point will be, you can brainstorm first and then decide what unifying statement your details will support.)

- Brainstorm items to include.

- Sort the items into logical groups.

- Organize an informal outline.

You'll be using this material throughout the rest of the chapter to create a complete essay, so be sure to keep it.

1. Growing up on a farm or in a small town is a much different experience from growing up in a metropolitan area of several million people. What were the advantages or disadvantages of growing up in a community the size of yours? (If you lived in many places as a child, choose one that you remember especially well.) Give specific, concrete details in your answer.

2. All over the world, people have pets even though these animals cost money and take time to care for. Why do you think people keep pets? Support your opinion with specific examples.

3. From time to time it has been suggested that all young Americans should be required to perform a period of public service similar to the military draft. Between the ages of eighteen or nineteen and twenty-one, they would spend a year working in places like nursing homes, hospitals, or community centers. Do you favor or oppose a policy of required public service? State your opinion and back it with reasons and examples.

4. A lot of people are concerned about the environment. They say we're spoiling the earth so fast there will be no clean air or water left for our children. They're worried about how many species of plants and animals are dying out. Others say that the effects of pollution are exaggerated, recycling is a hassle, and it's natural for species to die out. What do you think? Support your opinion with concrete details and examples.

ANSWERS WILL VARY.

WRITING A DRAFT

WHAT IS A ROUGH DRAFT?

After you have completed an outline, the next step in writing an essay is to write a draft. At this point, you expand the words and phrases in the outline into sentences and paragraphs. The draft won't be a finished product, but it will give you some material to examine and polish by revising and editing.

Write carefully when you're writing the first draft of a piece of writing, but don't labor over a spelling problem or tricky grammar question. You'll have plenty of time to come back and fix up your work later. When you're writing a rough draft, your goal should be simply to get your ideas down on paper.

Next comes the introduction. Continuing with the essay on television, the writer could create a short introduction like this:

> Television has benefited my life in many ways. It offers relaxation after a hard day's work. It provides me with a variety of inexpensive entertainment, and it gives me information about the world around me.

This paragraph accomplishes three things: First, it identifies the topic: *television*. Second, it presents the main point: *has benefited my life*. Third, it previews content and organization: *relaxation, entertainment, and information*. (As you know from the outline on page 182, these are exactly the points that will be covered.)

When you are writing an introduction, keep these points in mind:

1. **State your main point clearly.** If your readers know what point you are trying to make, they will find it easier to understand everything in the essay. In addition, stating your main point clearly is a good check for yourself to make sure you really know where your essay is going. As you write your essay, you can keep referring to your introduction to make sure everything you write supports your main point.

2. **Give your readers an idea of the content and organization of your essay.** If you have three major supporting arguments for your main point, you may want to list them in the introduction. Previewing content and organization in this way makes the essay easier for readers to understand. And, like stating your main point, it is a good check for you. If you can't describe the content and organization of your essay, maybe you're not quite ready to write yet.

3. **Arouse your readers' interest in your essay.** There are lots of ways to do this. Following are two examples of ways the writer of the essay on the benefits of television could modify his introductory paragraph to make it more interesting. The first example shows how he uses questions to get his readers interested in answers that he will include in his essay.

What do you do when you come home from work exhausted? What do you do when you want to see a good movie but don't have the money for a ticket? What do you do when you wonder whether Congress has voted to raise taxes today? If you're like me, you turn on your television set. Television is an important part of my life that provides relaxation, entertainment, and information about the world around me.

In the second example, he gives some background to show why his topic is important—showing that he has a sense of history or of social trends.

When television was introduced in the 1940s, few people guessed how quickly this invention would spread around the world. Today, nearly every American household has at least one television set, and satellites bounce programs from one continent to another. Some people may argue about whether this invention is worthwhile, but for me the answer is a definite yes. Television provides many benefits to me, including relaxation, entertainment, and information about the world around me.

Which introduction is the best? There is no one correct answer to this question. Your own preferences and the audience you're writing for will help you decide what kind of introduction to write.

Problems to Avoid

There are some standard traps to avoid when writing an introduction:

1. Don't announce your plans. Your ideas and organization should speak for themselves. Avoid sentences like these:

   I am going to discuss the benefits of television in this essay.
   My first paragraph will show how television relaxes me.

2. Don't apologize for your essay. You want to convince your reader that you have something to say. Never make an excuse like this one:

   This is a hard essay to write because I really don't watch much television, so here goes nothing.

3. Don't use empty words just to sound important and don't repeat yourself just to make the introduction longer. Can you see the problem below?

   Television has had many important effects on me. Its impact on my life has been tremendous. In fact, I've been influenced a great deal by television.

4. Don't assume that your reader has read the essay question or the title of your essay. Restate or summarize the subject of the essay in your introduction. After the question "How has television affected your life?" or the title "Benefits of Television," don't begin your introduction like this:

   For one thing, it helps me relax.

EXERCISE 3

Directions: Using the unifying statement and outline that you prepared in Exercise 2 on page 185, write two possible introductory paragraphs for your essay. Write on every other line so you will have room to revise later.

Check each paragraph to make sure that it identifies the topic, indicates your main point about the topic, predicts the content and organization of the essay, and arouses your reader's interest.

ANSWERS WILL VARY.

WRITING THE BODY

With your informal outline in front of you, you can draft the body of the essay fairly quickly. Each main heading in the outline will become the topic sentence of a paragraph. The details under the heading will become supporting sentences. Here's what the writer produced for the body of his television essay:

1. Provides an easy way to relax
   - When I'm tired, makes no demands on me
   - Sit down in comfortable chair
   - Doze off if I want to

Watching television is an easy way for me to relax at the end of a long, hard day. I don't have to stay alert as I would at a game of cards or use any physical energy as I would in football. I can just sit back in a comfortable chair and watch. If I doze off in the middle of a program, no one will be annoyed.

2. Provides variety of entertainment
   - Sports
     - Basketball
     - Wrestling
     - Gymnastics
   - Movies
     - Classics—*High Noon*
     - More recent movies—*Dick Tracy*
   - Music
     - Rock groups
     - Country
     - Jazz, classical

When I want to be entertained, television provides a variety of choices. All kinds of sports programs are available, from pro wrestling to gymnastics, and I can get a better view of the athletes on television than I could if I were sitting in the bleachers. Movies are another option, whether they are classics like *High Noon* or more recent films like *Dick Tracy*. Television also offers plenty of musical programs by rock, country, and jazz musicians. All this entertainment comes directly to my home at no cost.

3. Provides information about world
  - News
    - Local—city council
    - National—presidential press conference
    - International—war, arms race
  - Documentaries
    - Science
    - History
    - Other countries

Thanks to television, I know much more about the world around me. Each evening I can watch news about local, national, and international events. I can find out what the city council did at its last meeting, watch a presidential press conference live, or even find out about wars and famines in other parts of the world. Documentaries about science, history, and other countries further broaden my understanding.

Notice that the outline has been used as a guide, not a straitjacket. The writer added a few details that weren't in the outline. Compare the paragraphs to the outline in the margin. These ideas occurred during the actual drafting; since they're all relevant to the unifying statement, the writer decided to include them. If new ideas occur to you at any stage, it's fine to put them in. Just make sure they are relevant to the unifying statement.

EXERCISE 4

Directions: Choose the introduction you like best from Exercise 3, page 188. Using the outline you developed in Exercise 2 on page 185, write the body of your essay. Turn the main headings of your outline into topic sentences and the details under the headings into supporting sentences. Add more details as they occur to you. Don't worry too much about spelling or grammar. Write on every other line so you will have room to revise later.

ANSWERS WILL VARY.

WRITING THE CONCLUSION

Now that the introduction and body of the essay are written, it's time to draw your writing to a close with a concluding paragraph. But you've made your main point and you've used up the entire outline. What is left?

Don't worry. The last paragraph of an essay isn't intended to cover new material. In most cases, the concluding paragraph has two main purposes: one, to give the essay a sense of completeness, and two, to help the reader remember your main point.

To accomplish these purposes, you can use as your conclusion a reworded version of the unifying statement. If the writer of the television essay had chosen this approach, he might have ended this way:

> By helping me unwind, entertaining me, and educating me, television has made my life more pleasant and more interesting. This is one appliance that I would hate to do without.

Note that this summarizing conclusion touches on the main idea— "television has provided several benefits to me"—and the three groups of benefits discussed in the body: relaxation, entertainment, and information. Only the wording has been changed to keep from sounding monotonous.

A second kind of conclusion goes one step beyond summarizing and opens out to discuss the broader importance of the subject.

> Clearly, my reaction to television is positive. My favorable opinion isn't unique. Millions, perhaps billions, of people have had their lives enriched by this magic box. By watching it, we can relax, we can laugh and cheer, and, most important, we can better understand one another and the world we live in.

This time the unifying statement has been expanded to apply to television viewers in general rather than just the writer.

Problems to Avoid

Avoid the following traps when writing your conclusion:

1. Don't announce your plans. Avoid concluding like this:

I would like to end this essay by saying that I prize my television set.

2. Don't apologize for your essay like this:

I'm sorry this wasn't very good, but at least I tried. Of course, if I watched television more, I would have better examples.

3. Don't bring up new topics like this writer did:

My television set is my second most important possession. Only my car is more important because it gets me to work, takes me wherever I want to go on vacations, and lets me get together with my friends.

EXERCISE 5

Directions: Complete the draft that you worked on in Exercises 2, 3, and 4 by writing a conclusion. To get a running start, reread the introduction and the body. Remember, it's fine if you reword your unifying statement for the conclusion. Write on every other line so you will have room to revise later.

ANSWERS WILL VARY.

THE COMPLETED ROUGH DRAFT

Now the writer has a working draft, with an introduction, body, and conclusion tied to a unifying statement. He's accomplished a great deal!

However, this probably won't be his final version of the essay. He may need to revise it to link the paragraphs more smoothly and to provide more specific examples. He may want to change the wording in a few places. And what about editing considerations: spelling, punctuating, capitalizing? We'll look in detail at the revising and editing stages of the writing process in Chapter 6.

EXERCISE 6

Directions: When you complete your entire draft, use the following checklist to evaluate it. Make some notes about any changes you would like to make in your essay. Don't make the changes now; you'll revise the essay in Chapter 6.

- ☐ Does the introduction contain a unifying statement? Put an asterisk (✱) in the margin next to it.

- ☐ Does the introduction help arouse the reader's interest? Does it avoid common traps?

- ☐ Does each paragraph in the body support the unifying statement with specific details?

- ☐ Does each paragraph in the body contain a topic sentence?

- ☐ Are the paragraphs in the body arranged logically?

- ☐ Does the conclusion restate the main idea of the essay? Does it avoid common traps?

ANSWERS WILL VARY.

CHAPTER HIGHLIGHTS: WRITING AN ESSAY

1. An essay is a group of related paragraphs about one topic. It consists of an introduction, supporting paragraphs, and a conclusion.

2. Begin prewriting your essay by writing a unifying statement and brainstorming a list of details to support it.

3. Group brainstormed details in an outline from which you will write a working draft.

4. Use the unifying statement as the basis for the introduction to your essay. The introduction might begin with a question, an incident, a contrast, a general statement, or background information.

5. In the body of the essay, expand the outline in sentence and paragraph form. Turn each main heading in the outline into the topic sentence of a paragraph.

6. Restate your main point in the conclusion. You may also show the broader importance of the subject.

7. Expect to revise and edit the rough draft.

As they gain writing experience, writers develop their own versions of this writing process. Often the steps aren't nearly as clear-cut as they have been presented here. Writing a rough draft can turn into revising as a writer notices how the wording of a sentence can be clarified. Drafting may even give way to more planning when the writer temporarily gets stuck on a paragraph and decides to brainstorm more details. Don't hesitate to modify this process to suit your own writing style.

EXERCISE 7

Here is your second sample writing topic to help you practice for Part 2 of the GED Writing Skills Test. Try writing on this topic within the forty-five-minute time limit that you will have on the actual test. Put all the writing skills to use that you have learned so far in essay and paragraph construction, sentence structure, word choice, punctuation, and spelling.

Be sure to take ten minutes or so to plan your essay. Look for clue words in the question to help you identify topic, purpose, and the kinds of details to include. Make a unifying statement and brainstorm a list of details. Although you may not have time to make a formal outline, do try to group your details logically. Check for relevance, completeness, and organization.

When you begin drafting, don't worry if you can't think of a catchy introduction. Just use your unifying statement and fill out the paragraph with another sentence or two.

Save the last five to ten minutes for revising and editing your essay. Apply the checklist on page 191 as a revising guide.

Playing the "if only" game seems to be a natural human activity. We often imagine what our lives would be like if only one circumstance were changed. Even young children play the game: "If only I had a little brother, there would be someone to play with around here," or "If only I didn't have a little brother, I wouldn't have to share my toys."

Pick one circumstance in your life—past, present, or future—that you would like to change and describe the effects that change would have on your life.

POSSIBLE ANSWERS ARE ON PAGE 359.

JOURNAL WRITING

Have you written in your journal recently?

Here are some suggestions of things you could write about in your journal. Choose one or more of them to write about, or think of some topics on your own.

- Write about something wonderful about yourself that you wish everyone knew.

- Write about something that is very important to you.

- What are your biggest complaints about life?

Read each pair of sentences below and place a check beside the one that you think is written correctly.

_____ Hurrying to leave for work on time, the toast burned and coffee spilled on Michelle's white blouse.

_____ Hurrying to leave for work on time, Michelle burned the toast and spilled coffee on her white blouse.

_____ She hated starting her day with an empty stomach and food stains on her clothes.

_____ She hated starting her day with an empty stomach and staining her clothes.

_____ Michelle was so disgruntled that she hardly spoke to Maria, which rode to work with her.

_____ Michelle was so disgruntled that she hardly spoke to Maria, who rode to work with her.

Did you find the choice difficult? If so, don't worry. The errors weren't nearly as obvious as a sentence fragment or a misused verb. Instead, they involved questions of logic in word order and word choice. By studying the material in this chapter, you'll learn to recognize and write clear sentences with wording that doesn't confuse your readers or distract them from the point you want to make.

You'll be working with three problem areas in sentence structure: use of modifiers, parallel structure, and pronoun reference. This work in sentence structure will be helpful in both Parts 1 and 2 of the GED Writing Skills Test.

MODIFIERS

HOW ARE MODIFIERS USED?
Prepositional Phrases

In Chapter 4 you learned how to combine ideas in sentences by connecting *clauses,* which you learned are groups of words that contain subjects and verbs. Sometimes ideas can be combined without using entire clauses. How might you combine the following pair of sentences?

Governor Morrison won reelection yesterday. He won by a margin of seventy thousand votes.

Here are two possibilities:

Governor Morrison won reelection yesterday **by a margin of seventy thousand votes**.

By a margin of seventy thousand votes, Governor Morrison won reelection yesterday.

In both cases, the prepositional phrase from the second sentence *(by a margin of seventy thousand votes)* was inserted into the first sentence. (If you need to refresh your memory about prepositional phrases, review pages 110–112.) The phrase answers the question "By how much did the governor win?" In other words, it modifies, or describes, the word *win*.

A ***modifier*** is a word or phrase that describes another word in the sentence. A modifier answers a question: *when? where? why? how? how much? which one? what kind?* or *how many?*

Try combining a second pair of sentences in the same way: insert the modifying phrase from the second sentence into the first sentence.

The city's recreation department will hold a summer festival. The festival will be at Oak Park on June 24 and 25.

_____

_____

Again you have two choices:

The city's recreation department will hold a summer festival **at Oak Park on June 24 and 25**.

At Oak Park on June 24 and 25, the city's recreation department will hold a summer festival.

Verb Phrases

A prepositional phrase is only one kind of modifier. Other modifying phrases begin with verbs. Watch how the following pairs of sentences can be combined.

> Sid swerved to avoid a squirrel. The squirrel was scampering across the street.
>
> Sid swerved to avoid a squirrel **scampering across the street**.
>
> Teresa wanted to learn how to protect herself. She enrolled in a karate class.
>
> **To learn how to protect herself**, Teresa enrolled in a karate class.
>
> Jim was angered by my sarcastic comments. He turned and left.
>
> **Angered by my sarcastic comments**, Jim turned and left.

In each combined sentence above, the phrase in bold type is a modifier. *Scampering across the street* tells you which squirrel Sid swerved to avoid. *To learn how to protect herself* explains why Teresa enrolled in a karate class. *Angered by my sarcastic comments* explains why Jim turned and left.

◉ FOCUS ON PUNCTUATION

Introductory Phrases

When a modifying phrase begins a sentence, separate it from the rest of the sentence with a comma. Usually, no comma is needed when the phrase appears at the end of a sentence.

> **At 12:01 A.M. on June 28,** her first grandchild was born.
> Her first grandchild was born **at 12:01 A.M. on June 28**.
>
> **In order to annoy her parents,** Christine popped her knuckles and swore.
> Christine popped her knuckles and swore **in order to annoy her parents**.

EXERCISE 8

Directions: Combine the following pairs of sentences by turning one sentence into a modifying phrase. Be sure to insert commas after introductory phrases.

Example: Something happened in the middle of the night. The bed collapsed.

In the middle of the night, the bed collapsed.

1. Samantha was smiling seductively. Samantha sauntered toward Steve.

2. Something happened in the middle of the president's speech. A reporter shouted a question.

3. The governor wanted to prevent looting after the shopping mall fire. The governor called out the National Guard.

4. The campers were awakened by a bear. It was rummaging through the food supplies.

5. Vandals smashed the windshields of twelve cars. The cars were in the vicinity of West High School last night.

6. The crowd were shouting and whistling their approval. The crowd gave Slime Green a standing ovation.

7. The trucker drove an alternate route. The trucker wanted to avoid the weigh station.

8. Dick's Get 'n' Go was robbed. The incident occurred for the third time in less than a year.

9. Some people want to reduce the chances of catching a cold. Some people take large doses of vitamin C.

10. Smitty and Josh stared in fascinated horror at the tarantula. It was crawling across their sleeping friend's face.

11. Joey planted tulips and daffodils in his garden. Joey liked flowers.

12. Jorge's sweater was torn and stained. Roberto hid it before Jorge came home.

13. Inez enjoys working with wood. Inez has taken classes in carpentry and cabinet-making.

14. Something happened while Ed was burning leaves in the backyard. The garage caught fire.

POSSIBLE ANSWERS ARE ON PAGE 359.

PLACEMENT OF MODIFIERS

In the following sentence, who was dangling from a window: Mavis or her husband? How can you tell?

Dangling from a seventh-story window, Mavis dimly heard her husband yelling.

The answer to the question is based on word order. Since the modifying phrase *dangling from a seventh-story window* appears directly before *Mavis*, you can assume that she is the person it describes.

> To avoid confusing or unintentionally amusing your reader, place a modifying phrase as close as possible to the word it describes.

Here's an example of what may happen if this rule is violated:

Wearing nothing but a diaper, Mrs. Craig worried that the baby would catch cold.

Who was wearing the diaper? Although common sense tells you that it was the baby, the sentence structure implies that it was Mrs. Craig.

> A *misplaced modifier* can be corrected in two ways:
>
> • Move the modifier closer to the word it describes.
>
>   Mrs. Craig worried that the baby wearing nothing but a diaper would catch cold.
>
> • Turn the modifying phrase into a dependent clause.
>
>   Because the baby was wearing nothing but a diaper, Mrs. Craig worried that he would catch cold.

Underline the misplaced modifier in the following sentence.

Teetering up the driveway in a pair of high-heeled shoes, we smiled at the little girl.

Who was wearing the shoes: *we* or *the little girl*? The misplaced modifier is the introductory phrase.

Try correcting the sentence both ways. First, place the modifier directly after the word it describes.

_____

_____

Second, leave the modifier in its original position but turn it into a dependent clause by adding the words *As she was* at the beginning.

_____

_____

We smiled at the little girl teetering up the driveway in a pair of high-heeled shoes.

As she was teetering up the driveway in a pair of high-heeled shoes, we smiled at the little girl.

EXERCISE 9

Directions: Underline the misplaced modifying phrase in each sentence below. Then rewrite the sentence to correct it either by moving the modifier or by changing it to a dependent clause. Be sure to punctuate the new sentence correctly. If a dependent clause begins the sentence, follow it with a comma.

1. Stuck under his chair, Morris felt a large, moist blob of bubble gum.

2. Destroyed by hail, Larry Gunderson stared gloomily at his wheat field.

3. Swinging effortlessly from branch to branch, the children watched the chimpanzee.

4. The prisoner was escorted to Death Row by four guards screaming for mercy.

5. Gasping for air, the fans encouraged the marathon runner to complete the last hundred yards.

6. Hidden behind a layer of dense brown smog, we could barely see the outlines of the mountains.

7. A suave gentleman strolled through the park with a neatly trimmed mustache and beard.

8. Sonja draped her boa constrictor around the trunk of the apple tree with a slight smile.

9. Eager to recruit top athletes, promising high school seniors are offered full scholarships by some colleges.

10. Fuzzy and shriveled, we finally found the decaying orange in Will's top file drawer.

POSSIBLE ANSWERS ARE ON PAGE 360.

DANGLING MODIFIERS

Read the sentence below and answer this question: Who is driving on mountain roads?

Driving on mountain roads, the scenery is spectacular but the curves can be tricky.

You couldn't answer the question, could you? Sentence structure tells you that the phrase *Driving on mountain roads* modifies one or both of the subjects, *scenery* and *curves*. But common sense tells you that neither scenery nor curves can drive. The modifier just dangles at the beginning of the sentence without anything to modify.

Dangling modifiers are describing phrases and clauses that have no word to describe in a sentence. They can be corrected in one of two ways:

- Add a person or thing for the modifier to describe. (Be sure to place it near the modifier.)

  Driving on mountain roads, I find the scenery spectacular but the curves tricky.

- Turn the modifying phrase into a dependent clause.

  When I drive on mountain roads, the scenery is spectacular but the curves can be tricky.

Underline the dangling modifier in the following sentence.

Exhausted after a twelve-hour shift, a hot meal and a bath sounded good.

Did you mark the introductory phrase as the dangling modifier?

Now correct the sentence in two ways. First, revise the main sentence to include a word for the phrase to modify.

_____

_____

Second, turn the modifying phrase into a dependent clause. (Hint: You could start the dependent clause with *Because.*)

_____

_____

You might have corrected the sentence like this:

> Exhausted after a twelve-hour shift, **Kelly thought** a hot meal and a bath sounded good.

> **Because Kelly was exhausted after a twelve-hour shift**, a hot meal and a bath sounded good.

Not all dangling modifiers appear at the beginning of a sentence. Find and underline the dangling modifier in the sentence below.

> Taking a test is not difficult when well rested and prepared.

Did you mark *when well rested and prepared*?

Try revising this sentence. _____

_____

You might have corrected the sentence like this:

> Taking a test is not difficult **when you are well rested and prepared**.

EXERCISE 10

Directions: Underline the dangling modifier in each sentence below. Then correct the sentence by adding a word for the modifier to describe or by turning the modifier into a dependent clause. Be sure to punctuate the new sentence correctly.

1. Rewinding the VCR, the tape got stuck.

2. Hanging the picture, the frame slipped and hit Juanita on the head.

3. Returning my library books two weeks late, the fine was $1.20.

4. The getaway car sped down Highway 37 unaware of the road block.

5. Eager to break for cocktails and dinner, the meeting was adjourned until eight o'clock the following morning.

6. Stumbling over a fallen log, the rifle discharged.

7. Despondent about losing his job and filing for bankruptcy, suicide was a tempting prospect.

8. Screeching around the corner with its horn blaring, Josef was hit.

9. Singing along with the radio, the dog winced at Sharon's voice.

10. Giggling uncontrollably, the room seemed to spin around me after my fourth glass of champagne.

POSSIBLE ANSWERS ARE ON PAGE 360.

RENAMING PHRASES AS MODIFIERS

So far you've looked at sentence combining using prepositional phrases and phrases formed from verbs. A third kind of modifying phrase is a renaming phrase (sometimes called an *appositive*). Here are some examples of how the renaming phrase can be used.

"The Edge of Disaster" features plots about divorce, disease, and drug addiction. "The Edge of Disaster" is my favorite soap opera.

becomes

"The Edge of Disaster," my favorite soap opera, features plots about divorce, disease, and drug addiction.

Circle the phrase *my favorite soap opera* in the new, combined sentence and draw an arrow to the word or phrase it describes.

Did you extend the arrow to "The Edge of Disaster"?

Try a second example:

One successful halfway house for juvenile offenders is run by Dave Jackson. Dave is a former reform school resident.

becomes

One successful halfway house for juvenile offenders is run by Dave Jackson, **a former reform school resident**.

Circle the phrase *a former reform school resident* in the combined sentence and draw an arrow to the word or phrase it describes.

Notice that, once again, the modifying noun phrase describes another noun: *Dave Jackson*.

Just like the other modifying phrases you've been studying in this chapter, renaming phrases must be placed carefully in a sentence. Renaming phrases always come right after the noun they refer to.

> A ***renaming phrase*** supplies additional information about another noun (person, place, thing, or idea) in the sentence. A renaming phrase appears directly after the noun it describes.

◎ FOCUS ON PUNCTUATION

Renaming Phrases

Renaming phrases are separated by commas from the rest of the sentence. If a renaming phrase comes in the middle of a sentence, put commas before and after it.

Tim Baysinger, **my sister's ex-husband,** simply quit his job and disappeared.

My vote goes to Pennington, **a person with experience and integrity**.

EXERCISE 11

Part A
Directions: Punctuate the renaming phrases in the following sentences.

1. The Statue of Liberty a gift from France stands at the entrance to New York Harbor.

2. Bone strength depends on an adequate supply of calcium a mineral found in dairy products and some vegetables.

3. This week's lottery winner a mother of ten from the Bronx will receive twenty thousand dollars a year for the next twenty years.

4. Use Dazzle a revolutionary new detergent to get your clothes sunshine clean.

5. Our store detective is Farley Finck a man who can spot a shoplifter at fifty paces.

Part B
Directions: Combine the following pairs of sentences by using renaming phrases as modifiers. Be careful to punctuate the phrases correctly.

Example: For dinner we're having your favorite meal. Your favorite meal is spaghetti and meatballs.

For dinner we're having your favorite meal, spaghetti and meatballs.

1. The movie being shown tonight is *Rocky*. *Rocky* is a film about a common man who makes his dream come true.

2. Unfortunately, my fiancé's favorite vegetable is cauliflower. Cauliflower is the one food I'm allergic to.

3. Stephen King's novels are popular with young adults. Stephen King's novels are fast-paced horror stories.

4. Paula Hansen owns the hardware store on Second Street. Paula is my next-door neighbor.

5. The plane crashed while attempting to make an emergency landing. The plane was a B-17.

6. I've always wanted to visit New Orleans. New Orleans is a city with a reputation for fine food and great jazz.

7. Dr. Sidney Boldt had never developed a smooth bedside manner. Dr. Boldt was a sour man with a persistent frown on his face.

8. The band was playing "You Ain't Nothin' But a Hound Dog" when Angelo realized he'd forgotten to feed his poodle. The song was an old Elvis Presley hit.

9. Our next speaker is Sharon Moser. She is a woman with a keen sense of justice and a determination to protect the rights of all our citizens.

10. Maggie may have been a Scot, but she refused to eat haggis. Haggis is a disgusting concoction of oatmeal and the vital organs of sheep.

ANSWERS ARE ON PAGE 360.

PARALLEL STRUCTURE

WHAT IS PARALLEL STRUCTURE?

In Chapter 2, you learned that a sentence may contain compound elements connected by a conjunction such as *and* or *or*.

Pam likes water skiing, swimming, and sailing.

In this sentence there are three compound elements connected by the conjunction *and*: *water skiing, swimming,* and *sailing.* Notice that the three elements are consistent in form: each one ends in *ing*.

> Compound elements that are all in the same form have ***parallel structure***. Using parallel structure makes a sentence easier and smoother to read.

Compare the sample sentence above with a sentence lacking parallel structure.

NONPARALLEL: Pam likes water skiing, to swim, and sails.

This time each element has a different form. The first contains an *ing* verb, the second *to* plus a verb, the third a simple present-tense verb. The sentence could be corrected in either of two ways. The writer could use all *ing* verbs, as in the original example, or she could use *to* plus a verb for each element.

PARALLEL: Pam likes **to water ski, to swim,** and **to sail.**

Always use parallel structure with compound elements, whether they are single words, phrases, or clauses. Here are some examples of sentences that lack parallel structure, followed by their corrected parallel form. In each pair, circle the element that is changed to make the sentence correct.

Single Words

NONPARALLEL: Morris was so surprised by the question that he **paused** and **was stammering**.

PARALLEL: Morris was so surprised by the question that he **paused** and **stammered**.

In the incorrect sentence above, one verb is in simple past tense *(paused)* and the other is past continuing *(was stammering)*. In the corrected sentence, both verbs are in simple past tense.

NONPARALLEL: The qualities I admire most in a man are **honesty, courageous,** and **compassion**.

PARALLEL: The qualities I admire most in a man are **honesty, courage,** and **compassion**.

In the incorrect sentence above, there are two nouns and one describing word among the elements that should be parallel. In the corrected sentence, all the elements are nouns.

Phrases

NONPARALLEL: The goal of American democracy is a government **of the people, by the people,** and **that is run for the people**.

PARALLEL: The goal of American democracy is a government **of the people, by the people,** and **for the people**.

In the incorrect sentence above, there are two prepositional phrases and one clause among the elements that should be parallel. In the corrected sentence, they are all prepositional phrases.

NONPARALLEL: He's returning to school **to retrain for a higher-paying job** and **as an example for his sons**.

PARALLEL: He's returning to school **to retrain for a higher-paying job** and **to set an example for his sons**.

In the incorrect sentence, one phrase begins with *to* plus a verb and the other is a prepositional phrase. In the corrected sentence, both phrases begin with *to* + verb.

Making Elements Parallel

To check for parallel structure, you must first identify the compound elements. Look for the conjunction *and, but, or,* or *nor*; then decide which words the conjunction joins. After you've located the compound elements, check to be sure that the word forms are alike.

Remember, you're looking for similarity in form, not meaning. *Journalist, lawyer,* and *engineering* are related in meaning: all deal with occupations. However, the first two nouns refer to people, while the third refers to a career. A parallel list would be *journalist, lawyer,* and *engineer* (all people) or *journalism, law,* and *engineering* (all careers).

Underline the compound elements in the following sentence. Then circle the element that is not parallel to the others.

Jo draws attention to herself by dyeing her hair lavender, wearing green fingernail polish, and she speaks with a fake French accent.

The first two elements are phrases beginning with *ing* verbs, while the third is a clause. There is no need to repeat the subject in the third compound element.

Now rewrite the sentence using parallel structure.

_____

_____

Jo draws attention to herself by dyeing her hair lavender, wearing green fingernail polish, and speaking with a fake French accent.

EXERCISE 12

Part A

Directions: Underline the compound elements in each sentence below and circle the element that is not parallel in structure to the others. Then rewrite the sentence to create parallel structure.

Example: That man is <u>arrogant,</u> (a snob,) <u>and selfish.</u>

That man is arrogant, snobbish, and selfish.

1. A gymnast must be well coordinated, agile, and have strength.

2. Knitting nose warmers and to play Wahoo were Albert's hobbies.

3. Mr. Bubany was brave, honest, and a compassionate man.

4. We can solve arithmetic problems by adding, subtracting, multiplication, and dividing.

5. Why does Elizabeth love to cook but she hates to do dishes?

6. When Felicia had the flu, she took aspirin, drank plenty of liquids, and she slept a lot.

7. Long ago I discovered that I could relax by sipping a cup of hot tea or if I listened to soft music.

8. The kids tracked mud in the hallway, through the kitchen, and they got it on the living room carpet.

9. Malcolm stopped, was scratching his head, and wondered what to do next.

10. One of life's greatest sorrows is to have a child, to care for him lovingly as he grows, and then when you lose him to drugs.

Part B

Directions: Use parallel structure to complete the following sentences.

1. Three character traits that I admire in a person are _____, _____, and _____.

2. _____, _____, and _____ are all careers that interest me.

3. In my spare time I like to _____ or _____.

4. I would like to find out _____, _____, and _____.

5. Yesterday morning I _____, _____, and _____.

6. This country will be a better place to live when our citizens _____ and _____.

7. An effective speaker talks _____ and _____.

8. _____, _____, _____, and _____ are good ways to pass the time on a rainy Saturday.

POSSIBLE ANSWERS ARE ON PAGE 361.

PRONOUN REFERENCE

NOTICING CONFUSING PRONOUNS

How would you react to a friend who walked up to you and began a conversation like this?

"It was incredible! I've never seen anything like it! You could see them coming, but we couldn't tell how fast. And then it happened! You can't begin to describe it! They said I would be in shock for a while, and they're right!"

Probably you would respond by firing questions back as fast as you could: "What was incredible? What haven't you seen anything like? Who was coming? Was I really there? What happened? Who said you would be in shock?"

The problem with your friend's speech is the confusing use of pronouns. You'll remember from Chapter 2 that pronouns (words like *I, him, this,* and *it*) replace and refer to nouns. Used properly, they're certainly helpful little words. However, if they aren't used clearly and logically, communication can clank to a halt.

> To avoid confusing and frustrating your reader, follow two basic rules when using pronouns:
>
> **1.** Pronouns must refer clearly to their antecedents.
>
> **2.** Pronouns must agree with their antecedents.

AVOID CONFUSING PRONOUNS

As you learned in Chapter 2, an antecedent is the word a pronoun refers to. If there is any possible confusion about the antecedent of a pronoun, don't make your reader guess. Sometimes you can use a noun instead of one of the pronouns to make the sentence's meaning clear.

CONFUSING: Fumiko refused to share an apartment with Liyuh because **she** despised **her** taste in music.

CLEAR: Fumiko refused to share an apartment with Liyuh because **Liyuh** despised her taste in music.

CLEAR: Fumiko refused to share an apartment with Liyuh because she despised **Liyuh's** taste in music.

In the confusing sentence, you don't know whether Fumiko despised Liyuh's taste or Liyuh despised Fumiko's. You can't tell what the antecedents for *she* and *her* are. Notice that the meaning of the sentence changes depending on how you correct it.

A second way to eliminate confusion is to rephrase the sentence.

CONFUSING: Your wife is picking up your daughter at school, so **she** won't meet you at the office.

CLEAR: Your daughter won't meet you at the office because your wife is picking her up at school.

CLEAR: Your wife won't meet you at the office because she is picking up your daughter at school.

In the confusing sentence, you don't know who won't be at the office, the wife or the daughter.

Circle the confusing pronoun in the sentence below.

Jason will ride home with Dave if he gets off work early.

The problem pronoun is *he*. Will Dave or Jason get off work early? Rewrite the sentence, substituting one of the names for the confusing pronoun.

_____

EXERCISE 13

Directions: Rewrite each sentence containing a confusing pronoun to make the meaning clear. Either replace the confusing pronoun with a noun or rephrase the sentence. Mark any correct sentences with a *C.*

Example: _____ Tanya never saw Betina again after she moved to Los Angeles.

After Betina moved to Los Angeles, Tanya never saw her again.

_____ **1.** Sam and Ted got into a bitter argument after he called him a liar.

_____ **2.** As the dog approached the wounded bear, it was snarling menacingly.

_____ **3.** I like November much better than February; it's such a dreary month.

_____ **4.** Steven will probably never speak to James again now that he's a millionaire.

_____ **5.** I can't decide whether to buy the brown shoes or the black ones; they're

more expensive, but they'll probably last longer.

_____ **6.** Sonja never spoke to Maria again although she wanted to maintain their

friendship.

_____ **7.** Mrs. Perez smiled fondly as she watched her toddler playing in the wading

pool.

_____ **8.** Just as he was about to step from the curb, Sean glanced up and shouted,

"Tim, watch out!"

_____ **9.** Because fish is high in protein but low in cholesterol, it's better for most

people than beef.

_____ **10.** The country music fans and the rock fans never got along because they

thought the others were stupid and crude.

POSSIBLE ANSWERS ARE ON PAGE 361.

AVOID VAGUE PRONOUNS

In the last section, you looked at pronouns that were confusing because they could logically refer to two antecedents. Pronouns can also be confusing if they have no antecedent at all.

> CONFUSING: Doyle Garrison insists that the welfare system is run poorly because **they** just don't understand what it means to be poor.
> CLEAR: Doyle Garrison insists that the welfare system is run poorly because **politicians** just don't understand what it means to be poor.

In the confusing sentence, who are _they_: members of Congress? state legislators? social workers? There is no antecedent for _they_ in this sentence. To avoid such vagueness, replace the pronoun with an appropriate noun, as the writer did in the clear sentence.

It, they, and *this* are the pronouns most likely to lack an antecedent. Whenever you see one of these words as you're proofreading, make sure that it clearly refers to a specific noun. If it doesn't, add the necessary noun.

Circle the vague pronoun in the following sample passage.

> Tom told Stephanie that he was going bowling with his buddies every Monday night. She found out later that he was spending the evening with an exotic dancer. This made Stephanie so angry that she promptly sued for divorce.

Did you circle *This*? The word has no clear antecedent. What made Stephanie angry: Tom's lie? his affair? his preference for exotic dancing over ballet? Rewrite the last sentence of the passage in whatever way you think is logical to make the meaning clear.

_____

_____

You might have answered like this:

> **Tom's lying and cheating** made Stephanie so angry that she promptly sued for divorce.

Try one more example. Circle the vague pronoun in the sentence below.

> Everyone in the hall, including the bride and groom, was drunk; it almost turned into a riot.

The word *it* is the vague pronoun this time. Replace it with a noun that summarizes the action.

_____

_____

You might have answered like this:

> Everyone in the hall, including the bride and groom, was drunk; the reception almost turned into a riot.

EDITING HINT: Always be sure to read the entire sentence or paragraph when you correct a confusing pronoun. Be sure you match the intended meaning of the sentence.

EXERCISE 14

Directions: In each of the following sentences, cross out the vague pronoun and replace it with a word or phrase that makes the meaning clear. Mark any correctly worded sentences with a *C*.

the soldiers

Example: _____ As the sergeant entered the barracks, ~~they~~ snapped to attention.

_____ **1.** You should have seen the children chasing each other around the playground; it was hilarious.

_____ **2.** With the growing importance of computers, they need more qualified instructors at all levels.

_____ **3.** Although the doctor lectured the teenagers on the dangers of smoking, it didn't stop them from experimenting.

_____ **4.** They say that animals grow thicker fur before an unusually harsh winter.

_____ **5.** When the father rocked and sang to his baby, it seemed to quiet the child.

_____ **6.** We asked Laura to get some counseling, but she insisted that they do more harm than good.

_____ **7.** Mr. Cutforth was notified last night that he'd won. This excited him so much that he nearly passed out.

_____ **8.** In the article they say that acid rain is endangering wildlife and forests in the Northeast.

_____ **9.** When Smith and Torriello wrote the book, they didn't expect it to sell fifty thousand copies.

_____ **10.** Marian wanted to go into engineering because they have an excellent income.

POSSIBLE ANSWERS ARE ON PAGE 362.

HUMANS AND NONHUMANS

Relative pronouns link two ideas within a sentence. Relative pronouns must agree with their antecedents. Look at a sample sentence:

> Jana, **who** is a successful local realtor, will present a workshop for prospective homebuyers next Tuesday.

In this sentence the pronoun *who* is used to link two ideas:

> Jana is a successful local realtor.
> Jana will present a workshop next Tuesday.

Let's look at another example:

> The Sears Tower, **which** is located in Chicago, is one of the tallest buildings in the world.

Here the pronoun *which* combines two ideas:

> The Sears Tower is in Chicago.
> The Sears Tower is one of the tallest buildings in the world.

Now study one final sentence:

> The speaker **that** we heard last night works for an insurance company **that** might relocate in San Diego.

The pronoun *that* links ideas in this third sentence:

> The speaker works for an insurance company.
> We heard the speaker last night.
> The insurance company might relocate in San Diego.

Why did the first sample sentence use *who*, the second one *which*, and the third one *that*? The answer lies in the antecedents. In the first example, the antecedent for *who* is a person, Jana. In the second sentence, the antecedent for *which* is an object, the Sears Tower. In the third sentence, *that* referred once to a person (the speaker) and once to a thing (the insurance company).

Relative pronouns (*who, which,* and *that*) must agree with their antecedents.

Relative Pronoun	*Refers to*
who (whom, whose)	humans
which	nonhumans (animals and objects)
that	humans or nonhumans

EXERCISE 15

Directions: In each sentence, circle the antecedent for the relative pronoun. Then underline the relative pronoun that agrees with it.

Example: My (Uncle Ben,) (<u>who</u>, which) is a retired carpenter, gave me some excellent advice on remodeling the kitchen.

1. The horror movie *(who, that)* we saw last night was too gruesome for me.

2. The shortstop fired the ball to the catcher, *(who, which)* tagged the runner out at home plate.

3. Soccer, *(which, who)* involves more running and less body contact than football, is becoming popular throughout the United States.

4. Zebra finches are small gray birds *(who, that)* sound like a child's squeeze toy.

5. Much outdoor furniture is made of redwood, *(who, which)* is highly resistant to variations in moisture and temperature.

6. Lyndon Johnson, *(who, which)* became president after John Kennedy's assassination, was elected to a full term in 1964.

7. I've always preferred cats to dogs, *(which, who)* seem totally lacking in self-respect and dignity.

8. A shift in Pacific Ocean currents, *(which, who)* occurs every few years, may dramatically change weather patterns in the United States.

9. The teller *(who, which)* was robbed at gunpoint yesterday is my sister.

10. A fire destroyed the house *(who, that)* the Bensons had been renting for years.

ANSWERS ARE ON PAGE 362.

AGREEMENT IN NUMBER

In Chapter 3, you learned that subjects and present-tense verbs must agree in number: singular subjects take verbs ending in *s*, and plural subjects take verbs with no *s*. A similar rule applies to pronouns.

> Pronouns must agree in number with their antecedents.

The hawk dipped **its** wings into the water as **it** skimmed across the surface of the lake.

The hawks dipped **their** wings into the water as **they** skimmed across the surface of the lake.

In the first sentence, *its* and *it* are singular because their antecedent, *hawk*, is singular. In the second sentence, the pronouns *their* and *they* are plural because their antecedent, *hawks*, is plural.

Study the following chart to remind yourself which pronouns are singular and which are plural.

Singular Pronouns	*Plural Pronouns*
I, me, my, mine	we, us, our, ours
you, your, yours	you, your, yours
he, she, it, him	they, them, their, theirs
her, his, hers, its	

To check for agreement in number, follow these three steps:

1. Find the antecedent of the pronoun.

2. Decide whether the antecedent is singular or plural.

3. Make sure that the pronoun agrees in number with the antecedent.

Use the three steps to decide whether the pronoun *they* is used correctly in the sentence below.

> The government became so huge that **they** didn't listen to the people anymore.

1. What is the antecedent of *they*?

The antecedent is *government*.

2. Is *government* singular or plural?

Government is singular.

3. Does the pronoun *they* match a singular noun?

No. *They* is a plural pronoun.

Here's how the sentence should be written:

> The government became so big that **it** didn't listen to the people anymore.

Be careful to maintain agreement in number with antecedents throughout a passage. As you check for errors in Part 1 and Part 2 of the GED Writing Skills Test, correct any incorrect shifts between singular and plural words.

Circle the pronoun that does not agree in number with the rest of the passage in the example below.

A taxicab driver is an independent person. He owns his own cab and sets his own work hours. The city usually licenses them to operate within the metropolitan area.

The first sentence refers to a singular subject: *a driver*. The pronouns *he* and *his* in the second sentence refer to *driver*; they are also singular. However, the pronoun *them* in the third sentence is plural. To agree with the antecedent *driver*, the pronoun should be *him*.

As you learned in Chapter 3, some words like *either*, *neither*, and *both* control whether a compound subject is singular or plural. Study the following examples:

Both Jeremy and his brother **enjoy** cooking.
Neither Jeremy nor his brother **enjoys** doing dishes.

In the first example sentence above, *Both* joins the subjects together to make a plural subject. In the second sentence, *Neither* separates the subjects. The subject closest to the verb, *brother*, is singular. The verb forms agree with the subjects accordingly.

Words like *both* and *neither* also control pronoun-antecedent agreement. Study the following examples:

Both Jeremy and his brother clean **their** rooms annually.
Neither Jeremy nor his brother cleans **his** room weekly.
Neither Jeremy nor his brothers clean **their** rooms weekly.

In the first example sentence above, the plural subject requires a plural pronoun. In the second sentence, the part of the subject closest to the pronoun, *brother*, is singular, so the pronoun is singular. In the third sentence, the part of the subject that is closest to the pronoun, *brothers*, is plural, requiring the plural pronoun *their*.

For further review on these special words, you may want to restudy pages 105–107.

EXERCISE 16

Part A

Directions: For each sentence, underline the pronoun that matches its antecedent in number. Circle the antecedent.

Example: Every ⟨recruit⟩ must make (*his*, *their*) bed by 6:15.

1. After World War II, Germany received millions of dollars in foreign aid to help rebuild (*their, its*) cities.

2. Neither woman wanted to spend (*her, their*) day off cooking and cleaning house.

3. Both Steve and Charles spent much of (*his, their*) leisure time fishing.

4. Either the cat or the dogs have left (*its, their*) footprints on my clean kitchen floor.

5. The dog and the cat have left (*its, their*) footprints on my clean kitchen floor.

6. When learning about metric measurements, think of an ordinary paper clip. (*They weigh, It weighs*) exactly one gram, and (*their, its*) wire is one millimeter thick.

7. The insurance company sent (*its, their*) agent to discuss a new policy.

8. Although finches are attractive little birds to keep as pets, (*it, they*) can't be taught to talk.

9. All of the staff members signed the petition to have (*their, his*) supervisor removed for incompetence.

10. When a man becomes a father, (*they begin, he begins*) to see life differently.

Part B

Directions: Proofread the following paragraph for errors in agreement in number. Make corrections by crossing out the error and writing in the correct word or words in the space above. Make sure that the paragraph maintains agreement in number from sentence to sentence. You may occasionally need to change a verb to agree with the new pronoun. The first error has been corrected as an example.

they have

Children are much less upset by hospital stays if ~~he has~~ been prepared

properly for the experience. If possible, he should be taken on a tour of the

hospital before he is admitted. Becoming familiar with these new

surroundings will reduce his anxiety and help them adjust more quickly to

being away from home.

ANSWERS ARE ON PAGE 362.

AGREEMENT IN PERSON

Personal pronouns can be grouped in three categories: first person, which refers to the speaker or writer (I); second person, which refers to the audience (you); and third person, which refers to the individual or group spoken about (he, she, they). Study the box below.

PERSONAL PRONOUNS

First Person: I, me, my, mine, we, us, our, ours

When I applied for the job, I stated my qualifications clearly.

Second Person: you, your, yours

When you applied for the job, Joan, you stated your qualifications clearly.

Third Person: he, she, it, him, her, his, hers, its, they, them, their, theirs

When Carol applied for the job, she stated her qualifications clearly.

Within a sentence or longer passage, don't shift from one category of pronouns to another. Maintain agreement in person.

> DOES NOT AGREE: When **we** finally reached the summit, **you** could see for miles in every direction.
>
> AGREES: When **we** finally reached the summit, **we** could see for miles in every direction.

In the first example sentence above, the pronoun shifts from first to second person. The second sentence correctly shows that the writer, not the reader, saw the view.

> DOES NOT AGREE: If **a worker** is injured on the job, **you** will receive worker's compensation.
>
> AGREES: If **a worker** is injured on the job, **he** will receive worker's compensation.

In the first example sentence above, the pronoun shifts from third to second person. The second sentence correctly shows that the worker, not the reader, should receive benefits.

Circle the pronouns in the following sentence. Do they agree in person?

When we walked into the kitchen, you could smell the aroma of freshly baked bread.

The pronouns *we* and *you* do not agree, since *we* is a first-person pronoun and *you* is second person. Write the sentence correctly in the space below.

_____

_____

You might have written the following sentence, or you might have used *you* instead of *we*:

As we walked into the kitchen, we could smell the aroma of freshly baked bread.

Just as you should check a passage for agreement in number, you should proofread for agreement in person. It's especially easy to slip from first or third to second person. Don't use *you* unless you're speaking directly to your reader.

Circle the pronoun that does not agree in person with the rest of the passage below.

When we heard a rumble of thunder, we looked out the window apprehensively. By the erratic flicker of lightning, you could see tree branches whipping back and forth. We scurried around the house, closing windows and hunting for flashlights in case of a power outage.

Did you circle the pronoun *you* in the second sentence? Cross it out and replace it with *we* to write the passage consistently in first person.

Circle the pronoun that does not agree in person with the rest of the passage below.

If you want to build a bookcase, first decide what kind of lumber to use. Then measure the place where you plan to put the bookcase. When you go to the lumberyard, the salesperson will help you figure out how much wood to buy. When you get it home, remeasure everything. Then cut where you have marked and assemble the pieces. They may want to use both glue and nails for stronger shelf joints.

Did you circle the pronoun *They* in the last sentence? Replace it with *You* to write the passage consistently in second person.

EXERCISE 17

Part A

Directions: Underline the pronoun that agrees in person with its antecedent. Circle the antecedent.

1. As our plane was crossing the Atlantic, *(we, you)* saw a magnificent sunrise.

2. If *(you're not, one isn't)* careful around farm machinery, you can be seriously injured.

3. Ramish's favorite actor is Steven Seagal because *(you, he)* always knows that in the end Seagal will overpower the forces of evil.

4. Most farmers and construction workers agree that plain water satisfies *(your, their)* thirst far better than any carbonated soft drink.

5. Alyssa and Cynthia are always worried about how *(your, their)* hair looks.

6. When I saw Fluffy chasing a butterfly, *(I, you)* thought it was cute—until she caught it.

7. You have to study pretty hard if *(he, you)* hope to pass Mr. Rodriguez's class.

8. When the twins were little, they had *(their, our)* own private language.

Part B

Directions: Proofread the passage below for agreement in person. Cross out and replace any underlined pronouns that do not agree with the rest of the paragraph. Some of the underlined pronouns are correct as written.

As we neared the seacoast, the fog enveloped us so thickly that <u>you</u> couldn't see two feet in front of <u>our car</u>. One felt as if <u>you</u> were moving in outer space, with no signposts, no trees, not even a roadway to orient <u>you</u>. Even the sounds were muffled. An occasional car droned past <u>us, its driver</u> <u>slowly feeling his</u> way in the opposite direction. Most of the time, though, all <u>you</u> could hear was the dull throb of the waves on the beach and the mournful foghorns warning ships away from hidden rocks.

ANSWERS ARE ON PAGE 362.

CHAPTER HIGHLIGHTS: KEEPING YOUR STORY STRAIGHT

1. You can use a modifying phrase to combine ideas in a single sentence. To make sure that the sentence is clear, place the modifying phrase as close as possible to the word it describes.

WRONG: The motorcycle gang intimidated the neighborhood roaring down the street in formation.

RIGHT: Roaring down the street in formation, the motorcycle gang intimidated the neighborhood.

2. Set off renaming phrases and introductory modifying phrases with commas.

Mortimer, my pet toad, just zapped a fly.
Having finished his lunch, Mortimer dozed on a rock.

3. Use parallel structure whenever you include compound elements in a sentence. That is, use a similar word form for all items in a list.

WRONG: Timothy was dishonest, crude, and a coward.

RIGHT: Timothy was dishonest, crude, and cowardly.

4. Make pronouns refer clearly to their antecedents. Avoid confusing pronouns that could logically refer to either of two antecedents, and avoid vague pronouns that have no antecedent at all.

WRONG: The couple was playing cards, but Todd thought it looked boring.

RIGHT: The couple was playing cards, but Todd thought the game looked boring.

5. Make pronouns agree with their antecedents.

a. Use the relative pronoun (*who*, *which*, or *that*) that matches its human or nonhuman antecedent.

The man who used to live here played the drums.
His pet cat, which still wanders by, is deaf.

b. Make pronouns agree with their antecedents in number and person.

WRONG: When we visited New York City, you couldn't go up in the Statue of Liberty.

RIGHT: When we visited New York City, we couldn't go up in the Statue of Liberty.

6. When correcting confusing pronouns, be sure to read the passage as a whole to make sure the correction fits in with the rest of the pronouns in the passage.

EDITING PRACTICE

Part A

Directions: Find and correct the twelve errors in the following passage. Five of these errors are related to skills that you learned in earlier chapters: subject-verb agreement, verb forms, fragments, and run-ons. You may want to review the checklists on pages 65, 117, and 169 to refresh your memory on what to look for. The other seven errors are related to problems you studied in this chapter. For these errors, use the checklist below as your proofreading guide.

☐ Are modifying phrases placed close to the words they describe?

☐ Are commas used to set off renaming phrases and introductory modifying phrases?

☐ Do pronouns refer clearly to their antecedents?

☐ Are pronouns consistent with their antecedents?

☐ Is parallel structure used for compound elements?

Break-ins, muggings, and rapes has increased dramatically in our community since 1960. With this increase in street crime we citizens have lost much of our freedom. Growing up, our front door was never locked. You simply didn't worry about someone walking in and stealing our property. At eight years old, my parents let me ride the bus downtown by myself. My mother always a protective person, had no qualms about my safety. A few years later when I was in high school, my friends and I would often meet at five o'clock in the morning and walk six blocks to the park, to play tennis. No reason to fear being robbed or raped.

My daughter, which is now ten, doesn't enjoy the same freedom I had. Our house is equped with plenty of locks for the doors and a burglar alarm as well. We don't allow Cindy to take the bus alone or walking around the neighborhood after dark, there are too many reports of robberies and rapes for us to feel safe. For her and for most other children, the fear of crime has taken some of the fun out of childhood.

ANSWERS ARE ON PAGE 362.

Part B

Directions: Revise the essay you wrote on pages 188, 189, and 191. Use modifying phrases where appropriate to add variety and to link ideas logically. Then apply the proofreading checklist dealing with modifiers, pronouns, and parallel structure that you used in Part A to check for errors.

ANSWERS WILL VARY.

GED Practice
EXERCISE 18

Questions 1–6 refer to the following paragraph.

(1) Calculators, once bulky and expensive machines have become much smaller and cheaper in the past twenty years; as a result, they are revolutionizing the way math is taught. (2) Because pocket calculators are now widely available at low prices, they say that elementary school students should spend less time drilling their addition and multiplication facts. (3) Instead, the children should be taught to analyze a word problem, they should select the information needed to solve it, and decide whether to add, subtract, multiply, or divide. (4) The calculators will perform the mechanical operations. (5) The children will be able to concentrate on the real thinking skills. (6) The danger in this shift from drill is that you may not recognize a simple error caused by hitting the wrong key on the calculator. (7) The best math students will continue to be the children which have good problem-solving skills and a strong command of arithmetic facts.

1. Sentence 1: **Calculators, once bulky and expensive machines have become much smaller and cheaper in the past twenty years; as a result, they are revolutionizing the way math is taught.**

    What correction should be made to this sentence?

    (1) remove the comma after *calculators*
    (2) insert a comma after *machines*
    (3) replace *cheaper* with *cheaply*
    (4) replace *they are* with *it is*
    (5) no correction is necessary

2. Sentence 2: **Because pocket calculators are now widely available at low prices, they say that elementary school students should spend less time drilling their addition and multiplication facts.**

    What correction should be made to this sentence?

    (1) remove *Because pocket calculators are*
    (2) replace *they* with *some educators*
    (3) replace *elementary school students* with *they*
    (4) replace *addition* with *adding*
    (5) no correction is necessary

3. Sentence 3: **Instead, the children should be taught to analyze a word problem, they should select the information needed to solve it, and decide whether to add, subtract, multiply, or divide.**

    Which of the following is the best way to write the underlined portion of this sentence? If you think the original is the best way, choose option (1).

    (1) they should select
    (2) selecting
    (3) to select
    (4) select
    (5) that they select

KEEPING YOUR STORY STRAIGHT ▼ 225

4. Sentences 4 and 5: **The calculators will perform the mechanical operations. The children will be able to concentrate on the real thinking skills.**

   The most effective combination of Sentences 4 and 5 would include which of the following groups of words?

   (1) While the calculators perform the mechanical operations, the children
   (2) By performing the mechanical operations, the children
   (3) Concentrating on the real thinking skills, the calculators
   (4) The mechanical operations performed by the children
   (5) When the calculators concentrate on the real thinking skills,

5. Sentence 6: **The danger in this shift from drill is that you may not recognize a simple error caused by hitting the wrong key on the calculator.**

   Which of the following is the best way to write the underlined portion of this sentence? If you think the original is the best way, choose option (1).

   (1) you
   (2) we
   (3) he
   (4) they
   (5) one

6. Sentence 7: **The best math students will continue to be the children which have good problem-solving skills and a strong command of arithmetic facts.**

   What correction should be made to this sentence?

   (1) change *which* to *who*
   (2) replace *have good problem-solving skills* with *are skillful at solving problems*
   (3) insert *possessing* after *and*
   (4) replace *strong command* with *commanding strongly*
   (5) no correction is necessary

Questions 7–11 refer to the following paragraph.

(1) As Dave was pulling on his hiking boots and Jack was filling his backpack, Dave asked me if I was prepared for pain. (2) Within the first few hundred feet of our climb I discovered what he meant. (3) With every step up the steep mountain trail, I felt my pack grow heavier, my legs grow more tired, and my lungs become more desperate for oxygen. (4) We climbed higher and higher. (5) My heart was beating faster. (6) We finally reached the peak, and the view from the peak made our struggle worthwhile. (7) You could see range after range of mountains marching to the horizon.

7. Sentence 1: **As Dave was pulling on his hiking boots and Jack was filling his backpack, Dave asked me if I was prepared for pain.**

   What correction should be made to this sentence?

   (1) replace *As Dave was* with *With Dave*
   (2) replace *was filling* with *filled*
   (3) replace *Dave asked* with *he asked*
   (4) insert a comma after *prepared*
   (5) no correction is necessary

8. Sentences 2 and 3: **Within the first few hundred feet of our climb I discovered what he meant. With every step up the steep mountain trail, I felt my pack grow heavier, my legs grow more tired, and my lungs become more desperate for oxygen.**

   What correction should be made to these sentences?

   (1) insert a comma after *climb*
   (2) insert a comma after *step*
   (3) omit the comma after *trail*
   (4) change *become* to *became*
   (5) no correction is necessary

9. Sentences 4 and 5: **We climbed higher and higher. My heart was beating faster.**

   The most effective combination of Sentences 4 and 5 would contain which of the following groups of words?

   (1) As we climbed higher, the faster
   (2) Climbing higher and higher, my heart
   (3) Although we climbed higher and higher, my heart
   (4) The higher we climbed, the faster
   (5) The higher we climbed, and my heart

10. Sentence 6: **We finally reached the peak, and the view from the peak made our struggle worthwhile.**

    If you rewrote sentence 6 beginning with

    Upon finally reaching the peak,

    the next words should be

    (1) the view
    (2) it made
    (3) our struggle
    (4) we decided
    (5) the peak's view

11. Sentence 7: **You could see range after range of mountains marching to the horizon.**

    Which of the following is the best way to write the underlined portion of this sentence? If you think the original is the best way, choose option (1).

    (1) You could see range after range of mountains marching to the horizon.
    (2) Marching to the horizon, you could see range after range of mountains.
    (3) We could see range after range of mountains marching to the horizon.
    (4) We could see range after range of mountains, marching to the horizon.
    (5) Marching to the horizon, range after range of mountains.

Questions 12–16 refer to the following paragraph.

(1) Frank's parents warned him not to overuse his first credit card, which he cheerfully ignored and bought a new stereo system. (2) An expensive car, buying a large television set, and a trip to Las Vegas were next on Frank's list of plastic purchases. (3) By the middle of the following month, financial reality began to catch up with him; as a result, his spending spree screeched to a halt. (4) Frank always a carefree person, became depressed, withdrawn, and irritable. (5) After being confronted with a bill for twenty thousand dollars, the credit card was cut into tiny pieces.

12. Sentence 1: **Frank's parents warned him not to overuse his first credit card, which he cheerfully ignored and bought a new stereo system.**

What correction should be made to this sentence?

(1) replace *his* with *your*
(2) replace *his* with *a person's*
(3) replace *card, which he cheerfully ignored* with *card. He cheerfully ignored it*
(4) replace *card, which he cheerfully ignored* with *card. He cheerfully ignored their advice*
(5) no correction is necessary

13. Sentence 2: **An expensive car, <u>buying a</u> large television set, and a trip to Las Vegas were next on Frank's list of plastic purchases.**

Which of the following is the best way to write the underlined portion of this sentence? If you think the original is the best way, choose option (1).

(1) buying a
(2) to buy a
(3) bought a
(4) he also bought a
(5) a

14. Sentence 3: **By the middle of the following month, financial reality began to catch up with him; as a result, his spending spree screeched to a halt.**

What correction should be made to this sentence?

(1) insert a comma after *middle*
(2) remove the comma after *month*
(3) replace *him* with *them*
(4) replace *his* with *your*
(5) no correction is necessary

15. Sentence 4: **Frank always a carefree person, became depressed, withdrawn, and irritable.**

What correction should be made to this sentence?

(1) insert a comma after *Frank*
(2) remove the comma after *person*
(3) change *withdrawn* to *withdrew*
(4) insert *he was* after *and*
(5) no correction is necessary

16. Sentence 5: **After being confronted with a bill for twenty thousand dollars, the credit card was cut into tiny pieces.**

What correction should be made to this sentence?

(1) remove the comma after *dollars*
(2) replace *the credit card was cut* with *Frank cut the credit card*
(3) insert a comma after *cut*
(4) insert *by Frank* after *pieces*
(5) no correction is necessary

ANSWERS ARE ON PAGE 363.

GED Practice
ESSAY-WRITING REVIEW

Questions 1–8 refer to the following paragraph.

(1) Although it may be less popular than softball or football. (2) Competitive swimming is an ideal summer sport for most children. (3) Certainly swimming provides healthful exercise. (4) Done regularly, it builds muscular strength in the upper body and the legs, increases flexibility, and will improve heart and lung capacity. (5) It provides this with minimal danger of injury. (6) Of course, a swimmer, like participants in other sports, risks an occasional pulled muscle. (7) However, there's no knee injuries from tackling and no concussions from unexpected contact with a line drive. (8) In addition to its physical pluses, swimming provides psychological benefits for children by promoting cooperation among team members as they cheered one another on, particularly in the relay events. (9) Equally important is the chance for each swimmer to chart their own progress. (10) Not everyone can earn a blue ribbon in an individual event. (11) Even swimmers who come in last can be satisfied if they have swum a second faster than they did in the previous meet.

1. Sentences 1 and 2: **Although it may be less popular than softball or <u>football. Competitive</u> swimming is an ideal summer sport for most children.**

Which is the best way to rewrite the underlined portion of these sentences? If you think the original is the best way, choose option (1).

(1) football. Competitive
(2) football; competitive
(3) football, competitive
(4) football competitive
(5) football, but competitive

2. Sentence 4: **Done regularly, it builds muscular strength in the upper body and the legs, increases flexibility, and will improve heart and lung capacity.**

What correction should be made to this sentence?

(1) change *builds* to *built*
(2) change *builds* to *is building*
(3) insert *your* after *increases*
(4) replace *will improve* with *improves*
(5) no correction is necessary

3. Sentence 5: **It provides this with minimal danger of injury.**

What correction should be made to this sentence?

(1) replace *It provides* with *By providing*
(2) replace *It* with *And*
(3) change *provides* to *provided*
(4) replace *this* with *these benefits*
(5) replace *this* with *that*

4. Sentence 6: **Of course, a swimmer, like participants in other sports, risks an occasional pulled muscle.**

What correction should be made to this sentence?

(1) replace *a swimmer* with *swimmers*
(2) change *risks* to *risk*
(3) change *risks* to *has risked*
(4) insert a comma after *risks*
(5) no correction is necessary

5. Sentence 7: **However, there's no knee injuries from tackling and no concussions from unexpected contact with a line drive.**

What correction should be made to this sentence?

(1) replace *there's* with *there is*
(2) replace *there's* with *there are*
(3) change the spelling of *tackling* to *tackleing*
(4) replace *tackling and* with *tackling. And*
(5) no correction is necessary

6. Sentence 8: **In addition to its physical pluses, swimming provides psychological benefits for children by promoting cooperation among team members as they <u>cheered</u> one another on, particularly in the relay events.**

Which of the following is the best way to write the underlined portion of the sentence? If you think the original is the best way, choose option (1).

(1) cheered
(2) cheer
(3) cheers
(4) will be cheering
(5) were cheering

7. Sentence 9: **Equally important is the chance for each swimmer to chart their own progress.**

What correction should be made to this sentence?

(1) change *is* to *was*
(2) change *is* to *will be*
(3) replace *each swimmer* with *swimmers*
(4) replace *their* with *your*
(5) no correction is necessary

8. Sentences 10 and 11: **Not everyone can earn a blue ribbon in an individual event. Even swimmers who come in last can be satisfied if they have swum a second faster than they did in the previous meet.**

The most effective combination of Sentences 10 and 11 would include which of the following groups of words?

(1) because even
(2) but even
(3) if even
(4) when even
(5) in addition, even

Questions 9–16 refer to the following paragraph.

(1) When automobiles and airplanes might symbolize the changes in American technology in the first half of this century, computers certainly symbolize the second half. (2) These electronic marvels once room-sized monstrosities full of wires and vacuum tubes, have been reduced in size and introduced into countless household and business settings. (3) In the home, computers control appliances as varyed as microwave ovens, cameras, and television sets. (4) Automobiles and trucks also contain computers. (5) The computers regulate their fuel and electrical systems. (6) Wherever financial transactions take place, computers is likely to appear. (7) They have replaced cash registers in supermarkets and department stores. (8) Not only do they print receipts listing the items sold, but they also maintain an inventory of merchandise on hand. (9) Automatic tellers allowed banks' customers to make deposits, withdrawals, and transfers by pressing a few buttons. (10) Even gas stations have became computerized as customers paying by credit card wait while a central computer thousands of miles away checks card numbers and records transactions.

9. Sentence 1: **When automobiles and airplanes might symbolize the changes in American technology in the first half of this century, computers certainly symbolize the second half.**

Which of the following is the best way to write the underlined portion of this sentence? If you think the original is the best way, choose option (1).

(1) When
(2) Because
(3) As though
(4) Wherever
(5) Whereas

10. Sentence 2: **These electronic marvels once room-sized monstrosities full of wires and vacuum tubes, have been reduced in size and introduced into countless household and business settings.**

What correction should be made to this sentence?

(1) insert a comma after *marvels*
(2) remove the comma after *tubes*
(3) replace *size and* with *size. And*
(4) insert a comma after *household*
(5) no correction is necessary

11. Sentence 3: **In the home, computers control appliances as varyed as microwave ovens, cameras, and television sets.**

What correction should be made to this sentence?

(1) change the spelling of *varyed* to *varied*
(2) change the spelling of *ovens* to *ovenes*
(3) remove the comma after *ovens*
(4) insert *have computers* after *cameras*
(5) no correction is necessary

12. Sentences 4 and 5: **Automobiles and trucks also contain computers. The computers regulate their fuel and electrical systems.**

The most effective combination of Sentences 4 and 5 would include which of the following groups of words?

(1) computers, and the computers regulate
(2) computers that regulate
(3) computers, they regulate
(4) computers although they regulate
(5) computers who regulate

13. Sentence 6: **Wherever financial transactions take place, computers is likely to appear.**

What correction should be made to this sentence?

(1) replace *Wherever* with *Even though*
(2) insert a comma after *Wherever*
(3) remove the comma after *place*
(4) change *is* to *are*
(5) no correction is necessary

14. Sentence 8: **Not only do they print receipts listing the items sold, but they also maintain an inventory of merchandise on hand.**

Which of the following is the best way to write the underlined portion of this sentence? If you think the original is the best way, choose option (1).

(1) they also maintain
(2) also maintaining
(3) to be maintaining
(4) also to maintain
(5) also maintains

15. Sentence 9: **Automatic tellers allowed banks' customers to make deposits, withdrawals, and transfers by pressing a few buttons.**

Which of the following is the best way to write the underlined portion of this sentence? If you think the original is the best way, choose option (1).

(1) allowed
(2) allowing
(3) allows
(4) allow
(5) are allowed

16. Sentence 10: **Even gas stations have became computerized as customers paying by credit card wait while a central computer thousands of miles away checks card numbers and records transactions.**

What correction should be made to this sentence?

(1) change *became* to *become*
(2) replace *computerized as customers* with *computerized, customers*
(3) insert a comma after *wait*
(4) change *wait* to *waits*
(5) change *checks* to *check*

ANSWERS ARE ON PAGE 363.

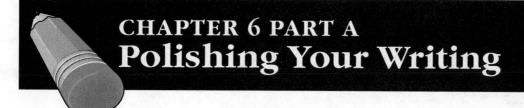

When you complete a rough draft of an essay, does an enormous sense of relief sweep over you—a "Whew! That's done!" sort of feeling? Finishing a draft should give you a sense of accomplishment. Prewriting and drafting an essay require a great deal of mental effort.

But before you set your essay aside as a finished product, remember the final stages in the writing process: *revising* and *editing*. Like the difference between a rough-cut gem and a diamond gleaming in a jewelry store window, the difference between a promising piece of writing and a fine essay lies in the polishing.

You've been editing throughout this book. You've learned to check for complete sentences, clearly combined ideas, consistent verbs and pronouns, and correct punctuation and spelling. By correcting these surface features of your writing, you'll make sure that your reader can concentrate on your ideas.

Revising, however, is different. Revising is the process of strengthening the content, organization, and wording of a piece of writing. In this step, you'll be putting yourself in the reader's place in order to decide what changes will sharpen meaning and make your writing more convincing.

It isn't easy to shift from viewing your paper as the writer to viewing it as a reader. After all, *you* know exactly what you mean! If possible, let your first draft rest a few days before you revise it. This breather will help give you a new perspective on the paper—fresh eyes to use in the task ahead.

By now, at least a few days will have passed since you finished your essay on page 223 of Chapter 5. Take the draft out and reread it, imagining that you are seeing it for the first time. Can you find the unifying statement? Is the meaning clear throughout? Does the paper move logically from one point to another? Is the material convincing? Take a few minutes right now to jot down ideas for any changes that would make your paper clearer to your reader.

There is no one correct way to revise an essay. You'll find yourself adding, removing, replacing, and moving material in order to strengthen meaning. In this chapter you'll study three possible ways to improve an essay through revision: using specifics, using sentence and paragraph links, and tightening the wording.

As you study each section, you'll see how one writer revised parts of an essay written in response to a question in Chapter 5: "Should young adults be required to perform a year of public service?" Then you'll revise your own Chapter 5 essay.

The original draft of the sample essay is printed below. As you read through the essay for the first time, notice how you respond to it. Are you convinced by the writer's arguments? Do you notice errors? How could this essay be improved?

America needs the help and assistance of its young adults during times of peace as well as during times of war. The drafting of young people shouldn't be limited to military purposes. At least one year of public service should be required. This requirement would be beneficial and helpful in many ways.

Public service jobs would provide automatic employment for young adults. They would no longer be causing trouble because they were bored. Young adults would be learning skills that they needed them to be good workers.

If the public service program were set up like the military service program, young adults could earn educational benefits by completing their year of duty. The money could be used for further training toward the career of their choice.

Required public service it would emphasize the importance our society places on helping others. Young people would learn how important it is to provide care for various groups who need help.

Required public service is an idea that its time has come. It will help the youth who work in the program, and it will help American society as a whole.

USING SPECIFIC REASONS

When someone is trying to persuade you, what makes the person's argument convincing? Usually you'll be willing to consider someone else's point of view if the person offers good reasons to back up his or her opinions.

> Use specific reasons to explain your opinions.

Many writers make the mistake of circular reasoning when they attempt to persuade their readers. That is, rather than providing a specific reason to support their opinion, they restate the opinion in other words.

PROBLEM: Teenagers are too young to drink alcoholic beverages because they aren't mature enough to handle alcohol.

BETTER: Teenagers are too young to drink alcoholic beverages because they tend to be daredevils. They're willing to drink to excess because they're still testing their limits.

The problem sentence is saying "Teenagers are too young to drink because they're too young to drink." Can you see that *aren't mature enough* means the same thing as *are too young*? In the revised version, the writer added two specific reasons why teenagers are too young to drink. Now look at another example.

PROBLEM: *Sacred Ruby of the Ganges* is the most exciting film I've ever seen. Every other film was boring in comparison.

BETTER: *Sacred Ruby of the Ganges* is the most exciting film I've ever seen because of the suspenseful chases, the romantic tension between the lead characters, and the constant danger from jungle animals.

The problem sentences are saying "The film was the most exciting because it was the most exciting." Can you see that *the most exciting film I've ever seen* says the same thing as *Every other film was boring in comparison?* The revised version gives specific reasons why the film was exciting.

Test the reasons you provide for each of your opinions in an essay. If you discover that you've restated something in other words, revise that section to make your support more convincing.

One of the three sentences below displays circular reasoning. Find it and correct it in the space provided.

Japanese cars are better than American cars because Japanese cars are more sturdily made and use less gas.

That book is boring because it simply doesn't interest me.

A tax increase is needed because the county needs to raise wages to keep up with inflation.

_____

_____

Did you revise the second sentence? *Boring* and *doesn't interest me* are two ways of saying the same thing.

EXERCISE 1

Directions: Read each of the following sentences. If a sentence provides a specific reason to support an opinion, write *OK*. If it uses circular reasoning, revise to add specific reasons.

Example: The mandatory retirement age should be raised because sixty-five is too low.

> *The mandatory retirement age should be raised because most sixty-five-year-old people are in better physical and mental health than older people were thirty-five years ago.*

1. City life is more stressful than farm life because city life has more tension.

2. In my opinion, the federal government wastes taxpayers' money by spending it on overpriced goods like two-hundred-dollar hammers.

3. Cigarette smoking is a harmful habit because cigarettes are dangerous.

4. The automobile is one of the most useful inventions of this century; it has provided many benefits.

5. The telephone has brought the world closer together by allowing people thousands of miles apart to communicate instantly.

6. I believe that water pollution is a serious environmental problem in this country because it is a threat to our surroundings.

7. America needs tougher gun control legislation because too many people are killed each year in accidental shootings and shootings related to domestic arguments.

8. Elementary school children should be required to learn a foreign language because learning a foreign language should be part of every child's education.

9. College athletes should be paid for playing because they deserve money for their services.

10. The minimum wage should be increased by at least one dollar per hour because the current wage is too low.

POSSIBLE ANSWERS ARE ON PAGE 364.

USING SPECIFIC EXAMPLES

Which of the following passages creates a clearer image in your mind?

Old people in nursing homes are often neglected. Their relatives ignore them, and the staff is too busy to attend to anything but their basic survival needs.

Old people in nursing homes are often neglected. Their relatives ignore them, and the staff is too busy to attend to anything but their basic survival needs. Imagine an eighty-six-year-old man strapped into his chair for hours, staring vacantly at the nurses hurrying past without a glance in his direction. In the eight years since he entered the nursing home, his son has visited twice.

Without a doubt, the second passage is more vivid. Notice that the writer has not just added more words that say the same thing. What makes the difference is the use of specific examples. Note the specific illustrations for the general statements summarized in the chart below.

General	Specific
old people	an eighty-six-year-old man
neglected	strapped in his chair for hours
relatives ignore them	son has visited twice in eight years
staff too busy	nurses hurry by without a glance

Using examples like these can make your writing interesting and convincing to your reader. You can draw examples from your own personal experience and that of your family and friends. You can also draw examples from the newspaper, what you have seen on television or in movies, or just your imagination.

How could you add a specific example to the general statement below?

People are obsessed with money.

You can probably think of a lot of examples of how people are obsessed with money. You could write about yourself or someone you know, like these:

People are obsessed with money. My friend Carl walks three miles to work and back every day just to save $1.20 in bus fare.

Or you could use less personal examples, like these:

People are obsessed with money. Every day you hear stories of families feuding over who's going to get Grandpa's money.

People are obsessed with money. I've read that most marital problems are caused by couples arguing about money.

EXERCISE 2

Directions: Add a specific example to each of the following general statements. You can draw on personal experience, your general knowledge, or your imagination.

1. High school students drop out of school for a variety of reasons.

2. We could learn a lot from older people if only we spent more time with them.

3. Many workers are dissatisfied with their jobs.

4. Having a lot of money does not always make people happy.

5. Big cities can be dangerous.

POSSIBLE ANSWERS ARE ON PAGE 364.

USING SPECIFIC DETAILS

USE SPECIFIC WORDS AND PHRASES

You can add detail and color to your writing in several ways. One easy way to dress up your writing is to use specific nouns and verbs to create a sharper picture for your reader. For example, a general sentence such as *A man walked into the building* might become *A trucker strode into Todd's Diner*, or *A drunk staggered into the hotel bar*, or even *General Patton marched into the Pentagon.* By giving specific people, places, and actions, these new sentences create very different events for the reader.

On the lines below, make up two more revisions of your own of the sentence *A man walked into the building.*

_____

_____

You can also add describing words and phrases to help your readers see what you want them to. Include details that answer the questions *what kind? which one? how many? where? when? how?* and *why?* about the nouns and verbs in the sentence. You could rewrite the sentence *A trucker strode into Todd's Diner* like this:

At eight o'clock last night, a two-hundred-fifty-pound trucker with a tattoo of a snake on his left forearm strode menacingly into Todd's Diner to confront his ex-girlfriend, Sadie, who's a waitress there.

How about the sentence *A drunk staggered into the hotel bar*? You could rewrite it like this:

> **Nearly tripping over the doorsill, a disheveled drunk in a rumpled business suit staggered into the Starlight Hotel's bar at midnight for one last shot of whiskey.**

Don't you get a better picture when the writer uses more describing words and phrases? Revise the two sentences that you wrote on page 238. Add at least three describing words or phrases to each—more if you can.

_____

_____

_____

_____

SHOW, DON'T TELL

Another way to add specifics to your writing is to show your readers what you mean. Don't just tell them what you think. Provide the specific details that allow your readers to reach the same conclusions you've made.

TELLING: My daughter was delighted.
SHOWING: My three-year-old daughter danced around the room, clapping her hands and giggling.

TELLING: The garden was beautiful.
SHOWING: The garden contained banks of golden and copper chrysanthemums flanked by dark green juniper hedges.

TELLING: The proposed freeway will destroy the neighborhood.
SHOWING: The proposed freeway will slice through King Memorial Park and require the demolition of St. Mary's Church, a one-hundred-year-old structure.

As you can see, specific observations will make your writing much more interesting and convincing. Try revising the following sentence by changing from telling to showing.

The dog was incredibly ugly.

(Imagine an ugly dog. Describe it so the reader can picture it, too.)

_____

_____

_____

EXERCISE 3

Part A

Directions: Revise the sentences below by using specific nouns and verbs, adding describing words and phrases, or replacing telling statements with showing statements to make the reader see what you see. Use your imagination!

Example: Two vehicles collided in an intersection.

A dump truck smashed into a motorcycle at the intersection of State Street and Tenth Avenue last Friday night.

1. The victim was upset.
2. A dog attacked the woman.
3. This neighborhood is run-down.
4. The new father was obviously nervous.
5. Vandalism is a problem in this community.
6. The musician played an instrument.
7. The teenager spoke to his parent.
8. The shopping mall was crowded.
9. Grocery prices have increased.
10. The federal government is wasteful.

Part B

Directions: Revise the paragraph below by adding "showing statements" to support the writer's conclusions. You may replace some sentences with specific sentences of your own, or you may choose to add sentences that provide supporting examples.

> Joe's Cafe is the worst place to eat in town. The building is filthy inside and out. Whether there is only one other customer or ten, the service is poor. Worst of all, the food tastes terrible. Even so, it's expensive.

POSSIBLE ANSWERS ARE ON PAGE 364.

STRENGTHENING AN ESSAY WITH SPECIFICS

To see how specifics can strengthen an essay, study some changes made by the writer of the essay on required public service for young people. Notice how the use of specifics has made this part of the essay clearer, more interesting, and more convincing.

EDITING HINT: Note that the writer hasn't recopied the essay in the following example. He has made changes by using carets (∧) to show where new material has been inserted. You'll find this revising technique especially useful when you're working under timed conditions, such as when you take Part 2 of the GED Writing Skills Test.

If the public service program were set up like the military

service program, young adults could earn educational benefits by ~~One year's worth of tuition at a public community college or university could be earned for one year of~~ completing their year of duty. ∧~~The money could be used for public service.~~ *Americans would be investing their money to produce well-trained engineers, auto* ~~further training toward the career of their choice.~~ *mechanics, police officers, nurses, and teachers.*

EXERCISE 4

Directions: Revise the essay you wrote in Chapter 5 by making your writing more specific. You may want to use more specific nouns and verbs, add describing words and phrases, use showing statements, and include specific reasons.

Rather than rewriting the essay at this point, cross out material you want to delete and use carets (∧) to show where insertions belong.

ANSWERS WILL VARY.

SENTENCE AND PARAGRAPH LINKS

ORGANIZATION AND PARAGRAPHING

When you are revising an essay, you should look carefully at the overall organization of the piece. In what order are your main points presented? Does that order make sense? Each of your main points should be developed in a separate paragraph. Have you sorted details, examples, or reasons that support each main point into the right paragraph?

Take a few minutes now to look at your essay from Chapter 5 again. Are there places where a new paragraph should start? If so, use the symbol ¶ to show the start of a new paragraph. Should the paragraphs be rearranged in a more logical order? If so, use arrows or numbering to show the new order.

TRANSITIONS

Making the relationships among your ideas clear to the reader is the key to more readable writing. You've already worked with patterns of organization for paragraphs in Chapter 4 and the overall structure of an essay (introduction, body, and conclusion) in Chapter 5. In this section, you'll look closely at how to help your reader follow the organization of your essay by using transition words and phrases.

Transitions help your reader follow your thoughts from sentence to sentence and from paragraph to paragraph. In the chart below, you'll find a few of the most common transitions and their uses.

Transitions	*Use*
first, second, next, then, later, finally	to show time order
one, another, also, in addition, the most important	to separate and rank items in a list
also, both, similar, like, on the other hand, different, disadvantage, advantage	to compare and contrast

You may also want to use the connectors you studied in Chapter 4 as transitions. To refresh your memory, some connectors are listed below. You will probably think of others to use in your writing.

Connectors	*Use*
moreover furthermore in addition	adds related information
however nevertheless	shows a contrasting or unexpected situation
therefore consequently	links cause to effect
otherwise	shows an alternative
for instance for example	gives specifics to illustrate a general idea

TRANSITIONS BETWEEN SENTENCES

Now let's take a look at how to choose transitions when you're revising your writing. This writer wants to explain why, with all its problems, she prefers living in a large city. She has written the two sentences below, and she wants to use a transition between them that will help her readers see the point she's making. Think of a transition she could use.

> Small towns may be quiet and peaceful. I prefer the excitement and variety of a big city.

She should choose a transition that shows contrast, such as *however* or *on the other hand*. Read the sentences again with the transition *however* inserted. Can you see how much easier it is to understand the writer's point?

> Small towns may be quiet and peaceful. However, I prefer the excitement and variety of a big city.

● FOCUS ON PUNCTUATION

Transitions

When connectors are used as transitions between sentences, they should be separated by commas from the rest of the sentence.

> Candy and carbonated soft drinks provide nothing but empty calories to the consumer. **However,** fruits and vegetables provide important vitamins and minerals with fewer calories.

The transition doesn't always appear at the beginning of the sentence. Here is the same example with the transition embedded in the second sentence. Notice that commas come before and after *however*.

> Candy and carbonated soft drinks provide nothing but empty calories to the consumer. Fruits and vegetables, **however,** provide important vitamins and minerals with fewer calories.

Many other common transitional words and phrases are probably familiar to you. They are all set off by commas. Circle the transitional phrases in the following example.

> In my opinion, Congress should pass a tax reform bill. The Senate, as a matter of fact, is debating the issue this week. Of course, the chances for passage are slim in an election year.

Did you circle *In my opinion, as a matter of fact,* and *of course*?

EXERCISE 5

Directions: Insert transitional words in the sentences below to show the logical links between ideas. Punctuate the sentences correctly.

Example: Sylvester insisted that his friends call him Rocky.

His parents *, however,* _____ continued to use his given name.

1. One hundred years ago settlers needed guns to protect themselves from wild

   animals. _____ those frontier days are long past.

2. The migration of people to the Southwest has created some serious problems.

   States like Arizona and New Mexico _____ may run short of water for their new residents.

3. _____ shake the can vigorously. _____ point

   it at your target before pulling the tab to open it. _____ laugh your head off and run away.

4. Many immigrants face a language barrier when they try to find jobs here.

   _____ they must adapt to unfamiliar interviewing practices.

5. The scenery in *The Secret of Machu Pichu* is breathtaking. The acting

   _____ is terrible.

POSSIBLE ANSWERS ARE ON PAGE 364.

TRANSITIONS BETWEEN PARAGRAPHS

Below are two paragraphs from the essay on living in a big city. How could the writer use a transition to link the two paragraphs? Think of at least one good transition.

Small towns may be quiet and peaceful. However, I prefer the excitement and variety of a big city. Big city entertainment ranges from live blues bars to ethnic street festivals. I can go see old movies for $2 or go to a fancy nightclub. No matter how much or how little money I have in my pocket, there's always something to do.

Job opportunities are better in a big city. New businesses are opening all the time here, and the "help wanted" ads on Sundays fill two whole sections of the paper. No matter what part of the nation's economy is growing, the growth is likely to happen in a big city.

What relationship do these two paragraphs have? They both give information about the advantages of living in a big city. The writer could revise the topic sentence of the second paragraph in any number of ways to make a smoother transition. Here are a few examples:

Furthermore, job opportunities are better in a big city.
In addition, job opportunities are better in a big city.
More important, job opportunities are better in a big city.
Another advantage is that job opportunities are better in a big city.

Two paragraphs of the sample essay on public service appear below, revised to include transitional words and phrases to emphasize overall organization and to link ideas clearly.

One benefit of a public service program would be
~~Public service jobs would provide~~ automatic employment for young

adults. They would no longer be hanging around street corners,

getting drunk, and vandalizing property because they were bored.
Instead, young
~~Young~~ adults would be learning skills that they needed to be good

workers such as being prompt, following directions, and serving clients

courteously.

In addition to gaining employment,
~~If the public service program were set up like the military service~~

~~program,~~ young adults could earn educational benefits by completing
If the public service program were set up like the military service
their year of duty. ~~A~~ year's worth of tuition at a public community *program, a*

college or university could be earned for one year of public service.

Americans would be investing their money to produce well-trained

engineers, auto mechanics, police officers, nurses, and teachers.

EXERCISE 6

Part A

Directions: Rewrite the following passages, adding transitional words and phrases wherever possible to make the relationships between ideas clearer to the reader.

1. You can make Tante Hanne's Apple Macaroons for dessert in forty-five minutes if you follow these simple directions. Butter a pie tin and slice four or five medium apples into it. Cover the apples with half a cup of sugar and as much cinnamon as desired. Cream together four tablespoons of margarine and half a cup of sugar. Beat in one egg. Mix in half a cup of flour and a dash of salt. Spoon the batter over the apples and bake for half an hour at 350 degrees.

2. High school students should not be allowed to drive for several reasons. They're not mature enough to handle the responsibility. Every Friday night one seventeen-year-old I know downs a six-pack of beer and then challenges his classmates to drag race down Main Street.

   Cars detract from schoolwork. Most students who own cars work to pay for gas and insurance. They spend less time on the schoolwork that should be their primary concern.

   Cars give them too much freedom. Instead of cruising the streets looking for parties to crash or girls to pick up, they should be with their families, where more adult supervision is provided.

POSSIBLE ANSWERS ARE ON PAGE 365.

Part B

Directions: Continue revising the rough draft of the essay you wrote in Chapter 5. This time revise for smooth links among sentences and paragraphs.

ANSWERS WILL VARY.

REVISING FOR SMOOTH WORDING

REPETITION

Does your writing seem to repeat itself? Perhaps you've overused a word or phrase, as in the following paragraph. Read the passage and circle the repetitive words and phrases.

> Masho is one of the most versatile people I know. Masho teaches math, chemistry, and electronics for a living. Masho plays the banjo and sings in a bluegrass band on the side. Masho writes his own computer programs as a hobby. Masho also paints as a hobby.

Each sentence in the paragraph uses the standard subject-verb pattern; in fact, each begins with the same subject: Masho. In addition, the phrase *as a hobby* is used twice.

If repetition is a problem, look for ways to rephrase the writing. You'll remember from Chapter 2 that pronouns like *he, they, our,* and *it* can take the place of nouns. Another way to avoid repetition is to use words or phrases that have similar meanings.

> Substituting **synonyms** (words and phrases that have the same meaning) and pronouns can eliminate repetition.

Here's a revised version of the repetitive paragraph, with synonyms, pronouns, and varied sentence structure making the passage much more pleasant to read.

> Masho is one of the most versatile people I know. **He** teaches math, chemistry, and electronics for a living, **and he plays** the banjo and sings in a bluegrass band on the side. **As a hobby,** Masho writes his own computer programs. **Another of his pastimes is painting.**

> **EDITING HINT:** Read your draft aloud to hunt for repetitive wording. Your ear is likely to detect what your eye might miss.

EXERCISE 7

Directions: Rewrite the following paragraph to eliminate repetition. Delete words, substitute synonyms or pronouns, and revise sentence structure as necessary to improve the sound of the paragraph. The first change has been made as an example.

Frank was annoyed with Lisa because ~~Lisa~~ *she* never became angry with ~~Frank.~~ *him* Whenever Frank complained to Lisa about anything, Lisa apologized to Frank instead of becoming angry in return. Frank found it impossible to have a good argument with Lisa because Lisa refused to argue. Lisa's refusal to argue simply made Frank even angrier than Frank was to begin with.

POSSIBLE ANSWERS ARE ON PAGE 365.

WORDINESS

Even if no words are repeated unnecessarily in a passage, it still may suffer from wordiness. What idea is repeated unnecessarily in the following sentence? *A great big huge dog attacked the mail carrier.* Three words are used to describe the size of the dog when one is enough. You could revise the sentence like this: *A huge dog attacked the mail carrier.*

> **Wordiness** is the unnecessary repetition of ideas in a passage or the use of more words than necessary to express a thought.

As you revise, look for ways to reduce the number of words in your essay without losing important ideas. This process, called **tightening**, will make your writing clearer and more forceful. When you cut words, don't cut interesting details or reasons or examples that support your argument. Just look for ways to make your points in fewer words.

Note the changes made to tighten each of the following sentences.

WORDY: Ricardo is a man who has great strength.
TIGHT: Ricardo is very strong.

WORDY: The doctor took a look at the patient's leg.
TIGHT: The doctor looked at the patient's leg.

WORDY: In this day and age computers are a significant and important part of our lives.
TIGHT: Computers are now a significant part of our lives.

WORDY: It is a fact that our bodies need vitamin A to prevent night blindness.
TIGHT: Our bodies need vitamin A to prevent night blindness.

How can the sentence below be tightened? Rewrite it in the space provided.

Substances that are hazardous or dangerous shouldn't be dumped near locations that are residential areas.

_____

_____

You might have rewritten the sentence like this:

Hazardous substances shouldn't be dumped near residential areas.

EDITING HINT: As you check your essay for wordiness, be especially careful to look for unnecessary pronouns.

INCORRECT: My father **he** was born in the Netherlands.
CORRECT: My father was born in the Netherlands.

Sentences using *who*, *which*, or *that* are especially likely to contain these errors.

INCORRECT: The milk that we bought **it** at the store yesterday is sour.
CORRECT: The milk that we bought at the store yesterday is sour.

Cross out the unnecessary pronoun in the following sentence.

The silver dollars that she gave him they were worth fifty dollars each.

You should have crossed out *they*.

EXERCISE 8

Part A

Directions: Revise the sentences below to eliminate wordiness. Change the wording as necessary. Be sure that as you revise you don't cut out important details. If a sentence does not contain any wordiness, write *OK*.

Example: The house that was old and rickety was on the market for sale.

The old, rickety house was for sale.

1. The dress is blue in color and cotton in fabric.

2. Acid rain is a serious problem in the Great Lakes region.

3. The chicken wings in the refrigerator they can be warmed up for supper.

4. The sign that the vandals destroyed it last night will cost a thousand dollars to replace.

5. At last we finally found an apartment that is large in size but inexpensive in cost.

Part B

Directions: Revise the paragraph below to eliminate wordiness. Change the wording as necessary.

At this particular point in time, heating costs are dangerously high for people living near or below the poverty level. Retired people who aren't working anymore must rely on a fixed income that doesn't change from month to month. As a rule, their social security checks they just aren't large enough in amount to cover higher utility bills when the weather is cold in the wintertime. Congress should pass a bill or law that it would offer some relief and assistance for such people who are in this type of situation.

POSSIBLE ANSWERS ARE ON PAGE 365.

TIGHTENING IN AN ESSAY

Here, one last time, is a part of the sample essay with which we began this chapter. Note the changes made by the writer to eliminate unnecessary repetition and wordiness.

One benefit of the public service program would be automatic

employment for young adults. They would no longer be hanging

around street corners, getting drunk, and vandalizing property

because they were bored. Instead, ~~young adults~~ *they* would be learning

skills that they need~~ed them~~ to be good workers, such as ~~being~~ *promptness, accuracy, and courtesy.* ~~prompt, following directions, and serving clients courteously.~~

EXERCISE 9

Directions: Complete your revision of the draft of your essay from Chapter 5 by checking for unnecessary repetition and wordiness.

☐ Delete unnecessary words (check especially carefully for excess pronouns).

☐ Replace repetitive phrases with synonyms and pronouns to improve the sound of the writing.

☐ Simplify the phrasing of bulky sentences.

You may be able to make these changes neatly by crossing out the words you want to remove and using carets (∧) to signal insertions.

ANSWERS WILL VARY.

EDITING

After revising your essay, your next step is to edit. You have practiced editing throughout this book. As you already know, editing is proofreading your writing for mistakes in grammar, punctuation, capitalization, and spelling. In the second half of this chapter, you'll be learning important rules that will help you edit for capitalization and spelling errors.

Following are some editing strategies that experienced writers use to find mistakes in their writing. Take a few minutes now to test each one. Pick a paragraph or essay of your own and try to find errors using each of the strategies listed.

1. Read your writing out loud. Listen carefully to how it sounds. Does anything jar your ear or sound awkward or incorrect? Mark problems to come back to after you have finished reading the whole piece.

2. Look at each sentence carefully, isolated from the rest of the writing. This technique is especially helpful in locating fragments.

3. Read your writing several times, each time looking for a different type of error. Choose two to four errors that you most commonly have trouble with to search for. For example, if you have trouble with subject-verb agreement, you might look at the subject and verb of each sentence in turn to make sure they agree.

PUBLISHING

After editing, the final step in the writing process is publishing. When your work is as polished as you can make it, share it with your family, friends, or classmates. This is the point at which you find out how successful you were at conveying your idea. Do the people you show your writing to understand what you're trying to say? Do they agree with your points, or does your statement get them to voice opposing opinions? Either one is good; the important thing is that you made them think. Any time you share your writing with an audience, you're publishing it.

CHAPTER HIGHLIGHTS: POLISHING YOUR WRITING

1. Revising is the process of strengthening the content, organization, and wording of a piece of writing.

2. Use specifics to help your reader get the picture. Use specific nouns and verbs. Add describing words and phrases. Show your reader what you mean; don't just tell what you think. Add examples and reasons that reinforce your points.

3. Use transitional words and phrases to show the logical links between paragraphs and sentences.

4. Eliminate unpleasant repetition by substituting synonyms and pronouns.

5. Eliminate wordiness by deleting unnecessary words and revising sentence structure to simplify phrasing.

6. Edit your writing for errors in grammar, punctuation, spelling, and capitalization.

7. Publish your writing by sharing it with an audience.

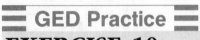 GED Practice

EXERCISE 10

Here is your third sample writing topic to help you practice for Part 2 of the GED Writing Skills Test. Try writing on this topic within the forty-five-minute time limit that you will have on the actual test. Put all the writing skills to use that you have learned so far in essay and paragraph construction, sentence structure, word choice, punctuation, and spelling.

Be sure to take ten minutes or so to prewrite, or plan, your essay. Look for clue words in the question to help you identify the topic and the kinds of details and examples to include. Write a unifying statement and brainstorm a list of details. Although you may not have time to make an outline, do try to group your details logically. Check for relevance, completeness, and organization.

Be sure to save the last five to ten minutes for revising and editing. This time, emphasize the revising skills that you've learned in this chapter. Use the following checklist as a revising guide.

☐ Does the essay contain an introduction, body, and conclusion?

☐ Does the introduction contain a clear unifying statement?

☐ Does the body develop the unifying statement with reasons and specific supporting details?

☐ Do transitional words show the logical links between sentences and paragraphs?

☐ Has unnecessary repetition of words and ideas been eliminated?

Make any changes you want by neatly crossing out words and by using carets (⋏) or asterisks (✶) to show insertions.

Finally, publish your writing by reading it to someone or giving it to a classmate or a friend to read.

Drunken driving is a serious problem in the United States. To help solve the problem, some people have proposed that anyone convicted of drunken driving be given an automatic thirty-day jail sentence, with no possibility of probation or parole. Write a statement supporting or opposing the proposal. Explain your reasons.

POSSIBLE ANSWERS ARE ON PAGE 365.

JOURNAL WRITING

Have you been writing in your journal a few times each week? If you have, you have been getting valuable practice in putting your thoughts down on paper. Here are some topics you might want to write about in your journal. Or you might want to come up with more ideas of your own.

- Everyone has a "job," although not everyone brings home a paycheck. What is your job? What do you do? Do you like your job? Why or why not?

- Whom do you think of when you think of your family? You may think of a lot of people or just a few. What is your family like?

- When you were little and people asked you what you wanted to be when you grew up, you may have said a firefighter or a baseball player. Now that you are older, how have your goals changed? What answer would you give to that question today?

- If you had to pick one person to be stranded on a desert island with for a week, who would it be? It might be the person you love most in the world. Or it might be somebody who knows how to build a boat or harvest coconuts or has some other useful skill. Describe in your journal the person you would choose and why.

Based on the revision techniques you learned in the first section of this chapter, the following paragraph is well written. It contains plenty of specific details, clear transition words, and no unnecessary repetition. Yet it needs further polishing; in fact, it contains twenty-four errors! As you read it, circle any mistakes you notice.

The two-hour special episode of "The Edge of Disaster" wensday nite was excelant. Frist, doctor Rasmussen discovered that his cancer was to advanced to be treated. Then his freind Joshua returned form a trip to thailand with a rare form of asian flu, barley able to breath. The hole emergency room staff at Blackhawk county hospital got food posioning from the Eggnog served at the new year's Eve Party. Finaly, a suprise blizzard left Tina and Rick stranded on highway 34.

If you had trouble locating all twenty-four errors, read on! They're all connected to capitalization and spelling. Although errors like these are unrelated to the meaning of a piece of writing (they would go undetected by a listener if the paragraph were read aloud), they distract readers from the writer's message. Instead of concentrating on Joshua's rare disease, for instance, they'll be thinking about the correct spelling of *friend* or wondering why the writer didn't capitalize *Thailand.*

Editing for standard capitalization and spelling won't make a bad piece of writing good, but it will make good writing better. You can use these final polishing skills to good advantage on your essay for Part 2 of the GED Writing Skills Test. In addition, you'll find capitalizing and spelling tested in Part 1.

CAPITALIZATION

You already know two important capitalization rules: the first word of every sentence and the pronoun *I* are always capitalized. In addition, when you practiced making sentences more specific in the first section of this chapter, you may have used some nouns beginning with capital letters. How can you be sure what to capitalize and what not to? Try to decide what rules explain the use of capital letters in the passage at the top of page 256.

Early yesterday morning a house at the northwest corner of Walnut Street and Fifth Avenue burned to the ground. Its owners, Doctor and Mrs. James H. Turner, were out of the state vacationing in Texas. According to Captain Thomas, the cause of the fire has not yet been determined. Neighbors reported seeing a car with an Indiana license plate stopped in the street right in front of the house moments before the fire broke out. Fire inspectors will issue a full report late next week.

You may have noticed that the capital letters were used for special names and titles. In fact, capitalization rules can be summarized in one broad principle.

CAPITALIZE NAMES OF SPECIFIC PEOPLE AND PLACES	
Specific	*General*
Doctor James H. Turner	owner
Captain Thomas	inspector
Texas	state
Fifth Avenue	street
Walnut Street	

Fill in the blanks in the following sentences, being sure to capitalize specific names.

My name is _____.

I live in the state of _____.

The name of the street I live on is _____.

Now that you know the basic rule for capitalizing, this second one will make sense.

Words derived from the names of specific people and places are also capitalized.

Natives of Italy speak **Italian**.
A family born in China has opened a **Chinese** restaurant here in town.
Do people in Denmark enjoy **Danish** pastries as much as I do?
Many **American** business representatives wish they spoke **Japanese** as well as people in Japan speak **English**.

Answer the following questions, making sure to capitalize properly.

What language(s) do you speak? _____

What nationalities were your ancestors? _____

What kinds of ethnic food do you enjoy? _____

EXERCISE 11

Directions: Proofread the following sentences for words that should be capitalized. Cross out each incorrect lowercase (small) letter and place a capital letter above it.

Example: The first people in this part of the ~~u~~nited ~~s~~tates were ~~i~~ndians, followed by ~~s~~panish and ~~f~~rench explorers.

1. Although margaret was born in london, her parents were german citizens.

2. The largest continent in both geography and population is asia, but the highest standards of living are enjoyed by europeans and north americans.

3. What a different world this would be without the inventions of thomas a. edison and alexander graham bell!

4. Thanks to vaccines, potentially dangerous childhood diseases like mumps and german measles have been almost eliminated in the united states.

5. The relations between this country and our latin american neighbors have not always been friendly.

ANSWERS ARE ON PAGE 366.

PROBLEMS IN CAPITALIZATION
Stick to the Basic Rule

Now that you are familiar with the most basic rule of capitalization, look more closely at a few potentially troublesome capitalization rules. As you study these rules, notice that each one still follows the basic rule: capitalize names of specific people and places. If you're ever in doubt about whether to capitalize something, apply that rule.

Titles

Words used as titles should be capitalized.

> My physician's name is **Doctor** Bone.
> As I was growing up, **Uncle** David was my favorite relative.
> In my opinion, **Mayor** Sly should be soundly defeated in the next election.

In these examples, the title is used as part of a person's name. Sometimes, when speaking directly to a person, you use the title as the whole name.

> You're just in time, **Doctor**.
> I'm sorry, **Mayor**, but I can't support you for reelection.

Doctor and *Mayor* are used like first names in the examples you just saw, so they are capitalized. You could say, "You're just in time, Anne," or "I'm sorry, Alfonso" instead.

Don't capitalize words like *doctor* and *mayor* when they're simply used as occupational labels.

> The **doctor** is running an hour late on appointments.

In the example above, *doctor* is not used as a first name. Try substituting your own name, and you'll see that it doesn't make sense. You wouldn't say, "The Anne is running an hour late."

Capitalize the first word and all important words in the titles of written materials.

> *I Know Why the Caged Bird Sings* is my favorite book.
> Raoul wrote an essay called "Life After Marriage."

Places

Capitalize geographical labels when they are part of a specific name.

GENERAL: I love to hike in the **mountains**.
SPECIFIC: I love to hike in the Rocky **Mountains**.

GENERAL: We saw a deer lying beside the **highway**.
SPECIFIC: We saw a deer lying beside **Highway** 415.

This rule also applies to *north, south, east,* and *west.* Don't capitalize them when they refer to a direction, but do capitalize them when they name a specific place such as a section of the country (the South, the Northwest).

GENERAL: We were hiking **north** on the trail, but when we got in the car, we drove **south**.
SPECIFIC: The old-timer said that the **North** Star Dance Hall is the oldest hall in the **Southwest**.

Dates

Capitalize days of the week and months, but not seasons.

Last **Thursday** I missed my dentist's appointment.
Workers can expect a two-week layoff in **August**.

but

Early **spring** is one of the dreariest seasons.
My favorite season is **autumn**, with its bright colors and crisp weather.

Capitalize names of holidays.

The **New Year's Eve** party got out of hand when someone began shooting off fireworks in the kitchen.
Some Americans use **Thanksgiving Day** as an excuse for overeating.

> **EDITING HINT:** When you are looking for capitalization errors in your own writing or in Part 1 of the GED Writing Skills Test, look for capital letters that should be small letters as well as small letters that should be capitalized.

EXERCISE 12

Directions: Four words are in bold type in each of the following sentences. Cross out the error in capitalization (either a missing capital letter or an unnecessary one) and write it correctly in the space above.

Example: Later this *m*~~M~~onth or early in **July**, we're planning a trip to **Niagara Falls**.

1. Last week a **Laotian** couple moved into the red brick **house** on **Oakdale road**.

2. On **Monday** morning **governor O'Reilly** will begin a campaign swing around the **state**.

3. When it's time for **Spring** cleaning, **Aunt Gladys** and her **neighbor** roll up their sleeves and scour from attic to basement.

4. Two **senators** and a **Judge** were indicted on **April** 26 for accepting **bribes**.

5. The **Mississippi** is the longest **River** in the **United States**, but not the longest in the world.

6. Both **Hannukah** and **Christmas** are **Winter holidays**.

7. Turn right off the **county road** when you reach **highway** 75 and drive five miles until you see the sign for Spring Lake **Park**.

ANSWERS ARE ON PAGE 366.

SPELLING

SPELLING CORRECTLY

You know now that there is much more to writing than correct spelling. Stating your ideas clearly and supporting them thoroughly are the essential skills for good writing. The best spelling skills in the world won't compensate for lack of thought in an essay.

On the other hand, a well-planned, well-supported essay deserves the final polishing that correct spelling provides. If you care about the piece you've written, you'll want to present it to your reader in the smoothest possible form.

What, then, can you do to improve your spelling skills? First, maintain a positive attitude. You've already learned how to spell many words correctly. (In addition to the words you knew before you opened this book, you've learned how to spell plurals and how to add *s, ed*, and *ing* endings to verbs.) You can learn more. Second, follow a logical plan for spelling improvement.

GENERAL HINTS FOR BETTER SPELLING

1. **Analyze your spelling problems.** With the help of your instructor or a friend who spells well, make a list of the words you've misspelled in your writing so far. In one column place your original spelling of the word, and in a second column, place the correct spelling. Save a third column for a note on the kind of error you've made. For instance, did the problem occur when you added a suffix (word ending)? Did you substitute one word for another that sounds like it? Did you use the wrong vowel? reverse letters? leave some letters out? Just put down an explanation that makes sense.

SAMPLE SPELLING LIST		
My Spelling	*Correct Spelling*	*Type of Error*
to	to<u>o</u>	soundalike word
prefered	prefe<u>r</u>red	adding suffix
goverment	gover<u>n</u>ment	omitted letter
diffrence	diff<u>e</u>rence	omitted letter
telavision	tel<u>e</u>vision	wrong vowel

This list has several uses. For one thing, it will help you concentrate on learning words that *you* use. For another, by identifying words with similar spelling errors, you'll be able to work on spelling patterns that apply to a whole group of words, not just one at a time. Finally, you'll be more sensitive to the kinds of words that give you trouble, so you'll know when to reach for a dictionary to check your work.

2. **Learn the rules that apply to the greatest number of words first.** Some of the most important rules apply to words to which prefixes (beginnings) and suffixes (endings) have been added; they're presented on pages 263–266. Learning them may immediately solve many of your spelling problems. Another very important rule is the Ie-Ei rule on page 267.

3. **Learn to distinguish the meanings of soundalike words.** Find out what the difference is between words like *too* and *to*, *course* and *coarse*, *advice* and *advise*. Soundalike words are presented on pages 269–272. Practice using them correctly in your own sample sentences.

4. **Learn to use pronunciation as an aid to spelling.** For practice, you may even want to mispronounce a word to make it sound more like the way it's spelled. For instance, make *attendance* rhyme with *dance* to help you remember the *ance* ending.

5. **Practice, practice, practice.** How do basketball players learn to make free throws consistently? How do typists learn to key eighty words per minute with no errors? How do cooks learn to get the vegetables, potatoes, and meat done at the same time? How do writers improve their spelling? They practice.

WORD PARTS

When you want to learn to spell a long word, you'll find it helpful to divide the word into parts. Which of the following ways to separate a word makes its spelling easier to remember?

c-h-a-r-a-c-t-e-r-i-s-t-i-c
char-ac-ter-is-tic

Like most people, you probably find the second kind of division more useful. It reduces the number of separate items to remember. Instead of memorizing fourteen separate letters in *characteristic*, you learn five chunks. In addition, you can connect the sound of each part of the word with its spelling. This method is called dividing words into syllables.

> A *syllable* is a word part containing a single vowel sound.

Say the word *delicious* aloud. How many syllables do you hear? There are three: *de-li-cious*. Even though there are three vowels in the last syllable, it has only one vowel sound: *uh*.

Notice that in the word *delicious*, the second syllable receives more punch than the others: *de-LI-cious*. This stress is called the **accent** in the word. Identifying accented syllables is sometimes useful in deciding whether to double a letter or not, as you'll see in a later section.

Write the number of syllables you hear in the following words. Then rewrite the words in syllables, capitalizing the letters in the accented syllable.

apparatus
cafeteria
scientific
exhilaration
temperament

You might have written the words like this:

4 ap-pa-RAT-us
5 ca-fe-TER-i-a
4 sci-en-TIF-ic
5 ex-hil-a-RA-tion
4 TEM-per-a-ment

You may sometimes have divided the words in slightly different places (such as *ap-pa-RA-tus* instead of *ap-pa-RAT-us*). That's all right, as long as you have only one vowel sound per syllable.

Many students have found this five-step process useful in memorizing words of more than one syllable.

1. Say the word aloud and count the number of syllables you hear.

2. Write the word in syllables.

3. Trace over each syllable, pronouncing it as you write. Repeat this step until you feel you know the word.

4. Fold your paper over so that you can't see the word, and quiz yourself by writing it syllable by syllable.

5. Check your work. If you misspelled it, go back to the tracing step. If you spelled it correctly, fold the paper over once more and try it again.

Writing the word correctly twice without looking means that you're well on your way to mastering it. You'll want to review it periodically to set the correct spelling permanently in your mind.

The method works well because it lets you use so many of the ways to learn to spell—seeing, saying, and writing—a triple whammy for your brain!

EXERCISE 13

Directions: From the following list, choose at least seven words that you can't spell. Use the five-step process described on pages 261–262 to learn to spell the words. If you can't find seven words on this list that you can't spell, turn to the list on pages 285–289 and find words that you don't know on that list.

approximate	conscientious	fundamental	perpendicular
association	consequently	guarantee	prescription
auxiliary	efficient	intelligence	significant
calculator	eligibility	kindergarten	symmetrical
congratulate	emphasize	miscellaneous	tremendous
communicate	exaggeration	monotonous	versatile
concentration	exhilaration		

ANSWERS WILL VARY.

COMPOUND WORDS

You'll find it more useful to learn the spelling of some words by dividing them into their meaningful parts than by dividing them into syllables.
Compound words are combinations of two words. Don't change the spelling of either when you combine them.

room + mate = roommate   him + self = himself

news + stand = _____

over + coat = _____

police + man = _____

news + paper = _____

PREFIXES AND SUFFIXES

Not all meaningful word parts can be used as separate words. Instead, ***prefixes*** (beginning word parts) and ***suffixes*** (ending word parts) may be added to a base word.

	PREFIX	BASE	SUFFIX
independence =	in +	depend +	ence
unusual =	un +	usual	
changeable =		change +	able

Here are a few of the most commonly used prefixes and suffixes in the English language and their meanings.

Prefix	Meaning	Example
anti	against	antifreeze
dis	apart, not	disappear
im, in	in	ingrained
im, in, ir, il, un	not	irrelevant, independent
inter	between	interstate
mis	wrongly	misspelled
pre	before	presoak
re	again	rewrite
trans	across	transatlantic

Suffix	Meaning	Example
able, ible	able to	irresistible, acceptable
ability, ibility	ability to	eligibility, respectability
al	relating to	personal
ance, ence	state of	maintenance, permanence
er, or, ar, ist	someone or something that performs an action	visitor, propeller, scientist
er, est	more, most	heavier, heaviest
ful, ous	full of, having	beautiful, ridiculous
ic	nature of	scientific
ity	state or quality	electricity
ive	tending toward	persuasive
ly	in a certain manner	mournfully
ment	result of, act of	government
tion, sion	act, process	repetition, persuasion

Learning the following rules for combining these prefixes and suffixes with base words will take care of many spelling problems.

Adding Prefixes

When you add a prefix to a base word, don't change the spelling of the prefix or the base.

dis + appoint = disappoint   ir + relevant = irrelevant

im + migrant = _____

mis + spelled = _____

As you can see, this rule explains why some words have double consonants. If the prefix ends with the same letter that the base word begins with, the word will have a double consonant (*unnatural, dissatisfied*).

Adding Suffixes

In general, when you add a suffix to a base word, don't change the spelling of the suffix or the base.

care + ful = careful   affection + ate = affectionate

counsel + or = _____

real + ist + ic = _____

However, unlike the prefix rule, the suffix rule doesn't always hold. Here are some common exceptions:

1. When the base word ends in *y* preceded by a consonant, keep the *y* before a suffix beginning with *i (ism, ist, ing)*, but change the *y* to *i* before adding any other suffix.

   study + ing = studying   happy + ness = happiness

   carry + ing = _____

   carry + age = _____

   marry + age = _____

2. When the base word ends in a silent *e*, keep the *e* before adding a suffix beginning with a consonant.

   care + less = careless   immediate + ly = immediately

   require + ment = _____

   sincere + ly = _____

   Exceptions:

   true + ly = truly

   judge + ment = judgment

3. When the base word ends in a silent *e*, drop the *e* before adding a suffix beginning with a vowel.

adventure + ous = adventurous   please + ure = pleasure

write + er = _____

like + able = _____

fascinate + ing = _____

Exceptions:

peace + able = peaceable   courage + ous = courageous

notice + able = noticeable   change + able = changeable

Notice that, in these exceptions, the base word ends in *ce* or *ge* and the suffix begins with an *a*. The *e* is needed to protect the "soft" sound of the *c* ("s" sound) or *g* ("j" sound) ahead of it.

4. The final consonant of a base word must be doubled if all of the following are true:

- the base word ends in a single vowel and a single consonant other than *h*, *w*, or *x*.

- the accented syllable of the root word is on the last (or only) syllable

- the suffix begins with a vowel

occur + ence = occurrence   commit + ed = committed

prefer + ed = _____

refer + ed = _____

propel + er = _____

but

quarrel + ing = quarreling *(accent not on last syllable)*

accustom + ed = accustomed

prefer + ence = _____

interpret + ed = _____

equip + ment = equipment *(suffix begins with a consonant)*

develop + ment = _____

embarrass + ment = _____

Ie-Ei Words

The following rhyme won't win a lyrics-of-the-year award, but it will help you remember the correct spelling of a large group of troublesome words.

> I before E
> Except after C
> Or when sounding like A
> As in *neighbor* and *weigh*.

Let's look at the rules presented in each part of the rhyme.

1. In most words using an *i* + *e* combination, *i* comes before *e*.

niece   field   believe   friend

2. If the combination appears immediately after the letter *c*, *e* comes before *i*. (This rule does not apply when the *ci* together make a *sh* sound as in *ancient* or *conscience*.)

receive   ceiling   conceit   conceive

3. When the combination sounds like an *A*, *e* comes before *i*.

weight   eight   neighbor   reign

There are only a few common exceptions to these rules. You'll find most of them in this nonsense sentence: *Neither weird foreign financier seized their height at leisure.*

EXERCISE 14

Directions: Proofread each group of phrases below. Circle the misspelled word in each group and then write the correct spelling of the word in the space provided. If all the words are spelled correctly, place a *C* in the space.

Example: reference books
preferred to be alone
strange (occurence)
quarreled constantly

occurrence

1. interrupt the discussion
interference with a police officer
dissection of a grasshopper
disappear into the sunset

_____

2. newspaper delivery
newstand robbery
tomorrow afternoon
kindergarten classrooms

_____

3. immediatly left
sincerely yours
truly sorry
severely burned

_____

4. manageable problem
valuable jewelry
peaceable nature
noticable difference

_____

5. in the beginning
equipped to serve
committed to a mental ward
preference for chocolate

_____

6. second marrage
carriage is waiting
carrying on like a baby
buried the bone

_____

7. propellers whirled
commitment to finish
occasionnal showers
performance of duties

_____

8. mournfull sound
hopeless situation
careful study
successful completion

_____

9. customer is dissatisfied
dissapprove of the decision
diseased parakeet
severe disappointment

_____

10. in my judgment
courageous act
flower arrangment
advantageous position

_____

11. either man
deceived his fiancée
everybody's freind
height of six feet

_____

12. beleive in yourself
file a grievance
ten-year reign
shriek of terror

_____

13. receive a call
seize the opportunity
foriegn currency
mischievous child

_____

14. wrecked her bycicle
boundary line
artificial sweeteners
ridiculous analysis

_____

15. voted for the governor
a carless mistake
the dictator died
conceal her prejudice

_____

ANSWERS ARE ON PAGE 366.

SOUNDALIKE WORDS
The Most Commonly Confused Words

One of the most frustrating experiences in learning to spell in English is to have someone cheerfully tell you, "It's easy to spell. Just sound the words out." That well-intentioned advice might lead to a paragraph like this:

> I've **waisted** a **hole** year of my life on you, and now you say **your board. Write** now I don't **no weather** to laugh or cry. **Its plane** to me you haven't learned to **except** responsibility for your **personnel** life. I've **weighted** in **vein** for you to grow up. We're **threw**!

Every one of the words in bold type is "spelled the way it sounds." Every one is wrong.

The problem is that the English language has many ways to spell the same sound. This problem leaves us with many words that sound alike or almost alike but have different spellings and different meanings. To improve your spelling, you need to master these confusing word pairs. Learn how to spell and when to use each word.

In Chapter 2 you studied one group of soundalikes: possessive pronouns and contractions like *its-it's* and *theirs-there's*. You may want to review the list on page 63 again. Here are some other commonly confused words:

affect (act upon)	The new plan will affect everyone.
effect (result)	The effect of the plan will be disaster.
a lot (many, much)	You have a lot of nerve.
allot (set aside)	Please allot ten minutes to plan your paper.
all ready (completely ready)	I'm all ready to leave for vacation.
already (previously)	We've already eaten.
all right (there is no such spelling as *alright*)	Do you feel all right?
brake (stopping device)	Step on the brake fast!
break (fall to pieces; take a rest)	Don't break the vase.
	Take a coffee break.
coarse (rough; not fine)	Use coarse sandpaper first.
course (classroom subject; path; of course = naturally)	She's taking a computer course.
	The course is too wet for the race.
	Of course I'm right.
knew (was aware of)	He knew how to drive.
new (fresh, not old)	I want a new car.
know (be aware of)	I know my limits.
no (none, opposite of yes)	No sane person would do that.
loose (not tight)*	These trousers are too loose.
lose (misplace; fail to win)	Don't lose your money.
	They'll lose the game.

passed (went by; succeeded)	Their car passed ours.
past (before the present; by)	He passed the test.
	The past was forgotten.
	We drove past the cemetery.
personal (belonging to an individual)*	She has personal problems.
personnel (referring to a group of workers)	The personnel department is taking applications.
principal (main; head of school)	Is smoking the principal cause of lung cancer?
principle (theory; belief)	The principal spoke to her students.
	Our government is based on democratic principles.
quiet (silent)*	Please be quiet.
quite (very)	This house is quite old.
right (opposite of left; correct)	Turn right.
write (put words on paper)	This answer is right.
	Write an essay.
their (belonging to them)	Their dog's in our yard.
there (in that place)	The flashlight is over there.
they're (they are)	There are three peaches.
	They're five minutes late.
thorough (careful, complete)*	Do a thorough job.
through (finished; into at one place and out at another)	I'm through with this saw.
	The dog ran through the yard.
threw (did throw)	She threw the baseball.
to (word before a verb; in a direction)	He loves to play football.
	Drive to the next corner.
too (more than enough; also)	He's too tired to think.
two (number after one)	Let me go, too.
	I want two helpings.
weather (atmospheric conditions)	Hot, humid weather makes me sick.
whether (if)	Do you know whether I'm working tomorrow night?
which (a pronoun)	Which do you want?
witch (performer of black magic)	The witch cackled hideously.

*Note the differences in pronunciation in this set.

More Soundalikes

The list on pages 269–270 barely scratches the surface of English soundalikes, but it does include some of the most commonly confused word pairs. Concentrate on them first. Once you've learned that list, you may want to master a second group presented below. Look up the meanings of any word pairs that you're unsure of.

accept—except	moral—morale*
advice—advise*	pair—pear
all together—altogether	plane—plain
angel—angle*	precede—proceed*
board—bored	role—roll
breath—breathe*	sight—site
capital—capitol	sole—soul
council—counsel	stationary—stationery
desert—dessert*	sweat—sweet*
diner—dinner*	vain—vein—vane
heroin—heroine	weak—week
hoarse—horse	whole—hole
later—latter*	wholly—holy
lessen—lesson	

*Note the differences in pronunciation in this set.

EXERCISE 15

Directions: Underline the word in parentheses that will correctly complete the sentence.

Example: Minneapolis is *(to, too, two)* far north for orange trees to grow outside.

1. I'm *(quiet, quite)* sure that the *(principle, principal)* ingredient in this pie crust is cardboard.

2. Please *(write, right)* a letter of application to the *(personal, personnel)* department.

3. Have you *(all ready, already)* *(accepted, excepted)* the nomination for treasurer?

4. A *(thorough, through)* inspection of the syringe revealed a trace of *(heroin, heroine)*.

5. I hope you'll learn your *(lesson, lessen)* before you *(break, brake)* *(your, you're)* poor mother's heart!

6. The *(whole, hole)* team was *(week, weak)* after a bout with the flu.

7. Don't be *(to, too)* quick to *(loose, lose)* your temper.

8. For *(desert, dessert)* we ate some *(sweet, sweat)* *(rolls, roles)*.

9. With one last *(horse, hoarse)* *(breath, breathe)*, *(their, they're, there)* gerbil died.

10. *(Its, It's) (passed, past)* time for *(diner, dinner)*.

11. Please give me some *(advice, advise)* on *(weather, whether)* or not to *(break, brake)* my contract.

12. *(They're, There, Their) (wasting, waisting) (they're, there, their) (desert, dessert)* by feeding it to the parrot.

13. Is it *(all right, alright)* to leave the *(board, bored) (they're, their, there)* until *(latter, later)* tonight?

14. Did you *(no, know)* that this is the *(dessert, desert)* where a *(plane, plain)* crashed last *(week, weak)*?

15. The father was awarded *(sole, soul)* custody upon the *(advise, advice)* of a child psychologist.

    After you check your answers, restudy the meanings of any words you missed. Then practice using them and their soundalikes in sentences of your own.

ANSWERS ARE ON PAGE 366.

USING PRONUNCIATION AS A SPELLING AID
Pronounce Carefully

    Although "sound it out" is not always a very helpful suggestion in spelling, you will find it easier to spell some words if you pronounce them carefully. People do tend to spell words as they sound. If they mispronounce a word by omitting or adding sounds, they're likely to misspell the word, too.

Omitted Sounds

    Some words are typically mispronounced and misspelled by leaving out parts: letters or syllables. For instance, people who say "libary" are likely to omit the *r* when they spell *library*. Practice pronouncing the following words carefully, paying special attention to the underlined letters.

February	quantity	characteristic
length	comfortable	conscientious
environment	government	laboratory
particular	probably	separate
sophomore	surprise	Wednesday
sandwich	representative	strength
literature	mathematics	miniature
recognize	interest	temperature

Added Sounds

Other words are mispronounced by adding sounds, and they're also misspelled as a result. The word *pronunciation*, for example, is often incorrectly spoken and spelled *pronounciation*. Can you see the difference? Study the following list, making sure you pronounce the underlined sections carefully—without adding anything extra.

equi<u>p</u>ment (not equiptment)

expl<u>a</u>nation (not explaination)

mischiev<u>ous</u> (not mischievious)

griev<u>ous</u> (not grievious)

p<u>e</u>culiar (not perculiar)

per<u>s</u>evere (not perservere)

simil<u>ar</u> (not similiar)

Make Sound Match Spelling

If you do tend to spell words as they sound, make that strategy work for you by pronouncing words as they're spelled when you practice spelling. Pronounce the *table* in *acceptable*, for example, to help you remember that it ends in *able*, not *ible*. Say *conSCIENCE* (like the study of nature) when you're learning how to spell *conscience*.

Here are a few words that might be learned more easily by changing the pronunciation to mimic the spelling. You'll be able to find more of your own. (Remember to do this for spelling practice only! Be sure you pronounce the word correctly in ordinary conversation.)

a bun DANCE
ac CI DENT (make the second syllable rhyme with *my*)
ac KNOW LEDGE
ad E QUATE (make the third syllable rhyme with *date*)
a GAIN, a GAINST, bar GAIN (make the vowel sound in the second
    syllable like the *ai* in *rain*)
assist ANT (like the insect)
DE scribe (make the first syllable rhyme with *me*)
ca LEN DAR, dol LAR (make the last syllable rhyme with *car*)
per sis TENT
sig nif I CANT
shep HERD (pronounce the silent *h* in the second syllable)
ve GE TABLE
vis IT OR

RECOGNIZE DIFFERENT SPELLING PATTERNS

The following chart summarizes the different spelling patterns for English sounds. Use it to learn what the spelling options are when you look words up in a dictionary and to categorize the words you're learning to spell.

Sound	Spelling Pattern
s	syllable, aggressive, miscellaneous, cereal, psychology
z	analyze, arouse, possess
sh	sheriff, chef, surely, efficient, association, possession
zh	usual, revision
ch	choose, catch, natural
h	hideous, whose
j	general, journal, exaggerate, badge
k	comedy, panicky, ache, kitchen, quart
m	moral, autumn
n	knock, narrative, gnat
f	factory, telephone
a	mistake, available, portrayal, neighbor, steak
e	employee, repeat, niece, deceive, precede
i	guidance, sight, by, aisle, island
o	loaf, associate, know
u	university, few
uh	aggravate, dozen, medicine, renovate, prejudice
er	dollar, doctor, cylinder
ense	absence, resistance, suspense
able	profitable, possible
el	nickel, natural, bicycle
ize	recognize, analyze, exercise
shun	appreciation, physician, session

COMMONLY MISSPELLED WORDS

In the back of this chapter on pages 285–289, you'll find a list of commonly misspelled words, some of which follow specific spelling rules and some of which do not. A page number following a word indicates the page where the spelling rule that applies to it can be found. All misspelled words in GED Test questions will be drawn from this list.

You will see from the list that there are many words that simply must be memorized because no rule applies. To study these words, use the strategies you've learned in this chapter, such as dividing the words into syllables, altering the pronunciation, and grouping words with similar spelling patterns. Perhaps a patient friend will dictate fifty words at a time to you so that you can find out which ones you already know and which need further study.

EXERCISE 16

Part A

Directions: The spelling words in this exercise will check your knowledge of plurals, basic spelling rules, soundalikes, and commonly misspelled words from the list on pages 285–289. Be sure you study the list before trying this exercise. Circle the misspelled word in each group and write it correctly in the space provided. If all the words are correct, place a *C* in the space.

Example: a beautiful sunrise
in (plane) sight
amateur boxing
expense account

plain

1. everything's all right
ripe strawberries
advertize for jobs
awkward landing

_____

2. wiegh the odds
against all odds
whether
studying for a test

_____

3. truly sorry
asociated with
severely scolded
unusually cheerful

_____

4. in late Febuary
Wednesday night
sometime next week
tomorrow morning

_____

5. disastrous descent
unnecessary advice
irritable baby
dissappointed child

_____

6. become a soldier
under seige
seized her arm
from arteries to veins

_____

Part B

Directions: Proofread the following paragraph for spelling errors. Cross out each misspelled word and write the correct spelling above it. The first correction has been made as an example.

Organizing

~~Organizeing~~ a suprise party for a freind requires alot of planing. You'll

need to attend to usal matters like invatations and refreshments, but you'll

have to keep your activitys a secret. To prevent the guest of honor from

gessing that anything's up, you must deside on a logical reson for inviting

her to the place where the party will be held. Anouther concern is how to

hide the rest of the guests until the proper moment. For the party to be

successfull, you're timeing must be perfect.

ANSWERS ARE ON PAGE 367.

CHAPTER HIGHLIGHTS: CAPITALIZATION AND SPELLING

1. Capitalize the first word of every sentence and the pronoun *I.*

2. Capitalize the names of specific people, places, days, and months.

3. Analyze your spelling problems to determine the types of errors you make most often.

4. To make words easier to spell, break long words into syllables; break compound words into their bases; and identify bases, prefixes, and suffixes.

5. Remember, it's *I* before *E* except after *C* or when sounding like *A* as in *neighbor* and *weigh.*

6. Learn the differences between soundalike words.

7. Use pronunciation as a spelling aid.

EDITING PRACTICE

Part A

Directions: Find and correct the sixteen errors in the following passage. Six of these errors are related to skills that you learned in earlier chapters: verb and pronoun forms, fragments, and punctuation. You may want to review the checklists on pages 65, 117, 169, and 223 to refresh your memory on what to look for. The other ten errors are related to capitalization and spelling. For these errors, use the checklist below as your proofreading guide.

☐ Are specific names of people and places capitalized?

☐ Are general names not capitalized?

☐ Are all words spelled correctly? Look especially carefully at words with prefixes and suffixes and at soundalike words.

EDITING HINT: You may find it easier to check for spelling errors if you read from the end to the beginning of the passage. This technique lets you temporarily ignore meaning in order to concentrate on spelling.

Some physcologists suggest that pepole can reduce tension by

imagining themselves in a peaceful setting. Whenever I use this advice. I

remembered Cave Point, a Park in Wisconsin on the shore of lake Michigan.

I picture myself sitting on top of a cliff overlooking the water. Despite the

cool lake breeze, the sun shinning on my back makes a sweater

unecessary. Closeing my eyes I soak in the warmth and listen to the

rythemical thumping of water in the limestone caves carved by centuries of

waves. Once agen this oasis of calm, works its magic and you can return to

the hassles of everyday life with renewed inner strenth.

ANSWERS ARE ON PAGE 367.

Part B

Directions: Edit for capitalization and spelling the essay that you revised in the first part of this chapter. Use the checklist above to help you locate errors.

If you want further practice, edit as many of your earlier writings as you have time to correct.

ANSWERS WILL VARY.

GED Practice
EXERCISE 17

Questions 1–7 refer to the following paragraph.

(1) Its becoming increasingly difficult for American political leaders to make national policies without considering their international effects. (2) Approving price supports for wheat grown in Kansas may mean that African Nations will look elsewhere for cheaper grain. (3) Reducing pollution controls for industries in the Ohio river region may anger Canadians because of environmental damage from acid rain. (4) Although raiseing the minimum wage may please labor unions here, it will also affect the balance of trade. (5) Competition from companys in countries with lower wages will reduce the number of goods exported from the United States. (6) The time has come for our government leaders to realize that their is no neat distinction between foreign and domestic affairs. (7) Befor they choose a policy position, they should remember that they're citizens of the world.

1. Sentence 1: **Its becoming increasingly difficult for American political leaders to make national policies without considering their international effects.**

   What correction should be made to this sentence?

   (1) replace *Its* with *It's*
   (2) replace *American* with *american*
   (3) replace *leaders* with *Leaders*
   (4) replace *their* with *there*
   (5) replace *effects* with *affects*

2. Sentence 2: **Approving price supports for wheat grown in Kansas may mean that African Nations will look elsewhere for cheaper grain.**

   What correction should be made to this sentence?

   (1) change the spelling of *Approving* to *Approveing*
   (2) replace *Kansas* with *kansas*
   (3) replace *African* with *african*
   (4) replace *Nations* with *nations*
   (5) no correction is needed

3. Sentence 3: **Reducing pollution controls for industries in the Ohio river region may anger Canadians because of environmental damage from acid rain.**

What correction should be made to this sentence?

(1) change the spelling of *Reducing* to *Reduceing*
(2) change the spelling of *industries* to *industrys*
(3) replace *river* with *River*
(4) change the spelling of *environmental* to *enviormental*
(5) no correction is necessary

4. Sentence 4: **Although raiseing the minimum wage may please labor unions here, it will also affect the balance of trade.**

What correction should be made to this sentence?

(1) change the spelling of *Although* to *Altough*
(2) change the spelling of *raiseing* to *raising*
(3) change the spelling of *minimum* to *mininum*
(4) change the spelling of *unions* to *unnions*
(5) replace *affect* with *effect*

5. Sentence 5: **Competition from companys in countries with lower wages will reduce the number of goods exported from the United States.**

What correction should be made to this sentence?

(1) change the spelling of *Competition* to *Compitition*
(2) change the spelling of *companys* to *companies*
(3) change the spelling of *countries* to *countrys*
(4) replace *States* with *states*
(5) no correction is necessary

6. Sentence 6: **The time has come for our government leaders to realize that their is no neat distinction between foreign and domestic affairs.**

What correction should be made to this sentence?

(1) change the spelling of *government* to *goverment*
(2) change the spelling of *realize* to *realyse*
(3) replace *their* with *there*
(4) change the spelling of *foreign* to *foriegn*
(5) no correction is necessary

7. Sentence 7: **Befor they choose a policy position, they should remember that they're citizens of the world.**

What correction should be made to this sentence?

(1) change the spelling of *Befor* to *Before*
(2) replace *choose* with *chose*
(3) replace *they're* with *their*
(4) replace *world* with *World*
(5) no correction is necessary

Questions 8–14 refer to the following paragraph.

(1) After the dreary darkness of January and February, I'm always relieved when March arrives with its first breath of Spring. (2) At last the season of snowstorms, overcoats, bare branchs, and cold remedies is over. (3) The robins return on schedule, hopping accross our lawn in search of nesting material. (4) Children hurry home from kindergarten to balance awkwardly on their new bicycles. (5) Once again I awake with the sun shinning through my bedroom window. (6) With the flip of a calendar page to this new month, my hole existence takes an optimistic turn. (7) No longer am I bored, exausted, and depressed. (8) My appetite for living has suddenly returned.

8. Sentence 1: **After the dreary darkness of January and February, I'm always relieved when March arrives with its first breath of Spring.**

What correction should be made to this sentence?

(1) change the spelling of *February* to *Febuary*
(2) change the spelling of *relieved* to *releived*
(3) replace *breath* with *breathe*
(4) replace *Spring* with *spring*
(5) no correction is necessary

9. Sentence 2: **At last the season of snowstorms, overcoats, bare branchs, and cold remedies is over.**

What correction should be made to this sentence?

(1) replace *season* with *Season*
(2) change the spelling of *overcoats* to *overcoates*
(3) change the spelling of *branchs* to *branches*
(4) change the spelling of *remedies* to *remedys*
(5) no correction is necessary

10. Sentence 3: **The robins return on schedule, hopping accross our lawn in search of nesting material.**

What correction should be made to this sentence?

(1) change the spelling of *schedule* to *scedule*
(2) change the spelling of *hopping* to *hoping*
(3) change the spelling of *accross* to *across*
(4) change the spelling of *nesting* to *nestting*
(5) no correction is necessary

11. Sentence 4: **Children hurry home from kindergarten to balance awkwardly on their new bicycles.**

What correction should be made to this sentence?

(1) change the spelling of *kindergarten* to *kindergarden*
(2) change the spelling of *balance* to *ballance*
(3) change the spelling of *awkwardly* to *akwardly*
(4) change the spelling of *bicycles* to *bycicles*
(5) no correction is necessary

12. Sentence 5: **Once again I awake with the sun shinning through my bedroom window.**

What correction should be made to this sentence?

(1) change the spelling of *Once* to *Ones*
(2) change the spelling of *again* to *agen*
(3) change the spelling of *shinning* to *shining*
(4) change the spelling of *through* to *throught*
(5) no correction is necessary

13. Sentence 6: **With the flip of a calendar page to this new month, my hole existence takes an optimistic turn.**

What correction should be made to this sentence?

(1) change the spelling of *calendar* to *calander*
(2) replace *hole* with *whole*
(3) change the spelling of *existence* to *existance*
(4) change the spelling of *optimistic* to *optomistic*
(5) no correction is necessary

14. Sentences 7 and 8: **No longer am I bored, exausted, and depressed. My appetite for living has suddenly returned.**

What correction should be made to these sentences?

(1) replace *bored* with *board*
(2) change the spelling of *exausted* to *exhausted*
(3) change the spelling of *appetite* to *appatite*
(4) change the spelling of *suddenly* to *sudenly*
(5) no correction is necessary

ANSWERS ARE ON PAGE 367.

GED Practice
REVISING AND EDITING REVIEW

Questions 1–9 refer to the following paragraph.

(1) In no other country on earth does citizens have as great a variety of national backgrounds as in America. (2) In the five hundred years since Christopher Columbus set sail from Italy, the Native americans have been joined by wave after wave of newcomers from Europe, Africa, Asia, and Latin America. (3) Each of these groups has enriched our culture with its unique customs, food, music, and language. (4) Jazz, for example, is part, of our African heritage. (5) The tradition of Santa Claus a contribution of Holland. (6) Going out for dinner in most cities, you can choose among Italian, Mexican, Chinese, and French restaurants. (7) Although this mixing of cultures has benefited us in numerous ways, it has also caused problems. (8) Each new group has had to face discrimination in housing, education, and jobs. (9) This problem is due to the prejudice of people who have forgotten their immigrant roots. (10) Unfortunately, the suspicion of anything or anyone diffrent sometimes overpowers appreciation of the advantages of a multicultural society.

1. Sentence 1: **In no other country on earth does citizens have as great a variety of national backgrounds as in America.**

   What correction should be made to this sentence?

   (1) change *does* to *do*
   (2) change the spelling of *citizens* to *citazens*
   (3) change the spelling of *variety* to *veriaty*
   (4) insert a comma after *variety*
   (5) no correction is necessary

2. Sentence 2: **In the five hundred years since Christopher Columbus set sail from Italy, the Native americans have been joined by wave after wave of newcomers from Europe, Africa, Asia, and Latin America.**

   What correction should be made to this sentence?

   (1) replace *set* with *has set*
   (2) remove the comma after *Italy*
   (3) replace *americans* with *Americans*
   (4) replace *newcomers from* with *newcomers. From*
   (5) remove the comma after *Asia*

3. Sentence 3: **Each of these groups has enriched our culture with its unique customs, food, music, and language.**

   Which of the following is the best way to write the underlined portion of this sentence? If you think the original is the best way, choose option (1).

   (1) has enriched
   (2) have enriched
   (3) has been enriched
   (4) have been enriched
   (5) enriching

4. Sentence 4: **Jazz, for example, is part, of our African heritage.**

   What correction should be made to this sentence?

   (1) remove the comma after *jazz*
   (2) remove the comma after *example*
   (3) remove the comma after *part*
   (4) replace *African* with *african*
   (5) replace *heritage* with *Heritage*

5. Sentence 5: **The tradition of Santa Claus a contribution of Holland.**

Which of the following is the best way to write the underlined portion of this sentence? If you think the original is the best way, choose option (1).

(1) Claus a
(2) Claus, a
(3) Claus, which is a
(4) Claus being a
(5) Claus is a

6. Sentence 6: **Going out for dinner in most cities, you can choose among Italian, Mexican, Chinese, and French restaurants.**

What correction should be made to this sentence?

(1) remove the comma after *cities*
(2) replace *you* with *we*
(3) change *choose* to *chose*
(4) change the spelling of *restaurants* to *restraunts*
(5) no correction is necessary

7. Sentence 7: **Although this mixing of cultures has benefited us in numerous ways, it has also caused problems.**

If you rewrote this sentence beginning with

This mixing of cultures has benefited us in numerous

the next words should be

(1) ways, it
(2) ways, so
(3) ways; however,
(4) ways; therefore,
(5) ways; for instance,

8. Sentences 8 and 9: **Each new group has had to face discrimination in housing, education, and jobs. This problem is due to the prejudice of people who have forgotten their immigrant roots.**

The most effective combination of these sentences would contain which group of words?

(1) Because of the prejudice of people
(2) Because each new group
(3) Although each new group
(4) Because they are prejudiced, each new group
(5) Being prejudiced, each new group

9. Sentence 10: **Unfortunately, the suspicion of anything or anyone diffrent sometimes overpowers appreciation of the advantages of a multicultural society.**

What correction should be made to this sentence?

(1) change the spelling of *diffrent* to *different*
(2) insert a comma after *diffrent*
(3) change *overpowers* to *overpower*
(4) change the spelling of *appreciation* to *apreciation*
(5) no correction is necessary

Questions 10–16 refer to the following paragraph.

(1) Technical advances in medical care, have raised new ethical questions for our society. (2) In the past, there were few remedies for patients with severe brain injuries and they died within a few days at most. (3) Today however, doctors can sustain life indefinitely by using artificial respirators and intravenous feedings. (4) Some patients lie in comas for years. (5) They're unable to respond to their environment. (6) There physicians and families must decide whether to prolong life-sustaining procedures that carry no hope of cure. (7) Family members were torn between a desire to end a loved one's suffering and the dread of imposing a death sentence. (8) Doctors, too, are understandably reluctant to withdraw life support, they've been trained to save lives, not end them.

10. Sentence 1: **Technical advances in medical care, have raised new ethical questions for our society.**

    Which of the following is the best way to write the underlined portion of this sentence? If you think the original is the best way, choose option (1).

    (1) care, have
    (2) care have
    (3) care has
    (4) care, has
    (5) care, having

11. Sentence 2: **In the past, there were few remedies for patients with severe brain injuries and they died within a few days at most.**

    What correction should be made to this sentence?

    (1) replace *there* with *their*
    (2) change *were* to *was*
    (3) change the spelling of *remedies* to *remedys*
    (4) insert a comma after *injuries*
    (5) no correction is necessary

12. Sentence 3: **Today however, doctors can sustain life indefinitely by using artificial respirators and intravenous feedings.**

    What correction should be made to this sentence?

    (1) insert a comma after *Today*
    (2) remove the comma after *however*
    (3) replace *indefinitely by* with *indefinitely. By*
    (4) insert a comma after *respirators*
    (5) no correction is necessary

13. Sentences 4 and 5: **Some patients lie in comas for years. They're unable to respond to their environment.**

    The most effective combination of these sentences would contain which of the following groups of words?

    (1) years they're
    (2) years, they're
    (3) years, so they're
    (4) years, or they're
    (5) years, unable

14. Sentence 6: **There physicians and families must decide whether to prolong life-sustaining procedures that carry no hope of cure.**

    What correction should be made to this sentence?

    (1) replace *There* with *Their*
    (2) replace *families* with *family's*
    (3) replace *whether* with *weather*
    (4) change the spelling of *procedures* to *proceedures*
    (5) replace *procedures that* with *procedures. That*

15. Sentence 7: **Family members <u>were</u> torn between a desire to end a loved one's suffering and the dread of imposing a death sentence.**

Which of the following is the best way to write the underlined portion of this sentence? If you think the original is the best way, choose option (1).

(1) were torn
(2) was torn
(3) were tore
(4) are tore
(5) are torn

16. Sentence 8: **Doctors, too, are understandably reluctant to withdraw life support, they've been trained to save lives, not end them.**

What correction should be made to this sentence?

(1) replace *too* with *to*
(2) insert a comma after *reluctant*
(3) replace *support, they've* with *support. They've*
(4) change *trained* to *train*
(5) no correction is necessary

ANSWERS ARE ON PAGES 367–368.

FREQUENTLY MISSPELLED WORDS

All misspelled words on the GED Test will be taken from the following list. Other forms of most of these words, including plurals and forms requiring suffixes, also may be tested.

A page number in parentheses tells you where you can find a spelling rule or hint to help you with the spelling of that word.

a lot (269)	address	although	apply
ability	addressed	altogether (271)	appreciate (262)
absence (274)	adequate (273)	always	appreciation (262)
absent	advantageous (266)	amateur	approach
across	advantage	American	appropriate (262)
abundance (273)	advertise (274)	among	approval (266)
accept (271)	advertisement (265)	amount	approve
acceptable (273)	advice (271)	analysis (262)	approximate (262)
accident	advisable (266)	analyze (274)	argue
accommodate (262)	advise (271)	angel (271)	arguing (266)
accompanied (265)	advisor (273)	angle (271)	argument (265)
accomplish	aerial	annual	arouse
accumulation (262)	affect (269)	another	arrange
accuse	affectionate (265)	answer	arrangement (265)
accustomed	again (273)	antiseptic (265)	article
ache (273)	against (273)	anxious	artificial (262)
achieve (267)	aggravate (273)	apologize (274)	ascend (273)
achievement (265)	aggressive	apparatus (262)	assistance (265)
acknowledge (273)	agree	apparent (273)	assistant (265)
acquaintance (273)	aisle (273)	appear	associate (262)
acquainted (273)	all right (269)	appearance (265)	association (262)
acquire	almost	appetite	attempt
across	already (269)	application (262)	attendance (273)

attention
audience
August
author
automobile (263)
autumn (273)
auxiliary (272)
available
avenue
awful
awkward
bachelor (273)
balance
balloon
bargain (273)
basic
beautiful (273)
because
become
before
beginning (266)
being
believe (267)
benefit (273)
benefited (265)
between
bicycle (265)
board (271)
bored (271)
borrow
bottle
bottom
boundary (273)
brake (269)
breadth
breath (271)
breathe (271)
brilliant (272)
building
bulletin
bureau (273)
burial (265)
buried (265)
bury (273)
bushes
business (273)
cafeteria
calculator (273)
calendar (273)
campaign

capital (271)
capitol (271)
captain (273)
career
careful (265)
careless (265)
carriage (265)
carrying (265)
category (262)
ceiling (267)
cemetery (273)
cereal
certain
changeable (266)
characteristic (261)
charity
chief (267)
choose
chose
cigarette
circumstance
congratulate (263)
citizen
clothes
clothing
coarse (269)
coffee
collect
college
column (274)
comedy
comfortable (265)
commitment (265)
committed (266)
committee
communicate (262)
company
comparative (266)
compel
competent (266)
competition (266)
compliment
conceal
conceit (267)
conceivable (266)
conceive (267)
concentration (262)
conception
condition (274)
conference (272)

confident (273)
conquer
conscience (273)
conscientious (273)
conscious (273)
consequence (273)
consequently
considerable (262)
consistency (273)
consistent (273)
continual
continuous (272)
controlled (266)
controversy (262)
convenience (272)
convenient (272)
conversation
corporal (272)
corroborate (262)
council (271)
counsel (271)
counselor (273)
courage
courageous (266)
course (269)
courteous
courtesy
criticism
criticize
crystal
curiosity
cylinder
daily
daughter
daybreak (263)
death
deceive (267)
December
deception
decide
decision (273)
decisive (273)
deed
definite
delicious (261)
dependent (273)
deposit
derelict
descend (273)
descent (273)

describe (273)
description (262)
desert (271)
desirable (266)
despair
desperate (273)
dessert (271)
destruction
determine (273)
develop
development (266)
device
dictator (273)
died
difference (272)
different (272)
dilemma
dinner (271)
direction
disappear (265)
disappoint (265)
disappointment (266)
disapproval (266)
disapprove (265)
disastrous
discipline
discover
discriminate (262)
disease (273)
dissatisfied (265)
dissection (265)
dissipate
distance (273)
distinction
division
doctor (273)
dollar (273)
doubt
dozen (273)
earnest
easy
ecstasy
ecstatic
education (272)
effect (269)
efficiency (273)
efficient (273)
eight
either
eligibility (262)

eligible
eliminate (262)
embarrass
embarrassment (266)
emergency
emphasis
emphasize
enclosure
encouraging (266)
endeavor (273)
engineer
English
enormous
enough
entrance
envelope
environment (272)
equipment (272)
equipped (266)
especially (272)
essential
evening (272)
evident
exaggerate (262)
exaggeration (262)
examine
exceed
excellent (273)
except
exceptional (265)
exercise (273)
exhausted (272)
exhaustion (272)
exhilaration (272)
existence (273)
exorbitant (272)
expense
experience (272)
experiment (272)
explanation (273)
extreme
facility
factory
familiar (272)
fascinate (273)
fascinating (266)
fatigue
February (272)
financial (273)
financier (267)

flourish
forcibly
forehead (263)
foreign (267)
formal
former
fortunate (273)
fourteen (263)
fourth
frequent
friend (267)
frightening (272)
fundamental (262)
further (272)
gallon
garden
gardener (272)
general (272)
genius
government (272)
governor (273)
grammar (273)
grateful (265)
great
grievance (267)
grievous (273)
grocery (272)
guarantee
guess
guidance
half
hammer
handkerchief (272)
happiness (265)
healthy
heard
heavy
height (267)
heroes
heroine (271)
hideous
himself
hoarse (271)
holiday
hopeless (265)
hospital (273)
humorous
hurried (265)
hurrying (265)
ignorance (273)

imaginary (266)
imbecile
imitation
immediately (265)
immigrant (273)
incidental
increase
independence (273)
independent (273)
indispensable (273)
inevitable (273)
influence
influential (262)
initiate (273)
innocence (273)
inoculate (262)
inquiry
insistent
instead
instinct
integrity
intellectual (262)
intelligence (262)
intercede
interest
interfere
interference
interpreted
interrupt
invitation
irrelevant (273)
irresistible (273)
irritable (273)
island (273)
its (63)
it's (63)
itself
January (272)
jealous
judgment (265)
journal (273)
kindergarten
kitchen (273)
knew (269)
knock (273)
know (269)
knowledge (273)
labor (273)
laboratory (272)
laid

language
later (271)
latter (271)
laugh
leisure (267)
length (272)
lesson (271)
library (272)
license (273)
light
lightning (272)
likelihood (265)
likely (265)
literal
literature (272)
livelihood (265)
loaf
loneliness (265)
loose (269)
lose (269)
losing (266)
loyal
loyalty
magazine
maintenance (272)
maneuver
marriage (265)
married (265)
marry
match
material (272)
mathematics (272)
measure (273)
medicine (273)
million
miniature (272)
minimum
miracle (273)
miscellaneous (262)
mischief (267)
mischievous (273)
misspelled (265)
mistake
momentous
monkey
monotonous (262)
moral (271)
morale (271)
mortgage (273)
mountain (273)

mournful (265)
muscle (273)
mysterious (265)
mystery
narrative
natural (273)
necessary (262)
needle
negligence
neighbor (267)
neither (267)
newspaper (263)
newsstand (263)
niece (267)
noticeable (266)
o'clock
obedient
obstacle (273)
occasion
occasional
occur
occurred (266)
occurrence (266)
ocean
offer
often
omission
omit
once
operate
opinion
opportune
opportunity (266)
optimist
optimistic (262)
origin
original (265)
oscillate (273)
ought
ounce
overcoat (263)
paid
pamphlet (272)
panicky
parallel
parallelism (265)
particular (262)
partner
pastime
patience

peace
peaceable (266)
pear
peculiar (273)
pencil
people
perceive (267)
perception
perfect
perform
performance (272)
perhaps (272)
period
permanence (273)
permanent (273)
perpendicular (262)
perseverance (266)
persevere (273)
persistent (273)
persuade
personality
personal (270)
personnel (270)
persuade
persuasion (274)
pertain
picture
piece (267)
plain
playwright
pleasant (273)
please
pleasure (266)
pocket
poison
policeman (263)
political (273)
population (274)
portrayal (265)
positive (273)
possess
possession (265)
possessive (265)
possible
post office
potatoes
practical (272)
prairie
precede
preceding (266)

precise
predictable (273)
prefer
preference (265)
preferential
preferred (265)
prejudice (273)
preparation (274)
prepare
prescription (274)
presence
president (273)
prevalent (273)
primitive
principal (270)
principle (270)
privilege (273)
probably (272)
procedure (273)
proceed
produce
professional (265)
professor (273)
profitable (273)
prominent
promise
pronounce
pronunciation (273)
propeller (266)
prophet
prospect
psychology (273)
pursue
pursuit
quality
quantity
quarreling (266)
quart
quarter
quiet (270)
quite (270)
raise
realistic
realize
reason
rebellion (266)
recede
receipt
receive (267)
recipe

recognize (272)
recommend
recuperate (262)
referred (266)
rehearsal
reign (267)
relevant (273)
relieve (267)
remedy
renovate
repeat
repetition
representative (272)
requirements (265)
resemblance
resistance (273)
resource
respectability (262)
responsibility (262)
restaurant (272)
rhythm
rhythmical
ridiculous
right
role (271)
roll (271)
roommate (263)
sandwich (272)
Saturday
scarcely (265)
scene
schedule (273)
science (273)
scientific (273)
scissors (273)
season
secretary (272)
seize (267)
seminar
sense
separate (272)
service
several (272)
severely (265)
shepherd (272)
sheriff
shining (266)
shoulder
shriek (267)
siege (267)

sight (271)
signal
significance (262)
significant (262)
similar
similarity
sincerely (265)
site (271)
soldier (272)
solemn
sophomore (272)
soul (271)
source
souvenir
special
specified
specimen
speech
stationary (271)
stationery (271)
statue
stockings
stomach (273)
straight
strength (272)
strenuous (272)
stretch

striking (266)
studying (265)
substantial (273)
succeed
successful
sudden
superintendent (272)
suppress
surely (265)
surprise (272)
suspense
sweat (271)
sweet (271)
syllable
symmetrical (262)
sympathy
synonym
technical
telegram
telephone
temperament (272)
temperature (272)
tenant
tendency (273)
tenement (273)
therefore
thorough (270)

through (270)
title
together
tomorrow
tongue
toward (272)
tragedy
transferred (266)
treasury
tremendous
tries (265)
truly (265)
twelfth (272)
twelve
tyranny
undoubtedly (272)
United States
university
unnecessary (265)
unusual (265)
vacuum
useful (265)
usual
valley
valuable (272)
variety (273)
vegetable (273)

vein (267)
vengeance
versatile (273)
vicinity
vicious (272)
view
village
villain (273)
visitor (273)
voice
volume
waist
weak (271)
wear
weather (270)
Wednesday (272)
week (271)
weigh (267)
weird (267)
whether (270)
which (270)
while
whole
wholly (271)
whose
witch (270)
wretched

7 Test-Taking Strategies

If you are ready for this chapter, you should be nearly ready for the GED Writing Skills Test. Either you have focused on a few weaknesses indicated by the Pre-Test, or you've worked carefully through this book, building your skills to improve your chances for success. Whichever category you're in, you should realize that you've already acquired the most important test-taking skills for this portion of the GED Tests: you've learned how to write and how to edit both your own writing and the writing of others.

In this chapter, you'll focus on putting these skills to work as efficiently as possible in a testing situation. Knowing what the test will be like and how best to attack each part should hold any butterflies of uneasiness to a manageable flutter when test day arrives.

Part 1 of the GED Writing Skills Test is multiple choice. Part 2 is the essay.

PREPARING FOR THE MULTIPLE-CHOICE TEST

WHAT IS THE TEST LIKE?

In Part 1 of the Writing Skills Test you'll have 75 minutes to answer 55 multiple-choice questions based on a series of six or seven short passages, each ten to twelve sentences long. These questions will check your knowledge of sentence structure, standard usage, punctuation, capitalization, and spelling. You're already familiar with this format; you've seen it in the Pre-Test and almost every chapter review and cumulative review exercise in this book.

HOW WILL IT BE SCORED?

The score you get is based on the number of correct answers. There is no penalty for guessing. The number of items you answer correctly will be converted to a standard score. The number of points in your standard score for Part 1 will be combined with your score on Part 2 of the Writing Skills Test (the essay). This combined score will apply to the 225 points you need to pass the entire GED Test battery.

HOW SHOULD I APPROACH THE TEST?
Read Each Passage Carefully

Before you start answering questions on the test, first read carefully the passage that the questions are based on. There are two good reasons for reading a passage in advance. First, it gives you a head start on locating errors. You may not identify a specific mistake, but you'll often be able to point out the part of a sentence where something seems wrong. Second, you'll see what the passage as a whole means and how the ideas fit together in it. Seeing overall meaning will help you answer questions about connecting words and identify sentences in which verbs or pronouns don't agree with the rest of the passage.

Each paragraph will contain a variety of errors. The following list will remind you of the main possibilities to keep in mind as you preview the passage.

TYPES OF ERRORS

1. Sentence fragments

   TYPICAL ERROR: Because we left the party early.

2. Run-on sentences or comma splices

   TYPICAL ERROR: Many Americans are **thoughtless, they** litter the highways with wrappers and beer cans.

3. Illogical connecting words

   TYPICAL ERROR: Computers are easy to use; **therefore,** many people are afraid of them.

4. Misplaced or dangling modifiers

   TYPICAL ERROR: **Sitting in front of a computer for hours,** her eyes began to burn.

5. Lack of parallel structure

   TYPICAL ERROR: On his days off Rodney enjoys sleeping, watching game shows, and **to play pool**.

6. Missing or misplaced commas

   TYPICAL ERROR: Whenever Robert loses at **pool he** breaks his cue.

7. Verb tenses used incorrectly

   TYPICAL ERROR: After the players returned to the locker room, the coach **scolds** them.

MORE TYPES OF ERRORS

8. Lack of subject-verb agreement

TYPICAL ERROR: Jim and Mary **was** at our apartment yesterday.

9. Lack of pronoun agreement with antecedents

TYPICAL ERROR: If a person drinks too much alcohol, **you** shouldn't drive.

10. Incorrectly spelled words (plurals, verb endings, soundalikes, and commonly misspelled words)

TYPICAL ERROR: Who bought **there** old house?

11. Incorrectly capitalized words

TYPICAL ERROR: The **united states** is a relatively young country.

The following passage is a sample of the paragraphs you'll encounter on the Writing Skills Test. Can you find any errors as you preview it? For practice, circle the errors you find.

(1) Far more than any European nation, our country has became a throwaway society. (2) Italians lovingly preserve structures that are hundreds of years old, some even date back to Roman times. (3) Americans, on the other hand, are more likely to bulldoze an old building down to make room for a skyscraper or even a parking lot. (4) In other countries you buy sturdy clothes and keep them until they wear out. (5) Restitching ripped seams and patching worn elbows. (6) In the United States, styles that were fashionable six months ago may well be outdated tommorow. (7) This throwaway mentality even extended to our political attitudes. (8) We have a short interest span. (9) Burning political issues have an average life expectancy of six months. (10) Physical fitness of young people, hunger in America, energy conservation, oil pollution of the oceans, and space exploration, have all come and gone as newsstand fads. (11) Our passion for whatever is new and exciting have too often led us to ignore enduring values and concerns.

Read Each Question Carefully

Before you try to answer a question, read it carefully. Test all possible answers. You'll find three types of questions used in Part 1 of the Writing Skills Test: sentence correction, sentence revision, and construction shift. You have practiced all three in the review tests at the end of each chapter and in the Pre-Test.

QUESTION TYPES
Sentence Correction

Four to five questions for each passage (about half of the questions) will have a sentence correction format. In this type, you'll see a sentence from the passage, followed by the question "What correction should be made to this sentence?" The five possible answers will focus on different parts of the sentence. One choice might deal with a spelling change, another with punctuation, a third with usage, and a fourth with sentence structure. Sometimes the fifth choice will be "no correction is necessary." That choice occasionally will be correct.

Example: Sentence 1: **Far more than any European nation, our country has became a throwaway society.**

What correction should be made to this sentence?

(1) replace *European* with *european*
(2) replace *nation* with *Nation*
(3) change *has* to *have*
(4) change *became* to *become*
(5) insert a comma after *became*

You may realize what the error in the sentence is right away. In that case, you should look for the answer that corrects that error.

Otherwise, the key to answering this kind of question is flexibility. Look carefully at the change suggested in each choice and see how it will fit into the sentence. Sometimes you also need to check the paragraph as a whole for verb tense or pronoun choice. Can you tell what rule is being tested in each of the five choices above?

Both (1) and (2) are checking your knowledge of capitalization. Choice (3) gives two present-tense forms of the same verb, so it's testing subject-verb agreement. Is *our country has* or *our country have* correct? Choice (4) presents two verb forms, too: past tense and past participle of *become*. Should it be *has became* or *has become*? The last choice offers a punctuation change. Is there any rule to support placing a comma after *became (our country has became, a throwaway society)*?

Can you eliminate any of these choices as clearly wrong? If you can, you'll increase your chances of picking the correct answer. Circle the answer that you think is correct.

Answer: The correct answer is choice (4). The helping verb *has* must be combined with the past participle *become*. The corrected sentence would read *Far more than any European nation, our country has become a throwaway society.*

Sentence Revision

Three or four of the questions for each passage will be in sentence revision form. This time a sentence from the passage will be presented with one section underlined, and you'll be asked to choose the best wording for the underlined portion. The first choice will repeat the original wording; the other four give you alternative revisions to choose from. You will choose choice (1) if the sentence is correct as written.

Example: Sentence 2: **Italians lovingly preserve structures that are hundreds of years <u>old, some</u> even date back to Roman times.**

Which of the following is the best way to write the underlined portion of this sentence? If you think the original is the best way, choose option (1).

(1) old, some
(2) old some
(3) old. Some
(4) old, in fact some
(5) old, for example, some

Since only one part of the sentence is used, this kind of question will probably focus on one or two rules rather than several. In the above example, you can see that the question deals with the correct way to connect the two halves of the sentence. Is the original sentence correct, or is it a comma splice? Which of the alternatives are punctuated correctly? See if you can eliminate the wrong answers. Now circle the correct choice.

Answer: Choice (3) is correct. One way to revise the sentence is to make two complete sentences. All other choices would create a run-on sentence or a comma splice. The revision would read like this: *Italians lovingly preserve structures that are hundreds of years old. Some even date back to Roman times.*

Construction Shifts

One or two of the questions for each passage will be construction shifts. This type of question will ask you to choose the best way to rewrite a sentence or to combine two sentences. There are two kinds of construction shift items.

Example 1: Sentences 8 and 9: **We have a short interest span. Burning political issues have an average life expectancy of six months.**

The most effective combination of Sentences 8 and 9 would include which of the following groups of words?

(1) Since we have
(2) Although we have
(3) span; however, burning
(4) span, yet burning
(5) span because burning

Notice that in this question format, the original sentences contain no error. Your job is to decide how the ideas in these sentences are related and combine them logically. The most likely topic to be tested by a construction shift question is sentence structure.

To answer this type of question, test each possible response by thinking of the complete sentence in which it would appear. Then decide whether the sentence makes sense. Eliminate any alternatives that don't preserve the meaning of the original sentences.

(1) Since we have a short interest span, burning political issues have an average life expectancy of six months.

(2) Although we have a short interest span, burning political issues have an average life expectancy of six months.

(3) We have a short interest span; however, burning political issues have an average life expectancy of six months.

Write the complete sentence for choices (4) and (5) below.

(4) span, yet burning

_____

(5) span because burning

_____

Now circle the number of the correct answer.

Answer: Choice (1) is correct. The word _Since_ makes sense as a link. It shows that our short interest span is the reason why political issues have such a short life expectancy.

Follow the same process—think of the whole new sentence—when you're asked to rewrite a sentence, as in the following example. Suppose Sentence 8 were written as follows.

Example 2: Sentence 8: **We have a short interest span; therefore, burning political issues have an average life expectancy of six months.**

If you rewrote sentence 8 beginning with

Burning political issues have an average life expectancy of six months

the next word should be

(1) which
(2) consequently
(3) because
(4) and
(5) but

Here again the original sentence contains no error. You must understand the relationship between the ideas in the sentence; then recombine them in a new way. Just as you did in the previous example, test each choice. Decide which one preserves the meaning of the original sentence.

LOOK AT THE WHOLE PASSAGE

Consider the context of the entire passage before choosing the correct answer. One or two questions from each passage will require you to think about passage meaning as well as sentence meaning. These questions deal with consistent verb and pronoun choice.

Example: Sentence 7: **This throwaway mentality even <u>extended</u> to our political attitudes.**

Which of the following is the best way to write the underlined portion of this sentence? If you think the original is the best way, choose option (1).

(1) extended
(2) had extended
(3) extend
(4) extends
(5) will be extended

Several of the choices would make a grammatically correct sentence. However, only one fits in with the rest of the paragraph. Is the passage as a whole written in past, present, or future tense? The answer to that question will determine the correct verb for sentence 7. Look back at the passage on page 293; then circle the correct answer.

Answer: The rest of the passage is written in present tense; therefore, the correct answer is choice (4). Pages 99–100 and 215–222 will refresh your memory on consistent verb and pronoun choices within a passage.

ANSWER ALL FIFTY-FIVE QUESTIONS

Be sure to answer all the questions. There's no penalty for guessing, so a wrong answer won't count against your score any more than a blank answer. Don't take too long on any one question. If you find a confusing question, you may want to mark it to return to after you've finished the rest of the test. Be sure, however, to choose an answer for each question before turning in your test paper.

When you skip a question, put a mark on your answer sheet next to the space for the question you skipped. Keep checking throughout the test to make sure that the number of the questions in the test booklet matches the number you fill in on the answer sheet.

USE YOUR TIME WISELY

Since both parts of the Writing Skills Test are given together as one test, you will be allowed to go on to Part 2, the writing sample, as soon as you finish Part 1, the multiple-choice section. However, *avoid the temptation to rush through Part 1 so that you will have a longer time to write the essay*. If you have worked carefully through this book, you now know that 45 minutes is plenty of time to prewrite, draft, and revise your writing sample. The best test-taking strategy is to work carefully through Part 1 and, if you have time, go back and check your work in that section. Be sure you are satisfied with your work on Part 1 before you go on to Part 2.

Remember that your final writing skills score comes from both parts of the test; in fact, Part 1 counts for a little bit more of the total score than does Part 2. It's important that you do well on both parts of the test. Although you may be concerned about the writing sample time limit, don't rush through Part 1 and do less than your best.

GETTING READY FOR THE ESSAY

WHAT IS THE ESSAY TEST LIKE?

In Part 2 of the GED Writing Skills Test, you'll have forty-five minutes to prewrite, draft, revise, and edit an essay on a topic given to you at that time. The assignment will be to explain some everyday problem or occurrence. This topic won't require any specific background knowledge on your part; just being an adult should give you enough knowledge to handle it.

The instructions for the essay will suggest that you write an essay of about two hundred words. However, don't worry about the length of your essay. As long as you have written a good essay, its length will not affect your score at all.

HOW WILL THE ESSAY BE SCORED?

Your completed essay will be scored by two readers trained to use a process called ***holistic scoring***. With this method, readers don't mark misspelled words and misplaced commas, nor do they write comments about the content and structure of your writing. They read your paper once; then they use a six-point scale to record their overall impression of the quality of your writing, 1 being the lowest score and 6 the highest. The two readers' scores are added to produce the final score for your essay. That means your final score is actually between two and twelve. This score is combined with your score from Part 1 to produce a single score for the Writing Skills Test.

WHAT DO THE SCORES MEAN?

Part 2 of the Writing Skills Test checks your ability to state a point clearly and support it convincingly in well-organized paragraphs. Although serious problems with capitalization, punctuation, and spelling will detract from the overall quality of your paper, you're not expected to produce a mechanically perfect piece of writing under testing conditions. The essay readers will realize that your essay was produced within a strict time limit and that you weren't able to use a dictionary or a grammar book for proofreading.

Briefly, here's what the numerical scores mean:

6 The essay shows evidence of mature thinking, with a clear, appropriate organizational plan. Support for the author's opinions is thorough, specific, and relevant. Although there may be an occasional error in mechanics, the writing is smooth and graceful.

5 The essay is clearly organized and well supported throughout. Ideas are meaningful, but they may not be expressed as gracefully as those in a 6 paper. Although the writer has generally good control of sentence structure and mechanics, there may be an occasional problem.

4 The essay has been organized, but not as clearly as a 5 or 6 paper, and the support is not as thorough or as convincing. More errors in standard written English appear, but they aren't serious enough to interfere greatly with the meaning of the essay.

3 Although the essay shows some evidence of development, it is often a listing of unsupported statements about the topic. Many weaknesses in sentence structure, usage, and mechanics reduce the effectiveness of the paper.

2 The essay is poorly developed and inadequately supported, with problems in unity and little evidence of mature thinking. Errors in standard written English are so numerous that they seriously damage the effectiveness of the paper.

1 The essay is rambling, lacking a main point and an organizational plan. The writer has little control over the sentence structure, usage, and mechanics of standard written English.

0 The paper is blank, illegible, or completely off the assigned topic.

In general, scores of 6, 5, or 4 mean that the essay is:

- clearly organized

- well supported

- correctly written according to the rules of standard written English

Scores of 3, 2, or 1 mean that there are serious flaws in one or more of these areas.

HOW SHOULD I APPROACH THE ESSAY?

If you've studied the first six chapters of this book, you should have a good start on answering this question. The writing exercises you've done so far, particularly the timed writings, have given you practice in responding to assigned topics. Here is a summary of the test-taking tips you've learned so far.

Budget Your Time

Don't begin scribbling in a panic the second the testing official says, "You may begin." Remember that you have forty-five minutes to plan and write your essay; use this time effectively. Here's one possible plan:

- 10 minutes to plan your essay

- 30 minutes to write it

- 5 minutes to revise and edit it

What division of time feels comfortable to you?

Read the Question Carefully

The first step in planning a piece of writing is analyzing. Ask yourself two questions: What is the topic? What kinds of ideas and details does the essay question suggest? The essay question will contain clues as to what to include in your essay. Suppose you were given the following essay question:

> A female secretary may make $15,000 per year, while a male administrative assistant with the same skills may make $25,000 per year. In general, men have higher average incomes than women. Discuss the causes of this income difference between the sexes.

What is the topic? The topic is *the income difference between the sexes.* You may be tempted to write an essay comparing the salaries and job skills of the female secretary and the male administrative assistant mentioned in the essay question. Be careful not to fall into this trap. The essay topic is more general: the income difference between the sexes. Your essay should react to this essay topic, not to the introductory statements that lead up to it.

What kinds of ideas and details does the question suggest? Look for clues in the question. The most important clue in the question is the word *causes.* What **causes** the income difference between the sexes?

Different essay questions will give you different clues. Are you being asked to **describe** the **effects** of something, or to **compare** two items?

Carefully read the essay topics below. Underline clues that tell you the kinds of ideas and details to include in your essay.

> Debates about the effects of television on children have raged for years. In particular, some groups have suggested that commercials be banned from children's programs. Describe some effects that television commercials can have on children.

Did you underline the word *effects*? Good. An essay on this topic should discuss the effects of TV commercials on children. It should not discuss whether commercials should be banned from TV. This statement is part of the introductory material, not part of the essay topic.

> More and more mothers of preschoolers are entering the work force. As a result, their children spend large parts of the day in day-care centers or with babysitters. How do you think this child-care arrangement affects small children as compared to children whose mothers stay at home? Give specific examples to explain your opinion.

Did you underline *affects* and *compared*? *Specific examples, explain*, and *opinion* also can suggest what to include in your essay.

> In every society in the world, ceremonies are used to mark major events in people's lives. Installations of government leaders, marriages, deaths, even sports events are all accompanied by certain rituals. Why do you think that ceremonies are so important to people? Use specific examples to support your reasons.

Did you underline *why* and *reasons*? You might also underline *specific examples* and *support*. All these words suggest ways to answer the essay question.

Prewriting Your Essay

In the actual test, scratch paper is provided for planning. Use it. You learned how to brainstorm ideas in Chapter 2 and how to write a unifying statement and organize your essay in Chapter 5. Use those skills. Remember to consider your audience (reader) and your purpose during this stage.

1. **Use the clues in the essay to focus your brainstorming.** Keeping these clue words in mind will help you think of relevant ideas. Underline the clues in the following essay question.

> Throughout the history of art and literature, romantic love has been an enduring theme. Today, people are still enchanted by lovers—stories about lovers, movies about lovers, songs about lovers, and pictures of lovers.
>
> Write a composition of about two hundred words explaining why people are so fascinated by love. Use specific details and examples in your answer.

Did you underline *explaining why*? Did you underline *specific details and examples*? Clue words can help you define your purpose for writing:

"Why am I writing this?"

To describe the effects of _____.

To compare _____.

To explain how/why _____.

2. Write a unifying statement. Writing a preliminary unifying statement also helps focus your brainstorming. Here's an example of a unifying statement for this essay topic:

> People are fascinated by romantic love because they can see their own dreams acted out by other people.

Can you see that this unifying statement could begin an essay *explaining why* people are so fascinated by romantic love?

How would you approach this essay topic? Write your own unifying statement for this topic. The unifying statement should tell the reader:

- the topic

- the direction in which the writer is taking the topic

_____

_____

Writing your unifying statement before you begin to brainstorm can help you get ideas down that are really relevant. However, you may not be sure right away what your main point will be. If so, brainstorm first and develop a unifying statement by figuring out how you could pull together ideas in your brainstorm list.

3. Make a brainstorm list. How many items are enough for your list? For a two-hundred-word essay, you can expect to write a brief introduction, two to three well-developed supporting paragraphs, and a brief conclusion. So your brainstorming list should contain at least two main points (one for each supporting paragraph) and as many related details as you can think of (even though you may decide not to use all of them later). In addition, if you think of an effective introduction for your essay, make a note of it.

4. Organize your list. You may not have time to make an outline, but do make an effort to group the details that you want in each paragraph. Use arrows and circles, or clusters, if you want, as a visual aid to your grouping. Check to make sure that each main idea is clearly related to the unifying statement and that each detail is clearly related to its main idea. Cross out any irrelevant material.

Since your time limit won't allow you to make extensive revisions of organization and content, the planning stage is doubly important. Use a little of your planning time to decide on the overall structure of your essay. How will you group your details? What order will make your ideas clear to your readers? Look once again at your brainstormed list of details. Are they specific enough? Are there enough to be convincing?

You may want to review the example of organizing a brainstorm list on pages 181–182.

EXERCISE 1

Directions: Prewrite your responses to the following essay questions. Taking ten minutes for each question, write a unifying statement, brainstorm a list of ideas, group the items in the list, and number your groups to indicate the order in which you plan to write your paragraphs.

1. Debates about the effects of television on children have raged for years. In particular, some groups have suggested that commercials be banned from children's programs. Describe some effects that television commercials can have on children.

2. More and more mothers of preschoolers are entering the work force. As a result, their children spend large parts of the day in daycare centers or with babysitters. How do you think this child-care arrangement affects small children as compared to children whose mothers stay at home? Give specific examples to explain your opinion.

3. In every society in the world, ceremonies are used to mark major events in people's lives. Installations of government leaders, marriages, deaths, even sports events are all accompanied by certain rituals. Why do you think that ceremonies are so important to people? Use specific examples to support your reasons.

POSSIBLE ANSWERS ARE ON PAGE 368.

Draft Quickly and Carefully

If you have done justice to the prewriting stage, the drafting stage shouldn't be too rough. You already know what your purpose is and what your major supporting points will be. Just put the information into sentence and paragraph form.

Write an introduction. Be sure the introduction contains a unifying statement and previews the organization of your essay for the reader. Then move on to the first supporting paragraph.

Write the body. As you write your supporting paragraphs, keep your unifying statement and overall organizational plan in mind. Write two or three supporting paragraphs. Work in appropriate transitions (*first, in addition, however,* etc.—the list is on page 242) to link the supporting paragraphs to the introduction and to one another. And remember, the more specific your supporting details are, the better.

If you think of new ideas as you write, feel free to include them as long as they're relevant and they fit in logically.

Write a conclusion. Like the introduction, the conclusion can be just a sentence or two. If your time is nearly up, simply rephrase the unifying statement.

Write quickly. Use your budgeted writing time wisely. If you get stuck because you can't think of the word you want to use or you can't remember how to spell it, leave a space and move on. Be sure, though, to fill something in before you hand in your paper. Again, your readers understand that you don't have access to a dictionary during the test. It won't hurt to take a stab at the spelling of the precise word you want to use rather than rewording your entire sentence to avoid the problem. The readers who will score your paper will not expect a polished piece of writing.

Write carefully. The instructions for this part of the Writing Skills Test will say nothing about the format of your writing. However, you should be sure to indent at the beginning of each paragraph and to leave side margins wide enough for adding a sentence or two if you decide to revise. Printing rather than cursive writing is perfectly acceptable, but if you print, use both capital and lowercase letters.

EXERCISE 2

Directions: Choose **one** of the topics in Exercise 1 and write an essay based on your unifying statement and brainstorming list. Set a thirty-minute time limit for yourself.

POSSIBLE ANSWERS ARE ON PAGE 368.

Revise and Edit Your Essay

Revise for content and organization first. Forty-five minutes won't allow you much time for revising and editing, so you'll need to have your priorities clear when you reach the last few minutes of the testing period. Study the revising checklist below to see what to concentrate on.

Revising Checklist

☐ Is the introduction worded clearly? If not, make some changes to clarify it.

☐ Will it be clear to the readers that the supporting paragraphs help prove the unifying statement? If not, change the wording to make the supporting points clearer.

☐ Are the details in each paragraph clear, specific, and relevant? Cross out irrelevant details and add details to make vague or general statements clear.

☐ Does the conclusion tie the essay together? You may just want to restate the unifying statement in slightly different words.

☐ Are paragraphs and sentences organized logically and linked smoothly? Add transition words to show connections clearly. You can also move material that seems to fit better in a different place.

Make any revisions neatly. Cross out material that is irrelevant to the paper and use a caret (λ) or an asterisk (✱) to show where inserted words belong. If you decide to move a sentence, circle it and draw an arrow to its new location. If you've forgotten to indent a new paragraph, use the symbol ¶ to show where it should begin.

Edit for sentence structure, usage, and mechanics. Check for the most serious problems first. Since sentence structure and punctuation errors can sometimes interfere with meaning, attend to them before you hunt for spelling or capitalization errors. Study the following editing checklist to help you maintain your priorities as your testing time draws to a close.

Editing Checklist

☐ Are sentences complete—no fragments or run-ons?

☐ Is wording clear? Are any words missing?

☐ Are endmarks and commas used correctly?

☐ Are verbs and pronouns used correctly and consistently?

☐ Are words spelled correctly? Look especially at plurals, verb endings, and soundalikes.

☐ Are words capitalized correctly?

EXERCISE 3

Directions: Take five minutes to revise and edit the essay you wrote for Exercise 2.

POSSIBLE ANSWERS ARE ON PAGE 368.

EXERCISE 4

Directions: If you need more practice writing essays before you move on to take the Post-Test, use any of the following topics. Remember to work for only forty-five minutes on each essay. Put into practice all you have learned about prewriting, drafting, revising, and editing.

1. American society is a mixture of races, religions, languages, and customs. This mixture has brought many benefits to our country, but it has caused problems not found in nations where the citizens have similar backgrounds.

Write a composition of about two hundred words describing the effects that our mixture of backgrounds has had on American society. You may describe the positive effects, the negative effects, or both. Be specific and use examples to support your view.

2. Many people in the United States are having smaller families. Rather than having three or four children, many parents choose to have only one or two children.

   Do you think this trend toward smaller families is good or bad? In a composition of about two hundred words, state your opinion and support it with specific reasons and examples.

3. The invention of the airplane has brought about a number of changes in American life. Although air travel has improved our lives in many ways, it has also brought new problems.

   Write a composition of about two hundred words describing the effects of the airplane on modern life. You may describe the positive effects, the negative effects, or both. Be specific and use examples to support your view.

4. Most people seem to think they don't have enough money. No matter how much they have, they always want more.

   Write a composition of about two hundred words explaining why, no matter how much money they make, people usually want more money. Be sure to support your views with specific reasons, details, and examples.

5. Even though fear and anxiety are unpleasant emotions, people regularly spend money to watch horror movies. What makes these movies so appealing?

   Write a composition of about two hundred words explaining why people go to horror movies. Use specific reasons and examples in your answer.

6. Fifty years ago, computers were unknown. Today these machines, from tiny pocket calculators up through room-sized mainframes, are used in schools, businesses, government, and homes. They check our tax returns and print out our bank statements and utility bills. They even ring up the sales at many supermarkets. The widespread use of computers has brought many benefits to our society, but it has also caused some problems.

   Write a composition of about two hundred words describing the effects of computers on modern life. You may describe the positive effects, the negative effects, or both.

ANSWERS WILL VARY.

Writing Skills Post-Test, Part 1

Directions: The following items are based on paragraphs that contain numbered sentences. Some of the sentences may contain errors in sentence structure, usage, or mechanics. A few sentences, however, may be correct as written. Read the paragraph and then answer the items based on it. For each item, choose the answer that would result in the most effective writing of the sentence or sentences. The best answer must be consistent with the meaning and tone of the rest of the paragraph.

POST-TEST ANSWER GRID

1 ① ② ③ ④ ⑤	15 ① ② ③ ④ ⑤	29 ① ② ③ ④ ⑤	43 ① ② ③ ④ ⑤
2 ① ② ③ ④ ⑤	16 ① ② ③ ④ ⑤	30 ① ② ③ ④ ⑤	44 ① ② ③ ④ ⑤
3 ① ② ③ ④ ⑤	17 ① ② ③ ④ ⑤	31 ① ② ③ ④ ⑤	45 ① ② ③ ④ ⑤
4 ① ② ③ ④ ⑤	18 ① ② ③ ④ ⑤	32 ① ② ③ ④ ⑤	46 ① ② ③ ④ ⑤
5 ① ② ③ ④ ⑤	19 ① ② ③ ④ ⑤	33 ① ② ③ ④ ⑤	47 ① ② ③ ④ ⑤
6 ① ② ③ ④ ⑤	20 ① ② ③ ④ ⑤	34 ① ② ③ ④ ⑤	48 ① ② ③ ④ ⑤
7 ① ② ③ ④ ⑤	21 ① ② ③ ④ ⑤	35 ① ② ③ ④ ⑤	49 ① ② ③ ④ ⑤
8 ① ② ③ ④ ⑤	22 ① ② ③ ④ ⑤	36 ① ② ③ ④ ⑤	50 ① ② ③ ④ ⑤
9 ① ② ③ ④ ⑤	23 ① ② ③ ④ ⑤	37 ① ② ③ ④ ⑤	51 ① ② ③ ④ ⑤
10 ① ② ③ ④ ⑤	24 ① ② ③ ④ ⑤	38 ① ② ③ ④ ⑤	52 ① ② ③ ④ ⑤
11 ① ② ③ ④ ⑤	25 ① ② ③ ④ ⑤	39 ① ② ③ ④ ⑤	53 ① ② ③ ④ ⑤
12 ① ② ③ ④ ⑤	26 ① ② ③ ④ ⑤	40 ① ② ③ ④ ⑤	54 ① ② ③ ④ ⑤
13 ① ② ③ ④ ⑤	27 ① ② ③ ④ ⑤	41 ① ② ③ ④ ⑤	55 ① ② ③ ④ ⑤
14 ① ② ③ ④ ⑤	28 ① ② ③ ④ ⑤	42 ① ② ③ ④ ⑤	

Questions 1–9 refer to the following paragraph.

(1) The invention of the X-ray machine in 1895 gave medical personnel a way to see inside a patients body without performing surgery. (2) This new tool enabled doctors to diagnose and treat ailments ranging from broken bones to tumors more efficiently. (3) In recent years, the X-ray machine and the computer has been combined to produce new data-gathering possibilities for doctors. (4) The new equipment produces three-dimensional images. (5) The images are produced when it takes a series of X-ray scans and reassembles them for viewing. (6) Some versions of this technology actually takes moving pictures of internal organs like a beating heart. (7) Surgeons particularly pleased with the computerized X-rays. (8) By discovering the exact size and shape of a tumor before surgery they can reduce the amount of time that a patient is on the operating table. (9) This saves lives. (10) Pediatricians too found the equipment useful. (11) Because it can produce exact images within a few seconds, the doctors can recieve the information they need even when their young patients squirm around.

1. Sentence 1: **The invention of the X-ray machine in 1895 gave medical personnel a way to see inside a patients body without performing surgery.**

   What correction should be made to this sentence?

   (1) change *gave* to *give*
   (2) change the spelling of *personnel* to *personal*
   (3) replace *patients* with *patient's*
   (4) change the spelling of *performing* to *preforming*
   (5) no correction is necessary

2. Sentence 3: **In recent years, the X-ray machine and the computer has been combined to produce new data-gathering possibilities for doctors.**

   What correction should be made to this sentence?

   (1) insert a comma after *computer*
   (2) change *has* to *have*
   (3) replace *combined to* with *combined. To*
   (4) change the spelling of *possibilities* to *possibilitys*
   (5) no correction is necessary

3. Sentences 4 and 5: **The new equipment produces three-dimensional images. The images are produced when it takes a series of X-ray scans and reassembles them for viewing.**

   The most effective combination of Sentences 4 and 5 would include which of the following groups of words?

   (1) By producing three-dimensional images, so it
   (2) By taking a series of X-ray scans and reassembling them for viewing, three-dimensional
   (3) After three-dimensional images are produced, the new equipment takes
   (4) images by taking a series of X-ray scans and reassembling
   (5) images, but it takes

4. Sentence 6: **Some versions of this technology actually <u>takes</u> moving pictures of internal organs like a beating heart.**

   Which of the following is the best way to write the underlined portion of this sentence? If you think the original is the best way, choose option (1).

   (1) takes
   (2) take
   (3) takeing
   (4) taking
   (5) taken

5. Sentence 7: **Surgeons particularly pleased with the computerized X-rays.**

What correction should be made to this sentence?

(1) replace *Surgeons* with *Surgeon's*
(2) insert *are* after *Surgeons*
(3) change the spelling of *particularly* to *paticularly*
(4) change *pleased* to *please*
(5) insert a comma after *pleased*

6. Sentence 8: **By discovering the exact size and shape of a tumor before surgery they can reduce the amount of time that a patient is on the operating table.**

What correction should be made to this sentence?

(1) change the spelling of *discovering* to *discoverring*
(2) insert a comma after *tumor*
(3) insert a comma after *surgery*
(4) change the spelling of *operating* to *operateing*
(5) no correction is necessary

7. Sentence 9: **This saves lives.**

Which of the following is the best way to write the underlined portion of this sentence? If you think the original is the best way, choose option (1).

(1) This saves lives.
(2) Thus saving lives.
(3) This procedure saves lives.
(4) A life-saving procedure.
(5) As a result, lives being saved.

8. Sentence 10: **Pediatricians too found the equipment useful.**

Which of the following is the best way to write the underlined portion of this sentence? If you think the original is the best way, choose option (1).

(1) too found
(2) to found
(3) too find
(4) to find
(5) to finding

9. Sentence 11: **Because it can produce exact images within a few seconds, the doctors can recieve the information they need even when their young patients squirm around.**

What correction should be made to this sentence?

(1) replace *Because* with *Although*
(2) remove the comma after *seconds*
(3) change the spelling of *recieve* to *receive*
(4) replace *need even* with *need. Even*
(5) no correction is necessary

Questions 10–17 refer to the following paragraph.

(1) Today many married women with children under two work outside the home. (2) With infants and toddlers, the presence of so many working women has caused new strains in the workplace. (3) For instance employers may be requested to grant maternity leaves that extend several months beyond the birth or adoption of a baby. (4) Although in many European countries businesses routinely grant such leaves, they are expensive to employers because of the costs of finding and retraining temporary replacement help. (5) In addition, some employers in the United States argue that the policy discriminates against men by granting benefits exclusively to women. (6) Their opponents insists that since only women become pregnant, a law requiring maternity leaves is not unfair to men. (7) One compromise may be to develop a law guaranteeing parental leaves. (8) The law would allow either mothers or fathers to spend time with their new babies. (9) While parental leaves after childbirth occupy much National attention, a related issue affects many more working parents. (10) Should mothers and fathers be permitted to stay at home with sick children, or should sick leaves be used only when the workers themselves become ill? (11) Both issues pitted the financial interests of employers, who want to save money on employee benefits, against the physical and psychological well-being of children and parents.

10. Sentence 2: **With infants and toddlers, the presence of so many working women has caused new strains in the workplace.**

Which of the following is the best way to write the underlined portion of this sentence? If you think the original is the best way, choose option (1).

(1) With infants and toddlers, the presence of so many working women has caused new strains in the workplace.

(2) With infants and toddlers in the workplace, the presence of so many working women has caused new strains.

(3) The presence with infants and toddlers of so many working women has caused new strains in the workplace.

(4) The presence of so many working women with infants and toddlers has caused new strains in the workplace.

(5) The presence of so many working women in the workplace with infants and toddlers has caused new strains.

11. Sentence 3: **For instance employers may be requested to grant maternity leaves that extend several months beyond the birth or adoption of a baby.**

What correction should be made to this sentence?

(1) insert a comma after *instance*
(2) change *requested* to *request*
(3) insert a comma after *extend*
(4) insert a comma after *birth*
(5) no correction is necessary

12. Sentence 4: **Although in many European countries businesses routinely grant such leaves, they are expensive to employers because of the costs of finding and retraining temporary replacement help.**

    If you rewrote Sentence 4 beginning with

    In many European countries, businesses routinely grant such leaves;

    the next word should be

    (1) moreover
    (2) therefore
    (3) then
    (4) otherwise
    (5) however

13. Sentence 6: **Their opponents insists that since only women become pregnant, a law requiring maternity leaves is not unfair to men.**

    What correction should be made to this sentence?

    (1) replace *Their* with *There*
    (2) change *insists* to *insist*
    (3) remove the comma after *pregnant*
    (4) change the spelling of *requiring* to *requireing*
    (5) change *is* to *are*

14. Sentences 7 and 8: **One compromise may be to develop a law guaranteeing parental leaves. The law would allow either mothers or fathers to spend time with their new babies.**

    The most effective combination of Sentences 7 and 8 would contain which of the following groups of words?

    (1) leaves, who would allow
    (2) leaves, which would allow
    (3) leaves which it would allow
    (4) leaves, and the law
    (5) leaves, but the law

15. Sentence 9: **While parental leaves after childbirth occupy much National attention, a related issue affects many more working parents.**

    What correction should be made to this sentence?

    (1) insert a comma after *childbirth*
    (2) change *occupy* to *occupies*
    (3) change *National* to *national*
    (4) remove the comma after *attention*
    (5) no correction is necessary

16. Sentence 10: **Should mothers and fathers be permitted to stay at home with sick children, or should sick leaves be used only when the workers themselves become ill?**

    What correction should be made to this sentence?

    (1) change the spelling of *permitted* to *permited*
    (2) remove the comma after *children*
    (3) insert a comma after *or*
    (4) insert a comma after *only*
    (5) no correction is necessary

17. Sentence 11: **Both issues pitted the financial interests of employers, who want to save money on employee benefits, against the physical and psychological well-being of children and parents.**

    What correction should be made to this sentence?

    (1) change *pitted* to *pit*
    (2) change the spelling of *interests* to *intrests*
    (3) replace *who* with *which*
    (4) insert a comma after *physical*
    (5) no correction is necessary

Questions 18–25 refer to the following paragraph.

(1) Quality circle programs have been adopted in a number of American businesses and industries in the last twenty years. (2) They were originally used in Japan. (3) These programs are design to improve production efficiency and working conditions. (4) They operate on the principal that many problems in the workplace can best be solved by the workers themselves. (5) The circles consisted of groups of six to ten employees from the same work area who meet on a regular basis. (6) They choose the problems that they want to attack, identify possible causes, test to discover whether their analysis was accurate, and they consider possible solutions. (7) When they've settled on a workable solution, they make a formal management presentation to their supervisors. (8) The success of quality circles can be measured in reduced production costs, fewer industrial accidents, and greater output, in addition, the programs result in more satisfied employees. (9) Gaining some control over his working environment leads to a greater interest in making the company a success.

18. Sentences 1 and 2: **Quality circle programs have been adopted in a number of American businesses and industries in the last twenty years. They were originally used in Japan.**

The most effective combination of Sentences 1 and 2 would include which of the following groups of words?

(1) Originally used in Japan, quality
(2) years so they were originally
(3) Originally used in Japan, but
(4) When quality circle programs in Japan
(5) By using them in Japan, quality

19. Sentence 3: **These programs <u>are design</u> to improve production efficiency and working conditions.**

Which of the following is the best way to write the underlined portion of this sentence? If you think the original is the best way, choose option (1).

(1) are design
(2) are designed
(3) design
(4) designed
(5) designing

20. Sentence 4: **They operate on the principal that many problems in the workplace can best be solved by the workers themselves.**

What correction should be made to this sentence?

(1) change *operate* to *operates*
(2) change the spelling of *principal* to *principle*
(3) insert a comma after *workplace*
(4) replace *workers* with *worker's*
(5) no correction is necessary

21. Sentence 5: **The circles consisted of groups of six to ten employees from the same work area who meet on a regular basis.**

What correction should be made to this sentence?

(1) change *consisted* to *consist*
(2) insert a comma after *employees*
(3) change *who* to *which*
(4) insert a comma after *meet*
(5) no correction is necessary

22. Sentence 6: **They choose the problems that they want to attack, identify possible causes, test to discover whether their analysis was accurate, and they consider possible solutions.**

Which of the following is the best way to write the underlined portion of this sentence? If you think the original is the best way, choose option (1).

(1) they consider
(2) to consider
(3) considering
(4) consider
(5) considers

23. Sentence 7: **When they've settled on a workable solution, they make a formal management presentation to their supervisors.**

Which of the following is the best way to write the underlined portion of this sentence? If you think the original is the best way, choose option (1).

(1) they make
(2) then they make
(3) and they make
(4) so they make
(5) making

24. Sentence 8: **The success of quality circles can be measured in reduced production costs, fewer industrial accidents, and greater output, in addition, the programs result in more satisfied employees.**

What correction should be made to this sentence?

(1) change the spelling of *measured* to *mesured*
(2) change the spelling of *accidents* to *accedents*
(3) replace *output, in* with *output; in*
(4) remove the comma after *addition*
(5) change *result* to *results*

25. Sentence 9: **Gaining some control over his working environment leads to a greater interest in making the company a success.**

What correction should be made to this sentence?

(1) change *his* to *their*
(2) change the spelling of *environment* to *enviornment*
(3) insert a comma after *environment*
(4) change *leads* to *lead*
(5) change the spelling of *interest* to *intrest*

POST-TEST

Questions 26–33 refer to the following paragraph.

(1) Are you looking, for a form of exercise that keeps your heart and lungs in good shape without endangering the rest of your body? (2) Do you need a sport that doesn't require any expensive equipment or a special place to play? (3) If so, consider walking. (4) This form of exercise is an equal opportunity sport. (5) If you stretch your muscles before you begin and cooled down slowly after you stop, you'll find that a brisk pace provides all the conditioning you want without the stress to bones and joints that jogging causes. (6) In fact, his swinging arm movement may actually provide more exercise than jogging does. (7) For maximum benefit, plan to walk at least two or three times a week. (8) Because you live near your place of work, you may decide to walk there instead of driving or using public transportation. (9) On the other hand, you may prefer to map a route around your neighborhood or down a quite country road for an early evening stroll. (10) Regardless of where you going, there will be a noticeable new spring in your step after only a few weeks of regular walking.

26. Sentence 1: **Are you looking, for a form of exercise that keeps your heart and lungs in good shape without endangering the rest of your body?**

What correction should be made to this sentence?

(1) remove the comma after *looking*
(2) insert a comma after *heart*
(3) replace *shape without* with *shape? Without*
(4) insert a comma after *without*
(5) no correction is necessary

27. Sentence 2: **Do you need a sport that doesn't require any expensive equipment or a special place to play?**

What correction should be made to this sentence?

(1) change *Do* to *Did*
(2) change the spelling of *equipment* to *equitment*
(3) insert a comma after *equipment*
(4) change the spelling of *special* to *speshal*
(5) no correction is necessary

28. Sentences 3 and 4: **If so, consider walking. This form of exercise is an equal opportunity sport.**

The most effective combination of Sentences 3 and 4 would contain which of the following groups of words?

(1) If so, this form
(2) being an equal opportunity sport, consider
(3) walking, but this form
(4) walking, which this form
(5) walking, an equal

29. Sentence 5: **If you stretch your muscles before you begin and <u>cooled</u> down slowly after you stop, you'll find that a brisk pace provides all the conditioning you want without the stress to bones and joints that jogging causes.**

Which of the following is the best way to write the underlined portion of this sentence? If you think the original is the best way, choose option (1).

(1) cooled
(2) cooling
(3) cool
(4) have cooled
(5) will cool

30. Sentence 6: **In fact, <u>his</u> swinging arm movement while walking may actually provide more exercise than jogging does.**

Which of the following is the best way to write the underlined portion of this sentence? If you think the original is the best way, choose option (1).

(1) his
(2) their
(3) our
(4) your
(5) my

31. Sentence 8: **<u>Because</u> you live near your place of work, you may decide to walk there instead of driving or using public transportation.**

Which of the following is the best way to write the underlined portion of this sentence? If you think the original is the best way, choose option (1).

(1) Because
(2) If
(3) Although
(4) Until
(5) After

32. Sentence 9: **On the other hand, you may prefer to map a route around your neighborhood or down a quite country road for an early evening stroll.**

What correction should be made to this sentence?

(1) remove the comma after *hand*
(2) change the spelling of *prefer* to *perfer*
(3) insert a comma after *neighborhood*
(4) change the spelling of *quite* to *quiet*
(5) no correction is necessary

33. Sentence 10: **Regardless of where you going, there will be a noticeable new spring in your step after only a few weeks of regular walking.**

What correction should be made to this sentence?

(1) change *going* to *go*
(2) change the spelling of *there* to *their*
(3) change the spelling of *noticeable* to *noticable*
(4) replace *step after* with *step; after*
(5) no correction is necessary

POST-TEST

Questions 34–41 refer to the following paragraph.

(1) As oil and coal supplies dwindle and with the shrinkage of available farmland, people may increasingly turn to the ocean for fuel and food. (2) Scientists are already conducting encouraging experiments in the Pacific ocean off the coast of Hawaii. (3) In one project, the scientists are pumping warm ocean water around pipes containing ammonia, a substance that has a very low boiling point. (4) When the ammonia boiled, its evaporation into a gas turns a turbine. (5) As it cools, it returns to its liquid state and it is recycled through the system. (6) Another group of scientists working with aquaculture, or ocean farming. (7) They've found that the icy water two thousand feet below the surface is rich with nutrients; however, it's too far from sunlight to harbor harmful bacteria. (8) Abalone is a shellfish considered a seafood delicacy, and this environment is ideal for growing it. (9) In a third experiment, farmers are pumping the cold ocean water through pipes lain in strawberry fields. (10) These experiments are just the beginning of a variaty of ocean industries that will develop in the twenty-first century.

34. Sentence 1: **As oil and coal supplies dwindle and <u>with the shrinkage of available farmland,</u> people may increasingly turn to the ocean for fuel and food.**

Which of the following is the best way to write the underlined portion of this sentence? If you think the original is the best way, choose option (1).

(1) with the shrinkage of available farmland
(2) with shrinking available farmland
(3) with available farmland shrinking
(4) available farmland shrinks
(5) available farmland shrank

35. Sentence 2: **Scientists are already conducting encouraging experiments in the Pacific ocean off the coast of Hawaii.**

What correction should be made to this sentence?

(1) replace *already* with *all ready*
(2) change the spelling of *encouraging* to *encourageing*
(3) change *Pacific* to *pacific*
(4) change *ocean* to *Ocean*
(5) change *coast* to *Coast*

36. Sentence 4: **When the ammonia <u>boiled,</u> its evaporation into a gas turns a turbine.**

Which of the following is the best way to write the underlined portion of this sentence? If you think the original is the best way, choose option (1).

(1) boiled
(2) was boiling
(3) boiling
(4) boils
(5) boil

37. Sentence 5: **As it cools, it returns to its liquid state and it is recycled through the system.**

    What correction should be made to this sentence?

    (1) change *cools* to *cool*
    (2) remove the comma after *cools*
    (3) insert a comma after *state*
    (4) change the spelling of *through* to *threw*
    (5) no correction is necessary

38. Sentence 6: **Another group of <u>scientists working</u> with aquaculture, or ocean farming.**

    Which of the following is the best way to write the underlined portion of this sentence? If you think the original is the best way, choose option (1).

    (1) scientists working
    (2) scientists are working
    (3) scientist's working
    (4) scientists' working
    (5) scientists' are working

39. Sentence 8: **Abalone is a shellfish considered a seafood delicacy, and this environment is ideal for growing it.**

    If you rewrote Sentence 8 beginning with

    This environment is ideal for growing abalone,

    the next word should be

    (1) a
    (2) who
    (3) being
    (4) they
    (5) it

40. Sentence 9: **In a third experiment, farmers are pumping the cold ocean water through pipes lain in strawberry fields.**

    What correction should be made to this sentence?

    (1) remove the comma after *experiment*
    (2) replace *farmers* with *farmers'*
    (3) change *are pumping* to *pumped*
    (4) insert a comma after *water*
    (5) replace *lain* with *laid*

41. Sentence 10: **These experiments are just the beginning of a variaty of ocean industries that will develop in the twenty-first century.**

    What correction should be made to this sentence?

    (1) remove *are*
    (2) change the spelling of *variaty* to *variety*
    (3) replace *industries that* with *industries. That*
    (4) replace *that* with *who*
    (5) change the spelling of *develop* to *develope*

POST-TEST

Questions 42–48 refer to the following paragraph.

(1) Few houses built before 1970 were designed to be energy efficient. (2) Because natural gas and other petroleum products were cheap and abundant, builders can easily reduce construction costs by using little or no insulation. (3) Furnaces also fuel wasters. (4) In fact, 30 percent or more of the heat produced went strait up the chimney. (5) During the 1970s, political and economic events in the Middle East raised the price of oil imported from Arab countries, and suddenly energy conservation became important. (6) Faced with skyrocketing costs for heating and cooling their homes, many homeowners began searching for ways to increase energy efficiency. (7) They discover that weatherstripping around windows and doors reduced both drafts and fuel bills. (8) Adding an extra layer of insulation in the attic kept homes warmer in Winter and cooler in summer. (9) Although the initial cost was high, blowing insulation behind the outside walls brought long-term energy savings. (10) Looking back, American homeowners realized that the energy crisis had made them wiser energy consumers.

42. Sentence 1: **Few houses built before 1970 were designed to be energy efficient.**

What correction should be made to this sentence?

(1) change *built* to *build*
(2) change the spelling of *before* to *befor*
(3) insert a comma after *1970*
(4) change *were* to *was*
(5) no correction is necessary

43. Sentence 2: **Because natural gas and other petroleum products were cheap and abundant, builders can easily reduce construction costs by using little or no insulation.**

What correction should be made to this sentence?

(1) change *were* to *was*
(2) remove the comma after *abundant*
(3) change *can* to *could*
(4) change the spelling of *easily* to *eazily*
(5) replace *costs by* with *costs. By*

44. Sentence 3: **<u>Furnaces also</u> fuel wasters.**

Which of the following is the best way to write the underlined portion of this sentence? If you think the original is the best way, choose option (1).

(1) Furnaces also
(2) Furnaces
(3) Furnaces being also
(4) Furnaces were also
(5) Furnaces that were

45. Sentence 4: **In fact, 30 percent or more of the heat produced went strait up the chimney.**

What correction should be made to this sentence?

(1) remove the comma after *fact*
(2) insert a comma after *percent*
(3) change *went* to *gone*
(4) change the spelling of *strait* to *straight*
(5) no correction is necessary

46. Sentence 5: **During the 1970s, political and economic events in the Middle East raised the price of oil imported from Arab countries, and suddenly energy conservation became important.**

If you rewrote Sentence 5 beginning with

Energy conservation suddenly became important during the 1970s

the next word should be

(1) when
(2) if
(3) until
(4) although
(5) unless

47. Sentence 7: **They discover that weatherstripping around windows and doors reduced both drafts and fuel bills.**

Which of the following is the best way to write the underlined portion of this sentence? If you think the original is the best way, choose option (1).

(1) They discover
(2) They discovered
(3) They will discover
(4) They have been discovered
(5) Discovering

48. Sentence 8: **Adding an extra layer of insulation in the attic kept homes warmer in Winter and cooler in summer.**

What correction should be made to this sentence?

(1) insert a comma after *attic*
(2) change *kept* to *keeped*
(3) change *Winter* to *winter*
(4) change *summer* to *Summer*
(5) no correction is necessary

Questions 49–55 refer to the following paragraph.

(1) An experienced renter considers far more than monthly rates when you're searching for a new apartment. (2) He checks the location of the unit to determine whether its close to his work or to a public transportation system. (3) Availability of stores and recreational facilities, is another consideration. (4) To find out if parking spaces are regularly available. (5) He visits the street at various times of the day and night. (6) Of course, the apartment building and the actual rental unit are closely inspected, are the entryway and hallways well maintained and well lit? (7) Most important, the renter makes a point of talking to the landlord or manager of the building. (8) Does the person seem interested and helpful? (9) Does the person seem bored and impatient? (10) It may be a good predictor of the response a tenant with a complaint will get.

49. Sentence 1: **An experienced renter considers far more than monthly rates when you're searching for a new apartment.**

   What correction should be made to this sentence?

   (1) change the spelling of *experienced* to *expirenced*
   (2) change *considers* to *consider*
   (3) insert a comma after *rates*
   (4) replace *you're* with *he's*
   (5) insert a comma after *searching*

50. Sentence 2: **He checks the location of the unit to determine whether its close to his work or to a public transportation system.**

   What correction should be made to this sentence?

   (1) insert a comma after *unit*
   (2) replace *whether* with *weather*
   (3) replace *its* with *it's*
   (4) insert a comma after *work*
   (5) no correction is necessary

51. Sentence 3: **Availability of stores and recreational facilities, is another consideration.**

   What correction should be made to this sentence?

   (1) change the spelling of *Availability* to *Availibility*
   (2) insert a comma after *stores*
   (3) change the spelling of *facilities* to *facilitys*
   (4) remove the comma after *facilities*
   (5) change *is* to *are*

52. Sentences 4 and 5: **To find out if parking spaces are regularly <u>available. He</u> visits the street at various times of the day and night.**

Which of the following is the best way to write the underlined portion of these sentences? If you think the original is the best way, choose option (1).

(1) available. He
(2) available, so he
(3) available he
(4) available, he
(5) available, and he

53. Sentence 6: **Of course, the apartment building and the actual rental unit are closely inspected, are the entryway and hallways well maintained and well lit?**

What correction should be made to this sentence?

(1) remove the comma after *course*
(2) replace *are closely* with *is closely*
(3) replace *inspected, are* with *inspected. Are*
(4) insert a comma after *hallways*
(5) no correction is necessary

54. Sentences 8 and 9: **Does the person seem interested and helpful? Does the person seem bored and impatient?**

The most effective combination of Sentences 8 and 9 would include which of the following groups of words?

(1) helpful although does
(2) helpful, but does
(3) helpful, and does
(4) helpful, or he seems
(5) helpful or bored

55. Sentence 10: **It may be a good predictor of the response a tenant with a complaint will get.**

Which of the following is the best way to write the underlined portion of this sentence? If you think the original is the best way, choose option (1).

(1) It may be
(2) This may be
(3) This being
(4) This general attitude being
(5) This general attitude may be

ANSWERS BEGIN ON PAGE 323.

POST-TEST

Directions: This part of the test is designed to find out how well you write. The test has one question that asks you to present an opinion on an issue or to explain something. In preparing your answer for this question, you should take the following steps:

1. Read all of the information accompanying the question.
2. Plan your answer carefully before you write.
3. Use scratch paper to make any notes.
4. Write your answer on a separate sheet of paper.
5. Read carefully what you have written and make any changes that will improve your writing.
6. Check your paragraphing, sentence structure, spelling, punctuation, capitalization, and usage and make any necessary corrections.

Take forty-five minutes to write on the assigned topic. Write legibly and use a ballpoint pen.

TOPIC

Every year, companies spend billions of dollars to advertise their products and services. We see advertising everywhere we look—on television, in magazines, on signs.

Write a composition of about two hundred words describing the effects of advertising on modern life. You may describe the positive effects, the negative effects, or both. Be specific and use examples to support your view. Two sample essays on this topic appear on pages 325–326.

POSSIBLE ANSWERS BEGIN ON PAGE 325.

Post-Test Answer Key

PART 1

1. (3) The possessive form must be used to show that a patient has a body.

2. (2) The verb must agree with the compound subject *machine* and *computer*. Since the subjects are joined by *and*, the verb must be plural to agree in number: *They have.*

3. (4) The new sentence is formed by shortening Sentence 5 into a modifying phrase that shows how the equipment works. The complete sentence would be "The new equipment produces three-dimensional images by taking a series of X-ray scans and reassembling them for viewing."

4. (2) By crossing out the interrupting phrase *of this technology*, we see that the subject of this sentence is the plural noun *versions*. The plural verb *take* agrees with this subject.

5. (2) The original word group is a fragment because it lacks a complete verb. The helping verb *are* provides the rest of the sentence skeleton. *Surgeons* is the subject, and *are pleased* is the verb.

6. (3) Use a comma to separate an introductory phrase from the main part of a sentence.

7. (3) The pronoun *This* is vague in the original sentence because it lacks an antecedent. Adding the word *procedure* makes clear what *This* refers to.

8. (3) From Sentence 3 on in this paragraph, present-tense verbs are used: *have been combined, produces, take, can reduce, saves.* Therefore, the verb in this sentence should also be present tense.

9. (3) The rule that applies is *I before E except after C.*

10. (4) The phrase *with infants and toddlers* should be placed directly after the word it modifies, *women.*

11. (1) Use commas to separate transitional words and phrases from the rest of the sentence.

12. (5) The two clauses in the original sentence were linked by the conjunction *although*, which shows contrast. The new sentence also needs a linking word to show contrast. It should read, "In many European countries, businesses routinely grant such leaves; however, they are expensive to employers because of the costs of finding and retraining temporary replacement help."

13. (2) The verb must agree with the plural subject *opponents: They insist.*

14. (2) The sentences can be combined by using the relative pronoun *which* to introduce a clause describing the law. Since the antecedent *law* is nonhuman, *which* must be used instead of *who*. The new sentence should read, "One compromise may be to develop a law guaranteeing parental leaves, which would allow either mothers or fathers to spend time with their new babies."

15. (3) Capitalize words that refer to specific places, like *American*, not general words like *national.*

16. (5) The sentence is correct as written.

17. (1) Except for the first sentence, every sentence in the paragraph is written in the present tense. Notice such present-tense verbs as *has caused, grant, are, occupy,* and *affects.* These verbs, as well as the other verb in Sentence 10, *want,* are clues that a present-tense verb must be used.

18. (1) The sentences can be combined by turning Sentence 2 into an introductory phrase that modifies *quality circle programs* in Sentence 1. The new sentence should read, "Originally used in Japan, quality circle programs have been adopted in a number of American businesses and industries in the last twenty years."

19. (2) The passive form is used to show that someone designs these programs. This form requires the past participle of the main verb: *designed.*

20. (2) The word that fits the meaning of the rest of the sentence is *principle*, meaning "theory" or "basic idea."

21. (1) Other verbs in the paragraph, such as *operate* and *choose,* as well as the other verb in this sentence, *meet,* are clues that the present tense is needed to show a general truth.

22. (4) For parallel structure, use the same word form for compound elements: *attack, identify, test,* and *consider.*

23. (1) The sentence is correct as written. The conjunction *When* in the first clause links the two parts of the sentence. No other linking word is needed.

24. (3) To avoid a comma splice, use a semicolon to separate two independent clauses connected by a linking word or phrase like *in addition.*

25. (1) The rest of the paragraph uses plural pronouns to refer to the employees: *they choose, they consider, they make.* The plural pronoun *their* fits the same pattern.

26. (1) Don't use commas before phrases that follow the word they modify.

27. (5) The sentence is correct as written.

28. (5) The sentences can be combined by turning Sentence 4 into a renaming phrase that describes *walking.* The complete sentence should read, "If so, consider walking, an equal opportunity sport."

29. (3) The present-tense verb *cool* matches the other verb in the dependent clause, *stretch.*

30. (4) The second-person pronoun *your* must be used because the rest of the paragraph is written in the second person: *you stretch, you live, you may prefer.*

31. (2) The first clause in this sentence shows under what conditions the second clause will be true, so the logical link between the two clauses is *If.*

32. (4) The word *quiet,* meaning "silent," fits the meaning of the whole sentence. *Quite,* meaning "very," makes no sense in this context.

33. (1) When the verb in the independent clause is in the future tense *(will be),* the verb in the dependent clause is in the present tense.

34. (4) For parallel structure, use the same word forms for compound elements: *coal supplies dwindle* and *available farmland shrinks.*

35. (4) Capitalize the name of a geographical feature when it is part of the name of a specific place.

36. (4) To show a general truth, the verbs in both the independent clause *(turns)* and the dependent clause *(boils)* must be in the present tense.

37. (3) Place a comma before *and* when it joins two independent clauses.

38. (2) The original word group is a fragment because it lacks a complete verb. The helping verb *are* makes the idea complete.

39. (1) The sentence can be rewritten by turning the second clause into a renaming phrase describing *abalone.* The complete sentence should read, "This environment is ideal for growing abalone, a shellfish considered a seafood delicacy."

40. (5) Since the pipes were *placed* in strawberry fields, a form of the verb *lay* must be used. The past participle form is needed here: *laid.*

41. (2) The unaccented vowel *e* in this word can cause spelling problems.

42. (5) The sentence is correct as written.

43. (3) Because the verb in the dependent clause, *were,* is in the past tense, the independent clause must also contain a past-tense verb.

44. (4) The original word group is a fragment because it lacks a verb. Choice (4) adds the verb *were.*

45. (4) To fit the meaning of this sentence, *straight,* meaning "directly," must be used. A *strait* is a narrow channel of water.

46. (1) The linking word *when* shows the time relationship between the two clauses. The complete sentence should read, "Energy conservation suddenly became important during the 1970s when political and economic events in the Middle East raised the price of oil imported from Arab countries."

47. (2) Because the rest of the paragraph is written in the past tense *(became, kept, wore, were replaced),* a past-tense verb should also be used in this sentence.

48. (3) Don't capitalize the names of seasons.

49. (4) The pronoun must agree with its antecedent in person. Since the antecedent in this sentence is *renter,* the third-person pronoun *he* is correct.

50. (3) By substituting *it is* in the sentence, you can see that the contraction *it's* makes sense, not the possessive pronoun *its.*

51. (4) Don't separate the subject from the predicate with a comma.

52. (4) Sentence 4 is a fragment lacking both a subject and a verb. It should be attached to Sentence 5 as a modifying phrase and separated by a comma because it appears before the main part of the sentence.

53. (3) Sentence 6 is a comma splice consisting of two complete thoughts not joined by a coordinating conjunction. These ideas can be written correctly as two separate sentences.

54. (5) The conjunction *or* shows that alternatives are being presented. *Bored and impatient* is parallel in form to *interested and helpful.* The complete sentence should read, "Does the person seem interested and helpful or bored and impatient?"

55. (5) In this sentence, *it* is a vague pronoun with no clear antecedent. *What* is a good predictor? The phrase *This general attitude* makes the meaning clear.

PART 2

Evaluating Your Essay

If at all possible, ask your instructor to read and evaluate your essay. At this point some advice from an experienced reader would be a great help to you! However, if you don't have access to an instructor, you might want to ask a friend or relative to read your paper. Choose someone whose reading and writing skills are at least as strong as yours—perhaps another member of your GED class who's been studying this book too.

A third possibility is to evaluate your essay yourself. This is a very difficult task, since it's hard to be objective about your own writing. If you do choose this alternative, be sure to set your work aside for a couple of days so that you can look at it from a fresh point of view.

Although the readers on the actual GED Writing Skills Test will have no specific set of questions to use as grading standards, the following evaluation checklist should help you or another reader predict the general range of scores in which your paper might fall.

Essay Evaluation Checklist

Yes   *No*

_____ _____ **1.** Does the essay answer the essay question?

_____ _____ **2.** Does the main point of the essay stand out clearly?

_____ _____ **3.** Does each paragraph contain specific examples and details that help prove the main point?

_____ _____ **4.** Can you follow how the writer has arranged and linked the ideas in paragraphs and sentences?

_____ _____ **5.** Are errors in sentence structure, word choice, and mechanics (punctuation, capitalization, and spelling) minor enough and few enough that they don't distract you from the ideas in the essay?

If you or your reader can answer yes to these five questions, your essay would probably earn an upper-half rating (4, 5, or 6) in the Writing Skills Test. You should be ready to try the actual test. Good luck!

A *no* on one or more of these questions indicates that your essay might earn a lower-half rating (1, 2, or 3). If you receive any *no* answers, study your essay carefully to see how you could strengthen it. You may also want to review sections in the text related to problem areas in your essay:

- Essay organization—Chapter 5
- Unifying statements—Chapter 5
- Paragraph development—Chapters 3 and 4
- Linking paragraphs and sentences—Chapter 6
- Sentence structure—Chapters 2, 4, and 5
- Punctuation—Chapters 2, 4, and 5
- Capitalization—Chapter 6
- Spelling—Chapters 2, 3, and 6

For more practice in essay-test writing, choose one or more of the topics from the list on pages 305–306. Write your essay under timed conditions and apply the evaluation checklist to your finished product. With each practice session, you should feel more confident that you can pass this section of the GED Writing Skills Test.

Here are two sample essays that show how different writers might have responded to the essay topic.

Sample Essay A

Like so many other complex issues, advertising has both good and bad effects on society. Advertising can provide you with information, and it also helps publishers and television stations stay afloat financially. However, advertising may also glamorize activities that could be harmful to you.

How did you discover your favorite kind of beer? Maybe you saw it in a television commercial. How did you know where to go to get your toaster on sale at 50 percent off? You probably saw an ad in the paper. Advertising gets information to you, whether a new product is coming out or an old product is being marked down. In addition, the television show and the newspaper that brought you those ads wouldn't be there without the ads. Advertising revenue brings you the six o'clock news, your favorite comedy, and Monday night football. It also pays newspaper reporters and editors whose job is to keep you up to date on the world around you. And what about your magazines? Your subscription or the price you pay in a store doesn't begin to cover the cost of those glossy publications.

However, advertising is not always performing a service to society. In fact, some advertising may be downright harmful. Ads for alcoholic beverages, for example, give you the impression that everyone drinks and that you are part of the "in" crowd if you drink, too. However, this impression may add to the problems of alcoholism and drunken driving that hurt so many people. Similarly, cigarette advertisements are designed to encourage you to smoke. You can be a macho Marlboro man, a liberated Virginia Slims woman, or any other brand you choose. However, the cigarette ads would rather not tell you that smoking is a proven health hazard to both smokers and nonsmokers. These and other advertisements for harmful or useless products encourage you to do damage to yourself and others and waste your money.

While there may be some good reasons to sing the praises of advertising, you should always look at ads with a critical eye. Use them as a good source of information and appreciate them for the services they make possible, but don't get seduced by the pretty pictures.

Sample Essay B

Every day, advertising shows us everything we need to lead the good life. We see new cars, exotic foods, gorgeous women, and handsome men, but these desirable things are not ours. They are in the ads. Advertising makes us less appreciative of the things we have and of the people around us. We can't escape the effects of its influence. Advertising may well hurt both our pocketbooks and our relationships with one another.

We have all seen a child throwing a temper tantrum because she can't have some new toy. No matter how many Barbie outfits a little girl already has, she must have the newest one, too. Advertising robs children of their pleasure in toys they already own by telling them they need new and different ones. It also strains the parent-child relationship, forcing the parent either to anger the child by saying "no" or to give in to expensive whims and spoil the child.

This problem is not limited to children. In a similar fashion, we adults see a new kind of lawnmower or a new clothing style advertised in our favorite magazine. Suddenly, no matter what condition our old lawnmower or old clothes are in, they look outdated. As a result, we often buy items we can't afford.

Perhaps the worst aspect of advertising is that it constantly bombards us with images of beautiful people. It's hard to appreciate a plain-looking but friendly and hard-working receptionist after staring at the sex goddess in a Seagram's ad. Seeing the beautiful people in the ads may also make us more self-conscious and less confident in relationships. After all, the ads tell us that we need the right cologne, the right clothes, and the right car in order to be attractive. We may throw away chances to meet people or make friends because we're afraid we don't measure up.

All in all, we may never be able to really measure the influence of advertising on our society. However, advertising clearly places many strains on both our bank accounts and our mental health. We would be better off without it.

Post-Test Evaluation Chart

On the following chart, circle the number of any item you got wrong. Next to each item you will see the pages you can review for those items that gave you the most difficulty. Pay particular attention to skill areas where you missed half or more of the questions.

Skill Area	Item Number	Review Pages
Complete sentences and fragments	5, 38, 44, 52	35–40
Parts of a sentence	51	41–49
Nouns, pronouns	1, 50	50–64
Verb tense/form	8, 17, 19, 21, 29, 33, 36, 40, 43, 47	79–100
Subject-verb agreement	2, 4, 13	163–168
Independent and dependent clauses	12, 23, 24, 31, 37, 46, 53	138–157
Modifiers	3, 6, 10, 18, 26, 28, 39	195–205
Parallel structure	22, 34, 54	205–208
Pronoun reference	7, 14, 25, 30, 49, 55	209–222
Sentence and paragraph links	11	241–246
Capitalization, spelling	9, 15, 20, 32, 35, 41, 45, 48	255–276
No error	16, 27, 42	

Writing Skills Practice Test

Directions: The following items are based on a paragraph that contains numbered sentences. Some of the sentences may contain errors in sentence structure, usage, or mechanics. A few sentences, however, may be correct as written. Read the paragraph and then answer the items based on it. For each item, choose the answer that would result in the most effective writing of the sentence or sentences. The best answer must be consistent with the meaning and tone of the rest of the paragraph.

Please note that for this Practice Test, there is no essay topic. Teachers may choose to assign an essay topic at their discretion.

PRACTICE TEST ANSWER GRID

1 ① ② ③ ④ ⑤	15 ① ② ③ ④ ⑤	29 ① ② ③ ④ ⑤	43 ① ② ③ ④ ⑤
2 ① ② ③ ④ ⑤	16 ① ② ③ ④ ⑤	30 ① ② ③ ④ ⑤	44 ① ② ③ ④ ⑤
3 ① ② ③ ④ ⑤	17 ① ② ③ ④ ⑤	31 ① ② ③ ④ ⑤	45 ① ② ③ ④ ⑤
4 ① ② ③ ④ ⑤	18 ① ② ③ ④ ⑤	32 ① ② ③ ④ ⑤	46 ① ② ③ ④ ⑤
5 ① ② ③ ④ ⑤	19 ① ② ③ ④ ⑤	33 ① ② ③ ④ ⑤	47 ① ② ③ ④ ⑤
6 ① ② ③ ④ ⑤	20 ① ② ③ ④ ⑤	34 ① ② ③ ④ ⑤	48 ① ② ③ ④ ⑤
7 ① ② ③ ④ ⑤	21 ① ② ③ ④ ⑤	35 ① ② ③ ④ ⑤	49 ① ② ③ ④ ⑤
8 ① ② ③ ④ ⑤	22 ① ② ③ ④ ⑤	36 ① ② ③ ④ ⑤	50 ① ② ③ ④ ⑤
9 ① ② ③ ④ ⑤	23 ① ② ③ ④ ⑤	37 ① ② ③ ④ ⑤	51 ① ② ③ ④ ⑤
10 ① ② ③ ④ ⑤	24 ① ② ③ ④ ⑤	38 ① ② ③ ④ ⑤	52 ① ② ③ ④ ⑤
11 ① ② ③ ④ ⑤	25 ① ② ③ ④ ⑤	39 ① ② ③ ④ ⑤	53 ① ② ③ ④ ⑤
12 ① ② ③ ④ ⑤	26 ① ② ③ ④ ⑤	40 ① ② ③ ④ ⑤	54 ① ② ③ ④ ⑤
13 ① ② ③ ④ ⑤	27 ① ② ③ ④ ⑤	41 ① ② ③ ④ ⑤	55 ① ② ③ ④ ⑤
14 ① ② ③ ④ ⑤	28 ① ② ③ ④ ⑤	42 ① ② ③ ④ ⑤	

Questions 1–10 refer to the following paragraph.

(1) If you're a woman have you ever wondered why your boyfriend won't ask for directions even after he's been driving around lost for hours? (2) If you're a man, have you ever wondered why your girlfriend keeps wanting to talk about you're relationship, even though things are going fine? (3) Believing that men and women speak different languages, there's scientific evidence that you may be right. (4) Often it's not what people says but how they say it that counts. (5) Boys grow up thinking that the main purpose of talking is to give someone information. (6) Girls grow up thinking that the main purpose of talking is to build emotional closeness. (7) Therefore, it's not surprising that when they grow up and try to talk to each other, they can wind up confused frustrated, and angry. (8) For example, most men don't like to ask directions because they feel it made them inferior to the person who knows the answer. (9) Most women feel that a relationship is working as long as they can talk about it, but most men feel that only if it's not working does he need to talk about it. (10) Before getting angry, the solution is to remember that the other person is not trying to drive you crazy. (11) It's just that his or her language be different from yours.

1. Sentence 1: **If you're a woman have you ever wondered why your boyfriend won't ask for directions even after he's been driving around lost for hours?**

   Which of the following is the best way to write the underlined portion of this sentence? If you think the original is the best way, choose option (1).

   (1) If you're a woman have you
   (2) If you're a woman, have you
   (3) If your a woman have you
   (4) If you're a women have you
   (5) If you're a woman you've

2. Sentence 2: **If you're a man, have you ever wondered why your girlfriend keeps wanting to talk about you're relationship, even though things are going fine?**

   What correction should be made to this sentence?

   (1) change the spelling of *wondered* to *wandered*
   (2) remove the comma after *man*
   (3) change *girlfriend* to *Girlfriend*
   (4) change the second *you're* to *your*
   (5) no correction is necessary

3. Sentence 3: **Believing that men and women speak different languages, there's scientific evidence that you may be right.**

   Which of the following is the best way to write the underlined portion of this sentence? If you think the original is the best way, choose option (1).

   (1) Believing that
   (2) A belief that
   (3) If you believe that
   (4) Believers that
   (5) People who believe that

4. Sentence 4: **Often it's not what people says but how they say it that counts.**

   What correction should be made to this sentence?

   (1) replace *it's* with *its*
   (2) change the spelling of *people* to *poeple*
   (3) change *says* to *say*
   (4) insert a comma after *says*
   (5) no correction is necessary

5. Sentences 5 and 6: **Boys grow up thinking that the main purpose of talking is to give someone information. Girls grow up thinking that the main purpose of talking is to build emotional closeness.**

The most effective combination of Sentences 5 and 6 would include which of the following groups of words?

(1) information, and girls
(2) information, so girls
(3) information as opposed to girls
(4) information; however, girls
(5) information, therefore girls

6. Sentence 7: **Therefore, it's not surprising that when they grow up and try to talk to each other, they can wind up confused frustrated, and angry.**

What correction should be made to this sentence?

(1) replace *it's* with *its*
(2) change the spelling of *surprising* to *surprizing*
(3) change *grow* to *grew*
(4) insert a comma after *confused*
(5) no correction is necessary

7. Sentence 8: **For example, most men don't like to ask directions because they feel it <u>made them inferior to the person who knows the</u> answer.**

Which of the following is the best way to write the underlined portion of this sentence? If you think the original is the best way, choose option (1).

(1) made
(2) makes
(3) has made
(4) are making
(5) were made

8. Sentence 9: **Most women feel that a relationship is working as long as they can talk about it, but most men feel that only if it's not working does he need to talk about it.**

What correction should be made to this sentence?

(1) insert a comma after *women*
(2) change *feel* to *felt*
(3) change *it's* to *its*
(4) change *does he* to *do they*
(5) no correction is necessary

9. Sentence 10: **Before getting angry, <u>the solution is to remember that</u> the other person is not trying to drive you crazy.**

Which of the following is the best way to write the underlined portion of this sentence? If you think the original is the best way, choose option (1).

(1) the solution is to remember that
(2) remember that
(3) one should remember
(4) remembering that
(5) people should remember

10. Sentence 11: **It's just that his or her language be different from yours.**

What correction should be made to this sentence?

(1) change *It's* to *Its*
(2) change *his or her* to *their*
(3) change the spelling of *language* to *langauge*
(4) insert a comma after *language*
(5) change *be* to *is*

Questions 11–20 refer to the following paragraph.

(1) Looking for a job is hard work in the best of times. (2) There are things you can do to improve your chances of getting hired. (3) First, spend some time, figuring out what kind of job you want. (4) Decide what skills you have, what work interests you the most, and whether a good salary, convenient hours, a good location, co-workers you like, or personal fulfillment are most important to you. (5) The next step is for one to apply for the right jobs. (6) Read the want ads, pound the pavement, and tell everybody you know that you're looking for work, you'd be surprised how many people have found jobs through a friend of a friend. (7) Show up on time dress neatly, and be friendly but not pushy. (8) Be ready to answer questions about your past jobs. (9) Why did you leave them? (10) When the interviewer asked if you have any questions, don't say, "How many sick days do I get?" (11) Employers like to think youll care about the company and the job, not just about what they can do for you. (12) After acing the interview, your new boss will welcome you aboard.

11. Sentences 1 and 2: **Looking for a job is hard work in the best of times. There are things you can do to improve your chances of getting hired.**

    The most effective combination of Sentences 1 and 2 would contain which of the following groups of words?

    (1) times, if there are
    (2) times, and there are
    (3) times, since there are
    (4) times, but there are
    (5) times, even though there are

12. Sentence 3: **First, spend some time, figuring out what kind of job you want.**

    What correction should be made to this sentence?

    (1) change *spend* to *spent*
    (2) remove the comma after *time*
    (3) change the spelling of *figuring* to *figgering*
    (4) change *want* to *wants*
    (5) no correction is necessary

13. Sentence 4: **Decide what skills you have, what work interests you the most, and whether a good salary, convenient hours, a good location, co-workers you like, or personal fulfillment are most important to you.**

    What correction should be made to this sentence?

    (1) remove the comma after *have*
    (2) change *interests* to *interest*
    (3) change the spelling of *convenient* to *convenent*
    (4) change *are* to *is*
    (5) change *like* to *liked*

14. Sentence 5: **The next step is for <u>one</u> to apply for the right jobs.**

    Which of the following is the best way to write the underlined portion of this sentence? If you think the original is the best way, choose option (1).

    (1) one
    (2) him or her
    (3) you
    (4) a person
    (5) he

15. Sentence 6: **Read the want ads, pound the pavement, and tell everybody you know that <u>you're looking for work, you'd be surprised</u> how many people have found jobs through a friend of a friend.**

    Which of the following is the best way to write the underlined portion of this sentence? If you think the original is the best way, choose option (1).

    (1) you're looking for work, you'd be surprised
    (2) you're looking for work. You'd be surprised
    (3) your looking for work, you'd be surprised
    (4) you're looking for work. You be surprised
    (5) you looked for work, you'd be surprised

16. Sentence 7: **Show up on time dress neatly, and be friendly but not pushy.**

    What correction should be made to this sentence?

    (1) change *show* to *showed*
    (2) insert a comma after *time*
    (3) change *neatly* to *neat*
    (4) change the spelling of *friendly* to *freindly*
    (5) no correction is necessary

17. Sentences 8 and 9: **Be ready to answer questions about your past jobs. Why did you leave them?**

    The most effective combination of Sentences 8 and 9 would contain which of the following groups of words?

    (1) about leaving your past jobs.
    (2) about why you left your past jobs.
    (3) Are you ready to answer
    (4) answer why you left your past jobs.
    (5) questions about your past

18. Sentence 10: **When the interviewer asked if you have any questions, don't say, "How many sick days do I get?"**

    What correction should be made to this sentence?

    (1) replace *interviewer* with *Interviewer*
    (2) change *asked* to *asks*
    (3) change *don't* to *dont*
    (4) change *get* to *got*
    (5) no correction is necessary

19. Sentence 11: **Employers like to think youll care about the company and the job, not just about what they can do for you.**

    What correction should be made to this sentence?

    (1) change *like* to *liked*
    (2) insert a comma after *think*
    (3) change *youll* to *you'll*
    (4) change the spelling of *company* to *companie*
    (5) replace *they* with *he*

20. Sentence 12: **<u>After acing the interview,</u> your new boss will welcome you aboard.**

    Which of the following is the best way to write the underlined portion of this sentence? If you think the original is the best way, choose option (1).

    (1) After acing the interview,
    (2) After the interview is aced,
    (3) After the interview,
    (4) After you ace the interview,
    (5) After the interview is over,

Questions 21–28 refer to the following paragraph.

(1) Doctors have knew for years that smoking is bad for your health. (2) However, Doctors recently have learned that even breathing someone else's smoke can be very dangerous. (3) Tobacco smoke contains more than forty chemicals. (4) The chemicals in tobacco smoke cause cancer, breathing problems, and heart disease. (5) Nonsmokers who live with smokers has a much greater risk of lung cancer than people who aren't exposed to smoke. (6) Breathing secondhand smoke will kill more than 50,000 people in the united States this year. (7) Secondhand smoke is especially hard on children. (8) Whose lungs are not yet fully formed. (9) Parents should not smoke in the same rooms where their kids is. (10) The only safe amount of tobacco is none, people who smoke are hurting not just themselves but their families.

21. Sentence 1: **Doctors have knew for years that smoking is bad for your health.**

What correction should be made to this sentence?

(1) change *Doctors* to *Doctor's*
(2) change *knew* to *known*
(3) insert a comma after *years*
(4) change the spelling of *health* to *helth*
(5) no correction is necessary

22. Sentence 2: **However, Doctors recently have learned that even breathing someone else's smoke can be very dangerous.**

What correction should be made to this sentence?

(1) change the spelling of *Doctors* to *doctors*
(2) change the spelling of *Doctors* to *Docters*
(3) change *learned* to *learn*
(4) insert a comma after *learned*
(5) change *can be* to *are*

23. Sentences 3 and 4: **Tobacco smoke contains more than forty chemicals. The chemicals in tobacco smoke cause cancer, breathing problems, and heart disease.**

The most effective combination of Sentences 3 and 4 would include which of the following groups of words?

(1) chemicals, of which there are forty, cause
(2) chemicals in tobacco smoke, which
(3) smoke causes cancer,
(4) heart disease are caused by
(5) forty chemicals that cause

24. Sentence 5: **Nonsmokers who live with smokers has a much greater risk of lung cancer than people who aren't exposed to smoke.**

What correction should be made to this sentence?

(1) insert a comma after *smokers*
(2) change *has* to *have*
(3) change *greater* to *greatest*
(4) insert a comma after *people*
(5) change *aren't* to *arent*

25. Sentence 6: **Breathing secondhand smoke will kill more than 50,000 people in the united States this year.**

What correction should be made to this sentence?

(1) change the spelling of *Breathing* to *Breatheing*
(2) insert a comma after *smoke*
(3) replace *will* with *would*
(4) replace *united* with *United*
(5) no correction is necessary

26. Sentences 7 and 8: **Secondhand smoke is especially hard on children. Whose lungs are not yet fully formed.**

Which of the following is the best way to write the underlined portion of these sentences? If you think the original is the best way, choose option (1).

(1) children. Whose lungs
(2) childrens. Whose lungs
(3) children. Who's lungs
(4) children, whose lungs
(5) no correction is necessary

27. Sentence 9: **Parents should not smoke in the same rooms where their kids is.**

Which of the following is the best way to write the underlined portion of this sentence? If you think the original is the best way, choose option (1).

(1) where their kids is
(2) where their kids are
(3) where they kids is
(4) where they're kids are
(5) wear they're kids is

28. Sentence 10: **The only safe amount of tobacco is none, people who smoke are hurting not just themselves but their families.**

Which of the following is the best way to write the underlined portion of this sentence? If you think the original is the best way, choose option (1).

(1) is none, people who smoke
(2) is none. People who smoke
(3) are none, people who smoke
(4) is none, however people who smoke
(5) is none, although people who smoke

Questions 29–37 refer to the following paragraph.

(1) Did you know, that you have several dreams every night? (2) If you don't usually remember your dreams you can teach yourself to. (3) You can even teach yourself to dream about a particular subject and rewrite the dream so they turn out the way you want it to. (4) A method called "lucid dreaming" can help you solve real-life problems, and get rid of nightmares. (5) For example, suppose your boss is getting on your nerves. (6) He's always telling you to do things you were just about to do on your own. (7) Here's what you do: first, just before falling asleep at night, imagine your boss is nagging you to doing something. (8) When in your dream your boss starts to nag them, change the script. (9) Rewind the dream and start doing the task he wants you to do before he show up so that when he walks into the room, he'll have nothing to complain about. (10) The next day, the same thing in real life.

29. Sentence 1: **Did you know, that you have several dreams every night?**

What correction should be made to this sentence?

(1) change *know* to *knew*
(2) remove the comma after *know*
(3) change *have* to *has*
(4) change *dreams* to *dream*
(5) no correction is necessary

30. Sentence 2: **If you don't usually remember your dreams you can teach yourself to.**

What correction should be made to this sentence?

(1) insert a comma after *dreams*
(2) change *don't* to *doesn't*
(3) change the spelling of *usually* to *usally*
(4) change *your* to *one*
(5) no correction is necessary

31. Sentence 3: **You can even teach yourself to dream about a particular subject and rewrite the dream so they turn out the way you want it to.**

What correction should be made to this sentence?

(1) change *teach* to *taught*
(2) change *yourself* to *oneself*
(3) insert a comma after *subject*
(4) change *they turn* to *it turns*
(5) change *it* to *them*

32. Sentence 4: **A method called "lucid dreaming" can help you <u>solve real-life problems, and get rid</u> of nightmares.**

Which of the following is the best way to write the underlined portion of this sentence? If you think the original is the best way, choose option (1).

(1) solve real-life problems, and get rid
(2) solved real-life problems, and get rid
(3) solve real-life problem, and get rid
(4) solve real-life problems and get rid
(5) solve real-life problems, and got rid

33. Sentences 5 and 6: **For example, suppose your boss is getting on your nerves. He's always telling you to do things you were just about to do on your own.**

The most effective combination of Sentences 5 and 6 would include which of the following groups of words?

(1) on your nerves although he's
(2) on your nerves because he's
(3) on your nerves unless he's
(4) on your nerves, therefore he's
(5) on your nerves so that he's

34. Sentence 7: **Here's what you do: first, just before falling asleep at night, imagine your boss is nagging you to doing something.**

Which of the following is the best way to write the underlined portion of this sentence? If you think the original is the best way, choose option (1).

(1) is nagging you to doing something
(2) were nagging you to be doing something
(3) is nagging you to have done something
(4) was nagging you to do something
(5) is nagging you to do something

35. Sentence 8: **When in your dream your boss starts to nag them, change the script.**

What correction should be made to this sentence?

(1) change *your* to *you're*
(2) change *starts* to *start*
(3) change *them* to *you*
(4) remove the comma after *them*
(5) no correction is necessary

36. Sentence 9: **Rewind the dream and start doing the task he wants you to do before he show up so that when he walks into the room he'll have nothing to complain about.**

Which of the following is the best way to write the underlined portion of this sentence? If you think the original is the best way, choose option (1).

(1) before he show up
(2) before, he show up
(3) before he's show up
(4) before they show up
(5) before he shows up

37. Sentence 10: **The next day, the same thing in real life.**

What correction should be made to this sentence?

(1) Remove the comma after *day*
(2) insert *do* after the comma
(3) change *same* to *some*
(4) change *life* to *Life*
(5) no correction is necessary

Questions 38–46 refer to the following paragraph.

(1) You can have muscles like Mr. or Ms. Universe. (2) If you can't function in everyday life, you're not fit. (3) The three elements of fitness are strenth, endurance, and flexibility. (4) For a real-life test of strength, try carry a two-year-old in one arm and a bag of groceries in the other. (5) You can test endurance by running a 10K race or trot up three flights of stairs to your apartment. (6) Flexibility your body's range of motion. (7) Can you do a backbend or touch you're knees with your nose? (8) The real-life test of all three is whether you can bend over to tie your shoes, then make it up three flights of stairs while carrying a toddler and groceries, and not collapse the minute one gets in the door. (9) You don't have to be the sleekest-looking person at the gym to be fit. (10) You just have to be able to make it through an overscheduled, overstressed day and still has enough energy left to enjoy life.

38. Sentences 1 and 2: **You can have muscles like Mr. or Ms. Universe. If you can't function in everyday life, you're not fit.**

The most effective combination of Sentences 1 and 2 would include which of the following groups of words?

(1) Universe, so if
(2) Universe, nor if
(3) Universe, then if
(4) Universe, but if
(5) Universe, therefore if

39. Sentence 3: **The three elements of fitness are strenth, endurance, and flexibility.**

What correction should be made to this sentence?

(1) change *elements* to *element*
(2) change *are* to *is*
(3) insert a comma after *are*
(4) change the spelling of *strenth* to *strength*
(5) no correction is necessary

40. Sentence 4: **For a real-life test of strength, try carry a two-year-old in one arm and a bag of groceries in the other.**

Which of the following is the best way to write the underlined portion of this sentence? If you think the original is the best way, choose option (1).

(1) test of strength, try carry
(2) test of strenth, try carry
(3) test of strength, tried carry
(4) test of strength, try carrying
(5) test of strength, try carried

41. Sentence 5: **You can test endurance by running a 10K race or trot up three flights of stairs to your apartment.**

What correction should be made to this sentence?

(1) change *You* to *One*
(2) change *can test* to *could have tested*
(3) change *running* to *run*
(4) change *trot* to *trotting*
(5) change *your* to *you're*

42. Sentence 6: **Flexibility your body's range of motion.**

    What correction should be made to this sentence?

    (1) insert a comma after *Flexibility*
    (2) insert *is* after *Flexibility*
    (3) change *your* to *you're*
    (4) change *body's* to *bodies*
    (5) no correction is necessary

43. Sentence 7: **Can you do a backbend or touch you're knees with your nose?**

    Which of the following is the best way to write the underlined portion of this sentence? If you think the original is the best way, choose option (1).

    (1) touch you're knees
    (2) touched you're knees
    (3) touches you're knees
    (4) touched your knees
    (5) touch your knees

44. Sentence 8: **The real-life test of all three is whether you can bend over to tie your shoes, then make it up three flights of stairs while carrying a toddler and groceries, and not collapse the minute one gets in the door.**

    Which of the following is the best way to write the underlined portion of this sentence? If you think the original is the best way, choose option (1).

    (1) the minute one gets in the door
    (2) the minute one get in the door
    (3) the minute you'll gets in the door
    (4) the minute you gets in the door
    (5) the minute you get in the door

45. Sentence 9: **You don't have to be the sleekest-looking person at the gym to be fit.**

    If you rewrote Sentence 9 beginning with

    To be fit,

    the next word should be

    (1) you
    (2) the
    (3) don't
    (4) person
    (5) at

46. Sentence 10: **You just have to be able to make it through an overscheduled, overstressed day and still has enough energy left to enjoy life.**

    What correction should be made to this sentence?

    (1) change *You* to *He*
    (2) remove the comma after *overscheduled*
    (3) change *has* to *have*
    (4) insert a comma after *energy*
    (5) change *enjoy* to *enjoyed*

Questions 47–55 refer to the following paragraph.

(1) Scientists have recently discovered a problem called sick building syndrome (SBS) which is caused by indoor pollution. (2) People who get headaches and sniffles when they were cooped up indoors may not have colds at all. (3) He may be suffering from SBS. (4) Inadequate ventilation a major cause of SBS. (5) Air must circulate from outdoors to keep harmful chemical fumes from building up. (6) These fumes come from unexpected places, like carpets curtains, and paneling. (7) The very products someone uses to clean house can make them sick. (8) Animal dander, dust mites, and molds can also cause indoor pollution, the best solution is good ventilation. (9) Fresh air reduces or even eliminates the things in the air that make people sick.

47. Sentence 1: **Scientists have discovered a problem called sick building syndrome (SBS) which is caused by indoor pollution.**

Which of the following is the best way to write the underlined portion of this sentence? If you think the original is the best way, choose option (1).

(1) (SBS) which is caused by
(2) (SBS) which causes
(3) (SBS), which is caused by
(4) (SBS) which are caused by
(5) (SBS) which will cause

48. Sentence 2: **People who get headaches and sniffles when they were cooped up indoors may not have colds at all.**

What correction should be made to this sentence?

(1) change *People* to *One*
(2) change *get* to *gotten*
(3) insert a comma after *sniffles*
(4) change *were* to *are*
(5) change *have* to *has*

49. Sentence 3: **He may be suffering from SBS.**

What correction should be made to this sentence?

(1) change *He* to *They*
(2) remove *may*
(3) change *suffering* to *suffered*
(4) insert a comma after *suffering*
(5) no correction is necessary

50. Sentence 4: **Inadequate ventilation a major cause of SBS.**

What correction should be made to this sentence?

(1) change the spelling of *inadequate* to *inadeqate*
(2) insert *is* after *ventilation*
(3) insert *was* after *ventilation*
(4) change *cause* to *causes*
(5) no correction is necessary

51. Sentence 5: **Air must circulate from outdoors to keep harmful chemical fumes from building up.**

If you rewrote Sentence 5 beginning with

If air cannot circulate from outdoors,

the next word should be

(1) but
(2) so
(3) then
(4) and
(5) moreover

52. Sentence 6: **These fumes come from unexpected places, like carpets curtains, and paneling.**

What correction should be made to this sentence?

(1) change *These* to *This*
(2) change *come* to *came*
(3) change *places* to *place*
(4) insert a comma after *carpets*
(5) no correction is necessary

53. Sentence 7: **The very products someone uses to clean house can make them sick.**

Which of the following is the best way to write the underlined portion of this sentence? If you think the original is the best way, choose option (1).

(1) products someone uses to clean house
(2) products someone uses to clean their house
(3) products someone use to clean house
(4) products people use to clean house
(5) products people use to clean one's house

54. Sentence 8: **Animal dander, dust mites, and molds also cause indoor pollution, the best solution is good ventilation.**

Which of the following is the best way to write the underlined portion of this sentence? If you think the original is the best way, choose option (1).

(1) pollution, the best solution is
(2) pollution, the best solutions is
(3) pollution the best solutions is
(4) pollution. The best solution is
(5) pollution the best solution are

55. Sentence 9: **Fresh air reduces or even eliminates the things in the air that make people sick.**

What correction should be made to this sentence?

(1) change *eliminates* to *eliminate*
(2) insert a period after *air*
(3) change *reduces* to *reducing*
(4) change *make* to *made*
(5) no correction is necessary

ANSWERS BEGIN ON PAGE 340.

Practice Test Answer Key

1. **(2)** The first four words are a dependent clause, so they need to be followed by a comma.

2. **(4)** *You're* means *you are*. *You are relationship* makes no sense, so replace the contraction *you're* with the pronoun *your*.

3. **(3)** The subject of the sentence is *you*, so the clause has to modify *you*. The original version is a dangling participle.

4. **(3)** *Says* is a singular verb, but *people* is a plural noun. Change *says* to its plural form, *say*.

5. **(4)** The word *however* expresses the contrast between the two parts of the sentence. The rewritten sentence would read, "Boys grow up thinking that the main purpose of talking is to give someone information; however, girls grow up thinking that the main purpose of talking is to build emotional closeness."

6. **(4)** Always separate three or more items in a series with commas: *confused, frustrated, and angry*.

7. **(2)** The verb *made* is past tense, but the rest of the sentence (and the rest of the paragraph) is in the present tense. Change the verb to present tense ("it makes . . .") to agree.

8. **(4)** The verb and the pronoun refer back to the plural noun *men*. For agreement, they should be plural too: *do they*.

9. **(2)** The introductory phrase (*Before getting angry*) must modify the subject of the sentence. In the original sentence, the subject is *solution*, and a solution can't get angry. In the rewritten sentence, the understood subject is *you*: "Before getting angry, (you) remember that the other person is not trying to drive you crazy."

10. **(5)** *Be* is an incomplete form of the verb. The present tense singular is *is*: "It's just that his or her language is different from yours."

11. **(4)** *But* expresses the contrast between the two parts of the sentence: "Looking for a job is hard work in the best of times, but there are things you can do to improve your chances of getting hired."

12. **(2)** No comma is required after the word *time* since the phrase *spend some time* is not a renaming phrase, extra information, or a form of direct address.

13. **(4)** Because of the word *or*, the verb should agree only with the noun closest to it. *Fulfillment* is singular, so the verb form should be the singular *is*.

14. **(3)** The sentences before and after this one use the second person ("co-workers *you* like," "*you're* looking for work"), so this sentence should be in the second person as well. The pronoun *one* is third person.

15. **(2)** The original sentence contains two complete thoughts run together. Choice (2) correctly makes them two separate sentences.

16. **(2)** A comma is needed to separate three or more items in a series: *Show up on time, dress neatly, and be friendly*.

17. **(2)** The new sentence would read, "Be ready to answer questions about why you left your past jobs." It's more specific than any of the other choices.

18. **(2)** The rest of the paragraph is in the present tense (*say*, not *said*), so the past-tense verb *asked* should be changed to the present-tense *ask*.

19. **(3)** *You'll* is a contraction for *you will*. Therefore, it should be spelled with an apostrophe.

20. **(4)** In the original sentence, the introductory clause incorrectly modifies the subject of the sentence, *boss*. Choice (4) rewrites the clause so it has its own subject, *you*.

21. **(2)** This sentence is in the past perfect tense. The helping verb *have* needs the verb form *known*.

22. **(1)** The word *doctors* is not a proper noun, so it should not be capitalized.

23. **(5)** The new sentence would read, "Tobacco smoke contains more than forty chemicals that cause cancer, breathing problems, and heart disease." Some of the other choices would be grammatically correct but awkward.

24. **(2)** The subject, *nonsmokers*, is plural, so it takes a plural verb, *have*.

25. **(4)** *United States* is a proper noun, so *United* should be capitalized.

26. **(4)** Sentence 8 is a fragment lacking a subject. It should be attached to Sentence 7 as a dependent clause: "Secondhand smoke is especially hard on children, whose lungs are not yet fully formed."

27. **(2)** The noun, *kids*, is plural, so the plural verb *are* should be used.

28. **(2)** The original sentence contains two complete thoughts run together. Choice (2) correctly makes them two separate sentences.

29. (2) The first three words should not be set off with a comma because that would separate the verb, *know*, from its object.

30. (1) *If you don't usually remember your dreams* is an introductory clause that should be set off with a comma.

31. (4) The pronoun refers back to *dream*, which is a singular noun. So the pronoun should be singular (*it*), not plural (*they*).

32. (4) The verbs *solve* and *get rid of* are two parts of a compound predicate. They should not be separated by a comma.

33. (2) The new sentence would read, "For example, suppose your boss is getting on your nerves because he's always . . ." The word *because* shows that the second part of the sentence is the reason for the first part.

34. (5) *To doing* is not a correct verb phrase. *To do* is a correct verb phrase in the present tense, which is consistent with the rest of the sentence (and the rest of the paragraph).

35. (3) *Your boss* is the subject of this clause; *starts* is the verb. The object pronoun that receives the action should agree with the rest of the paragraph: *you*.

36. (5) *He* is singular, so the verb should be *shows* to agree in number.

37. (2) The original word group is a fragment because it lacks a verb. The verb *do* makes the idea complete.

38. (4) The word *but* expresses the contrast between the two parts of the sentence. The rewritten sentence would read, "You can have muscles like Mr. or Ms. Universe, but if you can't function in everyday life, you're not fit."

39. (4) The *g* in *strength* can cause spelling problems.

40. (4) The original sentence has an incomplete verb form. *Carry* must be changed to the *ing* form, *carrying*. (Of course, "Try to carry . . ." would also be correct.)

41. (4) The two verbs must be parallel in form: "by running . . . and [by] trotting."

42. (2) The original word group is a fragment because it lacks a verb. Adding *is* changes it from a fragment to a complete sentence.

43. (5) *You're* is short for *you are*, and "touch you are knees" makes no sense. Change it from the contraction to the pronoun *your*.

44. (5) The original sentence contains a pronoun shift from *you* to the indefinite pronoun *one*. *One gets* should be changed to *you get*.

45. (1) The new sentence would read, "To be fit, you don't have to be the sleekest-looking person at the gym." The dependent clause *To be fit* modifies the subject of the sentence, *you*.

46. (3) The verb must agree with the subject: "You . . . *have* enough energy . . ."

47. (3) The clause "which is caused by indoor pollution" is an explanatory (nonrestrictive) clause, so it must be set off with a comma. If it were a limiting (restrictive) clause, that part of the sentence would read, "(SBS) that is caused by . . ."

48. (4) The sentence is in the present tense, as are all the sentences that follow. The verb *were* must be changed from past tense to present (*are*).

49. (1) The paragraph is written in the plural. The pronoun that is the subject of this sentence refers back to *people* in the previous sentence. Thus, it should be *they*, not *he*.

50. (2) The original word group lacks a verb. Adding *is* changes it from a fragment to a complete sentence. *Is* also agrees in tense with the rest of the paragraph.

51. (3) The new sentence would read, "If air cannot circulate from outdoors, then harmful chemical fumes may build up." The transition word *then* tells you that the idea in the first part of the sentence causes the action in the second part.

52. (4) Always separate three or more items in a series with commas: *carpets, curtains, and paneling*.

53. (4) The paragraph is written in the third person plural. This sentence must be rewritten to agree ("people use . . .").

54. (4) To avoid a comma splice, separate the two independent clauses with a period to create two sentences.

55. (5) The sentence is correct as written.

Practice Test Evaluation Chart

On the following chart, circle the number of any item you got wrong. Next to each item you will see the pages you can review for those items that gave you the most difficulty. Pay particular attention to skill areas where you missed half or more of the questions.

Skill Area	Item Number	Review Pages
Complete sentences and fragments	15, 26, 28, 37, 42, 50, 54	35–40
Parts of a sentence	6, 16, 29, 32, 52	41–49
Pronouns	2, 19, 43	50–69
Verb tense/form	7, 10, 18, 21, 34, 40, 48	79–100
Subject-verb agreement	4, 13, 24, 27, 36, 46	101–119
Independent and dependent clauses	1, 5, 11, 12, 17, 23, 30, 33, 38, 47, 51	137–177
Modifiers	3, 9, 20, 45	195–205
Parallel structure	41	205–208
Pronoun reference	8, 14, 31, 35, 44, 49, 53	209–231
Capitalization, spelling	22, 25, 39	255–276
No error	55	

Answer Key

CHAPTER 2

EXERCISE 4
page 39

Part A
1. F This group of words does not contain a subject. *Who* hunted?
2. F This group of words does not contain a predicate. *What* did the teenager do?
3. ?
4. .
5. F This group of words does not contain a predicate. *What about* the greatest movie ever made?
6. F This word group lacks a predicate. *What about* pink and purple plaid?
7. !
8. .

Part B
1. ?
2. F This group of words has no predicate. *What about* divided opinions?
3. .
4. F The word group has neither a subject nor a complete predicate. *What comes* from a balanced diet?
5. F The word group is a list of items lacking a subject and a complete predicate. *What* includes several servings of these foods?
6. .
7. .
8. F This group of words has no subject. *Who* substitutes empty calories?
9. F This word group is a list of items. It needs either a predicate (*what about* candy, cookies, and soft drinks?) or a whole sentence to be attached to.
10. ?

Part C
1. ?
2. .
3. .
4. F This word group lacks a subject and a complete predicate. *What happens* in the parking lot?
5. .

6. F The group of words lacks a subject. *Who* needs to learn?
7. F This word group lacks a subject and a complete predicate. *What happens* for stop signs and traffic lights?

EXERCISE 5
page 40

Part A
Here is one possible way to correct each of the fragments. Check to make sure your new sentences are complete, containing both a subject and a predicate.
1. Gary frantically hunted for his billfold.
2. The teenager gossiped on the phone for hours.
5. *King Kong Eats Rhode Island* is the greatest movie ever made.
6. Pink and purple plaid clashes with orange.

Parts B and C
Here is one way to rewrite the paragraphs in order to eliminate fragments. Check to be sure that each of your sentences is complete, containing both a subject and a predicate.

Do most Americans need to take vitamin pills? Opinions are divided on this question. Some nutritional experts say that we can easily get all the vitamins we need from a balanced diet, including several servings of bread and cereals, fruits and vegetables, dairy products, and meat. Others feel that many Americans don't eat properly. They skimp on vegetables. They substitute empty calories from junk food like candy, cookies, and soft drinks. Could both sides be correct?

What mistakes are typical of beginning drivers? One important error is misjudging distances. It takes practice for a driver to estimate correctly how far his car is from the one beside him in the parking lot. A related error is misjudging braking distance. A driver needs to learn how to slow down smoothly for stop signs and traffic lights.

EXERCISE 6
page 46

1. program is
2. truck hit
3. snake slithered
4. (you) leave
5. newspaper is
6. Milk is
7. bills were
8. Statue of Liberty is

EXERCISE 7
page 49

Part A

1. Do you want **scrambled eggs, oatmeal, or grits** for breakfast?
2. **Torrid romances and fatal illnesses** are featured in soap operas.
3. **Sam Abramowitz and Donna Tatum** are studying to become lawyers.
4. The batter **swung blindly, connected, and sprinted** for first base.
5. The food at Bob's Greasy Spoon is **filling but tasteless.**
6. He printed his name at the top of the application form **and began to list his qualifications.**

Part B

You might have answers similar to the examples below. Check to make sure that your sentences are complete and punctuated correctly.
1. On weekends I enjoy sleeping late, working on my motorcycle, and bowling.
2. Two of my favorite television programs are "Your Moment in Court" and "Rancid Romances."
3. I would go to China, Norway, and Brazil.
4. Brian Madden and Jorge Garcia live near me.
5. Writing skills, social studies, science, literature, and mathematics are covered on the GED Tests.

EXERCISE 8
page 51

The following words in each sentence are nouns.
1. plates, mugs, saucepan, vase, sink
2. hook, fights, round
3. earthquake, sections, Mexico City, rubble, thousands, people
4. boundary, United States, Canada, frontier, world
5. western, man, John Wayne
6. team, World Series, years
7. society, wisdom, courage, Americans
8. stare, Suwardy, marriage, trouble
9. Ace Manufacturing Company, plans, employees, month
10. Parenthood, patience, hope
11. vase, roses, daisies
12. changes, countries, world, mapmakers
13. Monica, frustration, anger, George, work

EXERCISE 9
page 54

Part A

The rules referred to in these answers are on pages 52–53.
1. countries (Rule 3)
2. needs (Rule 1)
3. homes (Rule 1)
4. businesses (Rule 2)
5. days (Rule 3)
6. nights (Rule 1)
7. cars (Rule 1)
8. trucks (Rule 1)
9. factories (Rule 3)
10. products (Rule 1)
11. fabrics (Rule 1)
12. people (Rule 6) or persons (Rule 1)
13. lives (Rule 4)

Part B

1. People
2. cities
3. wagons
4. highways
5. coaches
6. Lives
7. men
8. women

EXERCISE 10
pages 56-57

Part A

The rules referred to in these answers are on page 55.
1. **The boy's friend** moved away. (Rule 1)
2. **James's friend** moved away. (Rule 1)
3. **The boys' friend** moved away. (Rule 2)
4. **The ladies' hats** are on sale. (Rule 2)
5. **The firefighters' helmets** are worn for protection. (Rule 3)
6. **Hakkim's dog** is a collie. (Rule 1)
7. In Alaska, **the moose's food supply** ran short last winter. (Rule 3)
8. **The players' mascot** is a chicken. (Rule 2)

Part B

1. My **dog's** favorite ball was out of reach behind her house.
2. In the last two seconds, the **team's** final chance to score appeared.
3. **Chicago's** skyscrapers now rival **New York City's** skyline.
4. **Men's** coats and **women's** sweaters are on sale this weekend only.
5. The **girls'** argument ended when their mothers called them for supper. (We can tell that the word *girls* is plural because of the clue words *their mothers* and *them*.)
6. **Lawyers'** and **doctors'** fees have skyrocketed in recent years.

7. Caroline's last letter arrived only yesterday.

8. The **newspaper's** headline this morning read "Plane Crash Kills 257."

Part C

1. What **men's** or **women's** clothing has been on sale recently?

2. Are **doctors'** fees charged in your local clinic reasonable?

3. What do you think is this **country's** biggest problem?

4. In your opinion, who is the **world's** greatest athlete right now?

5. What is your **region's** major tourist attraction?

6. What do you think is **America's** best musical group?

7. Which of the **newspaper's** job listings do you read?

8. In your opinion, what is your **town's** best restaurant?

EXERCISE 11
page 59

3. John and Sarah
4. lake
5. John and Sarah
6. motorboat
7. John and Sarah
8. John and Sarah
9. John
10. John and Sarah

EXERCISE 12
page 61

1. *She* The pronoun is the subject of the verb *is.*

2. *him* *President Kennedy* should be replaced by an object pronoun since *leaders* is the subject of the verb *challenged.*

3. *My* The possessive pronoun is required here to show that Chun has favorite vegetables.

4. *it* No possession is shown in the sentence.

5. *They* The pronoun is the subject of the verb *voted.*

6. *them* An object pronoun is needed to replace *the senators,* since the subject of the sentence is *What.*

   their The possessive pronoun is used to replace *the senators'* to show that the senators have actions.

7. *your* Use the possessive form to show that the friends have trust.

8. *we* The subject form is needed because it replaces *you and I,* the subject of *can make.*

9. *her* The object form is used to replace *that woman* since the subject of the sentence is *weddings.*

10. *us* The object is used to replace *my partner and me* since the subject of the sentence is understood to be *you.*

EXERCISE 13
page 62

1. *her* Leaving *Young-Soo and* out, we have *Keep an eye on her.* The object form is needed because the subject of the verb *Keep* is understood to be *you.*

2. *I* Leaving *Bob and* out, we have *I plan to be married.* The pronoun is the subject of the verb *plan.*

3. *me* Leaving *your father and* out, we have *Please let me know.* The object form is needed because the subject of the verb *let* is understood to be *you.*

4. *we* Leaving *the Kowalskis and* out, we have *If we will be late.* The pronoun is the subject of the verb *will be.*

5. *she* Leaving *Jessica and* out, we have *Where did she go?* The pronoun is the subject of the verb *did go.*

6. *him, me* Using one pronoun at a time, we have *The flu hit him* and *The flu hit me.* The object forms are needed because the subject of the verb *hit* is *flu.*

7. *They* Leaving *and their cousins* out, we have *They will hold a reunion.* The pronoun is the subject of the verb *will hold.*

8. *he* Leaving *and Scott* out, we have *When he passed.* The pronoun is the subject of the verb *passed.*

9. *them* Leaving *and their children* out, we have *The lottery winnings gave them a secure income.* The object form is needed because the subject of the verb *gave* is *winnings.*

10. *us* Leaving *the Johnsons and* out, we have *They met us.* The object form is needed because the subject of the verb *met* is *They.*

EXERCISE 14
page 64

1. *It's* Use the contraction to show *It is past time.*

2. *Who's* Use the contraction to ask *Who is hiding?*

3. *your* Use the possessive pronoun to show that you had a childhood.

   you're Use the contraction to say that *you are not going to believe.*

4. *theirs* Use the possessive pronoun to show that they have a choice.

5. *its* Use the possessive pronoun to show that America has a name.

6. *its* Use the possessive pronoun to show that the commission had a report.

7. *your* Use the possessive pronoun to show that you have a guess.

8. *Whose* Use the possessive pronoun to show that someone has a name.
9. *Who's* Use the contraction to ask *Who has been stealing?*
10. *There's* Use the contraction to say *There is a stranger.*
 theirs Use the possessive pronoun to say that they don't have a friend.

EDITING PRACTICE
page 65
Part A

 Janet's bedroom looks as though it's just been struck by a tornado. **Blouses,** sweaters, socks, and jeans form a crazy quilt pattern on the **floor**. A solid three-inch layer of old **newspapers** and magazines covers her desk. Half-empty pop cans and candy bar **wrappers** surround the overflowing wastebasket in the corner. **The bed is unmade**. Peeping out from under it are the moldy remains of a large pepperoni pizza that **she** and her best friend **shared two** weeks ago. Never in my life have I seen a room as messy as **hers**!

EXERCISE 15
pages 66-69

1. **(1)** The plural of *block* is *blocks*.
2. **(2)** Commas are used to separate the items in a series but not to separate a series from the rest of the sentence.
3. **(3)** Use the possessive noun to show that the driver had a fault.
4. **(3)** Leaving *John and* out, you can see that the pronoun *I* should be used as the subject of the verb *drove: I drove*.
5. **(5)** The sentence is correct as written.
6. **(5)** *Or lose them entirely?* is a fragment because it lacks a subject. *Who* was losing them? The fragment should be attached to the previous sentence with no comma because *or* connects only two items.
7. **(4)** The phrase *by it is incredible ugliness* doesn't make sense, so the contraction *it's* is incorrect. Use the possessive pronoun *its* to show that the monster had ugliness.
8. **(3)** Use commas to separate items in a series.
9. **(4)** The original is a fragment because it lacks a predicate. What about toxic wastes? Choice (4) adds the verb *are contaminating* to tell what the toxic wastes are doing.
10. **(1)** Leaving *You and* out, we have *I may picture*. Use the subject pronoun as the subject of the verb *may picture*.
11. **(4)** The original is a fragment because it lacks a predicate. What about the picture? Choice (4) rearranges the words and adds the verb *is* to make a complete thought.

12. **(3)** Don't separate the subject from the verb of a sentence with a comma.
13. **(5)** The original word group is a fragment because it lacks a subject. *What* is creating problems? Choice 5 adds the subject *family pattern* and the verb *is* to make a complete statement.
14. **(1)** Nouns ending in *y* preceded by a consonant are made plural by changing the *y* to *i* and adding *es*.
15. **(2)** Use the possessive noun to show that women have salaries.
16. **(2)** By substituting *there is*, which makes sense (*there is no doubt*), you can see that the contraction *there's* is correct.
17. **(1)** The sentence is correct as written.

CHAPTER 3

EXERCISE 1
page 73

Compare your topic sentences to the examples below. Be sure that each sentence is complete and that it states the central point of the paragraph.
1. Money from the property tax increase could benefit our town in many ways.
2. Different exercises strengthen different muscles.
3. Sharon is a reckless driver.
4. Thomas Grosso has a huge appetite.

EXERCISE 2
pages 75-76

1. Cross out *c*. Other examples might include Christmas wrapping paper displays in December and turkeys promoted before Thanksgiving.
2. Cross out *a*. Other examples might include *sew-so, there-their, way-weigh,* and *bear-bare*.
3. Cross out *c*. Other examples might include tacos from Mexico and lasagna from Italy.
4. Cross out *b*. Other examples might include daytime soap operas with laundry detergent commercials and baseball games with beer commercials.
5. Cross out *b*. Other examples might include test condition of brakes and check body for dents that indicate an accident.

EXERCISE 3
page 76

A sample response for each paragraph appears below. Make sure each of your paragraphs has a topic sentence that identifies the problem and several supporting sentences that provide specific details about the problem.

Paragraph 1

Marge Watson deserves an award for her many hours of volunteer service to the elderly. For the last five years, she's been helping two older women who no longer drive. She takes them to the grocery store, the bank, and the doctor whenever they need to go. Every Sunday she picks them up for church. Two years ago she contacted our local Girl Scout and Boy Scout troops to arrange for youngsters to do free yard work for senior citizens who request help. Last year she organized a weekly current events discussion group for retired people.

Paragraph 2

Greenbelt Park Road is fast becoming the most dangerous street in town. During good weather, joggers and bicyclists by the dozens use the road. Small children, too, ride their little bikes or rollerskate along the edge of the park. But these people have to compete with motor vehicles traveling at a posted speed limit of forty miles per hour—sometimes faster. I've seen motorcycles doing at least eighty down that road. The street is also a truck route, so there's often a parade of semis, cement trucks, and dumpsters heading toward the highway. It's pure luck that so far no one's been killed there in a traffic accident.

EXERCISE 4
page 82

1. *satisfied* — The time clue *last night* tells you the verb should be in the past tense.
2. *asked* — The past-tense verb *toddled* tells you this verb should also be in the past tense.
3. *arrives* — The time clue *every day* and the present tense verb *leaves* indicate that this verb should be in the present tense.
4. *will picket* — The time clue *tomorrow* indicates the verb should be in the future tense.
5. *travels* — The sentence states a general truth, so the verb must be in the present tense.
6. *robbed* — The time clue *last year* tells you the verb should be in the past tense.
7. *will perform* — The time clue *next week* tells you the verb should be in the future tense.
8. *skips* — The time clue *usually* and the verb *makes* tell you that the sentence describes a usual action, so a present tense verb is needed.
9. *wanted* — The time clue *an hour ago* tells you the verb should be in the past tense.
10. *despise* — The time clue *now* tells you the verb should be in the present tense.

EXERCISE 5
pages 83-84

1. *will be flying* — The time clue *tomorrow at this time* indicates that the verb should be in the future continuing tense.
2. *am thinking* — The time clue *at present* tells you the verb should be in the present continuing tense.
3. *were shivering* — The time clue *at this time last year* indicates that the verb should be in the past continuing tense.
4. *will be visiting* — The time clue *next winter* indicates that the verb should be in the future continuing tense.
5. *am steaming* — The time clue *still* indicates that the verb should be in the present continuing tense.
6. *was returning* — The time clue *yesterday afternoon* indicates that the verb should be in the past continuing tense.
7. *was feeling* — The time clue *last night* tells you the verb should be in the past continuing tense.
8. *are continuing* — The time clue *at the present* indicates that the verb should be in the present continuing tense.
9. *were chirping* — The time clue *yesterday* tells you that the verb should be in the past continuing tense.
10. *will be going* — The time clue *Next fall* indicates that the verb should be in the future continuing tense.

EXERCISE 6
page 86

1. *had cleaned* — The time clue *By six o'clock last night* indicates that the action took place before a specific time in the past, so the past perfect tense is needed.
2. *has worked* — The time clue *since 1986* indicates that an action began in the past and is continuing. The present perfect tense is needed.
3. *had supervised* — The time clue *Before retiring last year* indicates that the action took place before a specific time in the past, so the past perfect tense is needed.
4. *will have passed* — The time clue *by this time next year* shows that an action will be completed before a specific time in the future, so the future perfect tense is needed.
5. *have missed* — The time clue *for the past week* indicates that an action began in the past and is continuing. The present perfect tense is needed.

6. *will have started* The time clue *By next fall* indicates that an action will be completed before a specific time in the future, so the future perfect tense is needed.

7. *had traveled* The time clue *long before Columbus's voyage in 1492* indicates that an action occurred before a specific time in the past, so the past perfect tense is needed.

8. *had* The time clue *before last week's race* indicates that an action occurred before a specific time in the past, so the past perfect tense is needed.

9. *has failed* The time clue *In the past five years* indicates that an action began in the past and is continuing in the present. The present perfect tense is needed.

10. *had degenerated* The time clue *last night* indicates that an action occurred before a specific time in the past, so the past perfect tense is needed.

EXERCISE 7
page 88

1. Millions of people watch soap operas.
2. The marketing department gathered the statistics.
3. The home team will crush the opposing team!

EXERCISE 8
pages 90-91

Part A

1. *played* Spelling rule 1. The time clue *last summer* indicates that the past tense is needed.

2. *hated* Spelling rule 3. The helping verb *has* indicates that the present perfect tense is needed.

3. *earning* Spelling rule 1. The present continuing tense is needed to show that the action is occurring now.

4. *carried* Spelling rule 2. The time clue *in the past* indicates that the past tense must be used.

5. *hoped* Spelling rule 3. The time clue *last month* indicates that the past tense should be used.

6. *studying* Spelling rule 2. The time clue *at the moment* tells you that the verb should be in the present continuing tense.

7. *comparing* Spelling rule 3. The helping verb *were* indicates that the past continuing tense is used.

Part B

1. *is filming* The time clue *at this moment* tells you the verb should be in the present continuing tense to show that the action is occurring right now.

2. *will announce* The time clue *tomorrow morning* indicates that the verb should be in the future tense.

3. *had gained* The time clue *before 6:20* indicates the action occurred before a specific time in the past, so the past perfect tense is needed.

4. *has purchased* The time clue *since 1980* indicates that the action began in the past and is still continuing. The present perfect tense is needed.

5. *will be earning* The time clue *within six months* indicates that the action will occur in the future.

6. *drop-kicked* The past tense verb *snarled* is a clue that this verb should also be in the past tense.

7. *overuse* The sentence expresses a general truth, so the verb should be in the simple present tense.

8. *will be shipped* The time clue *within two weeks* indicates that the action will occur in the future. The passive form is used to show that someone will ship the package.

9. *were loitering* The time clue *last night* indicates that the action was occurring in the past.

10. *is picked* The time clue *every Wednesday* indicates a usual action, so the verb should be in the simple present tense. The passive form is used to show that someone picks up the garbage.

11. *will have completed* The time clue *By next week* indicates that the action will be completed before a time in the future, so the future perfect tense is needed.

12. *remark* The time clue *often* indicates a usual action, so the simple present tense is needed.

EXERCISE 9
page 93

1. *gone* The helping verb *have* indicates that the past participle will be used.
2. *saw* There is no helping verb.
3. *run* The helping verb *have* indicates that the past participle will be used.
4. *brought* You must memorize this irregular past tense.
5. *done* The helping verb *have* (part of the contraction *I've*) indicates that the past participle will be used.
6. *came* There is no helping verb.
7. *were* Without a helping verb in the sentence, the simple past tense must be used.
8. *run* The helping verb *has* indicates that the past participle will be used.
9. *seen* The helping verb *have* (part of *I've*) tells you that the past participle will be used.
10. *come* The helping verb *has* tells you that the past participle will be used.
11. *did* There is no helping verb.
12. *went* There is no helping verb.
13. *brought* You must memorize this irregular past tense.
14. *did* Because there is no helping verb, the main verb must be in the simple past tense.
15. *saw* Because there is no helping verb, the main verb must be in the simple past tense.

EXERCISE 10
page 94

1. *began* Because there is no helping verb, the main verb must be in the simple past tense.
2. *swum* The helping verb *has* indicates that the past participle form must be used.
3. *sang* Because there is no helping verb, the main verb must be in the simple past tense.
4. *shrunk* The helping verb *have* indicates that the past participle form must be used.
5. *rang* Because there is no helping verb, the main verb must be in the simple past tense.
6. *sank* Because there is no helping verb, the main verb must be in the simple past tense.
7. *begun* The helping verb *has* indicates that the past participle form must be used.
8. *swum* The helping verb *have* (part of *I've*) indicates that the past participle form must be used.
9. *rung* The helping verb *has* indicates that the past participle form must be used.

EXERCISE 11
page 95

1. *taken* The helping verb *have* indicates that the past participle form must be used.
2. *chose* The time clue *at our last meeting* indicates that the verb should be in the past tense.
3. *stolen* The helping verb *has* indicates that the past participle form must be used.
4. *knew* The past tense of *know* is irregular.
5. *grown* The helping verb *has* indicates that the past participle form must be used.
6. *eaten* The helping verb *have* (part of the contraction *we've*) indicates that the past participle form must be used.
7. *wrote* Because there is no helping verb, the simple past tense must be used.
8. *broken* The helping verb *have* indicates that the past participle form must be used.
9. *ate* The verb *got* is a clue that the action occurred in the past.
10. *written* The helping verb *has* indicates that the participle form must be used.

EXERCISE 13
page 99

1. *lying* The subject is resting alone.
2. *sit* The subject is moving alone.
3. *raises* The subject is moving an object (the flag).
4. *set* The subject is moving an object (the cup).
5. *laid* The subject moved an object (the money).
6. *rose* The subject moved alone.
7. *lain* The subject rested alone.
8. *sitting* The subject is resting alone.
9. *laid* The subject is moving an object (plans).
10. *lying* The subject is resting alone.

EXERCISE 14
page 100

Before last night, neither the Mad Dogs nor the Spartans **had played** a good game all season. However, last night's football game **began** as a defensive battle and ended as a scoring free-for-all. During the first half, both teams ran the ball. The defensive lines on both sides **were** strong. At the end of the first half, the score was **tied** at 0-0.

In the second half, both teams **opened** with a new strategy. They passed the ball whenever they **saw** an opening. The quarterbacks **did** a superb job of setting up plays. The defensive lines, on the other hand, were **tiring**. They **weren't** blocking nearly as well. As a result, the final score **was** 47–39. By the end of that game, the Spartans **had won** their first victory of the season.

EXERCISE 15
page 104

Part A
1. *doesn't* The subject, *Alice*, is singular.
2. *were* The subject, *We*, is plural.
3. *move* The subject, *daughters*, is plural.
4. *live* The subject, *They*, is plural.
5. *doesn't* The subject, *It*, is singular.
6. *were* The subject, *They*, is plural.
7. *jogs* The subject, *Jim*, is singular.
8. *runs* The subject, *He*, is singular.
9. *don't* The subject, *thunderstorms*, is plural.
10. *think* The subject, *I*, does not take a verb ending in *s*.

Part B
Compare your paragraph with the following example. Be sure that you have written at least five complete sentences in the present tense. No verb should end in *s*, since the subject of each sentence is *I*.

Every day I <u>come</u> home from work exhausted. I <u>grab</u> a glass of iced tea. Then I <u>sink</u> down in an easy chair and <u>turn</u> on the TV. I <u>watch</u> the evening news. After that, I <u>switch</u> channels until I <u>find</u> a pro wrestling match. I always <u>cheer</u> for the underdog.

Part C
Compare your paragraph with the following example. Every verb should end in *s* this time, because the subject of each sentence is *he* or *she*.

Every day he <u>comes</u> home from work exhausted. He <u>grabs</u> a glass of iced tea. Then he <u>sinks</u> down in an easy chair and <u>turns</u> on the TV. He <u>watches</u> the evening news. After that, he <u>switches</u> channels until he <u>finds</u> a pro wrestling match. He always <u>cheers</u> for the underdog.

EXERCISE 16
pages 107

1. *wants* The subjects are connected by *nor*, so the verb agrees with the closer subject, *Damaris*.
2. *stop* The subjects, *subway* and *bus*, are connected by *and*, so the compound subject is plural. *They* stop.
3. *checks* The subjects are connected by *or*, so the verb agrees with the closer subject, *Dorothy*.
4. *provide* Because *lock* and *burglar alarm* are connected by *and*, the compound subject is plural. *They* provide.
5. *contain* Because *potatoes* and *carrots* are connected by *and*, the compound subject is plural. *They* contain.
6. *is* The subjects are connected by *nor*, so the verb agrees with the closer subject, *Montana*.

7. *offer* *San Francisco* and *Boston* are connected by *and*, so the compound subject is plural. *They* offer.
8. *stay* The subjects are connected by *or*, so the verb agrees with the closer subject, *parents*.
9. *interfere* *Spelling* and *handwriting* are connected by *and*, so the compound subject is plural. *They* interfere.
10. *appeals* The subjects are connected by *nor*, so the verb agrees with the closer subject, *skiing*.

EXERCISE 17
page 109

Part A
1. *are* The subject, *sponges*, is plural.
2. *is* The subject, *sock*, is singular.
3. *Are* The subject, *keys*, is plural.
4. *are* The subjects, *apple* and *sandwich*, are joined by *and*, so the compound subject is plural. *They* are.
5. *are* The subjects, *hat* and *coat*, are joined by *and*, so the compound subject is plural. *They* are.
6. *are* The subject, *you*, never takes a verb ending in *s*.
7. *are* The subjects, *the Bulls* and *the Pistons*, are joined by *and*, so the compound subject is plural. *They* are.
8. *Does* The subject, *anyone*, is singular.
9. *doesn't* The subject, *doctor*, is singular.
10. *doesn't* The subject, *government*, is singular.
11. *have* The subject, *two*, is plural.

Part B
Are Americans becoming more interested in physical fitness? There are many indications that they are. There **has** been an increase in the popularity of swimming, biking, and brisk walking. There **are** many companies that offer free use of gyms. They've found that it saves more money on health insurance than it costs them to provide wellness programs. **Do** you do anything special to keep in shape? What fitness activities **are** you interested in?

EXERCISE 18
page 112

1. *is* Crossing out the interrupter, *of butter cookies*, you see that *box* is the singular subject.
2. *knows* Crossing out the interrupter, *with the aid of a multitude of spies*, you see that *Santa Claus* is the singular subject.

3. *have*   Crossing out the interrupter, *of the commission*, you see that the subject, *members*, is plural.

4. *were*   Crossing out the interrupter, *about John Kennedy*, you see that the subject, *specials*, is plural.

5. *have*   Crossing out the interrupter, *of the Central City Chamber of Commerce*, you see that the subject, *members*, is plural.

6. *are*   Crossing out the interrupter, *in this carton*, you see that the subject, *eggs*, is plural.

7. *blows*   Crossing out the interrupter, *on open farmlands*, you see that the subject, *snow*, is singular.

8. *makes*   Crossing out the interrupter, *together with a healthy bank account*, you see that *smile* is the singular subject.

9. *melt*   Crossing out the interrupter, *in an insulated glass*, you see that the subject, *ice cubes*, is plural.

10. *crunches*   Crossing out the interrupter, *of potato chips*, you see that the subject, *package*, is singular.

11. *stops*   Crossing out the interrupter, *loaded with five passengers*, you see that *car* is the singular subject.

12. *does*   Crossing out the interrupter, *as well as the team members*, you see that *coach* is the singular subject.

EXERCISE 19
page 114

1. *wants*   The interrupter is *in the club*. The subject is *everyone*. This pronoun is always singular.

2. *belong*   The interrupter is *of the marbles*. The subject is *none*. This pronoun may be singular or plural, depending on its antecedent. The antecedent of *none* in this sentence is the plural noun *marbles*.

3. *melts*   The interrupter is *of the ice from the polar caps*. The subject is *some*. This pronoun may be singular or plural, depending on its antecedent. The antecedent of *some* in this sentence is the singular noun *ice*.

4. *understand*   The interrupter is *of the listeners*. The subject is *most*. This pronoun may be singular or plural, depending on its antecedent. The antecedent of *most* in this sentence is the plural noun *listeners*.

5. *like*   The interrupter is *of our neighbors*. The subject is *few*. This pronoun is always plural.

6. *has*   The interrupter is *in the audience*. The subject is *someone*. This pronoun is always singular.

7. *wishes*   The subject of this sentence is *nobody*. This pronoun is always singular.

8. *is*   The interrupter is *of the cake*. The subject is *all*. This pronoun may be singular or plural, depending on its antecedent. The antecedent of *all* in this sentence is the singular noun *cake*.

9. *are*   The interrupter is *of the pieces of cake*. The subject is *all*. This pronoun may be singular or plural, depending on its antecedent. The antecedent of *all* in this sentence is the plural noun *pieces*.

10. *bites*   The interrupter is *of these dogs*. The subject is *one*. This pronoun is always singular.

11. *knows*   The interrupter is *with an ounce of brains*. The subject is *anyone*. This pronoun is always singular.

12. *attend*   The interrupter is *of my friends*. The subject is *many*. This pronoun is always plural.

EXERCISE 20
page 115

1. *is*   Omitting the interrupter, *of my pet peeves*, you see that the subject is *one*. This indefinite pronoun is always singular.

   enter   The subject is the plural pronoun *they*.

2. *cause*   Omitting the interrupter, *like aspirin*, you can see that the subject is the plural noun *drugs*.

3. *is*   The compound subject is joined by *or*, so the verb agrees with the closer subject, *check*, which is singular.

4. *provide*   The subjects, *cotton* and *wool*, are joined by *and*, so the compound subject is plural. *They* provide.

5. *hopes*   Omitting the interrupter, *with a lottery ticket*, you see that the subject is *everybody*. This indefinite pronoun is always singular.

6. *do*   In this question, the verb comes before the subject. The subjects, *bride* and *groom*, are joined by *and*, so the compound subject is plural. *They* do.

7. *have*   Omitting the interrupter, *of the cookie crumbs*, you see the subject is *some*. This pronoun may be singular or plural, depending on the antecedent. The antecedent of *some* in this sentence is the plural noun *crumbs*.

8. *are*   In this sentence, the verb comes before the plural subject *cars*.

EXERCISE 21
pages 116-117

1. (4) The other verbs in the sentence, *slammed* and *shot*, indicate that the past tense of *throw* must be used. This is an irregular verb; its past tense is *threw*.

2. (1) This sentence is correct as written. The time clue *last night* indicates that the past tense of the verb should be used. Omitting the interrupter, *of the hottest rock groups in the country*, you see that the subject is *one*. The singular verb *was* agrees with this singular subject.

3. (5) The verb *is* in the first sentence is a time clue that the present tense is also needed in the second sentence. The verb *has* agrees with the singular subject *he*. Because the helping verb *has* is used, you need the past participle of the irregular verb *run* to form the present perfect.

4. (4) Drop the silent *e* on a verb before adding *ing*.

5. (2) The compound subjects, *Danita* and *brothers*, are joined by *nor*, so the verb agrees with the closer subject, which is the plural noun *brothers*.

6. (3) The time clue *later this year* indicates that the verb should be in the future tense.

7. (2) Because there is no helping verb, the past tense of the verb *ring* is needed, not the past participle.

8. (3) The cat was resting alone, so the verb should be a form of *lie*, not *lay*.

EDITING PRACTICE
page 117

As a child I loved having a yard full of trees. I climbed the smaller ones and **sat** for hours on the lower **branches munching** apples and reading. Often my friends and **I** used the trees for Wild West games. The outlaw **lay** in wait behind their broad **trunks and** prepared to spring out at unsuspecting settlers. During the long summer days, our laughter **mingled** with bird songs and the **chattering** of squirrels.

Now I stare out of my apartment onto a barren parking lot and **remember** those days with a sigh. **Are** some other children **having** the time of their lives in my old trees today?

PARAGRAPH REVIEW
pages 118-119

1. (3) Subject and verb must agree in number. In this question, the verb appears before the plural subject *dogs*.

2. (5) The sentence is correct as written.

3. (2) The word group *Like hamsters and parakeets* is a fragment, which must be attached to a complete sentence.

4. (3) When a verb ends in a single vowel and a single consonant and the accent falls on the last syllable, double the final consonant before adding *ed*.

5. (3) Subject and verb must agree in number. Omitting the interrupter, *for the popularity of dogs*, you see that the subject of this sentence is the singular noun *reason*.

6. (1) The original word group is a fragment because it lacks a subject. Who follows the leader? By replacing *following* with *they follow*, you add a clear subject and verb to make a complete sentence.

7. (4) Because the rest of the paragraph is written in the present tense, a present-tense verb is needed in this sentence. The verb must agree with the singular subject *leader*.

8. (2) The time clue *today* tells you that the verb should be in the present tense. The passive form is used to show that someone or something located the farmland.

9. (1) Use commas to separate items in a series.

10. (4) A form of the verb *rise* must be used to show that the subject is acting alone. Because the compound subjects, *trees* and *silo*, are joined by *or*, the verb must agree with the closer subject.

11. (4) Form the plural of a noun ending in a consonant followed by *y* by changing the *y* to *i* and adding *es*.

12. (2) The word *ancestors* is a time clue that this sentence needs a past-tense verb.

13. (2) When adding *ed*, double the final consonant of a verb only if the accent falls on the last syllable of the verb. In *covered*, the accent is on the first syllable.

14. (5) The sentence is correct as written.

CHAPTER 4

EXERCISE 1
page 123

1. **d.** 5
   e. 4
2. **a.** 5
   b. 2
   c. 1
   d. 3
   e. 4
   f. 6
3. **a.** 2
   b. 1
   c. 3
4. **a.** 5
   b. 3
   c. 1
   d. 4
   e. 2

EXERCISE 3
page 127

Here is a sample brainstorm list for topic 3.
3. Reasons for owning a car:
   protection from weather
   ~~cars are expensive to maintain~~
   can carry cargo/passengers
   desire for status symbol
   gives flexibility

EXERCISE 4
pages 127

Here is a sample paragraph for topic 3 from Exercise 3. Make sure both of your paragraphs include a topic sentence that states the cause-effect relationship you are discussing. Then check to be sure all your supporting sentences are relevant to your topic sentence.

Many people want to own a car because of the advantages it gives them. Since it provides protection from the environment, a car allows them to carry out their business regardless of the weather. A car also allows them to carry extra passengers and cargo; therefore, they can make fewer trips to accomplish a task. Moreover, owning a car gives them the flexibility to go where they want, when they want. In addition to all these practical reasons, some people really want to own a car to impress the neighbors.

EXERCISE 5
pages 130-131

Here is a sample chart and paragraph for the second topic.

Items to Discuss	Me	My Best Friend
1. Hobbies	playing piano	photography
2. How we both act	quiet, a loner	likes to be around people
	good listener	good listener
3. How we both look	tall; dark hair	tall; light hair
4. Background	urban	rural

My best friend and I have a few characteristics in common, but in many ways we're very different. She and I are both tall; however, her hair is almost blond while mine is very dark. We have different hobbies, too. She enjoys photography, while I prefer to play the piano. We are both good listeners, but I enjoy time alone while she loves to be in a crowd. Our backgrounds are quite different. She comes from a rural farm family; on the other hand, I was born and raised in the city. Despite our differences, we get along very well.

EXERCISE 7
page 133

Pattern of Organization	Clue Words You Should Have Circled
1. Comparison-Contrast	more
2. Cause-Effect	why
3. Time Order	Explain, how to
4. Cause-Effect	effect
5. Comparison-Contrast	Compare, advantages
6. Simple Listing	List
7. Simple Listing	examples
8. Cause-Effect	causes of

EXERCISE 8
page 135

Part A
1. (5)
2. (2)
3. (5)
4. (3)

Part B

Here is a brainstorm list used in writing the sample paragraph that follows it.

Topic: Effects of TV on my life

watching
TV makes
me too
passive

makes me less sociable (don't want to answer phone or talk to friends/ family while engrossed in TV)

makes me less creative (vegetate in front of TV; don't play piano or read as much as when not watching)

makes me feel sluggish

don't do things I need to (laundry, work, balance checkbook)

eat too much when I watch TV

don't exercise enough (TV makes me passive)

Television has had a negative effect on my life. *by making me too passive for my own good.* ~~It has made me much more passive than when I'm not~~ *This passivity not only affects me as I watch* ~~watching it, and therefore has caused me to miss out on~~ *TV but affects other aspects of my life as well.* ~~some positive aspects of life.~~ For example, vegetating in front of the TV keeps me from doing more creative and satisfying things such as playing the piano, reading, or talking with friends. Moreover, the sluggishness I feel *after* ~~while during~~ I've watched TV for a period of time *taking care of necessities like* prevents me from ~~doing necessary tasks such as~~ laundry, work, and balancing my checkbook. ~~(Maybe that's why I do so much of it!)~~ Because of my passivity from watching the tube, I'm also less prone to exercise *Combined with my tendency to* regularly like I should. ~~In addition, I~~ nibble while I watch TV, this has caused me to gain weight. ~~With~~ *Therefore* ~~these combined factors, I am noticing that I gain weight. As a result of the above,~~ television has caused me to retreat from the world in a negative way, which *has proven* in the long run ~~is~~ detrimental to my well-being.

EXERCISE 9
pages 140–141

Here are some sample answers. Does the conjunction you chose make sense in the new sentence? Make sure your sentences are punctuated properly. Also check each independent clause to make sure it has a subject and a predicate.

Part A

1. Color photographs are bright at first, but they begin to fade in a few years.
2. Do you want spaghetti for supper tonight, or would you prefer pizza?
3. X
4. The crowd roared its approval, and the cheerleaders jumped for joy.
5. The walls of the living room are magenta, and the carpet is daffodil yellow.
6. Andrea was afraid to dive off the high board, for she knew she would do a belly flop.
7. Neither Sam nor Barbara had finished high school, yet they managed to put their three children through college.
8. It was the first warm spring day, so Kelly begged to go outside.
9. X
10. We might look for work in the Minneapolis area, or we might move to Phoenix.

Part B

Your new sentences will vary. Below are some examples. Test the clauses you added to make sure each contains a subject and predicate and expresses a complete thought.

1. The Amadeos wanted a new car, but they couldn't afford to pay Slick Rick's prices.
2. I may decide to move to Texas, or I may stay right here in the Blue Ridge Mountains of Virginia.
3. He wanted to be respected, yet he insulted his employees.
4. Dr. Brady didn't make house calls, nor did he work on Saturdays.
5. Tua is studying computer science, for she wants to invent a new computer program that will make her rich and famous.
6. Mrs. Perez painted her bathroom, and her glasses got speckled with hot-pink paint.
7. Frank Cataldo wants his son to do well in school, so he keeps the dog from chewing up his son's homework.

EXERCISE 10
page 143

1. Correct as written
2. A cup of coffee, a piece of toast, and an orange were all she ate that day.
3. Correct as written

4. Tuan politely requested an application form, and after that he sat down to fill it out.

5. Julio plans to become a diesel mechanic, and Michael wants to play drums in a rock band.

6. Correct as written

7. Automatic transmission, power steering, and power brakes are standard on most models.

8. Job openings are available in restaurants, clothing stores, and lawn care.

9. Maria was watching her favorite soap, and Toni was studying a racing form.

10. The squirrel glanced up, froze momentarily, and darted for the tree.

EXERCISE 11
pages 145-146
Part A

For any connector you missed in the following sentences, go back and review the chart on page 144. Study the meaning of both the correct answer and the connector you chose. Also check the punctuation in each of your sentences.

1. **b** The bus driver was frequently late to work; therefore, she lost her job.

2. **a** I can't stand your cooking; moreover, I despise your taste in music.

3. **b** The rear license plate was missing; however, the police officer didn't give Leon a ticket.

4. **c** Catch up on your child support payments by next month; otherwise, we'll garnishee your wages.

5. **d** Cynthia is sometimes forgetful; for instance, once she bought three bags of groceries at the supermarket and drove home without them.

6. **a** Popcorn is a tasty snack; moreover, it's more nutritious than candy.

7. **c** Our ambassador spoke only English; consequently, he needed an interpreter with him at all times.

8. **a** Eric was placed on probation for two years; in addition, he was ordered to pay back the money he stole.

9. **d** She deeply distrusted his motives; nevertheless, she gave him her address.

10. **c** We hate hot, humid weather; however, we plan to stay in tropical Florida.

Part B

Here are some sample answers. Make sure your sentences are punctuated correctly and make sense.

1. Shan loves to stay up late; however, she went to bed after dinner last night.

2. I want to earn $50,000 a year; therefore, I'm not going to volunteer for the Peace Corps.

3. Kelly bakes the best pies in town; moreover, her cakes take first prize at the local bazaar every year.

4. You should cut down on your drinking; otherwise, you're going to pickle your liver.

5. Theodore is the meanest kid on the block; for example, he pushed Mrs. Brantley off the curb instead of helping her across the street.

EXERCISE 12
page 149
Part A

Here are some sample answers. Make sure your ideas are connected properly, your sentences are punctuated correctly, and you used all three methods at least once each.

1. Harvey couldn't believe his eyes. There was an iguana in the bathtub.

2. He tried to trap the iguana in his old guitar case; however, it had other ideas.

3. Harvey stared thoughtfully at the iguana, and the creature stared back.

4. Suddenly Harvey slapped his forehead. Then he jumped up and ran away.

5. The iguana waited patiently for round two, for it was in no hurry to leave its porcelain palace.

6. Falling in love can be delightful, but it can also be total hell.

7. Women think they have to be gorgeous, and men spend all their time trying to be tough.

8. Some couples manage to give up the pretenses and just love each other. Those are the best relationships.

Part B

Here is an example of how to rewrite the following paragraph. Remember that there is more than one way to correct the run-ons and comma splices. Make sure your sentences are punctuated correctly and make sense.

Used cars are fairly cheap to **buy, but they're** not always cheap to run. We bought a car with seventy thousand miles on the **odometer, and it** ran just fine for three **months. Then** our troubles began. The car began to gulp two quarts of oil a **week; in addition, there** was always a cloud of black smoke following us. Then the transmission started to **go, and we** had to swear at it to get it out of reverse. The electrical system was the last straw. We would turn the heater on, and the lights would go off. We'd had **enough, so we** sold our bargain to a junk collector for ten dollars.

EXERCISE 13
pages 153-154

For each conjunction missed, study its meaning in the chart on page 151. Then reread the sentence to yourself, substituting the correct conjunction for the underlined words.

1. (2) The sentence refers to place, not contrast.

2. (1) The first option, which shows similarity, is correct.

3. (4) The sentence specifies a condition.

4. **(3)** This shows cause and effect.
5. **(1)** Option (1), which shows contrast, is correct.
6. **(4)** Both the original conjunction (*Unless*) and the correct option (4) (*If*) are conditional, but the original doesn't make sense.
7. **(3)** This shows contrast.
8. **(4)** This shows contrast rather than the original's cause and effect.
9. **(1)** The original choice, *After*, is correct because it shows a time relationship.
10. **(5)** Both the original (*Until*) and the correct choice (*Before*) show time, but the original doesn't make sense.

EXERCISE 14
page 155

1. C
2. When he tried to speak, he was pelted with rotten eggs.
3. After his constituents had booed him for the tenth time in fifteen minutes, he wadded up his speech and left the platform.
4. C
5. Although he had done his best, there was no chance for reelection.
6. C
7. While she waited for the store to open, she planned her shopping strategy.
8. Although she was the only customer waiting outside, she stayed close to the door.
9. C
10. Since this clearance sale happened only once a year, she was determined to take advantage of it.

EXERCISE 15
page 157

Part A

1. S	10. S
2. F	11. S
3. S	12. F
4. S	13. S
5. S	14. S
6. F	15. F
7. S	16. S
8. S	17. F
9. F	

Part B

Riding the bus to work is an adventure in people watching. Each morning after I get on at 7:30, the same motley cast assembles. At the first stop after mine, a teenaged couple gets on. They hurry to the back of the bus so that they can hug and kiss undisturbed. Then the sports enthusiast appears. He sits across from the driver and talks nonstop about the latest game. If the driver tries to change the subject, he simply interrupts. My favorite character is the tiny old lady with the shopping bags. Although she never says anything, she observes the other passengers with as much interest as I do. I wonder what she's thinking as she watches our commuting companions. I'm always kind of sorry when the time comes to get off the bus and start working.

EXERCISE 16
page 158

Make sure you punctuated each of your sentences correctly.

1. **a.** After the last guest left, we cleaned the apartment.
   b. The last guest left; then we cleaned the apartment.
2. **a.** When the wind blows hard, the windows rattle.
   b. The wind blows hard; then the windows rattle.
3. **a.** Although Rosa wants to lose weight, she can't resist buttered popcorn.
   b. Rosa wants to lose weight; however, she can't resist buttered popcorn.

EXERCISE 17
page 159

Here are some possible ways you could have correctly combined these pairs of sentences. You should have written at least three combinations for each pair.

1. At fifty-six Leroy mastered fractions, decimals, and percents although he had had difficulty with math as a child.

   Leroy had had difficulty with math as a child, but at fifty-six he mastered fractions, decimals, and percents.

   Leroy had had difficulty with math as a child; however, at fifty-six he mastered fractions, decimals, and percents.
2. Harvey called the dogcatcher when an iguana climbed out of his bathtub.

   An iguana climbed out of Harvey's bathtub, so Harvey called the dogcatcher.

   An iguana climbed out of Harvey's bathtub; then Harvey called the dogcatcher.
3. Bridget has lost twenty-five pounds, and she is determined to lose fifteen pounds more.

   Although Bridget has lost twenty-five pounds, she is determined to lose fifteen pounds more.

   Bridget has lost twenty-five pounds; furthermore, she is determined to lose fifteen pounds more.

EXERCISE 18
page 160

Here are some possible ways to rewrite the sentences. You should have rewritten each sentence three different ways.

1. Tom did not tell Jill about losing the airline tickets; therefore, she was angry with him.

    Jill was angry with Tom because he did not tell her about losing the airline tickets.

    Since Tom did not tell Jill about losing the airline tickets, she was angry with him.

2. Since Gigi needed to feed her cats, she was anxious to get home.

    Gigi needed to feed her cats; consequently, she was anxious to get home.

    Gigi needed to feed her cats, so she was anxious to get home.

3. After Sarah ordered lunch for the department, she made us all watch a soap opera.

    Sarah made the department watch a soap opera after she had ordered us lunch.

    Sarah ordered lunch for the department, and she made us all watch a soap opera.

4. Ann dialed a wrong number, and she got the city morgue.

    Ann got the city morgue when she dialed a wrong number.

    Ann dialed a wrong number; as a result, she got the city morgue.

EXERCISE 19
page 162

1. **(1)** *After Joan put the baby to bed, she poured herself a cup of coffee.* Choices (2), (3), and (5) contain double signals. Choice (4) does not express the correct time order.

2. **(5)** *The grocery store was closed, so we couldn't buy more milk.* This answer is correct because it is the only choice that shows the cause-effect relationship indicated by the word *because* in the original sentence.

3. **(1)** *Although the vandals kicked in the door, they didn't steal anything.* Choice (1) expresses contrast and uses only one conjunction.

4. **(3)** *The clock struck twelve; then the guests decided to leave.* This is the only choice that shows the proper time order relationship.

5. **(2)** *The patient is in critical condition; however, the doctors expect him to recover.* Only this choice shows the contrast expressed in the original two sentences.

EXERCISE 20
page 166

1. **(3)** Putting both clauses in the simple past shows two actions happening at the same time in the past.

2. **(1)** The sentence is correct as written.

3. **(2)** Putting both clauses in the present tense shows that the statement is always true.

4. **(1)** The sentence is correct as written.

5. **(3)** Putting both clauses in the present tense shows that the statement is always true.

6. **(2)** Putting the first clause in the past perfect shows that the action in the first clause happened before the action in the second clause.

7. **(5)** Putting both clauses in past continuing shows that both actions were happening at the same time.

8. **(2)** Putting the first clause in the past perfect shows that the action in the first clause happened before the action in the second clause.

9. **(5)** *Would* is incorrect in this sentence because it is past tense. The verb in the first clause is in the present tense, so the verb in the second clause must be in the present or future. See the list of special helping verbs on page 165.

10. **(4)** Putting both clauses in the present tense shows that the statement is always true.

EXERCISE 21
pages 167-168

Part A

Here are some sample sentences. Make sure your sentences use correct punctuation and the proper verb tense.

1. If we move next year, it will take three semis to transport all of our possessions.

2. His parents were divorced because they had discovered they couldn't get along.

3. Although the lake is shallow, we dive into it headfirst.

4. Hortense coughed whenever Archibald wore his cheap cologne.

5. After the alien spacecraft had landed, we invited the extraterrestrials in for dessert.

6. The nation will be in trouble if we elect those sleazy politicians on the ballot.

7. When David became furious, steam came out of his ears.

Part B

Here are some more sample sentences. Make sure that at least half of your sentences begin with a dependent clause. Check all your verb tenses to make sure they are correct.

1. Although I love to eat a spoonful of peanut butter, it makes my tongue stick to the roof of my mouth.

2. I'm afraid to go to the dentist because I always have a cavity.

3. Whenever my son practices his trumpet, the dog rolls over and plays dead.

4. I won't be able to finish my laundry if I run out of quarters.

ANSWER KEY

5. He ran the marathon as though his life depended on it.

6. Despite the fact that she had butterflies in her stomach, Hildegarde was looking forward to the piano recital.

7. It's not wise to eat a big meal before you go swimming.

8. Until the cows come home, we won't have any milk for supper.

EDITING PRACTICE
page 169

Part A

Do you remember when being a child meant **having red** measles, German measles, mumps, and whooping cough? If you **do, you're** probably at least thirty, for in the last few decades scientists **have** developed vaccines that immunize children against all of these diseases. Although many people thought they were **harmless, they** could actually be quite dangerous. If a pregnant woman **caught** German **measles, her** child might have severe birth defects. Another serious disease was **mumps. It** could cause sterility in adult males. Today **because** the medical community has worked so hard to eliminate them, these diseases are not likely to bother you or **your** children.

EXERCISE 22
pages 170–173

1. **(2)** The ideas in this sentence are related by time, which eliminates choices (1), (4), and (5). Choice (3) does not make sense.

2. **(5)** This is the only choice that expresses the cause-effect relationship indicated in the original sentence.

3. **(3)** This choice is correct because you must use a comma after a dependent clause that begins a sentence.

4. **(1)** Correct as written

5. **(4)** This is the only choice that corrects the double signals in the original sentence.

6. **(3)** Only this choice correctly links the two ideas in the sentence.

7. **(3)** This choice corrects the comma splice in the original sentence.

8. **(5)** Correct as written

9. **(1)** Check: *If you have an inherited tendency toward a specific disease, there may be good news for you.* The other choices make no sense in the new sentence.

10. **(5)** This choice corrects the dependent clause fragment in the original passage.

11. **(3)** In the original sentence, *however* wrongly implies a contrast between the clauses. *In addition* tells you that the second clause adds information to the first.

12. **(2)** This choice both corrects the run-on sentence and preserves its original meaning.

13. **(2)** No comma should follow a conjunction in a dependent clause.

14. **(2)** *For instance* shows that the second clause gives an example of the idea in the first clause.

15. **(4)** The second clause should be in the future tense. The sentence looks into the future with the action in the first clause occurring first.

ORGANIZATION REVIEW
pages 174–177

1. **(5)** The subject of this verb is *reputation and freedom*, a plural compound subject. *Were* agrees with a plural subject.

2. **(1)** *Seen* is a past participle and requires a helping verb. The correct simple past form is *saw*.

3. **(4)** The object pronoun *me* should be used because this pronoun is not the subject of a verb.

4. **(3)** This choice uses the proper punctuation for the connector *then*.

5. **(5)** Correct as written

6. **(4)** The original sentence is a fragment. Choice (4) is a complete sentence and uses the correct verb form.

7. **(2)** This choice separates with a comma the two compound elements *sworn in* and *questioned*.

8. **(5)** Correct as written

9. **(1)** This choice shows the contrast between the two original sentences.

10. **(3)** The verb tense in the first clause is in the past tense, and the two clauses are happening at the same time. The helping verb *would* shows past tense.

11. **(2)** This choice corrects the misspelled plural *storys*.

12. **(1)** This choice correctly puts the verb in the past tense.

13. **(3)** Use a comma after a dependent clause that begins a sentence.

14. **(1)** Correct as written

15. **(4)** This choice corrects the misspelled verb form *writting*.

16. **(1)** Check: *When schoolteacher Christa MacAuliffe was chosen to be the first civilian in space in 1986, space travel became big news again.* The other choices do not express the relationship between the two original sentences.

17. **(2)** The subject of this sentence is *the crew, MacAuliffe, and the shuttle*, a plural compound subject. *Were* agrees with a plural subject.

18. **(3)** The time clue *for years to come* tells you the sentence should be in the future tense.

CHAPTER 5

EXERCISE 1
pages 183-184

One possible outline for each set of items appears below. Your organization may be different. Be sure that your outline contains logical groupings with clear headings to cover the items in each group.

1. Outdoor sports
1. Summer sports
   - Water skiing
   - Baseball
   - Golf
   - Tennis
2. Winter sports
   - Hockey
   - Ice skating
   - Cross-country skiing

2. Transportation
1. Land—private
   - Motorcycles
   - Bicycles
   - Cars
2. Land—public
   - Buses
   - Trains
3. Air
   - Planes
   - Helicopters

3. How to Lose Your Job
1. Don't get along with others
   - Argue with boss
   - Get in fights with coworkers
   - Treat customers rudely
2. Cheat on work hours
   - Regularly arrive late for work
   - Take long breaks
   - Leave work early
3. Steal on the job
   - Steal office supplies
   - Steal store merchandise

EXERCISE 7
page 193

This question asks you to choose *one* aspect of your life that you would like to change and to discuss the *effects* of that imaginary change on your life. The introduction of your essay should identify what you want to change, and the body should contain an explanation of the effects, grouped in a logical way. A sample essay in response to this question appears below.

Brainstorming

Married too young—if I'd married later in life, I would have developed a greater sense of independence.
1. didn't learn to budget my own money
2. didn't make decisions on major purchases—car, home
3. didn't develop my own hobbies—music
4. no chance to travel
5. no chance to develop my talents in hair cutting

Essay

When I was eighteen, Jeff and I had been going steady for two years. My idea of living happily ever after was to get married right away, settle down in a house of our own, and start a family. That's exactly what we did. But now, ten years later, I'm convinced that marrying later in life would have given me a much greater sense of independence.

Marrying early kept me from having a career outside the home. For years, I'd wanted to go to barber school, but after we married there wasn't enough money for both schooling and house payments. When the twins were born, our finances became even tighter. I had no choice but to stay home.

Without the chance to earn my own money, I never got to practice money management. Jeff was the one with the full-time job, so he kept the checkbook and paid the bills. Whenever we made a major purchase, like a new car or a refrigerator, Jeff made the final choice. Without bringing home a paycheck, I never felt that I had the right to share in the financial decision making.

Some people say that getting married makes people grow up in a hurry. For me, though, an early marriage made it harder to grow up in terms of choosing a career and handling money. If I had it to do over again, I would still marry Jeff, but I would postpone that walk down the aisle for a few more years.

EXERCISE 8
page 198

Possible answers appear below. Be sure that your sentences are punctuated correctly. All introductory phrases should be followed by commas.

1. **Smiling seductively,** Samantha sauntered toward Steve.
2. **In the middle of the president's speech,** a reporter shouted a question.
3. **To prevent looting after the shopping mall fire,** the governor called out the National Guard.
4. The campers were awakened by a bear **rummaging through the food supplies.**
5. Vandals smashed the windshields of twelve cars **in the vicinity of West High School last night.**
6. **Shouting and whistling their approval,** the crowd gave Slime Green a standing ovation.
7. The trucker drove an alternate route **to avoid the weigh station.**
8. Dick's Get 'n' Go was robbed **for the third time in less than a year.**
9. **To reduce the chances of catching a cold,** some people take large doses of vitamin C.
10. Smitty and Josh stared in fascinated horror at the tarantula **crawling across their sleeping friend's face.**

11. **Because Joey liked flowers,** he planted tulips and daffodils in his garden.
12. Roberto hid Jorge's sweater, **which was torn and stained,** before Jorge came home.
13. **Because Inez enjoys working with wood,** she has taken classes in carpentry and cabinetmaking.
14. **While Ed was burning leaves in the backyard,** the garage caught fire.

EXERCISE 9
page 200

Sample corrections appear below. Be sure that your corrected sentences have commas following introductory modifiers and that all modifiers are placed near the words they describe.

1. Stuck under his chair
   Morris felt a large, moist blob of bubble gum **stuck under his chair.**
2. Destroyed by hail
   Larry Gunderson stared gloomily at his wheat field **destroyed by hail.**
3. Swinging effortlessly from branch to branch
   The children watched the chimpanzee **swinging effortlessly from branch to branch.**
4. screaming for mercy
   Screaming for mercy, the prisoner was escorted to Death Row by four guards.
5. Gasping for air
   The fans encouraged the marathon runner **gasping for air** to complete the last hundred yards.
6. Hidden behind a layer of dense brown smog
   We could barely see the outlines of the mountains **hidden behind a layer of dense brown smog.**
7. with a neatly trimmed mustache and beard
   A suave gentleman **with a neatly trimmed mustache and beard** strolled through the park.
8. with a slight smile
   With a slight smile, Sonja draped her boa constrictor around the trunk of the apple tree.
9. Eager to recruit top athletes
   Promising high school seniors are offered full scholarships by some colleges **eager to recruit top athletes.**
10. Fuzzy and shriveled
    We finally found the **fuzzy and shriveled** decaying orange in Will's top file drawer.

EXERCISE 10
page 202

Sample corrections appear below; your sentences might be different. Be sure that every modifier clearly describes a specific word in the sentence and that it is placed near the word it describes. In addition, be sure to place a comma after every introductory modifier or clause.

1. Rewinding the VCR
   As I was **rewinding the VCR,** the tape got stuck.
2. Hanging the picture
   While Juanita was **hanging the picture,** the frame slipped and hit her on the head.
3. Returning my library books two weeks late
   Because **I returned my library books two weeks late,** the fine was $1.20.
4. unaware of the road block
   Unaware of the road block, the driver of the getaway car sped down Highway 37.
5. Eager to break for cocktails and dinner
   Because the members were **eager to break for cocktails and dinner,** the meeting was adjourned until eight o'clock the following morning.
6. Stumbling over a fallen log
   As he **stumbled over a fallen log,** the rifle discharged.
7. Despondent about losing his job and filing for bankruptcy
   Despondent about losing his job and filing for bankruptcy, Jim found suicide a tempting prospect.
8. Screeching around the corner
   Screeching around the corner with its horn blaring, a car hit Josef.
9. Singing along with the radio
   The dog winced at Sharon's voice when she **sang along with the radio.**
10. Giggling uncontrollably
    Giggling uncontrollably, I felt the room spin around me after my fourth glass of champagne.

EXERCISE 11
pages 204-205

Part A

1. The Statue of Liberty, a gift from France, stands at the entrance to New York Harbor.
2. Bone strength depends on an adequate supply of calcium, a mineral found in dairy products and some vegetables.
3. This week's lottery winner, a mother of ten from the Bronx, will receive twenty thousand dollars a year for the next twenty years.
4. Use Dazzle, a revolutionary new detergent, to get your clothes sunshine clean.
5. Our store detective is Farley Finck, a man who can spot a shoplifter at fifty paces.

Part B

Sample sentences using renaming phrases appear below. Be sure that in your sentences the renaming phrases appear directly after the word they describe and that they are separated by commas from the rest of the sentence.

1. The movie being shown tonight is *Rocky*, **a film about a common man who makes his dream come true.**
2. Unfortunately, my fiancé's favorite vegetable is cauliflower, **the one food I'm allergic to.**

3. Stephen King's novels, **fast-paced horror stories,** are popular with young adults.
4. Paula Hansen, **my next-door neighbor**, owns the hardware store on Second Street.
5. The plane, **a B-17**, crashed while attempting to make an emergency landing.
6. I've always wanted to visit New Orleans, **a city with a reputation for fine food and great jazz.**
7. Dr. Sidney Boldt, **a sour man with a persistent frown on his face**, had never developed a smooth bedside manner.
8. The band was playing "You Ain't Nothin' But a Hound Dog," **an old Elvis Presley hit**, when Angelo realized he'd forgotten to feed his poodle.
9. Our next speaker is Sharon Moser, **a woman with a keen sense of justice and a determination to protect the rights of all our citizens.**
10. Maggie may have been a Scot, but she refused to eat haggis, **a disgusting concoction of oatmeal and the vital organs of sheep**.

EXERCISE 12
pages 207-208

Part A

Your sentences may differ from the samples below. Be sure that all compound elements are written in the same form.

1. well coordinated, agile, *have strength*
   A gymnast must be well coordinated, agile, and **strong.**
2. knitting, *to play*
   Knitting nose warmers and **playing** Wahoo were Albert's hobbies.
3. brave, honest, *a compassionate man*
   Mr. Bubany was brave, honest, and **compassionate.**
4. adding, subtracting, *multiplication*, dividing
   We can solve arithmetic problems by adding, subtracting, **multiplying**, and dividing.
5. love, *she hates*
   Why does Elizabeth love to cook but **hate** to do dishes?
6. took, drank, *she slept*
   When Felicia had the flu, she took aspirin, drank plenty of liquids, and **slept** a lot.
7. sipping, *if I listened*
   Long ago I discovered that I could relax by sipping a cup of hot tea or **listening** to soft music.
8. in the hallway, through the kitchen, *they got it on the living room carpet*
   The kids tracked mud in the hallway, through the kitchen, and **on the living room carpet.**

9. stopped, *was scratching*, wondered
   Malcolm stopped, **scratched** his head, and wondered what to do next.
10. to have, to care, *when you lose*
    One of life's greatest sorrows is to have a child, to care for him lovingly as he grows, and then **to lose** him to drugs.

Part B
Possible answers appear below. Be sure that all items in each list use the same word form.
1. Three character traits that I admire in a person are **honesty, gentleness,** and **wit.**
2. **Nursing, repairing cars,** and **drafting** are all careers that interest me.
3. In my spare time I like to **cook Chinese food** or **read westerns.**
4. I would like to find out **where my ancestors were born, why they left their homeland,** and **whether they were happier in America.**
5. Yesterday morning **I bought a sack of doughnuts, took them to work,** and **ate all but one.**
6. This country will be a better place to live when our citizens **stop carrying handguns** and **start trusting the police to enforce the law.**
7. An effective speaker talks **slowly** and **clearly.**
8. **Munching popcorn, watching TV, cleaning the attic,** and **talking on the telephone** are good ways to pass the time on a rainy Saturday.

EXERCISE 13
pages 210-211

Sample answers appear below. If your sentences differ, be sure that your wording eliminates any confusion about which word a pronoun might refer to.
1. After **Sam** called **Ted** a liar, they got into a bitter argument.
2. As the dog approached the wounded bear, **the bear** was snarling menacingly.
3. I like November much better than February; **February** is such a dreary month.
4. Steven will probably never speak to James again now that **James** is a millionaire.
5. I can't decide whether to buy the brown shoes or the black ones; **the brown ones** are more expensive, but they'll probably last longer.
6. Although **Maria** wanted to maintain their friendship, Sonja never spoke to her again.
7. C
8. Just as **Tim** was about to step from the curb, Sean glanced up and shouted, "Tim, watch out!"
9. C
10. The country music fans and the rock fans never got along because **the country music fans** thought the others were stupid and crude.

EXERCISE 14
page 213

Sample answers appear below. Be sure that the noun you've substituted in each incorrect sentence makes the meaning clear.

1. You should have seen the children chasing each other around the playground; **the scene** was hilarious.
2. With the growing importance of computers, **schools** need more qualified instructors at all levels.
3. Although the doctor lectured the teenagers on the dangers of smoking, **the warning** didn't stop them from experimenting.
4. **Some people** say that animals grow thicker fur before an unusually harsh winter.
5. When the father rocked and sang to his baby, **his voice** seemed to quiet the child.
6. We asked Laura to get some counseling, but she insisted that **counselors** do more harm than good.
7. Mr. Cutforth was notified last night that he'd won. **The news** excited him so much that he nearly passed out.
8. In the article **scientists** say that acid rain is endangering wildlife and forests in the Northeast.
9. C
10. Marian wanted to go into engineering because **engineers** have an excellent income.

EXERCISE 15
page 215

	Antecedent	Relative Pronoun
1.	movie	that
2.	catcher	who
3.	Soccer	which
4.	birds	that
5.	redwood	which
6.	Lyndon Johnson	who
7.	dogs	which
8.	shift	which
9.	teller	who
10.	house	that

EXERCISE 16
page 218

Part A

	Antecedent	Pronoun
1.	Germany	its
2.	woman	her
3.	Steve, Charles (connected by *and*)	their
4.	cat, dogs (connected by *or*)	their
5.	dog, cat (connected by *and*)	their
6.	paper clip	It (weighs) its
7.	company	its
8.	finches	they
9.	all (members)	their
10.	man	he (begins)

Part B

Children are much less upset by hospital stays if **they have** been prepared properly for the experience. If possible, **they** should be taken on a tour of the hospital before **they are** admitted. Becoming familiar with these new surroundings will reduce **their** anxiety and help them adjust more quickly to being away from home.

EXERCISE 17
page 221

Part A

	Antecedent	Pronoun
1.	our	we
2.	you	you ('re not)
3.	Ramish's	he
4.	farmers, workers (connected by *and*)	their
5.	Alyssa, Cynthia (connected by *and*)	their
6.	I	I
7.	You	you
8.	twins	their

Part B

As we neared the seacoast, the fog enveloped us so thickly that **we** couldn't see two feet in front of our car. **We** felt as if **we** were moving in outer space, with no signposts, no trees, not even a roadway to orient **us**. Even the sounds were muffled. An occasional car droned past us, its driver slowly feeling his way in the opposite direction. Most of the time, though, all **we** could hear was the dull throb of the waves on the beach and the mournful foghorns warning ships away from hidden rocks.

EDITING PRACTICE
page 223

Part A

Break-ins, muggings, and rapes **have** increased dramatically in our community since 1960. With this increase in street **crime, we** citizens have lost much of our freedom. **When we were growing up**, our front door was never locked. **We** simply didn't worry about someone walking in and stealing our property. **When I was eight years old**, my parents let me ride the bus downtown by myself. My **mother, always** a protective person, had no qualms about my safety. A few years later when I was in high school, my friends and I would often meet at five o'clock in the morning and walk six blocks to the **park to** play tennis. **We had no** reason to fear being robbed or raped.

My daughter, **who** is now ten, doesn't enjoy the same freedom I had. Our house is **equipped** with plenty of locks for the doors and a burglar alarm as well. We don't allow Cindy to take the bus alone or **walk** around the neighborhood after **dark. There** are too many reports of robberies and rapes for us to feel safe. For her and for most other children, the fear of crime has taken some of the fun out of childhood.

EXERCISE 18
pages 224-227

1. **(2)** Use commas to separate renaming phrases from the rest of the sentence.
2. **(2)** The pronoun *they* is unclear in this sentence because there is no antecedent for it. The noun phrase *some educators* tells you who says that children should spend less time on drill.
3. **(4)** The sentence contains a series of things that children should be taught to do. For parallel structure, the items in the series should have the same word forms: analyze, *select*, and decide.
4. **(1)** The complete sentence would read, "While the calculators perform the mechanical operations, the children will be able to concentrate on the real thinking skills." This wording avoids misplaced modifiers by making clear what the calculators do and what the children do.
5. **(4)** Previous sentences refer to *the children*. The pronoun that agrees in number and person with this antecedent is *they*.
6. **(1)** The human antecedent *children* requires the human relative pronoun *who*.
7. **(5)** Correct as written
8. **(1)** Separate an introductory modifier from the rest of the sentence with a comma.
9. **(4)** The combined sentence should read, "The higher we climbed, the faster my heart beat." The two parts of the sentence are parallel, because the same word forms are used: *the higher, the faster*.
10. **(4)** If a sentence begins with a modifying phrase, the next word should tell what the phrase describes. Otherwise, the sentence will contain a dangling or misplaced modifier. The complete sentence should read, "Upon finally reaching the peak, we decided that the view made our struggle worthwhile."
11. **(3)** The pronoun *we* used in earlier sentences indicates that first person pronouns should be used throughout the paragraph.
12. **(4)** In this sentence, *which* is a vague pronoun because it has no clear antecedent. What did Frank ignore? The correct version replaces *which* with the noun phrase *their advice*.

13. **(5)** For parallel structure, each item in a series should use the same word form: an expensive car, *a* television set, a trip.
14. **(5)** The sentence is correct as written.
15. **(1)** Use commas to separate renaming phrases from the rest of the sentence.
16. **(2)** The original sentence contains a dangling modifier. *Who* was confronted with a bill? Choice (2) makes clear that Frank was confronted and that he cut up the card.

ESSAY-WRITING REVIEW
pages 228-229

1. **(3)** The first word group is a dependent clause fragment. It should be attached to the second sentence with a comma because it is an introductory clause.
2. **(4)** All items in the series should be made parallel by using the same word forms: builds, increases, and *improves*.
3. **(4)** There is no clear antecedent for the pronoun *this*, so it should be replaced by a noun to eliminate confusion.
4. **(5)** Correct as written
5. **(2)** The subject of the sentence, *injuries* and *concussions*, is plural, so the plural verb *are* must be used.
6. **(2)** The other verb in this sentence, *provides*, is the time clue that this verb should also be in the present tense. *Cheer* agrees with the plural subject *they*.
7. **(3)** The plural pronoun *their* must have a plural antecedent in this sentence. *Swimmers* chart *their* progress.
8. **(2)** The word *but* shows the contrast between not winning a ribbon and still feeling satisfied.
9. **(5)** The word *whereas* shows the contrast between the technology of the first half and that of the second half of the century.
10. **(1)** Use commas to separate renaming phrases from the rest of the sentence.
11. **(1)** If a verb ends in a consonant followed by *y*, change the *y* to *i* when adding *ed*.
12. **(2)** Since the second sentence describes a noun in the first sentence, the sentences can be combined using a relative pronoun. The pronoun *that* must be used instead of *who* because it refers to an object, *computers*. The complete sentence should read: "Automobiles and trucks also contain computers that regulate their fuel and electrical systems."
13. **(4)** The plural verb *are* agrees with the plural subject *computers*.
14. **(1)** The sentence is correct as written. This version maintains parallel structure in the two parts of the sentence by using the same word forms: not only do they *write*, but they also *maintain*.

15. (4) Because the rest of the paragraph is written using present-tense verbs to discuss the use of computers (for example, *take, print, maintain*), this sentence should also use a present-tense verb. The plural verb *allow* agrees with the plural subject *tellers*.

16. (1) Because the main verb follows the helping verb *have*, the past participle form, *become*, must be used.

CHAPTER 6

EXERCISE 1
page 236

The sentences that used circular reasoning in this exercise have sample answers. Make sure that your sentences include specific reasons and don't restate the first clause.

1. City life is more stressful than farm life because the city's extra noise, crowded conditions, and pollution make relaxing very difficult.
2. OK
3. Cigarette smoking is a harmful habit because it causes lung cancer, emphysema, and other life-threatening illnesses.
4. The automobile is one of the most useful inventions of this century; it has made transportation cheaper and more accessible to a broad cross section of the population.
5. OK
6. I believe that water pollution is a serious environmental problem in this country because it contaminates our drinking water and poisons our fish and wildlife.
7. OK
8. Elementary school children should be required to learn a foreign language because it teaches them about a culture other than their own.
9. College athletes should be paid for playing because colleges make a lot of money on ticket sales from games.
10. The minimum wage should be increased by at least one dollar per hour because the current wage does not take the rising cost of living into account.

EXERCISE 2
page 238

Here are some possible examples for each of the general statements.

1. I dropped out of high school because I wanted to earn money to help my mother, who was raising six kids on her own.
2. For instance, we could find out what happened in our families during the Great Depression of the 1930s.
3. For example, assembly line workers often find their work dull because they do the same thing over and over.
4. Day after day, you read stories in magazines and newspapers about rich film stars getting divorced or being hooked on alcohol or drugs.
5. For example, fires can spread very fast when buildings are close together.

EXERCISE 3
page 240

Part A

Here are sample answers to the first five sentences. Make sure your sentences use specific nouns and verbs to show, not just tell, what's happening.

1. Standing in the ticket line of the downtown bus terminal, the elderly grandmother sobbed uncontrollably when she discovered that her wallet had been stolen.
2. Mrs. McGillicuddy's German shepherd, Matildabelle, lunged at her yesterday when she tried to pet the protective dog's newborn pups.
3. The increase in the number of abandoned buildings, vacant lots, and litter-covered streets in Laketown has caused many shopkeepers to move their businesses to better-kept areas of the city.
4. James was so nervous when he changed his newborn daughter Lisa's diapers that he almost poked her with the diaper pin.
5. Seventy-five percent of the apartment buildings in Laketown have been sprayed with graffiti over the last year.

Part B

Here is a sample paragraph. Make sure you have used specific examples to show what you mean.

Joe's Cafe is the worst place to eat in town. First of all, the place is filthy inside and out. When you drive into the lot, you have to dodge empty beer cans, trash, and broken bottles in order to park. Walking in the front door is no improvement. Flies swarm around your head, and cockroaches run for cover with every step you take on the frayed, threadbare carpet. The service is lousy, too. About an hour after you've been seated, Joe waddles out of the kitchen in his grimy apron to clear off the table and take your order. After another hour, he plops an unrecognizable cut of meat swimming in gravy under your nose. Not only does it *look* unappetizing, but it tastes terrible as well. However, the worst is yet to come—the check. Not only have you subjected yourself to horrible abuse, but you now have to pay a fortune for it!

EXERCISE 5
page 244

The following sentences contain sample transition words or phrases. Make sure you use a transition word that links or shows the relationship of the ideas in the two sentences. Also make sure that you use the correct punctuation with your transition word or phrase.

1. **However,** those frontier days are long past.

2. States like Arizona and New Mexico, **for example,** may run short of water for their new residents.
3. **First,** shake the can vigorously. **Next,** point it at your target before pulling the tab to open it. **Finally,** laugh your head off and run away.
4. **In addition**, they must adapt to unfamiliar interviewing practices.
5. The acting, **on the other hand,** is terrible.

EXERCISE 6
page 246

Part A
The following paragraphs use sample transition words and phrases to make clear the relationship between ideas. Be sure to use the correct punctuation with your transitions.

1. You can make Tante Hanne's Apple Macaroons for dessert in forty-five minutes if you follow these simple directions. **First,** butter a pie tin and slice four or five medium apples into it. **Second,** cover the apples with half a cup of sugar and as much cinnamon as desired. **Next,** cream together four tablespoons of margarine and half a cup of sugar. **Then** beat in one egg. Mix in half a cup of flour and a dash of salt. **Finally,** spoon the batter over the apples and bake for half an hour at 350 degrees.
2. High school students should not be allowed to drive for several reasons. **First,** they're not mature enough to handle the responsibility. **For example,** every Friday night one seventeen-year-old I know downs a six-pack of beer and then challenges his classmates to drag race down Main Street.

   Second, cars detract from schoolwork. Most students who own cars work to pay for gas and insurance. **Therefore,** they spend less time on the schoolwork that should be their primary concern.

   Finally, cars give them too much freedom. Instead of cruising the streets looking for parties to crash or girls to pick up, they should be with their families, where more adult supervision is provided.

EXERCISE 7
page 247

Here is a sample paragraph. Read your paragraph aloud to check for repetitive wording.

Frank was annoyed with Lisa because **she** never became angry with **him**. Whenever **he** complained to **her** about anything, Lisa apologized to **him** instead of **getting mad** in return. Frank found it impossible to have a good argument with **her** because **she** refused to **fight back**. Lisa's **unwillingness** to argue simply made Frank **more irritated** than **he** was to begin with.

EXERCISE 8
pages 249-250

Part A
Here are some sample answers.
1. The dress is blue cotton.
2. OK
3. The chicken wings in the refrigerator can be warmed up for supper.
4. The sign that the vandals destroyed last night will cost a thousand dollars to replace.
5. We finally found a large but inexpensive apartment.

Part B
Here is one way to eliminate the wordiness in the original paragraph.

Today's heating costs are dangerously high for poor people. Retired people must rely on a fixed income. Their social security checks just aren't large enough to cover higher utility bills when the weather is cold. Congress should pass a bill to assist people in this situation.

EXERCISE 10
pages 252-253

Here is a sample essay. Notice how the writer has revised it by adding transition words and specifics and by tightening the wording.

Because drunken driving ~~is a serious problem~~ *claims countless lives* in the U.S., I believe something needs to be done to get drunk drivers off the streets and ~~to impress on them the~~ ~~serious nature of their crime. I don't, however, believe~~ *both to try to treat this addiction to alcohol. But simply punishing them for their behavior won't solve the problem. Therefore,* ~~that~~ the proposal to give a mandatory thirty-day jail sentence to those convicted will *not* have a lasting effect in reducing the incidence of drunken driving.

Statistics show that many drunk drivers are repeat offenders ~~, some even having~~ *. Some have even* spent ~~several terms~~ *time* in jail for their crime *, but without result. Doing time fails*. ~~Yet such jail terms don't keep them~~ *to keep them* ~~from going out on the road drunk again because they~~ *from driving drunk because it doesn't* ~~fail to solve~~ *address* the underlying problems causing their dependence on alcohol *, such as job- or family-related stress or fear of inadequacy*

A more effective solution would be to require ~~those~~ *first-time offenders* ~~convicted of drunken driving for the first time~~ to enter a ~~Such a program~~ residential drug/alcohol rehab program. ~~In the~~ *would enable these drivers to* ~~program, they would~~ get the assistance they need to *problems behind* deal with the ~~underlying causes of~~ their alcohol abuse. ~~such as job and family related stress, loneliness, feelings~~ *Addressing* ~~of inadequacy, etc. Such attention to~~ these underlying *is the best way to bring about a lasting* causes ~~would have longer lasting effects than a~~ *solution to drunken driving.* ~~mandatory jail sentence.~~

EXERCISE 11
page 257

1. Although **Margaret** was born in **London**, her parents were **German** citizens.
2. The largest continent in both geography and population is **Asia**, but the highest standards of living are enjoyed by **Europeans** and **North Americans**.
3. What a different world this would be without the inventions of **Thomas A. Edison** and **Alexander Graham Bell**!
4. Thanks to vaccines, potentially dangerous childhood diseases like mumps and **German** measles have been almost eliminated in the **United States**.
5. The relations between this country and our **Latin American** neighbors have not always been friendly.

EXERCISE 12
page 259

1. Last week a Laotian couple moved into the red brick house on Oakdale **Road**.
2. On Monday morning **Governor** O'Reilly will begin a campaign swing around the state.
3. When it's time for **spring** cleaning, Aunt Gladys and her neighbor roll up their sleeves and scour from attic to b̲a̲s̲ement.
4. Two ___ and a **judge** were indicted on April 26 fo___ ___es.
5. ___ he longest **river** in the United ___ gest in the world.
   ___ ristmas are **winter** holidays.
   ___ oad when you reach
   ___ miles until you see the

EXERCISE 14
pages 267-268

Here is the correct spelling of the word you should have picked.

1. C
2. *newsstand* — This correct spelling follows the rule of combining compound words: don't change the spelling of either word when you combine them.
3. *immediately* — Follow the rule of keeping the silent *e* of the base word when you add a suffix that begins with a consonant.
4. *noticeable* — This word keeps its silent *e* before adding a suffix beginning with *a* in order to keep the soft *c* sound.
5. C
6. *marriage* — This word follows the rule of changing the *y* to *i* before adding any suffix other than one beginning with *i*.
7. *occasional* — This word follows the general suffix rule of not changing the spelling of the suffix or the base.
8. *mournful* — Look at the correct spelling of the suffix *ful* in the chart on page 264.
9. *disapprove* — When adding a prefix to a word, don't change the spelling of either the prefix or the base word.
10. *arrangement* — This word follows the rule of keeping the *e* before adding a suffix beginning with a consonant.
11. *friend* — *I* before *E* except after *C*.
12. *believe* — *I* before *E* except after *C*.
13. *foreign* — This word is one of the exceptions (found in the nonsense sentence on page 267) to *I* before *E* except after *C*.
14. *bicycle* — The base word is *cycle*, the prefix is *bi*.
15. *careless* — In general, don't change the spelling of the suffix or the base.

EXERCISE 15
pages 271-272

If you missed any of these, go back and restudy the meanings.

1. quite, principal
2. write, personnel
3. already, accepted
4. thorough, heroin
5. lesson, break, your
6. whole, weak
7. too, lose

 8. dessert, sweet, rolls
 9. hoarse, breath, their
10. It's, past, dinner
11. advice, whether, break
12. They're, wasting, their, dessert
13. all right, board, there, later
14. know, desert, plane, week
15. sole, advice

EXERCISE 16
pages 275-276

Part A

1. *advertise*   You must memorize this spelling.
2. *weigh*   This spelling follows the rule that says "E before I when sounding like A as in neighbor and weigh."
3. *associated*   You must memorize this spelling.
4. *February*   This word is commonly misspelled because the first r is often not pronounced when the word is spoken.
5. *disappointed*   When you add a prefix, don't change the spelling of either the prefix or the base word.
6. *siege*   I before E except after C.

Part B

    Organizing a **surprise** party for a **friend** requires **a lot** of **planning**. You'll need to attend to **usual** matters like **invitations** and refreshments, but you'll have to keep your **activities** a secret. To prevent the guest of honor from **guessing** that anything's up, you must **decide** on a logical **reason** for inviting her to the place where the party will be held. **Another** concern is how to hide the rest of the guests until the proper moment. For the party to be **successful, your timing** must be perfect.

EDITING PRACTICE
page 277

Part A

    Some **psychologists** suggest that **people** can reduce tension by imagining themselves in a peaceful setting. Whenever I use this **advice, I remember** Cave Point, a **park** in Wisconsin on the shore of **Lake** Michigan. I picture myself sitting on top of a cliff overlooking the water. Despite the cool lake breeze, the sun **shining** on my back makes a sweater **unnecessary. Closing** my **eyes, I** soak in the warmth and listen to the **rhythmical** thumping of water in the limestone caves carved by centuries of waves. Once **again** this oasis of **calm works** its **magic, and I** can return to the hassles of everyday life with renewed inner **strength**.

EXERCISE 17
pages 278-281

 1. **(1)** This choice replaces the incorrect possessive pronoun *its* with *it's*, the contraction for *it is*.
 2. **(4)** The word *nations* in this sentence is general, so it should not be capitalized.
 3. **(3)** The specific name *Ohio River* should be capitalized.
 4. **(2)** Drop the silent *e* when adding a suffix beginning with a vowel.
 5. **(2)** To form the plural of a word ending in *y* preceded by a vowel, drop the *y* and add *ies*.
 6. **(3)** *Their* and *there* are commonly confused.
 7. **(1)** You need to memorize this commonly misspelled word.
 8. **(4)** Do not capitalize names of the seasons.
 9. **(3)** To form the plural of a word ending in a hissing sound, add *es*.
10. **(3)** You need to memorize this commonly misspelled word.
11. **(5)** Correct as written
12. **(3)** Drop the silent *e* when adding a suffix that begins with a vowel. Do not double the consonant.
13. **(2)** This choice replaces the incorrect use of the word *hole*, meaning "a gap," with *whole*, meaning "total."
14. **(2)** You need to memorize this commonly misspelled word.

REVISING AND EDITING REVIEW
pages 282-285

 1. **(1)** The subject of the sentence, *citizens*, requires a plural verb, *do*.
 2. **(3)** A word derived from the name of a specific place must always be capitalized.
 3. **(1)** The sentence is correct as written. The singular indefinite pronoun *each* takes a singular verb, *has*.
 4. **(3)** A modifying phrase at the end of a sentence is not set off by a comma.
 5. **(5)** Adding the verb *is* makes this fragment a complete sentence.
 6. **(2)** Sentences 3, 4, and 7 use the first person pronouns *we* and *our*, so this pronoun should also be in first person.
 7. **(3)** This choice uses a connector that correctly shows the contrast indicated by *Although* in the original sentence.
 8. **(1)** Check: *Because of the prejudice of people who have forgotten their immigrant roots, each new group has had to face discrimination in housing, education, and jobs.* This sentence shows the cause-effect relationship.
 9. **(1)** This word is often misspelled becau[se] people don't pronounce the s[econd]

10. (2) Don't separate the subject of the sentence from the predicate with a comma.

11. (4) A comma must precede the conjunction *and* when it connects two independent clauses.

12. (1) A transition word like *however* needs to be set off from the rest of the sentence.

13. (5) Check: *Some patients lie in comas for years, unable to respond to their environment.*

14. (1) This sentence calls for the possessive pronoun *their*.

15. (5) The passage is written in the present tense.

16. (3) This choice corrects the comma splice in the original sentence.

CHAPTER 7

EXERCISE 1
page 303

A sample brainstorming list for the third topic appears below. Your ideas may be completely different. Check to be sure that you have a clear unifying statement, that your details will help explain your point to your reader, and that they are logically arranged.

Unifying statement: Rituals give participants a sense of belonging, importance, and control.

3 gives sense of control over natural forces
birth—christening
death—funeral

1 unifies participants who come together
singing National Anthem at game
saying prayer together in church

2 adds to sense of importance of an occasion
music, oath of office for president
official awarding of medals at Olympics
exchange of vows in wedding ceremony

EXERCISE 2
page 304

The sample essay below builds on the brainstorming list from Exercise 1. It still needs work on revising and editing.

Why ... ore people just move in together instead ... wedding ceremony? Why did teams hol... ...nies for athletic games instead of ... ... does a president have an ... ...ply moving into the Oval ... ...portant part of our lives. ... sense of belonging to ...nts, and to give ... ...icipants in an ...nem is sung ... players are ...ngregation

in a church are brought together when they sing a hymn or recite a prayer. Performing a ritual together gives you a sense of belonging.

Ceremonies also add to the sense of importance of an occasion. Couples which repeat wedding vows making a public, solemn statement of their intention to live together permanently. There decision seems much more significant than an offhand "Let's share an apartment" would be. In the same way, when a president swears in public that he will uphold the Constitution of the united states the whole country realizes the importance of the job and of his commitment to it.

Finally, at a basic level, rituals give people a sense of control over their lives, and this function is especialy evident in funerals. We can't prevent the death of a loved one, but we can organize a ceremony to mark the event. This ritual helps us feel that we are not totally at the mercy of natural forces.

On the surface, ceremonies may seem like a waste of time, empty words repeated unthinkingly. But rituals do have underlying importance. By serving such basic human needs as the desire to belong, to see our actions as important, and to feel in control of our world, these rituals have a real function in our lives.

EXERCISE 3
page 305

Here is a revised and edited version of the sample essay from Exercise 2.

Why don't more people just move in together instead of having a wedding ceremony? Why **do** teams hold opening ceremonies for **athletic** games instead of just starting to play? Why does a president have an inauguration instead of simply moving into the Oval Office? Ceremonies are an important part of our lives. We use these rituals to create a sense of **belonging, to** emphasize the importance of events, and to give ourselves a feeling of control.

Ceremonies help to unify the participants in an event. For the time that the National Anthem is sung before a baseball game, the crowd and the players are performing as a **unit. In** the same way, the congregation in a church are brought together when they sing a hymn or recite a prayer. Performing a ritual together gives **people** a sense of belonging.

Ceremonies also add to the sense of importance of an occasion. Couples **who** repeat wedding vows **are making** a public, solemn statement of their intention to live together permanently. **Their** decision seems much more significant than an offhand "Let's share an apartment" would be. In the same way, when a president swears in public that he will uphold the Constitution of the **United States, the** whole country realizes the importance of the job and of his commitment to it.

Finally, at a basic level, rituals give people a sense of control over their **lives. This** function is **especially** evident in funerals. We can't prevent the death of a loved one, but we can organize a ceremony to mark the event. This ritual helps us feel that we are not totally at the mercy of natural forces.

On the surface, ceremonies may seem like a waste of time, empty words repeated unthinkingly. But **they do have a deeper meaning**. By serving such basic human needs as the desire to belong, to see our actions as important, and to feel in control of our world, these rituals have a **valuable** function in our lives.

Index

ENCYCLOPEDIA OF
GARDENING
TECHNIQUES

American Horticultural Society Editors

DAVID J. ELLIS • FIONA GILSENAN • RITA PELCZAR • GRAHAM RICE

Additional contributors

SIMON AKEROYD • PAUL ALEXANDER • JIM ARBURY
GUY BARTER • HELEN BOSTOCK • LENKA COOKE • MARTYN COX • COLIN CROSBIE
ANDREW HALSTEAD • BEATRICE HENRICOT • LEIGH HUNT • DAVID JEWELL
NICK MORGAN • DEAN PECKETT • ROSEMARY WARD

MITCHELL BEAZLEY

CONTENTS

AHS Encyclopedia of Gardening Techniques

First published in Great Britain in 2008 by Mitchell Beazley,
a division of Octopus Publishing Group Limited,
Endeavour House, 189 Shaftesbury Avenue, London WC2H 8JY
www.octopusbooks.co.uk
www.octopusbooksusa.com

in association with the American Horticultural Society.

An Hachette UK Company
www.hachette.co.uk

This paperback edition published in 2013

Design and layout copyright © Octopus Publishing Group Ltd 2008, 2013
Text copyright © The Royal Horticultural Society 2008, 2013

Distributed in the US by Hachette Book Group USA
237 Park Avenue, New York NY 10017 USA

Distributed in Canada by Canadian Manda Group
165 Dufferin Street, Toronto, Ontario, Canada M6K 3H6

ISBN-13: 978 1 84533 770 4

AMERICAN HORTICULTURAL SOCIETY EDITORS
David J. Ellis, Fiona Gilsenan, Rita Pelczar, Graham Rice

ADDITIONAL CONTRIBUTORS
Simon Akeroyd, Paul Alexander, Jim Arbury, Guy Barter, Helen
Bostock, Lenka Cooke, Martyn Cox, Colin Crosbie, Andrew
Halstead, Beatrice Henricot, Leigh Hunt, David Jewell, Nick
Morgan, Dean Peckett, Rosemary Ward

MITCHELL BEAZLEY
PUBLISHER Alison Starling
COMMISSIONING EDITOR Helen Griffin
SENIOR EDITOR Joanna Chisholm
ART DIRECTOR Tim Foster
ART EDITOR Victoria Burley
PRODUCTION MANAGER Peter Hunt
INSTRUCTIONAL ILLUSTRATIONS Peters and Zabransky Ltd,
Ivan Hissey, Richard Peters, and Coral Mula
LINOCUT CHAPTER OPENER ILLUSTRATIONS Jeremy Sancha
DECORATIVE SCRAPER BOARD ILLUSTRATION Jane Smith

Created and produced for Mitchell Beazley by The Bridgewater
Book Company Ltd

A Cataloging-in-Publication record for this book is available from
the Library of Congress

Typeset in 10pt Caslon

Printed and bound in China

CHAPTER ONE

GARDENING BASICS

7

ASSESSING YOUR YARD AND PLANNING TO MAKE THE best of it can seem daunting, but help is all around. Sometimes research is needed, but often all you need to do is to look at the surrounding yards and neighborhoods to see what grows well in the area and form ideas for yourself based on what you see.

Designing a garden to suit your style and needs can be an exciting opportunity to make a real difference in your life. This chapter includes tips for helping you develop a plan that is both practical and pleasing by designing not only garden areas but also walkways and paths, and other functional aspects of the landscape.

Before you get started you will need to evaluate the soil. This can be a bit tricky, even for experienced gardeners, but it is crucial to do this if you are to grow plants successfully, as soil is the medium in which all garden plants grow. Fortunately, the simple rules in this chapter provide the basic knowledge, sufficient for practical purposes.

Putting theory into practice

Once you have discovered what kind of soil you are gardening on, the next step is to act. Amending the soil is the vital first step in making a successful garden, and the most important soil amendment is organic matter. Getting, making, and retaining organic matter should be central to your gardening work. Fertilizers quickly feed plants, but they will not work unless good soil structure allows roots to take up the nutrients.

Unfortunately what is good for garden plants is also good for weeds. Gardeners have to vigorously eradicate unwanted plants—it cannot be helped and is not always a joyous task, but the methods advocated in this chapter will make reasonably light work of an onerous job.

❧ Mastering pests & diseases

Although well-grown plants that have good root systems and sufficient nutrients are much less likely to suffer pest and disease damage than plants that have not, troubles arise in all yards sooner or later. Some problems are instantly recognizable—if you know the tell-tale signs to look for. The giveaway symptoms and treatments for several common pests and diseases of garden plants are described in this chapter.

Unfortunately, not all problems are easy to diagnose. Plants have limited ways of expressing stress. As a result, you may find it hard to discern the origin of brown or falling leaves, for example, which could be due to a multitude of causes. Gardeners have to be 'plant detectives', and this chapter offers you guidance on what clues to look for and how to interpret each one of them.

Not only are powerful chemical remedies becoming less widely available to gardeners, but many people are uneasy about using them in case harm is done to wildlife or people. Fortunately, prevention is much easier than cure, and if problems do crop up the emphasis in this chapter is on managing rather than eliminating them. Management depends on some understanding of the ways problems and garden plants interact, and the life cycles of pests and diseases. Modern gardeners find this understanding interesting—not only does it help them garden better, but it is also another facet of the fascinating interaction with nature that gardeners can enjoy. Even slugs and snails can be interesting once you know what makes them tick!

CLIMATE & YOUR GARDEN

Understanding your garden in the context of its environment is the key to successful gardening. A garden's environment directly affects what plants will thrive and when tasks should be carried out, so you need to be familiar with the local climate, prevailing weather conditions, and microclimates within your yard—such as sheltered walls, dry shade under trees, and exposed borders—as well as what type of soil you have. Forearmed with all the facts you are likely to find gardening a much more rewarding experience as you work with, rather than against, nature's will.

Hardiness & heat

The 'weather' is what happens day-to-day, while 'climate' refers to the general conditions experienced in an area over a long period. This actually makes life simpler for the gardener. Rather than needing to become an expert at interpreting the weather each day, you only need an understanding of the climate in your garden to get on with many gardening tasks. For example, gardeners who know a little about their local climate will know when the last frost of spring is likely to be, and will plant tender plants outdoors accordingly. With climate change, such predictions will become more difficult; the only advice is to watch the weather and adapt as necessary.

Select plants that are well adapted to the temperatures and rainfall typical of your region; they will thrive and require less care than plants better suited to other climates.

Climate

The climate across North America varies enormously. In some areas it is as warm in winter as it is in summer at the other end of the country. The result, of course, is that gardeners in different parts of the U.S. may grow entirely different plants or, if they cultivate the same plants, grow them in an entirely different way. In California oleanders brighten the median of the freeway from year to year. On the other hand, in Pennsylvania, for example, they must be grown in containers and moved into a protected environment in order to survive winter.

A suburban yard in Arizona or Texas will look entirely different from the same space in Washington state or Maine so giving gardeners good, reliable information about how to grow ornamental and food plants is a challenge. Two crucial factors are tolerance of winter cold and of summer heat.

Zone maps

The United States Department of Agriculture (U.S.D.A.) has created a Hardiness Zones map (*see page 12*). This divides the U.S., Canada, and Mexico into 11 winter hardiness zones based on average annual minimum temperatures. Zone 1, below -50°F, is the coldest; zone 11, above 40°F, is the warmest. This has allowed the American Horticultural Society to rate garden plants according to the coldest zone in which they will grow, or sometimes the range of zones in which they thrive. Details can be found in the American Horticultural Society's *A–Z Encyclopedia of Garden Plants*. These ratings are very widely used in books and magazines, online, in nursery catalogs, and on plant tags.

Hardiness refers to a plant's ability to withstand cold temperatures, but its adaptability to summer conditions, including heat and humidity, significantly impacts on your garden. Light is another critical factor; shade-loving plants would perform poorly in this sunny garden.

Annuals raised from seed are not rated because they are usually grown only for a single growing season.

Winter temperatures, however, are only part of the story. Summer heat is also a factor, influencing the growth of many plants, so the American Horticultural Society created its Heat Zones map (*see page 13*), which divides the country into 12 heat zones. These are not based on the annual maximum summer temperatures but on a more important summer measure for garden plants—the average number of 'heat days' (days with a temperature above 86°F) in a given region. Increasingly, plants' Heat Zone ratings are also now part of the standard information provided.

You can find out the appropriate hardiness zone for your area by visiting the United States Department of Agriculture website or the American Horticultural Society website.

Hardiness & heat tolerance

Although these zones maps are vital sources of basic information about which plants are likely to thrive in your area, they do not tell the complete story. Local and seasonal factors also have an impact.

Plants growing in areas that receive regular deep winter snow cover are insulated against the lowest temperatures, while with less snow cover, or variable cover across the winter, plants are more vulnerable. A plant growing in shade that is kept consistently moist will tolerate more frequent high summer temperatures, and higher temperatures overall, than the same plant growing a few feet away in full sun and dry soil.

THE WEST & CANADA

In the West, publishers Sunset have created a different zone system based on a wider range of factors: not only summer heat and winter cold but also the length of the growing season, the amount of rainfall, and humidity and wind levels. Although used almost exclusively in the West, the whole of the U.S. and southern Canada has been mapped into 45 zones. Although this system has the advantage of being based on more factors that influence plant growth, many gardeners find the large number of zones confusing.

Canada, while rated by the U.S.D.A. for its Hardiness Zone map, also has its own system. Natural Resources Canada first developed a hardiness zone map based on a range of climatic conditions. More recently it has begun to augment this information with reports from gardeners on the plants that actually survive in their area.

Hardiness zones

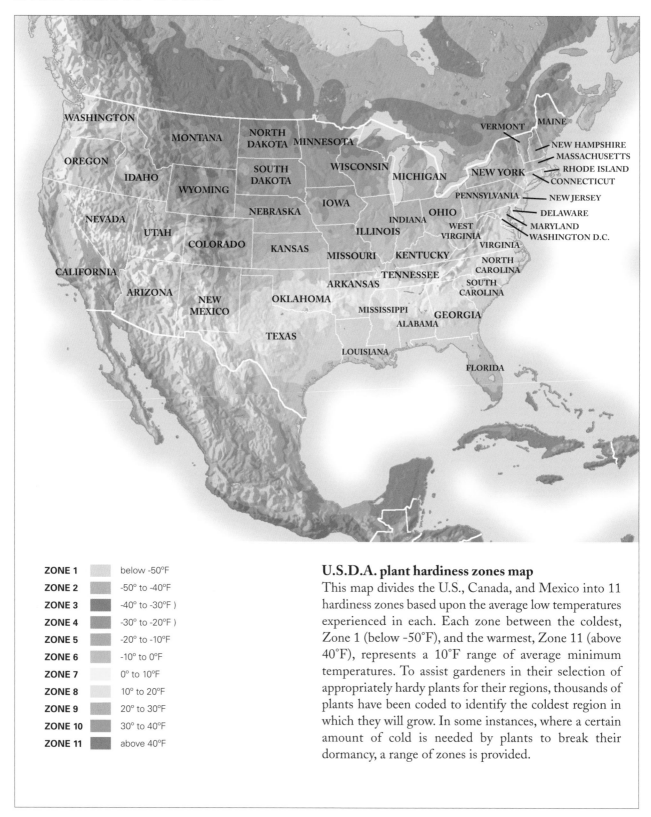

ZONE 1		below -50°F
ZONE 2		-50° to -40°F
ZONE 3		-40° to -30°F)
ZONE 4		-30° to -20°F)
ZONE 5		-20° to -10°F
ZONE 6		-10° to 0°F
ZONE 7		0° to 10°F
ZONE 8		10° to 20°F
ZONE 9		20° to 30°F
ZONE 10		30° to 40°F
ZONE 11		above 40°F

U.S.D.A. plant hardiness zones map
This map divides the U.S., Canada, and Mexico into 11 hardiness zones based upon the average low temperatures experienced in each. Each zone between the coldest, Zone 1 (below -50°F), and the warmest, Zone 11 (above 40°F), represents a 10°F range of average minimum temperatures. To assist gardeners in their selection of appropriately hardy plants for their regions, thousands of plants have been coded to identify the coldest region in which they will grow. In some instances, where a certain amount of cold is needed by plants to break their dormancy, a range of zones is provided.

Heat zones

Average number of days per year above 86°F	ZONE
< 1	1
1 to 7	2
> 7 to 14	3
> 14 to 30	4
> 30 to 45	5
> 45 to 60	6
> 60 to 90	7
> 90 to 120	8
> 120 to 150	9
> 150 to 180	10
> 180 to 210	11
> 210	12

A.H.S. heat zones map

The American Horticultural Society (A.H.S.) developed this map to assist gardeners in their selection of plants that will withstand the summer conditions experienced in their region. The map is divided into 12 zones according to the average number of 'heat days'—days where temperatures reach or exceed 86°F. The number of heat days range from less than one in Zone 1 to more than 210 in Zone 12. Thousands of plants have been assigned a heat zone range that indicates the regions with minimum and maximum amounts of heat necessary to promote healthy growth for the given plant. Like hardiness, a plant's tolerance to heat is influenced by many factors including soil, light, wind, rainfall, and humidity. To check your particular heat zone, enter your zip code on http://www.ahs.org/publications/heat_zone_finder.htm

Know your yard

Zone maps will give you a pretty good idea of the general climate in your area but more local factors can also have a noticeable influence.

Local features

In urban areas temperatures are generally higher (*see page 16*) and your local topography and landscape may also be a significant influence on the growing conditions in your yard. If your area is shaded from the early morning sun or the setting sun by a hill or nearby tall buildings, frost and snow will fade more slowly in spring.

However, in some circumstances, shade from early morning sun can be an advantage; often it is not the cold which damages buds or new shoots on a frosty night, but the early sun thawing them too quickly. So providing shelter from the early morning sun can protect fragile flowers from damage.

If your home is on or near a lake that freezes in winter, that mass of water acts like a heat reservoir in fall and keeps the temperatures in your yard a little higher than in yards farther away; in spring that vast sheet of ice will keep temperatures lower and delay spring a little.

Day length & sunlight

Before you plant, consider the amount of sunlight different parts of the garden get each day. This is a very important determining factor on the type of plants that will grow there. For many plants, sunshine and the accompanying warm temperatures encourage the maximum amount of fruit, flowering, and growth, but there are a great many other plants that thrive in cooler, more shady conditions.

Day length is also worth considering. Not only can it trigger, among other things, leaf fall in fall and flowering, but the angle of the sun differs greatly during short winter and long summer days, casting more or less shade. You will need to judge the amount of sunlight different parts of your garden get and plant accordingly.

Frost

Frost can damage plants by freezing the water in the cells, causing them to burst. In the case of plants that are not hardy to frost, such as begonias and petunias, it will cause the leaves to blacken and die.

Altitude affects how cold it is. For every 1,000ft. rise in altitude, average temperatures drop by 1°F. This makes

MIXED CLIMATE

In this localized climate, the lake shore ❶ has a mild climate due to the water's influence. Slope ❷, which faces south, gets more sun than northfacing slope ❸. Frost pockets ❹ form as cold air flows downhill and is trapped by the ridge. The hilltop ❺ is cooler due to the effect of altitude and wind. The woodland shelters the field ❻ as it filters the prevailing wind. Similar variables will be at play in your own locality.

hilltops and mountainous areas naturally colder, and more frosts can be expected. This is a local factor that may not always be reflected in the zone rating for your area.

Water

When there is insufficient rain or not enough water provided by the gardener, many plants are unable to keep their cells fully inflated with water and they wilt. Where too much rain causes waterlogging, the roots may rot.

You can improve the situation to a certain extent—by watering during drought, by improving the drainage of damp soils. The best solution is to choose plants that suit your local conditions. Plants vary dramatically in the moisture they require, from drought-tolerant succulents and bulbs to plants that only grow in or near water.

Wind

New developments and subdivisions, and many older ones, often have no fence or hedge between properties. The result is that in windy areas it can be less comfortable to sit outdoors. Plants also need more support, and large fragile foliage of plants like bananas, for fruit or ornament, may be damaged more often than if shelter is provided.

So consider not only the windbreaks shown here but also planting an attractive hedge (*see page 121*), or erecting a wall or fence. Be sure to reassure your neighbors about the reason for your decision. As you can see, hedges filter the wind but they also dampen down sound from neighbors. Choose a formal clipped hedge or an informal flowering hedge according to the style of your yard.

Although it is true that a wall or fence can cause turbulence (*see below*) this can be mitigated by planting

TYPES OF WINDBREAK

The best windbreaks allow some wind to filter through. They can be hedges or natural screens (*top*), or porous walls (*center*) or fences (*bottom*). Such barriers are also useful at the bottom of slopes as they stop cold air accumulating to form frost pockets.

wall shrubs and vines so they grow up and over the wall. And of course without a wall or fence on which to train vines, wall shrubs and trained fruit trees, you will be denied the opportunity to choose from the extraordinary range of lovely varieties available.

WIND FLOW

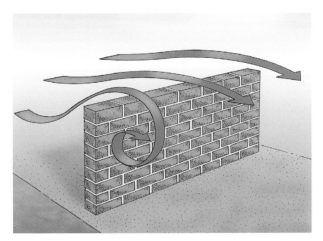

Solid barriers cause turbulence on the lee side. In extreme cases, this can knock plants over and cause walls and fences to collapse.

Porous barriers, like screens of trees and shrubs, are ideal for shelter. They filter the wind, reducing its force and slowing it down.

Microclimates

Once the general climatic conditions are known, you will need to assess what the microclimate is like—the conditions that are unique to your particular yard. Events such as flooding, severe droughts, and hard, late frosts may only occur every five to ten years, and it is these that will set the limits of what can be regarded as truly hardy plants for your yard. But do look out for what grows locally, as this should provide a good indication of what will thrive in your garden.

To begin with, work out the aspect of the yard. South- and westfacing sites are warmer than those that face north or east. Then take into consideration that urban areas often create a 'heat island'. This is where the hard surfaces such as roads and buildings collect heat from the sun and release it at night, raising the temperature. This can mean that a city is as much as 7°F warmer than the surrounding area. Although this sounds good in principle, the high temperatures endured by urban yards in summer, exacerbated by drought, can make the conditions difficult for many.

Planting microclimates

Careful planting to suit the different microclimates of your yard will ensure you get the most out of the conditions. Typical microclimates in suburban gardens include sheltered areas under trees, shrubs, houses, fences, and walls (which are often very dry as they not only get shelter from the wind but also the rain), cold, shady areas along north- and eastfacing walls, and southfacing walls that retain heat in the day and then give it off at night, providing extra protection for tender plants growing against them. Solid fences and walls at the bottom of slopes, dips, and hollows can accumulate cold air in winter, turning them into frost pockets.

MICROCLIMATE

A typical westfacing backyard shows many variations in microclimate that can all be exploited by the gardener. In the example above there are two warm and sunny, sheltered walls: one at the back of the house ❶, which is ideal for tender plants in containers; and another along the side of the garage ❶, which is home to a wall-trained apricot tree. The sunniest spots away from the walls are reserved for the patio, lawn, greenhouse, vegetable garden, and small wildlife pond.

The large tree ❷ at the front of the house casts a lot of early morning shade, while the entry ❸ at the side of the yard acts as a wind tunnel, affecting the garden on the right of the yard. The fence on this side casts shade most of the day, so the border ❹ is filled with shade-loving plants. The compost pile ❺ occupies a cool, shaded position at the top corner of the yard, away from the house.

FROST PROTECTION

Across the country our winters vary from never dropping below freezing all winter to never rising above freezing for months. But in all these areas gardeners try to stretch the limits and grow plants that are on the margins of being tough enough to survive the winter outdoors. A deep 6in. mulch will be enough to protect some plants in your area, while in many yards digging up plants like cannas and dahlias and storing them in a frost-free place like a basement works well.

But you may need to protect larger specimens, even large plants in containers that are too heavy to move, where they grow outdoors. Create a layer of insulation. A wrapping of row cover fabric or plastic over straw packed close to the plant works well or, ideally, create an insulating barrier by setting up two skins of wire netting with straw, burlap, bubble wrap, or packaging air bags in between the two layers.

Gardening with the environment

The aim of any gardener must be to preside over an attractive, healthy, and productive yard that has a minimal impact on the wider environment. This does take more thought, but the result is that resources are saved, and you will have made a positive contribution to the environment. As part of the wider environment, yards can also be of great benefit to wildlife.

A sustainable approach

To garden in an environmentally sensitive way, you can adopt methods pioneered by organic gardeners. These are all fairly easy to put into practice and will minimize your impact on the wider environment, while at the same time promoting all it has to offer.

One of the biggest steps you can take in this direction is to maintain a healthy soil through good cultivation and the regular addition of natural fertilizers, compost, and mulch. Your soil should be teeming with life, which helps aerate the soil so plants can grow strongly, and encourages natural predators that keep pest populations under control.

External inputs to the garden should be naturally derived and, if possible, locally sourced, reclaimed, or recycled. Synthetic pesticides and herbicides should state how best to use them and possible environmental hazards; they are not approved for use in organic systems.

A garden can be built around sustainable principles. Even in this tiny yard, space is found for a bird feeder, a nest-box, a woven fence made from local wood, a compost pile, and a rain barrel.

WATER CONSERVATION

Efficient use of water is essential if plants are to grow well. Most plants, unless they are cacti or succulents, need a continuous supply from the soil, which often means that you will need to irrigate—particularly for container plants during summer and in dry summer climates—when there are long periods between rainfall. It is important, therefore, to understand how and when to water to get the most efficient results and prevent water being wasted, especially with the threat of longer, hotter summers and diminishing water resources due to a changing climate.

Apply the water at the base of a plant, rather than over its leaves and branches, and aim to wet the top 12in. of soil. This moistens the soil around the roots but does not provide excessive amounts that simply drain out of reach of the roots. Water is most needed by plants in containers, new plantings, seedlings, leafy greens, and gardens next to walls and fences. Established trees, shrubs, lawns, and drought-tolerant plants should not need any extra water, even in the driest summer. Lawns will look very bare after a drought, but they usually green up quickly when rain returns.

Aim to conserve water further by digging organic matter, such as well-rotted garden compost, into the soil. This fibrous matter tends to act like a sponge and hold the water in, rather than letting it drain away. The addition of a thick layer of mulch over the surface of the soil will keep the soil underneath moist by reducing evaporation.

Timer systems (*shown above*) can be connected to irrigation pipes that feed water to sprinklers, soaker hoses, or drip irrigation for container plants. Programmable and rain-detecting devices are also available, which makes watering even more efficient.

Store rainwater in rain barrels, where possible, and use this on the soil rather than turning on the outdoor faucet. Gray water collected from bathing and showering can be used on all plants except seedlings, fruit, and vegetables.

GARDEN DESIGN

A garden must be functional as well as beautiful to be enjoyed to the full. Early planning is critical in creating a yard that is practical and cohesive. Visit public gardens and shows with a notepad to jot down ideas and features that you like, and read magazines for ideas and inspiration. Creating a new yard can be expensive, so you should set a realistic budget from the start when choosing materials to avoid disappointment later on. Buying plants and hardscaping material, hiring machinery, or paying for the skills of electricians for lighting or water features all add up financially.

Making a start

From a design point of view, it is easiest to begin with a blank canvas, but most people will be starting with an existing garden and hoping to make changes that will suit their lifestyle and taste.

Deciding what to keep
Begin by making a list of key features in the existing garden that could be tweaked, salvaged, or incorporated into your own plans. There will be no choice but to include some existing features in the design, including

septic drainage fields, surrounding buildings, and dimensions of the site. Consider how these can be worked into the design of the new garden. Check also that there are no legal or homeowners-association restrictions that might influence your plan, such as limits on the height of fences, trees, and hedges.

Avoid committing to anything until you have seen the garden in each of its different seasons; gardens look very different in winter and summer. What might appear to be a private and secluded garden in summer might suddenly

PLANNING A REDESIGN

Before redesign

After redesign

KEY
❶ Shrub beds squeezed against boundary of yard
❷ Unsafe retaining walls
❸ Badly-laid paving slabs
❹ Washing line dividing garden at eye level
❺ Central path dividing garden into unrelated sections
❻ Existing tree
❼ Unsafe steps, not matching other materials
❽ Open corner for trashcans

KEY
❶ Mixed shrub and perennial garden with enough depth for generous planting
❷ New tree
❸ Bed for salad and herbs
❹ Seat under tree providing focal point for yard
❺ Raised beds for annuals, shrubs, and trailers
❻ Curved path around mixed border for easy maintenance
❼ Picnic table with umbrella
❽ Play area with sandbox
❾ Trashcan storage

LOCATION & DESIGN

Small city or urban yards can have unappealing views or be overlooked. It may be necessary to enclose the space using fences, walls, or evergreen hedges and trees.

Suburban gardens allow for a broader canvas and may have features in the background that either need screening or—if they are attractive—incorporated into the view.

Rural gardens may back onto fields or other beautiful views. Keep fences or walls low to incorporate the large sweep of scenery into your yard.

be overlooked in winter when the leaves have fallen from the trees. Make a note of all the plants that flowered throughout the year, which you want to save or remove.

Planning your new yard

Consider where the garden is predominantly going to be viewed from. This is usually from one or more of the windows in the house, so study these views before committing a design to reality.

Your location will influence your design. In rural locations you may borrow views, while in urban spaces you may need to block them. Yards near busy roads may need screening from the noise, and fences and gates incorporated to keep children and pets safe.

It is important that the style of the garden is in keeping with the design of the house. Contemporary, chic gardens work with a modern house but can look out of place around a colonial-style cottage. Use bricks, slabs, and other hardscaping materials that blend in with the architectural features of the surrounding buildings.

Making a sketch

The next stage is to make a simple aerial plan of the garden. Outline the boundaries, the edge of the house, and any features that are definitely staying. Then fill in the additional features that you would like to include, such as paths, lawns, flowerbeds, patios, focal points, and utility areas such as sheds and compost piles. Keep the

sketch simple—detailed planting plans can be created of individual features. Add notes about color, style, and season of interest.

You can use a computer design program, which is easier to manipulate as you develop your plans. Otherwise, draw a sketch of the site using graph paper for scale and proportion. The plan will be a work in progress and will probably need frequent tweaking when the work starts.

Yards are viewed from the ground, either from seating outdoors or from windows. Take your plan and visualize it from these vantage points, perhaps using sketches or drawing on photographs.

Styles & themes

Personal taste will be the main driving force when choosing a style or theme for your garden, but it is worth being aware of options before starting a design.

A yard for a family should be as spacious as possible. Lawns provide a soft surface for play, ideally near the house. A deck or patio for dining is useful, as is outdoor storage for toys, bikes, and garden furniture; and you should install secure gates and fences. Avoid poisonous or spiky plants and water features.

Urban yards and courtyards are usually surrounded by buildings. The design is often contemporary or formal, with modern hardscaping material and decking, and low-maintenance architectural plants rather than lawns. Vines are useful to clothe walls and fences.

Wildlife gardens are increasingly popular. Informal native planting encourages local wildlife: shrubs, hedges, and trees for nesting, meadow grass for a host of insects, and ponds with sloping edges for drinking holes.

Romantic English-style gardens use informal drifts of relaxed planting in wide beds along informal paths, and vines scramble over walls, fences, or rustic arbors. With the addition of fruit trees planted against walls, and vegetables and herbs informally mixed into borders, an ornamental garden can be wonderfully varied as well as useful in your yard.

FAMILY

Many landscapes have designated spaces for outdoor entertaining. This inviting dining area, paved with stone and surrounded by a well-maintained lawn and attractive plantings, provides a relaxing retreat for both informal family meals or special gatherings.

URBAN

Urban yards are often small, so designing to maximize the limited garden area is important. Lawns may be reduced or eliminated altogether to allow more space for ornamental plants. Hardscaping features, such as fences and pathways, can be integrated into the planting design, and should be appropriate for the size of the garden and the style of the house.

WILDLIFE

Sharing a garden with wildlife provides interest beyond plants. The movement of squirrels and chipmunks, the song of birds, the buzz of bees, and the dancing flight of butterflies all contribute to an environment that is alive with activity. Create a habitat for wildlife by selecting a wide variety of plants that provide beauty as well as food and shelter.

ROMANTIC

Romantic landscapes combine lush vegetation and an abundance of flowers to create an intriguing area that begs closer inspection. Such gardens often include old-fashioned shrubs and perennials, vines that ramble over fences and arbors, and windows trimmed with boxes of flowers. Although this type of landscape involves significant maintenance, working in it can be a real joy.

Function & practicality

Your garden should be not only beautiful but also practical. Keep in mind the principle that 'form follows function' and create the design around the practical requirements. Otherwise your yard may well become unusable.

Some basic requirements, such as a shed, a compost pile, or place for the trashcans, are not very attractive. If a yard is large enough, designate one area as the 'working' part of the garden. Screen it with trellis or hedging and tuck it out of sight where it does not impinge on the overall design. Avoid placing it at the back of the yard, because it will be a long walk to put out the trash, and try to avoid creating straight, purely functional paths to these utility areas.

Simplicity

Start by concentrating on the composition as a whole before focusing on the smaller design details. A well-designed yard should flow together as a single entity with all the elements in the right place. Simplicity is key to a relaxing and pleasurable space, and is most important in small spaces. Complicated spaces with too many features become disjointed and messy.

Harmony & balance

Objects or plants placed randomly without relation to the overall style lose their alluring qualities and look cluttered and awkward. In a garden of any size, harmony is

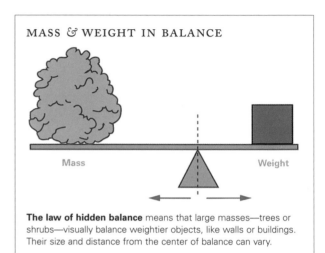

MASS & WEIGHT IN BALANCE

Mass

Weight

The law of hidden balance means that large masses—trees or shrubs—visually balance weightier objects, like walls or buildings. Their size and distance from the center of balance can vary.

important. A garden without it exudes a sense of conflict and clashes with the senses. Keep a simple continuous or cohesive theme, such as using the same paving materials for the paths throughout.

Balance is also important (*see below*). Without it, a space feels awkward. A simple example of balance is using two upright trees in containers on either side of an entrance; a tree on just one side would be incongruous. Sometimes balance is more subtle than such mirror symmetry, with the height of a tree on one side balanced by a mass planting on the other (*see box, above*).

BALANCE IN PLANTING DESIGN

Sparse planting allows hardscaping materials and expanses of grass to dominate and draw the eye. It creates a dull, unbalanced space with little foreground interest.

Massed planting balances the tree and large areas of grass, holding attention on the path. The tree now balances the weight of the foreground planting, drawing the eye beyond them.

Lawns *see page 280* | **Water gardening** *see page 306* | **Container gardening** *see page 342*

FOCAL POINTS

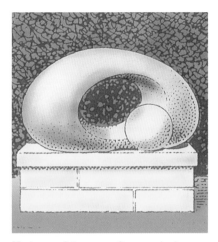

Modern sculptures are often organic shapes that look perfectly at home in a garden.

Gazebos and summerhouses provide a focal point as well as a vantage point.

Individual specimen trees or dramatic foliage plants can be planted as natural focal points.

Focal points & intrigue

Every yard should have focal points to give a sense of purpose to a space and draw you from one area to another. Have only one focal point in any vista, and just one centrally placed focal point in a small courtyard. Simple focal points could include a water feature, a statue or sundial, a tree, a view, or even a splash of color from a strategically placed flower garden. Design the surrounding areas to blend in and reinforce this focus, with paths, low hedges, and walls leading up toward the focal point.

Remember that if all features of a yard can be seen at once, the space can feel dull. Partially conceal areas of the yard to create a sense of intrigue and excitement.

Garden rooms

Divide large areas, especially long, narrow spaces, into 'rooms' to add structure and create different areas of interest. They should never be completely independent but flow from one to another. Create partitions with trellis, arches, or even just a change in planting style. In a small space, low walls divide areas without restriction.

SCREENING

Vertical and horizontal screening can provide both privacy and protection from the elements, whether wind or overhead sun. Here, overhead lumbers, fencing, and planting enclose the dining area.

CREATING INTRIGUE

Create a little intrigue by strategically planting trees and shrubs, erecting a screen to hide the end of a path, or creating alcoves or garden rooms using a trellis and low walls. A suggestion of a hidden space entices people to explore, and even hiding a functional area behind a screen makes a yard seem more complex and interesting.

Walkways & pathways

The walkways and paths that accommodate foot traffic through your yard are important parts of your landscape. These features offer a welcoming entrance to your home and the opportunity for viewing gardens at close range. They can also divide your yard into discrete sections or provide easy passage to utility areas. The material you select for your walkways as well as their dimensions will depend on their intended uses.

Primary walkways

The walk leading to your front door from the street, garage, or parking area should provide an attractive and safe approach to your home. The surface should be smooth and sharp curves avoided so that it is easy to negotiate in any weather, day or night. Ideally it should be at least 5–6ft. wide, to accommodate two people walking side by side or an individual with an armload of groceries. Concrete, flagstone, brick, or manufactured pavers are good choices of material for primary walkways.

Secondary walkways & service paths

Paths that provide access to outlying parts of the yard—a gazebo, pond, play area, garden shed, or vegetable garden—are often less formal and, if space allows, may be less direct. A meandering path can provide planting opportunities along its length, affording visitors the chance to experience the surrounding gardens more intimately. A secondary walkway can also delineate areas of the yard, separating flower borders from a lawn or play area, for example. The same materials used for primary walkways can be used for secondary walks, although a strip of lawn, packed gravel, ground stone, and shredded wood mulch are other options.

If your yard includes a wooded area, woodland paths can provide a relaxing, shady retreat from the more formal or open areas of the yard. The direction these paths follow is often influenced by the presence of existing trees and shrubs. Woodland paths are commonly covered with pine needles, bark, or shredded hardwood mulch and may be attractively edged with ferns and woodland flowers.

A simple service path 3ft. wide will accommodate a single person carrying a load as they travel to and from a compost bin, garbage can, or woodpile. Keep service paths as direct and smooth as possible. To facilitate the maintenance of deep borders, strategically place stepping stones through the planted area. The stones make it easier to reach plants without trampling them. Space them evenly, the distance of a comfortable stride between each stepping stone.

Steps

A significant slope is easier to negotiate with steps. The rise—the height of each step—should range between 4in. and 8in.; the tread or depth of each step should be a minimum of 12in. The most important aspect of these dimensions is that they are consistent so that they do not require uncomfortable, uneven strides or increase the risk of tripping. If steps cover a long incline, consider providing a landing after each series of steps as a spot to pause. Steps can be wide or narrow, depending on the space available and the material used.

Stepping stones create an informal walkway to outlying parts of the yard. The broad curves provide interest as well as the opportunity to see garden areas at closer range.

Garden lighting

Adding light to a garden extends its use and beauty by illuminating areas where you can relax after the sun goes down. Candles and torches are appropriate for an evening party. More permanent lighting options include fixtures using standard household current (120 volts), for which you will need to contract with an electrician, or low voltage (12 volts) kits which are available in a variety of styles and are relatively easy to install without professional assistance. Low voltage kits include a 'step down transformer' to convert household current to a safer 12 volts.

Another option is solar lighting. These units absorb energy from the sun during the day and most turn on automatically at dark. Although solar lights, or at least their collectors, are limited to sunny areas, they offer several advantages: they are easy to install, can be moved from place to place as desired, and they require no electricity other than that provided by the sun. Regardless of the type of lighting you select, fixtures are available to suit a variety of uses and styles.

Pathway lighting

Paths and walkways are more difficult to follow in the dark, particularly when they include steps; pathway lights are bright enough to facilitate safe passage. Place them along the length of the path, especially near turns and steps. In addition to enhancing safety, illuminated pathways can draw visitors farther into the evening garden, leading them from one area to another.

Garden pathways are easier to navigate at night when they are lighted. Most pathway light fixtures are low to the ground and shine their beams where needed, at foot level.

Landscape lighting invites visitors to experience the magic of the evening garden. Spotlights illuminate single plants or small areas, while floodlights cast much wider beams.

Most pathway light fixtures are low-to-the-ground; some are even incorporated into the walk as illuminated stepping stones or as strip lights that are secured to the risers of steps. Other fixtures are designed for attachment to railings or posts.

Area lighting

Some fixtures are designed to showcase areas of your garden at night. Spotlights produce focused beams while floodlights illuminate a broader area. Either type can be secured to the eave of the house or garage or the branches of a tree to shine on garden areas below. This style, known as downlighting, mimics natural light, although shadows and the surrounding darkness add intrigue.

The same fixtures can be placed at ground level to 'uplight' an area of the garden or to illuminate a piece of garden art. This technique can also be used to create a living sculpture by directing the light beam upward through the branches of a tree.

A wall can be employed to create some exciting lighting effects. If a flood- or spotlight is placed in the foreground of a garden that is backed by a wall, the plants are illuminated and their shadows are cast against the wall. By placing the light fixture between the plants and the wall behind them and directing the beam toward the wall, dramatic plant silhouettes are created that stand out against the illuminated surface.

Designing utility

You can incorporate convenient solutions to a variety of practical landscaping issues as you construct your garden. But even with careful planning utility issues may arise that will require your attention.

Utility camouflage

Some parts of the yard, such as the area where you keep your garbage cans and the external parts of your heating and cooling system, are necessary, but not ornamental. If surrounded by a fence or lattice wall these necessary items can be easily hidden from view, and the fence or lattice provides a space for growing ornamental vines.

Another functional area in many yards is the woodpile. Be sure its access allows for the passage of a wheelbarrow or cart for loading and unloading wood.

Composters

Both the placement and style of a compost bin or pile require special consideration. It should be convenient so that kitchen scraps and garden wastes can be easily added. At the same time, it should be placed where it does not detract from your garden or attract vermin. Fortunately,

A garden shed is an ideal place to store tools and supplies so that they can be kept clean and handy. The planted pathway leading to this shed helps make it part of the overall landscape.

many styles of composters have been designed for suburban use that are relatively inconspicuous and will discourage unwanted pests. If pests are a serious problem, consider composting only leaves to produce leafmold.

Water access

Be sure to provide easy, safe access to your outdoor faucets or rain barrel for watering. This may require the placement of stepping stones through a garden as well as hose guides to prevent damage to plants. And consider where your hose will be stored when it is not in use; bowls, brackets, and stands are available to keep your hose tidy between uses.

Tool storage

Establish a convenient place to store your garden tools and equipment. A tool shed is ideal, but depending on the size of your yard and the number of tools a corner of the garage or a large closet can do as well. Wall racks can be employed to save space; they also help keep tools organized so that they are easy to find when needed. If you use garden chemicals, be sure to store them in a safe place, out of reach of children and pets.

Access to garden areas for maintenance is an important consideration. A wheelbarrow travels easily over this smooth, paved surface, and the path is wide enough to accommodate it with a full load.

Working with your topography

In addition to the size and shape of your yard, the topography or 'lay of the land' will have a significant impact on your gardening options and requirements. Level lots are generally easier to maintain than sloping sites, which offer a variety of challenges and rewards.

Level landscapes

A yard that has no significant slope is generally easy to plant and maintain. Depending on its size, a level yard can provide space for a variety of outdoor recreational activities from picnicking to playing Frisbee or croquet, so a lawn area may be important. Fortunately, mowing grass is easier when no hills are involved. Level walkways and paths need no steps. The construction of patios and other hardscaping features requires significantly less site preparation than the same construction on a sloping site.

Large planters and window boxes can be strategically placed to add height and visual interest to a level landscape. Another effective strategy is to create a raised bed. If the raised bed is constructed with sides—usually stone or timbers—the planting depth will be approximately the height of the sides. If the soil is not contained by sides, the center height of the bed will rise several inches to 2–3ft. above the existing ground level, gradually tapering toward the ground on all sides. Raised beds usually provide excellent drainage for plants.

Sloping sites

Sloping sites are often more visually interesting than level sites. However, depending on the steepness of the slope, they may require significantly greater effort to design, develop, and maintain.

Gentle slopes are similar to level sites, although some grading may be necessary for the construction of a level patio or planting area, and low steps may be needed along a pathway.

A landscape built on a steeper slope presents a variety of challenges. For example, steps are usually needed for walkways. Erosion may be a problem on banks, and mowing grass on steep hillsides can be dangerous. Planting deep-rooted ground covers or shrubs is one solution for both of these problems.

Steep slopes often require significant grading for garden, deck, or patio construction. A retaining wall, or a series of retaining walls, can be built to create terraces along a slope. In addition to creating level areas that are easier for planting and maintenance, terraces help reduce erosion. If the slope is significant, consider two or more

Sloping sites often offer opportunities to create intriguing landscapes. Steep slopes can be reduced by constructing retaining walls that create planting areas on different levels.

retaining walls rather than a single tall wall, which can seem imposing. Retaining walls are commonly constructed of stone, formed concrete blocks, or timbers. Recycled plastic timbers are available in some areas. To integrate the walls into the rest of the landscape, consider growing plants that cascade over the wall or filling crevices between stones or timbers with small, creeping plants.

Dealing with runoff

In some yards, heavy rains cause serious erosion. In others, water collects, creating areas that remain damp most of the time.

Providing above-ground drainage by digging a swale or drainage ditch is a practical solution to accommodate the movement of water on a sloping site. It is a good idea to coordinate the construction of the swale with neighbors so that the your runoff solution does not create problems for others.

On a level or gently sloping site, drainage tiles can be installed to carry water away from areas where it collects. Be sure all diverted water is directed away from the house. If your site includes an area that remains wet for most of the time, you may want to consider planting a bog garden or rain garden for water-loving plants.

The spring garden

Bulb-filled borders are almost essential in spring. When planted with perennials to carry on the display, bulbs can die down naturally.

To give structure and good value at other times of the year, choose spring-flowering trees and shrubs that also offer fall color, berries, or ornamental bark. For color, plant bulbs to flower throughout spring. The bulb flowers will show through the bare branches of deciduous shrubs and, later, their dying foliage will be hidden by the shrubs' newly emerging leaves. It is best to avoid slightly tender plants, such as camellias and magnolias, in areas where sudden late frosts are likely, as their buds or flowers may be blackened by frost. Use natural materials like twigs for staking emerging summer perennials.

PLANTS FOR SPRING

PERENNIALS & BULBS

Crocus These low-growing spring or fall flowers can be planted either in containers, at the front of a border, or naturalized in drifts on lawns. Z3

Daffodil (*Narcissus*) Every garden should make room for this spring favorite. They will tolerate damper conditions than tulips. Z3–Z7

Hyacinthus Prized for their spikes of scented tubular flowers, hyacinths need fertile, well-drained soil in sun or light shade. Z5

Primula These are beautiful naturalized in damp, grassy meadows and banks. There is a wide range of colors. Z3–Z9

***Tulipa* (shown)** Plant these in sunny, well-drained soil; the bright colors of the hybrids will put color into any border. Z4

TREES & SHRUBS

Amelanchier lamarckii Shrub or small tree with profuse, star-shaped, white flowers, followed by purple-black berries and vibrant fall color. Z5

Camellia Evergreen spring-flowering shrub requiring acid soil and a sheltered spot. It can be trained against a shady wall. Z6–Z8

***Chaenomeles* x *superba* 'Crimson and Gold'** An early-flowering shrub that produces deep red flowers. Suitable for training against a wall or growing as a lawn specimen; ornamental quinces also produce attractive, although unpalatable, fruit in fall. Z5

Crabapple (*Malus*) Ornamental apple trees such as 'Golden Hornet' are ideal for a small yard, providing masses of blossom in spring and attractive crabapples in fall. Z5

Flowering currant (*Ribes sanguineum*, shown) These ornamental currants produce abundant, deep reddish pink flowers in pendulous clusters with little maintenance. The strong aroma of the leaves can be too pungent for some. Z6

Forsythia* x *intermedia Providing a bright splash of gold when its flowers appear in spring on the bare branches, this deciduous shrub can also be used as attractive hedging. Z6

***Laburnum* x *watereri* 'Vossii'** Deciduous tree that provides a spectacular display of long clusters of bright yellow flowers. Z6

***Magnolia stellata* (shown)** This compact magnolia has white, star-shaped flowers and can be grown on alkaline or acid soil. Z5

Rhododendron Mostly evergreen woodland plants, although deciduous azaleas also belong to this group. Z5–Z9

***Tulipa* 'China Pink'** and others are best planted in large groups for maximum impact.

Magnolia stellata eventually makes a wonderful specimen flowering tree.

***Ribes sanguineum* 'King Edward VII'** is compact with dark red flowers and bluish fruit.

Garden design *see page 18* | **Roses** *see page 125* | **Container gardening** *see page 342*

The summer garden

Give planting schemes a twist by thinking about shapes, heights, textures, and foliage colors, as well as the flower color palette.

The vibrant colors and textures of annuals, bulbs, and perennials take center stage as the garden fills out in summer. Annuals are used not just for single beds but also as quick gap fillers, or in hanging baskets and containers. Shrubs and trees become less prominent in summer, with the exception of roses.

Formal rose beds are less common nowadays; instead, you can let ramblers sprawl through trees, and mix soft-colored old roses with traditional border perennials such as catmints (*Nepeta*), penstemons, and delphiniums for a contemporary, vibrant feel.

PLANTS FOR SUMMER

ANNUALS, PERENNIALS, & BULBS

***Allium hollandicum* 'Purple Sensation'** This ornamental onion produces large, purple, globe-shaped flowers. Plant them in drifts in sunny borders. Z4

***Astrantia major* 'Claret'** Classic perennial producing claret-colored, pincushion flowers during summer. Z4

Daylily (*Hemerocallis*) The combination of showy red, orange, or yellow flowers and long, straplike foliage make the daylily an outstanding perennial for the front of the border. Z3

***Echinacea purpurea* 'White Swan'** Coneflowers are perennials popular for prairie-style planting. This one bears white flowers with deep yellow centers from late summer to fall. Z3

Echinops ritro A tall architectural, thistlelike plant for the border with metallic-blue, spherical flowerheads in late summer. Z3

***Geranium* (shown)** These hardy perennials flower from midsummer to fall in shades of white, pink, and blue. Z4–Z9

Lantana Bright, often multicolored flowerheads attract butterflies. Sprawling or trailing growth. Z9

Lobelia erinus Popular summer annual for edging and containers. Trailing varieties are useful for hanging baskets. Z9

***Miscanthus sinensis* (shown)** The many varieties of this deciduous, perennial grass have impressive green foliage and tassels of flowers in late summer that last well into winter. Z4

Phlox paniculata Popular perennial in a wide range of varieties and colors, including blue, pink, and red. Z4

***Salvia* x *sylvestris* 'Mainacht'** Many tender salvias are used as annuals, but this is a hardy perennial; it produces purple spires of flowers. Z5

TREES & SHRUBS

Calluna vulgaris There are a wide range of heather varieties available, producing spikes of small, bell-shaped flowers from midsummer into fall. Z5

Fuchsia magellanica This easy, hardy shrub produces abundant red and purple hanging flowers from midsummer to fall. Z9

Hibiscus rosa-sinensis Huge flowers in vibrant colors and color combinations make a dramatic spectacle. Z9

***Rosa filipes* 'Kiftsgate'** Popular rambling rose producing large clusters of scented, cream flowers. Train over a large healthy tree or a wall in good condition. Z6

Rose varieties come in almost every color so can be included in most planting schemes.

***Miscanthus sinensis* 'Zebrinus'** has sturdy, green foliage banded with yellow stripes.

***Geranium* 'Philippe Vapelle'** flowers profusely from midsummer to fall.

The fall garden

Late border color from echinaceas, rudbeckias, and asters is one reason for the popularity of prairie-style planting.

With careful planning you can create a yard where the fiery color from flowers, berries, and spectacular foliage lasts through the fading light of fall into winter. For large yards, *Nyssa sylvatica* or *Liquidambar styraciflua* are ideal trees; for smaller yards use birches (*Betula*), sorbus, or Japanese maples (*Acer palmatum*). Aim for a varied range of berries, from white to red, perhaps from hedges of evergreens such as holly (*Ilex*). Clumps of late-flowering perennials can replace the fading flowers of summer, and many will provide structure and texture with seedheads that persist throughout winter.

PLANTS FOR FALL

PERENNIALS & BULBS

***Aster amellus* 'King George' (shown)** This classic border perennial provides purple daisy flowers with yellow centers. Z5

Colchicum fallale Ideal bulbs for underplanting, called naked ladies because the pale pink flowers appear before the leaves. Z4

***Rudbeckia fulgida* var. *sullivantii* 'Goldsturm'** Flowering well into fall, the golden flowerheads with black centers are ideal for extending color in the border. Z4

***Schizostylis coccinea* 'Sunrise'** Perennial with spikes of large, salmon-pink flowers in fall; ideal for the front of the border. Z7

Sedum spectabile This popular perennial produces bright pink flowers above succulent-looking foliage. Z4

TREES & SHRUBS

***Cornus kousa* var. *chinensis* (shown)** Superb tree in all seasons, ideal for the back of a flower garden. In fall, it produces an impressive display of foliage and fruit. Z5

Crabapple (*Malus*) Fruiting trees with yellow, orange, or red fruit in fall after spring blossom; ideal for a small yard. Z5

Firebush (*Hamelia patens*) Easy, drought-tolerant tropical shrub with long, orange tubular flowers which are superb for butterflies and hummingbirds. Flowers from spring to early winter. Z9

Ginkgo biloba Suitable for a larger yard, the unusually shaped leaves turn an attractive buttery yellow in fall. Z5

Japanese maple (*Acer palmatum*) Ideal for small yards with dappled shade. The green leaves of 'Sango-Kaku' turn pale yellow in fall; others turn purple or red. Z6

Nyssa sylvatica A medium to large deciduous tree providing spectacular fall leaf color. Z5

Sumac (*Rhus typhina*) A tall shrub with unusual velvety shoots. It provides fiery fall colors on the large leaves made up of many leaflets; female plants also bear red fruit. Z3

Viburnum Deciduous shrubs equally suitable for borders or woodlands, with colorful fall foliage and colorful berries. Z2–Z7

***Vitis* 'Brant' (shown)** Ornamental grape vine with black, edible grapes and purple fall foliage. Train it on an arbor in sun. Z5

Yellow birch (*Betula alleghaniensis*) Like many other birches, the leaves turn a mellow, buttery yellow in fall, lasting well in sheltered sites. Z4

Cornus kousa* var. *chinensis bears unusual strawberrylike fruit and spring flowers.

***Aster amellus* 'King George'** flowers from late summer until midfall.

***Vitis* 'Brant'** provides some of the best fall foliage of all the grape vines.

The winter garden

On frosty mornings, grasses such as miscanthus are magical, but even without such icy highlights they provide structure and shades of gold.

In many areas all there is to see in the winter garden is snow while at the other extreme there is a much less dramatic difference between the seasons. In cooler areas that are not under snow for months, winter-flowering plants and evergreen foliage give welcome color and plant skeletons provide structural beauty. Evergreen textures range from fine pine needles to glossy leaves, and may be green, golden, or variegated. Deciduous dogwoods (*Cornus*) or willows (*Salix*) with colored stems are at their best, while birches (*Betula*) look superb. Most winter-flowering shrubs are scented; underplant with early bulbs.

PLANTS FOR WINTER

PERENNIALS & BULBS

Erica carnea 'Springwood White' Lime-tolerant heather that produces white flowers for most of the winter months. Z5

Helleborus (shown) Cup-shaped flowers in late winter make these clump-forming perennials ideal for winter borders. Z6

Snowdrop (Galanthus) The delicate, white, nodding heads of snowdrops appear in late winter and signify the start of another growing season. 'Flore Pleno' has double flowers. Z3

TREES, SHRUBS, & VINES

Christmas box (Sarcococca confusa) Like box (*Buxus*), but with small, fragrant flowers. Makes a good low hedge in shade. Z6

Clematis cirrhosa var. purpurascens 'Freckles' Vine with bell-shaped, creamy flowers with red speckles during winter. Z7

Cornus alba 'Sibirica' Deciduous shrub grown for its bright red winter stems. Yellow and orange varieties are available; they make most impact when densely planted in large groups. Z2

Daphne bholua 'Jacqueline Postill' Slow-growing, evergreen shrub unsurpassed for the winter fragrance of its pink flowers. Z8

Euonymus fortunei 'Emerald 'n' Gold' Grown for its bright gold-variegated foliage, which takes on pink hues in winter, this can be grown as a low-growing shrub or trained up walls. Z5

Garrya elliptica Evergreen shrub with leathery, gray-green foliage, which sets off long, fluttering catkins in similar shades. Z8

Mahonia x media 'Charity' Shrub producing yellow flower spikes with a heady scent from late winter onward. Evergreen foliage is an ideal backdrop for winter-flowering bulbs. Z8

Paper-bark maple (Acer griseum) (shown) Several maples have colored shoots and patterned or flaky bark, continuing to draw attention even after their leaves have fallen. Z4

Silver birch (Betula utilis var. jacquemontii) Peeling, white trunk that may be multistemmed or single. Z5

Viburnum x bodnantense 'Dawn' A deciduous shrub that produces scented, pink flowers on its bare stems all winter. Z7

Wintersweet (Chimonanthus praecox) Deciduous shrub known for the delicate perfume of its pale yellow flowers. Z7

Witch hazel (Hamamelis x intermedia, shown) This deciduous shrub produces scented, yellow to red flowers on its bare branches in winter. 'Pallida' has sulfur-yellow flowers. Z5

Hellebores flower from winter to spring in many shades, often speckled.

Witch hazels often stand out better if evergreens are planted behind them

Paper-bark maple has cinnamon-colored, flaky bark, which makes a superb focal point.

LOOKING AFTER YOUR SOIL

Healthy soil supplies your plants with water, air, and nutrients—essential ingredients for growth. If the soil in your yard is not ideal, there is usually a solution close to hand and most soils can be amended with just a little time and effort. This may mean increasing the water-holding capacity of a light, sandy soil by digging in well-rotted organic matter, or reducing the acidity of a soil by adding powdered lime. In this section you will also learn how to make compost and leafmold—both of which are very useful soil additives that you can make at home for free.

Know your soil

There is a complex world below the surface of the soil. The soil has been formed over thousands of years from the breakdown of rocks into mineral particles of sand, silt, and clay. However, this only describes its 'skeleton', usually making up only about half the volume of the soil. The rest is made up of air, water, living creatures, and organic matter (also known as humus), which is derived from plant and animal waste, dead matter, plant roots, soil bacteria, and fungi. The character of the soil is largely determined by the nature of the parent bedrock.

Soil profile
The layered pattern a soil forms above the bedrock is known as the soil profile. The top shallow layer is mostly decaying humus, which helps to retain moisture, improve aeration, and provide nutrients. On cultivated soils humus can decompose quickly, so regular additions of well-rotted organic material are required. Below the humus is the topsoil, ideally 24–36in. in depth but often less, which should be kept well drained, aerated, and fertile. Below the topsoil is the subsoil, containing less organic matter and nutrients.

Types of soil
Garden soils can be defined by the proportion of sand, silt, or clay particles they contain and their pH (*see facing page*). It's important to know your garden's soil type as it is one of the factors determining what plants will grow well.
Clay soils: These tend to be described as 'heavy' and can be sticky when wet, hard when dry, and slow to warm up in spring, but they do retain useful concentrations of nutrients. The addition of organic matter has the effect of improving drainage and increasing the amount of air in the soil. The chemical action of powdered lime can help in the same way if it is added to a clay soil.
Sandy soils: These are easy to cultivate and will warm up quickly in spring, but they dry out quickly and leach nutrients easily. Adding organic matter to sandy soils will improve water and nutrient retention.

A TYPICAL SOIL PROFILE

Key
❶ humus layer ❸ subsoil ❺ bedrock
❷ topsoil ❹ bedrock fragments

Digging techniques *see page 34* | **Amending the soil** *see page 35* | **Making compost** *see page 37*

SOIL TYPES

Clay soils are made up of very small particles that stick together and make drainage and air penetration slow and cultivation difficult. In your hand, they can be rolled into sausages.

Sandy soils consist of relatively large particles surrounded by air spaces. Water drains easily, and there is plenty of air for plant roots. They feel gritty between thumb and forefinger.

Silty soils contain medium-sized particles that can be sticky and heavy but are also quite nutrient rich. When rubbed between fingers they have a silky feel.

Silty soils: These can be improved by adding organic matter, which helps the texture and workability greatly.

The ideal soil for gardeners is loam, a relatively balanced mixture of clay, sand, silt, and humus. Loam soils are easy to cultivate and retain moisture and nutrients well.

Plant nutrients

A good soil should provide all the nutrients for healthy plant growth. Those required in relatively large quantities are nitrogen, phosphorus, and potassium. Nitrogen stimulates rapid leaf and shoot growth, phosphorus stimulates root development, and potassium encourages flowering and fruiting. Other equally important nutrients, such as calcium, sulfur, iron, and boron, are required in lower amounts. The nutrient content of any soil can be boosted by soil additives, particularly fertilizers.

Earthworms, insects, slugs, snails, bacteria, fungi, and many other forms of life all contribute to the nutrient content of the soil and should be encouraged unless their presence is a severe nuisance.

TESTING SOIL PH FOR ITS ACIDITY OR ALKALINITY

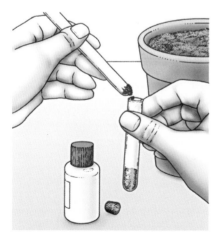

1 **Take small, random samples** of soil from different parts of your yard. Test each one by inserting it into the tube provided with a soil-testing kit. Such kits are available in most garden centers.

2 **Shake up each soil sample** in the solution included with the kit. Allow the soil to settle. The solution changes color depending on the soil pH; this is largely determined by the bedrock and vegetation of your yard.

3 **Soil pH is measured** on a scale of 0 to 14. Most plants suit soils between pH 6.0 and pH 7.5. Higher readings indicate alkaline soil and lower readings acid soil; always check if plants will tolerate your soil pH before you buy.

Digging techniques

Digging can bring real benefits: it helps control weed growth, is a means of incorporating compost, fertilizers, or other additives into the soil, and also relieves compaction and improves soil texture.

Digging the ground is the most effective method of soil cultivation. Generally, you should undertake this in fall or winter, depending on conditions in your area, to allow the frost and winter weather to work on the roughly turned soil. Ground that is frozen, snow covered, or very wet should never be dug.

To reduce the effort of digging, keep the spade held vertically as it is the most efficient method, and try to lift small manageable amounts of soil each time as it will be quicker and less effort in the long run. Finally, you don't have to dig over the whole site at one time; it is easier to do a little each day over several days.

Single digging

It is usually sufficient to dig just to the depth of one spade blade. By turning the blade over, you will bury annual weeds; you can remove perennial weeds by hand with their roots intact. Organic matter can be mixed in as the soil is turned over.

No-dig gardening

Some gardeners believe digging can be harmful to both soil structure and the activity of bacteria and earthworms within the soil. They also argue that digging can unearth dormant weed seeds. No-dig gardening uses copious amounts of organic material applied to the surface of the ground as thick mulches, and it is left to soil organisms to incorporate the material. There is no doubt this technique works, and it also saves labor.

SINGLE DIGGING

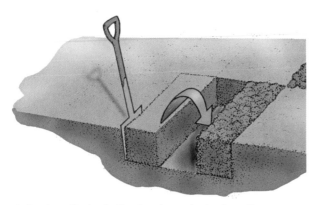

1 **Dig out a trench** one spade blade deep across one half of the site to be dug. Pile the soil removed from this trench nearby so that it can eventually be used to fill the final trench. Tip any compost or other organic matter that is to be added into the bottom of the trench.

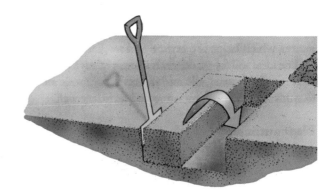

2 **Lift a spadeful of soil** from behind the trench, turning it over into the trench. Work along the trench until a second trench has been created. Turn the spade over as you tip off the soil and mix in any organic matter that has been added.

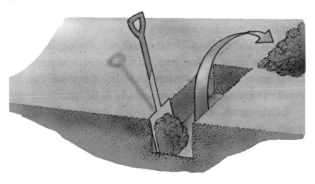

3 **Continue digging further trenches** as in step 2, working backward and backfilling the previous trench each time, and mixing in any organic matter.

4 **Continue until the end** of the first half of the site, then turn around and work your way back along the second half. When you come to the final trench, backfill it with the soil removed at the very beginning, which should be right next to where it needs to be.

Amending the soil

Soil additives can be used either to amend the soil or feed the plants. Compost and mulches work on the soil and also release a limited quantity of plant foods while the sole use of fertilizers is to nourish plants.

Fertilizers

All fertilizers are labeled to show their nutrient content in terms of nitrogen (N) which stimulates leafy growth, phosphorus (P) to help root and flower production, and potassium (K) which helps plants resist disease and tolerate cold. All-purpose fertilizers vary in the quantities they include of each nutrient. Fertilizers for specific uses may have high levels of one or two ingredients. They do not amend the soil, but act quickly on the plants.

Bulky organic material

This not only improves soil but also retains moisture and can contain minor nutrients often lacking in fertilizers. It is advisable to compost bulky materials, especially animal manure, before use. Garden compost is the most useful (and free) resource (*see page 37*) and can be used to amend the soil or as a mulch. A range of other bulky materials, like fallen leaves, may be available in your area.

Modifying pH

Changing soil pH is an important way of suiting the soil to specific plants. To raise the pH add lime as advised on

Inorganic fertilizers are loaded with nutrients and they are easy to handle and apply to the soil. A few, however, can be toxic or caustic, and you should always wear gloves and a mask when handling these.

the bag or by your soil test; never apply fertilizers at the same time. To reduce the pH add bulky organic materials that are naturally acid, including leafmold and peat moss, or apply sulfur.

PREPARING ANIMAL MANURE

1 **If animal manure is available,** find a place where it can be left to rot before use. This will stabilize the nutrients, reduce any toxins it may contain, and make it easier to handle.

2 **Stack up the manure** into a pile and water it very well if dry. Firm it down gently in order to get rid of excess air.

3 **Cover the pile** with black plastic or a tarp to keep moisture in and rain out. It should be ready to use within 2–3 months.

Mulching

A mulch is a loose covering of material on the surface of the soil. Mulches can be either biodegradable—loose organic materials such as compost, shredded bark and wood waste, and leafmold, all of which will eventually break down—or nondegradable, such as landscape fabric or gravel, which do not add organic matter to the soil.

Most mulches are applied to suppress weeds, but they help retain moisture in the topsoil, too. They can also help to regulate soil temperature, buffering against extreme high temperatures and providing invaluable winter protection in cold areas. Dark mulches absorb sunlight and radiate heat at night, while light-colored materials reflect heat rather than store it. The temperature above light mulches can thus be much lower at night.

Biodegradable mulches

It is biodegradable mulches that play the most important role in soil management. As they gradually decompose on the soil surface, they are absorbed into the soil by rain and the activities of worms and other soil-living creatures, and are eventually broken down completely. This improves the soil structure and supplies plant nutrients. The quantity and rate at which the nutrients become available depends on the particular mulch.

How to apply a mulch

It is essential that the soil is wet before you apply a mulch: dry soils are difficult to rewet once covered with a mulch as it acts as a barrier to rainwater. For the same reason, it is also vital that the soil is warm, since the mulch can act as an insulating barrier. This is particularly the case with light-colored mulches. Once in place on a warm, moist soil, a mulch helps to keep it warm and moist but prevents it getting too hot or wet. This moderating effect is very good for plant roots and soil life.

Spread the mulch evenly over the surface of the soil with a garden fork or rake or by hand. How thickly you apply it depends on the size of the plants and how much material that you have available. Even a ½in. layer will help to improve the soil structure, but it will take mulch 3–4in. thick to control weeds effectively and provide some frost protection.

In most cases, particularly for trees and shrubs, you should maintain a space between the mulch and the plant stem, as contact can encourage rotting and cause a grafted tree or shrub to shoot from the rootstock. Occasionally, however, mulching up to the stem can be beneficial; for example, tomato and cabbage plants will root into mulch mounded around their stems, helping them grow.

APPLYING A LOOSE MULCH

1 **Water the soil well** before mulching if it is dry. This moisture will be locked in by the mulch once it is applied.

2 **Spread the mulch out** by hand around small plants, leaving a little space around their stems. Ensure an even coverage.

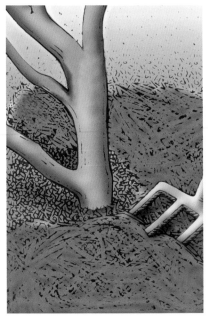

3 **Keep the mulch clear** of the stems of trees and shrubs. Use a garden fork or rake to spread mulch around large plants.

Making compost

Garden compost is a superb source of bulky organic matter that can be made for free from garden and kitchen waste. A good compost pile will readily turn these waste products into an invaluable soil conditioner.

How to make good compost

To make good, friable compost your pile must be well constructed so that the organic material can decompose rapidly and not turn into a pile of stagnant vegetation. Air, moisture, and nitrogen are all necessary if bacteria and fungi are to break down the raw materials efficiently. Air should be allowed in through the base and the sides of the pile. Water can be applied with a can or hose if the pile shows signs of drying out. Moisture can be retained by lining the pile with black plastic. The nitrogen should be provided in the mix of materials added to the pile (*see following page*). The ideal position for the pile is in a sheltered, shady place where it is less likely to dry out in the sun and wind.

Well-rotted, friable compost is dark brown in color and is crumbly in texture. It should be sweet-smelling and is often inhabited by countless soil organisms, such as worms and centipedes. When spread as a mulch or dug in, it makes an excellent soil conditioner.

TYPES OF COMPOST BIN

Compost can be broken down simply by stacking it in a spare corner of the yard. Such piles, however, may become untidy and the outside of the pile can dry out. Decomposition will take place more rapidly in a home-made or commercial compost bin that allows air in and retains moisture.

Home-made bins vary in design. One of the simplest is a square cage of plastic or wire netting ❶, supported by four stout posts driven into the ground. Make sure the front is removable to allow the rotted compost to be easily extracted and turned. Make a false floor by placing a layer of twiggy branches in the base, or support a few sticks on bricks; this will allow air to flow into the pile. Line the inside of the cage with newspaper to reduce drying out.

A piece of burlap or plastic can be placed on top of the pile and weighed down with bricks to help retain moisture. The disadvantage of a bin with netting sides is that most of the heat generated by the composting process escapes.

A more solid structure can be made from wooden boards ❷, with small gaps to allow in air. These retain more heat so the pile rots more quickly and weed seeds and diseases are killed. The internal structure of the pile is the same as with a cage. You can use bricks or blocks, provided that occasional vertical joints are left unmortared to allow air in. The front of such bays can be equipped with removable wooden slats.

Commercial compost bins ❸ come in all shapes and sizes. Some have sliding sides

to allow the compost to be shoveled out and lids to keep in moisture. Check that the bin is robust and large enough for your compost needs, bearing in mind the length of time it takes material to decompose. For good results, compost bins should be around 4ft. tall and at least as wide.

A series of two or three compost bins is useful, particularly in large yards. When one bin is full, the compost can be left to rot and another bin brought into use, keeping a cycle of composting going.

If you do not have room for a compost bin, try worm composting (*see following page*). Alternatively, some local municipalities collect green waste for composting, which is eventually resold.

TURNING THE COMPOST PILE

All plant and animal remains decay naturally without our interference—the composting process is not something that the gardener has invented. The key players are countless micro-organisms, and when suitable materials are worked together in a compost pile, their numbers build up and the rate of decomposition increases. You can help the composting process by turning the pile regularly to allow air to penetrate, giving micro-organisms the oxygen they need.

1 **When adding new material**, break up large clumps with a fork to allow air to penetrate.

2 **Introduce more oxygen** months later by removing the material from the pile and mixing it with a fork.

Compostable materials

All sorts of garden and kitchen waste make good compost if properly mixed. One of the secrets of ensuring rapid and effective decomposition is not to allow large quantities of one particular material to build up in the pile. Try to get a good balance of approximately one third soft and green, sappy (nitrogen-rich) materials to two thirds hard, brown (carbon-rich) materials. Nitrogen-rich materials include lawn-mowings, annual weeds, raw vegetable peelings, tea leaves, and hedge clippings. Carbon-rich materials include plant stems, woody twigs, straw, scrunched-up newspaper (not glossy magazines), and corrugated cardboard. Do not use any material that has been treated with herbicides (for example lawn-mowings) or that is affected by diseases or pests. Shred tough, large, or woody prunings to enhance their rates of decomposition.

WORM COMPOSTING

Compost worms are known as 'tiger' worms because they are striped. They differ from earthworms by living in decaying organic matter. At least 100 worms are needed to start a worm compost bin. You can buy them mail order or gather them from existing compost piles. The bin can be home-made or bought. It should be rainproof and maintain a damp environment, but be well drained with a sump or drainage holes so excess moisture can escape. It needs to have a wide surface area and be insulated and portable. The worms are most productive at 64–77°F; try not to let them get too cold over winter or too hot over summer.

A simple wormery can be made from a wooden box with holes in the base or you can buy a purpose-made wormery. Introduce the worms onto a moist bed of leafmold or compost mixed with shredded paper or card, then begin to add food in small quantities; worms are more likely to be killed by overfeeding than starvation. Cover the contents with wet newspaper or black plastic. Worms eat anything that decomposes: annual weeds, tea leaves, vegetable scraps, coffee grounds, food scraps, crushed egg shells, citrus peel (in small quantities), and shredded newspaper are all suitable. Avoid weed seeds, perennial weeds, and diseased material. Cover the bin with a heavy lid to exclude light, flies, and vermin.

Building up the compost pile

Add as much material as possible all at once, thoroughly mixing the green and brown materials or filling with thin, alternating layers. Ensure sufficient moisture is present, but don't allow the pile to become waterlogged.

If you fill the pile all at once with a good balance of materials you may be able to encourage hot composting. Hot piles compost more quickly, producing useful compost in around six months; they can also kill some weed seeds and diseases. If the pile is filled bit by bit the pile may or may not heat up. Cold composting is slower than hot composting as the compost can take around a year to mature, and weed seeds and diseases often survive. The pile can be turned at intervals to suit you; this can enhance the rate of decomposition and produce a more uniform finished compost.

Once the material has broken down to form a dark and crumbly texture, the compost should be ready to use as a soil amendment. The longer you leave it to decompose, the better the finished compost will be.

Leafmold

Fallen leaves, once broken down into leafmold, make one of the best soil amendments. The dying leaves from any deciduous tree or shrub can be used, but it is best to avoid diseased leaves, which can pass on infection (such as rose blackspot or apple scab); leaves with thick veins (such as some maple leaves) will take longer to rot. Do not use evergreen or conifer foliage. In many communities, leaves are raked into a pile at the curb near the street, or bagged in paper sacks, for the municipality to collect.

If possible, keep your fallen leaves and make your own leafmold. Also, in some municipalities and cities, leaves and other organic materials are collected, composted, and then bagged for sale, which is a good scheme for gardeners with no space for bins.

Collect the fallen leaves after rain, as it saves watering them later, and pack them into a wire bin or black sacks (with a few air holes punctured in the sides with a garden fork, for aeration). Leave them to break down in an out-of-the-way corner of the yard. Decomposition is a slow process, taking one to two years, but partially rotted leafmold can be used as a soil amendment or mulch after a few months.

Leafmold contains few nutrients but is an excellent soil amendment, improving soil texture and aeration. Mature leafmold makes an excellent potting soil. It is often used as a peat moss substitute in potting mixes as it has similar characteristics: low pH, good aeration, and excellent water retention.

MAKING LEAFMOLD

1 **Collect leaves after rain** when they are moist. Rake them up, or run a mower over them, which will also shred them and mix them with lawn-mowings, both of which enhance the rate of decomposition.

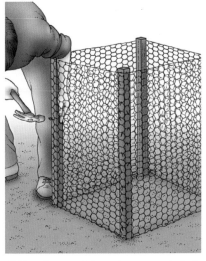

2 **To make a container**, choose a cool, shady place, hammer 4 posts into the ground and staple wire or strong plastic netting to them.

3 **Fill the container** with leaves, pressing them down and watering well if dry. They decay slowly by fungal action over 1–2 years to form a dark, friable material that makes an excellent soil conditioner or mulch.

PESTS, DISEASES, & OTHER PROBLEMS

The healthy growth of plants may be disrupted by a pest or disease attack, a nutrient deficiency, or a disorder caused by climatic or environmental conditions. The easiest way of dealing with a problem is to prevent it occurring in the first place, which entails selecting vigorous plants and growing them in the right place, making sure your soil is healthy, and encouraging natural predators. In such conditions, the majority of your plants will remain healthy, although it is always worth keeping an eye out so that you can act quickly when the system fails and specific treatment is required.

Know your friends

Although you should encourage a whole range of wildlife into your garden, creatures that are predators of garden pests are particularly welcome. It is useful to recognize these creatures and learn their habits, as this can help you tip the balance between friend and foe in your favor.

Some predators have a limited diet and target specific pests. Flower fly larvae, for example, feed mainly on aphids. Others, like centipedes, have a more wide-ranging diet, consisting of what is most available; they will eat more pests during a pest outbreak and thus help to restore the natural balance within a garden.

Sometimes the dividing line between friend and foe is not clear cut. Earwigs, for example, can be pests if you have prize dahlias, but they also prey on aphids and moth eggs. The best strategy is to tolerate such creatures and protect vulnerable crops when necessary.

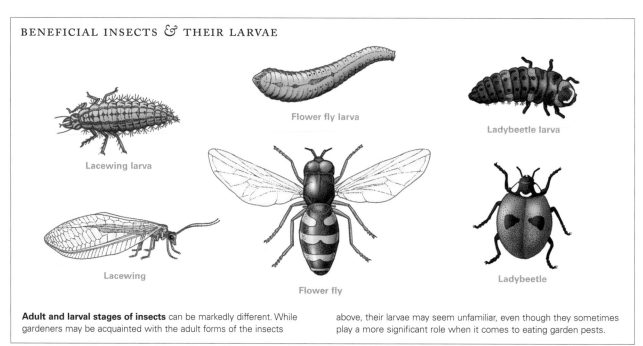

BENEFICIAL INSECTS & THEIR LARVAE

Flower fly larva

Ladybeetle larva

Lacewing larva

Lacewing

Flower fly

Ladybeetle

Adult and larval stages of insects can be markedly different. While gardeners may be acquainted with the adult forms of the insects above, their larvae may seem unfamiliar, even though they sometimes play a more significant role when it comes to eating garden pests.

KNOW YOUR FRIENDS

Gardening with the environment *see page 17* | **Preventing problems** *see page 42* | **Understanding problems** *see page 43*

PEST PREDATORS

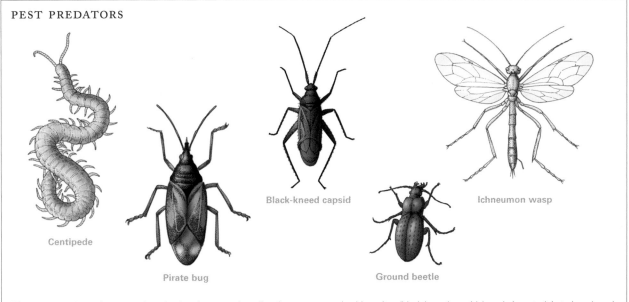

Centipede

Pirate bug

Black-kneed capsid

Ground beetle

Ichneumon wasp

These common predators can be mistaken for pests, but all make a contribution to gardens, feeding on caterpillars (ichneumon wasps), red spider mites (black-kneed capsids), scale insects (pirate bugs), and small slugs (ground beetles and centipedes).

Garden insects, spiders, & centipedes

Praying mantis are familiar garden insects in many parts of the country (*see page 46*) and will consume an enormous quantity of pests. Most of us are also familiar with ladybeetles, flower flies, ground beetles, earwigs, spiders, and centipedes, but there are countless other creatures that go unrecognized. Many of these also have larvae that are completely different from their adult forms, which makes identification even harder. The larvae of ladybeetles, for example, have tapering bodies that are segmented, grayish black with orange markings; like the adults, they feed on aphids, mites, scale insects, mealybugs, and small caterpillars. As a general rule, check when you come across something you do not recognize—beneficial insects can easily be mistaken for pests.

Flower fly and lacewing larvae are keen predators of aphids, and may also eat other small insects. Ground beetles are seen all year round and are important predators of slugs. They also eat the eggs and larvae of various root flies and lettuce root aphids. Spiders catch flies and other small insects.

Garden vertebrates

The more easily identified garden friends are the vertebrates. Garter snakes, although alarming to some people even though they are harmless, are invaluable predators which feed on many pest insects. Frogs and toads also perform a useful service and providing damp habitats helps keep them in your yard. Insect-eating birds not only make appealing residents but also consume a wide range of insects, although not all may be pests. Robins and chickadees are widespread; other birds will be especially helpful in your area, too. Every garden should have a bird feeder, which should be kept well filled. Bats too, although less visible, should be encouraged by providing bat boxes as they catch many insects, including moths and aphids.

BENEFICIAL AMPHIBIANS

Frog

Toad

Garden amphibians include frogs, toads, and turtles. They rely on water for breeding and eat, among other things, slugs and snails.

Preventing problems

Choose plants and varieties that are suitable for your yard; give them a good start and they will grow strongly. Plants do, however, vary in their susceptibility to pests and diseases and growing those that are known to have resistance is an invaluable means of preventing a specific, recurring problem, such as black spot on roses.

Buying healthy plants

Young, vigorous plants will establish more quickly than those that are old and rootbound. While plants in flower may look more attractive, those not yet in flower are in fact a better buy because the plants will be able to put all their energy into settling in before flowering.

Inspect all new plants for pests and disease. Bulbs should be firm and show no sign of mold. Always buy certified virus-free seed potatoes and fruit trees and bushes where available. Seeds should be as fresh as possible. Seek pest- and disease-resistant varieties.

Preventative gardening

With experience, gardeners can learn to incorporate preventative techniques as they cultivate plants, in order to avoid problems later. Amending the soil with organic matter will improve its water-holding potential and lessen the effects of drought, which can cause stress to plants.

THINNING TO THE CORRECT SPACING

Planting vegetable plants or thinning seedlings to their recommended spacing will provide proper air circulation, which will reduce the incidence of disease.

Planting at the correct spacing will encourage good airflow and thwart disease. Sowing times can be adjusted to avoid the periods when certain pests and diseases are most active, while mixed or interplantings can confuse pests, and so reduce large-scale infestations.

Greenhouse whiteflies are common pests in greenhouses and are often introduced to gardens and homes on infested, greenhouse-raised plants. These small, white, sucking insects can cause serious damage to both vegetable and ornamental plants in summer. To avoid introducing them to your garden, inspect greenhouse-grown plants carefully before purchasing. Fortunately, where winters are cold, whiteflies do not survive outdoors.

Understanding problems

Despite our best endeavors, plants may suffer from pest damage or diseases. Adverse environmental conditions and nutrient imbalances can also cause unwanted symptoms. Whatever the problem, it is important to identify the cause correctly. Having done so, it is useful to know when the problem first appears, when it leaves, how it spreads, the range of plants it will attack, how and where it survives the winter, and what level of infestation or infection can be tolerated. This information will help in planning a control strategy.

PESTS

This is the term given to any creature that affects a plant in a way we do not approve of. The aim of the gardener is to keep pests at a manageable level.

Many different creatures can act as pests, and they vary considerably. Some, such as slugs and certain aphids, attack a variety of plants; others, such as the lily beetle and potato nematode, restrict their activities to one or a few plants. Pests may look more or less the same from birth to death, like slugs, or go through several very different stages of growth during their life cycles, like moths. Some creatures are active all year while others may be active only in certain seasons or during the 'pest' stage of their life cycles.

Symptoms & identification

If the pest is visible, identification is relatively easy, although the presence of a creature does not mean that it is the guilty party. Often, symptoms are the only clues the gardener has to go on.

Holes in foliage, stems, or roots, or plants disappearing completely, are caused by pests with biting or rasping mouthparts. Curled leaves and distorted growth are caused by creatures that feed on plant sap, either by piercing the plant tissue or by living within the plant. Be aware that similar symptoms can have different causes. For example, the red blisters that appear on the leaves of red and white currants in early summer are caused by a pest, known as the currant blister aphid. Similar red blisters on peach leaves in the spring, on the other hand, are caused by a disease—peach leaf curl.

KNOWING PESTS FROM DISEASES

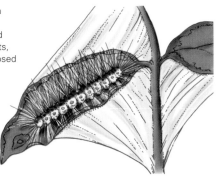

Webworms build an unsightly webbing around branches and stems of many plants, feeding on the enclosed leaves. Control by removing and destroying the webs or spraying with a biological insecticide.

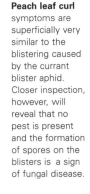

Peach leaf curl symptoms are superficially very similar to the blistering caused by the currant blister aphid. Closer inspection, however, will reveal that no pest is present and the formation of spores on the blisters is a sign of fungal disease.

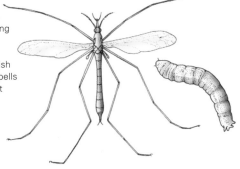

Leatherjackets are garden pests, feeding on grass roots and causing patches of lawn to turn yellowish brown during dry spells in summer. Its adult form, the crane fly, however, does not harm plants.

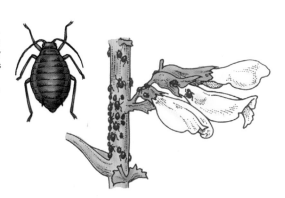

Black bean aphids, or blackfly, are common pests of fava beans. They overwinter as eggs on garden plants such as viburnums and philadelphus when the fava bean food supply is finished.

DISEASES

Disease symptoms are caused by fungi, bacteria, and viruses, all of which are mainly too small to be seen. Diseases also tend to be known by the symptoms they produce, such as 'white rot' or 'downy mildew'.

Fungal diseases

The majority of plant diseases are caused by fungi, even though the majority of fungi do not cause diseases. Fungi spread from plant to plant mainly in the form of spores, which are spread by wind, rain, or soil contact. Some disease-causing fungi can live on both dead and living plants, so dead plant material can act as a source of further infection. A few, including rusts and powdery mildews, can survive only in living plants. Some fungi, including clubroot and onion white rot, produce tough resting bodies, which are difficult to eradicate.

The myriad effects of fungal diseases range from mild to life-threatening. Some affect just a localized area, while others are systemic, meaning they spread throughout the plant. Typical symptoms include death of plant tissue (spots), abnormal increase in tissue (peach leaf curl, clubroot), change in color such as silvering or yellowing (silver leaf), wilting (wilts, foot rots), wet rots (damping off), and powdery and fluffy molds (mildews, botrytis).

Bacterial diseases

These tiny, simple organisms cause few diseases but those they do are difficult to control. Symptoms include soft rots, leaf spots, and cankers. Bacteria are spread in soil water, in and on planting material, and by wind and rain. Their main point of entry is through a wound.

Viral diseases

The majority of viruses are moved from plant to plant by aphids, nematodes, hands, or pruners. Infected plants may not show obvious symptoms, so it is advisable to buy plants that are certified virus free.

Symptoms include mottling or mosaic patterns on leaves or flowers, sometimes confused with mineral deficiencies; a virus is initially likely to appear on one or two plants only, whereas a deficiency is more likely to affect a whole row. Once a plant is infected with a virus there is no cure.

IDENTIFYING DISEASES

Viruses on tulips cause the flower color to 'break', with the petals having either white streaks or streaks darker than the normal color. Destroy any plant showing these symptoms unless the plant was bought specifically to exhibit such coloration.

Canker affects a wide range of ornamental and fruit trees and shrubs such as apple, pear, ash, beech, gardenia, and sorbus. It shows as sunken and discolored patches on the bark. The branch usually becomes swollen around the canker, which can cause die-back.

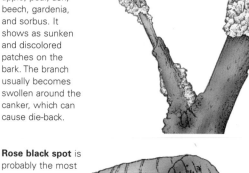

Botrytis causes affected tissues to become covered with a gray, fluffy growth of fungus, which should be cut off as soon as it is seen. In severe cases, whole plants will need to be destroyed.

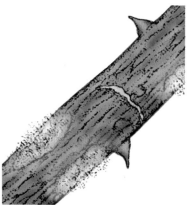

Rose black spot is probably the most common disease of roses. Circular dark brown or black spots develop on the leaves, surrounded by yellowing tissues. As they increase in size, the whole leaf becomes discolored and falls prematurely.

IDENTIFYING DISORDERS

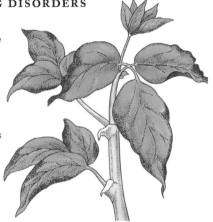

Potassium deficiency causes the scorching of leaves, which may also start to curl, as seen on this bean plant. Such mineral deficiencies are most likely on light, sandy, peaty, or alkaline soils on plants that require lots of potassium, such as tomatoes, beans, and fruit.

Splitting of fruit, such as tomatoes, and vegetables like carrots and cabbages, as well as the bark of trees, is caused by an irregular supply of water. Heavy rain after drought, for example, will cause very rapid growth, which can lead to splitting.

Edema is caused by an excess of water in the plant, brought about by a wet soil or overly moist atmosphere. The symptoms are small warty growths on the stems and undersides of leaves, typically seen on eucalyptus, ivy-leaved pelargoniums, peperomias, camellias, and vines.

Frost can cause considerable damage to the leaves, stems, buds, and flowers of plants. Typical symptoms are sudden browning of the leaves overnight on frost-sensitive plants, such as potatoes or annuals.

DISORDERS

Problems caused by environmental conditions, such as low temperature, day length, or herbicide drift, are known as plant disorders. They can also result from shortages of particular plant foods. Knowing the underlying cause usually makes it easy to correct the problem.

Poor fruit set: Poor pollination will result in a poor crop on vegetable and fruit plants. This may be due to cold, wet, and windy weather preventing the work of pollinating insects, frost killing the flowers, or lack of pollen. Providing windbreaks and choosing later-flowering varieties can help to solve the first two problems. Lack of pollen can be due to the absence of flowers of a compatible variety (many fruit trees need a partner nearby). Water shortages and high temperatures can also reduce fruit set, as can poor flowering caused by overfeeding or hard pruning.

Bolting: This is the term used when a plant flowers prematurely, usually a problem with vegetables that are normally picked before they flower. It can be caused by adverse temperatures, day length, root disturbance at transplanting, or shortage of water.

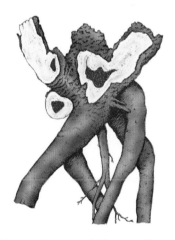

Crown rot often occurs where the soil is too wet or waterlogged. Such conditions promote infection by a soil-borne bacteria, which rots the tissue. Seen on hostas, daylilies, orchids, and other plants.

Distorted growth: This can be caused if spray from a herbicide finds its way onto other plants. Once a plant is damaged in this way there is no cure. Distorted growth may also be the result of frost or pest damage.

Mineral deficiencies: These are caused by shortages of nutrients in the soil, and can be rectified simply by applying the missing mineral to the plant or to the soil. Examples include potassium deficiency (*see above*), lack of iron causing yellowing between the leaf veins, and magnesium deficiency—typically seen on sandy soils.

Taking action

Good cultural practice is not always enough to keep pests at bay. Some, like slugs and snails, are persistent, and defensive action will have to taken if susceptible plants are to survive. The main control measures are biological control agents, barriers, traps, repellents, and chemicals.

Biological control

This method of control uses natural predators and parasites to keep certain pests in check. Most biological control agents, except the fearsome-looking praying mantis, are tiny or even microscopic creatures and they are often very specific in the pests they attack. Biological controls are rarely seen in stores as many have a limited 'shelf life' so are supplied by specialty mail-order suppliers. Different predators and parasites are suitable for different pests; consult your local cooperative extension service.

Tips on using biological control

If you plan to introduce biological control, do not use any persistent pesticides. The aim of biological control is to

Copper barriers are one of many products available for the exclusion of slugs and snails. It is wise not to rely on just one method of control against these determined pests. Traditional methods, such as baited traps, slug pellets, and hand-picking at night, should not be overlooked.

BIOLOGICAL CONTROLS

Cards bearing whitefly scales killed by *Encarsia* larvae can be hung on greenhouse plants to control whiteflies. The larvae develop into small wasps that emerge and lay eggs to parasitize more whiteflies. You are unlikely even to notice the tiny wasps themselves.

Nematodes (microscopic worms) for controlling vine weevil larvae can be watered onto the soil of individual container plants.

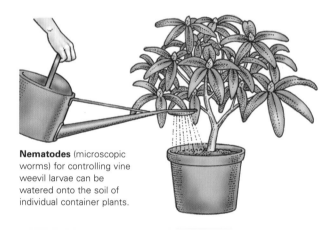

Aphidoletes pupae help control aphids. Leave them under an upturned pot to hatch, and after a couple of days small flies emerge. The orange larvae are voracious predators of aphids and will kill and eat their prey until fully grown and ready to pupate.

Praying mantis feed voraciously on moths, beetles, aphids, cutworms, and other pests. Egg cases containing about 200 eggs each can be bought by mail order for introduction to your yard.

reduce pest levels and related damage rather than to eliminate pests completely. In some cases this can be achieved with one application, but sometimes you may need a further batch of biological control agents.

There is no advantage in introducing the agent before pests are present. If pest levels are high, try to reduce them using other nonchemical means before using the agent.

Before ordering, check that you can meet the required conditions of temperature, humidity, and daylight. Try to use the agents as soon as they arrive, and read the instructions carefully before opening.

Barriers & crop covers

The age-old technique of placing a barrier between a plant and its pest can be highly effective. Tree guards are the classic example, protecting newly planted trees and shrubs from deer, rabbits, and other mammals. Large soda bottles with the bases removed can be used to protect seedlings from pests, particularly slugs and snails.

A nondrying glue is available for making sticky barriers on pots and legs of greenhouse benches, which will protect against vine weevils, ants, and sowbugs. Wrap

a strip of wide sticky tape around first, then smear it liberally with the nondrying glue. The glue can then be removed easily at the end of the growing season by peeling off the tape.

Grease bands can help to protect fruit and ornamental trees from moths and ants, which both climb up trunks. Copper bands are available to deter slugs and snails.

For food crops, very fine mesh netting is available to protect plants against small pests such as flea beetle, root flies, and caterpillars. These floating row covers are very lightweight and some can be placed directly over a growing crop without the need for any framework for support. They allow air and rain to penetrate.

When using a crop cover it is important to put it in place before the pest is present—usually as soon as the plants are sown. Covers can, if necessary, be left in place for the life of the crop. Be sure to check for weeds and diseases, which can thrive in the sheltered environment.

Keeping out large pests

The only effective control for large pests, such as deer or rabbits, is to erect a stout, mesh or electric fence. Plastic

BARRIERS

A mini greenhouse made from the top end of a large soda bottle will protect vulnerable young plants from many pests and the weather. Bell cloches perform a similar function. In both cases, water and air cannot penetrate easily, so they will have to be removed every time the plant needs to be watered, or when there is a risk of overheating.

Cabbage root fly mats are made from 6in. squares of any thick material, such as carpet underlay. Lay the squares flat on the soil around the bases of newly planted brassica plants. They form simple barriers, preventing female cabbage root flies from laying their eggs in the soil near the roots.

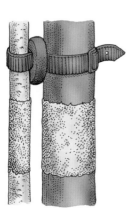

A grease band applied to a tree trunk will prevent wingless female moths from climbing up to lay eggs on vulnerable trees. If the plant has a stake, either apply the band above the point where the stake is attached or grease band the stake too, as shown.

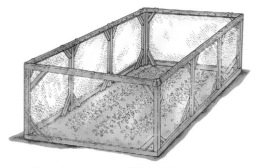

A carrot fly barrier comprises a 30in. tall, fine-mesh net erected around carrots. This gives effective protection as the flies do not fly above this height. The barrier can also be made of clear plastic, but this may get toppled by strong winds.

netting is usually sufficient to keep out birds and smaller mammals, and, for fruit growers, fruit cages are available in many sizes. Deer can be excluded by sturdy fences that are at least 7ft. tall.

Grouping soft fruit plants together within a fruit cage is an efficient method of protecting ripening fruit from birds. The netting should be removed when fruiting has finished and should not be replaced until after the blossom has set. This allows access for pest-clearing birds and pollinating insects and also avoids the danger of snow bringing down the roof. Individual fruit trees can be protected by draping netting over them. This is much simpler where the plants are trained against a wall.

Traps

These can be used in the yard to reduce pests in a small area. Traps baited with pheromones (sex hormones) are useful to control codling moth, for example, while sticky yellow traps are good for controlling whiteflies and aphids, and sticky blue traps are hung up to catch leafhoppers and thrips.

As well as trapping the pests, they are also sometimes used to provide an indication of when an infestation is on the rise and so allow the introduction of a biological control agent or a chemical spray to be timed accurately.

Scaring & repelling devices

Various devices for scaring and repelling deer, cats, rabbits, and moles are available. Most are not that effective but may be worth a try if you have a persistent problem and other methods have failed.

Chemical control

Garden chemicals can give rapid and effective control of pests and diseases that would otherwise destroy or badly spoil the appearance of plants. Before their use, make sure that the correct treatment is applied, and follow the manufacturer's instructions carefully. Only apply chemical controls when necessary, and avoid days that are windy, frosty, hot, or wet. In this way, garden chemicals are used efficiently and only as needed.

Wear rubber gloves when handling pesticides. Garden chemicals must be treated with respect at all times, since incorrect use may harm the user or damage plants. After use, they must be locked away where children and pets cannot reach them.

COVERING CROPS

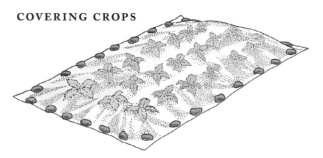

Floating row covers are made of a finely woven material and are placed directly over a crop and held in place with stakes or stones. They also protect plants from frost.

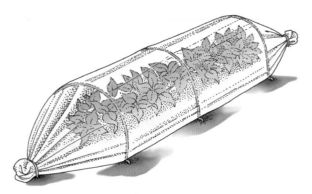

Row cover material or clear plastic can be stretched over hoops, which will support the material over the crop. Anchor the hoops well.

TRAPS

Yellow or blue sticky traps control a range of pests. Each is a plastic card covered with a nondrying glue, which flying insects adhere to if they settle on it. Several traps may be required in a greenhouse, many in a yard, and you will need to replace them periodically.

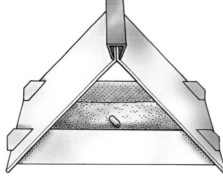

A pheromone-baited trap attracts male moths. Hang traps from tree branches when the moths are active in late spring.

Common pests

The range of pests that devour our plants is enormous. These are some of the most common.

Slugs & snails

Seedlings and new shoots on vegetables, perennials, and annuals are particularly vulnerable to slugs and snails. In wet weather they are more active. Some species live in the soil, where they damage potato tubers and bulbs.

Use nontoxic slug baits or physical barriers, such as copper strips. Biological control using a nematode is effective against slugs, but not against snails.

Aphids

Most plants are attacked by these sap-feeding insects. Infested plants may suffer distorted growth and become sticky with the honeydew that aphids excrete, which becomes blackened with a sooty mold.

Use a hard stream of water to knock aphids off the host plant. Insecticidal soaps and several botanical insecticides are available for controlling heavy infestations.

Japanese beetle

This voracious beetle, with its distinctive green and copper coloring, feeds on a wide variety of ornamental and food plants. Adults eat the leaves and flowers; grubs eat the roots of lawn grasses. Pyrethrum or neem insecticides are effective against the beetle. Treating lawns with milky spore bacterium reduces the grub population.

Leaf miner

Tiny larvae of various moths burrow just under the leaf surface, creating a pattern of small tunnels. Many different plants are attacked. The damage is unsightly more than damaging. Pick off the infested leaves.

Spider mites

Tiny creatures, less than $\frac{1}{25}$in. long, suck the sap, usually on the undersides of foliage, and create a silky protective web. Plants can quickly become debilitated. Infestations are especially common when humidity is low. Keep the air surrounding plants damp; control with predators.

Gophers & groundhogs

Gophers (5–12in.) and the much larger groundhogs or woodchucks (17–26in.) are destructive burrowing rodents which can cause havoc in vegetables gardens in particular. The most reliable control is live trapping, releasing the creature some miles from your property.

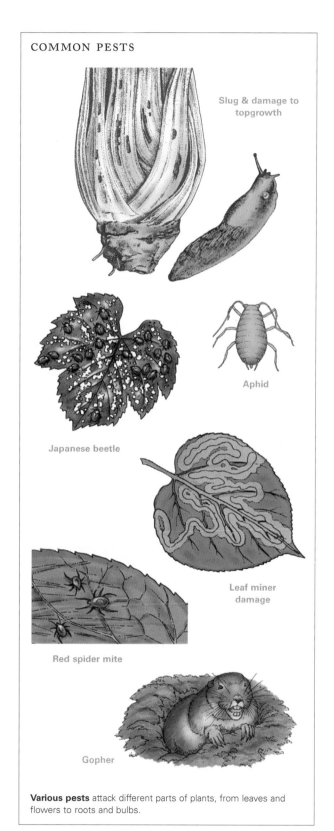

COMMON PESTS

Slug & damage to topgrowth

Aphid

Japanese beetle

Leaf miner damage

Red spider mite

Gopher

Various pests attack different parts of plants, from leaves and flowers to roots and bulbs.

Rabbits, deer, & squirrels

New plants are particularly vulnerable to rabbits and deer, which gnaw bark, especially in winter, causing young trees and shrubs to die. Some plants are less appetizing to deer; selecting these for your garden may help reduce deer browsing. However, if deer are hungry enough, they will eat almost anything. Squirrels eat flower buds and shoot tips, ripening fruits and seeds, and bulbs and corms. They also strip bark from the trunks of trees. Wire netting is an effective barrier: For rabbits, use small mesh netting 3ft. tall with another 12in. below soil level angled outward to prevent burrowing. Deer need robust fencing, at least 7ft. tall. Repellent substances and scaring devices give only short-term protection.

Vine weevil

Both the adult beetles and the grubs damage many plants. The adult weevils are active at night when they crawl up plant stems and eat notches in leaf edges. The larvae are creamy white, legless grubs with brown heads; they feed on roots, especially those growing in containers. In cold areas damage may only occur between spring and fall, and a hard winter may kill many grubs. In areas with no or little frost, damage may occur year-round. Search by flashlight for adult weevils on plants showing leaf damage and destroy them. Insecticides are not very effective against adults; control the larvae using biological control.

Deer often visit yards at dusk or early in the morning when there is nobody about. They may jump fences to get in and out, and their grazing can cause serious damage.

Caterpillars

Many caterpillars feed on the foliage and flower buds of garden plants. Damage is often limited to unsightly holes in the leaves but some cause more extensive defoliation. Hand removal is feasible for light infestations. Vegetables can often be protected from caterpillars by using floating row covers. Spraying with *Bacillus thuringiensis* (Bt) may be effective, or choose an appropriate insecticide.

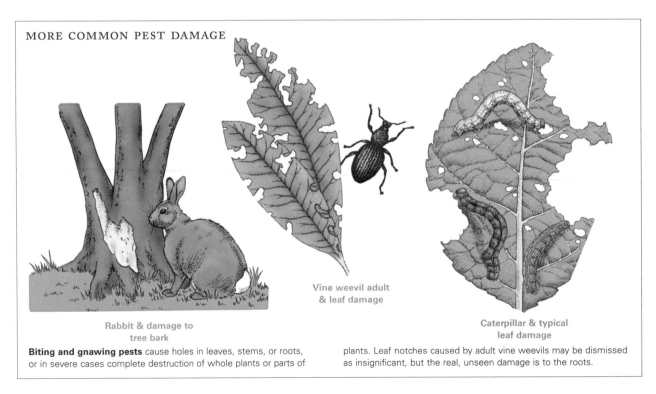

MORE COMMON PEST DAMAGE

Vine weevil adult
& leaf damage

Rabbit & damage to
tree bark

Caterpillar & typical
leaf damage

Biting and gnawing pests cause holes in leaves, stems, or roots, or in severe cases complete destruction of whole plants or parts of plants. Leaf notches caused by adult vine weevils may be dismissed as insignificant, but the real, unseen damage is to the roots.

Common diseases

As with pests, there are many diseases that can infect plants. Listed below are some of the most common, wide-ranging diseases that you are likely to encounter at one time or another in your own yard. Diseases that affect particular plants are listed in the relevant chapters.

Armillaria root rot

This fatal disease can affect all woody plants and some perennial ones too. Typical symptoms include thinning of the canopy, branch die-back, or the sudden death of a plant. Examination of the stem base or larger roots reveals a white sheet of fungal growth between the bark and wood, which smells strongly of mushrooms. Sometimes, but not reliably, clumps of honey-colored mushrooms may appear at the base of the trunk or along root runs in midfall. The mushrooms have honey-colored caps, with white gills and collars on the stalks.

It is not possible to eradicate an established infection, and ultimately affected plants will die. Armillaria root rot mainly infects new plants by root contact using rhizomorphs (bootlacelike structures that grow through the soil). You should therefore destroy infected plants, taking care to remove as much of their root systems as possible. Severed rhizomorphs in the soil can cause new infections, so leave soil fallow for several months before

replanting. Where armillaria root rot is known to be present, it is wise to choose plants that are less susceptible to infection, such as bald cypress, beech, boxwood, American holly, ginkgo, and yew.

Verticillium wilt

This disease attacks a wide range of plants including potatoes, tomatoes, and peppers; maples, cotinus, and catalpa are also commonly affected. Individual branches wilt and eventually die back, often over successive years. Typically, dark streaking is evident within the vascular tissue of these branches. Sometimes plants may recover.

The disease is soil borne, so badly affected plants and their roots should be removed. You will also need to sterilize tools. When verticillium wilt occurs in vegetable gardens, the only remedy is crop rotation. Conifers, cacti, and ferns are immune and many varieties of plants and crops are resistant.

Phytophthora

There are many species of phytophthora (pronounced 'fi-top-thora'), some of which are highly specific (such as holly blight), while others have a wide host range. Trees and shrubs seem especially susceptible. Infected plants most commonly suffer from a root or stem rot,

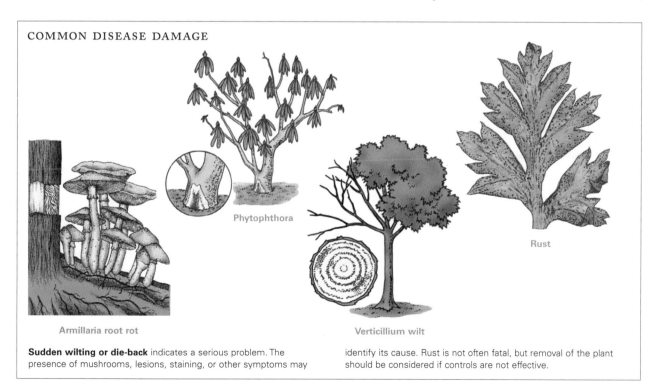

COMMON DISEASE DAMAGE

Phytophthora

Rust

Armillaria root rot

Verticillium wilt

Sudden wilting or die-back indicates a serious problem. The presence of mushrooms, lesions, staining, or other symptoms may identify its cause. Rust is not often fatal, but removal of the plant should be considered if controls are not effective.

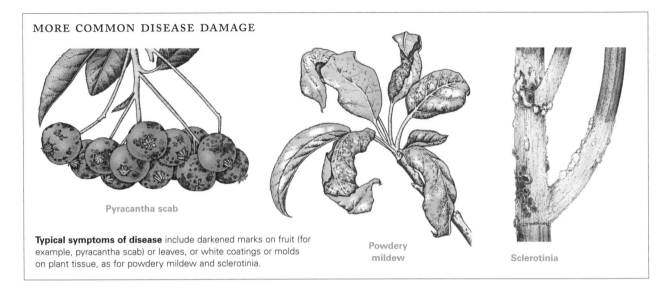

MORE COMMON DISEASE DAMAGE

Pyracantha scab

Powdery mildew

Sclerotinia

Typical symptoms of disease include darkened marks on fruit (for example, pyracantha scab) or leaves, or white coatings or molds on plant tissue, as for powdery mildew and sclerotinia.

characterized by an inverted V-shaped lesion beneath the bark at the stem base, together with rotten roots. Dieback of the canopy becomes evident as infection of the root system advances.

Prevention is the only method of control as the disease can remain dormant in the soil for many years in the form of resting spores. On soil that is known to be infected, you should take measures to improve drainage, and it is important to sterilize garden tools and use clean water for irrigation to limit the amount of cross infection. Avoid using high-nitrogen fertilizers.

Remove affected plants promptly, including their root systems and soil. Choose a nonsusceptible species. Keep the affected area free of woody plants for three years.

Rusts

The first sign of infection is the appearance of pustules of powdery, orange or brown spores on stems and leaf undersides. Corresponding pale spots on upper surfaces of leaves may appear, and the leaves may fall prematurely.

Hygiene is important in controlling an outbreak of rust. Pick off diseased material and destroy it promptly, and at the end of the season remove dead material. Several fungicides are available to protect against infection or to eradicate existing disease. If rust occurs despite these measures, resistant varieties of plants are often available.

Scabs

Apple, crab, and pyracantha fruit are susceptible. The fruits develop brown or black scabs, although on pyracanthas they may be reduced to clusters or small, blackened ruts. Prevent infection of crabapples by raking

and removing infected leaves and applying appropriate fungicides. Resistant varieties are also available.

Powdery mildews

This large group of related fungi affects a very wide range of plants. Typically, a powdery white coating appears on any part of the plant and infected tissue becomes distorted. The leaves may drop, buds die, or stems die back. Outbreaks are most severe on dry soil and in low humidity. Promptly remove infected tissue to reduce further spread.

If available, grow resistant varieties; improving soil conditions and watering regularly will reduce drought stress. It is equally important to encourage good air circulation around the foliage by proper pruning, and ventilation if in a greenhouse. Spraying infected plants with an appropriate fungicide may also help.

Sclerotinia diseases

These affect many vegetables and ornamentals. Symptoms include sudden wilting, yellowing of basal leaves, and a brown rot of the stem. This is associated with white mold, often containing hard, black structures called sclerotia. These fall into the soil to germinate the following spring and cause new infections. Typically, the stem base is attacked, but bulbs, carrots, and parsnips in storage can also be affected.

Destroy infected material before sclerotia can be released into the soil, where they may survive for years. Material should not be composted. The potential host range is very wide, so control weeds that could act as hosts. If infected soil cannot be changed, avoid growing susceptible plants there for up to eight years.

Digging techniques *see page 34* | **Lawn weeds** *see page 296* | **Aquatic weeds** *see page 335*

WEED CONTROL

Successful weeds tend to be fast-growing and colonize new ground rapidly. They must not be allowed to invade ornamental or food-growing areas as they out-compete the plants we want to grow by depriving them of water, nutrients, and light. Understanding how weeds grow can help us to control them. Annual weeds survive long term by producing large quantities of seed, while perennial weeds build up food reserves underground; not only do these reserves make perennial weeds harder to pull out but they also allow them to regrow when the topgrowth is killed. Always aim to remove weeds before they set seed.

Removing weeds

Annual weeds tend to have short, fibrous root systems so are relatively easy to pull up by hand. Their roots rarely survive if the leaves and shoots are killed, so removal with a hoe works well over large areas and between rows of vegetables. Move the blade parallel with the ground, cutting the tops off the weeds just below soil level. It takes immense persistence to control perennial weeds this way.

Digging can be a good way to clear tap-rooted perennials if you are careful to remove the whole root. Unfortunately, it is very difficult to eradicate weeds with creeping underground stems, or storage tubers, by digging alone as any tiny pieces left in the soil will regrow.

Using herbicides

There are many herbicides on the market. Before you buy, check that the product is suitable for the type of weeds you want to kill and the area you want to treat.

Contact herbicides: These act quickly to kill the parts of the plant they touch. They are not carried down to the roots so are effective only against annual weeds.

Systemic herbicides: These tend to act more slowly, but they are carried down to the roots to kill both annual and perennial weeds. Selective systemic herbicides are effective against many broad-leaved weeds, but do not affect grasses, so are useful for lawns.

PERENNIAL WEED ROOT SYSTEMS

Taproots The carrotlike taproots of dandelions, thistles (*shown above*), and docks grow straight down into the soil. They can be removed by deep digging.

Rhizomes Bindweed, bishop's weed, and quack grass (*shown above*) grow from these underground stems. They break into pieces and can be difficult to dig out.

Tubers The numerous tiny bulbils that develop around the tuberous roots of some oxalis (*shown above*) and lesser celandine break off easily and grow into new plants.

FORKING OUT WEEDS

Weeding by hand is effective against most small weeds and many large annuals. If the ground is dry, or the weeds brittle, use a handfork to help. Hand weeding paths and patios is effective only if weeds are caught while small and easy to pull out.

Pre-emergent herbicides: These are applied to an area prior to weed seed germination and are effective against annual weeds such as crabgrass. They kill the young seedlings as they emerge. Do not apply to lawns that are being seeded because the herbicide does not distinguish between weed and grass seed. Corn gluten, a by-product of corn processing, is a natural pre-emergent herbicide. It both suppresses seed germination and supplies nitrogen.

Smothering weeds

Mulches and low-growing or spreading ornamental plants are commonly used to provide a cover over the soil to exclude weeds. Loose mulches, such as lawn-mowings, composted bark, shredded wood products, or gravel, will smother small annual weeds and make it easier to pull out any weeds that do emerge, although they will not stop perennials. Bark and gravel have the added bonus of looking attractive. Loose mulches work well between established plants, but will require regular topping off. For maximum effectiveness in smothering weeds, apply a layer of mulch at least 3in. deep.

Woven or spun landscape fabric, or black plastic, will quickly kill annual weeds. They can also be successful against many perennial weeds, including bishop's weed, if left in place for two growing seasons. Laid under paths and patios, they will help to prevent perennial weeds from pushing through, and they are a good long-term solution between permanent plants, around trees, and for unplanted areas.

Where appearances matter, landscape fabrics can be disguised with a thin layer of bark or other mulch. The best time to lay landscape fabric is when planting a new bed, so the soil can be well cultivated, compost added, and weeds removed before the mulch goes down.

Make sure the soil is moist before you lay a plastic sheet, as water will not easily penetrate once the

USING A LANDSCAPE FABRIC

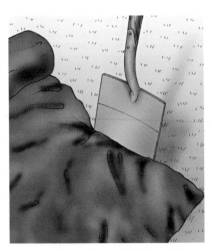

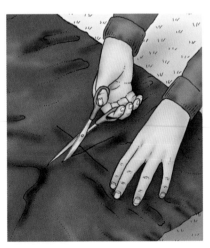

1 **Anchor the landscape fabric** in position by pushing the edges into the soil or weighting them with bricks. If the fabric is to be planted through, then ensure that the ground underneath has been well cultivated, and well watered if it is not already moist.

2 **Cut a cross** in the fabric with sharp scissors or a knife and, using a hand trowel, make a small planting hole in the soil beneath to plant in the normal way. Make the cut no larger than it needs to be as weed seeds will settle and germinate on exposed soil.

3 **Put the plant** through the cut in the landscape fabric and into the planting hole. Firm the soil around it and repeat until all the bed is planted. The fabric can then be covered with a loose mulch of chipped bark, gravel, or pebbles, for example, so it looks attractive.

Mulching *see page 36* | **Lawn weeds** *see page 296* | **Aquatic weeds** *see page 335*

Kudzu vine, originally from Asia, grows so fast that it is sometimes known as the foot-a-night vine. Its smothering growth is now seen across the entire Southeast.

Japanese knotweed is an aggressive weed in Europe and North America. It is very difficult to eradicate as its roots spread widely and up to 10ft. deep underground.

Pampas grass, an attractive and well-behaved ornamental grass in some areas, has become a noxious weed in California where it has spread extensively by seed.

covering is laid. Black plastic is a cheap option for short-term situations, such as vegetable gardens. Landscape fabric is much longer lived, and porous to water, so is suitable for long-term planting such as shrub beds or under paths.

Biodegradable mulches that last only a few months, such as cardboard, newspaper, and straw, can be very useful to help clear weedy ground, such as an overgrown vegetable garden. Cut down all the weeds, spread the mulch over the top, and plant through it. Weeds and mulch will rot down together, and the ground will be much more manageable at the end of the season, when it is cleared.

Ground cover

The most satisfying way to discourage weeds is to cover the ground with attractive plants. In ornamental areas you can use ground-cover plants that are low-growing and vigorous, spreading out to form a dense carpet that prevents weed seeds from germinating. Sadly, ground-cover plants will not prevent perennial roots from regrowing, so it is vital to clear the ground of weeds first. Weeds will also need to be removed until the ground-cover plants have knitted together. Alternatively, plant through a suitable landscape fabric. Evergreen shrubs or perennials make the best plants for ground cover.

In the vegetable garden, bare areas can be planted with cover crops to exclude weeds. Intercropping, making short-term use of the gaps between widely spaced young plants, also helps deny access to weeds. For example, lettuces or radishes can be planted between rows of brassicas or squashes.

Invasive weeds

However bad they are in gardens, many of our weeds are native plants and cause no problems in their natural habitats. Unfortunately, some garden plants have not only become a problem in yards but have also escaped into the wild. Here they can do real damage by smothering native plants, blocking waterways, and depriving wildlife of its natural food or habitat. Sometimes the damage is obvious, where large areas of Japanese knotweed or Japanese barberry prevent anything else from growing. Many problems with these invasive escapees could be prevented if gardeners composted, dried, or burned excess plants, rather than dumping or planting them in the wild.

Noxious weeds

Across the country, states cite various introduced and native plants as noxious weeds. The state-by-state details are available at the U.S.D.A. website, and your state agricultural agencies will be able to provide good local information. Many states and regions also have not-for-profit groups dedicated to raising awareness of this issue.

Never buy plants of any species listed as noxious in your area, never buy seed of them, and never plant them. If you find some in your garden, dig them up to prevent them escaping. Never put them out in the trash or discard them in wild places.

However, if new plants arrive unexpectedly in your yard, do not automatically assume they are invasive weeds. As our climate changes, they may prove to be native plants that are simply moving into the climatic conditions they prefer.

CHAPTER TWO

WILDLIFE GARDENING

57

ENTHUSIASM FOR WILDLIFE AND NATIVE-PLANT GARDENS, derived perhaps from a desire to reconnect with the natural world in an era when technology is so dominant in our lives, has never been stronger, as gardens are the place where most people experience their closest and often most frequent encounters with nature. As a reason to be active outdoors and a simple source of pleasure, gardening for wildlife can enrich your life and your world.

The lure of the wild

The satisfaction of something as simple as seeing your shade garden sparkle with native forest flowers or driving past a statuesque native palm in your graveled front yard every day is only the start of the rich experience of connecting with nature in your own yard.

Plants native to your local area, of course, will connect with your local landscape in a way that garden plants from across the world can never do. And whether you devote your entire yard to native plants, replicate natural habitats in some areas, or integrate native plants into your flower gardens with other plants, they represent a powerful connection between wild nature and the cultivated yard.

When forest is felled to make way for a new development, the gardens created on the cleared land may be the only refuge for wildlife displaced by construction. Your yard could prove to be an invaluable wildlife refuge for all manner of interested creatures.

But before you rush to make changes, ripping out existing garden features, and replacing them with a 'wildlife garden', it is better to begin wildlife gardening by observing what is already there. An understanding of the existing ecosystem allows a sensitive approach to managing the yard.

❧ How to be wildlife friendly

This chapter focuses on how to maximize the wildlife potential of your yard. The first thing to understand is that all yards are, to some degree, wildlife habitats. Even a Japanese-style gravel garden or a yard dominated by hardscape is still likely to harbor insects, spiders, and soil organisms. Once these low-level food chain species are present, higher-level species such as mice, chipmunks, and insectivorous birds will be attracted. These then attract other predators, including foxes, hawks, and owls. Gardens that extend the range of habitats and introduce varied plants as a food source will therefore see biodiversity soar accordingly.

Native plants are always viewed as the premier connection between the garden and wild insects, birds, and other creatures that are attracted by the pollen and nectar, the seeds, the water, or other features. But many garden plants introduced from other countries can be as attractive to wildlife; just count the butterflies on your fall sedums in the flower garden.

Adding a water garden to your yard makes a dramatic difference, especially if it is not maintained too diligently! Even a small pond will add to your yard's attractiveness to wildlife as more insects arrive, insect-eating birds follow them, and amphibians which enjoy the moisture take up residence. 'If you build it, they will come.' Take a step further, add a bird feeder to the scene, and icy winters without flowers will be full of daily joy and entertainment, and you will ensure that birds that would otherwise not survive the rigors of a cold winter make it through the year.

So a combination of local native plants, carefully chosen garden plants, thoughtful adaptation of your yard, and bird feeders will bring a wealth of wildlife very close to home. You could even have your garden certified as a Wildlife Habitat by the National Wildlife Federation.

WILDLIFE IN YOUR YARD

To create a suitable environment in your yard for wildlife to thrive, you must take into account two elements: habitat creation and habitat improvement. For the first, consider your property as a whole and think about features that will attract insects, birds, and other animals. You might want to create a woodland area, a bog garden, or redesign your garden entirely. For the second, assess your garden or part of it and work on ways to develop existing habitats. For example, you could put up nest-boxes, replace a fence with a hedge, make a ladybeetle refuge, or add a green roof to a shed.

Garden wildlife

You can attract wildlife to your garden by providing the necessities of life: food, water for bathing and drinking, and accommodation for nesting and protection. Keep in mind that by extending a welcome to wildlife you may also attract some unwanted visitors, including those who will prey on the very creatures you have encouraged. Knowing how to discourage the predators common in your area will help you to create the right balance for a successful garden habitat.

Birds

Loved by most gardeners, birds are readily attracted by a year-round supply of clean, ice-free water and food. You should site both in an open area, so the birds are not so vulnerable to predators like cats and hawks, but with the shelter of shrubs nearby.

For water, a shallow bowl or pond edge makes it easy for birds to drink and bathe. Heated bowls are available if your winters are icy. For food, put out a variety of bird seed mixes to attract the greatest diversity. Also use a range of feeders: wire-mesh peanut dispensers, seed feeders, bird tables, ground-feeding tables, and suet block holders in winter.

Natural foods are equally important (*see page 68*). Grow berry- and seed-producing trees, shrubs, perennials, and vines. Keep some areas of short grass so that robins can probe for ants and worms. Attract hummingbirds by growing perennials, vines, and shrubs with trumpet-shaped flowers such as bee balm (*Monarda*), trumpet creeper, and columbine. Where safe to do so, leave cavities in trees and walls to allow birds such as owls, nuthatches, woodpeckers, and even ducks to nest.

PLANNING A WILDLIFE GARDEN

Key
1. Seat
2. Shade garden
3. Mown path
4. Shelter/summerhouse
5. Meadow
6. Rotting logs
7. Mixed hedge
8. Pond visible from all angles
9. Log piles
10. Berry-producing trees
11. Family terrace or deck
12. Butterfly garden
13. Bird table in view of window
14. Shrubs with winter berries

Many wildlife-friendly features can be included in any yard. The gardener's needs must be considered alongside the main wildlife theme, so that the yard is also ornamental and practical.

Know your friends *see page 40* | **Wildlife plants** *see page 68* | **Growing ornamentals** *see page 70*

ARTIFICIAL & NATURAL WILDLIFE HABITATS

Wooden bird box

Woodpecker & tree hole

Sunbathing lizard on rock

Hibernating ladybeetle cluster

Stag beetle on log

Caterpillar hidden by leaf

Native bee box

By improving your garden habitat you can attract a great diversity of wildlife to your yard. Bird and bee boxes are straightforward enhancements, as are long grass and stones for reptiles and amphibians, and piles of old logs for beetles. If you grow a good range of garden plants it allows any wildlife to make a home for itself, in and among trees and shrubs, often in uncultivated areas.

Bats

Position bat boxes (*see right*) in trees or on walls, at least 10ft. above ground level. Face them out of the prevailing wind and rain, sited in the shade to reduce temperature fluctuations. Cavities in trees are often used by bats as a protected wintering site, while you may also have them hibernating under your siding.

Grow nectar- and pollen-rich plants, particularly those that attract moths, as these will provide ready meals for bats. Some bats are becoming rare, so gardeners can really contribute to their survival.

Bees

The lure of pollen and nectar is enough to attract bees to your garden, and as long as there are plants in flower they will continue to visit. Avoid applying insecticides, as they will kill bees and other beneficial and predatory insects.

Provide nesting sites for native bees in the form of open-ended hollow tubes; you can buy them ready-made, or use bundles of drinking straws. Undisturbed hedge bases or sunny banks also make good nesting sites. Bees need a source of shallow water for drinking.

MAKING A BAT BOX

1 Use 6 pieces of waste lumber to make a simple box, about 8in. tall and 4in. wide. It needs to be rough sawn with ridges ½in. apart on the inside of the back panel, as this helps the bats to cling. Try to use untreated wood for the box.

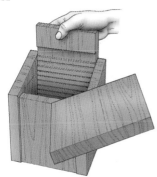

2 Piece the box together with screws or nails and make holes in the back panel so the box can be fitted to a wall or tree in the same way. Between the bottom and back panels, leave a gap of about ¾in. wide so that the bats can gain access.

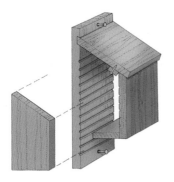
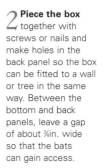

Hummingbirds feed on nectar and are attracted to plants with tubular, often red, flowers such as agastache, columbine, monarda, penstemon, salvia, trumpet vine, and yucca. You can provide additional food by hanging feeders filled with a mixture of 1 part sugar dissolved in 4 parts water. Avoid the use of food coloring in hummingbird feeders.

Lacewings, flower flies, & ladybeetles

Tolerate some aphids in your garden to ensure sufficient food for these natural predators. Leave stems of perennial plants standing through the winter to provide cover and protection for overwintering adults, or make a lacewing and ladybeetle refuge. Many species of adult flower fly (also known as hoverfly) visit pollen- and nectar-bearing flowers, particularly those with open centers.

Beetles & centipedes

Ground beetles, identifiable by their black bodies and scurrying habit, are ferocious predators of slugs and other soil pests, as are centipedes. To provide them with cover and good hunting territory, mulch beds with organic matter, grow ground-cover plants, leave the soil as undisturbed as possible, and place stones and logs around the garden. Centipedes require a similar habitat.

Butterflies & moths

To enjoy adult butterflies and moths, there must be some tolerance of their caterpillars, which eat plants. It is worth planting swathes of both caterpillar-food plants and nectar plants, the latter attracting the largest number of butterflies if planted in full sun. Some butterflies will also feed on fallen fruit, such as apples and pears, if it is left to rot.

Night-flowering plants are needed to attract most moths, although 'sugaring' is also effective. This involves smearing a tree trunk or wooden post with a thick, sugary compound such as a molasses solution.

Snakes & lizards

Although venomous snakes are an occasional hazard in gardens, harmless species such as the common garter snake are found all over North America and help to keep down the numbers of insects in the garden. Lizards are likewise beneficial; encourage them by providing log and rock piles so they can shelter and sun themselves.

Chipmunks

Delightful and entertaining, although they sometimes eat flower bulbs and plant roots, chipmunks tend to prefer nuts, mushrooms, seeds and fruits, insects, and worms. Their burrows can be annoying, but the minor irritations of having chipmunks in the yard are more than compensated for by the pleasure of watching them.

Squirrels

The gray squirrel and, in areas where conifers are common, the red squirrel are entertaining garden residents or visitors. The ingenuity of the gray squirrel in stealing from bird feeders is well known and fascinating, but genuinely squirrel-proof feeders are now available. More serious is their love of corn ears and flower bulbs.

Frogs & toads

Although some people find their peeping and croaking annoying, frogs and toads are an invaluable component of the garden habitat; a garden pond will act like a magnet to them. Frogs tend to eat insects, toads are less particular.

Deer

Deer are found eating our gardens more and more often. As new homes are built in the woods and the deer become braver in their search for food, even in cities our flowers and vegetables are under attack. Some plants are deer resistant; sprays and other deterrents sometimes work; a lively dog can help. The only sure way to protect your yard from deer is a tall fence (*see box, right*).

Foxes

The red fox is the most widespread mammal in the world and native to almost all of North America. Its tolerance of a wide range of climates and habitats allows it to make use of our yards everywhere, and red foxes are increasingly living in suburbs, moving into yards from golf courses, cemeteries, and other open spaces. They are a delight to see; watch carefully from your deck at night.

Opossums

Familiar in both suburbs and rural areas, the strange-looking, marsupial opossum has a very varied diet including insects, worms, and fruit. They can damage lawns as they dig for grubs. Often itinerant, at times they may take over a burrow or nest under a deck, then move on when food runs out. Cats seem to coexist with them happily; dogs are less tolerant.

Raccoons

The endearing, black-and-white striped face of the raccoon distracts us from two unfortunate problems. Raccoons can cause havoc in garden ponds, and in fruit and vegetable gardens, digging up root vegetables, eating unripe fruit and anything else that takes their fancy. They also carry rabies; while people are very rarely infected, dogs and cats are more susceptible although vaccination is very effective.

Bears

Brown and black bears are widespread in America, and while primarily rural animals they are sometimes seen in cities and suburbs, and often found in yards when in search of food after they emerge from hibernation in spring. Bird feeders are especially attractive, and bears have a great fondness for black-oil sunflower seed and for sugared hummingbird water. In some states, attracting bears to your yard—even as a side-effect of having bird feeders—is illegal. As well as damaging shrubs and other plants, garden furniture, and trashcans as they search for food, bears can break down deer fences, allowing the deer to do their worst.

SOME COMMON WILDLIFE

Leafy and twiggy shrubs and hedges provide places for birds to escape predators and to nest. Encourage birds to nest by hanging loose bits of string or wool nearby. Avoid pruning hedges during the birds' nesting season.

Foxes and coyotes are scavengers rather than garden pests, but they can pose a threat to household pets and pond life. A large guard dog or a secure fence may be the only means of deterrence.

Raccoons, skunks, armadillos, and opossums can be trapped and relocated but there is no effective way to prevent their return. Eliminating food sources such as lawn grubs may make your yard less attractive.

Physical barriers are the best way to protect your garden plants from deer. Cage individual plants or build a fence at least 8ft. tall, or try two shorter fences spaced 5ft. apart. Wire mesh is the best fencing material.

In suburban or rural areas where bears are present, never leave garbage or sources of food such as bird feeders where bears can reach them. In a small garden, a very sturdy or electric fence may deter bears.

Wildlife ponds

A good wildlife garden has a variety of water features to provide the greatest range of habitats; these may include a pond, a small cascade with drop pools, a stone trough or barrel, a pebble fountain, or simply a bird bath. Even small balconies can accommodate an old sink filled with rainwater, a couple of pond plants, or a dwarf waterlily. Building a wildlife pond in your garden is the single most worthwhile addition in terms of attracting wildlife.

Siting & design

A flexible liner, such as E.P.D.M. (*see page 313*), gives much more scope to a wildlife-friendly design. Preformed and formal ponds often have steep edges, poorly suited to wildlife—they must be fitted with ramps to allow animals that have fallen in to escape.

You will attract the greatest amount of wildlife if at least part of your pond is in sun. A dense marginal planting on at least one side will give young frogs some protection from predators when leaving the pond. A log pile or bog garden (*see page 322*) that adjoins the pond also makes an excellent wildlife shelter and provides a more natural transition between land and water.

Deep-water areas for amphibians to breed and a shallow zone or beach are essential. The latter not only provides good access for birds and amphibians but also

Multifaceted, informally designed ponds are the best for wildlife as they include a diversity of niches and habitats. This pond has small waterfalls, dense marginal plantings, lots of hiding places between the rocks, and waterlilies covering part of the water surface.

creates the best habitat for small aquatic creatures that live in the pebbles, mud, and shallow water. The pond edge is also important. Hide the liner by tucking it under sod (*see page 321*). This allows the grass to grow into the pond, providing cover to the water's edge. Large stone

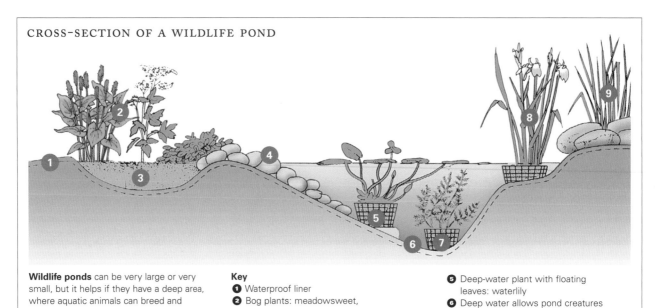

CROSS-SECTION OF A WILDLIFE POND

Wildlife ponds can be very large or very small, but it helps if they have a deep area, where aquatic animals can breed and overwinter, and a shallow shelf or beach so creatures can enter and exit the pond. A bog garden area is not essential, but it does make a useful transition zone from land to water for frogs and toads.

Key
1. Waterproof liner
2. Bog plants: meadowsweet, pickerel weed
3. Bog area filled with soil
4. Shallow slope with pebble beach to give animals a place to enter and exit the water
5. Deep-water plant with floating leaves: waterlily
6. Deep water allows pond creatures to overwinter
7. Submerged plants: American water milfoil
8. Marginal plants: water iris
9. Long grass gives creatures cover

slabs or logs also make a good edge, particularly where a few gaps are left to allow frogs to shelter under the overhang. Lay an old tree branch part in and part out of the water. Dragonflies and damselflies use mossy structures like this for laying their eggs.

Fish

Fish eat algae and insects, including mosquitoes. Any pool with a depth of 1½ft. in mild climates can accommodate small fish, but in cooler climates such small ponds may freeze solid in winter. You'll need a pond at least 3–4ft. deep for larger, more vigorous fish.

Children

Gardens where young children play can still be host to a pond; metal grids can be fitted to make them safe (*see page 311*). Alternatively, you could create shallow rills or a bog garden, perhaps by filling in a preexisting pond with soil. Children should always be supervised around water.

Planting a wildlife pond

Even though this should be left to natural colonization, most gardeners prefer to plant directly, as this gives them control over how the pond will look. Choose a range of aquatic plants (*see page 324*). Although it can appear more attractive to leave a big expanse of clear water in the center of a pond, remember that most aquatic wildlife prefers the security of complex, underwater planting.

Introducing plants and animals from other ponds should only be attempted if you are confident that the material is noninvasive and disease free. Never take samples from the wild, or from any pond without the owner's permission. Avoid introducing invasive aquatic weeds (*see page 335*).

Maintaining a wildlife pond

Fill and top up the pond where possible with rain or well water, but do not be afraid to allow the pond to occasionally dry out, since many invertebrate creatures will survive in the mud at the bottom. Municipal water should be used only as a last resort as it can lead to a pH imbalance in the pond.

A few leaves falling in the pond is no bad thing, but excessive amounts release toxic compounds into the water as they rot. If netting is used to keep out leaves, ensure it is kept taut to prevent birds from getting caught. Clear out excessive vegetation and silt in late summer when the water level is at its lowest. Aim to clear only a section or half of the pond in one year to allow recolonization of wildlife from the undisturbed areas.

ENCOURAGING POND WILDLIFE

Overhanging branches make good perching spots for birds. Larger branches double up as ramps on straight-sided ponds.

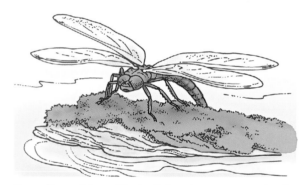

Dragonflies and damselflies lay their eggs on moss-covered surfaces, such as half-submerged logs and rocks.

An area of long grass and tall plants at the pond edge is an important haven for young amphibians as they venture out of the pond.

Creating a wildflower meadow

By devoting an area of your yard to wildflowers, you create a haven for wildlife and enhance the overall sustainability of your garden. Although wildflower meadows vary greatly from one region to another, a functioning meadow is a mixture of flowering perennials, grasses, and grasslike plants—often but not always native to the area—enhanced with annuals and bulbs. Meadow plantings in general require less irrigation than traditional borders and turfgrass, and there should be no need for the use of pesticides and herbicides. However, meadows are not maintenance free; good preparation of the site and proper plant selection are essential and will help to prevent future problems.

Wildflower plants

Before planting wildflowers, it's best to consult with a knowledgeable local source about which plants will grow well in your area. Some meadow favorites, such as coreopsis, rudbeckias, coneflowers, lupines, daisies, and many grasses and sedges, are suitable for wildflower plantings in many parts of the country, but a local native plant society and your cooperative extension service can tell you more about species suitable for your climate and soil, as well as which ones to blend in a seed mix and which to start from plugs or container-grown plants.

Spring meadows make use of spring-flowering bulbs and perennials. The area is left uncut until they flower, then left to die down naturally after flowering. The meadow is then kept mown until fall.

Adapting an existing lawn

Although it's possible to kill an existing lawn with herbicide, it's preferable to dig up the turf. Then you must eliminate any remaining grass and weeds by covering the ground with dark plastic or newspaper covered with mulch and leaving them in place for up to several months.

CREATING A WILDFLOWER MEADOW FROM SCRATCH

1 **Remove the topsoil** from the area and fill with less-fertile subsoil 4–6 weeks before sowing. Remove any weeds that appear by hand or with herbicide, then prepare the ground as for sowing a lawn (*see page 288*).

2 **Bulk up the seed mix** with an equal amount of sand. A typical meadow seed mix consists of 85 percent grass species and 15 percent wildflower species.

3 **Sow the seeds** evenly in early fall, or spring for heavier soils. Sow half the batch in one direction and half in the opposite direction, before lightly raking in. Water the seeds after sowing and during dry spells.

CONVERTING LAWNS TO MEADOWS

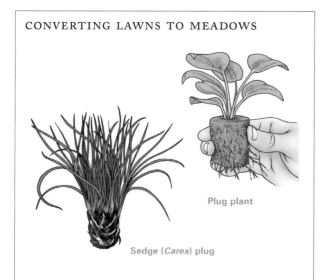

Plug plant

Sedge (*Carex*) plug

Plugs are the quickest and most economical method of establishing a mix of meadow grasses, perennials, and grasslike plants such as sedges. These will quickly establish and help to crowd out weeds.

MOWING A MEADOW

Mow from early fall to early spring for summer meadows. For spring-flowering meadows, leave them unmown from spring to midsummer, then cut. For an even mix of seasonal flowers, cut just once in early fall. The height of cut for routine mowing should be no less than 3in.

A weed trimmer is the best tool for cutting back long grasses. Grasses with softer foliage can be cut with a string trimmer. Many perennial grasses have tough stems and leaf stalks; for these, fit the weed trimmer with a sawblade attachment. Always wear protective eyewear when cutting back long grasses.

A quicker alternative is solarization—covering the ground with clear plastic for several weeks during the summer. The temperature under the plastic will quickly rise, killing off weeds as they germinate.

Establishing a meadow

Unlike most garden soil, a wildflower meadow should be low in fertility, so do not amend before planting. Spring and fall are the best times to establish the meadow. Lightly loosen the soil with a rake and then scatter wildflower seeds (*see facing page*). Cover the seedbed with a light mulch. If planting plugs or container-grown plants, loosen the soil in the planting hole but do not add fertilizer. Plant in clumps or broad swathes. Use a bulb planter to add a few groupings of bulbs. Irrigate the new meadow regularly.

Mowing & maintenance

Weeding is the major task in a wildflower meadow. As the plants become established, learn to identify desirable wildflowers and remove weeds by hand. Most meadow perennials will not flower until their second season, but annuals such as Californian poppy or cornflower may bloom in the first season. Most meadows are mown once or twice a year (*see box, above right*), but you can define the edges with a closely mown strip and increase interest by mowing a winding path through the center. Take care when mowing not to disturb nesting birds or other creatures that have found a home in the meadow.

Summer meadows come into their own toward the end of spring as the flowers appear. They are mown once the display is over.

WILDLIFE PLANTS

Wildlife is incredibly adaptable to even the harshest environment, but remove plants from the equation and the majority of animals would struggle to survive. From providing organic material for soil organisms to offering nesting sites for birds, plants perform a myriad of roles. In fact, the act of simply growing plants is probably more important than any other single wildlife gardening activity, and the wider the diversity of plants you grow, the more wildlife you are likely to attract to your yard. Plants are also used to link green areas together, making your yard part of a larger and greater wildlife entity.

Choosing plants

You could say that all gardens are wildlife gardens, but some plants provide more resources for wildlife than others. Instead of worrying about choosing the 'right' plants, start by deciding on how to use plants to create the most diverse habitats. One way to do this is by varying the heights of planting (*see below*), from low-lying lawns and pond plants through to long meadow grasses, perennial plants, small shrubs, vines, and finally trees.

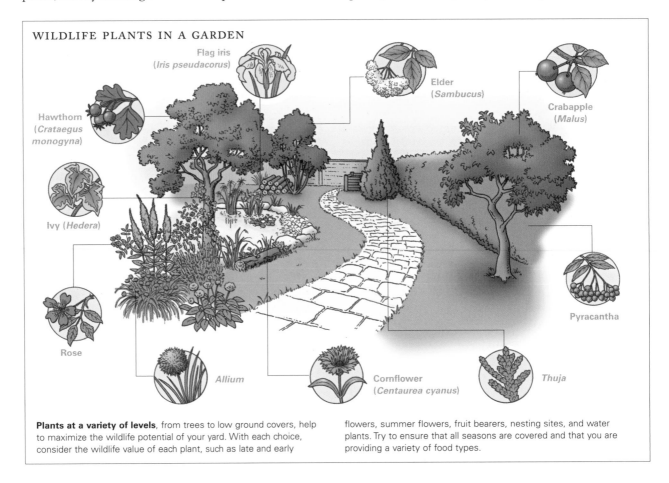

WILDLIFE PLANTS IN A GARDEN

Flag iris (*Iris pseudacorus*)

Hawthorn (*Crataegus monogyna*)

Ivy (*Hedera*)

Rose

Allium

Cornflower (*Centaurea cyanus*)

Thuja

Pyracantha

Elder (*Sambucus*)

Crabapple (*Malus*)

Plants at a variety of levels, from trees to low ground covers, help to maximize the wildlife potential of your yard. With each choice, consider the wildlife value of each plant, such as late and early flowers, summer flowers, fruit bearers, nesting sites, and water plants. Try to ensure that all seasons are covered and that you are providing a variety of food types.

Purple coneflower is an attractive native which attracts butterflies such as swallowtails.

Sweet rocket is a weed in some areas but invaluable for wildlife in others.

Red valerian flowers all summer long, attracting butterflies to its bright flowers.

Native versus introduced species

An increasing number of gardeners choose to restrict themselves to growing native plants. However, studies have shown that there are many introduced species that attract wildlife and, unless there is a desire to attract a highly specialized insect or animal, then the need to plant natives at the exclusion of all other plants is not justified. The good news is that plants known to be useful to wildlife include a good proportion of ornamentals, which means wildlife gardens can be packed with attractive plants.

The need for trees

Trees, by their very size, are vital to a good wildlife garden. If there are trees in neighboring gardens and your yard is very small, then leave it at that. But if there is a dearth of trees in the area, see if you can make room for one. Oaks host an exceptional range of wildlife, but grow quite large; maples come in a range of sizes. Consider the impact on your neighbors when planting trees close to property lines.

Nectar & pollen

Hummingbirds, butterflies, moths, bees, flower flies, and pollen beetles all feed from flowers. Hummingbirds prefer tubular flowers, but most wildlife are attracted to open, single flowers. Look for plants with a long season of bloom, or those that flower early or late when other food sources are scarce.

Berries, fruit, & seeds

Relieve some of the time and expense of feeding garden birds with bird food by stocking your garden with plants that offer berries, fruit, and seeds. It is a joy to watch goldfinches eating seeds from your evening primroses. The principles are very simple: Check before you plant to see if a shrub or tree needs separate male and female plants to fruit, and avoid cutting back seedheads until late winter. Other creatures such as chipmunks, mice, voles, and even foxes also enjoy these natural meals.

Larval food plants

It is leaf-eating creatures, especially the larvae of moths and butterflies, that are perhaps most fussy about their food plants. If you want to attract a particular butterfly, for instance, it is best to do your homework and find out which plants are needed for the caterpillar stage. Some of these plants may be grasses, so it would make sense to plan a wildflower meadow (*see page 66*) with the desirable grass species in the mix. Plant dense groups of the same plant in large numbers to convince the egg-laying females that your site will support many hungry mouths. And, of course, be prepared to tolerate some leaf damage.

Planting for small yards

In urban areas, where yards are smaller, plants need to be high performers. Those that provide multiple resources—for example by producing not just nectar and pollen but also seeds, foliage for herbivores, and a nesting habitat—are worth including in even the smallest of spaces.

For height, plant fruit- and seed-bearing trees such as dogwood, holly, or mulberry. Cover walls and arbors with vines such as virginia creeper. Lavender and chives are good wildlife plants for pots, while colorful annuals such as cosmos and bachelor's buttons are simple to grow along with perennial sedums and salvias in order to attract hummingbirds.

CHAPTER THREE

GROWING ORNAMENTALS

PLANTS GROWN FOR THEIR BEAUTY ARE KNOWN AS ORNAMENTALS. They are planted so that their flowers, scent, foliage, fall color, berries, or winter bark can be admired and make our outdoor living spaces beautiful places to be. Some gardeners also deliberately include plants that attract, or create habitat for, birds, butterflies, and other beneficial wildlife. These are often a mixture of flowering plants favored by nectar gatherers, fruiting plants that provide berries or nuts, and evergreen plants that provide cover and nesting places. Creating an ornamental garden is simple if you follow a few basic design rules. Any size of yard, even a balcony, roof space, or tiny courtyard, can accommodate ornamentals.

Types of plants

An understanding of different plant types is required if a design is going to be attractive all year. Some modern designs use planting schemes like single beds of one type of flower, but yards are usually more exciting if there is a mix of plants that either complement or contrast in shape, color, and texture.

Annuals grow from seed to flower and then die all in one year; in addition to ornamentals, many vegetables fit into this category. Biennials produce foliage in the first year, flower in the second year, and then die. Plants known as perennials are essentially nonwoody plants that live for at least two years—ornamental grasses and ferns are usually considered part of this group. Most die back to ground level in winter and reappear in spring. Some plants that are perennial in warm-climate regions but are killed by frost are known as tender perennials; these include tropical and subtropical plants such as cannas and elephant's ear.

Often referred to as the 'bones' of the garden, long-lived trees and shrubs have a permanent, woody structure that serves as a framework for the garden's design. They may be deciduous or evergreen, and their key features can include flowers, berries, bark, and foliage. Trees tend to have one central trunk, while shrubs are often multistemmed or branch very near the ground.

Climbing plants, commonly known as vines, can be either woody-stemmed or herbaceous. Some are annuals and need to be replanted every year, but many are perennial and can grace walls, trellises, or other structures for years.

A plant group that is rapidly gaining in popularity among American gardeners is succulents. Often native to arid regions, these plants store water in thick, fleshy leaves and are often drought tolerant. Succulents, which include cacti, range from statuesque and sculptural agaves to tiny, geometric wonders such as hens-and-chicks (*Sempervivum*).

The key to growing any of these plants successfully is choosing the right plants for the location. Select plants compatible with the soil in your garden; basic soil-testing kits can be bought from garden centers. Some plants are sun-lovers while others prefer shade, so check which areas of your garden receive sunlight and at what time of day.

Winter hardiness also varies, so the average minimum winter temperatures in different regions, based on the U.S. Department of Agriculture's plant hardiness zone map (*see page 12*), should be used as a guide to determining which plants can be grown in your area. Plants also differ in their tolerance of high summer temperatures and high humidity. More detailed information about the hardiness and heat tolerance of individual plants can be found in the American Horticultural Society's several plant encyclopedias and on the A.H.S. website.

PLACING PLANTS

Choosing the right plant for the right place should be the guiding principle when buying any plant for your yard. Plants for a sunny location will have to endure baking hot conditions all day long. Even in cool climates, heatwaves are not unusual, and plants need to tolerate drought if they are to stand any chance of survival. Every yard also has shaded areas, and many gardeners are inclined to see these as problem areas. It is true that profusely flowering annuals will not perform in such conditions, but shade-loving plants range from elegant to dramatic, so a shady spot need never be dull.

Gardens in sun

Plenty of plants revel in hot sun, but some can be tender and may require protection from the elements over winter. Drought-tolerant plants are a good choice, but they may struggle with wet fall and winter weather. Add grit and sand to the soil to alleviate this problem.

Look beyond bright summer flowers

Many gardeners instantly think of brilliantly colored summer annuals, such as marigolds, for summer color in sunny gardens. But there is also an increasing range of annuals in more subtle and more stylish colors that blend in with each other more successfully. Many sun-loving perennials also bring softer, more restful tones as well as

Drifts of color that extend to both sides of the border are key to prairie-style perennial planting. In all styles, perennial plants look most natural planted in odd-numbered groups of 3 or more.

a huge range of flower shapes, while vines and shrubs add height and screening capabilities.

Many fruit trees thrive in sunny places that help the fruit ripen and develop its full sweetness and flavor; apples and peaches make attractive trees with the bonus of blossoms, and grape vines can be grown over arbors.

Foliage plants

Many plants that flourish in the hot sun have silvery or velvety foliage to cope with the heat, and most of the herbs with edible or aromatic foliage are sun lovers. Many ornamental grasses can cope with dry weather and also offer interest through winter months. The same is true of dramatic foliage plants such as yuccas, cordylines, agaves, bananas, and palms. Many evergreen shrubs and conifers tolerate drought and give structure and color during winter even when covered in snow.

Style & structure

Look to naturally sunny places for design inspiration. Prairie-style plantings combine ornamental grasses and hot-colored perennials. Mediterranean styles use silvery foliage shrubs and herbs with arbors, trees, and outdoor dining areas, but these plants need good drainage and may not survive in colder zones. Subtropical gardens, with luxuriant growth, foliage, and exotic flowers, are better for heavier, more moisture-retentive soils.

Create height at the back of borders with shrubs and tall perennials such as delphiniums or sunflowers. Train vines like sweet peas, which adore the sun so long as they have nutrient-rich soil, on structures of bamboo canes or elegant steel frames (*see page 139*). Place these taller plants carefully to avoid casting shade on other plantings.

PLANTS FOR SUN

PERENNIALS & ANNUALS

Black-eyed Susan (*Rudbeckia fulgida*, shown) Daisylike, yellow flowers bloom all summer. Z4

***Calamagrostis* x *acutiflora* 'Karl Foerster'** Tall grass for prairie planting with perennials. Summer flowerheads last well into winter. Z5

Delphinium Back-of-the-border favorite for its blue spires. Needs fertile soil. Z3

Eryngium bourgatii Silver bracts on branching blue stems last well for winter displays. Prefers a poor soil. Z5

Eschscholzia californica Intense orange and yellow annuals for well-drained, poor soil.

***Perovskia* 'Blue Spire' (shown)** Spires of bright blue flowers and silvery gray foliage. Z6

***Phlox paniculata* 'David'** White flowers bloom on 3ft. stems. Z4

Red hot poker (*Kniphofia*) Retain foliage over winter to protect from cold. Z4–Z7

Salvia argentea Rosettes of velvety silver leaves make a perfect foil for bright annuals. Remove flowers for best foliage display. Z5

Sunflower (*Helianthus annuus*) Wide range of colors and heights to choose from.

BULBS

Allium cristophii Globes of purple flowers are held aloft in spring; they dry well. Z5

***Crocosmia* 'Lucifer' (shown)** Clumps of searing red flowers in summer. Z6

***Tulipa* 'Queen of Night'** Dark maroon-black blooms; likes well-drained, sunny sites. Z4

VINES

***Campsis* 'Madame Galen'** Grow against a wall for orange, trumpetlike blooms. Z5

Coral honeysuckle (*Lonicera sempervirens*) Prolific, reddish orange flowers attract hummingbirds. Z4

***Passiflora caerulea* (shown)** Glossy foliage, exotic flowers, and occasional yellow fruit. Z6

Rose climbers and ramblers Hundreds available; most perform best in full sun. Z5

Trachelospermum jasminoides Self-clinging evergreen with scented, white flowers. Z9

TREES & SHRUBS

Abelia* x *grandiflora Fragrant, white flowers on arching, semievergreen stems. Z6

***Artemisia* 'Powis Castle' (shown)** Silvery foliage for rock garden or border. Z7

Bottlebrush (*Callistemon*) Evergreen with red flowers and attractive seeds. Z8–Z10

Calluna vulgaris Varieties of this popular heather require an acidic soil. Z5

Ceanothus Deciduous or evergreen shrubs with blue flowers. Z4–Z9

Crape myrtle Multistemmed, large shrub has late-summer flowers in pastel colors. Z7

Euphorbia characias* subsp. *wulfenii Shrub with lime-green flowers. Z7

***Lavandula angustifolia* 'Hidcote'** Scented, bright blue flowers and silvery foliage. Z5

Phlomis fruticosa Evergreen shrub with gray-green, aromatic foliage and yellow flowers. Z8

Pittosporum tobira Handsome evergreen with fragrant, white flowers. Z9

Rock rose (*Cistus*) Drought-tolerant shrub with large, pink or white flowers. Z9

Rosemary (*Rosmarinus*, shown) Ideal for dry conditions, with usually blue flowers. Z8

Sweet pepperbush (*Clethra alnifolia*) Deciduous shrub has fragrant, white to pink flowers. Z5

***Crocosmia* 'Lucifer'** enjoys the sun but also appreciates moist soil in summer.

Black-eyed Susans are heat- and drought-tolerant perennials.

Artemisia 'Powis Castle' is a striking foliage plant, pruned in spring to keep it compact.

Passiflora caerulea may be evergreen or semievergreen in warmer climates.

***Perovskia* 'Blue Spire'** prefers a soil that is well drained but fertile. Prune hard in spring.

Rosemary is a shrublike herb with glossy, aromatic leaves, widely used in cooking.

Gardens in shade

An area of shade in a garden should be treated as an asset. There are many plants suitable for these conditions, offering a diverse palette of textures and colors. In lower light levels, the flower colors are usually softer and more subdued than those of sun-loving plants, creating tranquil havens from the heat of the midday sun.

Types of shade
Light levels range from the dense shade cast by large buildings and evergreen trees to the dappled shade of a deciduous canopy, which can be underplanted with woodland spring bulbs. Canopies can be lightened by thinning tree crowns. Experiment with plants and work with the conditions to create drama and intrigue.

Dry shade is found near buildings or under trees and shrubs that leach moisture from the soil; it creates challenging conditions. Add organic matter to the soil to retain moisture, and water young plants frequently to get them established. For ground covers, try dead nettles (*Lamium*), epimediums, heucheras, hardy geraniums, and low-growing shrubs such as *Mahonia aquifolium*.

Most woodland bulbs prefer slightly damp or moisture-retentive soil in dappled sunlight, where ligularias and primroses are worth trying. Only moisture-loving plants such as *Trollius europaeus* or *Caltha palustris* enjoy sitting permanently in water in moderate shade.

Large, lush leaves are characteristic of shade-loving plants, so exploit them to make a garden composed of texture rather than vibrant color.

Not many plants flower in deep shade. Evergreen conifer woods are challenging environments where little or nothing can grow, and in deciduous forests woodland plants flower early in the year, before trees are in full leaf.

Flowers & fruits in shade
Plant bulbs in large clumps, and—for temporary displays—annuals like polyanthus primroses, impatiens, and begonias. These can also be grown in containers and placed in shade, with new containers replacing them when the display is over.

Cyclamen, winter aconites (*Eranthis*), hellebores, and snowdrops provide a late-winter floral display, while mahonia and daphne flowers provide an intoxicating fragrance at the shrub level. The highlight of the year is spring, with shrubs such as camellias and rhododendrons, while bluebells (*Hyacinthoides*) and anemones carpet the ground. Even species daffodils like *Narcissus bulbocodium* work well in light shade. Nothing is more spectacular in a woodland garden than *Cardiocrinum giganteum*, with its display of white summer flowers, and the late-summer flowerheads of *Hydrangea paniculata*. For decorative fruit that will provide food for birds and other wildlife, try wintergreen (*Gaultheria procumbens*), salal (*G. shallon*), and viburnums.

Foliage interest
The glossy leaves of evergreen shrubs such as camellias and rhododendrons provide year-round interest; for a more exotic look try the palm-shaped leaves of *Fatsia japonica*. Distribute evergreens throughout the planting scheme so that shades of green create a backdrop to the flowers. Japanese maples are also wonderful foliage plants for areas in dappled shade. Hostas and ferns are popular foliage perennials, adding texture and a splash of subtle color to any planting. Vibrant color can be added with golden-variegated Japanese forest grass (*Hakonechloa macra* 'Aureola'), which spreads slowly to form a ground cover.

Structure & seasonal change
Creating tiers of interest is easier in a shade garden than a sunny garden, because you do not need to worry about taller plants casting shade over smaller ones.

Trees and shrubs such as maples or viburnums can provide the backbone to any design. If possible, clothe shade-creating trees or buildings with shade-loving vines such as climbing hydrangea or winter jasmine. Perennials and bulbs create seasonal interest.

Know your yard *see page 14* | Know your soil *see page 32* | Container gardening *see page 342*

PLANTS FOR SHADE

PERENNIALS & BULBS

Cardiocrinum giganteum Dramatic, 6ft. tall, bulbous plant with white trumpet flowers. Z7

Cyclamen coum (shown) Tuberous perennial with white to pink flowers in late winter to spring. Z5

Erythronium 'Pagoda' Slender stems carry pale yellow flowers; for moist areas. Z4

Galium odoratum Ground-cover perennial with clusters of narrow leaves and small, white, starry flowers in summer. Z5

Hosta (shown) Perennial for moist conditions, with bold foliage and spires of white or lilac flowers. Z3

Japanese painted fern Decorative, small fern with silvery blue fronds. Z5

Kirengeshoma palmata Large divided foliage and yellow, bell-shaped flowers. Z5

Lamium maculatum 'White Nancy' Ground cover with silver leaves and white flowers. Z4

Lenten rose (*Helleborus* x *hybridus*, shown) Low-growing perennial that bears large nodding flowers in many colors in early spring. Z6

Lily-of-the-valley (*Convallaria majalis*) Scented, white flowers; can be vigorous. Z2

Pachysandra terminalis Perennial evergreen with dark green leaves and small, white, spring flowers. Prefers moist soil. Z4

Polystichum munitum Clumping fern with leathery, dark green fronds. Z3

Solomon's seal (*Polygonatum* x *hybridum*) White, bell-shaped flowers, hanging from arching stems in spring. Z6

Trillium (shown) Spring-flowering perennials for slightly acid, moist but well-drained soil. Z5

Waldsteinia ternata Ground cover for dry site, with toothed foliage and yellow flowers. Z3

Winter aconite (*Eranthis hyemalis*) Ground cover with golden flowers; ideal in winter. Z4

SHRUBS & TREES

Aucuba japonica 'Variegata' Tough evergreen with gold-marked foliage; creates a splash of lighter color in the shade. Z6

Camellia Shrubs with glossy, dark evergreen leaves and white to pink or red flowers. Z6–Z8

Dicksonia antarctica Tree fern with attractive fronds and a tall, fibrous trunk. Z9

Fuchsia A useful and colorful shade plant with a long flowering season. Z9

Garrya elliptica Spectacular, silvery gray catkins in winter and early spring. Tolerates moderate shade and poor, dry soil. Z8

Hydrangea paniculata (shown) Huge, cone-shaped flowerheads in pinks and white. Z4

Itea ilicifolia Evergreen shrub ideal for planting against shady walls, with hollylike foliage and long catkins. Z7

Japanese maple (*Acer palmatum*, shown) Spectacular foliage in fall. Z6

Osmanthus Evergreen shrub bears fragrant, white flowers. Z7

Rhododendron Woodland shrubs, including azaleas, for dappled shade and acidic soil. Z5–Z9

Rubus cockburnianus Ornamental bramble with ghostly white stems, at its best during winter. Z5

Ruscus aculeatus Evergreen with spine-tipped leaves, suitable for dry shade. Female plants produce small, reddish berries. Z7

Sarcococca confusa Evergreen shrub with highly fragrant, white, winter flowers. Z6

Skimmia japonica Evergreen shrub has small, white flowers and red berries. Z7

Trillium grandiflorum flowers usually open white but sometimes fade to pink or lilac.

Japanese maples (*Acer palmatum*) prefer a sheltered spot in dappled shade.

Hydrangea paniculata stems should be cut back to 2 buds in spring for the best flowers.

Lenten roses (*Helleborus* x *hybridus*) have early spring flowers in a range of colors.

Hosta 'Gold Standard' is typical of a wide range of strongly marked, large-leaved hostas.

Cyclamen coum flowers in varied shades of pink above mottled, heart-shaped leaves.

Plant qualities

Plants are usually selected for their flower color, but they can also provide interesting foliage, seedheads, texture, and architectural qualities. When creating a planting list, select a range of plants that provide interest year-round.

Shrubs and trees form the framework, usually at the back of a mixed border behind smaller perennials. Trees also make superb focal points. Choose carefully, because some trees quickly outgrow their allotted space.

Generally, larger perennials are placed at the back of a border and lower ones in front, using groups of odd numbers (usually three and five). The rules are not rigid; a yard is far more interesting if occasional, larger plants are closer to the front or partially obscure the view.

Clever color

Color planning is essential, because some colors clash, so use a color wheel to work out which work well together. Colors can create moods and atmospheres. Hot, fiery colors tend to excite emotions, while paler colors appear tranquil or can lighten dense plantings.

Bright, hot colors, such as reds and oranges, tend to seem closer than they really are, while cool, pale colors, such as pastels, blues, or whites seem farther away. Pale colors farther away from the house can make a yard seem larger, while placing hot colors at the fsrthest end of a long, narrow space makes it appear shorter.

DESIGN TRICKS

- **Make narrow yards** look wider by using horizontal or diagonal lines that break up the length. These can be in the form of paths, flowerbeds, or even low walls. A path leading straight up the middle will make a yard look even longer and narrower.
- **Yards look bigger** when filled with sweeping curves that will lead the eye alternately from one side to the other. Staggered features, such as shrubs and containers that are placed alternately down the yard, achieve the same effect.
- **Make your borders** as wide as possible. Plants look awkward and cluttered in narrow borders, which do not give enough room for creating depth to the design with tiers or drifts of planting.
- **Avoid haphazard planting** by working always from a plan. Keep your initial planting plan to refer to later, because you will add plants when they (and their neighbors) are not flowering.
- **Vary the shapes** of flowers in a design. For example, break up lots of round, daisy-shaped flowers with spiky forms, such as kniphofias, delphiniums, or lupines.

Restful green & lawns

Green is a neutral background color and in foliage or lawns can be used as a foil for many brighter colors. There are many shades of green, and interest can be created with foliage alone.

The soft surface of a lawn is an attractive feature in any yard, and in larger yards lawns can unify a whole area. Consider interesting shapes, such as circles or ellipses, or plant another type of ground cover. Or install hardscape materials, such as gravel, decking, or paving.

Emphasize long borders and focal points through careful use of color. Placing warm colors at the front and pale colors farther away may seem too simple to work, but the subtle shift lengthens the vista.

A lush, tropical feel in this courtyard is created by a range of foliage textures and shades of green. The overall effect is increased by the splash of hot red crocosmia flowers.

Invasive weeds *see page 55* | **Creating a wildflower meadow** *see page 66* | **Wildflower plants** *see page 68*

Native plants

Many gardeners now like to include native plants in their gardens, or even to grow native plants exclusively. Plants that are naturally native to your area are suitable for your local climate and are likely to attract beneficial insects and other wildlife. Natives are often more informal and less garish in appearance than nonnatives. Your local cooperative extension service, and also local nurseries, will be able to advise you on plants that are native to your area.

Remember that, like nonnative garden plants, natives can sometimes be too vigorous, or even invasive, when grown in rich garden soil. Do not expect them all to be naturally well behaved.

Choosing native plants

Few plants that are native to California are also native to Maine—each region has its own natives that are found naturally in local woods and fields, along creeks, and in other wild places. It is important to know which plants are native to your area and there are a number of sources of good information.

Native plant nurseries: There are more and more nurseries specializing in native plants, and they will provide knowledgeable advice on the best plants for your area—and also, of course, provide the plants themselves.

Conservation groups and regional native plant societies that wish to discourage the planting of nonnative invasive plants and encourage native plantings often provide handouts, talks, and practical demonstrations.

Cooperative extension services: Extension services often offer free leaflets or booklets with information on local natives and may also organize native plant sales and talks on native plants.

Garden clubs: Other local gardeners with experience of growing native plants will be able to give advice.

Books and magazines: Look for locally-based garden magazines and books that are focused on your state or region for the most appropriate advice.

Radio and TV shows: Gardening shows on local radio and TV often include segments on native plants—and if there is a gardening call-in radio show in your area, call and ask about natives.

Online: There is a wealth of advice available on the internet, but the region on which websites are focused is not always obvious. Check carefully and find sites that relate specifically to your area.

Sources of native plants

Never dig up plants from fields and forests and take them back to plant in your yard. Even if you have the landowner's permission to do this, you may well bring back new pests and diseases, and it is often difficult to dig plants up with enough roots for them to survive. In some areas, there may be prohibitions against the removal of threatened, vulnerable, or endangered plant species; you can be fined for removing such plants from their native habitats. Try to visit a specialist native plant nursery or find an online mail-order specialist in your region.

Mountain laurel (*Kalmia latifolia*) is a spring-blooming shrub native to eastern North America.

Tiarella cordifolia is a vigorous, spreading perennial native to the Northeast.

Scarlet clematis (*Clematis texensis*) is a 4–8ft. vine native to Texas.

ANNUAL PLANTS

Annuals create an almost instant splash of color in the garden. Whole borders can be grown in a matter of weeks, or individual plants can be used to fill gaps. As their name suggests, annuals are sown and grown, then flower, set seed, and die all in a year. This may make them seem transient, but many annuals will self seed, some of them abundantly. To fuel their accelerated life cycles, these plants use considerable energy: while many will grow in poor soil, annuals tend to need full sun. Some plants grown as annuals are truly perennials, but they are treated as annuals in areas where winters are too cold for them to survive.

Growing annuals

There are many advantages to growing annuals from seeds yourself. The cost of a few packets of seeds is far smaller than that of buying plants. Also, most annuals grow rapidly and quickly transform an area in a few weeks. Annuals bring flexibility to any design, where changes are easy to make and a different choice of flowers can be selected the following year to suit personal taste.

Creating an annual border
To make an entire border of annuals, rather than use them as gap fillers, start by drawing up a planting plan. Ensure that taller plants are toward the back and smaller plants at the front, but occasionally allow taller ones to drift forward. Consider repeating the same plants at intervals to create a sense of unity and balance.

SOWING AN ANNUAL BORDER

1 **Prepare the ground** by weeding thoroughly, removing all perennial roots. Many annuals prefer a light, well-drained soil, so incorporate well-rotted compost if the soil is heavy. Rake the soil level, lightly tread it over, and then give it a final rake.

2 **Use sand to outline** where the blocks of different annuals are going to be sown. Use soft contours to shape the planting areas into natural drifts, avoiding straight lines.

3 **Sow in straight lines.** This helps to differentiate weeds from sown plants, and so make maintenance easier. Once plants grow, the straight lines will not be distinguishable, but do vary the angles of furrows in each section to avoid rigidity.

4 **Once growth is established**, thin out the seedlings according to the instructions on the packet. It is tempting to leave more than specified, but crowded plants will not grow as well and are prone to disease.

Growing annuals from seed

Annuals vary in the temperature they need for germination to start. Some, such as poached egg plant (*Limnanthes*), larkspur (*Consolida*), annual poppies (*Papaver*), and love-in-a-mist (*Nigella*), germinate at relatively low temperatures, even as low as 40°F, while petunias, zonal geraniums (*Pelargonium*), and impatiens, for example, germinate best at a temperature of 70°F.

So in some areas, especially those with long winters and cool summers, most annuals may need to be started in a protected environment—perhaps on a windowsill or on the sun porch—in order to receive enough warmth for germination to begin. Starting them in a protected environment also allows the plants to get ahead of the season, so when conditions warm up outdoors you can plant young plants that are already a few weeks old. This is especially important in areas with short summer seasons.

In areas with a longer spring season, annuals that germinate at low temperatures can be sown outdoors where they are to flower, while only those needing high temperatures are sown in warm conditions.

But there is one other factor to consider when deciding whether to sow seed outdoors or indoors. Seed of some annuals is relatively cheap, and each packet may contain hundreds of seeds. Others are much more expensive and your packet may only contain 20 seeds, or perhaps as few as four or six seeds. Losses to diseases and other mishaps are far more frequent outdoors, so expensive seed is best sown in a protected environment.

Sowing annuals outdoors

Sow at the depth and spacing recommended on the packet. Pressing a bamboo cane into the soil is the simplest method of forming a shallow furrow. Cover the seeds with soil, and water using a fine rose. Protect the bed with nets or twiggy sticks to deter birds from removing the seeds. You can leave spaces where other plants can be slotted into the scheme later.

In areas with mild winters, seed of some annuals can be sown in fall. Larkspur and love-in-a-mist are in this category. They soon germinate, produce a rosette of leaves and deep roots, and may continue to develop in winter. In spring, they surge into growth and develop into larger and more prolific plants than if sown in spring.

Sowing annuals in containers

Seeds can be sown in most types of containers, from shallow propagation trays to plant pots or cell packs. The

SOWING IN POTS

1 **Scatter seeds** on the surface of the potting mix and sieve a thin layer of mix over them. Lightly firm the soil. Maintain humidity by laying a sheet of glass over the pot or securing a plastic bag over it with a rubber band.

2 **When seedlings emerge**, remove the glass or bag. Once true leaves appear and the seedlings are large enough to be safely handled, transplant them into individual pots. Only ever handle seedlings by the seed leaves.

SOWING IN CELL PACKS

1 **Cell packs** are ideal for large seeds that are sown individually. Place 1–2 seeds into each cell. Lightly firm the soil. Some small seeds can also be sown as small clumps that are transplanted intact into containers or borders.

2 **Push established seedlings** out of the cell packs from below, with their root systems intact and minimal disturbance. This is not only convenient but it also gets the young plants off to a good start.

GROWING SWEET PEAS FROM SEED

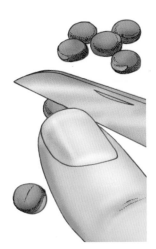   

1 **Nick the seeds** with a sharp pocket knife opposite the 'eye' or scar to let water in and improve germination rates.

2 **Sow into deep pots**, cell packs, or root trainers, as sweet peas like a deep root run. Cardboard tubes are ideal.

3 **Pinch back** the growing tips when the seedlings reach about 3in. This will encourage bushier plants.

4 **Train plants** up supports of canes or peasticks, allowing one plant per support. Tie in stems with twine as they grow.

container should be thoroughly washed before use. Fill it near to the top with new seed starter mix. Never reuse old soil or garden soil as it will have no nutrients and may carry disease. Tap to firm the mix and then lightly water and leave for an hour.

When sowing, mix fine, dustlike seeds with sand before sprinkling them thinly over the surface. Place pots or packs in trays of water until the potting mix feels moist. Keep the temperature at 64–70°F. It is especially important not to overwater seeds and seedlings as this quickly encourages disease. Try to keep the soil damp—but not wet.

Sowing sweet peas

Sow in fall for early flowering the following spring in warmer regions, but an early spring sowing is best for cooler areas. Plant seeds ½in. deep and about 1¼in. apart in potting mix. If using cardboard tubes, plant just one seed in each. Water well and keep the seeds at about 59°F until the seedlings emerge, then transfer them to a cold frame (*see page 399*). Keep the lid of the cold frame open most of the time to harden fall-sown seedlings, but always close it if frosts are forecast. Give spring-sown plants more protection. When seedlings reach 1½in., thin them into individual pots, being careful not to damage the roots. Plants in cardboard tubes can be set out without ever taking them from the tubes.

Sweet peas prefer a deep, rich, and well-drained soil, so add plenty of compost before planting. Plant out fall seedlings in midspring, and spring-sown plants a couple of weeks later. Pick regularly to prolong flowering.

Maintenance of annual borders

Looking after annuals is fairly simple. Hoe off emerging weeds, but remember some annuals produce seedlings, which can be left in place if wanted for the following year. Some of the taller plants may need staking, and removal of dead flowers encourages plants to continue flowering and not set seed. When the display is over, the plants can be removed and composted.

WHAT IS A BIENNIAL?

Biennials live for 2 years before dying. They are less popular than annuals, because they do not give the same 'instant' effect. Foxgloves (*Digitalis*) are probably the most widely grown. Some short-lived perennials such as wallflowers (*Erysimum*) are often treated as biennials, sold in the fall of their first year, and discarded after they have flowered in the second year.

HERBACEOUS PERENNIALS & ORNAMENTAL GRASSES

Perennials are the workhorses of the garden, providing the greatest opportunity for adding diverse colors, shapes, and textures to the overall design. By definition they are herbaceous (nonwoody) plants that live for more than two years. In temperate regions they typically die back to the ground in winter and reemerge in spring, but in warmer regions many perennials remain in active growth year-round. Most ornamental grasses and ferns are considered perennials.

Creating a perennial garden

These plants will remain in the ground for several years, so preparation of the soil is important. Perennials will tolerate either slightly acidic or alkaline soils, but ideally they prefer the former. Choose plants suitable for not only the soil but also the level of light.

Planting a perennial garden

Clear the ground of surface debris and dig it over, being careful to remove the roots of any perennial weeds. Most perennials prefer soil that is reasonably well drained but with a good moisture content, so amend the soil with

By integrating herbaceous perennials and grasses with different colors, sizes, and textures, a gardener can design an artistic planting that offers interest nearly year-round. Here, tall grasses provide a backdrop for geraniums, sedums, and a dwarf blue spruce.

83

plenty of compost, then rake the ground level. Unless the soil is already nutrient-rich, apply a topdressing of composted manure or a balanced slow-release fertilizer in the quantities recommended by the manufacturer. Lightly tamp down the soil before raking it over again.

Using a planting plan, set out the plants in position before taking them out of their pots. Allow for their size when mature. You need not splurge on the plants in the largest pots, because by the middle of summer those bought in slightly smaller pots reach the same size. Once you are happy with the positioning, they can be planted.

Most perennials are sold as container-grown plants. You can buy and plant them at any time of year (*see below*), although they are best planted during spring or fall when they are more likely to succeed.

With their attractive forms and graceful, feathery fronds, ferns such as this ostrich fern make elegant additions to shade or woodland gardens.

Clump-forming grasses such as blue fescue (*Festuca glauca*) look good when planted in geometric patterns.

Daylilies, available in hundreds of different flower color combinations, are versatile additions to sunny garden sites.

PLANTING A PERENNIAL

1 **Water container-grown plants** well and allow them to drain before sliding each one out of its container.

2 **Tease the roots** gently from the sides and bottom. This will encourage quicker root establishment in the ground.

3 **Place the plant** in the hole and adjust the height by adding or removing soil. Firm in using your fingertips, apply a thick layer of organic mulch, and water in well.

Maintenance through the year

There will be plenty of bare soil in the first year of a new perennial garden as the plants start to establish, so weeds will readily appear. Reduce these by interplanting with annuals (*see page 80*), or hoe them off as soon as they appear. The plants will need watering during any dry spells, particularly in the first year.

Mulching & fertilizing

Mulch beds each year with well-rotted manure or garden compost about 2in. deep in early spring. Keep the organic matter well away from emerging stems.

Inorganic mulches, such as gravel, add another texture to beds throughout the year and suppress the germination of weed seeds. They are most suitable for plants with low-nutrient requirements, such as those in Mediterranean gardens, prairie plantings, or dry garden beds.

Perennials may need fertilizing in spring before the mulch is renewed—organic mulches also help to nourish the soil. Alternatively, spot-treat plants looking pale with fertilizer or compost just before the growing season starts.

Staking

Staking (*see below*) is an important consideration for gardeners who plan to grow tall perennials, especially varieties that have topheavy flowers—such as peonies, lilies, dahlias, and some irises. Without sturdy support, such plants will often collapse or break when exposed to heavy rain or strong winds.

The key to successful staking is to get the support in place early so it will be as effective and as unobtrusive as possible. Put supports in position before the new growth has reached 4–6in. tall.

METHODS OF STAKING

Tie plants to stakes with soft twine in a figure 8. If using bamboo canes for staking, try to ensure that they are well weathered because new canes show up easily.

Metal supports last for years, so are good value despite their high initial cost. They are less attractive than supports made of natural materials, although dark green ones are less visible than shiny bare metal. Plant growth usually hides the supports by summer.

Natural woven supports are attractive in their own right, and the ideal option where a plant of delicate form may not completely conceal its support. Natural materials will need replacing every year.

Linking stakes are relatively costly if there are many plants to support, but they are sturdy and will last well. They can be put in place around a plant later in the season if you failed to put grow-through supports in place, but they may not be completely concealed.

Plants with upright, delicate flower spikes, such as delphiniums, need individual staking with canes. Other plants can grow through larger supports.

If using twiggy branches, push them into the ground around the plant, or group of plants. Bend the top of each branch over to its neighbor and twist them around each other. Create a second tier by twisting the branches around neighbors in the first tier. The most useful twigs for staking are red osier dogwood and witch hazel, due to their fan-shaped branches, followed by birch, which should be cut in winter before their buds develop.

An alternative is 4–6in. netting, ideally black, stretched over frameworks of stout wooden stakes painted black, leaving gaps to allow access. The stems of the plants will thread through the support, disguising the netting.

Division

After a few years, perennials often become congested and lose vigor. Sometimes the plant dies in the center, or it outgrows its space and invades that of its neighbors.

The best method of renovation is to dig the plants up, and divide them up into chunks with a sharp spade, knife, or saw (*see box, above right*). The traditional method of pulling them apart with two forks placed back to back is awkward. Replant divisions elsewhere or compost them. Fall is the usual time for dividing perennials, but early spring is best in cold, wet areas because plants have a better chance of recovering. Agapanthus, asters, and kniphofias prefer to be divided in spring.

Deadheading

Check flowerbeds regularly, removing faded flowerheads or stems and tidying the plants by removing tired foliage. Deadheading (*see right*) prevents plants from wasting energy on seed production, encouraging prolonged flowering and clean, fresh growth instead. Plants may need extra fertilizing and watering to encourage a second flush of flowers. Deadheading also prevents a prolific crop of seedlings from plants such as alliums.

Do not deadhead plants that produce attractive fruit or seeds, such as *Iris foetidissima*. It is also not worth deadheading those that have a profusion of tiny flowers. Plants such as astrantias and some geraniums can be cut to ground level to encourage more flowers.

Pinching & thinning

Pinching is a technique used to create a lower, slightly more study plant, less prone to collapse without support. It works particularly well on tall plants, such as heleniums, veronicastrums, and eupatoriums, as well as sedums.

DIVISION TO REINVIGORATE

Dividing plants is sometimes a delicate job and at other times a tough one. Fibrous roots can be teased apart, while harder, woody roots need to be cut with a spade or even a saw.

DEADHEADING

Cut entire flowering stems of plants such as delphiniums down to ground level to encourage a smaller, second flush of flowers. Apply an all-purpose fertilizer at the same time. Cut other plants, such as phlox, back to a lower set of clean leaves.

Remove the flowers of bulbs, complete with any swelling seedpods. Daffodils are best deadheaded to avoid energy being wasted on seed production, but allow bulbs such as snowdrops (*Galanthus*) to set seed and naturalize.

THINNING

Remove shoots of multistemmed perennials, such as phlox and heleniums, at the base. Thinning the new growth will produce larger flowers on a stronger and healthier plant, because fewer stems are sharing nutrients from the roots.

PINCHING BACK

The traditional way of pinching plants is to individually pinch back the growing tips when they are one third of their final height. This is often done on asters and helps to produce a denser plant. Plants may be sheared instead.

Cut back early luxuriant growth by one third with hedge shears or pruners when in active growth during late spring. In deep borders, chopping just the front part will enable the plants at the back to be seen.

Thinning to improve the flowering display is carried out on multistemmed plants, and involves removing about one in three stems at ground level when they are about 4–6in. tall.

Clearing away old growth

Cutting back perennials should take place from fall onward. If you leave it until late winter, much of the dead foliage will be well rotted, so there will be less to remove than if the borders are cut back in fall. The cut foliage can simply be raked up and added to the compost pile.

Waiting until spring is ideal for slightly tender plants, such as agapanthus and kniphofias, as their old foliage protects the crown over winter. It also suits plants that have attractive seedheads or architectural form, such as sedums or eryngiums, and woody perennials, such as asters and penstemons. If you intend to renovate a border in spring, old foliage will help to identify the position of the dormant plants. Cut deciduous ornamental grasses such as fountain grass (*Pennisetum*) and switch grass (*Panicum*) back to near ground level in late winter. Evergreen grasses can be groomed annually to remove dead stems.

CUTTING BACK IN FALL

Dead foliage can provide winter shelter for pests and diseases and is not needed by hardy plants. Cut back the old growth of perennials such as hostas (*far left*) in fall or early winter.

Not all stems last well through winter to provide striking skeletal forms. Those of rudbeckias (*left*) and other multistemmed plants can become a dark tangle, so cut them back to ground level or just above the basal leaves.

Gardening basics *see page 6* | **Pests, diseases, & other problems** *see page 40* | **Placing plants** *see page 74*

Pests & diseases of perennial plants

The usual common garden pests (*see page 49*) attack perennials, but some others especially love these plants.

Earwigs

Active from spring to fall, earwigs feed on young leaves and petals at night, hiding during the day. Place pots on the ground; dispose of earwigs that hide inside them.

Nematodes

Microscopic nematodes feed inside the leaves of many plants, including chrysanthemums and penstemons. Infested leaf parts, separated from uninfested parts by the larger leaf veins, turn brown or black, forming discolored islands in the leaves. Symptoms are mainly seen in late summer to fall. There are no effective pesticides available for garden use: tolerate the damage or remove the plants.

Cutworms

These fat, soft caterpillars live in the soil and eat through the stems of seedlings or feed on roots. Hand pick or turn over unplanted areas to expose the pests to birds.

Caterpillars & loopers

The larvae of moths and butterflies, caterpillars and loopers feed on buds, flowers, fruits, and especially leaves. Small infestations can be removed by picking them off by hand; biological and chemical sprays are also available. Garden birds can also be helpful.

Beetles

Cucumber beetles, Japanese beetles, Colorado potato beetles, and many other species feed on flowers or foliage; some have grubs that bore into the bark of trees. Reduce their numbers with appropriate biological or chemical controls. Scent traps are often effective.

Tobacco budworms

Tobacco budworm feeds on the developing flowerbuds of perennials such as geraniums and penstemons, leaving tattered petals or unopened flowers. Hand pick pests at dusk or treat with *Bacillus thuringiensis* (Bt).

Thrips

These tiny, winged insects are $^{1}/_{10}$in. long and cause pale or silvery flecking on the foliage and flowers of a wide range of ornamental and food plants, indoors and outdoors, as well as on pea and bean pods. A hand vacuum is a useful control measure.

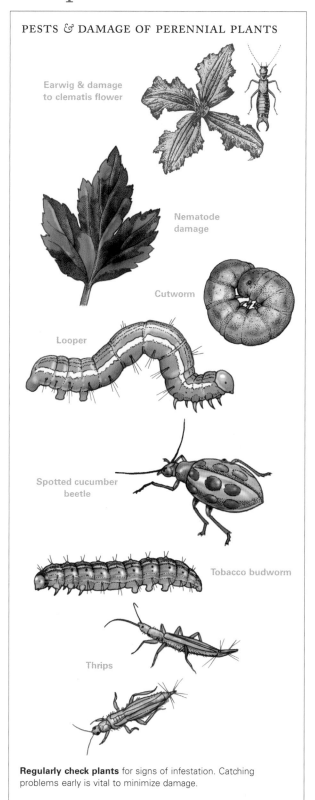

PESTS & DAMAGE OF PERENNIAL PLANTS

Earwig & damage to clematis flower

Nematode damage

Cutworm

Looper

Spotted cucumber beetle

Tobacco budworm

Thrips

Regularly check plants for signs of infestation. Catching problems early is vital to minimize damage.

Rusts

This group of fungi infects many species of perennials—asters, chrysanthemums, and daylilies, for example. Symptoms are yellow, creamy, buff, or rust-colored pustules on leaves and stems. Immediately destroy affected plants. Seek out resistant varieties, if available.

Aster yellows

Attacks a wide range of vegetables and flowers—and not just asters. Leaf veins lose their green coloring, then new foliage turns yellow and older leaves develop reddish tones. Infected plants often change their habits of growth, becoming upright and spindly; flowers may become green and distorted. This disease is caused by a viruslike organism called a phytoplasma and is spread by leafhoppers. There is no cure. Dig up infected plants and destroy. Do not compost the remains.

Peony wilt

In spring or early summer, shoots wilt and die. They have a brown area at the base, sometimes covered in gray, fluffy mold. Brown blotches appear on leaves, mainly at the tips. The fungus spreads by airborne spores and in the soil. Promptly cut back affected tissue, if necessary to below soil level, and do not compost. Ideally, carefully replace the soil around the plant crown. This common fungal disease thrives in humid air, so do not let clumps become too dense.

Powdery mildew

Perennials such as garden phlox and bee balm (*Monarda*) are susceptible to this fungal disease, which causes dusty white or gray patches on leaves and stems. Heat, humidity, and shady conditions are exacerbating factors. Select resistant cultivars, practice good sanitation, or treat with baking-soda based fungicides.

Stem & root rots

A range of fungal diseases cause rotting of roots and stems. Roots are softened by infection, then the rot spreads into stems, turning them black. Plants collapse and die. Garden soil or potting mix that remains overly wet for long periods may cause or aggravate the condition.

Delphinium black blotch

This bacterial disease starts on leaves but spreads to stems and flowers. Bacteria are splashed from the soil and infect the leaves, causing large, black blotches. Remove and destroy badly affected plants.

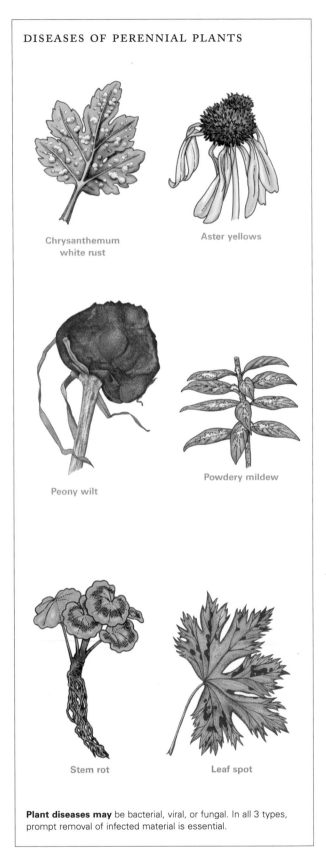

DISEASES OF PERENNIAL PLANTS

Chrysanthemum white rust

Aster yellows

Peony wilt

Powdery mildew

Stem rot

Leaf spot

Plant diseases may be bacterial, viral, or fungal. In all 3 types, prompt removal of infected material is essential.

BULBOUS PLANTS

Bulbous plants are some of the best-known flowers in the garden. Many are spring-flowering, including tulips, cyclamen, daffodils, crocuses, snowdrops, bluebells, and alliums. There are also many summer-flowering bulbs such as lilies and crocosmias, and late-performing dahlias, to name a few. This chapter includes not only true bulbs but also tubers, corms, and rhizomes. Essentially, these all have swollen or fleshy underground storage organs, which enable them to survive periods of dormancy.

Planting bulbous plants

Bulbs generally have only one season of interest. While in flower they provide a glorious display, from large flower spikes to drifts of smaller flowers, and their blooms are sometimes also fragrant. Once flowering is over, however, their foliage fades away and they retire below ground until their season comes again.

How to plant

As a rule of thumb, plant spring-flowering bulbs such as daffodils and tulips in early fall, summer-flowering bulbs in spring, and fall-flowering bulbs in late summer. There are exceptions to these guidelines: spring-flowering snowdrops establish most successfully if they are dug up while in leaf just after flowering, and are transplanted promptly. Pot-grown bulbs can be planted at any time, but they cost a lot more than dry bulbs.

PLANTING BULBS INDIVIDUALLY

Plant each bulb in a hole of the appropriate depth. This is usually 2–3 times the height of the bulb, although a few larger, less hardy bulbs prefer to be close to the surface for maximum heat.

PLANTING GROUPS OF BULBS

1 **Prepare the ground** well and dig a large hole. Place the bulbs randomly, at least twice their own width deep and apart.

2 **Draw the soil** back over the bulbs. Do this gently, with your hand rather than a spade, to ensure that the bulbs are not dislodged.

3 **Firm the soil** by tamping it gently with the back of a rake. Do not tread on the soil, as your weight may damage the bulb tips.

PLANTING BULBS IN GRASS

1 To create drifts of large bulbs like daffodils in rough grass, start by scattering the bulbs randomly over the planting area. Adjust those that are less than their own width apart, leaving the rest where they fall for a natural look.

2 Dig a hole with a trowel where the bulb fell. If you are planting a lot of bulbs, buy a bulb planter. This cuts out a core of sod faster and with far less effort than a trowel. Short-handled types and models with a long shaft that are pushed in with the foot, like a spade, are both available.

3 Remove the core of sod and check the hole is the correct depth for your bulb, crumbling some soil back into the hole if it is not. Scatter a little all-purpose fertilizer into the hole if the soil is poor.

4 Place the bulb into the hole and crumble some soil from the end of the core over the bulb so that it is completely covered with loose soil. Replace the plug of sod over it and firm in gently. Fill any gaps around the plug with loose soil.

The simplest method of naturalizing small bulbs, such as crocuses, in a lawn is to make holes with the prongs of a fork and insert the corms into them, backfilling with soil. Alternatively, cut away a section of sod with a spade or a half-moon edger and peel it back gently to reveal the bare soil. Lightly dig over the soil with a hand fork and press the bulb into it, then replace the sod and firm it in by tamping it down with the back of a rake. Large bulbs can be planted with a bulb planter (*see above*).

Where to plant

There are bulbs for every situation from sun to shade, and for soils from poor to rich, dry to damp. Most prefer well-drained conditions; such bulbs may rot in damp soil.

Bulbs can be planted in mixed borders or in pots that are moved into prominent positions while they flower, and then taken away once the display is over. Use low-growing, early spring-flowering bulbs at the front of flower gardens, giving them an opportunity to shine before the perennials and shrubs take center stage.

Tulips are frequently used in formal gardens, containers, and mixed borders. Hybrids are ideal for quick color, but most will rarely flower well for a second year. Robust species types, which require a well-drained soil, are suitable for more subtle planting schemes and can usually remain in the soil for years.

Later-flowering bulbous plants, such as gladioli and dahlias, add vibrancy to late summer and can be used for cut flowers. *Fritillaria imperialis* and *Crinum* x *powellii* 'Album' add architectural interest, while late-flowering eucomis brings a touch of the exotic to the border.

Bulbs in drifts give large shady areas a natural, long-established feeling. Most woodland bulbs, such as trilliums, snowdrops (*Galanthus*), winter aconites (*Eranthis hyemalis*), and wood anemones (*Anemone nemorosa*), prefer moist but well-drained soil. Fork the soil over lightly and add rotted leaves or old potting mix prior to planting. If you have specimen trees, naturalizing winter- and early spring-flowering bulbs at the base will create seasonal interest while the trees remain bare and dormant.

Crocuses can be commonly naturalized on lawns; daffodils are also popular, but when choosing a location remember that you cannot cut the grass until after the foliage of the bulbs has died back. Meadows are another area ideal for naturalizing bulbs (*see page 66*). Among the most popular plants are the snake's head fritillaries (*Fritillaria meleagris*), which thrive in damp conditions, and cowslips or primroses (*Primula*).

Looking after bulbous plants

Permanently planted bulbs generally need little care. Removing dead flowers can increase vigor in the following year, and staking may be necessary for tall or lush plants such as gladioli and dahlias. Allow foliage to die back before tidying the plants up. If flowering diminishes, it is likely that the clumps have become congested; simply lift them when dormant, remove some of the bulbs, and replant.

Storing bulbous plants

Most of the spring-flowering bulbous plants commonly grown in American gardens—such as daffodils, crocuses, snowdrops, and grape hyacinths (*Muscari*)—are hardy and can be left in the ground permanently.

However, there are a number of summer-flowering bulbs that are not tolerant of frost. When grown in areas that have cold winters, these plants need to be dug up in fall and stored over winter in a dry, frost-free place such as a garage or potting shed (*see below*). Such plants include dahlias, cannas, glory lilies (*Gloriosa*), caladiums, elephant's ears (*Colocasia*), and calla lilies (*Zephyranthes*). Even in milder regions, if these bulbs are planted in wet, heavy soil you should dig up and store them to prevent them from rotting. Some bulbs, such as tender cyclamen, amaryllis, and nerine lilies, are best grown in pots and brought under cover in regions that have cold winters.

LIFTING & STORING DAHLIAS

1 **When the first frost** blackens the leaves of the plants, cut down the stems to about 6in. above ground level. Loosen the soil carefully and ease the tubers out.

2 **Remove loose soil** and stand the roots upside down to ensure that any remaining moisture drains from the stems and top of the crowns. Keep the roots in a frost-free place for about 3 weeks.

3 **Place the tubers** right-way up in a wooden box and cover them with coconut fiber, perlite, or a similar medium to prevent them from drying out completely. Keep cool but frost free. Inspect the tubers regularly and remove any that shows signs of rot.

4 **Encourage new growth** by placing the box in a sunny spot in spring, and watering lightly. In late winter, you can force tubers into early growth by planting them in potting mix and placing them in a warm, light place. Plant outdoors once all risk of frost has passed.

Pests & diseases of bulbs

While bulbs are in growth, check them for any symptoms of pests and diseases. When lifting them, seasonally or to divide clumps, inspect the bulbs themselves and destroy any showing signs of infection or infestation. Many bulb problems are spread on the bulbs themselves, so never take a chance. If you have the slightest suspicion that a bulb may be infested, do not pass it along to a friend.

Lily beetle

This native of Asia and mainland Europe continues to spread, but so far only in the northeast. Adult beetles are ¼in. long and bright red with black legs and heads; they eat the foliage of lilies (*Lilium*) and fritillaries (*Fritillaria*) from spring to fall. The reddish brown grubs, which are covered in black excrement, feed from late spring to late summer. Damage reduces the bulb size and may prevent flowering next year. Remove the beetles and larvae by hand, or use a suitable spray.

Gladiolus thrips

Thrips are narrow-bodied, sap-feeding insects up to ¹⁄₁₆in. long. The adults are blackish brown and the immature nymphs pale yellow. They cause pale mottling of foliage and feed inside the developing flower buds. In heavy infestations the flower buds fail to open. Watch for the early signs of feeding damage on the foliage before flowering starts. Burn or otherwise destroy the foliage and stems in the fall to kill overwintering thrips.

Narcissus nematode

Microscopic nematodes within bulbs and foliage stunt and distort growth before killing bulbs. Bulbs cut across show concentric brown rings. Purchase firm, good-quality bulbs, and remove bulbs showing symptoms and any others growing within 3ft. of infested plants.

Narcissus bulb flies

Large bulb flies resemble small bumblebees and attack narcissus bulbs, cyrtanthus, hippeastrums, and snowdrops (*Galanthus*), from late spring to midsummer when the foliage is dying down. Infested bulbs are often killed or produce just a few thin leaves, and contain a plump grub up to ¾in. long. This eats the center of the bulb, filling it with muddy excrement. Small bulb flies produce many maggots up to ⅜in. long, but attack only bulbs already damaged by other pests or diseases. Cover valuable bulbs with floating row cover when flies are active. Bulbs in sunny positions are most vulnerable.

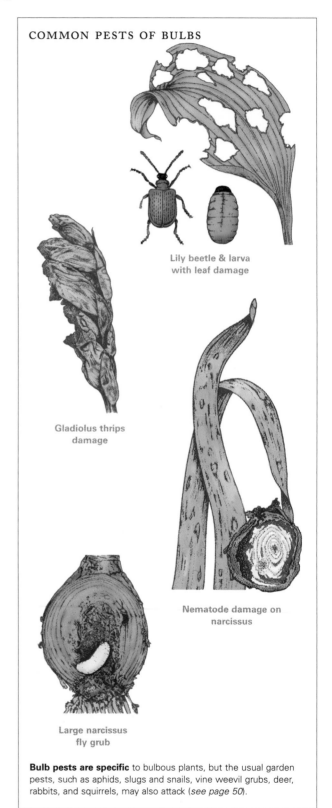

COMMON PESTS OF BULBS

Lily beetle & larva
with leaf damage

Gladiolus thrips
damage

Nematode damage on
narcissus

Large narcissus
fly grub

Bulb pests are specific to bulbous plants, but the usual garden pests, such as aphids, slugs and snails, vine weevil grubs, deer, rabbits, and squirrels, may also attack (*see page 50*).

Tulip fire

Brown scorching deforms shoots, and sunken yellow spots with green edges appear on nearby tulips. Affected tissue may have a gray mold. Inspect bulbs for lesions with small, black bodies before planting. Destroy affected plants and avoid planting tulips for three years.

Iris leaf spot

This fungal leaf spot also affects plants such as gladioli and daylilies (*Hemerocallis*), causing elliptical, yellow-edged brown spots or gray spots. Entire leaves may die, usually after flowering. Outbreaks are worst in wet conditions. Remove diseased leaves promptly and clear dead leaves in fall. Keep plants vigorous; moderate liming of soil and fungicidal sprays may help.

Lily disease

This fungal disease causes elliptical, water-soaked spots on the leaves, and may rot the entire leaf and spread to the stem or flowers. Remove and burn affected growth and ensure good air circulation.

Snowdrop gray mold

Usually worst in mild winters. Growth is stunted and the leaves and stalk rot, sometimes with gray, velvety mold. Small, black bodies may develop on rotting bulbs and survive in the soil to infect others, so check bulbs before planting. Destroy infected clumps, and do not replant.

Basal rot

Affects daffodils and crocuses when dying back, mostly in hot summers. The basal plate softens and red rot spreads inside, sometimes with pink mold. Bulbs in the soil rot and the disease spreads. Lift bulbs in early summer; store in a cool, airy place; inspect and remove soft bulbs. Triandrus, jonquil, and tazetta daffodils are resistant.

Narcissus leaf scorch

Leaf tips show a reddish brown scorch, which may spread, and leaves yellow and shrivel. Flowers may show brown blotches. Remove affected tissue. Avoid chilling bulbs or planting late. Poeticus, polyanthus, tazetta, and poetaz daffodils are vulnerable, but it is not limited to daffodils.

Viruses

A variety of viruses cause concentric rings, pale streaking or blotches on leaves, streaking in flowers, or distortion. Viruses can spread by vegetative propagation, but are carried mainly by insects, such as aphids or thrips, so pest control is important. Destroy infected plants promptly.

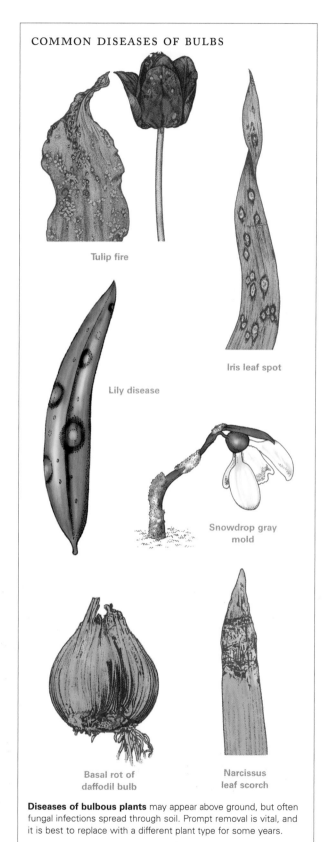

COMMON DISEASES OF BULBS

Tulip fire

Iris leaf spot

Lily disease

Snowdrop gray mold

Basal rot of daffodil bulb

Narcissus leaf scorch

Diseases of bulbous plants may appear above ground, but often fungal infections spread through soil. Prompt removal is vital, and it is best to replace with a different plant type for some years.

TREES & SHRUBS

It is hard to imagine a yard without trees and shrubs. They comprise a huge group of small to very large, evergreen and deciduous plants that can be planted on their own—to be enjoyed as stand-alone specimens—or in groups, if you have the space. The size and structure of many trees and shrubs make them an essential feature in most yards as they are a counterpoint to walls, buildings, and other hardscaping, giving balance to a garden's design. As hedges, trees also provide screening, boundaries, and filters to noise. Low-growing shrubs can be used to cover ground in an ornamental way.

Buying trees & shrubs

Many garden centers and nurseries sell container-grown trees and shrubs year-round; some will also have bare-root and balled-and-burlapped plants from late fall to early spring for planting at that time of year. Container-grown trees and shrubs are best planted during this period as well, but they can be planted year-round.

Planting in fall allows the plant to become established before winter and be ready to grow in spring. Container-grown trees and shrubs will require a lot of watering if planted in spring or summer, making them vulnerable to dry weather. Avoid planting during drought conditions or if the ground is frozen or waterlogged.

Selecting a healthy plant

If you want your plants to get off to a flying start, then choose healthy plants. Avoid any that show signs of pests and diseases, or those that have badly damaged branches.

Generally, if you are buying a shrub, make sure it has a good network of evenly spaced branches, and if you are buying a tree, check it has a straight, clear stem with a good head of branches.

When buying container plants, slide off the pot and check the roots. Reject any plant where the roots are spiralling or noticeably rootbound. The roots of bare-root plants should be damp and show no signs of damage.

WAYS TO BUY TREES & SHRUBS

Bare-root plants are available only during the dormant season, usually for fruit, hedging, or rose plants. Plant them immediately.

Balled-and-burlapped plants come with moist soil attached to the roots. Check that the wrapping is firmly in place before buying.

Container-grown plants should be checked to ensure they have not become rootbound.

Planting trees & shrubs

Before planting, remove any weeds from the site, either by hand or with a fork; if the site is covered with deep-rooted perennial weeds, treat with a herbicide (*see page 53*).

For bare-root plants, look for the flare of the trunk—the area where the upper roots grow from the base of the trunk—and plant just above this level. Do the same for container-grown plants by scraping off the surface of the potting mix, as some may have been planted too deeply in their pot. A tree or shrub that is planted too deeply may rot at the base of the trunk. As a general rule, however, you should plant container-grown trees and shrubs at the same level as they were in their containers.

The depth of each planting hole for trees and shrubs should be the same as the rootball. For most trees, you will need only a hole that is the depth of a spade's blade, but be guided by the rootball and dig the hole accordingly.

In the past, it was recommended that well-rotted manure or garden compost should be placed into the bottom of the hole. However, you should avoid doing this: Trees planted on top of a layer of organic matter can sink into the ground as this material starts to decay.

You should also avoid adding fertilizer when planting as this can harm and burn freshly forming roots. The addition of mycorrhizal fungi (available in garden centers)

PLANTING A SHRUB

1 Dig a round hole about twice the diameter of the root system, and to the same depth.

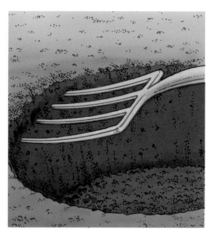

2 Pierce the sides of the hole with a fork. You can mix the dug soil with well-rotted compost, so long as this soil is used only to fill in around the roots, not below them.

3 Tease out roots that have grown around the rootball on container-grown plants. This encourages them to grow outward, rather than in a circle.

4 Position the shrub in the planting hole, making sure that it is at the right level.

5 Backfill the planting hole with the excavated soil. Firm it around the roots with your fingers so no air pockets remain.

6 Soak the soil around the base of the shrub, mulch thickly, and water regularly through the first growing season.

PLANTING A TREE

1 **Prepare a hole** as for a shrub (*see previous page*). Pierce the bottom with a fork—do not dig it over as the tree will sink after planting.

2 **Place the tree** into the hole, checking that the flare of the trunk is just below the level of the ground. Tease out the roots and backfill the hole with the excavated soil, firming gently.

3 **Drive in a wooden stake** at an angle for container-grown or balled-and-burlapped trees; point in the direction of the prevailing wind. Use a vertical stake for bare-root trees.

4 **Tie the tree** to the stake using a tree tie, about one third of the way up the trunk. Leave space between the stake and trunk.

5 **Soak the soil** around the base of the tree. Repeat regularly during the first year. Use a tree guard if necessary (*see page 100*).

6 **Mulch thickly** over the roots to hold moisture in the soil. Keep the mulch clear of the trunk to prevent rotting.

to the soil, however, can be beneficial, as it can help trees to establish. Mix in the mycorrhizal fungi granules with the soil before it is returned to the hole.

How to plant

Trees and shrubs are planted in much the same way (*see above and previous page*), except that trees need staking and the bottom of their planting holes need to be pierced with a fork to encourage deeper rooting.

Tease out the roots of container-grown plants before planting to boost speedy anchoring in the soil. If roots are very pot-bound, slice the roots several times with a spade to help them emerge upon planting. Failure to do this leads to spiraling roots, and the tree will not establish.

Staking a tree

If at all possible, choose small trees about 3ft. tall, which do not need staking. Apart from saving you time when planting, smaller trees also establish more quickly.

Larger trees will need a stake, the function of which is to help anchor the roots. Stakes are not there to prevent the stem from moving; in fact, stem movement in a breeze is good for the plant as it helps to make the trunk stronger. Put in a stake at 45 degrees for container-grown or balled-and-burlapped trees (*see facing page*) and a short, vertical stake for bare-root plants.

You often see trees that have been staked for many years. This is unnecessary, and if it is needed, then there is probably something wrong with the tree or in the way

STAKING A TREE

Diagonal stakes at 45 degrees are used for container-grown or balled-and-burlapped trees; the stake will not damage the root system when it is put in place.

Sturdy H-stakes are not often seen except in public spaces, where trees may be prone to vandalism. Like diagonal stakes, they avoid damage to the root system.

Use vertical stakes for bare-root trees only. They are unsuitable for container-grown or balled-and-burlapped plants as it is not possible to get the stake close enough to the tree.

it was originally planted. As a rule, leave stakes in the ground for 18 months after planting, and then remove them carefully so as not to disturb the roots.

To tie the tree to its stake, use a rubber tube or belt for small trees, and a plastic buckle tie for larger trees. Ties should not be so tight as to restrict the growth of stems, or too loose, which can cause the stem to rub against the tie or stake. From time to time, relax ties so they do not restrict growth, and tighten any that have come loose.

The life of a transplant

We often expect newly planted trees to thrive after planting, but newly planted bare-root transplants will take at least three years to grow vigorously (*see below*).

When trees are lifted from the nursery field, they can lose up to 90 percent of their original root system, so in the first year of planting, do not expect too much of the tree, when shoots are likely to be shorter and leaves smaller than normal.

THE FIRST YEARS IN THE LIFE OF A TRANSPLANT

FIRST YEAR
Roots gradually take hold, but as leaves and shoots are smaller and shorter in the first year, energy for root growth will be limited.

SECOND YEAR
Roots spread over a greater distance, so they will be able to take up more water and nutrients, promoting more topgrowth.

THIRD & SUBSEQUENT YEARS
Vigorous growth results now that the root system is fully recovered from transplanting and the roots are well established.

Tree & shrub aftercare

Immediately after you buy a tree or shrub, you need to follow a care program to ensure that it thrives. If you cannot plant it right away, container-grown specimens can be kept in their pots for a few weeks out of direct sun, and bare-root or balled-and-burlapped trees can be heeled in (*see below*). After planting, water thoroughly, then add a tree guard (*see right*) if it is necessary to protect a tree from large mammals such as deer or rabbits. Next, cover the ground under the plant with a layer of mulch (*see page 36*), no deeper than 3in., leaving a gap around the base of the tree so that the mulch does not come into contact with the bark; this can lead to rotting at the base of the trunk.

Water trees and shrubs attentively while they establish (*see below, right*), especially during periods of drought or if they have been planted in well-drained soil. Apply generous amounts of water every two weeks, rather than a sprinkling every few days, to encourage deep rooting.

Fertilizing & weeding

It is not necessary to fertilize trees or shrubs after planting. In subsequent years, a continuous-release, all-purpose plant food can help to boost the growth of trees planted in poor or very well-drained soil—apply this over the root area, which is under the canopy.

You should keep the root area under the tree free of weeds. A thick mulch should help with this, and it should be topped up as it rots away. If necessary, weed on a regular basis, rather than allowing a carpet of weeds to develop.

TREE PROTECTION

Protect the trunk of a young tree from mammals like deer, mice, or rabbits. They can strip the bark and easily kill the tree. Many types of tree guard are available; simple wrap-around guards made from plastic or wire mesh are usually sufficient and can be attached to the stake.

Heavy-duty tree guards are made from wire mesh, like chicken wire, or tough plastic. They give extra protection from large mammals. The guard should be supported independently of the tree stake, on 3 or 4 stakes of its own, forming a cage around the trunk.

HEELING IN

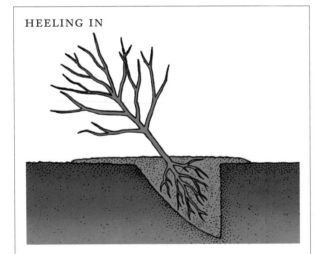

Bare-root or balled-and-burlapped trees and shrubs must be heeled in if they cannot be planted right away. To do this, dig a hole—or trench, if more than one plant—to the depth of the root system. Plant at the same depth as in the nursery (*see page 97*).

WATERING A TREE

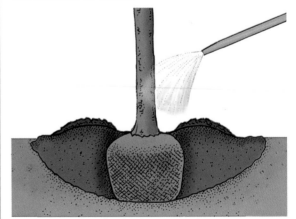

In the first year, watering is perhaps your most important job. To direct water over the roots, a good tip is to create a shallow dip around the trunk, to act as a reservoir, or lay a soaker hose over the root area and cover with mulch.

Moving trees & shrubs

Whether you are moving to a new home and want to take a certain tree or shrub with you, or you are planning on implementing a new planting scheme or simply think that a shrub has been planted in the wrong place, you can move a plant to a new position with a little effort.

When to move plants

Ideally, move deciduous trees and shrubs in fall as they become dormant. Evergreens are best moved in early spring, because at this time the plant will be entering its growing season and the roots will be able to soak up water and nutrients from the warming soil, helping it to establish quickly. In some areas it is tempting to move an evergreen in winter, but an evergreen plant can still lose water from its leaves, even though it is dormant, so if it is moved at this time it will dry out.

Preparing the plant

Dig a trench around the root area and undercut the roots (*see below*), with the aim of creating a large rootball with lots of roots. This will help the plant to reestablish itself quickly. Severing roots is unavoidable when you do this, but if done properly the plant will recover on replanting.

Moving the plant

You must keep the rootball damp and replant as soon as possible after lifting. Wrap the rootball tightly in wet burlap or an old blanket so it does not dry out.

While small shrubs are easily removed by one pair of hands, if you have a large plant you will end up with quite a sizeable rootball. Not only will this be heavy to move, but the digging will also be hard work. This is a job best done by two people.

MOVING A TREE FOR REPLANTING

1 **Dig a trench** 12in. wide and 24in. deep around the root area, which is measured by the spread of the canopy.

2 **Undercut the roots** with a spade and trim back any untidy roots with pruners. Prepare the new hole ready for replanting.

3 **Lift the tree** carefully, tilting it on its rootball so that an old blanket or burlap can be slipped underneath.

4 **Wrap up** the rootball tightly and tie in place. Spray it with water to keep it damp before replanting as soon as possible.

Pruning & training

The purpose of pruning and training is to influence the way a tree or shrub grows. By doing so, you can create some wonderful effects in the garden.

Some plants need very little pruning other than the removal of dead flowerheads, or the removal of crossing branches or those that spoil the shape. Other plants may be overgrown and require more work to restore them to their former glory. Some need annual pruning to ensure a good display of flowers, fruit, or ornamental stems, while formal hedges or topiary need pruning to maintain a crisp shape. Trees in particular require early training in their formative years (*see below right*) to produce a strong framework and an attractive shape.

Whatever your reason for pruning, your trees and shrubs are unlikely to grow, flower, and fruit in the way that you want without any pruning at all. This section shows you how to do it successfully. Do not worry if your plants look different to the illustrations—the basic principles and techniques can still be applied.

What happens when you prune

In general terms, if you remove part of a tree or shrub, you will encourage it to grow. At the end of each shoot is a terminal bud, which is dominant over the buds that grow to form side branches. If the terminal bud is cut off, it results in the growth of side branches below—hard pruning results in more vigorous growth than cutting back lightly. If you cut vigorous growth back hard, this may result in more vigorous growth, so as a rule of thumb weak growth should be pruned hard, while vigorous growth should be pruned more lightly (*see box, facing page*).

Pruning tools

It is important to buy good-quality tools for pruning. A pair of pruners is essential for cutting branches of pencil thickness, while a hand-held pruning saw will speedily cut through branches that are more than finger-thick. Fixed-blade models are available, but folding saws are handier as they can be stored in your pocket when not in use. If you have lots of tall trees in your garden, it may be worth buying pruning tools that can be mounted on a telescopic handle, which is safer than climbing a ladder.

For a small run of hedge you should not need anything more than a pair of hand-held shears. An electric hedge trimmer is ideal for more substantial hedges.

Make sure your tools are sharp and clean, as rough cuts or torn branches can result in disease. Cut just above a strong bud, or pair of buds (*see box, above*).

HOW TO MAKE A PRUNING CUT

Prune back to just above a strong bud or pair of buds, or a healthy sideshoot, as shown above. The cut should slope away from the bud or shoot. Pruning too close to the bud or shoot will cause it damage; pruning too far away will result in die-back.

EARLY TRAINING

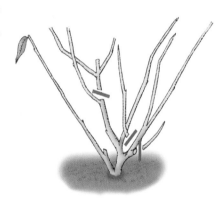

1 **Remove branches** that are crossing or crowded during the first few years after planting as these will spoil the symmetry of the plant. This is especially important for shrubs or trees that cannot be hard pruned when they are older, such as witch hazels, magnolias, or rhododendrons.

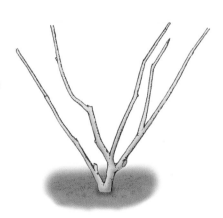

2 **After training** you are left with evenly spaced branches and a balanced, open habit. This forms the permanent woody framework from which the rest of the plant will develop; aim to maintain this open habit on new growth as the plant grows.

Formative pruning

Some trees and shrubs develop a well-shaped branch structure quite naturally, but many benefit from a little help in the early years (*see facing page*), particularly if they can only undergo minimal pruning when mature (*see page 112*).

If you intend to grow trees or shrubs as a restricted form, such as a wall-trained cordon or espalier, then you will need to prune them quite carefully in the first few years to form the shape that you need.

Formative pruning is less vital for shrubs that are pruned hard or for renewal (*see page 115*), but it still helps to create a balanced shape with evenly spaced branches.

Pruning for shape

After initial pruning and training, many trees and shrubs can be left to their own devices, with minimal pruning to remove dead, diseased, or damaged branches. By paying attention to detail, you can maintain an attractive shape through well-judged pruning.

Sometimes, however, branches develop that spoil the shape and symmetry of the plant, and these can be cut out. If one side of your tree has developed more vigorously than the other, giving a lop-sided look, you can lightly prune the stronger shoots and hard prune the weaker ones to restore the balance (*see box, below*).

PRUNING TO MAINTAIN A BALANCED SHAPE

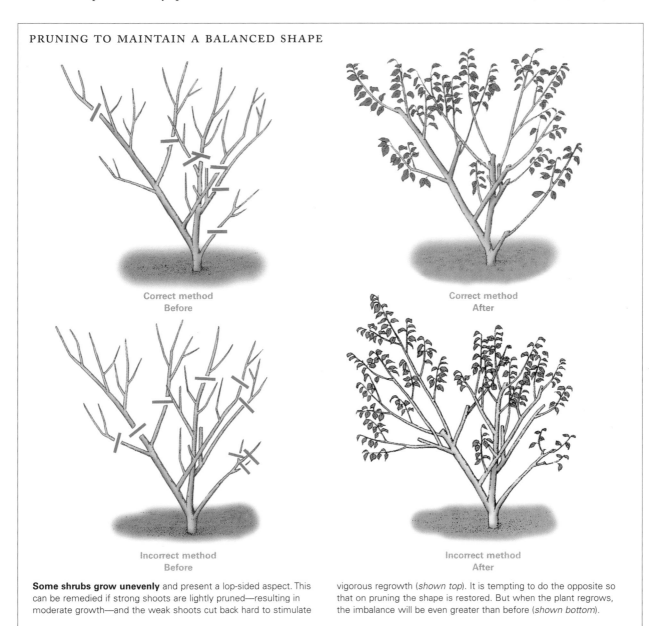

Correct method
Before

Correct method
After

Incorrect method
Before

Incorrect method
After

Some shrubs grow unevenly and present a lop-sided aspect. This can be remedied if strong shoots are lightly pruned—resulting in moderate growth—and the weak shoots cut back hard to stimulate vigorous regrowth (*shown top*). It is tempting to do the opposite so that on pruning the shape is restored. But when the plant regrows, the imbalance will be even greater than before (*shown bottom*).

WATER SHOOTS

Clusters of shoots can arise on tree trunks and main branches, often around an old wound. They should be cut out each year, in winter, back to the base, as they may weaken other growth.

Pruning to prevent disease

You will want your trees and shrubs to remain healthy, so always prune to remove dead, diseased, and damaged wood. These should be removed as soon as they are spotted to prevent any potential problems from spreading into other parts of the plant. Either cut out the affected branch completely or cut back into healthy wood. If the material is diseased, burn it if possible.

If dead or damaged wood is present, this can act as an easy entry point for disease, and a plant that is in poor health is much more susceptible to infection by further diseases or attack by pests.

You should always be on the lookout for dead, diseased, and damaged material. At the same time, you can also give the plant's health a boost by snipping out any very thin or crossing shoots from the center of the plant. These develop due to lack of light, and removing them will open the plant up and allow air to flow more efficiently through the crown.

Pruning to encourage flowers

Many shrubs are pruned for a better display of flowers. To be successful, the correct timing of pruning is essential and you need to know if the plant flowers on old wood or on shoots that are produced in spring of the same year.

For example, the many varieties of *Buddleia davidii* flower on new wood, and the best floral spectacle comes as a result of hard pruning the shrub in early spring to encourage lots of new branches, which will bear the

PRUNING A LARGE BRANCH

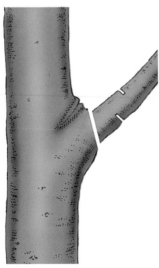

Remove in stages to reduce damage. Finish by sawing straight through the branch, outside the bark ridge and the branch collar.

WHERE TO CUT ON DIFFERENT TYPES OF BRANCHES

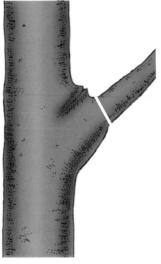

A swollen branch collar and raised bark ridge, above the branch, should be pruned outside the collar and ridge.

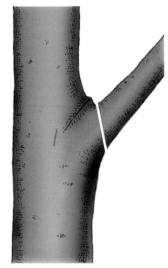

If there is no obvious bark collar, imagine an angled line starting from the outer edge of the bark ridge, running away from the trunk.

flowering wood. Closely related *Buddleia alternifolia*, however, flowers on one- and two-year-old wood, so if it was pruned heavily in the spring there would be no floral show at all that year.

Any good nursery or garden center will be able to supply you with this information when you buy a shrub. Established plants are less easy to ascertain; start by identifying the plant and go from there. Flowering trees, such as horse chestnuts or laburnums, tend to be left to their own devices.

Pruning for foliage

With flowering shrubs, it helps to understand what a plant is and how it grows before you start to prune. Golden-leaved elders, purple hazels, and Indian bean trees can all be cut back hard for maximum foliage effect (*see page 111*), whereas Japanese maples need only minimal work (*see page 112*). Where shrubs are grown for their flowers as well as their foliage, as with variegated-leaved philadelphus, practice renewal or minimal pruning.

Other reasons to prune

Further pruning that may be necessary includes removing large tree branches (*see below*), dealing with suckering and water shoots (*see boxes, right and facing page*), or cutting out any reverted shoots—seen on shrubs with variegated leaves, where shoots develop with pure green leaves. These should be cut back to the base, as they are more vigorous and will eventually dominate.

SUCKERING SHOOTS

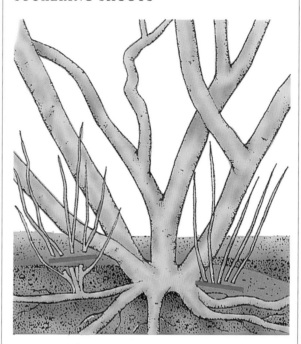

Shoots that arise directly from the roots of a woody plant are known as suckers. These can be a nuisance on trees like sumac (*Rhus*), as they spoil the look of the plant. Suckers that arise on trees and shrubs that are grafted onto rootstocks, such as roses, are more of a problem—they do not share the same ornamental qualities as the grafted plant, and if left will gradually take over. Pull off each sucker at its point of origin so that the dormant buds are removed at the same time (*right*). If suckers are simply cut off at ground level (*left*), further suckers will result.

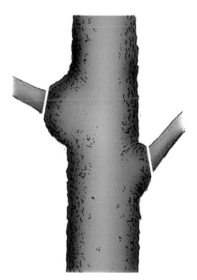

Obvious ridges and collars make branch removal straightforward. Cut just beyond the bark ridge and the swollen branch collar.

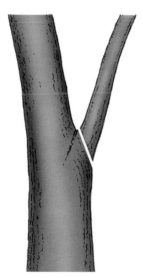

V-shaped branch junctions are weak and should be removed. Cut from the bottom of the branch to avoid damaging the trunk.

Steep branches may also need to cut from below. Judge the cut carefully so that you do not cut, or remove any material from, the trunk.

Pruning evergreen shrubs

Assuming that they are grown in the right place with plenty of space to develop, and that they have been pruned formatively to create a balanced framework (*see page 102*), most evergreen shrubs will grow happily with the minimum of pruning. You will only need to remove the dead heads of fading flowers (*see box, right*) and dead or diseased branches as they are seen.

If there are any wayward shoots, winter-damaged branches, or badly placed growths that spoil the shape of the shrub, these are best removed in spring. This gives plenty of time for regrowth to ripen before cooler weather returns in fall. Pruned earlier, new growth could be susceptible to frost, and if cut later, say in summer or fall, the resulting new growth will be soft and sappy, making it vulnerable to damage over winter.

Some evergreen plants can be cut back hard for foliage effect (*see page 111*). For example, eucalyptus plants

DEADHEADING

Removal of faded flowerheads after flowering, known as deadheading, prevents the plant from diverting energy into fruit production. It also improves the look of the plant.

COMPETING SIDESHOOTS

PRUNING TO STIMULATE SIDESHOOTS

Prune back sideshoots that compete with the main stem, in spring. If a double main stem develops, it can cause a point of weakness.

1 **Cut back** the tip of the main stem in spring by just a few leaves to stimulate growth of sideshoots from buds in the leaf bases (*inset*).

2 **Sideshoots develop** in summer, forming a bushier plant. Train the top sideshoot to continue the upward growth of the main stem.

develop oval leaves on mature growth, but can be pruned close to ground level each spring to promote lots of new stems that bear plenty of attractive, rounded, juvenile leaves. As well as looking good in a mixed border, the new shoots can be cut for indoor display.

Early training of young shrubs

Young evergreen shrubs sometimes need training to help develop a main stem and bushy growth. If the plant has a strong main stem, it may be necessary to reduce the length of any competing sideshoots (*see facing page, left*). Alternatively, if the main stem is weak with very few branches, it can be pruned to encourage the growth of sideshoots; the uppermost sideshoot then takes over as the main stem (*see facing page, right*).

Pruning lavender & heather

If left unpruned, lavender will develop a mass of leggy, woody stems and prove to be difficult to rejuvenate. It is best to keep plants compact, bushy, and attractive by trimming twice a year (*see below*). Heathers need minimal pruning (*see box, right*): lightly trim winter-flowering varieties in midspring after they have finished flowering. Prune summer- and fall-flowering heathers at the same time, as this allows you to enjoy their old flowerheads over

TRIMMING HEATHER

1 **Lightly trim** over the plant in midspring, removing the old flowerheads just below the base. Use shears, or scissors on small plants, to follow the natural growth of the plant—do not attempt to cut them into shapes.

2 **Flowering takes place** again the following summer, fall, or winter, depending on the species of heather. Do not trim again until midspring.

PRUNING LAVENDER

FIRST YEAR

1 **Prune back** young plants quite hard in midspring to remove untidy growth, to encourage new branches, and to start to create the required shape.

2 **Remove old flowerheads** after flowering by giving the shrub a light trim with shears. This improves the look of the plant and prepares it for winter. Avoid the temptation to trim plants back harder at this time.

SECOND & SUBSEQUENT YEARS

3 **Trim closely** in early spring with hand shears. You can cut back quite hard—it keeps the plants neat and compact—but do not cut back into the older, leafless wood, as this will not rejuvenate.

4 **Over the years**, lavenders will gradually fill out, despite close trimming each year. Eventually, they will need replacing, as will unkempt or badly shaped lavenders.

Pruning deciduous shrubs

It is a misconception that all deciduous shrubs need to be pruned. All will grow successfully without pruning, but from a gardener's perspective most will quickly begin to look untidy and their displays may lack quality.

It will be necessary, therefore, to prune from time to time. How regularly you do this depends on your needs as a gardener; if you are trying to achieve a naturalistic look, you can ease off a bit and maybe grow shrubs that only need minimal attention (*see page 112*). If you want the maximum performance from each and every one of your garden shrubs, you should prune attentively.

RENEWAL PRUNING

Shrubs that flower on stems produced the previous year can be pruned after flowering to promote a renewed supply of young and vigorous shoots. If done each year, lots of new shoots will grow farther down the plant, resulting in flowers nearer the ground, which are easily enjoyed by the gardener.

Renewal pruning not only maximizes the flowering potential of a deciduous shrub but it also keeps the shrub within bounds; if left unpruned, especially in a small garden, these shrubs can outgrow their space.

Shrubs that can be pruned by this method form a large group, mostly consisting of spring- or early summer-flowering shrubs like spring-flowering ceanothus, deutzias (*see below*), forsythias, kerrias (*see facing page*), kolkwitzias, hydrangeas (*see facing page*), philadelphus, flowering currants (*Ribes sanguineum*), *Buddleia alternifolia*, spring-flowering tamarix, weigelas, and *Spiraea* 'Arguta'.

If you do not want to prune annually, or if you have the space to let them grow naturally, philadelphus, deutzias, and spiraeas can be left to grow for four or five years before chopping them back hard to 6in. from the ground (*see page 110*). Allowed to grow like this, they will develop an attractive, natural shape that is similar to that obtained by the shrub in the wild; one drawback is that it may take them a couple of years to recover fully.

PRUNING DEUTZIAS

FIRST YEAR

1 Prune away all weak growth and the tips of all main shoots back to a pair of strong buds on planting, in fall to early spring. Aim to create a balanced, open framework (*see page 102*). Water the roots well and add a thick mulch over the root area.

SECOND & SUBSEQUENT YEARS

2 Let the plant flower and develop strong new shoots and branches in its first growing season. These new shoots and branches will become the renewal growth.

3 Cut back all the flowering stems to strong side branches lower down the stems as soon as the display is over. Prune out any weak growth and any other badly placed shoots to maintain the open, balanced framework.

4 In winter, you will see how the strong side branches have grown to replace the old flowering stems that were removed the previous summer. This is the renewal growth that will flower in the coming year, when the shrub should be pruned using the same method.

Pruning evergreen shrubs *see page 106* | **Hedges** *see page 121* | **Vines & wall plants** *see page 138*

PRUNING KERRIAS

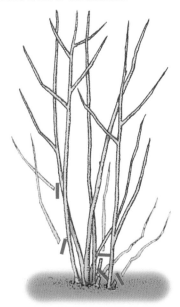

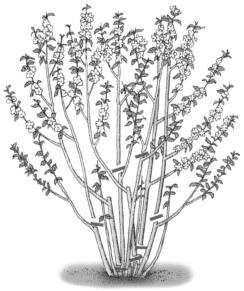

FIRST YEAR

1 **Cut back** all weak growth to a strong bud on the plant in fall to early spring, to create a balanced framework (*see page 102*).

2 **Remove all flowered shoots** at the base or low down on the branches where new shoots are forming. Mulch, if necessary.

SECOND & SUBSEQUENT YEARS

3 **Prune after flowering** each year in the same way as in step 2. New shoots that emerge will form the renewal growth.

Variations on a theme

Deutzia (*see facing page*) is a typical example of a shrub that benefits from renewal pruning. Branches that have flowered are cut back to strong new shoots that then flower the following year.

The new shoots of some shrubs, such as kerrias (*see above*), grow from or close to ground level rather than on existing branches. The main point of difference is that, after flowering, branches that have flowered are cut right back to the base or to a point low down on the stem where there is vigorous new growth.

Pruning hydrangeas

Bigleaf hydrangeas flower late in the growing season and they are often mistakenly pruned hard in spring in the belief that the resultant strong growths will flower that same year. With the exception of new varieties such as Endless Summer, this is not the case.

Only minor pruning is required of a mature hydrangea, and this should be delayed until spring as old flowers left on the plant over winter help to protect the vulnerable buds below from frost. In spring, remove the dead flowerheads back to a healthy pair of buds. Renewal pruning can be done on mature hydrangeas if they have become choked with lots of twiggy growth (*see right*).

PRUNING A MATURE HYDRANGEA

1 **Remove old flowerheads** by cutting them back to a strong pair of buds in midspring. On congested plants, remove one third to a quarter of the older branches to their bases at the same time; renewal growth will emerge in the coming season. Aim to keep a balanced framework (*see page 102*).

2 **On flowering**, in mid- to late summer, you will notice that new flowerheads form from the strong pair of buds that were below the old flowerheads. The renewal growth will have extended, but this will not flower until the next season.

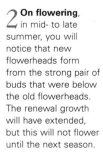

HARD PRUNING

Shrubs that flower on growth that develops during spring and summer can be pruned hard in spring, to produce vigorous new shoots for flowering.

Plants that can be pruned by this method consist of late summer- or fall-flowering shrubs like butterfly bush (*Buddleia davidii*), fall-flowering ceanothus, caryopteris, ceratostigmas, *Fuchsia magellanica*, *Hydrangea paniculata*, leycesterias, Russian sage (*Perovskia*), romneyas, and all varieties of *Spiraea japonica*.

There are various ways of hard pruning deciduous shrubs. Leycesterias, Russian sages, and hardy fuchsias, which do not form a woody framework, can be pruned almost to ground level. Fall-flowering ceanothus, and caryopteris can be allowed to develop a permanent framework of branches and then the old shoots cut back to within a few inches of this. Butterfly bush (*Buddleia davidii*), which is extremely vigorous, can be pruned back harder to a lower framework (*see below*).

Hard pruning for winter stems

A number of deciduous shrubs can be pruned down to the ground annually to showcase their colorful new shoots. Good choices for this technique include varieties of red osier dogwood (*Cornus stolonifera*), bloodtwig dogwood (*C. sanguinea*), small willows (*Salix*), and ghost bramble (*Rubus cockburnianus*). Known as coppicing or stooling, this straightforward procedure (*see facing page*) should be done in late winter or early spring, before new growth emerges.

Shrubs grown for their winter stems tend not to be particularly decorative otherwise, so pruning simply consists of cutting down all growth to ground level. New shoots sprout vigorously if the plant is growing under the correct conditions, and when the leaves drop in fall their ornamental stems are revealed.

A related but less commonly used technique, known as pollarding, involves pruning willows or dogwoods so that the new stems emerge at the top of a short, or tall, trunk (*see box, facing page*).

PRUNING A BUTTERFLY BUSH

1 **Prune back** all shoots by two thirds to vigorous buds, or emerging shoots, on planting. Remove weak shoots entirely.

2 **Vigorous new shoots** develop and flower at the tips in late summer. They should be deadheaded to prevent self seeding.

SECOND YEAR

3 **Prune back hard** all shoots to 1–2 buds from the base in spring. A permanent woody framework begins to develop.

4 **Remove tips** of flowered stems in early fall to prevent self seeding and damage during winter storms.

THIRD & SUBSEQUENT YEARS

5 **Prune back hard** all shoots to strong buds at the base in spring, as in step 3. Repeat this process in successive years.

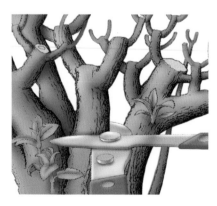

6 **Remove sections** of the permanent framework, with loppers or a pruning saw, when it becomes overcrowded.

HARD PRUNING DOGWOOD TO PRODUCE COLORFUL STEMS

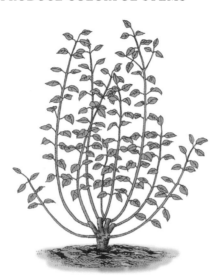

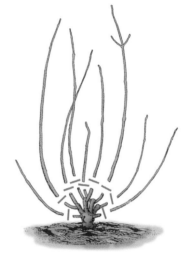

FIRST YEAR

1 Prune back hard all shoots close to their bases on planting. Mulch the plant and fertilize, if needed, around the roots.

2 Vigorous new shoots develop in spring and summer. When the leaves fall, the attractive stems will be revealed.

SECOND & SUBSEQUENT YEARS

3 Prune hard all shoots to near the base, as in step 1. Remove any weak stumps at their bases. Mulch well.

Hard pruning for maximum foliage effect

Like deciduous shrubs grown for their winter stems, some shrubs are hard pruned purely for their decorative foliage, which is a feature in summer and fall.

Shrubs that can be pruned this way include Indian bean trees (*Catalpa bignonioides*), smoke bushes (*Cotinus coggygria*), *Cornus alba* (some varieties), sumacs (*Rhus typhina*), golden elders (*Sambucus nigra* 'Aurea'), and purple-leaved hazels (*Corylus maxima* 'Purpurea').

Not all shrubs tolerate hard pruning; some will die if given such treatment. Those that can stand it are pruned in the same way as for winter-stem shrubs (*see above*). They will not flower given such treatment, and on most foliage shrubs this is of no importance.

If you want flowers as well as foliage, as you may well do with a smoke bush or a dark-leaved elder, you must prune less harshly; in the case of elders and smoke bushes, revert to minimal pruning (*see following page*).

Indian bean trees (*Catalpa bignonioides*) bear impressive foliage if hard pruned each spring, particularly this golden form 'Aurea'. The leaves are also often much larger than on unpruned specimens.

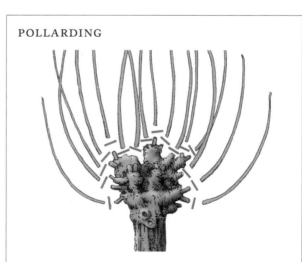

POLLARDING

The basic framework of coppiced shrubs can be varied in height if allowed to grow on a trunk, as a pollard. This is useful in raising the height of the display. New shoots are pruned in the same way.

MINIMAL PRUNING

There is a large group of shrubs or small trees that develop a permanent framework of branches and require very little pruning once established. Japanese maples (*Acer japonicum* and *A. palmatum*), euonymus, deciduous magnolias, smoke bushes (*Cotinus*), viburnums, cotoneasters, hibiscus, witch hazels (*Hamamelis*), and others produce their growth from the perimeter of the framework, unlike other shrubs that make lots of vigorous growth from the base and lower branches. Early training of these shrubs is needed to build up a framework (*see below*), with the aim of creating an attractive shrub with a well-balanced branch structure.

When mature, maintain these shrubs by cutting out any dead, diseased, or damaged branches. Wayward shoots can also be removed to maintain symmetry. If vigorous shoots do grow from the base or lower down the framework, either cut them out or train them in, if this is necessary to replace older branches.

Intricately branched Japanese maples may look as if they are the result of attentive pruning, but beyond the creation of the basic framework they are actually left unpruned. After leaf fall, the trees can be inspected for dead, damaged, or diseased branches.

PRUNING A DECIDUOUS MAGNOLIA

FIRST YEAR

1 **Remove crossing branches** and weak growth on planting, in fall to early spring. Aim to create a balanced, open framework (*see page 102*), here on *Magnolia stellata*.

SECOND YEAR

2 **Prune away** any badly spaced side branches in spring that have formed after the first season of growth. Leave all the other branches unpruned.

THIRD & SUBSEQUENT YEARS

3 **Prune only as required** to remove dead, diseased, or damaged branches as they are seen. Crossing branches that emerge must also be removed as they will cause damage when they rub together.

4 **Leave the plant unpruned** at flowering time so its display can be enjoyed. The spring flowers and new growth can be seen to emerge at the perimeter of the framework at this time of year.

Pruning a full-branched tree

A full-branched tree is easily recognized by its main stem, which is clad with a series of evenly spaced branches, almost to ground level. This naturalistic method of growth gives the most informal look, and is most often seen on birches, alders, and mountain ashes (*Sorbus*).

The aim with the early training is to develop a single, dominant topshoot, or leader (*see below*), avoiding a forked or double leader. You do this by removing any competing shoots that may form. Shoots that grow from the base of the tree need to be removed immediately for a similar reason: if they are left, you will end up with a multistemmed tree.

As the tree matures, it should form a symmetrical shape without any intervention. You can encourage this by pruning out any branches that ruin the symmetry or are badly crossing during late fall and early winter. Dead, diseased, and damaged branches can be taken out at the same time. Lower branches that will get in the way of the mower when cutting the grass or that are too overcrowded, can also be removed, if necessary.

A full-branched tree can easily be converted into a central-leader topbranched tree (*see following page*) by cutting back the lower branches over a number of years until the required height of the bare trunk is reached.

PRUNING A FULL-BRANCHED TREE

FIRST YEAR

1 **On planting**, stake and tie in the tree. Allow the tree to grow unpruned in its first spring and summer.

2 **Cut back** shoots that grow close to the base in mid- to late fall. If not removed, these may rival the main stem.

SECOND YEAR

3 **Remove the stake** after 18 months, in summer. Cut out any sideshoots that turn upward to compete with the leading shoot.

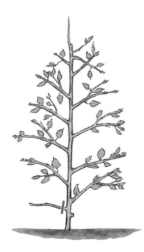

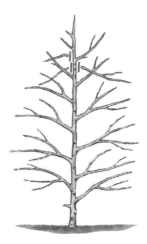

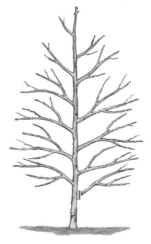

4 **Remove any low branches** that may interfere with mowing, in fall.

THIRD YEAR

5 **Remove any shoots** that might compete with the leader, in late winter.

FOURTH & SUBSEQUENT YEARS

6 **Let the tree develop** naturally, pruning in winter to remove badly placed branches.

Pruning a topbranched tree

Crabapples, cherries, and many other small garden trees are grown as topbranched standards. These trees have a stem that is clear of branches for the first 6ft. from the ground, followed by a well-branched crown. You can buy young trees from nurseries and garden centers that are already trained with a clear trunk.

These trees are not grown with a dominant central leader, unless they are grown as a central-leader standard (*see box, right*). The type of crown that forms depends on the natural growth of the plant, since there is very little intervention from the gardener.

Early training involves the removal of side branches until the desired length of clear stem has been reached. This stage can be skipped if you have bought a pretrained standard tree and these are often available from nurseries. Minimal pruning during late fall and early winter will then keep the tree in good shape—simply remove badly placed or crossing branches, along with any that spoil the symmetry of the tree. Dead, diseased, or damaged branches should be pruned out whenever you spot them. The aim is to create an open crown framework of well-spaced branches.

You should also remove any shoots that emerge on the clear trunk, as well as any vigorous upright shoots within the crown that may try and develop into dominant leaders during the first few years.

CENTRAL-LEADER STANDARD TREES

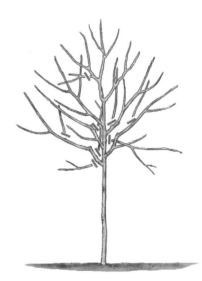

Large trees suit this branch structure. Prune initially as for a full-branched tree (*see previous page*), with lower branches removed gradually each year, until the clear stem is at the desired length.

PRUNING A TOPBRANCHED TREE

FIRST YEAR

1 **On planting**, stake and tie in the tree. Allow the tree to grow unpruned in its first spring and summer.

SECOND & SUBSEQUENT YEARS

2 **Allow further branches** to develop in the crown. No pruning is necessary, but if a leading shoot forms cut it back to a strong bud, to encourage branching in the crown.

3 **Prune out** crossing or crowded branches in mid- to late fall, to form an open, evenly spaced framework. Remove any shoots that appear on the main stem.

Shrub rejuvenation

If you inherit a new yard full of neglected shrubs, or you have a plant that has become too large for its position or is choked with branches, you may think that the only answer is to remove the shrub completely and start again. Before making such a decision, it is worth trying to rescue the plant through drastic pruning (*see right*).

This may sound brutal, and sometimes it is, but shrubs have remarkable powers of recovery and many respond well to such treatment. If you have a prized shrub, or one that you feel is not strong enough to recover from such a shock, then you can attempt the rejuvenation over two or more years (*see below*). With evergreens, however, you will find that it is best to tackle the shrub in one go, as partial pruning looks uneven, untidy, and unsightly.

There is a risk that a neglected shrub does not recover from such an operation, for whatever reason. If this is the case, consider it a failed experiment and replace the plant.

When to rejuvenate shrubs

Deciduous shrubs should be pruned between late fall and early spring while they are dormant. Tackle evergreen shrubs in late spring when they are coming into growth.

A high percentage of deciduous shrubs respond well to hard pruning, but among the evergreen shrubs there are some notable exceptions: most conifers and some woody herbs such as lavender and rosemary will not regrow from old wood. Rhododendrons, camellias, mahonias, hollies (*Ilex*), yews (*Taxus*), and cherry laurels (*Prunus*), however, should all recover rapidly.

RENOVATION BY DRASTIC PRUNING

1 **Cut back** all stems to 6–12in. from ground level in winter. Mulch and fertilize.

2 **Prune out** new shoots that emerge next year, leaving the strongest as renewal growth.

Aftercare

With so much woody material removed, shrubs must be well fed and mulched in spring for several years following rejuvenation pruning. It will also help if you water the plant well in summer, particularly during the first year. Emerging shoots may be nibbled by deer or rabbits, so protect the plants in gardens where these animals are present. Within three or four years, the rejuvenated shrub should be well recovered.

REJUVENATING A DECIDUOUS SHRUB OVER TWO YEARS

  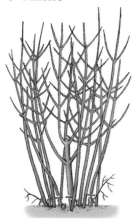 

FIRST YEAR

1 **Cut back** half of all old stems back to ground level from late fall to early spring.

2 **New shoots** emerge from the base and the remaining old stems flower. Mulch and fertilize the plant generously.

SECOND YEAR

3 **Remove the remaining** old stems back to the ground in fall to early spring. Cut back any new growth that is weak.

4 **One-year-old shoots** bear flowers, while new shoots grow from the base. Rejuvenation is complete.

Tree renovation

Large trees in need of renovation should be left to a qualified arborist, armed with the right tools, professional training, and safety equipment suitable for carrying out pruning high above the ground. Restoration of small deciduous trees, however, that have been neglected or poorly pruned in the past, is something that in many cases can be undertake by gardeners as long as appropriate safety measures are taken. The best time to tackle this kind of restorative pruning is in late fall through midwinter, which in most regions is when deciduous trees are dormant and evergreens are not in active growth.

The aim with pruning is to create a well-balanced tree. Most trees can be restored by removing dead, diseased, or damaged branches, followed by pruning out crossing branches and thinning a mass of upright branches to leave an open center. In some circumstances, it may be necessary to remove one or more large branches. Severe pruning like this is likely to result in the development of water sprouts—thin, fast-growing, upright stems—for several years afterwards (*see above right*). Water sprouts are weak stems that rarely flower or bear fruit. They also detract from the appearance of a tree, so they should be removed immediately.

WATER SPROUTS

Major pruning cuts on large branches often cause the formation of vigorous shoots from around the wound for several years after the cut was made. They should be removed as soon as they appear, at the base.

STUBBY SPURS

'Haircut' pruning results in a framework of stubby spurs. These need careful but heavy thinning over a number of years in order to return the tree to its former glory.

Most coniferous trees, such as pines, spruces, and firs, are not good candidates for major restorative pruning because they do not reliably send out new growth from old wood. Stick to light trimming of new growth and occasional removal of damaged or dead branches.

Corrective pruning

One response to poor pruning is a congested cluster of shoots or stubby spurs (*see above*). This follows drastic winter pruning in which trees have had all their new growth cut off. It is often seen on apple trees (*see page 274*); it looks ugly and stunts flowering and fruiting.

To restore the balance to trees like this, first remove any dead, diseased, or damaged branches, and any that are crossing or badly placed. Once this is done, you can tackle the stubby spurs that are left on the branches by thinning out the shoots that grow from them.

Fruit trees are another group of trees that are often inherited in a neglected state. If left to their own devices, they can soon become a mass of twiggy branches with lots of leafy growth but poor fruit yields (*see page 275*). Carry out rejuvenation work gradually, over a three-year period so as not to overly stress the tree. Fertilize, water, and mulch all renovated trees well.

Young hedges that are correctly pruned when young form dense growth that is evenly distributed from top to bottom. Such hedges look good and they are effective as boundaries and screens.

PESTS OF WOODY PLANTS

Pests, diseases, & other problems *see page 40* | **Rose pests & diseases** *see page 136* | **Fruit pests** *see page 276*

Pests of woody plants

As well as the common pests listed here, woody plants are also vulnerable to aphids, vine weevils, deer, rabbits, squirrels, and various caterpillars (*see page 49*).

Borers

Borers are often pests of fruit trees such as cherry, peach, and plum; other borers attack birch, eucalyptus, or palm trees. Look for holes in bark, raised bark where borers have tunneled, black gummy residue, or piles of sawdust. Controls vary according to the specific type of borer; your cooperative extension service can assist you with identification and offer advice on control.

Leafhoppers

Many species of these small, wedge-shaped pests attack a wide range of plants, including roses, rhododendrons, and apple trees. When disturbed, they may run sideways or leap away. Both adults and nymphs suck on plant juices, causing spotting or curling of leaves. They also spread diseases such as fireblight (*see page 120*). Use yellow sticky traps, or control with insecticidal soap.

Gypsy moth

Gypsy moths are a serious pest in eastern U.S. and Canada, and have spread west. Many tree species are affected, especially oaks. Gypsy moth caterpillars eat leaves and can defoliate an entire tree in short order. Hand pick caterpillars and egg masses, encourage natural predators, or use *Bacillus thuringiensis kurstaki* (Btk).

Tent caterpillars

Impossible to miss, these pests congregate in large nests, favoring fruit trees and feeding on foliage. Infestations tend to peak every few years; spray trees with horticultural oil as a preventive or remove by hand.

Scale

These small, sap-feeding insects cluster on leaves and stems. They attack many deciduous and evergreen tree species. Remove by scraping with a knife or nail file. Spraying with dormant oil may be effective for fruit trees.

Viburnum leaf beetle

Both adults and larvae feed on leaves between the midrib and larger veins, reducing them to a lacelike appearance. *Viburnum tinus* and *V. opulus* are most affected. Remove egg-infested twigs after fall leaf drop and/or spray larvae with insecticidal soap.

PESTS & DAMAGE OF WOODY PLANTS

Borer

Leafhopper

Gypsy moth & caterpillar

Tent caterpillars

Cushion scale with eggs

Viburnum leaf beetle damage

Pests of woody plants generally cause damage to soft tissues, such as stems, leaves, flowers, and fruit. But some insects can tunnel into the stems or trunk of a tree, causing serious damage.

Berberis sawfly

The caterpillarlike larvae of this insect are up to ³/₄in. long and creamy white with black and yellow blotches. They feed voraciously on the foliage of some deciduous berberis shrubs, especially *Berberis thunbergii*, and also mahonia shrubs. There can be two or three generations between late spring and early fall, and plants can be defoliated. The shiny, black adults, which have black wings and upswept antennae, can be seen between mid- to late spring for the first generation; the second generation is present in mid- to late summer.

Inspect vulnerable berberis and mahonia shrubs between late spring and early fall for young larvae. It may be a good thing if berberis sawfly feeds on invasive Japanese barberry, but it also damages noninvasive barberries and mahonia.

Boxwood psyllid

The overwintered eggs of this insect hatch in midspring and the flattened, pale green nymphs feed by sucking sap at the shoot tips of boxwoods during the rest of spring. Winged adults develop in late spring and early summer, but these cause no damage.

The feeding of the nymphs stunts normal shoot extension and causes leaves to be cupped, giving a cabbagelike appearance to the shoot tips of boxwood plants. A sugary liquid called honeydew is excreted. The droplets are coated with white wax secreted by the nymphs. These droplets cascade out of the shoot tips when disturbed, leaving white smears on the foliage. Boxwood psyllid is of consequence only on young plants, where they may slow the rate of growth.

Pieris lacebug

The host plants of this sap-feeding insect are *Pieris* species and some rhododendrons. From late spring, the upper leaf surfaces develop a coarse, pale mottling. By late summer, much of the green color may have been lost and the attractive bright gloss of the foliage is ruined. Plants will still bloom, perhaps less prolifically, but vigor is weakened and the overall impact of the plant is reduced.

Lacebugs live on the leaf undersides, which are covered in brown excrement spots. The adults are ¹/₈in. long and their wings, which are carried flat on their backs, are transparent, with distinctive, black markings. Check plants in late spring or early summer for recently hatched nymphs or signs of feeding damage on the new foliage. Spray with an insecticidal soap.

Adelgids

These aphidlike insects suck sap from various conifers. Some species live openly on the foliage or young stems, where they are covered by a fluffy, white wax secreted from their bodies; others develop inside swollen shoot-tip galls. Infestations can be unsightly and, in the case of the hemlock woolly adelgid, very destructive. On small specimens, adelgids can be rubbed off by hand or sprayed with horticultural oil.

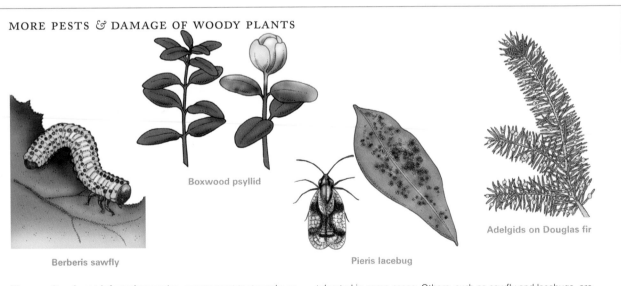

MORE PESTS & DAMAGE OF WOODY PLANTS

Boxwood psyllid

Berberis sawfly

Pieris lacebug

Adelgids on Douglas fir

The severity of pest infestations varies, so you must try to make an accurate identification of a pest before you make a decision about its treatment. Some pests, such as boxwood psyllid and adelgids, can be tolerated in some cases. Others, such as sawfly and lacebugs, are more serious in their nature and will need to be dealt with promptly if an infested plant is to survive without too much damage.

Pests, diseases, & other problems *see page 40* | **Rose pests & diseases** *see page 136* | **Fruit diseases** *see page 278*

Diseases of woody plants

Many diseases can infect trees and shrubs, and some of the most common are listed here. Die-back or death is often attributable to Armillaria root rot, phytophthora, or verticillium wilt (*see page 51*).

Tree rusts

Rusts are usually relatively harmless to mature trees, apart from white pine blister rust (*see below*). They predominantly attack the leaves to produce dusty, yellow or orange pustules, although some infect the bark and usually alternate between two hosts. These are some of the tree rusts that you may encounter.

Birch rust: This rust alternates on larch. Rust-covered birch leaves will defoliate prematurely.

Poplar rusts: These can alternate on alliums, arums, larch, or pine. Rust-covered poplar leaves die and remain hanging on the tree.

White pine blister rust: This alternates on currants (wild and cultivated) and on gooseberries. Black currants can defoliate severely, but this is usually late in the season and so does not affect plants adversely. This rust affects five-needled pines and infects the bark, forming swellings that can girdle and kill entire branches.

Willow rusts: These alternate on alliums, euonymus, and larch. The symptoms are similar to poplar rusts.

Control is difficult unless the trees are young and starting to get established. Sometimes it is practical to remove a known alternate host to break the life cycle, although other spores can still be blown in from some distance away.

Azalea gall

This common fungal disease can disfigure rhododendrons and azaleas, particularly the Indica azalea group. It causes dramatic swellings, or galls, on affected leaves. The green galls become covered in a white spore bloom, which will spread the infection. Remove the galls by hand before they become white.

Wood decay & bracket fungi

Many different fungi can cause wood decay. Some cause rots in upper branches, where airborne spores enter wounds in the canopy and cause branch decay. Others cause root and butt rots, and may be indicated by crown thinning and early leaf loss.

Often the first indication of decay will be the appearance of fungal fruiting bodies such as brackets. Removing the fruiting body does not stop the decay and

COMMON DISEASES OF WOODY PLANTS

Rust on a juniper tree

Azalea gall

Bracket fungi

Coral spot

Fungal diseases are common on trees and shrubs, often seen as galls on leaves, rusts or spots on branches, or elaborate outgrowths.

unfortunately they usually only appear when infection is well established. With an infected tree, it is wise to seek professional advice regarding its safety.

Coral spot

Coral spot is commonly seen on dead twigs of trees and shrubs, or on woody debris. It is weakly parasitic and causes problems on stressed plants that are suffering from poor establishment, root damage, or drought.

In damp weather, small, pink or red, cushionlike eruptions are evident on affected bark. Vast numbers of spores are produced from these 'coral spots'. They can infect through wounds and once established kill branches rapidly. Magnolias, elaeagnus, maples, figs, currants, and gooseberries are frequently affected.

Good hygiene in the garden will reduce new infections. Careful pruning of your trees and shrubs so that dead wood is removed cleanly is a good precaution against coral spot as it will limit points of entry. It is also worth investigating plants to ensure that there is no underlying cause that could be corrected culturally.

Citrus scab

This disease, caused by the fungus *Elsinoe fawcetti*, affects many types of citrus. The fungal spores overwinter on fruit and leaves, infecting new growth in spring. Warty spots develop on leaves and spots spread over the surface of the fruit. To reduce risk of infection, provide good air circulation and keep foliage dry in spring.

Verticillium wilt

Many trees can be affected by the verticillium fungus, including catalpas, redbuds, maples, roses, and fruit and nut trees. Water-conducting tissues become clogged, killing individual branches and, eventually, weakening the entire plant. Applying excessive nitrogenous fertilizer can encourage the disease. The fungus can be impossible to eradicate from the soil. Plant resistant varieties.

Fireblight

A bacterial disease that affects apples, pears, pyracanthas, hawthorns, and mountain ashes, fireblight causes leaves to turn black and die while still attached to the stem. Fruit may be spotted or blotchy. Oozing cankers may appear, spreading the disease to other plants. There is no chemical control; plant resistant varieties.

Camellia blight

Attacking only the flowers, the fungus *Ciborinia camelliae* causes tan or brown spots that turn the entire blossom brown within days. The fungus can survive for years in the soil. Plant only camellia plants that are certified blight free. Clean up fallen flowers, leaves, and mulch from under plants and discard; do not compost. Replace the mulch each year.

Willow anthracnose

This host-specific fungal disease can affect many trees, including ash, elm, maple, sycamore, and willow. Symptoms vary according to the host tree but include spots or blotches on leaves, twigs, stems, or fruit. Plant resistant varieties. Prune and discard affected twigs and branches. Your local cooperative extension service may recommend other control methods.

Canker

Cankers on trees and shrubs may be caused by bacteria such as *Pseudomonas syringae* or a fungus, including *Nectria* or *Coryneum*. Cankers may exude a brownish liquid. Fungal bodies may also be visible. There is no chemical treatment; prune out affected branches or remove the damaged area. Consult an arborist for severe cases.

MORE DISEASES OF WOODY PLANTS

Citrus scab damage
to fruit & leaves

Verticillium wilt

Fireblight on
ornamental pear

Camellia blight

Willow anthracnose
on dogwood

Canker

Diseases caused by bacteria and fungi can sometimes resemble cultural problems such as wounding, sun scorch, or drought stress. For help in identifying a potential disease, consult your local cooperative extension service or a knowledgeable local arborist or garden center. Take a sample and, if possible, a photo of the damage with you.

HEDGES

Hedges have many uses in the yard, but their main purpose is to provide an external boundary to your property. They can also be planted to provide shelter and privacy, as well as making a very good windbreak and filter against noise. Within the yard, they can be used as a device to create 'rooms', while dwarf hedges are ideal for intricate parterres or as an attractive border to beds. Formal hedges are often trimmed several times a year to keep a geometric shape and are grown for their foliage rather than flowers. Informal hedges are mostly left to grow more naturally, with the plants allowed to flower and fruit.

Planting a hedge

Deciduous hedges are best planted between late fall to early spring using bare-root plants. Use container plants for evergreen hedges, planting from mid- to late spring.

Choosing a hedge

What style of hedge you choose largely depends on your style of yard. Formal hedges are kept closely clipped, and hornbeam, beech, boxwood, holly, yew, arborvitae, and cypress are commonly used. Informal hedges are allowed to grow more naturally so plants flower or bear fruit. This suits a more naturalistic garden style.

Native hedges consist of several different trees and shrubs that will produce berries, flowers, fruit, and nuts that are attractive to birds, bees, insects, and mammals. They are ideal for a wildlife garden.

Spacing the plants

A single row of plants, spaced 12–24in. apart, is common for most hedges, but in some circumstances where a thicker hedge is required, it may be necessary to plant a double row. Allow 18in. between rows and stagger plants in the rows, spacing them 36in. apart.

PLANTING A HEDGE

1 Dig a trench along a planting line marked by a taut piece of string. The trench will need to be 16–24in. wide. Place the excavated soil to one side and remove any weeds as you find them.

2 Fork well-rotted manure or garden compost into the bottom of the trench, and then return the excavated soil to the trench, mixing it in with the manure or compost as you go. Break up any large clumps of soil with the fork.

3 Tease out the roots from the rootballs of container-grown plants to encourage them to grow outward after planting. Rake over the soil in the trench and mark planting holes with canes every 12–24in.

4 Firm in the plants after you have dug holes and planted them at the same depth they were in their pots—or, if they are bare-root plants, to the soil marks on the main stems. Prune back the tips of leggy plants and water each plant in well.

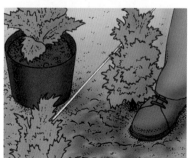

Pruning hedges

To grow into a dense hedge, young plants will need pruning in their early years to encourage thick growth. Formal hedges will need regular clipping to maintain their shapes, whereas informal hedges require only clipping once a year to keep them from getting overgrown. Treat wildlife hedges in the same way as informal hedges.

All established hedges are attractive to birds because they provide shelter, so try to avoid trimming them between spring and midsummer, the main nesting time for birds. Always check for nests before you cut.

Tools for hedge cutting

A pair of hand shears is perfect for maintaining a short run of hedge, while longer hedges are easier with a power trimmer. For most gardens, choose either an electric or lightweight, cordless model.

Initial pruning of a newly planted hedge

In the past, hedging plants were pruned hard upon planting, but this is unnecessary. The modern way of thinking is to save the first prune until the second growing season after planting.

Cut back deciduous plants to half their height in early spring and evergreen shrubs to about two thirds their height in spring (*see facing page, top*). If you forget to prune a young hedge, it will fail to 'knit' together and there will be a lack of shoots at the base of the hedge.

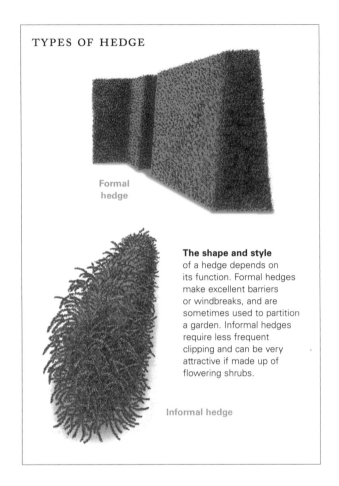

TYPES OF HEDGE

Formal hedge

The shape and style of a hedge depends on its function. Formal hedges make excellent barriers or windbreaks, and are sometimes used to partition a garden. Informal hedges require less frequent clipping and can be very attractive if made up of flowering shrubs.

Informal hedge

GETTING YOUR HEDGE TO THICKEN AT THE BASE

Hedges with no initial pruning tend to grow upward quickly, forming top branches at the expense of the lower ones. The base remains bare, while the topgrowth is dense.

Young hedges that are correctly pruned when young form dense growth that is evenly distributed from top to bottom. Such hedges look good and they are effective as boundaries and screens.

FORMATIVE PRUNING OF AN EVERGREEN HEDGE

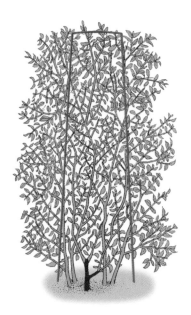

SECOND YEAR

1 **Hard prune** if growth is leggy (shown). If not, cut evergreens by one third in spring; deciduous hedges by a half in early spring.

THIRD & FOURTH YEARS

2 **Trim back** sideshoots lightly in summer and then harder in early spring, starting to form a shape with tapered sides.

SUBSEQUENT YEARS

3 **Let the hedge** gradually fill out to full size, all the while trimming twice a year to maintain the tapered shape.

Hedges made from shrubs that are naturally bushy at the base, such as hornbeam and beech (*see below*), should have their leading shoots pruned lightly in the second growing season after planting, along with some of the longer sideshoots. This should be repeated in the third and fourth years. Prune with a good pair of pruners, making a slanting cut just above a bud. The angle should be facing away from the bud.

After planting a coniferous hedge (*see following page*), simply trim any untidy side branches to encourage more sideways growth. In subsequent years, trim the sides to get the required shape and prune only the leading shoots when they reach the desired height for the hedge.

In a newly planted hedge, there will be a lot of competition at the roots. Apply a thick mulch of organic matter each year and water the new plants in well.

FORMATIVE PRUNING OF A NATURALLY BUSHY, DECIDUOUS HEDGE

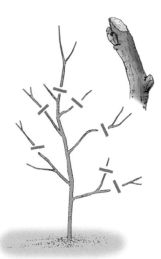

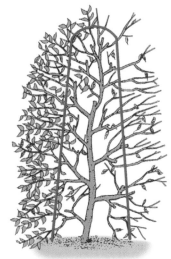

SECOND YEAR

1 **Trim back** the main stem and side branches by one third between fall and late winter. Cut each to a bud, using good pruners.

THIRD & FOURTH YEARS

2 **Shorten all new growth** by one third between fall and late winter. The hedge will begin to thicken.

SUBSEQUENT YEARS

3 **Cut the sides** with shears in early summer, and again in late winter, trimming back to a permanent framework with tapered sides.

Pruning established hedges

Once established, formal hedges are maintained by cutting every four to six weeks in summer, aiming to keep a neat shape with slightly tapered sides. Informal hedges are usually pruned after their display of flowers or berries.

Maintain coniferous hedges by pruning once or twice in summer. Fast-growing hedges must be cut regularly or they will get out of control; some such as Leyland cypress are not suited to warm-summer climates as they often get coryneum canker.

FORMATIVE PRUNING OF A CONIFEROUS HEDGE

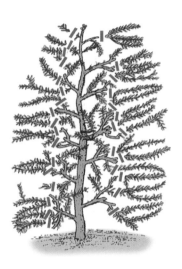

SECOND YEAR

1 Prune side branches by about one third in early spring. Tie the unpruned leading shoot to a stake as it lengthens.

THIRD & FOURTH YEARS

2 Trim back sideshoots in summer, gradually forming a tapered shape. Continue to tie in the leading shoot to the stake.

SUBSEQUENT YEARS

3 Prune the leading shoot when the hedge is at its required height. Trim in summer to maintain the tapered sides.

Renovation

Over time or through neglect, hedges can become too wide or overgrown. It is possible to restore these plants through some drastic pruning carried out over a two-year period (*see box, right*).

In the first year, treat one side of the hedge as normal, but cut back branches on the other side hard to the main stems. The following year, if growth on the hard-pruned side has been vigorous, cut the other side back hard and treat the restored side as normal. If new growth is not vigorous, sprinkle an all-purpose fertilizer around the base of the hedge at the recommended rate, mulch thickly with well-rotted organic matter, and wait another year.

Deciduous hedges can be treated this way in winter, when dormant, while evergreens should be pruned in late winter. Unfortunately, most coniferous hedges will not tolerate such hard pruning as they do not regenerate from old wood; yew is a notable exception. In such cases, it will be necessary to dig out the old hedge and replant with a new one. After pruning, give hedges a boost by watering, fertilizing, and mulching well.

RENOVATING A HEDGE

Cut back one side of the hedge, then repeat on the other side the next year. Not all hedges respond well to this, but it works with yew, holly, cotoneasters, pyracanthas, and many deciduous plants.

Garden design *see page 18* | **Amending the soil** *see page 35* | **Trees & shrubs** *see page 96*

ROSES

Of all the garden plants, roses are among the most versatile. They can be used in a variety of ways to bring color and fragrance to the yard, from bold displays in summer borders to climbing roses that adorn walls and arches, and rambling roses growing high into tree canopies. Patio roses may be grown in containers, and ground-cover roses will scramble over a bank or trail from a raised bed. The first steps in giving your roses a good start are to buy good stock from a reputable nursery, and to plant correctly. You can then keep your roses flourishing by following the basic maintenance advice.

Buying roses

Roses are sold either bare root or in containers. Bare-root roses are usually available by mail order. They are dug from the soil in the rose nursery in fall, or as needed until early spring. Container-grown roses are available in nurseries and garden centers and also by mail order, and are on sale right through the growing season.

Bare-root roses

The mail-order nurseries that supply bare-root roses often list a very wide range. But they can be planted only between late fall and early spring (and not when the ground is frozen) and need special care after planting.

Plant bare-root roses as soon as possible after they arrive. If you are unable to plant them at once, heel them in (*see page 100*) in a hole or trench. Never leave roses in their plastic-bag packaging after they arrive.

Container-grown roses

Some mail-order rose nurseries list a wide range of container roses, but they are much more expensive to ship, owing to their extra weight. Most roses seen in nurseries and garden centers are container-grown, but a more limited range is available than by mail order.

Plant container-grown roses at any time when it is neither frosty nor too hot; they usually make good-sized plants quickly. It is not necessary to plant container-grown roses immediately, but if they must wait to be planted place them in a shady spot.

Seeking out disease-resistant roses

There has been a sea change in rose breeding in the last decade, with the emphasis shifting from glamorous but chemically-dependent hybrid tea roses to vigorous and disease-resistant shrub and ground-cover roses that are better suited to today's gardens and today's gardeners.

These new roses, sometimes grouped under the term 'landscape roses', are available in a range of flower colors and plant forms. They combine well with herbaceous perennials and other shrubs in mixed borders and form attractive ground covers on shallow slopes. Most are quite hardy and heat tolerant, so they are suitable for gardens in much of North America. They bloom fairly continuously from spring through early fall. Among the most widely adaptable are the KnockOut shrub rose series; the Flower Carpet ground cover roses; the Oso Easy rose series; the Meidiland rose series; and the Carefree Wonder rose.

A huge range of roses is available, from bushes, ground covers, and climbers (*shown*) to different flower forms, colors, and scents.

Planting roses

Roses are prone to replant disorder, or soil sickness (*see box, below*). The first measure to combat this problem is deep soil preparation prior to planting. If preparing an old border that previously contained roses, remove the topsoil to a depth of 6in. Use this soil elsewhere in the garden—as long as you avoid growing roses in it, you should not encounter any problems. Cultivate the soil by single digging or with a rotary tiller. Amend the soil generously with organic material, then leave the ground fallow for a few weeks to allow the soil to settle.

How to plant

Soak the roots of bare-root roses, and check them for any injuries in case they have been damaged while being transplanted for sale. The graft union is typically planted just below soil level; on heavier soils, avoid the risk of rose canker by shallower planting.

Water container-grown roses with a soluble rose food a few hours before planting to help the plants start growing vigorously. Plant as for container-grown shrubs (*see page 97*) and mulch well.

PLANTING A BARE-ROOT ROSE

1 Prepare the plant by soaking the root system in a bucket of water for about an hour before it is planted. Remove any leaves or hips from the branches, and prune off any long or damaged roots.

2 Dig out a hole about 20in. deep and wide for each new plant. For a rose against a wall or fence, dig the hole 12in. away to avoid the soil drying out. Exchange the soil with soil from another part of the garden; mix in bagged garden soil and a handful of rose fertilizer.

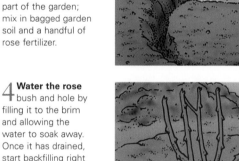

3 Place the plant in the hole and carefully spread out the roots. On heavy soils, the graft union should be planted about 1in. above soil level to prevent rotting. On lighter soils, plant it 1in. below soil level. Check this by laying a cane or spade handle across the hole.

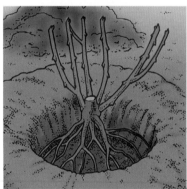

4 Water the rose bush and hole by filling it to the brim and allowing the water to soak away. Once it has drained, start backfilling right away, as a delay could lead to the roots drying out.

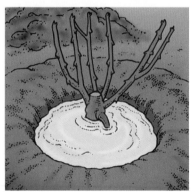

5 Backfill the hole with the amended garden soil, firming the soil around the roots as you go. Give the soil a final firm in with the heel of your boot and rake the soil over to tidy it up. Add a thick mulch.

REPLANT DISORDER

The causes of this disorder are not fully understood. It occurs when a rose is planted into soil previously occupied by rose plants. An affected rose may display stunted growth or a distinct lack of vigor. If you uncover the roots of the plant, you may discover signs of root rot; in severe cases, the plant may die rapidly (*see page 137*).

For most gardeners, the straightforward approach is to avoid planting roses on a site previously occupied by roses. Alternatively, the soil can be well prepared or even replaced with new topsoil. Mycorrhizal fungal spores can also be added to the soil on planting. These are beneficial fungi that form a symbiotic relationship with the plant.

Routine care of roses

Roses are not as difficult to grow and maintain as some people think, but if you want the best display of flowers and a strong, healthy plant there are a few tasks that you should carry out through the year.

Spring

Remove any die-back on shoots and branches. This may have occurred a few weeks after pruning or during periods of prolonged cold in winter.

Check plants for pests and diseases, referring to the list of common problems listed on page 136. Prune out diseased or damaged canes. When moving from rose to rose, sterilize pruners in alcohol to prvent spreading disease. Roses with serious disease problems should be dug out and replaced with disease-resistant varieties.

New growth on climbing and rambler roses should be tied in, as these roses do not have a natural twining habit and benefit from a bit of guidance.

Early to midsummer

Carry out light weeding and hoeing around the roots of your roses, and remove any suckers (*see right*). Remove dead blooms to encourage further flowering (*see following page*). If required, purchase container-grown roses now for immediate planting or planting in early winter.

Late summer to early fall

Tie in new growth on climbing and rambler roses while it is still supple and easy to bend into place. Continue removing dead blooms to prolong flowering.

In early fall, place orders for bare-root roses, ready for delivery in late fall, and heel in (*see page 100*) straight away unless you are ready to plant. Lightly prune hybrid tea and floribunda roses to prevent windrock.

Winter

Begin pruning and tying in climbing and rambling roses in early winter and prepare beds for planting of new roses on days that are frost free and dry.

In late winter or early spring, begin pruning hybrid tea, floribunda, standard, shrub, and patio roses. Once pruning is complete, rake over the bed to remove old foliage, rose stems, and old mulch. Apply a dressing of rose fertilizer around the base of each plant, and rake it in lightly. Apply a 3–4in. layer of mulch around each rose or cover the rose bed completely. This will help to suppress weeds and retain moisture during the forthcoming growing season.

ROSE SUCKERS

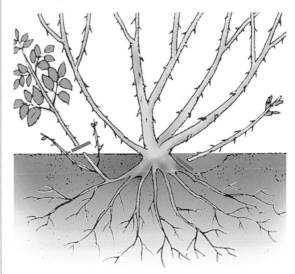

Standard roses are prone to suckering on their main stems, which is actually the rootstock of the grafted plant. As soon as you spot a sucker growing on the rose, put on a pair of thick gloves and pull it off or rub it away with your thumb.

Remove suckers growing from the ground as soon as they are seen. Carefully clear away the soil and trace the sucker back to the roots. Rip it off at its base—if you cut off a sucker with pruners, you will encourage more suckering growth to develop.

Check roses for suckers during summer. Suckers are shoots that sometimes develop from the rootstock of the rose, below the graft union. If left unchecked, suckers will eventually take over the plant and they become increasingly difficult to remove.

More and more rose nurseries are now growing own-root roses. These have a great advantage: when a shoot grows from the roots it is the same as the variety whose flowers you are trying to encourage. So instead of being a sucker that needs to be removed it adds to the growth of the plant.

Tools for rose pruning

It is well worth investing in good-quality pruners: bypass pruners are used by professionals and can be expensive but should last a lifetime. Use pruners only to cut stems of no more than ²/₃in. across—about the thickness of a finger. If you want to prune stems thicker than this, use a pruning saw or loppers. The latter come in various styles: select a pair with sturdy handles for good leverage when pruning, preferably with a bypass cutting blade. Folding pocket saws are great for pruning thicker stems and make a cleaner cut than loppers. They have pointed tips, which allow you to make pruning cuts close to the base of a plant. The blades cut on the pull stroke.

Pruning techniques

Pruning is a simple operation, but as roses range in size from miniatures, which are less than 12in. tall, to vigorous vines, which may reach 30–40ft., they require a variety of pruning techniques to keep them healthy, free flowering, and within bounds.

Use sharp tools to cut stems cleanly with no ragged edges to reduce the change of infection. Make a 45-degree, sloping cut above a healthy, outwardfacing bud to allow moisture to drain away (*see below*), reducing risk of die-back and rot in the bud. This should prompt new shoots to grow outward from the center of the bush, avoiding overcrowding of shoots, improving circulation of air, and reducing occurrence of diseases such as black spot. If you cut too high above the bud, the stem will die back due to a lack of sap flow.

Basic steps of pruning

First cut out all dead, diseased, and damaged wood to leave a framework of healthy wood to prune. Always be mindful of the shape with every pruning cut made and aim to create an open-centered or goblet-shaped plant. Deadhead flowers to prolong flowering (*see above right*).

PRUNING CUTS

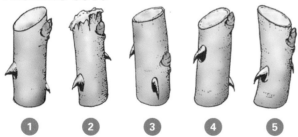

Pruning rules ❶ Make a sloping cut ¼in. above a bud. **❷** Ragged cuts lead to infection. **❸** Too high a cut leads to die back. **❹** Cutting too close damages a bud. **❺** A cut toward a bud causes it to rot.

DEADHEADING

Snap off dead flowers in summer at the abscission layer—the slightly swollen section of stem just below the bloom and the point where the bloom naturally falls off the plant. This technique encourages more flowers over a shorter period and promotes healthy foliage.

Basic tools needed to prune roses include loppers, a pruning saw, hand pruners, and a pocket knife.

Heirloom roses

When choosing an heirloom rose, take note of the plant's habit and eventual size, because you do not prune these roses as hard as bush roses, so it is not so easy to contain them. Pruning them is a matter of judgment; assess the shape, habit, and growth of each rose as you prune it in early spring year to year.

Prune lightly on planting, pruning the tips of each shoot to a healthy bud. Once they are established, the aim is to maintain a strong, open framework, gradually replacing old wood with new growth over a number of years to promote vigor and encourage flowers.

Continually assess the plant as you prune. Remove all dead, diseased, and damaged wood, and cut out up to three old stems. Prune sideshoots by up to a half. Take care not to remove too much wood, which may spoil the shape of the rose and cause it to splay apart.

Variations on a theme

There are many types of heirloom rose, all with slightly different flowering and growth habits. They can be divided into three main groups.

Once-flowering shrub roses: This group contains what are known as the old roses, such as alba, centifolia, moss, and damask roses. You can leave these unpruned, but after a few years you will have to thin them substantially in early spring to get rid of older, unproductive wood. Otherwise, prune as for general shrub roses (*see below*).

Repeat-flowering shrub roses: This group contains the 'English Roses', which flower through the summer. Prune these as for general shrub roses (*see below*).

Ground-cover roses: To cover large areas of bare soil, peg down strong stems with small wire hoops to prompt rooting. Cut back any upright stems in early spring.

PRUNING A SHRUB ROSE

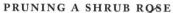

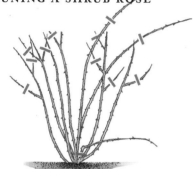

SECOND YEAR

1 **Cut main stems** by one third and sideshoots by up to a half, in early spring. Remove badly placed shoots.

2 **Flowering begins** in early summer, on the pruned sideshoots. Repeat-flowering shrub roses will flower through the summer.

3 **Prune back the tips** of tall stems in early fall to minimize windrock over winter, which loosens the roots.

THIRD & SUBSEQUENT YEARS

4 **Cut main stems** by up to one quarter, and sideshoots by up to a half, in early spring. Remove 1–3 older stems at the base.

5 **Flowering begins** again in early summer, more abundantly this time as there are more sideshoots to flower from.

6 **Prune back tips** of tall stems in early fall. Prune from now on to maintain a balanced, open framework.

Bush roses

Easy-care shrub and ground-cover roses are beginning to challenge hybrid tea and floribunda roses as the most popular bush roses for home gardens.

Pruning bush roses

As with all roses, pruning is a constant process of wood renewal, with the aim of encouraging vigorous, new growth and maximum flowering.

Look for potential buds, or eyes, on the shoots when deciding where to cut (*see page 128*). If you examine a rose bush, you will notice that the buds are positioned closer together if they are nearer the base of the plant.

New plantings of hybrid tea and floribunda roses should be pruned in the same way (*see below*). Reduce all shoots back to two to four buds—about 4–6in. above the ground. This promotes vigorous growth in the first year. After this, prune as for an established plant.

Pruning hybrid tea roses

Prune new hybrid tea roses relatively hard to encourage plenty of flowering shoots. When pruning established hybrid tea roses (*see below*), remove all dead, diseased, and damaged wood, then cut back all the remaining shoots, according to their relative vigor. This ensures that all old wood is renewed over a three-year period.

Pruning floribunda roses

Floribundas are more vigorous than hybrid teas, so are not pruned as hard. Remove all dead, diseased, and dying wood, then cut back all remaining shoots to five to seven buds or 6–8in. above the base of the plant.

Pruning easy landscape roses

For taller bush roses, trim off from one third to one half of their height with hedge clippers in early spring.

PRUNING A HYBRID TEA BUSH ROSE

  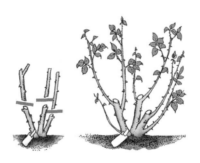 

FIRST YEAR

1 **Prune a bare-root rose** before planting by cutting back the main shoots slightly and pruning long, coarse or damaged roots.

2 **Cut back each shoot** in late winter or early spring, to leave 2–4 buds or 6in. of stem above soil level (*left*). By summer, new, shoots should have grown (*right*).

3 **Trim back flowered stems** at the end of the first season's growth to prevent windrock over winter. Also cut out any soft, unripe shoots.

SECOND & SUBSEQUENT YEARS

4 **Cut out wood** that is dead, diseased, weak, crossing, or inward-growing in late winter or in early spring.

5 **Prune strong stems** at the same time, cutting them back to 4–6 buds or 4–6in. of stem above soil level. Cut back the less vigorous stems to 2–4 buds.

6 **Trim back** flowered stems at the end of the season's growth in early fall. Also cut out any soft, unripe shoots.

Climbing & rambling roses

These are both excellent roses for covering structures like fences and walls. You can also train them to grow into the canopies of mature trees. Ramblers tend to have laxer habits and more pliable stems than climbing roses, and they usually flower only once, whereas climbers repeat flower throughout summer. Ramblers are also more vigorous and produce more basal growth once established. However, no two varieties are the same, so it is worth doing some research before purchasing new plants.

After planting, apply a rose fertilizer around the base of the plant; work it in with a fork and then apply a generous layer of mulch.

Pruning climbing & rambling roses

Most climbers and ramblers require support; this may be in the form of a tripod of posts, an arbor, an arch, or a wall or fence. Over the first two or three years after planting, concentrate on developing a basic framework of rose stems, which you can then tie into place on the support structure until it is covered.

Traditionally, climbers were pruned in late fall when dormant, and ramblers were pruned in late summer directly after flowering. However, you can prune climbers and ramblers at the same time of year, from late fall to early winter, to produce plenty of flowers (*see below*). The key is to replace old wood with new wood, while keeping a strong framework of stems.

Before beginning to prune, look carefully at the climber or rambler and identify any dead, diseased, or damaged wood; prune it out. Also look for new rose stems to replace the older stems. At this point, you may decide to remove one or two old stems completely if the rose has produced sufficient new growth since it was last pruned. This is often the case with ramblers.

PRUNING CLIMBERS & RAMBLERS

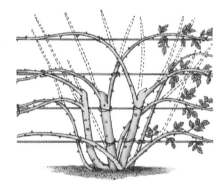

FIRST YEAR

1 **Prune before planting** to leave 3–4 stems 3½–6in. long. Trim coarse or uneven roots on bare-root plants.

2 **New shoots develop** in the first spring after planting to form the basic shape of the rose.

3 **Train the stems** into the supports from early summer to early fall, to prompt new sideshoots to develop along the stems.

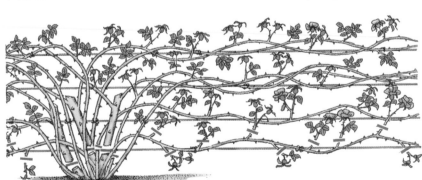

SECOND & SUBSEQUENT YEARS

4 **Tie in shoots** that develop horizontally, from early to midsummer. Flowers are borne on the previous year's sideshoots.

5 **Cut out a few flowered shoots** in late summer or early fall to the base, leaving some to fill in the framework. Prune sideshoots to 2–3 buds, then tie in all new growth to the supports, keeping the stems horizontal to stimulate more sideshoots.

Then prune all the remaining sideshoots arising from the main stems. Sometimes these are very vigorous, so it is worth considering them as replacements for older stems. Finally, tie in all pruned stems. Use garden twine worked in a 'figure eight' cross loop (*see box, right*). Remove the tips from the longest stems if they are outgrowing the support.

Climbers and ramblers growing against a fence or wall often tend to have a concentration of rose blooms at the top of the fence or wall. If you regularly bend the stems horizontal during pruning and training, they will produce more flowering laterals lower down on the plant. It is often easier to untie the plant from its support, then bend and twist the stems into place before tying them in with new twine. Take your time to ensure the best result.

Creating a floral wall

It is possible to train roses horizontally to form a fragrant wall. This can be achieved by erecting a series of wooden posts 4in. wide and 5ft. tall, at regular intervals along a boundary. Use several lengths of strong galvanized wire, spaced 16in. apart, fixed to strong bolts to connect the posts together.

Select fragrant varieties of climbing roses to plant along the length of the supports. Once the plants are established, train and tie in the stems to cover the support, pruning in the same way as against a wall or fence for a dense wall of flowers in summer.

Roses in trees

When growing roses through mature trees, it is important to provide an initial support, such as a thick rope or wooden stake. Anchor this to the ground and secure into

---

TYING IN A CLIMBING ROSE

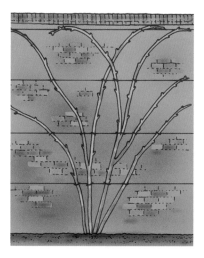

Tie in stems to the support with special ties or soft 3-ply twine, using a 'figure 8' cross loop to cushion the stem. Make sure it is not too tight, to avoid the twine cutting into the stem.

---

the lower branches of the tree to help the rose to establish quickly. Roses growing under trees have to compete with the root system of the tree for soil, water, and nutrients, so they will require the best possible care, with regular fertilizing and watering to help promote strong, vigorous growth, which will be more resistant to pests and diseases.

It is not necessary to undertake any pruning once the rose has grown into the lower branches of the tree—just let it grow and enjoy its beauty.

Summer maintenance

In late summer, loosely tie into the supports any vigorous new shoots as they develop. At this time of year, you will find that the stems are soft and pliable, making them less prone to damage when you bend them into place.

TRIPOD-TIED CLIMBERS

Train the stems of a climber or rambler growing up a tripod or obelisk by bending them gently and twisting them around the structure. This slows the flow of sap within the stems, encouraging the plant to produce more sideshoots and, eventually, flowers.

WALL-TIED CLIMBERS

Support roses grown against fences and walls with wires, fixed into place with eye bolts and tension bolts. Position the wires horizontally, spacing them about 16in. apart.

Standard roses

These are hybrid tea and floribunda bush roses that have been budded onto tall-stemmed rootstocks. They are used to give height to bush roses when they are grown with other plants. Given such a position, they can be extremely effective, particularly in a formal context.

Staking standards

Standard roses require some form of staking to help support the topgrowth. Use 1¼in. square posts and two rubber tree ties, each with a spacer, for each plant. Position the ties at equal distances along each post.

Pruning standard roses

Follow the pruning techniques as for bush roses, but take care not to overprune them; if this happens, the suckers from the rootstock can dominate (*see page 127*).

First remove all dead, diseased, and damaged wood; prune healthy stems to outwardfacing buds to promote an open center. Remove any suckering growth on the main stem below the crown, and from below soil level.

To prune a weeping standard (*see box, right*), first remove all dead, diseased, and damaged wood, then prune out two-year-old wood in early spring to leave strong, new, vigorous growth. Prune lightly to shape the canopy.

Pruning patio & miniature roses

Remove all dead, diseased, and damaged wood, and reduce strong shoots by one third in spring. Cut out twiggy growth and prune lightly to shape the plant.

WEEPING STANDARDS

This form of rose is created by budding a climbing rose onto a rootstock with a tall stem. The graft union is at the top of the stems, just below the topgrowth. This produces a weeping standard, with long and attractive, trailing shoots.

PRUNING A STANDARD ROSE

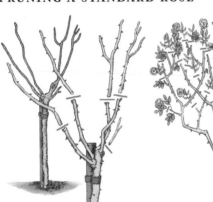

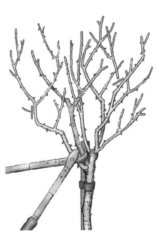

FIRST YEAR
1 **Cut back each branch** in early spring, to leave 4–7 buds on each branch. Remove spent blooms during summer.

2 **Trim back** the flowered stems in fall to prevent windrock over winter. Also cut out any soft, unripe shoots.

SECOND & SUBSEQUENT YEARS
3 **Cut out** dead, diseased, or damaged growth, and any badly placed stems, in early spring to create an open center.

4 **Prune branches** at the same time, to 4–6 buds. Cut back the weaker stems to 2–4 buds to promote vigor.

Rose renovation

Unpruned and neglected roses can flower quite happily for many years; however, after a period of time they will start to become less vigorous and produce weak stems and fewer blooms. Many of us inherit roses in such a state when we move house; this can be daunting, as you may be faced with a large, unruly plant that you need to prune but are unable to identify.

Pruning a neglected rose

Wait until the rose comes into flower, so you can see if it is worth keeping. If you decide to keep it, try to identify it, perhaps by sending a sample to a local rose nursery or ask your cooperative extension service.

To renovate a rose, aim to prune it in late winter or early spring, then encourage the plant to produce new growth by fertilizing it with a rose fertilizer over the soil and lightly raking it in. Apply a thick mulch around the base of the rose and water regularly through summer. Most bush and shrub roses will respond well to renovation pruning.

Neglected roses often have thick stems without any visible signs of buds. Do not be concerned by this when deciding where to cut stems; concentrate on making good, clean cuts with a pruning saw.

Revisit the rose a month after pruning and examine the stems. If your pruning has been successful, you will notice new buds emerging from the remaining stems. This is a good sign, indicating new vigor.

Overgrown roses such as this climber can be daunting to prune. In some cases it may take pruning over a couple of years to restore a rose to its ideal size and shape.

Continue to monitor the rose throughout summer and if growth still appears to be weak apply a liquid fertilizer at the manufacturer's recommendations.

Prune again in early spring, and remove one or two old stems, depending on the amount of new growth. Continue with this annual prune over the next few years until all or most of the original old wood is replaced.

RENOVATION PRUNING

FIRST YEAR

1 **Cut out half** the main stems to the base in early spring; leave the youngest and strongest. Cut sideshoots to 2–3 buds.

2 **Flowers should appear** by midsummer on sideshoots of older wood. Vigorous new shoots should grow from the base.

SECOND YEAR

3 **Cut out more** of the old stems in early spring. Prune all sideshoots to 2–3 buds.

4 **Flowers are borne** in early to midsummer on sideshoots. New, vigorous stems replace the old framework of the plant.

Rose pests & diseases

To reduce the chances of pest and disease problems, start out by selecting disease-resistant varieties suited to your climate. Although some problems are inevitable, even with resistant roses, few will seriously affect the plants. As well as the pests listed here, roses are also vulnerable to aphids, red spider mites, Japanese beetles, deer, rabbits, and caterpillars (*see page 49*).

Black spot

Dark brown or black blotches appear on leaves from late spring onward. Affected leaves usually turn yellow and fall prematurely, which can weaken the plant. Initially, the infection originates in spots on stems in which the fungus has overwintered.

Select disease-resistant varieties; avoid wetting the foliage when watering. When new infections arise, promptly remove diseased material (*see box, below*) to slow the spread of the disease. As a last resort, treat with a fungicide based on bicarbonate (baking soda) or some other low-toxicity control.

Large rose sawfly

The female has a yellow abdomen with a black head and body. Her eggs are laid in the soft, young shoots of wild and cultivated roses, and hatch into caterpillarlike larvae that are greenish white with many black and yellow spots. They cause extensive defoliation, with two or three generations between early summer and early fall. Pick off the larvae by hand or spray with insecticidal soap.

Rust

In spring, elongated patches of perennial rust appear on stems and leaf stalks. In summer, leaves become infected, with small, bright orange, dusty spots arising on the undersides of leaves. The spots multiply and turn dark brown by late summer. Often, plants are severely defoliated. The dark spores overwinter on plant debris, soil, and stems.

Cut out lesions when you see them on stems and destroy fallen leaves. For severe infections, use a sulfur-based fungicide; apply to stems in midspring before overwintering spores germinate.

Leaf-rolling sawfly

Small, black-bodied sawflies emerge in late spring and females insert eggs into rose leaves from late spring to early summer. Affected leaflets curl downward along their lengths until they are tightly rolled. Later, the eggs hatch

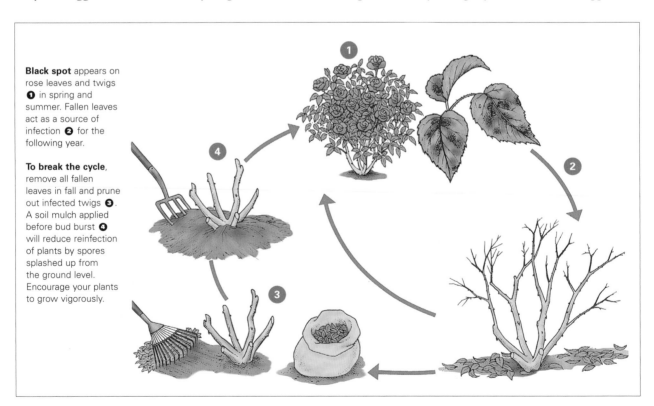

Black spot appears on rose leaves and twigs ❶ in spring and summer. Fallen leaves act as a source of infection ❷ for the following year.

To break the cycle, remove all fallen leaves in fall and prune out infected twigs ❸. A soil mulch applied before bud burst ❹ will reduce reinfection of plants by spores splashed up from the ground level. Encourage your plants to grow vigorously.

PESTS & DISEASES OF ROSES

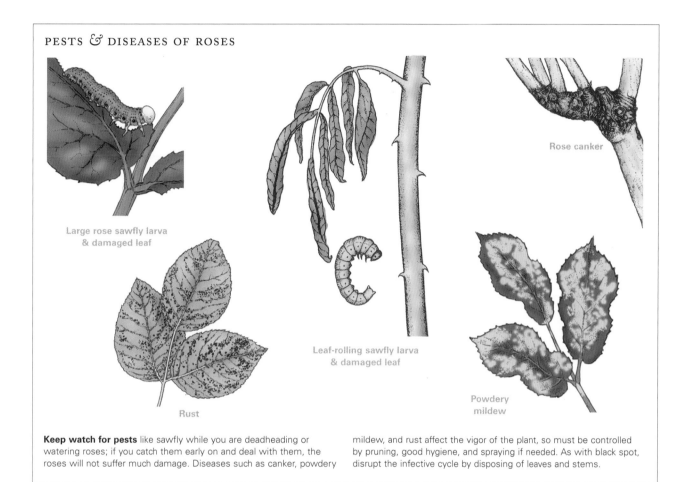

Large rose sawfly larva
& damaged leaf

Leaf-rolling sawfly larva
& damaged leaf

Rose canker

Rust

Powdery
mildew

Keep watch for pests like sawfly while you are deadheading or watering roses; if you catch them early on and deal with them, the roses will not suffer much damage. Diseases such as canker, powdery mildew, and rust affect the vigor of the plant, so must be controlled by pruning, good hygiene, and spraying if needed. As with black spot, disrupt the infective cycle by disposing of leaves and stems.

---

into pale green, caterpillarlike larvae, which eat the rolled leaves. It is difficult to prevent female sawflies from causing leaf curling, but you can control larvae by picking off rolled leaves on lightly infested plants. If many leaves are affected, spray with insecticide.

Rose canker

Various fungi cause canker and die-back of rose stems. Most infect through bad pruning cuts or wounds. Plant roses so that their graft unions are not covered by soil and make clean pruning cuts, close above buds. Keep roses vigorous by applying rose fertilizers. Prevent drought or waterlogging to avoid die-back.

Powdery mildew

White powdery patches appear on leaves, stems, thorns, and buds. The fungus commonly overwinters around the thorns and in dormant buds. Rambling and climbing roses are particularly susceptible, although this may be as a result of their location—soil near walls often remains dry and roses that suffer dryness at the roots are always more prone to mildew. Thorough mulching and regular fertilizing help to keep plants vigorous. Remove heavily infected stems during spring pruning, as well as any that appear later in the summer. Use bicarbonate-based fungicides to help control severe infections. Some varieties are resistant; check catalogs for details.

Replant disorder

This results in stunting of plants when they are planted in affected soil; the roots are found to be small and dark (*see page 126*). Change the soil before planting beyond the full spread of the roots.

Armillaria root rot

If established rose bushes suddenly die, inspect them for the presence of armillaria root rot (*see page 51*). Rose family plants are very susceptible to this fungal disease.

VINES & WALL PLANTS

Vines have adapted to grow vertically, clambering over rival plants in a search of sunshine. This habit is exploited by gardeners to cover unsightly garden features or brighten up dull walls and to add extra height to the yard by training vines on obelisks or arches. Fences clothed with vines provide a more natural backdrop to borders. Many shrubs are also suitable for wall training, in particular slightly tender plants that benefit from the warmth and shelter. Vines and wall shrubs take up very little soil space, which makes them invaluable for smaller yards where they can show off their foliage, flowers, and berries.

Methods of support

Choose a vine to suit the allotted space or support, thereby reducing the need to prune too often, and the exposure—sun-loving plants become straggly in shade.

Train wall shrubs or vines on taut, horizontal wires fixed to walls and fences. Use nails or eye hooks to hold the wires about 2in. away from the vertical surface to allow space for stems to twine and air to circulate.

Space wires 10–18in. apart, depending on the vine. Twining vines can be trained on trellis or netting, fixed to wooden battens to create a 2in. gap between the support and wall. Wooden trellis needs to be 12in. above soil level to prevent rotting. Free-standing screens made from trellis or netting on posts work in sheltered sites; large structures need good anchorage.

GROWTH HABITS OF VINES & WALL PLANTS

Natural clingers hold onto walls and fences by means of aerial roots or sucker pads, so no system of support is needed. Examples include ivy (*Hedera*) and Virginia creeper (*Parthenocissus*). The clinging parts may mark or damage soft brickwork.

Twiners are a large group of plants that climb by means of curling or twining leaf tendrils, leaf stalks, or stems. A support system, such as a trellis or wire netting, is needed for the tendrils to twine around. Typical plants include honeysuckles (*Lonicera*), clematis, and wisterias.

Scramblers and floppers clamber up neighboring vegetation by using hooked thorns (roses) or by rapid elongation of their willowy shoots, such as the potato vine (*Solanum crispum*). A support system is needed to which the growth can easily be tied in.

Wall shrubs are shrubs trained on wires fixed to a wall or fence, even though they do not climb naturally. This method is especially useful for growing species that are not reliably hardy in your area. Bottlebrushes (*Callistemon*) are often grown in this way in some areas.

GROWING VINES & WALL PLANTS

Gardening basics *see page 6* | **Pests of woody plants** *see page 117* | **Diseases of woody plants** *see page 119*

Growing vines & wall plants

Most vines are container grown, but some are available as bare-root plants. Look for healthy plants with well-developed roots and strong stems. Although container-grown plants can be planted at any time of year (as long as the soil is not frozen or waterlogged, or temperatures too high), plants tend to establish better if they are planted in fall or spring. Avoid planting in summer since plants will require regular watering. More tender plants are best planted in spring. Plant bare-root plants immediately after purchase.

Planting

Fix the support in place before planting. Do not plant right up against it, but leave an 8–12in. gap. Allow an 18in. gap if planting against a wall or fence to avoid the rain shadow (*see box, right*).

Dig a planting hole twice the size of the existing container and fork the bottom and sides to relieve any compaction. Water the plant well and place in the planting hole at a 45-degree angle, making sure that the top of the rootball is level with the soil surface. A few vines, such as most clematis, benefit from deeper planting. If the soil is poor, mix in topsoil or leafmold before planting, then firm well and water.

Pruning & training

The aim of formative pruning is to create a well-balanced framework that clothes the support. Remove any weak or damaged shoots and train the remaining stems into the support, spacing them evenly. If any stems are too short, tie them to canes fixed to the support. Tie in stems as they grow to cover the required area. Cut back sparse growth to encourage branching. Shorten or prune out stems that are badly placed.

Vines require regular pruning to stimulate new growth and flowering, as well as to restrict the size. The time of pruning depends on the age of the flowering wood. Early-flowering plants bloom on the previous season's wood; prune them straight after flowering. Plants that flower in mid- to late summer on the current season's growth are best pruned in early spring.

General care of vines

For healthy plants, apply an all-purpose fertilizer each spring around the base of the plant at the manufacturer's recommended rate. Water in dry spells, especially vines planted against walls. Mulch to improve moisture retention and reduce evaporation from the soil.

PLANTING VINES

Walls and fences create a certain amount of rain shadow, and this must be accounted for when planting at their bases. Site the plant about 18in. from the wall or fence. A short stake or cane can be used to guide the young growth so that it bridges the gap between the roots and the support. This can be removed once the plant has established itself on the support wires of the wall or fence.

Free-standing supports, such as pillars, trellis, or frames, do not create the same degree of rain shadow as a solid structure, so the planting distance needs to be only 8–12in. If you intend to grow a vine into a host plant, such as a tree, the root systems of the 2 plants will compete with each other for food and water, so plant the vine a good distance away from the host plant's roots, and water well to help the vine take root.

139

Clematis

Clematis are evergreen or deciduous vines that often use twining leaf stalks to attach to supports. There are also some shrubby and herbaceous clematis. The climbing varieties are very versatile: use them to clothe walls and fences, on arbors and frames, or to extend seasonal interest and complement shrubs such as roses.

Planting & initial training

Choose a site in full or partial sun, with fertile, moisture-retentive but well-drained soil. Plant the rootball 2in. below the soil surface to protect the crown from clematis wilt. Evergreen and perennial species do not need deep planting. Keep the base of the clematis cool, with shade cast by nearby plants and an annual mulch of organic matter, such as well-rotted compost.

To avoid lanky growth and ensure branching from the base, cut all clematis back to 6–12in. after planting (*see box, facing page*). Train in shoots if needed; handle them with care as new stems are brittle. Clematis are split into three groups, according to pruning needs.

Clematis group 1

This group includes evergreen and deciduous species that flower in winter or spring on the previous year's growth, for example *Clematis alpina*, *C. armandii*, *C. macropetala*, and *C. montana*. They do not need regular pruning, apart from trimming of overlong stems and removal of dead, diseased, or damaged wood.

If required, prune to shape after flowering; prune winter- and early spring-flowering species immediately after flowering. Older plants may benefit from congested growth being thinned and some older stems cut back to the main framework. You can completely renovate group 1 clematis by cutting them back to 6in. from the base, after flowering in spring. Do not do this again for at least three years.

Clematis group 2

This group comprises large-flowered, deciduous varieties, such as 'Nelly Moser', 'The President', and 'William Kennet', all of which produce spectacular flowers in early summer on the previous year's growth. A second flush follows in late summer, of fewer, medium-sized blooms on the current season's growth.

Prune to establish a framework of older wood and to stimulate new growth. In late winter or early spring, remove weak shoots, thin congested growth, and cut about one fifth to a quarter of the oldest stems to 12in.

Early-flowering clematis, such as these purplish pink flowers of 'Constance', are in group 1 and require only minimal pruning.

Midseason clematis, such as this variety 'H.F. Young', flower in early summer. Being in group 2, they can be renewal pruned or left unpruned.

Late-flowering clematis, such as 'Étoile Violette', are in group 3. They should be hard pruned each year in late winter or early spring.

FORMATIVE PRUNING OF CLEMATIS

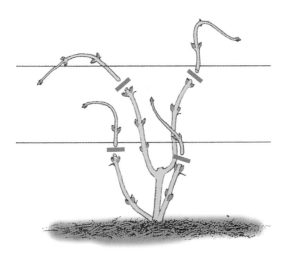

Initial pruning of all clematis

Prune the stem of a newly planted clematis as the buds start to swell, cutting it back to just above the lowest pair of strong, healthy buds. Mulch well around the base of the stem.

Second-year pruning

Cut back all main stems that have been trained during the previous year, reducing them by half their lengths to a pair of strong buds. Do this in mid- to late winter and mulch well.

above the base to encourage renewal growth. Trim back immediately after flowering to improve the second flush. This type of clematis can be left unpruned and cut hard back to the base every three or four years. The first flush of flowers will be lost, but it should flower in late summer.

Clematis group 3

Clematis that flower from midsummer to fall on the current season's growth fall into this category, and include 'Étoile Violette', 'Duchess of Albany', and *C. texensis* and *C. viticella* varieties.

The plants become topheavy, with bare bases, tangled growth and fewer flowers high up, if not cut back hard each year. Hard prune to a pair of buds 6–12in. above soil level in late winter or early spring, as the buds begin to break; only buds higher up might show signs of growth—pruning will stimulate breaking of dormant buds close to the base. To extend the season, prune late large-flowered clematis, such as 'Perle d'Azur', 'Rouge Cardinal', 'Star of India', and 'Jackmanii' varieties, by combining pruning methods from group 2; retain some older stems and cut others back to the base in early spring.

PRUNING MATURE CLEMATIS

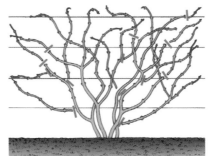

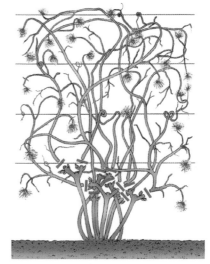

Group 1 clematis only need to be pruned to shape after flowering, in spring. Trim overlong stems and remove dead or damaged growth.

Group 2 clematis are pruned back to an established framework when dormant. A few of the older stems are cut back to the base.

Group 3 clematis are hard pruned back each year to 6–12in. above soil level. This keeps them tidy and prolific.

Wisteria

These deciduous, woody-stemmed, vigorous, twining vines flower in late spring, producing showy, hanging bunches of flowers that are frequently scented. Occasionally, a few flowers appear in summer.

Wisterias are ideal plants for covering sunny walls or growing on sturdy posts, arches, and gazebos; however, rigorous training and pruning are required to keep them within bounds. If space allows, and with a little help to start them off, they will cover entire structures or climb into large trees, giving a beautiful flowering display in spring in return for very little attention.

Choosing a wisteria

The most commonly grown wisteria is *Wisteria sinensis*. However, this species and also *W. floribunda* should be treated with great caution, because in the east and southeast in particular they are proving invasive in the wild. Instead, grow the American native *W. frutescens*. The flowers are best displayed when it is trained as an espalier.

Almost any wisteria, however, will look attractive, regardless of the structure on which it is grown or how it is trained. Where space is limited, *W. frutescens*, which is less vigorous and slower growing, is the only choice; it has shorter racemes of flowers later in the season. When buying a nonnative wisteria, choose a grafted, named

A properly trained wisteria over a gazebo is not only beautiful but it also doubles up as a shady canopy in summer. Although the spring flowers are the main feature, the deciduous leaves are elegant, too.

variety. There are many to choose from, with flowers in shades of blue, violet, pink, or white. Seed-raised plants are shy to flower, often have inferior blooms, or may not flower at all. Even a grafted, named variety may take three to five years to produce a worthwhile display.

ESPALIER PRUNING OF WISTERIA

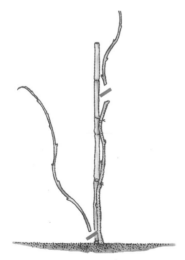

FIRST YEAR

1 **Prune the strongest shoot** after planting, cutting it to 30–36in. above soil level. Tie to a stake, taking care not to damage the plant. Cut back to the base all other shoots. Remove any sideshoots on the main shoot to promote new growth.

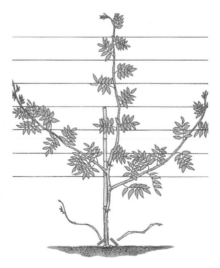

2 **Tie in the main shoot** vertically as it grows in summer. Select the two strongest sideshoots, on each side, and train them in at 45 degrees. Trim any secondary shoots on the sideshoots to 6in. Remove any growth from the base and the remaining sideshoots.

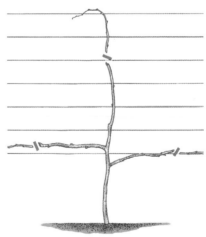

SECOND YEAR

3 **Cut the main shoot** in late winter or early spring to about 30in. above the topmost sideshoot. Carefully lower the sideshoots that were at 45 degrees and tie them horizontally to the supports. Cut them back by about one third.

Formative pruning

Wisterias are often trained as espaliers (*see below*), but they can be grown as fans, low standards, or as semiformal wall shrubs, so initial pruning will differ according to the required habit. It is best to train the main stems horizontally to encourage flowering. If growing an espalier, continue training until the vacant space is covered and the main framework is formed.

Maintenance pruning

Although wisterias bloom even if left unchecked, flowering on established plants can be encouraged and improved by regular pruning, once in late summer and again when dormant, to divert the plant's energy into producing flowering spurs (*see box, below*). This will also help to manage the vigorous extension growth. Even on plants that are trained informally, regular summer and winter pruning is beneficial to encourage flowering.

In late summer, prune back all the current season's growth to 6–12in., unless any growth is needed to extend the existing laterals or to replace damaged branches. Further growth should break from the pruned shoots, and flowering buds will form at the bases of the shoots. These buds should be easily distinguishable because they are rounder and plumper than the slim and pointy growth buds. In late winter or early spring, prune again to the lowest two or three buds from the main branch.

General care

The most common complaint about wisterias is a lack of blooms or poor flowering, despite regular pruning. Poor soil conditions may be to blame. Although established plants benefit from an annual application of all-purpose fertilizer in spring, avoid overfertilizing. The use of high-nitrogen fertilizers will encourage leafy growth at the expense of flowers. Feeding with a fertilizer high in potassium may encourage flowering.

Wisterias are fairly drought tolerant, but they may flower poorly if planted against a wall where the soil is in a rain shadow and very dry. Water the plant well during dry spells in summer and mulch to conserve soil moisture. Wisterias require plenty of sunshine to grow and flower well, making them unsuitable for north- and east-facing sites. They can be allowed to climb into mature trees, provided the trees are healthy.

Neglected plants

Renovation pruning of neglected plants is best spread over several years. In winter, select damaged, old, or unwanted main branches and cut each back to the base of another suitable branch, or remove branches completely at the base. You will probably have to cut and remove long branches in sections to free them from the dense growth without causing damage to the plant. Hard prune to stimulate vigorous growth; flowering may diminish for a while.

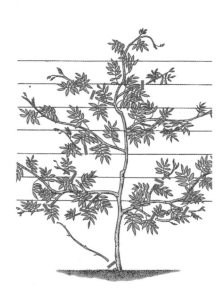

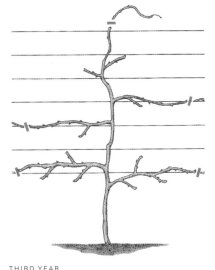

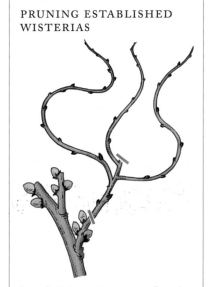

PRUNING ESTABLISHED WISTERIAS

4 **Train the main shoot** vertically as it grows in summer. As in step 2, choose further pairs of sideshoots and tie them in at 45 degrees, and trim secondary shoots. Remove other sideshoots and any growth at the base. Trim sideshoots so they fit the allotted space.

THIRD YEAR
5 **Prune the main shoot** in winter to about 30in. above the topmost sideshoot. Carefully lower the laterals that are at 45 degrees, tie horizontally, and reduce these and other sideshoots by about one third. Continue each year until the basic framework is formed.

Prune in 2 stages to encourage flowering spurs: in summer, cut extension growth to within 6in. of the framework (*top cut*). In winter, cut down again to 2–3 buds (*bottom cut*).

Honeysuckles

These woody, twining vines with fragrant flowers prefer full sun but tolerate light shade. After planting, reduce all stems by about a half to stimulate strong growth from the base. As the new shoots appear, train the strongest onto the support and remove the rest (*see below*). Mature plants are split into two groups for pruning.

Vigorous, evergreen honeysuckles like *Lonicera henryi* and *L. hildebrandiana* make up the first group. They produce flowers from summer to fall on the current season's growth. Established plants do not require regular pruning, but as they quickly fill the allotted space the growth will have to be controlled.

In early spring, prune back overlong branches, thin out congested growth, and remove weak or damaged shoots. Mature or neglected plants can be renovated by cutting all stems back to 24in. from ground level in late winter.

Into the second group fall deciduous and semievergreen honeysuckles that flower on the previous year's growth in summer. The most commonly grown honeysuckle from this group is common honeysuckle or woodbine (*Lonicera periclymenum*) and its varieties. Prune after flowering to encourage even growth (*see box, below*). Japanese honeysuckle (*L. japonica*) is sometimes recommended, but this vigorous, invasive species is listed as a noxious weed in some states.

TRAINING OF HONEYSUCKLES

Initial pruning at planting time is the same for all honeysuckles. Cut all stems by half to stimulate strong growth.

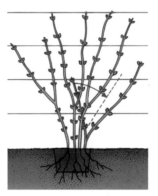

Train and tie in the shoots so that they evenly cover the support. If growth becomes too congested, prune hard in winter.

DECIDUOUS HONEYSUCKLE PRUNING

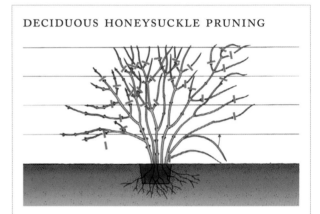

Prune back by one third after flowering to prevent plants becoming bare at the base. As for evergreen honeysuckles, they can be renovated in winter by hard pruning all shoots.

Wall shrubs

In cooler areas shrubs gain an extra dimension if they are grown against a wall or fence. Some, such as pyracantha, daphnes, cotoneasters, and variegated euonymus, enliven shady walls. Bottlebrushes (*Callistemon*), ceanothus, and fremontodendrons, flower well against a warm, sunny wall.

Ceanothus as a wall shrub

Evergreen ceanothus is often grown as a wall shrub, especially in areas too cold for it to thrive in the open, for its brilliant blue, spring flowers, which form on the previous season's growth. Fall-flowering ceanothus, such as 'Fallal Blue' and 'Burkwoodii', flower on the current season's growth in late summer.

After planting in spring, tie in the shoot that is to form the main stem. Space the side branches evenly on the support and remove any badly placed or competing shoots. Lightly shorten overlong branches and cut back any branches that are growing inward, toward the support, or outward and away from it. As growth progresses, tie in the extension growth and trim the unwanted branches to two buds after flowering.

In following years, tie in the new growth to form the framework. After flowering, trim back all flowered shoots to 4–6in. from the side branches. Shorten longer branches by about one third. Prune back some of the older side branches to a younger branch, as a replacement.

For fall-flowering ceanothus, prune the previous season's growth by about one third in spring. Prune all ceanothus regularly as it does not respond to renovation pruning. Neglected plants are best replaced.

PRUNING SPRING-FLOWERING CEANOTHUS

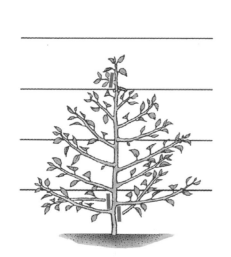

FIRST YEAR

1 **Tie the main shoot** vertically. Spread out the side branches and remove crossing, or inward- or outward-growing branches in spring.

SECOND YEAR

2 **Cut back branches** growing inwardly or outwardly from the support, after flowering. Let the framework fill out, and tie in.

THIRD & SUBSEQUENT YEARS

3 **Trim back all flowered shoots** to 4–6in. after flowering. Shorten long branches by one third at the same time.

Flowering quince as a wall shrub

Making a handsome wall shrub, flowering quince (*Chaenomeles* x *superba*) flowers in spring on one-year-old and older wood. Though it will grow in a shady situation, flowering is better when this shrub is planted against a sunny wall. It can be trained as an espalier, as described for wisteria (*see page 142*).

To train as a more relaxed wall shrub, follow the basic training as described for ceanothus (*see above*). Several evenly spaced main stems can be selected instead of just one to develop a multistemmed framework.

Pyracantha as a wall shrub

Pyracantha is often used to brighten up walls with its bright yellow, orange, or red fruits. It also bears attractive, white flowers in early summer on the previous season's growth, which need to be encouraged for their fruit.

To train pyracantha as a wall shrub, follow the method recommended for ceanothus. After the initial training, shorten extension growth in spring to retain the shape, even though some flowering wood will be pruned off. In late summer, shorten the new extension growth to display the developing berries and to enhance wood ripening. Pyracantha can be renovated in spring, by removing some of the old growth. It can also be trained formally, as an espalier, cordon, or fan.

PRUNING A MATURE FLOWERING QUINCE

1 **Shorten all** flowered sideshoots by pruning back to 3–6 leaves after flowering. On established plants, cut back long extension growth unless it is needed for further development of the framework.

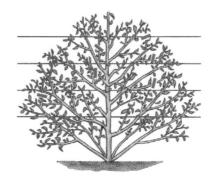

2 **Cut back** badly positioned, dead, diseased, damaged, or crossing branches, as well as any that grow in or away from the support, after flowering. This maintains an open and healthy, permanent framework.

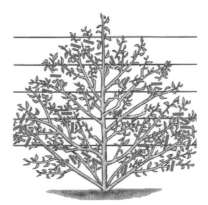

Succulents

Over the last decade, succulents have gained popularity in North American landscapes, aided by their increased use in drought-tolerant plantings in the desert Southwest, Texas, California, parts of Washington, British Columbia, and the Rocky Mountain region. Visionary nursery owners and succulent aficionados have expanded the diversity of succulents available to gardeners, introducing new varieties in an array of sizes, shapes, colors, and textures.

What is a succulent?

Succulents come from several plant families that have in common fleshy leaves and stems that store water and thus can survive extended periods of drought. Most are native to warm, arid areas worldwide, but others are found in alpine regions, Mediterranean climates, and tropical areas. Because of their wide distribution, succulents exhibit tremendous diversity, with plants ranging from tiny stonelike lithops to giant agaves and exotic flowering trees such as frangipani (*Plumeria*).

Most American gardeners' experience with succulents is through plants such as sedums and hens-and-chicks (*Sempervivum*), which are widely hardy. Most of the succulents native to this continent, however, are members of the cactus and agave families, located primarily in the Southwest and Mexico.

Planting & caring for succulents

Site succulents where they will receive at least eight hours of direct sun a day in summer. They resent having moisture build up around them in winter, when they tend to go dormant, so provide a site with well-drained soil. Gardeners in regions that get regular winter rainfall, and who have heavy clay or organic-rich soil, should build raised beds or amend soil liberally with fine gravel. Avoid planting succulents within range of sprinkler systems.

After planting, mulch with a layer of gravel. Wait a month before watering new plantings; in subsequent years, water sparingly and fertilize lightly once or twice.

With their upright clusters of sharp, pointed leaves, agaves make dramatic focal points in the garden. Patient gardeners must wait about 25–30 years for the emergence of a tall flower stalk; following this spectacular floral display, the primary plant dies.

Selecting succulents

Good starter succulents are hens-and-chicks, which come in a wide array of colors and are quite easy to grow in the garden or in containers. Creeping sedums, along with ice plants (*Delosperma*), are useful ground covers and have become a mainstay of green-roof plantings.

A few cacti are quite hardy, including eastern prickly pear (*Opuntia humifusa*), which has been found growing as far north as Massachusetts. Temperate zone gardeners looking for more statuesque succulents can grow *Yucca flaccida* and its variegated variety 'Golden Sword'.

Dry-climate gardeners have a much wider choice of succulents, including shrubby or treelike cacti called chollas (*Cylindropuntia*), dramatically spiked agaves, and agave relatives such as bear grass (*Nolina*).

Pests & diseases

If planted in an appropriate site with well-drained soil, succulents are not bothered by serious pests or diseases.

Agaves and other succulents should be planted in very well-drained soil and mulched with a layer of gravel or decorative stone.

TYPES OF SUCCULENT

Cacti come in a variety of shapes and sizes. Their spines—actually modified leaves—help protect them from animals.

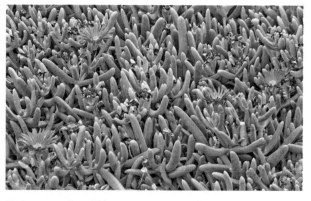

Native to southern Africa, coppery mesemb (*Malephora crocea*) form a spreading ground cover in well-drained soil.

Prickly pear cacti (*Opuntia*) have attractive, papery flowers available in a range of bright colors, from white to deep red.

A favorite of children, hens-and-chicks (*Sempervivum*) are easy to grow in containers or beds.

147

CHAPTER FOUR

Growing Vegetables & Herbs

149

More and more people are growing their own vegetables. It may even be their first attempt at gardening of any kind apart from cutting the lawn. Some are growing their own food simply to save money. Others realize that the only way to know for sure what chemicals have—or have not—been sprayed on their tomatoes is to be the one who holds the sprayer or who leaves it on the shelf. If you want to be 100 percent organic, you can be sure that your crops are never sprayed with chemicals. If you are happy to spray occasionally when you need to, you will know exactly what crops were sprayed and when.

Flavor and nutrition are also important reasons for growing your own vegetables. We are all realizing that the longer the time between harvesting and eating your vegetables the less flavor and fewer vitamins and minerals remain. And during those days trucking lettuce from California to Maine, flavor and vitamins seep away. At the same time, carbon emissions climb as the trucks thunder through the night. It is just not necessary when you can grow your vegetables outside your own kitchen window.

Growing vegetables can be great fun. The secret is to start simply, enjoy your success, and gradually broaden the range of crops you grow.

Getting started

The soil is the basis for success. Vegetables require a fertile soil that is capable of retaining moisture without becoming waterlogged. Additions of organic matter, such as well-rotted compost or manure, contribute to good soil structure and encourage beneficial soil organisms that provide a continuous supply of nutrients for your vegetables.

Most vegetables are planted as seeds or young plants. For some crops, seeds can be planted directly in the garden where they will grow. After the seedlings germinate, they often require thinning to assure proper spacing. An earlier start to the garden can be achieved by planting seeds of many vegetables indoors and growing them for several weeks before transplanting them into the garden.

There is something especially satisfying in raising plants from seed, and it gives you the widest choice, but you can just buy young plants instead— these are sold in nurseries or garden centers, and by mail order.

A successful harvest

Once plants and seeds are in the ground, their main need is water. It is difficult to grow good vegetables without watering, but most gardeners aim to protect the environment and conserve water. Target water when and where it is needed, and don't be afraid to take your trowel and look at the soil near the roots. Water if it is dry, wait a little if it is moist.

Beneficial insects can thrive in vegetable gardens with plentiful organic matter, close vegetation, and occasional watering. Naturally, gardeners do not want to harm beneficial creatures, but pests and diseases need controlling. Modern approaches manage rather than eliminate these: try to prevent conditions that favor problems, and treat any that do arise promptly, but don't waste time or money and upset the balance with heavy-handed use of remedies on lost causes. Scrap problem crops and move on to the next—safety lies in variety.

Finally, you will need to harvest your crops. Store or give away any surplus, and in times of shortage fall back on the supermarket to remind yourself how much better your home-grown produce tastes.

PREPARING TO GROW

Preparation of a vegetable and herb garden is not always the most popular task in the gardener's calendar, especially as most of the digging and clearing tends to be done when the weather is wintry and the soil can be cold, lifeless, sticky, and wet. A first-year garden requires a good deal of heavy work as you remove previous vegetation and amend the soil. In succeeding years, preparing your garden will become much easier. Looking ahead to a bountiful harvest makes forward planning a happy antidote to the cold work outdoors, as seeds are ordered, sowings planned, and beds organized.

Soil preparation

The ideal soil for vegetable crops is open in texture, allowing roots and water to penetrate it and holding moisture well, and is rich in nutrients, not too acid or alkaline, and free of weeds. Some soil preparation is essential, but the less that is done to achieve the ideal soil the better, both for the soil and for your back.

Raised beds or traditional digging?

Many gardeners find raised beds the easiest way to manage their vegetable garden. Beds should be 4–5ft. across, narrow enough so that you can reach the center; paths in between will need to be wide enough for a wheelbarrow. Raised beds drain and warm up more readily than in open ground, and need less frequent digging.

To make raised beds, you need to construct 6–16in. high sides of timber, brick, plastic, or recycled composite materials. Fill the beds with soil from the paths; this avoids importing soil that may contain diseases and weeds.

Double digging was widely practiced in the past. This allows deeper rooting and access to more soil moisture, but is only essential where compacted soil is encountered below the normal digging depth. Single digging (*see page 34*) is sufficient for most soils.

If your plot is free of perennial weeds, use a rotary tiller to give quick and satisfactory results, but do not use it when the soil is wet. Heavy soils are very vulnerable to damage if tilled when wet, and raised beds are an especially effective solution for such soils.

CONVERTING LAWN

1 **Divide the plot**, mark a line down the center and then mark individual trenches 24in. wide. Skim the sod from the first trench to a depth of about 2in. and put it, grassy side up, by the trench at the same end.

2 **Remove the soil** from the first trench to one spade's depth, placing it in a separate pile next to the skimmed sod. Fork over the bottom of the first trench to a depth of 12in. to break up the subsoil.

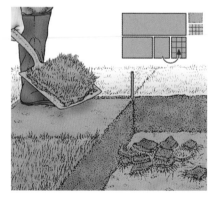

3 **Place the sod** from the second trench in the first and chop it. Dig the soil from the second trench into the first and fork over the bottom. Repeat across the plot, filling the last trench with the sod and soil from the first.

Clearing a new site

A grassy or overgrown site is often rich in nutrients and free of soil-borne pests and diseases, but you will need to clear the plot of its covering of grass or weeds before you can make a vegetable garden.

One way to do this is to kill all weeds by mowing overgrown plots very short, then covering the area with black or clear plastic, for at least six to eight weeks. As the sun shines down, a great deal of heat builds up beneath the plastic to a depth of several inches, killing not only existing weeds but dormant weed seeds as well. Deep digging and removing weeds are also very effective.

Raised beds are a good way of tackling an overgrown plot, because weeds, turf, and debris can be buried deep in the base of the raised bed. Here they will rot to release nutrients to support crops and will not regrow, although persistent weeds, such as bindweed and quack grass, should be carefully removed.

Amending the soil

The soil in a vegetable garden needs fortifying because crops take nutrients with them when harvested. Amend the soil of raised beds by incorporating lots of well-rotted organic matter such as compost, rotted leaves, animal manure, leafmold, old potting soil, or whatever well-rotted material is available.

Planning your crops

A constant supply of perfect produce often requires repeated or successional sowings, typically at intervals of two to four weeks. Salad greens, carrots, peas, summer squash, and snap beans are examples of crops that can be grown successionally.

Opportunities often arise to fit in crops either before and after the main crop (catch cropping) or between larger, slow-growing crops (intercropping). These techniques takes some planning, to avoid the main crop and the catch crop or intercrop getting in each other's way, but they can greatly increase your garden's productivity. For example, you might want to grow lettuce, but there is no need to set aside a separate space for it; instead, intercrop lettuce between early potatoes, or plant it as a catch crop before your main crop of tomatoes or peppers.

Crops also need to be rotated from year to year (*see box, above*) to prevent the buildup of pests and diseases in the soil. You can adapt systems of rotation, catch cropping, and intercropping to meet your individual circumstances.

CROP ROTATION

	Area 1	**Area 2**	**Area 3**
Year 1	Potatoes, peppers, eggplants, and tomatoes	Roots, peas, beans, and everything else	Brassicas
Year 2	Roots, peas, beans, and everything else	Brassicas	Potatoes peppers, eggplants, and tomatoes
Year 3	Brassicas	Potatoes, peppers, eggplants, and tomatoes	Roots, peas, beans, and everything else

Soil-borne pests and diseases can be damaging if susceptible crops are grown repeatedly in the same site. To help prevent this, divide the vegetable garden into sections and grow different crops each year on each section. A typical rotation plan has 3 crop groups, giving a 2-year gap between plantings. Problems can persist in the soil for far longer, but rotation helps to reduce losses; it is also a convenient and efficient way of working a plot.

The deeply dug soil prepared for the potatoes, peppers, eggplants, and tomatoes is ideal for the following year's root crops, peas, and beans, while the additional nitrogen provided by the peas and beans helps nourish the subsequent brassica crops. You may find that strict rotation is impractical in a small area: here, grow crops wherever is most convenient year after year. If troubles arise, and often they do not, grow the affected crop in a new place or in containers of fresh potting mix.

INTERCROPPING

The gaps between slow-growing crops that fill their space slowly can be planted with fast-maturing crops that are harvested before they present any competition. Slow-growing leeks and speedy spinach are ideal partners, as are parsnips and radishes.

Preparing a seedbed

Establishing a crop is the most important, yet trickiest part of growing vegetables. Sowing seeds directly into a seedbed is the cheapest method and is essential for crops that transplant poorly, such as carrots and parsnips. Thin out seedbed crops to their required spacing and leave them to grow, or transplant them to their final growing positions.

Working the soil

Prepare your seedbed in spring, but check first to ensure the soil is not wet and sticky. Working wet soil ruins the structure and will reduce crop growth and cause root crops to become distorted. Sometimes it is useful to dig the ground over the previous fall and expose the rough soil to the winter weather, to help break it down.

In wet conditions, stand on a plank as you work; seedbeds on raised beds are worked from the surrounding paths. To make the soil ready for early sowing in cooler regions, cover open ground with row covers or landscape fabric in midwinter or as soon as the snow is gone to warm the soil and keep it dry. You will soon have a warm, well-drained soil ready for early cultivation and sowing.

Creating a level surface for sowing

For good results when sowing, level and finely rake the soil surface. The lower layers of the soil need to be firm but not compact so that a drill (a shallow groove for sowing) can be drawn to a constant depth. You achieve this by raking the soil level and then lightly treading the surface if it appears to be 'fluffy'. After treading, rake the soil over again.

Generally, the less soil movement the better, but sometimes the soil has to be broken up beforehand, and debris, weeds, and stones removed. If you have raised beds, a light raking is usually all that is needed.

Raking has the side effect of exposing slugs and other soil pests both to birds and to drying out. It will also break up tiny crevices where pests may be hiding.

PREPARING THE SOIL

1 Spread a 2–3in. layer of organic matter, such as rotted compost, manure, or leaf mold and a slow-release, all-purpose fertilizer such as fishmeal, bonemeal, or worm castings, according to package directions over the soil surface in early spring.

2 Cultivate the soil, incorporating the organic matter and fertilizer. A hand cultivator, rake, or rotary tiller can be used to break up any large clods. Work to a depth of about 6–8in., using a backward-and-forward motion. Remove any surface weeds, debris, or stones as you do so.

3 Consolidate the soil by breaking up any remaining clods with the head of a rake. Use the rake to fill any depressions with soil, but do not overwork the soil at this stage. Where possible, do not walk on the soil unless it appears to be light and 'fluffy'.

4 Level the surface with the rake to produce a final, level texture. Move the rake backward and forward with as little soil movement as possible, keeping the teeth of the rake only just in the soil surface.

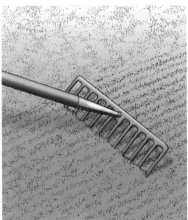

Looking after your soil *see page 32* | **Sowing & growing** *see page 156* | **Sowing seeds** *see page 405*

Cover crops

Growing crops for the sole purpose of digging them into the soil seems a waste, but growing a cover crop prevents soil erosion and leaching of nutrients, and it also smothers weeds. Dig in cover crops when young, before the plants become woody. They are not a substitute for compost, however, but they can improve soil structure and make the soil easier to work.

When to sow

In most regions, cover crops are sown from late summer to early fall to follow summer crops and cover the soil over winter. Good cover crops include mustard, ryegrass, and buckwheat, and especially those in the pea family including cowpeas, crimson clover, lupines, vetch, fava and field beans, alfalfa, and fenugreek. Sowing times vary according to climate, so check a local reference or your cooperative extension service for advice on growing cover crops in your area.

Dig in cover crops at least 2 weeks before the ground is needed for planting. Alternatively, add the material to the compost pile or spread it over the soil as a mulch.

GROWING A COVER CROP

1 **Sow seeds** in rows or scatter the seeds over the ground. They will grow quickly to cover the soil. Choose a cover crop to suit your climate; most are sufficiently hardy to keep growing all winter in mild areas. Spring and summer sowings may occupy ground better used for vegetable crops.

2 **Chop the foliage** down with a pair of shears or a weed whacker when the land is needed or when the crop is beginning to mature (whichever comes first). Leave the clippings to fall on the ground and wilt before digging them in.

3 **Dig the clippings** into the soil with a sharp spade or rotary tiller. As they rot down, they will release nutrients into the soil that can be used by the following crop. Alternatively, leave the clippings on the surface as a mulch. Cover crops that have become too mature to dig in easily can be added to the compost.

4 **Allow 2 weeks** or more between digging and any further sowing or planting, for the cover crop to decompose. The interval between cutting and planting should be longer if the crop has become tough or the soil is cold in winter or spring.

SOWING & GROWING

Fresh, high-quality seeds are an absolute necessity. Seeds that are stale or have been exposed to heat, damp, or sunlight are less likely to make a worthwhile crop than fresh seeds from a reputable supplier or your own garden. The difference between the best varieties and ordinary ones is often great, and varieties that thrive in one climate may perform poorly elsewhere. Seek varieties known to thrive in your area. Some gardeners favor flavorful old heirloom varieties; others prefer modern hybrid varieties which often produce heavier crops. Do not save seed from hybrid varieties because the characteristics of the resulting plants will vary.

Sowing seeds

Seeds can be sown either directly into the soil or in containers (*see page 405*). Direct sowing is much less time consuming, but in containers you have more control over the growing environment, where seedlings can be protected from pests, warmed for early crops, or given a head start if they need a long growing season.

Direct sowing into the ground

There are two methods: sowing into shallow grooves called drills (*see below*), or station sowing, also known as space sowing (*see facing page*). Always check the seed packet for sowing advice.

Sow as shallowly as possible; draw deeper drills for larger seeds with a hoe, and shallow drills of ½–¾in. for small seeds by pressing a length of broom handle into the soil. Stretch a string between two pegs to get a straight, easy-to-hoe drill. Ideally, run rows north–south to provide even light, but this is not essential.

A simple method of sowing fine seeds is to hold a little in the palm of one hand and then take pinches between thumb and forefinger of the other hand and gently trickle them into the drill. Sand sowing is another method for sowing small, hard-to-handle seeds.

In dry weather, water the bottom of the drill before sowing, and sow a little deeper than normal. Some soils form a crust after rain so that seedlings cannot break through. Where soil is prone to crusting, cover seeds with potting mix instead. Finally, firm down the soil with the

DRILL SOWING

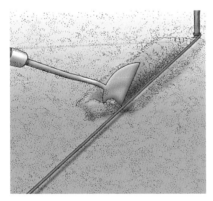

1 **Stretch some string** tightly between 2 pegs at the ends of the row at ground level. Hold the hoe against the line and draw out a drill with one of its corner edges.

2 **Water the bottom** of the drill and allow to drain. In very wet conditions, lay a line of sand in the bottom instead. Sprinkle seeds thinly and evenly, cover with soil, and firm in.

3 **Thin excess seedlings** as soon as possible, to avoid problems caused by overcrowding. Leave the strongest to grow: you may thin a row of seedlings several times.

head of a rake to keep the seeds and soil in close contact. A very shallow raking of the surface then conceals the drill from birds.

When seedlings emerge, thin them by removing surplus plants in stages. At first, leave four times the final number of seedlings, then half, and finally just those plants that are needed for the crop. This means that you must judge how many seeds to sow, which can be tricky. Sow too many and they may spoil from overcrowding before you can thin them, but sowing too few can result in gaps, wasting space and leading to shortages.

Thinning seedlings is very slow and tedious, so sowing sparsely is usually best. Sow a few extra seeds at the end of the row in order to give some spares in case any gaps need to be filled; mark the ends of the rows with short sticks to help avoid inadvertent damage later; bear in mind that some root crops do not transplant well.

Station sowing can speed up thinning and wastes fewer seeds. As it is impossible to be certain that each seed will germinate, place three to five seeds a finger-width apart wherever you want a single eventual plant.

If you only have a few, expensive seeds, you can pregerminate them (*see below*). Only those that germinate are sown, so the seed can be used more economically.

Growing from transplants

Transplanting—either from container-grown plants or those raised in a seedbed—is useful as plants can be raised in a small area before planting out. Transplants make efficient use of space and a small number of expensive seeds, but it is quite a lot of work to raise them, unless you buy them ready prepared from a nursery.

Bare-root transplants are the easiest to grow. These are plants raised in a seedbed outdoors in garden soil. They need to be carefully lifted with a fork and replanted with a trowel and plenty of water. This works well for cabbage family plants and for leeks. Most vegetable transplants, however, are raised in pots or cell packs just as ornamental plants often are; you will find that they are even easier to grow on than most ornamentals.

ESTABLISHING TRANSPLANTS

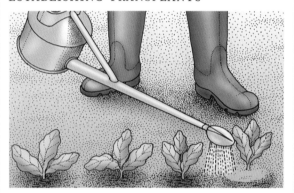

Water transplanted seedlings regularly as every day each transplant needs about 5fl. oz. of water until fully established. Use a waterbreaker, and apply water at the base of each plant, in the morning or evening to minimize wasteful evaporation.

VARIATIONS ON SEED SOWING

Station sowing
This is ideal for large seeds such as beans and corn. Sow 3–5 seeds per station at their final spacing, and later thin each station to one seedling.

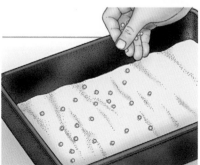

Pregermination
Place seeds on damp paper towel in an airtight box and keep at 64–72°F until the first signs of roots are visible, then sow immediately.

Protect newly transplanted seedlings on cold spring nights with floating row covers supported by wire hoops. This also protects seedlings from wind damage.

Watering & weeding

Sometimes you can grow vegetables without watering, but careful watering at key times can greatly improve results. Constantly wet soil from wasteful overwatering often encourages weeds, diseases, and slugs.

To maximize water efficiency, plant rows closer together and use a porous mulch such as straw to prevent evaporation; water only within the rows. Adding compost increases the water-holding capacity of the soil. 'Ponding'—drawing up low banks of soil around plants and along rows—can help water soak in. Weeds rob vegetables of water, so weeding is vital.

Water according to need

Ideally, you should water your seedbeds 24 hours before sowing, although watering into the bottom of drills is often enough. In dry weather, seedlings and transplants need regular, thorough watering. A fine spray is essential to avoid compacting soil or damaging young plants.

Most vegetable crops will flourish if given ½–1in. of water per week. It is a good idea to position a rain gauge near the garden to determine how much additional water is needed. Once plants are established, occasional deep, slow watering is more helpful than providing them with light, frequent applications.

To increase efficiency and reduce evaporation, water in the morning before temperatures rise and when the air is still. Consider using soaker hoses or trickle irrigation

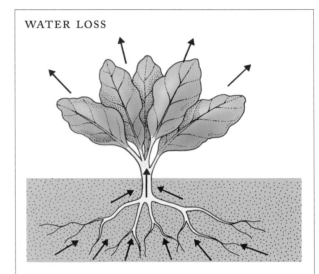

WATER LOSS

The water absorbed from the soil by roots is pulled up through the plant, carrying nutrients and fueling chemical processes, and is lost through transpiration from the leaves.

systems laid along the rows; these direct the water to the root zones of the plants where it is needed, without wasting water between rows. Avoid overhead watering, which is more subject to loss from evaporation and increases the spread of disease.

Water fruiting crops at regular intervals once they begin to flower to assure maximum crops and high quality.

WEED CONTROL METHODS

Dig out perennial weeds in winter. Remove every possible fragment of root, or they will regenerate. Annual weeds are easily controlled by hoeing.

Mulch with well-rotted compost after rain or watering to conserve water and suppress weeds. Planting through opaque plastic or paper landscape fabric is ideal for widely spaced crops or those that compete poorly with weeds.

Hoeing is best done on dry, warm days before annual weeds flower and set seed. Slice the stems with a sharp hoe, keeping the blade just below the soil surface and level with it.

Hand weeding is often the best way to remove individual weeds, especially those that are close to your garden plants. For larger weeds, use a hand fork to penetrate the soil and ease out the root system.

Weed control *see page 53* | **Preparing to grow** *see page 152* | **Using cold frames & cloches** *see page 382*

Row covers, cold frames, & hoop houses

Nothing can equal a good greenhouse for protection in cooler regions, but cold frames, hoop houses, and row covers can greatly increase productivity, providing shelter from the wind and a few extra degrees of warmth that can make all the difference to tender plants.

Floating row covers

Floating row covers are the most economical and convenient covering material. They keep off wind and mild frosts. Birds and many other pests are excluded, but weeds and slugs thrive if left unchecked. They do not give enough frost protection for tender plants, but can bring on early carrots, peas, and salad greens. Floating row covers can be draped right over plants or supported by hoops set at intervals along the length of the row. Covered plants generally produce about two weeks before uncovered ones.

In summer, a cover can make all the difference in preventing insect damage to cucumbers, squash, and bush beans. The cover will need to be removed from squash and cucumber plants once flowering begins, to allow insects access to the flowers for pollination.

Cold frames & hoop houses

Cold frames are essentially boxes with glazed lids that can be opened. They give more protection and much better control of temperature than row covers (*see box, right*) and may be heated. They are ideal for raising and hardening transplants in spring.

A hoop house is constructed of a clear plastic sheeting suspended over a frame. It can be sized to meet the needs of any garden. Hoop houses can provide heat-loving crops such as tomatoes with a head start on spring planting. They can also be used to acclimatize seedlings prior to transplanting into the garden.

Row cover fabric suspended over plastic or wire hoops is especially useful for advancing early crops. Often, these also offer protection from pests, such as the carrot root fly and flea beetles.

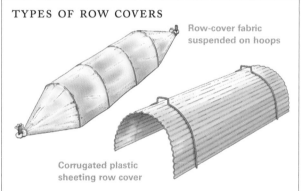

TYPES OF ROW COVERS

Row-cover fabric suspended on hoops

Corrugated plastic sheeting row cover

Row covers and hoop houses are useful for extending either end of the growing season. In spring, they provide protection from late frosts, allowing gardeners to get an early start on the season. In fall, covering crops can lengthen the harvest season by several weeks.

CONTROLLING VEGETABLE PESTS & DISEASES

There are several pests and diseases that plague each vegetable crop. Some, such as slugs or aphids, attack multiple crops. Others are host specific, attacking only one crop or crops within one family. Depending on the garden's location and the season, pests and diseases vary. Many vegetable problems can be avoided by selecting seed that is resistant to the diseases and pests that the crop is likely to encounter in your region. Other preventive measures include rotating crops, providing adequate air circulation, removing weeds that could be an alternate host of the problem, and removing infected plants or plant parts (sanitation).

For each vegetable covered in the following pages, major pests and diseases are covered; however, there are several others that can cause significant damage. Before attempting to control a pest or disease, it is important to accurately identify it and to determine if the damage it is likely to cause is sufficiently significant to warrant control. In many states, the cooperative extension service hotlines and Master Gardener plant clinics offer help in pest identification. Many nurseries and garden centers also provide similar assistance.

Once identified, learn about the life cycle of the pest or causal agent of the disease; this often suggests cultural methods of preventing or reducing its spread. Natural predators and introduced biological controls are available for many pests. Trapping is an option for others. If the pest or disease requires a pesticide for control, always look for the least toxic, effective material available. Consult your local extension agent for specific control recommendations. Remember that applying pesticides often reduces the population of natural predators. Always read the label of any pesticide and use only as directed.

LEAFY GREENS

Salad greens and leafy plants such as spinach are the very essence of freshness and flavor, and nothing can be fresher than those from your own garden. Salad greens and leafy crops often quickly 'bolt' or flower, so sowing little and often avoids waste and ensures absolute freshness. A 5ft. row is usually sufficient for a week's supply for a family of four. 'Baby leaf' salad greens can offer inspiration—the tasty contents of these are very quick and easy to grow yourself, and add wonderful fresh flavors to any salad. Mesclun mixes and cut-and-come-again greens are good choices and fit into any size of garden.

Lettuce

You can sow lettuce at intervals so that leaves, if not hearts, may be gathered over an extended season. There are many different lettuce types and varieties that offer different flavors, shapes, and sizes. Leaf colors in shades of green, yellow, and red are available.

Boston: Also called butter-head. Very easy-to-grow varieties that are smaller than most other types. They form soft, round hearts, with mild, almost buttery flavor.

Icebergs: Also called crisp-heads. These require a long,

cool season to mature. They produces firm heads of crisp leaves. In cool-climate regions, they are usually planted in early spring, but late-summer plantings that mature in the fall are often more successful.

Looseleaf: Many varieties available, with loose and brightly colored leaves, and varied shapes and textures.

Romaine: Medium or tall, upright varieties are available, with boat-shaped, flavorsome leaves and sweet hearts. They prefer rich, moist soils.

FROM SOWING TO HARVESTING LEAF LETTUCE

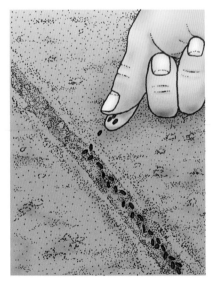

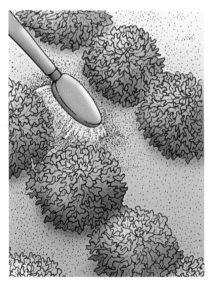

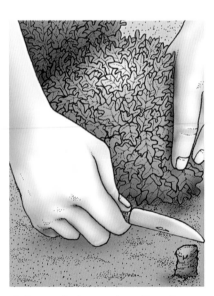

1 **Sow in drills** about ½in. deep as soon as soil can be worked in spring. Thin seedlings as soon as they can be handled, because crowded plants will not form proper hearts.

2 **Water well** as the leaves enlarge—and particularly as the weather warms, to prevent bolting. Mulching will help retain even soil moisture.

3 **Harvest the leaves** when still small, usually in 3–6 weeks. Cut outer leaves, allowing the inner leaves to continue growing, or cut the entire head, leaving a short stump with buds that may produce another crop.

SOWING PROTECTED LETTUCE

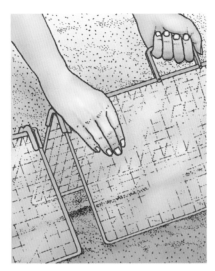

1 **Sow in midfall or early spring** in mild regions a prepared seedbed, in drills 8in. apart. Station or space sow, placing 3–4 seeds at 3in. intervals. Protect from hard frosts.

2 **Thin seedlings** when they are ½in. tall, leaving only the strongest plant growing at each station. Thinnings can be added to a salad for fresh flavor.

3 **Make final thinnings** to leave a plant every 2–10in., depending on eventual size. Plants should be ready to harvest from early winter to late spring, depending on your region.

Stem lettuce (celtuce): Grown for its cookable stems, but cultivated just like other lettuce.

Soil & site

Any fertile garden soil in full sun is suitable; summer crops can tolerate light shade. Before sowing, add some well-rotted compost and all-purpose fertilizer at the rate recommended on the package.

Sowing & cultivation

Lettuce can be sown directly into the garden (*see page 160*) in early spring and again in late summer in many regions of the country. In warmer regions, it can be grown throughout winter. Sow seeds in rows—10in. apart for small lettuce, 12in. for medium lettuce and 14in. for large romaine and icebergs—and thin seedlings to 2–10in. apart depending on the type. Avoid transplanting, but use surplus seedlings with under five leaves to fill gaps.

For convenience or an early start, sow in cell packs or propagation trays using good potting mix. Mild, but not warm, conditions and high light levels are essential—a cold frame or row cover will do, but windowsills are seldom suitable. Plant out as soon as the roots bind the growing mix, and water well before and after planting.

In warmer regions, seeds sown in late summer can be harvested in early winter, particularly if protected by cloches or row covers (*see above*). Mesclun mix is likely to be the most successful.

Common problems

Slugs and snails are the most damaging pests. Vigilant sanitation is the best control for caterpillars and viruses. You can control aphids with an organic insecticide, but try resistant varieties if root aphids cause wilt and stunted growth. In wet periods, downy mildew attacks older leaves; sow resistant varieties for fall crops.

Looseleaf lettuce brings varied color and texture to the salad bowl, and there is some evidence that the red-tinted types are less prone than most lettuce to slug and snail damage.

Endive

The leaves of this very bitter salad plant can be cut when young to add a different note to mixed salad greens (*see page 166*). Alternatively, it can be blanched to reduce the bitterness (*see below*). The curled- and plain-leaved forms are both grown in the same way.

Any fertile garden soil in full sun is suitable for endive cultivation. Before sowing, promote the fertility and the retention of moisture in the soil by adding some well-rotted compost and, unless the ground was amended for a previous crop in the same season, all-purpose fertilizer at the rate recommended on the package.

Mild, but not warm or hot, conditions and high light levels are essential for sturdy plants. Covering the planting with a floating row cover after sowing can advance harvesting by as much as two weeks. Spring sowings benefit from a site in partial shade, which will help to prevent them from bolting. If growth is slow and leaves are pale, apply additional fertilizer and water it in.

Common problems

Endive is easy to grow and suffers few significant problems. Slugs and snails are the most damaging pests and are dealt with as for other crops.

Endives may succumb to gray mold and other fungal diseases in wet weather, especially when the plants are covered for blanching. Good ventilation around the plants can help prevent this from happening, but prompt disposal of affected material is the only remedy.

FROM SOWING TO HARVESTING BLANCHED ENDIVE

1 **Sow the seeds** directly into the ground ½in. deep in drills 12in. apart. Where summers are mild, sow every 2 weeks from midspring to late summer so that leaves can be gathered continuously from summer until early winter.

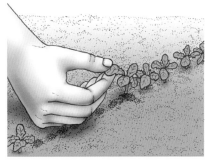

2 **Thin emerging seedlings** when the first 4 leaves appear, so they are 10in. apart. Water the growing plants regularly, especially during hot, dry weather, to prevent the plants from bolting.

3 **Loosely tie the plants** around their stems with twine when they are fully grown—about 3 months after sowing. The twine tie keeps the lower leaves off the ground, which reduces the risk of rotting.

4 **Begin to blanch** about 4 months after sowing, covering each plant with a large, light-proof container. Blanch 2–3 plants at a time for a supply over a long period, because blanched plants tend not to last long.

5 **Cover any holes** to exclude light. A slight gap between the rims and the soil allows for ventilation to prevent rotting. The blanched leaves should be free of bitterness within 2 weeks in mild weather.

6 **Harvest blanched plants** by cutting just above soil level. Use blanched endive immediately, because it does not keep well in the kitchen.

Chicory

There are various types of chicory. Radicchio and other hearting chicories form firm heads with a bitter flavor that are used in salad green mixtures, while sugarloaf chicory has only moderately bitter leaves. Roots of Belgian chicory can be forced in winter to produce buds of mild-tasting, firm leaves called chicons (*see below*).

Sowing, cultivation, & harvesting

Any fertile garden soil in full sun is suitable. Before sowing add plenty of well-rotted compost and all-purpose fertilizer at the rate recommended on the package.

Sow all chicories either directly where they are to grow or in containers, at intervals of two weeks, so that the leaves can be harvested from midspring to fall, depending on your region. Thin the seedlings as soon as they can be handled. The leafy chicories are suitable for growing as cut-and-come again salad leaves (*see page 166*), and these should be thinned to just ¹⁄₂in. apart; thin other types to

8in. spacings. Plant out seedlings raised in containers as soon as the roots bind the growing mix, and water the soil well both before and after planting.

Radicchios form heads about four months after sowing, but this period can be shortened by covering with a floating cover. Chicories have deep roots, and in many climates watering is usually only necessary for young plants during very hot, dry weather; in dry climates, regular watering may be necessary. Sidedress with fertilizer if growth is slow.

Harvest chicory when the hearts are firm or the leaves are usable. Radicchio is best harvested after it has been sweetened by a light frost. Cut-and-come again crops can make an interesting, bitter addition to salad greens, and a second crop may regrow from the stumps. Picking young leaves does not have an adverse affect on the development of Belgian chicory roots for forcing.

Chicory is easy to grow and suffers from no significant pest or disease problems.

FROM SOWING TO HARVESTING FORCED BELGIAN CHICORY

1 **Sow the seeds** directly into the ground, ¹⁄₂in. deep in rows 12in. apart, from midspring until fall, depending on your region. Thin plants when large enough to handle, allowing 8in. between plants.

2 **Lift the roots** when the leaves start to die down. Discard any thin or forked roots and retain those that are ¹⁄₂–1¹⁄₄in. in diameter at the top, because these are the most suitable for forcing.

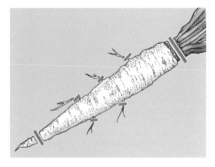

3 **Cut off remaining leaves** to within ¹⁄₂in. of the crown and discard unsuitable, damaged or diseased roots. Shorten the roots to 9in. and remove any side roots with a sharp knife.

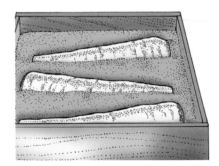

4 **Half-bury prepared roots** horizontally in boxes of dry sand so they are not touching. Keep in complete darkness in a cool but frost-free place, until you want to force them.

5 **Plant a few roots** in a pot of coarse sand or light garden soil, keeping ¹⁄₂in. of the crown above the surface. Water sparingly and keep in darkness. Creamy white chicons will appear in just a few weeks.

6 **Cut the blanched chicons** about 4 weeks after planting. Use them immediately. After harvesting, the roots will produce several smaller shoots that can be blanched in the same way.

Preparing to grow *see page 152* | **Sowing & growing** *see page 156* | **Common problems** *see page 220*

Spinach & chard

Spinach is a very nutritious crop, and there are similar, easier-to-grow crops that have their own special qualities. Any fertile garden soil in full sun or light shade is suitable. Before sowing, add plenty of well-rotted compost and all-purpose fertilizer, at the rate recommended on the package, to ensure good-quality leaf production.

Spinach

Growing spinach successfully requires cool temperatures. In many regions, it is planted in late winter or early spring for a spring harvest and again in early fall for a late fall harvest. In mild winter climates, it is grown as a winter crop. Sow seed where it is to grow, ³⁄₄in. deep in rows 12in. apart. As spinach tends to bolt quickly, sowing little and often is best.

Apply lots of water in hot, dry weather to reduce the chances that the plants will bolt. When leaves begin to enlarge, start cutting, removing no more than half the leaves at a time. A final sowing of hardy spinach in late summer or early fall will grow slowly over winter for gathering in spring in some areas.

Aphids, leaf miners, and cabbage worms can be controlled by protecting the crop with floating row covers. Downy mildew may infect plants in wet weather; resistant varieties are available.

New Zealand spinach & chard

These vegetables are good alternatives to spinach, and they are usually easier to grow. Robust, sprawling New Zealand spinach is suitable for any soil in full sun, or even hanging baskets. Unlike true spinach, it thrives in warm weather. Pests and diseases seldom trouble these crops.

Cultivation is as for chard (*see below*) and they are ready for harvest just as soon as leaves become big enough. New Zealand spinach and chard make good baby salad leaves if sown in rows 6in. apart with ¹⁄₂in. between plants.

FROM SOWING TO HARVESTING CHARD

1 Sow 3–4 seeds at 8in intervals in ³⁄₄in deep drills, from late winter for spring crops, in midspring for summer crops, and again in late summer for picking the following spring in suitable areas. For crops of baby leaves, sow seeds in rows 6in. apart with ½in. between plants.

2 Thin the seedling clusters when each seedling is big enough to handle. Leave 1 seedling per station. Thinning can be done over several weeks as the thinnings are useful eaten either cooked or raw.

3 Hoe regularly between the rows during the growing season. Water the growing plants liberally in hot, dry weather.

4 Harvest a few of the largest leaves after 60–80 days or as soon as the plants are large enough, picking or cutting them off as close to the ground as possible. Gather the the leaves regularly to encourage further production.

Arugula & exotic salad greens

Arugula is now a 'must-have' crop for any vegetable grower, but it has only become popular in recent years. This is surprising, given that it is so easy to cultivate and so well suited to the smallest yards, even if confined to a large container. Many other 'exotic' salad leaves are now available as seed, and are well worth trying for their interesting flavors.

Mixed seed packets offer variety; they are very easy to grow as cut-and-come-again crops (*see below*) and in spring and fall make a superior and cheaper alternative to mixed salad from the supermarket. In warmer regions, arugula can be grown throughout winter.

Growing arugula

Any fertile garden soil in full sun or light shade is suitable. Before you sow, apply plenty of well-rotted compost and all-purpose fertilizer at the rate on the package.

Sow every two weeks, ideally directly in the ground or else into containers, from midspring until late summer for a continuous supply. Sow seeds 1in. apart in drills about ¹⁄₂in. deep and 4–8in. apart; reduce spacing by ten percent on raised beds. For containers, simply sprinkle seed lightly on the soil surface. There should be no need to thin the young plants.

In hot, dry weather, apply lots of water regularly to reduce the likelihood of the arugula plants bolting. Take a few leaves from each plant as soon as they can be handled; the plants will continue to produce more foliage.

Special seed mixtures for cut-and-come-again crops can be bought. Each leaf type should grow at the same rate and will provide a spicy or Mediterranean flavor. Try experimenting with your own mixtures.

Leaves can be punctured by flea beetles; a floating cover usually excludes the beetle and the application of liquid fertilizer helps plants to outgrow the pest. In hot weather arugula leaves become bitter and the plants bolt.

FROM SOWING TO HARVESTING CUT-AND-COME-AGAIN SALAD LEAVES

1 **Sow salad seeds** directly where they are to grow in a container. Sow every 2 weeks for a steady supply of young leaves throughout the summer months.

2 **Lightly cover and water** and keep in a light, airy place; raise the container on bricks to deter slugs and snails. Plants take 3–6 weeks to produce the first usable crop.

3 **Cut the leaves** as required and leave the stem center to regrow. Water lightly to keep plants growing; they should produce further crops at 3–6 week intervals.

THE CABBAGE FAMILY

Plants of the cabbage family are also known as brassicas. They are a varied group of crops, ranging from leafy cabbages and kale to broccoli and cauliflowers, and they even include rutabaga (*see page 200*), found among the root crops. Most of these are cool-season crops, planted early in spring. By planting again in late summer for a fall crop, you can use brassicas to extend the productive season in the garden and provide healthy and tasty greens when plentiful summer crops come to an end. In warmer regions, brassicas can be grown in winter.

Growing brassicas

Brassicas produce abundantly in cool weather, and they should be harvested before the heat of summer arrives and reduces their quality. In many areas, it is easiest to grow brassica crops in the fall, where the weather grows cooler as the crops mature. Try to get some local advice. With a few exceptions all are cultivated in the same way: home-raised or bought young plants should be planted in fertile soil and protected from their numerous enemies.

Any fertile garden soil will support brassicas; if in doubt, add plenty of well-rotted compost and all-purpose fertilizer, at the rate recommended on the package, at least four weeks before planting. Check the soil pH (*see page 33*) and add lime if it is less than pH 6.5, to limit the severity of clubroot disease; avoid liming within two weeks of applying fertilizer. Try to rotate plantings with at least two years between brassica crops.

Raising plants

Start young plants indoors in containers for your spring crop; they can be started outdoors in midsummer for a fall crop. Alternatively, purchase young plants from a garden center. Sow twice as many seeds as you need for large plants, such as Brussels sprouts, and transplant seedlings into 3½in. pots as soon as they can be handled. If many plants are needed, as with spring cabbages, sow two seeds per cell in cell packs or propagation trays and discard the weaker one. Transplant seedlings when they have grown four or five leaves (*see right*). Plants need at least 1in. water per week throughout the growing season.

To exclude pests, especially flea beetles, and imported cabbage worms and cabbage maggots, cover plants with floating row cover until late spring; after this, it may overheat the plants, so use insect-proof mesh.

Biological controls are also effective for controlling several caterpillars that attack brassica crops. Brassicas are seldom badly damaged by their many leaf diseases, but, where disease is a problem, resistant varieties are available for use in your garden.

TRANSPLANTING BRASSICAS

Transplant when the roots bind the potting soil firmly together. Firm the soil, watering 24 hours before transplanting if it is dry, and rake level. Water, then ease out the seedlings. Set each one in the soil up to the lowest leaves and firm in very well. Water regularly until the plants are growing strongly.

Cabbages

Although botanically a biennial, cabbage is grown as an annual, forming a tight head of edible leaves that are rich in vitamins A, C, and K. It can be eaten raw or cooked and is included in many soup and stew recipes. It is also used to make sauerkraut.

Varieties include smooth leaf types that range from light to dark green and red-purple. Savoy types have crinkled leaves. Chinese cabbage also produces crinkled leaves and its heads are elongated. It is fast maturing and somewhat bolt resistant.

Varieties are also classified according to their season. Early varieties are generally smaller and mature in 60–75 days after transplanting. Late varieties are usually best for fall planting. They produce large heads that are suitable for winter storage.

Cabbage requires cool weather to mature, growing best when temperatures are 55–65°F. Its seeds are planted at different times of the year in various regions of the country. In cool regions, it can be planted as both a spring and a fall crop. As you head south to warmer regions, crops planted in late summer for fall harvest are usually more successful. As temperatures cool in the fall, the flavor of

Assorted cabbages are available: some produce smooth leaves, others are crinkled. Leaves may be pale to dark green, blue-green, or purple. Heads may be rounded, elongated, or pointed.

FROM PLANTING TO HARVESTING FALL CABBAGES

1 Pull up a little soil around the base of the young plants about 2 weeks after planting in late summer. This protects against windrock, which can loosen the roots and cause problems in later months. Firm any plants loosened later by adverse weather.

2 Spread fertilizer or well-rotted compost around each head of cabbage to encourage rapid growth. Alternatively, apply a liquid fertilizer, such as fish emulsion or compost tea, at 2-week intervals as the heads mature.

3 Hoe between the growing plants regularly to keep the rows free from competing weeds and maintain a good texture to the soil. Water during dry periods, but do not overwater because this can cause the maturing head to split.

4 Cut mature fall cabbages as required from midfall to early winter. Clear away the stumps and roots as this breaks the cycle of the whitefly pest, which may otherwise move onto other brassica plants in summer.

HARVESTING & STORING CABBAGE

1 **Lift winter cabbages** for storing as entire plants in late fall and early winter. If they are carefully stored and regularly checked, some varieties can last through winter.

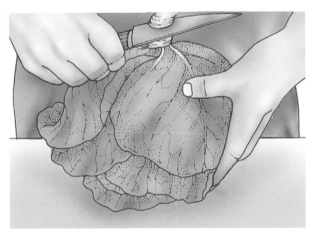

2 **Trim off the roots** and the bottom of the stem. Remove the coarse outer leaves to leave a clean, solid head. Varieties with the densest heads are most suitable for long storage.

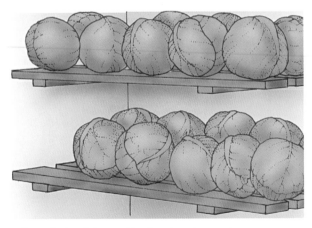

3 **Store the heads** in a cool but frost-free place, such as a garage, basement, or garden shed. Slatted shelving allows air to circulate, and the cabbages can be stacked if necessary.

the head becomes more mild and there is less chance of its splitting. In year-round mild regions, cabbage is often planted as both a fall and a winter crop.

Raising & planting out

Start young plants for spring planting indoors, in cell packs or propagation trays, six to eight weeks prior to the last expected frost. Planting for fall and winter cabbages can be done in the garden in late summer. Set plants into very fertile soil. Depending on the size of your variety, space cabbages 12–24in. apart. Water young plants well and mulch around their bases to help maintain even soil moisture.

Chinese cabbages can be raised in propagation trays, but sowing where they are to grow is often easier. Sow ³/₄in. deep, 2in. apart, in rows 12in. apart, and thin to 8–10in. apart as soon as they can be handled.

Cultivation & harvesting

As your plants grow, fertilize them by sprinkling extra nitrogen-rich fertilizer around the bases if growth appears to slow. Apply it at the rate recommended on the packet. Ideally, water your cabbages so that the soil stays evenly moist. However, if water and time are in short supply the most economical use of available water is to give a good soak when the head is just forming. Chinese cabbages in particular must be kept well watered during any extended dry spells or else they will bolt instead of forming edible heads.

You can cut heads whenever they are usable, although it is best to wait until firm, solid heads have formed. When the hearts are truly solid, cut and use immediately or keep in the vegetable compartment of the refrigerator. Some cabbage varieties, including some red ones, are especially solid and can be cut in fall and stored in a frost-free place until late winter. Allowing fall cabbage to remain in the garden until after several light frosts improves the flavor.

Common problems

Caterpillars can be very damaging; control them by thorough hand picking, by applying an appropriate biological control, or by covering with insect-proof mesh, which will form an effective barrier to the egg-laying adult butterflies without the need for pesticides. If a pesticide is needed, consult your local cooperative extension service. Mesh provides protection against all flying pests, but it can act as a hiding place for slugs. Minimize clubroot by liming, improving drainage, rotating crops, and by growing resistant varieties.

Cauliflower

This member of the cabbage family is perhaps the most difficult to grow well. It requires a long, cool season. If temperatures are too cold or too warm, a stunted head or no head at all will form. Although it tolerates some cold, it is not as hardy as cabbage. Cauliflower only does well in very fertile, moisture-retentive soils, and it is highly susceptible to clubroot, although resistant varieties are available. Cultivate in a well-limed, neutral to alkaline soil with a high level of organic matter, and apply a balanced fertilizer before planting.

The head of a cauliflower is made up of tightly packed flower parts called curds. These are typically white, but varieties are available in green, orange, and purple; romanesco types have minarets of pale green curds and a robust texture and flavor.

Raising & planting out

Sow in very early spring for an early summer harvest, or sow in midsummer to harvest in late fall or early winter. In regions with warm summers, planting summer-sown seed for a fall harvest provides the best growing conditions. In mild-winter regions, cauliflower can be grown throughout the year except in summer. Because cauliflower is so sensitive to adverse weather, planting it at weekly intervals during the appropriate season will improve the chances of harvesting a successful crop. Space it 18–24in. apart; some vigorous varieties do best at spacings of 28in. To reduce shock, water transplants with a dilute solution of water-soluble fertilizer.

When the head first begins to form, small leaves shade the developing curds, but as it expands the curds may become exposed. Shading the head from direct sun will keep the curds white and prevent them from developing off-flavors. Although some varieties are 'self blanching' with leaves that grow close to the head, providing shade, others will need to be blanched. This is accomplished by tying the leaves around the heads as they form. Begin when the heads are about 2in. across and secure the leaves with string, rubber bands, or clothespins. Check them frequently and adjust as the heads expand.

Cultivation & harvesting

Keep your cauliflower plants well watered and fertilized as they grow to assure quality head production. Regular applications of a liquid, all-purpose fertilizer, such as compost tea or fish emulsion, work well. Any stress or setback, such as being grown for too long in containers, poor planting, or a lack of water, can lead to open, poorly

Although somewhat more finicky in its growing requirements than other brassica crops, cauliflower can be grown in most areas of the country. Its head is composed of tightly spaced curds that are usually white, although green, purple, and orange varieties are available.

MINI-CAULIFLOWER

Small but perfectly formed mini-cauliflowers are ideal for small households or for freezing. Transplant seedlings or station sow seed (*see page 157*) 6in. apart in rows 10in. apart. Seed suppliers offer suitable varieties, and fall-grown plants often produce the highest-quality crop.

formed heads or disappointingly small curds or heads, which are called 'buttons'. Cultivate shallowly to control weeds, but take care not to damage the shallow roots. Alternatively, mulch the soil around plants to prevent weeds from growing and to reduce water loss.

Cut the head as soon as ready, when the head is firm and the curds tight. Home-grown cauliflower may only reach the size of a grapefruit at peak maturity. But heads left in the garden too long are prone to off-flavors and disease and insect damage. Use the cauliflower immediately for best quality, or freeze for later use.

Common problems

To exclude cabbage worms, flea beetles, cabbage whitefly, and many other pests, cover plants with a floating cover or an insect-proof mesh. Clear away stumps and roots of old crops before planting new crops to deter whiteflies and mealy cabbage aphids. Do not plant cauliflower where another brassica crop was grown the previous year.

Caterpillars can also be controlled by regular hand picking, by applying appropriate biological controls or an approved insecticide, or by growing plants under floating row covers.

FROM SOWING TO HARVESTING SUMMER-SOWN CAULIFLOWER

1 **Cultivate the soil** deeply in winter or when appropriate in your area, and dig in plenty of well-rotted garden compost.

2 **Rake in additional fertilizer** if the soil is still poor, in early to midspring, and add lime if necessary to increase the pH. Do this 1–2 weeks before sowing or planting out.

3 **Plant out seedlings** in midsummer at the desired spacings. Generously water both seedlings and planting site the day before transplanting.

4 **Water in** a dressing of nitrogen-rich plant food at regular intervals according to package directions.

5 **Water regularly,** particularly in dry weather. Unless the variety is self blanching, tie leaves around each developing head to shade it from direct sun.

6 **Cut each cauliflower** as it matures and as needed. The heads should be firm and well developed, but not yet beginning to open.

Broccoli & broccoli raab

Broccoli may be the easiest of all brassica crops to grow in a backyard garden. Most varieties form a large central head which is often followed by small sideshoots. It is a cool-season crop and can mature as little as 12 weeks after sowing. Plant in early spring to harvest before summer heat arrives; late-summer sowings produce well into fall.

Broccoli raab is also easy to grow, versatile to use, and in recent years new and much improved varieties have been released. Unlike normal broccoli, instead of producing one head similar to that of a cauliflower, broccoli raab develops a number of smaller heads, which are sometimes called spears or florets. These are like small broccoli heads on long, tender stalks and may be green, white, or purple. Each plant produces a succession of spears until the plants bolt or succumb to winter cold.

Depending on conditions in your area, broccoli raab can be harvested most of the year except in summer. It is hardy in areas where cauliflowers are not. Both broccoli and broccoli raab are very high in vitamins A and C, and are good sources of fiber.

Sowing & transplanting

Sow seeds for spring crops indoors, four to six weeks prior to the last expected frost, or purchase seedlings from a garden center. Sow seed for fall crops directly in the garden during midsummer.

Once spring seedlings are hardened, transplant them into the garden after the last hard frost, spacing them 24–30in. apart. These crops grow best in moderately fertile soil, which should be prepared as for most brassica crops (*see page 168*). Water broccoli regularly to assure good production of heads and sideshoots.

Cultivation & harvesting

Control weeds by cultivating shallowly, taking care not to damage the broccoli roots. Or mulch the soil around plants with compost or straw, which will also help maintain even soil moisture.

Cut the heads of broccoli when they are firm, before buds open to reveal yellow flowers. Cut broccoli raab shoots as soon as they can be handled, typically when they are about 4in. long, and before the buds open. Varieties vary in exactly how the crop develops: Some first produce a relatively large head followed by many smaller spears; others develop a continuing supply of small spears. Frequent picking will prevent any spears from becoming overmature, and will prolong harvesting.

Common problems

Broccoli suffers from the same pests as other brassicas, but broccoli raab is significantly less susceptible.

Cabbage worms and loopers, aphids, and flea beetles may cause problems. These can be largely avoided with the use of floating row covers, hand picking, or an approved insecticide. Plant where no cabbage family crops have grown for at least two years.

FROM PLANTING TO HARVESTING BROCCOLI RAAB

1 **Transplant seedlings** into the garden, spacing them 24–30in. apart. Water regularly and control weeds by cultivating shallowly or applying a mulch around the plants.

2 **Begin to harvest** as soon as spears can be handled. Cut the central and topmost shoots first. Water and fertilize to encourage continued spear development.

3 **Continue to harvest** by removing the sideshoots as they develop and before the flowers begin to open. Check them every couple of days.

Brussels sprouts

Brussels sprouts are far more popular in Britain than here, but now that varieties with improved flavor and improved disease resistance have been introduced American gardeners should give them another look. Purple varieties also make unusually attractive plants.

Brussels sprouts have a unique appearance; they grow taller than other brassica crops, often to 3ft. Their tiny cabbagelike heads develop along the central stem, covering it almost completely. Brussels sprouts take a long time to produce their crop. In most areas they are planted in early spring and not harvested until after frost sweetens the sprouts in the fall. Sprouts harvested too early are usually bitter. In mild regions, they can be harvested throughout winter.

Sowing, raising, & planting out

Sow seeds indoors four to six weeks before the last expected frost in spring, or in warm climates, start outdoors in a protected area. A floating row cover is best as it excludes mealy cabbage aphid, cabbage whitefly, and several leaf-eating caterpillars, which can all severely damage this crop. Use a root collar against cabbage maggot. Early sowings in late winter or early spring, for all varieties, produce the best crops.

Sow twice as many seeds as you require in small pots and transplant the seedlings into 3½in. pots—or 6in. pots in areas where clubroot is a problem—as soon as the young plants can be handled by their leaves. Plant into their final positions as soon as the roots bind the potting soil. Because they take time to fill out, intercrops of salad greens, spinach, and radishes can be grown between the rows of Brussels sprouts.

Although it is not true that planting in loose soil results in fluffy sprouts, you should firm the young plants in well to encourage good growth; when the leaves are gently tugged, you should not be able to uproot the whole plant.

Harvesting

Break off sprouts as soon as they are firm and before they become loose. They mature from the base of the stem

FROM PLANTING TO HARVESTING BRUSSELS SPROUTS

1 **Transplant young plants** into a well-prepared soil that has been amended with compost and an all-purpose fertilizer. Space the plants at about 24in. apart in rows 30in. apart. Plant them firmly with the lowest leaf at soil level.

2 **Water in** the young plants well and check that they are firmly planted by tugging each top leaf gently. Firm planting is essential, especially on light soils, as the plants can become topheavy and planting them in firmly helps them become more stable.

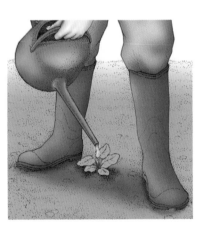

3 **Protect young plants** from cabbage maggot by positioning a tightly fitting root collar around the base of each plant at transplanting time. The collar prevents the female laying eggs in the soil.

4 **Continue to water** the young plants through late spring and early summer until they are well established. Further watering may not be necessary after this, unless they begin to suffer during prolonged dry weather.

upward. The tops can be cut for use as greens, but only after most of the sprouts are gathered as the leaves provide protection from severe weather. Remove and destroy spent crops promptly to prevent the carry-over of insect pests.

Common problems

Brussels sprouts can be tall and topheavy and need staking in exposed yards or where the soil is light. Deep and firm planting, however, as well as drawing soil into a low ridge around the bases of the plants in summer will often be enough to steady them in sheltered sites.

All parts of the crop are a favorite food of birds during lean times and plants need careful netting, with the net strongly suspended 12in. above the crop. Caterpillars are a serious pest and should be controlled by applying biological controls or an approved insecticide, or covering with row covers, which will keep out other flying pests.

Mealy cabbage aphid and cabbage whitefly can build up in late summer; control with an approved insecticidal soap or horticultural oil. Prevent reinfection by removing all old brassica crops before new plants are introduced.

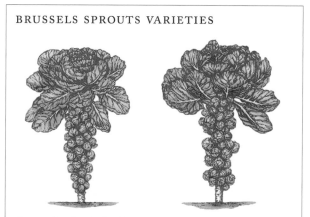

BRUSSELS SPROUTS VARIETIES

Conventional varieties (*right*) compare poorly to modern hybrids (*left*). They produce fluffy, poor-quality sprouts that are less abundant and have less resistance to disease.

Brussels sprouts are very susceptible to clubroot. Grow in well-drained, neutral to alkaline soil with a little lime placed in the planting hole. Raise transplants in 6in. diameter pots to obtain large root systems able to withstand infection. Do not compost any infected material.

5 Draw up some soil around the base of each stem during summer in light soils or exposed sites, to make the plants more stable. Hoe around the plants regularly to keep them free from weeds.

6 Apply a nitrogen-rich fertilizer around the bases of the plants during midsummer at a rate recommended on the package. To protect the crop from flying pests, such as cabbage white butterflies and birds, cover with a fine mesh netting.

7 Remove loose or open sprouts from the lower stems, and any yellowing leaves, from late summer onward, and put them in the compost pile. This will help reduce foliage disease and suppress slugs.

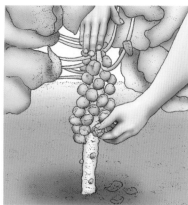

8 Gather the sprouts as soon as they are firm, harvesting them as required, starting from the bottom of the stem. The leafy tops of the plants can also be removed for eating, but not before most of the sprouts have been collected.

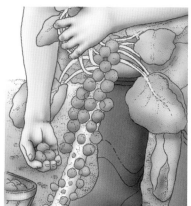

Kale

Kale is the hardiest of the brassicas and its nutritious and tasty leaves will stand summer heat and winter temperatures as low as 0°F. The flavor even improves after frost. Edible kales are usually green or red, although 'black' kales are also available. Brightly colored ornamental kales are botanically identical but, apart from the youngest leaves, are considered unrewarding to eat. Red curly kale and black kale are sufficiently attractive to be grown with flowers.

Kale is much less prone than other brassicas to pests and diseases, including clubroot, although mealy cabbage aphid may require control.

Sowing, cultivation, & harvesting

Sow plants for fall harvesting in early to midsummer; in mild-winter regions, sow kale in fall for winter harvest. Raise young plants in cell packs or pots and plant out 16–20in. apart, depending on whether dwarf or tall varieties are being grown. The soil need be only moderately fertile; use half the fertilizer needed for other brassicas, omitting fertilizer altogether if plenty of compost is applied.

Kale seldom suffers from drought so there is no need to water lavishly, except on planting. Firm planting is required and drawing soil up around the stem in late summer will help to steady the crop in exposed yards.

You can keep kale in reserve in case other winter brassicas are destroyed by especially severe weather in winter. The flavor of leaves is improved after they have

HARVESTING KALE

Pick only young leaves and shoots, pulling off and discarding yellowing or tough, old leaves. Sideshoots will form in response; again, harvest when young, from the top downward.

experienced cold temperatures. Young leaves and shoots can be gathered as needed, and old yellow foliage consigned to the compost pile. As spring approaches, sideshoots are produced continuously, but by early spring when flowering starts you should discard the plants.

KALE VARIETIES

Red curly kale is a curly, dark purple variety with ornamental qualities. 'Redbor' is a tall hybrid that overwinters well.

Italian black kale is famed for its delicious, strong flavor and is revered by cooks. 'Nero di Toscano' is a popular variety.

Red winter kale has purple stems with red, frilly leaves. Useful for salad greens or stir fry. It is very hardy.

STALKS & SHOOTS

There are few edible stalks, as stems have to be robust to support foliage in a potentially hostile environment and are therefore usually stringy and tough. What few there are, however, make a delicious addition to the vegetable garden. Asparagus and rhubarb, like many plants, put on a spurt of growth in spring to grab as much light and space as they can before the competition catches up. Until they toughen with age, the young shoots of these crops are tender and tasty. By lavish fertilizing and watering, celery stems (which are actually leaf stalks) can develop a crunchy but 'stringless' texture.

Asparagus

You could describe asparagus as the perfect vegetable crop: it produces delicious shoots from midspring until early summer when little else is available; it is expensive to buy in the supermarket; and it is a long-lived perennial, so it does not need sowing each year.

Preparing the site

Find a sunny site with good drainage. Raised beds provide perfect conditions where the soil is heavy or badly drained. Once asparagus is growing it is nearly impossible to remove perennial weeds, so choose a weed-free site or devote a season to eradicating all perennial weeds.

Thorough cultivation is essential, because the crop is likely to be in place for at least ten years. Dig in generous amounts of well-rotted compost to get the crop off to a good start, adding lime, if necessary, to ensure the pH is 6.5–7. As asparagus grows up to 5ft. tall, choose a spot sheltered from strong winds. Asparagus requires a cold period for dormancy, so it does not grow well in warm, frost-free regions.

Planting & cultivation

Modern hybrid varieties are very vigorous and are 'all male'. Male plants produce heavier crops than female plants and do not set seed, avoiding the problem of hard-to-remove seedlings between the rows. In fact, occasional female plants sometimes occur even where 'all-male' varieties are grown.

Planting one- or two-year-old 'crowns' (dormant roots) is the traditional way of starting asparagus, although modern hybrids grow very strongly and starting from seed (*see right*), or growing young plants in small pots, is often cheaper; consider, however that roots should be at least three years old before you begin to harvest.

Crowns are usually bought in spring. It is a good idea to soak the crowns overnight prior to planting. Space them about 16in. from each other in trenches 4ft. apart. Where space is short, you can use closer planting, but this will result in shorter-lived plants. Trenches should be about 12in. wide and 8in. deep. Set the crowns on a 4in.

FROM SOWING TO THINNING ASPARAGUS

1 Sow the seeds thinly in ½–¾in. deep drills, 18in. apart, in spring. Keep the bed completely free from weeds, and water in dry weather. Hybrid varieties tend to be more vigorous and productive than traditional, nonhybrid varieties.

2 Thin the seedlings when they emerge until they are eventually 6in. apart. The seedlings can be transplanted to the permanent bed in the following spring, but if you wait a year it allows you to identify and remove any less-productive female plants when they produce their berries.

GROWING ASPARAGUS: THE FIRST YEAR

1 Cultivate the ground to the depth of one spade blade in winter. Dig in plenty of well-rotted compost, and add lime as required so that the soil pH is between 6.5 and 7. Ensure the ground is clear of weeds before you plant.

2 Dig a trench about 12in. wide and 8in. deep, in spring. Lightly rake into the trench all-purpose fertilizer at the rate recommended on the package. Make a ridge 4in. high at the bottom of the trench.

3 Plant the crowns in spring at 16in. intervals. They have spidery roots that can be spread evenly over the ridge, with the pointed buds facing upward. Carefully pull back soil into the trench over the roots so that the tops of the crowns are just covered. As the plants grow, gradually fill in the trench.

4 Cut back in fall once the stems turn yellow and add to the compost pile. Remove any weeds by hand; do not dig too deeply as asparagus roots are easily damaged. Finally, apply a 2–3in. layer of well-rotted compost into the top of the trench and mound it up over the row.

ridge of soil at the bottom of the trench and cover them so that they sit just below the soil surface. As the stalks grow, gradually fill in the trench. Spears must not be cut until the third season after planting, as eventual heavy harvesting depends on a slow buildup of crown size, starting with the all-important first two seasons, when no cutting should be done.

Thorough weeding and watering in dry spells is essential in the first year to help really strong plants develop. You will need to weed and water the following year as well, taking great care not to damage the shallow roots when hoeing or lifting out weeds. Apply more all-purpose fertilizer in spring.

By the third spring, you can cut a light crop from the emerging spears of the young plants beginning in midspring, but limit your harvest to two weeks. The following year, harvest for three weeks. In succeeding years, a full crop can be taken.

Harvesting a mature crop

Asparagus spears are the emerging shoots that grow from the roots as they break dormancy in spring. After the fourth year, spears can be cut for about four to six weeks from midspring to early summer without harming the following year's crop. Use a small, sharp knife to carefully sever each one just below soil level, keeping in mind that other shoots are probably underground growing very close by; if they are damaged they will not produce spears.

Cut all shoots that are thicker than a pencil, but stop cutting completely in early summer so that the remaining shoots can feed and strengthen the roots for the next year's crop.

Subsequent management

Management of a mature crop is very easy. Remove any weeds by hand or carefully ease them out with a trowel as soon as they appear.

A mulch of weed-free, well-rotted compost or other organic mulch can be very effective in preventing annual weeds growing in the crop. It will also help fertilize the asparagus. An annual application of all-purpose fertilizer will be necessary as well; sometimes this is supplemented with an additional application immediately after the last spears are harvested.

MANAGING AN ASPARAGUS BED

1 **Apply all-purpose fertilizer**, at the rate recommended on the package, in early spring to nourish the coming growth of the asparagus plants.

2 **Cut the spears** with a sharp knife in midspring when they are 5–6in. above soil level. Cut each spear obliquely, 1–2in. below the soil surface. Take care not to damage any underground shoots as you do so.

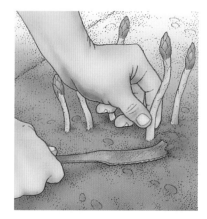

3 **After harvest,** apply an all-purpose fertilizer in early summer, at the same rate as in spring. This extra dose of fertilizer is not essential, but it ensures a high level of fertility as the plant builds up its energy levels for the next harvest. Allow the shoots to develop until fall.

4 **Cut down** the yellowed stems and foliage in fall and add to the compost pile. Remove weeds by hand or with a trowel, then apply a mulch of well-rotted compost.

After harvesting, leave the stems to grow, supported with stakes and string if necessary. In fall, the topgrowth turns yellow and strawlike; remove this by cutting near to soil level, and add it to the compost pile. At this stage the plant's resources are stored in the roots ready to support spear production the following spring. Before winter, apply a thick mulch to improve the soil and smother weeds. For additional weed control, before mulching, you can draw up soil with a hoe from between the rows of plants to form a ridge over the crowns.

Common problems

Asparagus is largely trouble free, but asparagus beetles can strip foliage in summer. On a small scale, these red beetles can be removed without resorting to approved insecticides, either by hand or with a carefully directed jet of water. Slugs sometimes feed on the emerging spears in spring and will need controlling.

Leaf and root diseases occasionally reach significant levels in asparagus. Plant resistant varieties and burn any infected foliage in fall; removing and destroying plants found to have diseased roots are the only remedies.

HOW ASPARAGUS GROWS

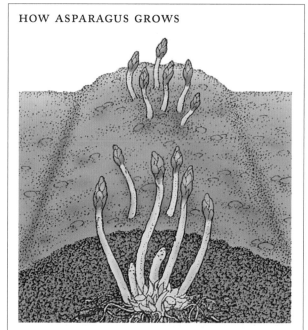

Emerging shoots or 'spears' grow from a rootstock deep underground. The plant dies back to this rootstock over winter.

Celery

Celery needs a long, cool season to produce a good harvest. It is grown as an early spring or fall crop in cool regions, as a winter crop in mild regions. Depending on the variety, it requires 90–120 days after transplanting to mature. Modern green-stemmed celery is full flavored, tender, and rich in vitamins; older varieties need blanching to produce pale stems, which many consider to be the finest. Self-blanching varieties, if closely planted, provide naturally pale stems.

Sowing & cultivation

Sow the fine seed indoors 12–16 weeks prior to the last expected hard frost. Soaking seed overnight will hasten germination. As soon as the seedlings are easily handled, transplant them into small pots. After all danger of frost has passed, plant them outdoors in highly fertile soil, spacing them 6–10in. apart. Add plenty of well-rotted compost and apply an all-purpose fertilizer.

Never let plants dry out, and add nitrogen-rich fertilizer, at the rate on the package, once they are growing well. For tender, sweet stems, exclude light by hilling (*see below*), by using light-excluding collars, or by placing boards along the rows of stems.

Celery is susceptible to a few viral diseases, so buy resistant varieties. Floating row covers can be used to exclude flying pests.

FROM SOWING TO HARVESTING CELERY

1 **Dig a trench** 16in. wide and 12in. deep in early spring, in full sun. Fork compost into the base and refill.

2 **Transplant young plants** grown from seed once they have a few leaves and are large enough to handle.

3 **Rake fertilizer in** at the rate recommended by the manufacturer just before planting. Check the package for details.

4 **Plant out** self-blanching types 10in. apart in a block for mutual shade, and other types 16in. apart in rows 18in. apart.

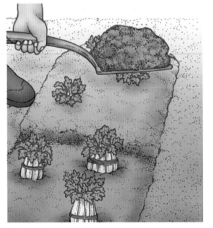

5 **Exclude light** to blanch the stems by tying them and hilling them; or simply wrap collars of opaque material around the stems.

6 **Cut whole heads** at the bases in late summer and early fall. Celery rapidly becomes pithy or rots as winter approaches.

Preparing to grow *see page 152* | **Sowing & growing** *see page 156* | **Common problems** *see page 220*

Rhubarb

This long-lived crop can remain productive for many years without replanting. In summer, its broad, lush leaves build up resources that, after the leaves die down in fall, are stored in the roots over winter. To produce well, roots must be subjected to freezing temperatures. In spring, buds expand rapidly into long leaf stalks that are cut for use.

Cultivation

Although container-grown plants are available from garden centers, it is very easy to take an offset from any mature plant. Rhubarb is rarely grown from seed.

Rhubarb grows on any good garden soil in full sun or light shade. Because it remains in the same place for several years, amend the soil thoroughly before planting. Leave new plants uncut for the first year. Once they are growing well, cut stalks of a worthwhile size in spring. Continue to fertilize and mulch each spring.

Although rhubarb may occasionally be damaged by viruses, fungus, or crown rot, most failures result from excessive shade and lack of generous fertilizing.

FORCING RHUBARB

The best and earliest stalks are produced in the dark. Cover the crown of the plant with a light-proof container, such as an upturned trashcan at least 20in. tall, in late winter, and gather the stalks as soon as they are large enough, generally within 5–6 weeks. They will be especially tasty and tender.

Leave the plants to rebuild their reserves uncovered and unpicked for 2 years after forcing them. Fertilize well in spring and add a thick mulch around the stems.

FROM PLANTING TO HARVESTING RHUBARB

1 **Take offsets** with a strong bud from the edge of a parent plant during winter or early spring. Replant 3ft. apart in soil amended with plenty of well-rotted compost and all-purpose fertilizer at the rate recommended on the package. Plant the offset with the bud just above the surface.

2 **Apply all-purpose fertilizer** in spring at the rate on the package, water well in dry spells, and keep weed free. A 3in. deep mulch of well-rotted compost in spring will help prevent weeds and improve growth.

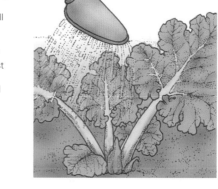

3 **Remove the old leaves** in fall, once they have turned brown and helped to build up reserves in the root. Apply an all-purpose fertilizer, to each plant.

4 **Harvest stems** the following spring by cutting them at their base or by gripping each near soil level and pulling and twisting. Discard the foliage: it is potentially harmful if consumed but safe to compost. Stems become stringy by midsummer; stop cutting and let the plants build up their reserves for the following year.

PODS & SEEDS

Bean and pea plants, otherwise known as legumes, are varied, attractive, and rewarding to grow. Some are eaten as pods, such as snap beans and snow peas, others grown for their protein-rich seeds, like lima beans and garden peas. All these plants share one characteristic: thanks to specialized bacteria in nodules on their roots, they can 'fix' nitrogen from the air. This means they need less nitrogenous fertilizer than other vegetables, and when the season is over their remains make an invaluable addition to the compost pile. Given sun and support, they provide crops from late spring to late fall.

Peas

This vegetable comes in three types. All are both tasty and highly nutritious.

Garden peas: Also known as English peas, these are grown for their immature seeds, which are removed from the pods for cooking. Some very small-seeded varieties are sold as 'petit pois' but, in fact, other shelled pea varieties harvested at an early stage are just as good.

Plant densely because each pea plant will produce only a few pods, and many closely spaced plants are required for a worthwhile crop. Successive sowings will also be needed to ensure continuity of supply throughout summer.

Snap peas: These peas have rounded, unusually thick pods and relatively small seeds. Snap peas have become very popular in recent years because they are productive and many disease-resistant varieties have been developed. The whole pod is cooked, often steamed, or eaten raw.

Snow peas: Again, the whole pod is eaten, but in this case the pods are flat and can be cooked or eaten raw.

Some peas have tendrils in addition to leaves. Bush peas need no support, but vining types should be provided with a trellis, fence, or other support to climb.

Peas are cool-season vegetables and can be grown for spring and fall crops in many areas. In mild regions they can be grown in winter. Bush varieties grow 18–24in. tall and are usually the earliest to mature, while vining varieties can reach 8ft. if provided with sufficient support. Snap and snow peas are ready more quickly than shelled peas because they are gathered before the seeds mature.

Growing conditions

If possible, provide fertile, well-drained soil in full sun. Acid soils of less than pH 6 are unsuitable. If growing where fertilizers or manures have been applied for previous crops, peas need no extra fertilizer; but if in doubt apply low-nitrogen fertilizer or plenty of well-rotted compost.

Successive sowing

In regions with a long spring season or cool summers, successive sowings will extend the pea harvest. The first spring planting can be made as early as mid March in many areas. As a rule of thumb for successive sowing, sow when the preceding sowing is 2in. high. In cool weather, however, seed may be slow to germinate; germination can

FROM SOWING TO HARVESTING PEAS

1 **Sow seeds** at about ½in. spacings, in drills 2in. deep and in rows that are 24–30in. apart. This gives a high plant population, but still allows easy weeding and picking.

2 **Cover the drill** by raking the soil back over it gently. Firm down with the head of the rake to ensure that the seeds are held in close contact with the soil.

3 **Place wire or plastic netting,** curved into hoop houses, over the rows immediately after planting. This will help to prevent damage by birds and rabbits, although mice may still present a problem.

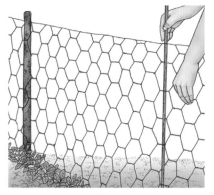

4 **Erect a netting support** on posts and wire when the plants are 3–4in. tall. The netting should be at least as tall as the expected height of the plants. Twiggy sticks or canes and string are other options.

5 **When the plants flower,** water thoroughly. For the best crops, never allow peas to dry out while in flower or when the pods are swelling.

6 **Pick the pods** of garden peas when well filled but still young and tender. Pick snap and snow peas as pods develop. Harvest regularly to keep the plants producing more flowers and pods.

be hastened by soaking seeds overnight. If your garden soil stays damp for long periods, consider growing peas in a raised bed.

Cultivation & harvesting

Water peas if the weather is dry, particularly once the peas flower. A thorough soaking when flowering begins and again two weeks later ensures a good crop in dry spells. Cultivate to remove weeds, but take care not to damage the pea's shallow roots.

To harvest, gently pull the pods from the plant without damaging the vine. Pods tend to develop at the base of the plant first. Gather snap and snow varieties as soon as the pods are big enough; harvesting usually can begin about a week after flowers first appear. Harvest garden peas when the seeds have swollen but before they

turn floury or the pods turn pale. Harvest frequently to assure best quality and to encourage further flower development. As summer temperatures rise, flowers will stop forming and vines begin to shrivel. When harvesting is over, compost the plants.

Peas suffer from a few pests including aphids, pea weevils, and rabbits. Aphid populations can be reduced with a hard stream of water or they can be treated with an insecticidal soap. Pea weevils are best avoided by crop rotation and removal of plants at the end of the season. Use wire cages to protect new plantings from rabbits. Bacterial and fungal blights can destroy pea plantings. Be sure to obtain disease-free seed from a reputable source and practice crop rotation. Other diseases such as fusarium wilt and powdery mildew can be avoided by growing resistant varieties and watering in dry periods.

Pole beans

Any vigorous bean that twines around poles or other supports as it grows is referred to as a pole bean. Local climate has a significant impact on which kinds of pole bean you will be able to grow—lima beans require much warmer conditions than runner beans. Sowing time and whether seed needs to be sown under protection will also depend on your local climate; seek local advice.

All pole beans thrive in full sun or in a little shade and in soil with a pH above 6. A sheltered position is essential as strong winds will topple these tall plants, damage developing pods, and impair pollination. Success also depends on lush growth, which can only be achieved with plenty of moisture. Before planting, dig plenty of well-rotted compost into the soil. In addition, apply an all-purpose fertilizer at the rate on the package.

Sowing

Sow pole beans outdoors in late spring or early summer after all danger of frost has passed. In mild areas, you can make a second sowing in mid- to late summer for a fall crop. Plants can be raised indoors in small pots of all-purpose mix from midspring; this is essential where the soil is cold, heavy clay.

By late spring the roots will be binding the growing mix and in mild districts the plants can be set out beneath a temporary row cover or under cloches. In colder areas, delay planting out until early summer.

TYPES OF BEAN

The naming of beans can be confusing.

Bush beans Kidney, lima, and snap beans, which grow as low bushes.

Butter beans *see* lima beans.

Fava beans Cool-climate beans usually making tall, upright bushes, grown for their immature seeds.

Filet beans Pencil-podded snap beans, bush or pole.

Kidney beans Bush beans grown for their dried seeds.

Lima beans Warm-climate bush or pole beans grown for their immature seeds.

Pinto beans A kidney bean with speckled seeds.

Pole beans Any vigorous vining bean, which twines around poles or other supports as it grows.

Runner beans Easy-to-grow pole beans cultivated for their flat, fleshy pods.

Snap beans Bush beans whose pods are eaten whole.

Soy beans Bush beans grown for their high-protein seeds, eaten fresh or dry.

Yard-long beans Pole beans with unusually long, slim pods that are eaten fresh.

With their pretty flowers and fast-growing habit, runner beans make an attractive and productive, temporary screen for the ornamental yard. Within a matter of weeks, these vigorous vines will have scrambled to the tops of their 8ft. supports.

SOWING & PLANTING OUT

Plant out young plants raised indoors, at the base of each support, as soon as the risk of frost has passed. As they will already be growing strongly, the crop will get off to a fast start. A second sowing from midsummer can give an extra crop in fall.

Supporting pole beans

A variety of supports can be used for pole beans. In some gardens, an existing fence can provide an ideal support. For a double row of beans, make two parallel drills, 24in. apart and 2¾in. deep. Space the seeds 6in. apart, thinning plants when they emerge to one every 12in. Push a 6–8ft. cane beside each plant, crossing and tying the poles at the top, then join them all together by tying a horizontal cane along the ridge (*see below*). Allow 4ft. between double rows.

Cultivation & harvesting

When the young plants are thinned, add an all-purpose fertilizer, at the rate recommended on the package, to the pole bean site, unless growth is very green and lush.

Hoe between plants to remove weeds, and if the shoots need encouragement to climb their supports gently twine them against the canes or tie them in until they are self supporting. When the plants reach the top of the canes, pinch back their growing tips.

When the plants are flowering, never let the soil dry out as this results in a poor yield of pods. You may need to water as often as every three days. Harvest the pods when they reach their mature length according to variety.

Common problems

Most pole beans are free of significant pests, although bean beetles cause problems in some areas. Delayed planting and sanitation can reduce bean beetle damage. Several biological controls are effective or consult your extension service for recommended pesticides. Most diseases are best controlled by using certified disease-free seed, selecting resistant varieties, and by crop rotation.

FROM SOWING TO HARVESTING POLE BEANS

1 **Dig a trench** and amend the soil with plenty of organic matter, such as well-rotted garden compost. Pole beans are deep rooting and like a moisture-retentive soil.

2 **Rake the soil level** and firm it in by treading over it lightly. Add a dressing of all-purpose fertilizer.

3 **Sow seeds** in drills 2¾in. deep, 6in. apart. Make a parallel drill 24in. from the first. When young plants emerge, thin them to 1 plant every 12in. Stake each plant.

4 **Tie the canes** together to form a length of triangular supports. Secure them at the top where they cross over, and lay a cane across the ridge, tying it to each support to give the whole structure rigidity.

5 **Fertilize young plants** with an extra application of nitrogen-rich fertilizer, unless the growth is very green and lush.

6 **Harvest the beans** when the pods have reached the mature length for that variety. Pick frequently to encourage and stimulate continued production.

Lima & fava beans

Lima and fava beans are grown for their seeds. Lima beans, also known as butter beans, are more suited to the south while fava beans appreciate cooler, northern conditions. Both are easy to grow, and are sweet and delicious. Both are best at a soil pH of 5.5–6.0.

Lima beans: The seeds are large and flat and are harvested while they are still green, or they can be left on the vine to dry for winter use. They grow quickly in hot, summer weather. Once night temperatures fall below 60°F, they cease producing. Some lima beans grow as bushes, others develop as vines and are similar to pole beans (*see page 184*) in the way they are grown.

Fava beans: With fatter seeds than lima beans, and a need for much cooler conditions, the beans are carried in unusually fleshy pods and harvested before they start to harden. The young pods can also be picked and eaten whole. The shoot tips can be eaten; their removal will revive plants whose production is slowing down. In parts of zone 7 and zone 8 fava beans may be sown in fall; generally they are sown in early spring.

If grown where previous crops have been fertilized and compost added there should be no need to add more nutrients; if in doubt, give the soil a boost with a low-nitrogen fertilizer at the rate recommended on the package. The general approach to growing these two beans can be similar, in spite of their regional preferences.

Sowing

Sow lima beans where they are to grow, at a temperature of 70°F; at lower temperatures many seeds may fail. Sow seeds 3in. deep and 3in. apart, in rows 2–3ft. apart; check the seed packet for the requirements of individual varieties. For a head start, plant seed indoors in individual pots.

In early spring, as soon as it is possible to cultivate the soil, sow fava beans where they are to grow. This can be before the last frost in your area. Grow in two rows 10in. apart, making drills 2¾in. deep and sowing beans 8in. apart. Leave 28in. between double rows. Dwarf varieties, at 20in. tall, are useful for small yards and windy sites. Sow these 8in. apart, in single rows 10in. apart. This recommended spacing will allow easy access from the paths for staking, weeding, pest control, and picking. It also ensures good ventilation. Check the seed packet for the requirements of individual varieties.

FROM SOWING TO HARVESTING FAVA BEANS

1 Sow seeds 3in. deep, every 8in,. in double rows set 10in. apart. This wide spacing ensures good air circulation between plants to discourage fungal disease.

2 Hammer strong stakes into the ground at each end of the row to support tall plants in exposed areas. Run lengths of string along the row and attach them to the stakes. You may need extra stakes if the rows are very long.

3 Weed between the rows with a hoe, taking care not to damage the bean plants. If left to grow, weeds compete with your crop for nutrients, moisture, and sunlight. They also reduce ventilation and may harbor pests.

Cultivation & harvesting

Hoe out weeds as the beans grow and, if necessary, support plants with stakes and string. If the soil is dry when the beans are flowering, they produce fewer pods. In dry spells, give the ground a thorough soaking as the beans come into flower.

Harvesting of lima beans starts 70–90 days after sowing in early summer, while fava beans are ready about 90 days after a spring sowing, depending on the variety that has been sown. As soon as the beans are big enough to use, you can gather them. If you pick too late, however, the pods will harden and become fibrous, making the beans hard and starchy.

Common problems

Blackfly on beans can be very damaging, especially to fava beans. Treat them with an approved insecticide as soon as you spot them. Horticultural oils and insecticidal soaps are effective and are likely to spare natural predators. Control of bean beetles is as for pole beans (*see page 185*).

In mild, wet weather, the fungal disease chocolate spot can be damaging. The only remedies are promoting air flow by wider spacing, a more open position, and increased ventilation.

FAVA BEAN TOPS

Pinch out the tips of fava bean plants once they have flowered to deter blackfly. They can be eaten as 'greens' and are something of a delicacy. Lightly steamed, they taste a little like spinach.

4 **Soak the ground** if the weather is dry when the flowers first appear. Repeat 2 weeks later. This will help the flowers produce a good yield of pods.

5 **Harvest fava beans** after 28–35 weeks for fall-sown plantings, or 12–16 weeks for spring-sown plantings. To dry the beans for storing, dig up a plant, shake off the soil, and hang it upside down in a frost-free site until dry.

6 **Dig spent plants** into the soil. Like other legumes, fava beans are an invaluable resource as they fix nitrogen in small nodules on their roots—digging old plants into the soil will boost nutrient levels for the next crop.

Bush beans

Although bush beans are less productive per square foot than pole beans, they are easier to grow and take much less work. Kidney beans, lima beans, snap beans, and soy beans all have many bush varieties, but lima and soy beans require much warmer conditions than other bush beans. All commonly grown bush beans, however, are warm-season crops; they do not tolerate frost. Bush snap beans are the most extensively grown and are discussed here.

Most bush snap beans have the usual green pods, but there are also some very attractive varieties with purple, yellow, and speckled pods, which make decorative ornamental plants. Yellow snap beans are commonly known as wax beans. Many of the purple-podded varieties turn green when they are cooked. The pods of most snap bean are thin and rounded, and tapered at either end. Some varieties, however, such as 'Romano', have flattened pods. Snap beans can be eaten raw or cooked. They can also be frozen, canned, or pickled for use in winter.

Prepare the soil in the same way as for fava beans (*see page 186*). If you are not sure about the fertility of your soil, incorporate an all-purpose fertilizer at the rate recommended on the package.

Sowing & planting out

Sow directly in the garden after all danger of frost has passed, sowing the seed 1in. deep and about 2in. apart. You can start sowing directly outdoors once the soil temperature has reached 60°F. Planting can be done a little earlier in sandy soils, which warm faster than clay soils. Planting before the soil has warmed sufficiently will result in poor germination. Depending on the soil temperature, seeds germinate in 8–14 days.

If you are planting beans in a new area, you may want to consider treating your seed with a 'bean inoculant'. This is a beneficial bacterium that grows on the bean roots and helps convert atmospheric nitrogen into a usable form for the plant. Once beans have been successfully grown in a location, the bacteria are usually present in sufficient numbers for many years.

Bush snap beans often have short harvesting seasons so successional sowing every 2–3 weeks until late summer will ensure continuous production until early fall. Sometimes high temperatures will cause beans to temporarily stop producing. Blossoms may drop from plants and they may stop forming altogether. When the temperatures moderate, flowering and pod formation will resume once again.

Dwarf bush beans grow well in containers. With their pretty flowers, lush foliage, and slender pods, they give good value in summer as a decorative and productive plant.

Cultivation & harvesting

As soon as the beans are growing well, thin the seedlings to 6–8in. apart. At the same time, if the beans are anything less than green and lush, it is advisable to fertilize them with a nitrogen-rich fertilizer at the rate recommended on the package. Support is not essential for bush varieties of beans, but a few twigs pushed in among the plants can prevent them from flopping.

Bush snap beans are less sensitive to dry soil at flowering time than other beans and peas. However, thorough watering every ten days during dry spells will greatly increase the quantity and quality of the crop. Mulching beans will help to maintain an even level of moisture in the soil and help prevent moisture loss through evaporation. It also discourages the growth of weeds. Once beans begin to flower, reduce watering. Overwatering at this time can result in a reduction in the development of pods.

Pick the beans as soon as they are usable and harvest every two or three days. Snap beans are ready to harvest before the seeds mature; the pod should be firm and snap when bent. Be sure not to let any beans mature on the plant as this inhibits further production. Gather kidney beans as late as possible, then dry shell, and store them.

Common problems

A number of pests can cause problems for bush beans, including aphids, blackflies, and Mexican bean beetles.

Spider mites can cause plants to turn bronze and dry up, particularly during hot, dry periods. Control aphids and blackflies by using a horticultural oil or insecticidal soap, as they do least harm to natural predators. Spider mites can often be successfully controlled with repeated sprays of cold water. Several biological controls are available for bean beetles; removal of crop debris can prevent their spread. If further control is necessary, consult your local cooperative extension service for recommendations.

Several diseases of beans, including bean common mosaic virus, rust, and anthracnose, can be avoided by selecting resistant varieties. Other diseases such as bacterial blight and halo blight are transmitted in infected seeds, so be sure to purchase disease-free seed from a reputable supplier. Because several diseases are spread by watering, avoid overhead sprinklers. Instead, use soaker hoses along the length of the row or a hose with a waterbreaker that directs the water to the plant roots rather than foliage. To further reduce the spread of diseases, avoid working near the beans or harvesting them when wet.

FROM SOWING TO HARVESTING BUSH SNAP BEANS

1 Sow seeds in drills 2in. deep and 2–3in. apart. Grow in fertile soil in full sun with a pH no lower than 6. If grown where previous crops have been fertilized, there should be no need to add extra nutrients. Wait until the soil temperature has reached 60°F before sowing outdoors. Thin seedlings to a final spacing of 6–8in. between plants.

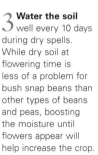

2 Hoe plants regularly to remove weeds before they compete with your crops for nutrients, moisture, and sunlight. Take care not to damage the roots or topgrowth of the young plants. Mulch to prevent weeds from regrowing.

3 Water the soil well every 10 days during dry spells. While dry soil at flowering time is less of a problem for bush snap beans than other types of beans and peas, boosting the moisture until flowers appear will help increase the crop.

4 Harvest beans regularly to encourage plants to keep producing pods. Snap beans have a relatively short, concentrated production season, so make successive sowings every 2–3 weeks to assure a continuous supply.

THE ONION FAMILY

The onion family, which includes garlic, leeks, onions, and shallots, are all easy to grow. They either store well or, in the case of leeks, are very hardy, which makes them invaluable in winter when other vegetables are in short supply. Their distinctive flavor comes from sulfur compounds produced by enzymes released when the plant tissue is cut. These compounds are not only flavorful but are also claimed to have medicinal properties. As all the onion family are susceptible to onion white rot, a persistent soil-borne disease, never grow them on the same piece of ground two years in a row.

Onions

Bulb onions can be grown from seed, young plants, or small bulbs called 'sets'. Initially, they concentrate their efforts on sending up leaves, then, when a certain critical day length is reached in late spring, the process of bulb formation is triggered. If left in the ground for a second year, the bulb sends up flowers and sets seed.

Onions do best in areas with cool spring weather that is not too dry, followed by drier, hotter summers. The cool, damp spring weather encourages good early growth and hotter summer weather ensures that the bulbs ripen well and are good for winter storage. Unfortunately, if sown or planted too early, onion plants 'mistake' cold weather in spring for winter, causing them to 'bolt', which means they flower in the first year. Your aim, therefore, is to plant onions out as early as possible to make a strong plant by midspring, but not so early that bolting occurs.

For salad greens, scallions are ideal although the thinnings of bulb onions can also be a good salad crop.

Sowing & planting

Choose a site in full sun, in fertile, well-drained soil. Onions will not grow well on acidic soils with a pH of less

FROM PLANTING TO HARVESTING ONION SETS

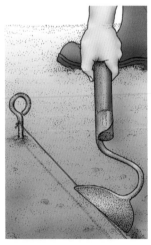

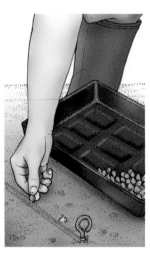

1 **Make a drill** ¾in. deep. To help keep it straight, run the edge of a hoe along a length of string held taut between two pegs knocked into the ground.

2 **Plant sets** 2–3in. apart. Push each bulb firmly into the soil, burying it so only the tip is visible. Cover with a row cover to deter birds and warm the crop.

3 **Water plants** during dry spells. They need little water at other times, but they are easily swamped by weeds, so hoe around the plants regularly.

4 **Harvest onions** after 12–18 weeks. Pull them as needed. For onions to store, wait until their leaves bend over before digging up. Leave to dry for about 10 days.

Preparing to grow *see page 152* | **Sowing & growing** *see page 156* | **Common problems** *see page 220*

FROM PLANTING TO HARVESTING SCALLIONS

1 **Sow seeds** a finger's width apart in rows 4in. apart. Make successive sowings every 3 weeks from early spring to summer for a continuous crop. Seed can be sown from late winter in mild areas, under a row cover. Alternatively, sow the seeds at the same spacing in 3in. wide blocks set 6in. apart.

2 **Thin out** the developing onions to 1in. apart. The thinnings can be used in a salad. Scallions are ready to harvest just 8 weeks after sowing. Lift them gently with a hand fork.

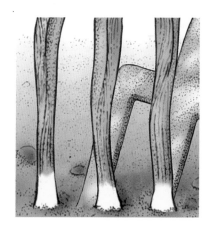

than 6. Be sure your soil is well drained, has been deeply cultivated, and is free of stones. Before sowing, add plenty of well-rotted compost, then an all-purpose fertilizer at the rate on the package.

In most gardens, onion sets are the best way to grow onions, but only a limited range of varieties are offered compared to seeds. Sets are miniature onion bulbs that are too small to form flowers if subjected to cold.

Plant onion sets in spring every 2–3in. in drills ³⁄₄in. deep. Make the rows 10in. apart. Bury the sets so that only their tips show. To prevent birds from dislodging them, cover your sets with a floating row cover until they are firmly rooted; the extra warmth will speed up growth.

In mild regions, onions can be raised from seeds sown outdoors (*see right*), in early spring in drills ¹⁄₂in. deep. Space seeds a finger-width apart and in rows 10in. apart; thin to 2–3in. between plants.

Seeds sown indoors in late winter in cell trays of all-purpose mix, however, are more reliable. Sow either two seeds per cell and thin later to one plant, or sow six or seven seeds per larger cell to get a clump of four to five plants. When the plant roots start to bind the growing mix, they can be planted out.

Cultivation

Onions have limited root systems so thorough watering after planting out and in dry spells is essential. To encourage strong growth in spring, scatter a nitrogen-rich fertilizer at the rate recommended on the package. Onion leaves cast little shade, so the ground around them is quickly colonized by weeds.

Onions are unusually susceptible to competition from weeds, so regularly hoe and hand weed carefully around the plants, especially in the early weeks when the young onions are particularly vulnerable.

Harvesting & storing

If bulbs begin to appear crowded, harvest every other one for fresh use. This will provide the required space for the remaining bulbs to develop.

As the bulbs mature in summer, the foliage topples; allow this to happen naturally. Once the tops have fallen over, the bulbs will not swell further and the crop can be lifted for drying. Loosen their roots with a fork if you intend to dry them in the sun, but in wet weather you

SOWING ONIONS OUTDOORS

1 **Sow seeds** in soil that has been previously amended with compost and fertilizer. Mark out a drill ½in. deep and sow seeds about ½in. apart. The rows should be 10in. apart.

2 **Fertilize plants** in spring with 1oz. of nitrogen-rich fertilizer. This will ensure bigger bulbs. Thin out plants to a spacing of 2–3in. apart. By late summer your onions will be ready to harvest.

DRYING & STORING ONIONS

1 Loosen ripe onions with a fork on a sunny day and let them dry for about a week. Onions are ripe once the foliage flops over. Let this process happen naturally; if you attempt to speed things up by toppling the foliage yourself, it will encourage disease.

2 Lift onions and spread them out to dry in a warm, dry, airy place—if the weather is damp or wet. If you have room indoors, bring them in to dry on racks. It can take up to 2 weeks.

3 Inspect each onion, checking whether the skins feel papery. If not, leave them for a few more days to dry out. Any onions with thick necks or those showing the first signs of rot should be used immediately for cooking; store only blemish-free onions.

4 Store onions by placing them carefully in layers in an open-sided wooden box. Place the box somewhere well ventilated. Cold will not harm them, but dampness and poor air circulation will lead to rapid deterioration. Examine them regularly and discard any onions that are blemished or showing signs of deterioration.

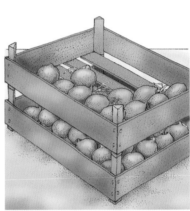

should lift the bulbs and dry them under cover. Once dried, onion bulbs should be stored in cool, dry, airy conditions (*see above*).

Common problems

Onions are damaged by onion fly and onion thrips, although these rarely prove too much of a problem in gardens. Insect-proof mesh will keep onion fly at bay. There are no reliable controls for onion thrips, but where they have been well watered and well fed crops seldom suffer serious damage.

In mild, persistently wet weather, onion downy mildew may develop on damp foliage. Crop rotation, removal of all infected material, and avoiding growing perennial onions nearby should reduce damage.

Onion white rot persists in the soil, so careful crop rotation and removal of all infected material are necessary to allow crops to grow. In severe infestations, grow in raised beds or pots filled with sterile potting mix.

Other pests and diseases may cause problems in some regions; consult your local cooperative extension service for advice on local onion pests and diseases.

After harvest, onions are usually dried as they are the ideal crop for storing for use in the kitchen through the winter. Put aside any damaged or less-than-perfect onions for immediate consumption.

Garlic & shallots

Both garlic and shallots are easy to grow. They are usually problem free, but onion white rot can be damaging (*see facing page*). Prepare soil as for onions (*see page 190*), but use half the fertilizer. If growth seems weak in spring, scatter a nitrogen-rich fertilizer at the rate on the package. Garlic and shallots seldom require watering. Weeding, however, must be done regularly as their leaves cast little shade and weeds soon exploit the space around them.

By early to midsummer their foliage yellows and dies back. The bulbs can then be eased out of the soil and dried and stored as for onions (*see facing page*).

Growing garlic

Split your garlic bulbs into separate cloves and plant them out in fall or early winter or, for certain varieties, in early spring. Depending on the planting time, they take 16–36 weeks to mature. Grow in rows 14–18in. apart, with 4–6in. between plants. Bury your cloves 1in. deep so the tip is just visible, then firm the soil around them to prevent them being dislodged by frost or birds. Rust occasionally covers and destroys the foliage—the only remedy is crop rotation, which prevents it from building up.

The ideal time to plant is in fall, 3–6 weeks before the first expected frost in your area. This allows the roots to grow before winter. In cold areas, provide a mulch 4in. deep to protect the crop over winter. Garlic can also be planted in spring. Set the cloves as soon as the soil is workable to allow the longest possible growing season.

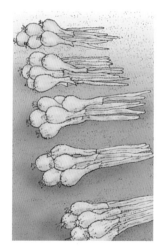

PLANTING GARLIC

Use your fingers to pull a garlic bulb apart, gently separating the individual cloves; damaged bulbs are susceptible to rotting. When planting, position the cloves pointed ends up.

Growing shallots

Shallots are exceptionally easy to grow (*see below*). Although they can be raised from seeds—sown as for onions (*see page 191*)—it is much easier to split the bulbs into segments, in the same way as garlic, and plant those.

In fall, early winter, or as soon the soil is workable in early spring depending on the climate in your area, plant the bulbs in drills ¾in. deep. Set them 4–6in. apart, barely covering them with soil but firming it around them to prevent them becoming dislodged by birds and frost. Make the rows 10–12in. apart. Onion downy mildew can be damaging (*see facing page*).

FROM PLANTING TO HARVESTING SHALLOTS

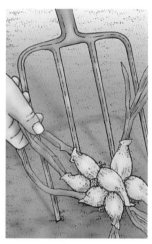

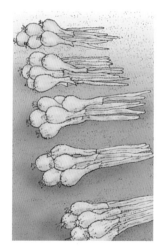

1 **Plant shallot bulbs** with their tips just showing. By early summer, each set will develop into a clump.

2 **Hoe regularly** between rows to keep the weeds at bay. You only need to water during prolonged dry spells.

3 **Harvest shallots** with a fork when the leaves die down and the bulbs are a good size.

4 **Dry bulbs** for storing by spreading them out on the ground in the sun for a few days. If it rains, dry them under cover.

Leeks

Leeks require good soil and a long growing season but are otherwise easy to grow, with few pest and disease problems. They are also among the hardier vegetables so can be harvested in winter in many areas. They are grown from seeds in the same way as onions.

Seed can be sown outdoors in areas with long, mild springs, but in many areas sowing in a protected environment is advisable.

Sowing & cultivation

Sow seeds outdoors in early spring, a finger's width apart in drills ½–⅜in. deep and 8in. apart. Indoor sowing is often more convenient, and essential in many areas. Sow in cell packs, either two seeds per small cell, thinning to one, or five to seven seeds per larger cell to make a clump of four to five plants. Plant out into a seedbed once the roots bind the growing mix together. After thinning in early to midsummer, transplant the seedlings when they are at least pencil thickness into deep planting holes or trenches.

Leeks are traditionally blanched by planting into deep holes or trenches 4in. deep and 4–6in. apart, in rows 12in. apart. It is easier to plant leeks from cells in the base of a drill, and space clumps 12in. apart. Draw soil around the plants in drills; watering washes enough soil into holes to cover the roots, and the holes gradually fill. As the leeks grow, pull soil around the plants to exclude light or steadily fill trenches.

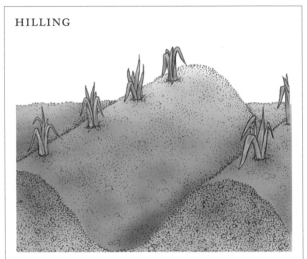

HILLING

Leeks grow perfectly well planted on the level, but excluding light increases the length of the tender white stem and controls weeds. Blanching with a collar of opaque material, such as cardboard, can supplement or even replace hilling.

Leeks appreciate generous watering in dry spells. Add nitrogen-rich fertilizer at the rate on the package in midsummer if growth appears to be flagging.

Careful weeding is needed in the early stages. Leeks can be affected by onion white rot, but usually suffer only from rust, and this seldom causes severe losses. Partially resistant varieties are available.

FROM SOWING TO HARVESTING LEEKS

1 **Sow** in a prepared seedbed in early spring in suitable areas. Otherwise sow in a protected environment.

2 **Thin** to ¾–1¼in. between plants in early summer, and firm back the soil around remaining plants.

3 **Transplant** from early to midsummer. Mulch around the plants or, for longer white stems, hill them (*see box, above*).

4 **Harvest** from late fall. Cover a few with several layers of row cover so that you can lift them even during heavy frost.

Preparing to grow *see page 152* | **Sowing & growing** *see page 156* | **Common problems** *see page 220*

ROOTS & TUBERS

Roots are not the most glamorous occupants of the vegetable garden, and gardeners with very limited space may feel inclined to omit them altogether. But most root crops can be grown in containers, and short-term crops such as carrots, early potatoes, and turnips can make good use of space, allowing for two harvests a year from the same ground. Young, freshly lifted roots are quite different from the fare found in supermarkets. Root crops come from a wide range of plant families and have varied requirements, but some needs are common to all: well-cultivated soil and crop rotation.

Carrots

Carrots are biennials, forming a fleshy root in the first year and flowering in the second. They are grown as annuals, harvested before they flower or produce seed. Gardeners are fortunate in having an amazing range of carrot varieties to choose from. Carrots are usually orange, but recently white, yellow, red, and purple roots that were once common have been reintroduced.

Over the years carrots have been classified in a confusing range of categories. However, there are three main types.

Finger carrots: Producing early slender roots, these are tender enough to be eaten raw or lightly steamed. May become tougher as they become thumb-thick and fatter.

Maincrop carrots: These varieties are fatter, producing heavy, fine-flavored yields later in the season. They are the best for winter storage.

Round carrots: Spherical, marble to golf-ball-sized roots, ideal for shallow stony soils and for containers.

Sowing, cultivation, & harvesting

Any friable, well-drained, sunny soil will support carrots. Dig over heavy soil in late fall or winter, or loosen lighter soils with a fork in spring, removing as many stones as possible to help reduce the number of 'fanged' roots. Soil fertility need only be moderate. Ideally, plant on ground that had compost or manure for a preceding crop, and rake in an all-purpose fertilizer at the rate on the package. Carrots dislike acid soils—a pH of 6.5–7 is ideal.

Sow carrots in rows ½–⅜in. deep, spacing seeds about a finger's width apart. Carrots are not damaged by light frosts. Sow in rows 8in. apart after the danger of heavy frost has passed for early carrots, and 12in. apart for later,

larger carrots. The first sowing is usually made in early spring, where the soil is light enough, as soon as the soil can be worked, to give a crop that is lifted in midsummer.

Gardeners with heavy clay soil can use raised beds or tubs for early spring sowings, using finger and round varieties. Sow in the ground in midspring for late summer and early fall lifting. Sow the larger varieties in late spring

Carrots have been bred in orange shades in the West for centuries, but the wider range of colors originally found is now being bred again. Red carrots in particular have 'superfood' status.

for use in late fall or winter. In some areas, carrots can also be sown from late summer to fall for winter harvest.

Thin carrots as soon as possible, to ³⁄₄in. apart for early carrots, 2–4in. for midseason and late crops. Watering is usually unnecessary, but in really dry spells a thorough soak every ten days will help swell the crop. Regular and careful hand weeding and hoeing are required. To prevent carrot shoulders from turning green, carefully mound soil over the tops of exposed roots.

Carrots can be used as soon as roots are a worthwhile size. A good soaking can make pulling carrots from the ground easier. They can be lifted and stored in boxes of sand for winter use; this is especially useful on wet, heavy clay soils and in very cold areas. In areas with milder winters, it is better to leave the crop in the ground and cover it with a frost-excluding layer of cardboard, topped with black plastic landscape fabric to keep the carrots dry.

Common problems

Garden carrots usually only suffer significant damage from carrot rust fly, and a few resistant varieties are now available. Covering with floating row cover will exclude carrot rust fly, but it must be replaced with insect-proof mesh, beginning in early summer, as the heat trapped by the floating row cover could harm the crop.

Alternatively, restrict your carrot crop to a space no more than 6ft. across and erect a vertical barrier 30in. tall around the area. This will largely exclude the carrot rust fly, which struggles to fly over the barrier and needs more than 6ft. to descend to the crop.

FROM SOWING TO HARVESTING CARROTS

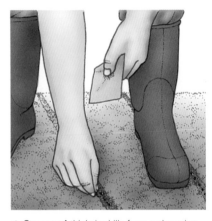

1 **Sow seed** thinly in drills from early spring after raking the ground to a fine texture. Row covers exclude carrot rust fly and greatly improve the reliability of early sowings.

2 **Thin seedlings** to the appropriate spacing when the first 4–5 leaves appear. Remove thinnings promptly and cover crops; the smell of bruised leaves attracts the carrot rust fly.

3 **Water deeply in dry spells** and hoe or mulch between the rows to keep down weeds, because the feathery foliage of carrots is not effective at suppressing them.

4 **Harvest carrots** from summer onward as they are ready. Soaking the soil makes pulling the roots easier.

5 **Protect from frost** with a loose mulch of straw in midfall if your soil and local conditions allow you to leave crops in the ground. The foliage will die back naturally.

6 **Lift for storage** if necessary. Twist off foliage and store sound roots in boxes of dry sand, spaced so that they do not touch, in a cool but frost-free place.

Preparing to grow *see page 152* | **Sowing & growing** *see page 156* | **Common problems** *see page 220*

Parsnips

Parsnips are an invaluable, late-season root crop and are easy to grow, but do require a long growing season. They occupy space for a considerable time, but to make the most use of the space they can be interplanted with quicker-growing crops such as radish or salad greens. The vigor and disease resistance of many hybrid varieties make them especially useful.

Sowing, cultivation, & harvest

Any friable, well-drained soil in full sun is suitable; a pH of 6.5–7 is ideal, but parsnips are not fussy. Choose ground that has had compost or manure applied for a preceding crop. Buy fresh seeds every year, because parsnip seeds are short-lived, and sow in early spring, as soon as the soil is warm and dry enough. Gardeners with heavy clay soils might have to delay sowing until midspring or grow parsnips and other crops in raised beds. Watering is seldom necessary, but in really dry spells a thorough soak every ten days will help swell the crop. Harvest as needed, beginning in late fall.

Parsnips can be damaged by carrot rust fly; control these as for carrots (*see facing page*). Where parsnip canker rots roots, use resistant varieties, exclude carrot rust fly to minimize damage to roots, and apply lime. Leaf miners cause damage that is more cosmetic than significant, and picking off the worst affected leaves is all that is required.

FROM SOWING TO HARVESTING PARSNIPS

1 **Dig heavy soils** in late fall or winter or loosen lighter soils with a fork in spring to provide the right structure. Remove stones to help reduce incidences of 'fanged' roots.

2 **Rake in an all-purpose fertilizer** at the rate on the package. Covering soil with clear plastic landscape fabric from midwinter assists successful germination.

3 **Sow seeds** ½–¾in. deep and a finger's width apart, or station sow at 4in. intervals, in rows 14in. apart. Cover with row covers to improve germination.

4 **When 4–5 leaves appear**, thin seedlings as soon as possible to 4in. If seeds were station sown, remove weaker seedlings to leave one strong plant at each station.

5 **Hoe and weed** by hand, taking care not to damage the 'shoulders' of the swelling roots because damage encourages canker. The thick foliage will suppress many weeds.

6 **Lift in fall** for storage when the foliage dies down. Alternatively, cover the crop with a cardboard box topped with plastic landscape fabric to repel rain, and lift as needed.

Radishes

Summer radishes are a well-known salad crop, while larger-rooted, hot-flavored winter radishes can be grated into salad greens, soups, or casseroles, and immature seed pods can be eaten raw. Oriental radishes, often called mooli or daikon, are grown as winter radish.

Sowing & cultivation

All radishes belong to the brassica family, but summer radishes grow too fast to suffer from soil-borne diseases. They can be grown in any part of the rotation, or as catch crops and intercrops. Winter radishes are slower to mature. Any fertile garden soil in full sun is suitable; if in doubt treat as for turnips (*see page 200*).

In most regions, summer radishes can be sown from late winter to late summer, in drills ½–¾in. deep and 6in. apart, leaving about a thumb's width between seeds. Protect early sowings before midspring with row covers. Thin seedlings to ¾–1¼in. apart if necessary. Water in dry spells: quick growth gives tender, crisp roots, and dry soils produce poor-quality roots. To produce seedpods, just let plants go to seed, which they do very quickly in summer. Long-podded or rattail varieties are available for the best seedpods, which are produced for several weeks throughout summer.

Sow winter radish in late summer, as for summer radishes (*see below*), but leaving 12in. between rows and thinning the young plants to 4–6in.

Common problems

Cabbage root fly is the only significant pest. Protect winter radish with insect-proof mesh; summer radishes may need protection but often grow too fast for serious damage. Flea beetles and aphids can cause minor damage.

FROM SOWING TO HARVESTING SUMMER RADISHES

1 **Sow seeds** in drills where they are to grow. Radishes soon become coarse and unpleasantly fiery, so sow every 2–3 weeks for mild, tender roots.

2 **Thin seedlings** as soon as they can be handled by their leaves, as they emerge rapidly in warm weather.

3 **Lift roots regularly** when they begin to mature. This takes 6–8 weeks for early sowings, or as little as 3–4 weeks for sowings in midsummer.

FROM SOWING TO HARVESTING WINTER RADISHES

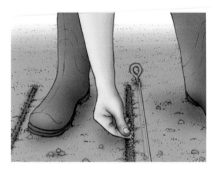

1 **Sow seeds** in drills in late summer. The seeds can be station sown (*see page 157*) n groups of 3–4 seeds at 4–6in. intervals.

2 **Thin seedlings** as soon as they can be handled, leaving one plant at each station if the seeds were station sown. Water the seeds afterward.

3 **Lift for storage** in midfall in cold regions. Elsewhere, winter radishes are very hardy, although you should protect Oriental winter radishes with a double layer of row covers.

Beet

Beets are quick growing and generally free of pests and diseases so can be used anywhere in the crop rotation plan. They can be prepared straight from the ground as well as stored for winter use. The round, red beet is the most familiar type, but there are also slower-growing varieties with cylindrical roots for winter storage, as well as varieties with white, yellow, or color-banded roots.

Sowing & cultivation

Beets can be grown as both spring and fall crops. In mild regions they can be planted in winter. Any well-drained, fertile, sunny soil that is not acid (below pH 6) is suitable. Add plenty of well-rotted compost, then rake in an all-purpose fertilizer at the rate recommended on the package. Sow beet seed ¾in. deep, spacing them about a thumb's width apart, in rows 14in. apart. What looks like a beet seed is usually a cluster of several seeds so more than one seedling may arise from the cluster. Many modern hybrid varieties, however, have only one seed in each cluster and so produce only one seedling.

On clay soils or in colder regions, raise plants indoors in cell packs or propagation trays. Sow two seeds per cell, thinning to one plant as soon as possible and planting out under row covers in late spring. For a fall harvest, sow outdoors in midsummer. Thin beet as soon as possible, with final spacings according to the variety size. Watering in really dry spells, with a thorough soak every ten days, will help to swell the crop.

Leaf miners are the only significant pest of beet: control by removing infested leaves as soon as seen. Aphids may sometimes need controlling with a hard spray of water or application of insecticidal soap.

FROM SOWING TO HARVESTING BEET

1 **Prepare the ground** in early spring and rake to a fine texture so it will be easy for the seedlings to grow in it.

2 **Sow thinly** or station sow (*see page 157*) when the soil is warm and dry enough. Protect earlier sowings with row covers.

3 **Thin seedlings** when 4–5 leaves appear. Spacings vary, from 3in. for small beets to 6in. for large ones.

4 **Hoe very carefully** or pull weeds by hand to avoid damaging the roots. The thick foliage helps to suppress weeds.

5 **Harvest roots** from summer onward for immediate use or storage. Lift carefully, and avoid breaking the skin.

6 **Store only undamaged roots** in boxes of sand for a ready-to-use, winter supply.

Rutabaga, turnips, & kohlrabi

Rutabaga and turnips are both members of the cabbage family, and should be included in the cabbage part of your crop rotation. Both are grown for their edible roots. The leaves of turnips can also be eaten. Kohlrabi is grown in the same way as turnips but the swollen stem is the edible part. Some varieties have purple coloring and are grown for their ornamental as well as culinary value.

Turnips are quick growing; both spring and fall crops can be grown in most regions. Young roots are amazingly succulent and sweetly flavored; older roots become woody and coarse flavored. Rutabaga grows slowly but is very hardy. It has harder, yellower flesh with a distinctive, sweet flavor, and its leaves usually arise from a 'neck'. Both are badly affected by drought; rutabaga in particular grows best in moist, cool soil. Kohlrabi is considered to be much less drought sensitive.

Site & soil

These crops are usually sown where they are to grow, but where convenient they can be grown in cell packs or propagation trays, sowing three seeds per cell and thinning to the strongest seedling as soon as possible. Any seed starter or all-purpose mix can be used.

Any fertile, well-drained garden soil in full sun suits rutabaga, kohlrabi, and turnips, while light shade is

RUTABAGA SHOOTS AS GREENS

Rutabaga can be lifted in midwinter, trimmed, and packed into boxes of compost or soil. If kept in a basement, garage, or shed in semidarkness, they will produce blanched greens.

acceptable for turnip tops. Dig in plenty of well-rotted compost or manure. For the best yields, rake in an all-purpose fertilizer at the application rate recommended on the package. Acid soils promote clubroot; where this disease is present liming to at least pH 6.5 is the best way of reducing damage. Resistant varieties are sometimes available, but these may not be resistant to all forms of

FROM SOWING TO HARVESTING TURNIPS

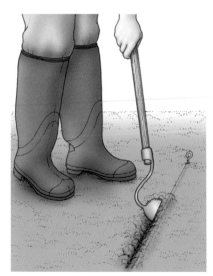

1 **Prepare the ground** and water the day before sowing. Draw out drills and water the bases of the drills if the soil is at all dry.

2 **Sow thinly**, allowing about a thumb's width between seeds. Cover each drill, firm the soil, and gently rake over.

3 **Thin seedlings** to 3in. apart as soon as they are large enough to be handled. Water after thinning, especially if the weather is dry.

clubroot. Cabbage root maggots may also be a problem; rotate crops to avoid a buildup of this pest.

Sowing, cultivation, & harvesting

Sow summer turnips (*see below*) from late winter or early spring, initially protecting with row covers in colder climates. The earliest sowings, gathered in early summer when few other vegetables are available, are the most valuable, but later sowings in summer produce a fall crop with a flavor that sweetens after exposure to frost.

Sow turnip and kohlrabi seeds a thumb's width apart, in drills ½–³⁄₈in. deep and 12in. apart. Thin as soon as possible. Where crops are not doing well, apply a nitrogen-rich fertilizer. Water in dry spells and mulch around plants. Harvest as soon as they are usable, that is, from about golf-ball size. Store turnips for winter use in boxes of sand in a frost-free basement, garage, or shed.

Slower-growing rutabaga is sown from late spring to early summer in the same way as turnips, but allowing 16in. between rows and thinning to 10in. Water in dry summer weather to swell the roots and help to prevent powdery mildew, which is especially damaging to drought-stressed crops. The roots are ready to use beginning in late fall. Rutabaga often survives unprotected in the soil in mild regions; elsewhere, store as for turnips.

Common problems

These crops suffer from the same pests and diseases as other brassicas. Cabbage root fly larvae in particular will

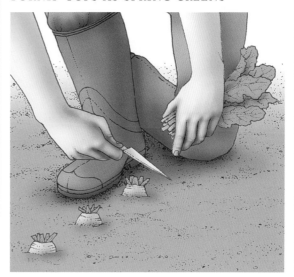

TURNIP TOPS AS SPRING GREENS

The roots of early-fall sowings will not swell before winter, but they may survive the winter to produce a crop of early greens in spring. These will sprout again to produce a further crop.

kill young plants and tunnel into maturing roots, making them unusable. Covering initially with a row cover, and then with insect-proof mesh in summer, prevents damage. Row cover also excludes flea beetles, which can damage young plants from midspring, and aphids and caterpillars, but slugs thrive beneath row cover and mesh and usually need to be controlled.

4 **Thin plants again** to 6in. when their leaves begin to touch those of their neighbors in the row. Firm the soil afterward.

5 **Hoe between rows**, taking care not to damage the developing roots. Ensure that the plants never dry out.

6 **Harvest young turnips** as needed, or by late fall in all but the mildest areas. Store in sand or dry soil in a frost-free basement.

Potatoes

Potatoes are a major source of energy in many people's diets, and contain high-quality protein and useful amounts of vitamins, especially vitamin C.

Although freely available in stores at good prices, it is well worth growing your own, not only for a far better flavor but also because commercially-grown potatoes are usually treated with more agricultural chemicals than most crops and you may wish to avoid food grown with these treatments. Potatoes are easy to grow, but unfortunately suffer from some serious pests and diseases.

Types of potato

Early potatoes: (short season) Maturing 60–80 days after planting and harvested in early to midsummer, new potatoes are the first crop of the new season and have exquisite texture and flavor. If space is limited in your vegetable garden, grow only new potatoes.

Maincrop potatoes: (midseason) Maturing 80–100 days after planting, the crop is usually heavier than that of early potatoes with more and larger potatoes, but slugs and blight will need to be controlled.

Storage potatoes: (long season) Maturing 100–130 days after planting, these are the varieties to grow for storage through the winter and to produce large potatoes for baking. Again, slugs and blight can be a problem.

Fingerlings: Maturing at various stages of the season, fingerlings have a long, slender shape and a superb flavor. They are more likely to suffer from pests and diseases.

A vast array of potato varieties is available, both old heirloom ones and modern introductions. Not all varieties

FROM PLANTING TO HARVESTING HILLED POTATOES

1 **Prepare the ground** well in advance with well-rotted compost, manure, and fertilizer, and cultivate the fine soil texture needed for hilling the soil.

2 **Dig drills** 4–6in. deep, spaced appropriately for the type of potatoes you are planting: earlies are closest together, storage potatoes the most widely spaced.

3 **Place the tubers** in the drills with the shoots of the rose end (*see facing page*) uppermost. Space the tubers according to the type of crop.

4 **Cover the drills,** using a draw hoe to pull back the earth. Mound it over the drills into a ridge 4–6in. high.

5 **Water during dry weather** through the growing season, particularly at the start of summer and when the plants flower. Hoe out weeds to prevent competition for water and nutrients.

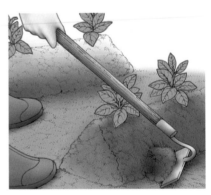

6 **Hill the rows** regularly, drawing soil up from the drill between, until the ridges are 12–15in. high.

Preparing to grow *see page 152* | **Sowing & growing** *see page 156* | **Common problems** *see page 220*

are suitable for all climates and their colors, flavors, and textures differ greatly, so try to grow two or three varieties of each type to discover those that suit you and your climate best.

Seed potatoes & presprouting

Potatoes are usually grown from 'seed potatoes', tubers grown specifically for farmers and gardeners to grow new crops. Do not try to grow store-bought potatoes as they are often treated to prevent shoots growing. Always buy seed potatoes that are certified disease free. Although good crops may be raised from tubers you have saved from your previous crop, they will seldom be as successful and carry the risk of spreading disease.

Most of the buds or 'eyes' present on the tuber are found at one end, called the 'rose end'. The buds are dormant when the tuber is harvested, but they are ready to start growing by spring when tubers are bought. Many gardeners simply plant their seed potatoes in the ground, but to get off to a flying start it pays to presprout them (also called greening). This simply means standing the tubers in a light, warm (70°F) place to encourage the buds to start to grow. Short, stubby shoots will develop and after about ten days the seed potatoes are ready to plant.

Site & soil

Any fertile, well-drained garden soil in full sun suits potatoes. Unlike most vegetables they don't object to acid soils, but common scab disease can disfigure potatoes grown in alkaline soils. Choose scab-resistant varieties where the soil has been limed. Leave at least two, and preferably three, full years between potato crops on the same soil, to prevent buildup of soil-borne pests and diseases.

PRESPROUTING POTATOES

Buy seed tubers as early as possible. Tubers the size of hen's eggs are best. Large potatoes can be cut into several pieces, each with at least 2 or 3 eyes. Allow pieces to cure for at least 24 hours prior to planting.

After purchasing, place each tuber pointed end uppermost in a tray or shallow box, rejecting any that are damaged. Place them in a warm, frost-free place in good light. Tubers soon get into a tangled mess if neglected and left in their packaging.

Organic matter not only fertilizes the plants but also helps to prevent scab and hold moisture, greatly increasing the yield. Therefore add masses of well-rotted compost in winter or early spring. Before planting the presprouted tubers, scatter on the soil an all-purpose fertilizer at the rate recommended on the package.

Planting & cultivation

In many regions, early potatoes are among the first crops to be planted, often around St. Patrick's Day. After that,

7 **Lift early potatoes** in early summer, when the flowers are fully open. Using a flat-tined fork will help to avoid damage.

8 **Lift maincrop and storage** potatoes from midsummer onward, when the foliage tops begin to die down.

9 **Store the tubers** in a frost-free place. Use sacks or trays, but make regular inspections and remove any rotten tubers.

Digging potatoes is always exciting. Use a fork to carefully turn the soil without piercing tubers. Use any damaged potatoes as soon as possible; dry undamaged tubers before storing in a cool, dry place.

weeds without harming the plants. As the shoots grow, lightly cover them with soil every week or so. This kills any weeds, encourages tubers to form at the stem bases, and ensures tubers are always covered with soil and protected from both light and blight spores falling from infected foliage. Exposure to light will cause potatoes to turn green and accumulate toxins in their skins.

A thorough soak in early summer if the weather turns dry can lead to more tubers being formed and will help to reduce scab infection. Ideally, potatoes should never be allowed to suffer from drought. Mulching rows with compost or straw helps retain soil moisture, suppresses weeds, and moderates soil temperature.

Harvesting

Begin harvesting as soon as early tubers are usable—usually when they are about the size of a chicken egg. Use your fingers to feel your way through the loose soil and remove the tubers you need without disturbing the roots too much. That way, the remaining tubers will continue to grow until the top of the plant dies back, then you can dig the rest. Maincrops can be dug and stored when their foliage dies back and as soon as their skins 'set'. Test this by pressing the skin firmly with finger and thumb—it should resist being rubbed from the flesh. Leave storage potatoes as long as possible to 'bulk up'.

When the time comes to lift, cut off remaining foliage and leave for two weeks to let the skins harden and any blight spores decline. Then ease the tubers from the soil with a fork, taking great care not to pierce them with the fork or bruise them by careless handling. Leave to dry on the surface for two hours before storing. Store sound, disease-free tubers in burlap or paper sacks, keeping them dry and cool but frost free and inspecting them every month to remove any diseased tubers. Diseased tubers should be burnt or consigned to the garbage.

Common problems

Colorado potato beetle (*see page 222*) and late blight (*see page 224*) are the greatest threats to your potato crop. Trapping the beetles is a good approach, while late blight can be controlled by organic and other fungicides, and resistant varieties are available.

Viral diseases (*see page 44*) can be crippling, but the danger is largely eliminated by buying only certified disease-free seed potatoes. Viral diseases are spread by aphids (*see page 49*), another reason to keep them under strict control. Potato cyst nematodes (*see page 222*) are especially damaging as they remain in the soil for many years to infect later crops.

determine your planting time by the number of the days your varieties need to be ready for harvesting. Navigating these variables in your own particular climate can be difficult if you are new to growing potatoes, so it is a good idea to get local advice.

The longer their growing season the more room they need, so space early potatoes 12in. apart, in rows that are 24in. apart; set maincrops 14in. apart in rows 28in. apart; and plant storage varieties 16in. apart in rows 30in. apart.

Tubers should be set in drills 4–6in. deep (*see page 202*). Cover the tubers and make a slight ridge over the drills, so you know where the potatoes will emerge and can hoe

Sweet potatoes

Sweet potato is a tropical, heat-loving crop that thrives in full sun and well-drained soils. Although it is an attractive, ground-covering vine, it can overtake a small garden. Some varieties are grown as ornamental foliage plants, but their roots are inferior for consumption. Many gardeners choose to grow their sweet potatoes in a separate area where the vining stems can spread freely. Bush types are more appropriate for smaller gardens.

Because they have a long growing season, sweet potatoes are most suitable for warmer regions. Recently, however, short-season varieties have been developed that produce good crops as far north as Maine and Canada.

Planting & cultivation

Sweet potatoes are usually grown from rooted cuttings called 'slips', which should be certified as disease free.

Prepare the soil and fertilize as you would for potatoes (*see page 202*). Pull soil up to form 12in. high, ridged rows before planting. After all danger of frost has passed, plant the slips 12–15in. apart along the ridge in rows that are spaced 3–4ft. apart.

Water thoroughly after planting and during dry periods, but stop watering about two weeks prior to harvest. Mulching plants with compost or straw will help suppress weeds and conserve moisture.

Harvesting

Sweet potatoes should be harvested before a hard frost, although a light frost will not injure the roots. Dig them carefully to avoid bruising and use damaged roots immediately. To cure, place sweet potatoes in a humid, well-ventilated area, at 55°F, for about ten days.

Common problems

Few pests and diseases bother sweet potatoes. To avoid sweet potato weevils, use certified insect-free slips, practice sanitation, and rotate crops. For sweet potato whiteflies use traps or biological controls.

GROWING SWEET POTATOES

Sweet potatoes grow from rooted cuttings called 'slips', which develop at one end of the tuberous root. An attractive indoor vine can be grown by placing the lower part of the potato in water.

Sweet potatoes are among the most nutritious vegetable crops. They are easy to grow, but they require a good bit of space. Bush varieties with their shorter stems are best suited to smaller gardens.

VEGETABLE FRUIT

Fruiting vegetables are some of the tastiest and most versatile vegetables. Many are attractive enough to be included in a patio garden, either grown among ornamentals in a bed or alone in containers. Most of these crops are easy to grow, and they are far more flavorful than those you can buy in the grocery store. Fruit forms only in warm and sunny conditions, so these are crops for the summer. In cooler regions, some of these vegetables should be given a head start indoors or in a greenhouse. However, some fruits store well and greatly extend your winter vegetable supplies.

Summer squash, winter squash, & pumpkins

These members of the cucumber family are closely related, but their cultivation and harvest differ. Zucchini and other summer squash produce soft, watery fruit that are usually consumed in summer as tender, immature fruit with a delicate flavor and texture. Pumpkins and winter squash develop solid, robust, and often ornamental fruit that can be stored during winter or even, for winter squash, until spring.

Zucchini all used to be elongated and cylindrical in shape, and eaten both as immature and mature fruits. You can now buy spherical zucchini to consume when immature. Other summer squash come in bottle shapes, with or without a neck, or as scalloped, disclike fruit. Colors range from dark green to yellow and white, and some are striped. The flowers are also edible.

Winter squashes and pumpkins are rewarding to grow, and pumpkins are of special interest to children. Their attractive, brightly colored fruit add a range of flavors and textures to winter meals. They can be used to make pies, cakes, bread, pudding, soups, and stews.

FROM PLANTING TO HARVESTING ZUCCHINI, PUMPKINS, & SQUASHES

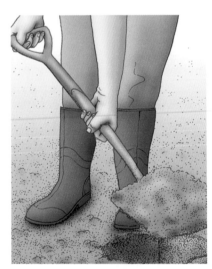

1 **Before planting, dig holes** a spade's width and depth at the desired spacings for either bush or trailing varieties.

2 **Water the soil** thoroughly once the holes have been filled with well-rotted compost. The excavated soil can be used to create a ridge around each planting hole, which can be used as a reservoir for water.

3 **Transplant young plants** into the top of the prepared soil once the risk of frost has passed. Alternatively sow 4–6 seeds; when a few leaves develop, remove plants as necessary so that 2–3 plants are left to grow.

Site & soil

All of these plants are grown in the same way (*see below*) and can have either a trailing or a bushy habit. They need a position in full sun and fertile, well-drained soil that is not too acid, with a pH greater than 6.

If possible, add plenty of well-rotted compost or manure, and rake in all-purpose fertilizer, at the rate recommended on the package, before sowing; double this rate of application if you are have been unable to add compost or manure. One traditional and very effective way of producing large fruit is to grow pumpkins and squashes on old compost or manure piles.

Sowing seed

Early crops can be grown from seeds sown indoors in midspring at 68–77°F. Sow in cell packs or propagation trays, allowing one seed per pot and inserting the seed on its thin edge. Any all-purpose potting mix is suitable, including soilless mixes. The large seeds produce large, vigorous plants that will be ready to grow outdoors when the risk of frost is passed. They are ready for transplanting when the roots hold the potting mix together and each plant has four or five leaves.

In most areas, you can sow the seeds where they are to grow in early summer. Sow several seeds per station and remove surplus plants later. A second sowing in midsummer for early-fall crops of zucchini can also be productive; sow seeds directly into the ground or in pots.

Growing & harvesting summer squash

Plant or set seeds of bush varieties 30in. apart in rows 3ft. apart, and trailing types 3ft. apart in rows 5ft. apart. Closer planting may suppress fruit formation and should therefore be avoided if at all possible. You could try growing trailing varieties up a fence—this is a very effective use of space in small yards and vegetable gardens as well as being quite ornamental.

Planting through a black plastic or landscape fabric is a good way to prevent weeds. Covering your plants with a floating row cover will greatly increase growth, but remove it when flowers begin to form. Weeding will be needed until the foliage spreads, but later the leaves will suppress most weeds. Water every ten days in dry spells to improve production and reduce powdery mildew.

Male flowers are formed before the females, and they can be removed and stuffed or fried. Female flowers follow, but they may spontaneously abort until the plant is large and growing well. Regular watering and scattering nitrogen-rich fertilizer, at the rate on the package, will increase growth and reduce loss of fruit.

Cut the fruit as soon as it is usable. Young zucchini are easily missed, and if allowed to mature will suppress further fruit formation. Removing some older leaves will help harvesting and make the developing fruit more visible. Keep maturing squash clean by using mulch or by placing them on tiles or pieces of wood, and for the best shape turn the fruit occasionally.

4 **Water developing plants** regularly, and begin to fertilize as soon as the first fruit start to develop. Liquid fertilizers are useful as they can be applied while you water.

5 **Pinch back the tips** of all sideshoots of trailing varieties once they reach 24in. long. Train all of the trailing stems evenly around the plant.

6 **Harvest the fruit** as soon as ready. Pick zucchini regularly when young and tender. Leave pumpkins and winter squashes to ripen in the sun and gather once the foliage has died down.

VARIED FRUIT

Summer squashes vary in shape and size. Some are elongated and hard skinned, with either plain or striped skins.

Pumpkins are usually trailing varieties. Allow at most 4 fruit per plant; the fewer there are, the larger they will be.

Zucchini plants are best picked when no more than 4–6in. long. There are yellow, green, and speckled types. The flowers are edible, too. Surplus crops can be grated and frozen.

Growing pumpkins & winter squashes

Winter squash and pumpkins are most commonly seeded in place in the garden, but in areas with a short growing season, it may be better to start seeds indoors a few weeks before the last expected frost.

Plant out bush and trailing varieties in the same way as summer squash, either weeding until the foliage spreads or growing through black plastic landscape fabric. Landscape fabric also protects the fruit from damage caused by soil contact. Alternatively, mulch with several sheets of newspaper covered with straw. If not using a mulch, place maturing fruit on tiles or pieces of wood, turning occasionally for the best shape and even ripening.

If growth appears weak, scatter nitrogen-rich fertilizer at the rate on the package, but be aware that excessive fertilizing can reduce production. The male flowers are produced first, and female ones follow often as much as several weeks later. Pumpkins and squashes often respond to close planting by failing to fruit. Consider growing trailing varieties up fences, or in other situations where they can wander freely.

Harvesting pumpkins & winter squashes

You can tell when the fruit are mature when they develop stout and woody stems and a fully colored and firm skin, and they ring hollow if gently tapped. Gather them as late as possible: typically, the first chilly nights of fall kill the foliage and expose the fruit, which can then be collected. If a very hard frost is expected, either cover the fruit with straw or similar material or bring them indoors before they freeze, because frozen fruit rots quickly. Fruit that are not fully colored can sometimes ripen if kept indoors at 54–68°F.

Store the fruit in a dry, airy, and frost-free place. If possible, store for a two week 'curing' period at about 59°F to heal any wounds, then at 50–54°F. You will need to use your pumpkins by midwinter, but many winter squashes will keep until early spring.

Common problems

Squash bugs and vine borers can be very destructive. Proper sanitation, crop rotation, and use of floating row covers can reduce the problem. Plantings can also be timed to avoid the pests. Viral diseases are spread by aphids and any affected plants should be immediately removed; resistant varieties are available. Powdery mildew often attacks plants in late summer, especially where plants are short of water. Fungicides give some protection, but watering and improving the soil with plenty of compost are more effective.

Corn

The superior quality of freshly picked sweet corn makes it well worth including in your garden, even though it takes a lot of space. Varieties may have yellow, white, or bicolored kernels; also available are super-sweet varieties and sugary-enhancer types that retain their sweetness for a longer time.

Corn is a warm-season crop. For ears to develop, they must be wind-pollinated, so it is important to plant corn in blocks of the same variety. Successive plantings, two weeks apart, will provide fresh corn over a long season.

Cultivation

Select a sunny site with fertile, well-drained, neutral (ideally, pH 6.5–7) soil. Incorporate compost and all-purpose fertilizer prior to planting. Sow seed 6in. apart in blocks of at least four rows, 2–3ft. apart. Thin young plants to 12in apart.

Apply an all-purpose fertilizer when plants are 12in. tall. Water regularly, particularly in dry spells. Harvest when ears have filled out and kernels are fully developed but not starchy (usually about 18 days after silks appear).

FROM SOWING TO HARVESTING CORN

1 **Plant seeds** 6in. apart in blocks of at least 4 rows, 2–3ft. apart, to assure good pollination between the plants.

2 **After germination**, thin seedlings to stand 12in. apart. Suckers and crop roots that form at the bases of stalks provide support.

3 **Cultivate to control** weeds and water regularly. Sidedress with an all-purpose fertilizer when stalks are 12in. tall.

4 **For kernels to develop**, pollen must be transferred from the tassels at the top of the stalk to the silks on each ear.

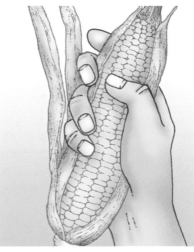

5 **Harvest ripe cobs** in late summer, when the tassels have withered and pressing a nail into a kernel yields creamy white juice.

6 **Twist the cobs** downward and pull away from the stem to detach them. Eat as soon as possible, before the sugars turn starchy.

Peppers

All peppers need hot, sunny conditions and are killed by frost, so they are usually grown as annuals. Peppers may be sweet, mildly hot, or very hot, according to the variety. Also depending on the variety and stage of ripeness, peppers may be green, yellow, orange, red, or purple. If there is room, grow several varieties for their different flavors.

The fruit of sweet peppers may be rounded, blocky, or elongated, and they commonly have thick walls. Some sweet peppers grow to the size of a grapefruit. Hot peppers are often smaller, although some grow quite long. They too come in many shapes, but generally have thinner walls.

Peppers can be used fresh in salads and salsas, or cooked in a variety of ways from stuffed and baked to stir fried or grilled. Many varieties are quite ornamental and can be grown in a flower garden or in a pot on a deck or patio.

Planting & cultivation

You can raise peppers indoors from seeds in spring as for tomatoes (*see page 214*), but they need even more warmth and light. They also take longer—at least 8–10 weeks to produce garden-sized plants. Using a heat mat to provide bottom heat will speed germination. Many gardeners prefer to buy 'plug plants' by mail order or larger plants from garden centers. The range of varieties is less extensive than with seed, but there are plenty to choose from.

Any fertile garden soil is suitable for pepper cultivation. Unless previously manured, add plenty of well-rotted compost and rake in an all-purpose fertilizer before sowing. To get peppers off to a faster start, use a black plastic landscape fabric to warm the soil.

Some gardeners grow their peppers in containers. During warm dry spells, plants may need to be watered as often as twice a day. Be sure the container has adequate drainage. Soilless mixes work well.

Harden off seedlings and transplant them into the garden after the risk of frost has passed. Space plants about 18in. apart in rows 24–30in. apart. Peppers should be watered regularly, especially during dry periods. Apply an all-purpose fertilizer as soon as fruiting begins.

Peppers grow very well in the warm soil of raised beds where the soil is well drained.

Harvesting

Although peppers can be harvested green, for the best flavors wait until the fruit develops its mature color, which varies by variety. Harvest fruit regularly to encourage continued production. Use garden shears or snips to cut peppers from the plant to avoid breaking any stems. Wear plastic gloves when handling hot peppers because they can cause skin to burn.

Peppers can be used fresh or cooked, and they can be preserved for winter use in a variety of ways. Hot peppers are often threaded onto strings and hung to dry.

Common problems

Peppers are largely trouble free, but biological controls or insecticidal soaps are sometimes needed for aphids. Pick off caterpillars if they are observed. Floating row covers can be used to prevent infestation by flying pests. Lack of water or irregular watering, especially in container-grown peppers, can lead to dark sunken patches (blossom end rot).

Peppers belong to the same family as tomatoes and eggplants, so do not plant these in the same space in consecutive years. A three-year rotation is even better.

FROM PLANTING TO HARVESTING PEPPERS

1 **Transplant young peppers** into the garden after the soil has warmed and the danger of frost has passed. Space plants 18in. apart within the row, allowing 24–30in. between rows.

2 **Combat pests** such as aphids or red spider mites with biological controls or a strong spray of water. Pick off caterpillars by hand. Continue to water, keeping plants moist but never soggy.

Preparing to grow *see page 152* | **Sowing & growing** *see page 156* | **Common problems** *see page 220*

Eggplants

These ornamental fruit, like peppers and tomatoes, are tropical perennials that are grown as annuals; they need hot and sunny conditions and are killed by frost. Eggplants produce purple flowers followed by fruit that ranges from white to purple-black in color. Many varieties produce rounded or oblong fruit. Italian and Asian types are long and thin. In the kitchen, eggplants can be grilled, fried, or baked and they are often combined with other vegetables in curries, stir fries, and stews.

Cultivation & harvesting

You can raise plants from seeds in spring, as for peppers. A very limited range of varieties can be bought as young plants, but a much wider selection is offered as seeds.

Any fertile garden soil suits outdoor plants. Unless already manured, add plenty of well-rotted compost and all-purpose fertilizer at the rate on the package.

Eggplants are well suited to growing in raised beds where the soil is well drained. Small-fruited types add interest to ornamental plantings. Growing eggplants in containers avoids verticillium wilt infection. Keep container-grown plants moist, but never soggy. Use an all-purpose liquid fertilizer every two weeks, or more often on plants that are growing weakly.

Harvest fruit when it reaches full size and its skin is shiny, by cutting it from the plant with snips or a sharp knife to avoid breaking a stem. Leave an inch of stem attached to the fruit. Eggplants do not keep well, so use them as soon as possible after picking.

Common problems

Eggplants are often attacked by aphids, flea beetles, whiteflies, and red spider mites. Floating row covers prevent problems with many of these. Biological controls are highly effective if introduced early, and horticultural oils or insecticidal soap can be used if the infestation is heavy and requires further treatment.

Verticillium wilt, a soil-borne fungal disease, is very damaging; growing eggplants in containers filled with potting mix is the only remedy.

Eggplants can be harvested at any time after the fruit develops until it reaches its full size, which varies among types. Its skin should be shiny and its flesh firm.

Pinch out growing tips when they reach 8–10in. tall, to make a bushy, freely producing plant. Support plants with canes if needed.

Cucumbers

Cucumbers require full sun and a fertile soil and thrive in warm weather. Most varieties produce long vines that can be trained on a trellis or fence, but compact bush varieties are also available. The cucumber fruit ranges in size from tiny gherkin types that are harvested when they are only 2–3in. long, to slender Armenian cucumbers that can grow 3ft. long. Slicing cucumbers, grown for fresh eating, bear straight, slender fruit and often have thick or warty skins. 'Burpless' cucumbers have been bred so that they do not become bitter, a trait that causes some people indigestion. Pickling cucumbers are typically smaller and thin-skinned; they can be used fresh or preserved as pickles and relishes. If you have room for only a single variety, choose a pickling type since they are more versatile.

Planting, cultivation, & harvesting

Before planting, incorporate plenty of compost or aged manure and some balanced fertilizer into the soil. Seed is usually sown directly in the garden, ½in. deep, although plants can be started in pots indoors about 4 weeks prior to your last expected frost for an earlier crop. Do not rush to plant cucumbers because they are very sensitive to cold. Sow seeds or transplant seedlings into the garden after all danger of frost has passed and the soil has warmed.

Thin vining varieties to 12in. apart, in rows 3–4ft. apart; bush varieties can be sown in hills of three or four plants each, with 3–4ft. between hills. Although cucumbers can be allowed to sprawl over the ground, you can make the most of your garden space by growing them on a trellis or fence. The climbing vines can reach 6ft. and are very attractive, and the fruit stays clean and grows straight. Bush varieties also grow well in containers.

Water cucumbers regularly for maximum production. Mulch them to maintain more consistent soil moisture and to prevent weeds. About a week after plants begin to flower, sidedress with a balanced fertilizer. Alternatively, apply a liquid fertilizer such as fish emulsion or compost tea. Once fruit begins to form—usually 50–70 days after planting—harvest frequently to prolong the season. Inspect vines every day or two and do not allow mature cucumbers to remain on the vine or production will slow.

Pollination

Most cucumbers produce both male and female flowers and fruit forms only when a female flower is pollinated. Female flowers can be distinguished from male flowers because the ovary behind the blossom looks like a tiny fruit.

Gynoecious hybrid varieties bear only female flowers and are very productive. Each package of gynoecious seeds typically includes a few nonhybrid seeds to provide sufficient male flowers for pollination. Be sure to plant the entire package, otherwise pollination may not occur. Incomplete pollination often results in distorted fruit. This may occur early in the season but often is resolved as more flowers form.

By training cucumbers to grow on a fence, trellis, or other vertical support, the fruit will hang from the vine, developing a straight shape and remaining clean.

Common problems

Cucumbers can be troubled by a number of pests including striped and spotted cucumber beetles, aphids, vine borers and pickle worms. They are also susceptible to several diseases such as bacterial wilt, anthracnose, and powdery mildew. Select resistant varieties and practice good sanitation and crop rotation.

Cucumber beetles, which vector bacterial wilt, can be discouraged with floating row covers until flowering when the covers must be removed to allow for pollination. Heavy mulching can prevent adult beetles from laying eggs in the ground. Biological controls are available for other pests. Consult your local cooperative extension office for other control recommendations.

Tomatoes

Tomatoes are the most widely grown vegetable in America, and for good reason. Store-bought tomatoes simply cannot compare with those that are home grown, vine ripened, and freshly harvested. In the kitchen, they are extremely versatile, both for eating fresh and for making sauces, juice, or soups.

Tomatoes come in a range of sizes and colors. Some dwarf varieties are suitable for growing in containers. Fruit sizes range from bite-sized cherry and grape tomatoes to large beefsteak types that are great for slicing.

Indeterminate varieties grow until frost kills the vine; in no-frost regions they can produce all winter. These types provide a steady supply of fruit for fresh eating, but because the plants tend to be large and sprawling they need to be staked or grown on trellises or in cages.

Determinate varieties produce fruit in clusters at the end of each stem. These plants tend to be bushier and to produce a more concentrated crop—an advantage if you like to can or freeze some of your crop. Determinate varieties can be grown in cages, staked, or left to sprawl on mulch-covered ground.

Sowing tomatoes

For the widest selection of varieties, you should purchase seeds to start indoors. Sow seeds indoors 6–8 weeks before your last expected frost. Sow thinly in shallow pots of seed starter mix, and lightly cover the seed. Provide them with lots of light—a greenhouse is ideal, but a

Tomatoes are delicious summer treats and they come in a huge range of flavors, shapes, and sizes. Some varieties make compact growth and can be grown in hanging baskets.

sunny window supplemented with grow lights can produce satisfactory results. If you do not have such facilities, a selection of tomato varieties are available as young plants from most garden centers.

Planting & cultivation

Tomatoes need a sunny, warm location. Amend the soil with well-rotted compost and an all-purpose fertilizer, at

FROM SOWING TO TRANSPLANTING TOMATOES

1 **Sow seeds** and transplant seedlings as soon as they have their first 4–5 leaves. Plant in individual, small pots of all-purpose mix and grow in bright light, at 54–64°F, spacing the plants so that their leaves do not touch.

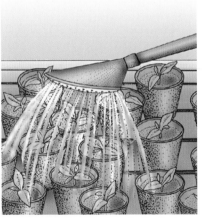

2 **Water plants** regularly, keeping plants moist but never soggy. Apply a dilute liquid fertilizer if the plants become pale.

3 **Plant out** after all danger of frost has passed and the soil has warmed. Water well before and after planting tomatoes in their final positions.

Preparing to grow *see page 152* | **Sowing & growing** *see page 156* | **Common problems** *see page 220*

GROWING TOMATOES

1 Plant out in early summer, once the risk of frost has passed, into well-cultivated and fertile soil. Choose a sunny spot and space plants 18–24in. apart. Water the soil well before and after planting.

2 Support vine or staking tomatoes securely with a sturdy wooden or metal stake. Some gardeners prefer growing tomatoes in wire cages. Place the stakes or cages soon after transplanting in order to avoid damage to plants.

3 In favorable climates, a number of sideshoots can be allowed to grow to increase the crop. In marginal areas, snap them off to concentrate the plant's energy on developing fewer fruits.

4 Pick the fruit individually as they develop full color, taking each one with the stalk intact. At the end of the season, pick unripe fruit as whole trusses and ripen indoors.

the rate recommended on the package. Use crop rotation to avoid any buildup of soil problems; potatoes, peppers, eggplants, and tomatoes occupy the same space in a rotation because they are related and share the same pests and diseases, especially cyst nematode (*see page 222*).

Large containers can be used for tomato cultivation if fertile garden soil or garden space is not available, but they do need more watering and fertilizing.

You can suppress weeds and keep your crop cleaner by mulching with straw or planting through black plastic landscape fabric, although this makes watering more difficult. Dwarf bush tomatoes don't require a stake, but you'll need to make a strong support for vine or staking tomatoes, enough to support the weight of a good 8lb. crop per plant. For staked tomatoes, you can remove sideshoots as they develop at leaf joints.

Tomatoes need about 1in. of water each week. Be sure to water well during dry spells. Topdress plants with an all-purpose fertilizer once a month throughout the growing season.

Common problems

Aphids and greenhouse whiteflies can be a problem, particularly early in the season. Biological controls and organic insecticides based on oils or soaps can reduce their infestations. Caterpillar damage can occur in late summer. Picking off the few caterpillars usually present is the best control measure.

Tomatoes are susceptible to a number of serious diseases, including several fungal leaf blights and wilts as well as viruses. Prevention is the best control for these. Practice crop rotation and sanitation. Do not add diseased plants to your compost pile. Select varieties that are resistant to the diseases common in your area.

Uneven watering can lead to blossom end rot, in which a lack of calcium in the fruit results in black sunken spots where the flower was attached to the fruit. Remember that plants need the equivalent of 1in. of water each week. Mulch plants to maintain more even soil moisture. This disorder usually disappears a once proper watering regime is resumed.

Sunscald can occur on fruit during periods where temperatures are high, especially on plants that are not protected by foliage. Again, this condition usually disappears when temperatures drop.

Mottling, streaking, and stunted growth may indicate viral diseases. There is no remedy, and early removal of infected plants is advisable as the viruses are spread from plant to plant on hands and tools.

HERBS

Nothing can compare to herbs fresh from the garden. Most herbs originate in the Mediterranean region and so thrive best in full sun with plenty of drainage and with shelter from the worst weather. Imagine a sun-drenched Mediterranean hillside with a coarse soil where deep roots sit out the summer heat and drought. If you can mimic this, your herbs will flourish. If there is nowhere in your garden with at least six hours of sun in midsummer, the range of herbs you can grow will be limited. Herbs grow very well in pots, and it is easy to make containerized herb gardens on patios and balconies.

Growing herbs

Easy access to your herbs is essential if you want to use them in the kitchen. Formal gardens edged with low-growing herbs are a traditional favorite, but in less formal gardens the herbs can be planted though gravel, perhaps with paving slabs for walking. Gravel suits herbs as it keeps soil from being splashed onto leaves by rain. Clay and other wet soils are often too badly drained for herbs to really thrive. Raised beds are the ideal solution.

Herbs are ideally grown for convenience near the kitchen door or on or under windowsills, near windows, or next to patios and seated areas for their summer scent. Many grow well in pots and can be positioned all around the garden for an interesting display.

Propagating herbs

Many herbs, such as parsley, are easily raised from seeds sown where they are to grow or in cell packs. They will need to be replaced at least annually: make several sowings each year for a regular, fresh supply. These herbs fit in well in the vegetable garden as intercrops and catch crops.

Other herbs, such as thyme, are perennial and need to be replaced every few years. These are easily raised from semihardwood cuttings (*see page 435*) taken in late summer and early fall and placed in equal parts all-purpose potting mix and coarse grit. Some herbs, such as mint, can be grown from divisions of older plants; simply pull off a young, vigorous part and replant it.

Cultivation

Most soils, especially sandy ones, benefit from the addition of plenty of well-rotted compost. Low-nutrient composted bark helps to open up clay soil; grit can help if the clay content is not too high, but too little grit can make matters worse. Try it in a small area first. Add lime, if necessary, to achieve a pH of at least 6.5.

Start your herb garden with a weed-free plot by covering the site for at least one growing season with black plastic landscape fabric. In established herb gardens, remove weeds rigorously, spot treating perennial weeds as soon as they are seen.

Herbs seldom need fertilizing or watering, but seedlings or new plants require water for their first few weeks. If growth is poor try a potassium-rich liquid fertilizer. Pests and diseases rarely cause problems. Insecticidal soap or horticultural oils will eliminate most pests and leave no residues. Remove diseased foliage or plants as soon as seen.

MAKING A HERB WHEEL

1 Mark a circle with pegs and string to a diameter of 24–48in., which is the traditional size for a herb wheel. However, you can tailor the size and sections, or even the shape, to suit your own needs.

2 Dig out the circle to a depth of half a brick's length. Place the bricks, stood on end, around the edge. This forms a slightly raised bed, which provides the warmer and better-drained conditions that many herbs enjoy.

3 Divide the bed into sections with double courses of bricks. Too many divisions will make the spaces both hard to build and too small to plant, so aim for no more than 6. A short section of ceramic drainage pipe makes an ideal center that can be planted. Mortar the bricks in place, if desired, and leave for a day to set.

4 Fill the sections with soil. You can adjust the soil in each to suit different herbs, but your plants should be well matched in their size, vigor, and needs if the wheel is to look good for more than a season. Lining a section with weed-proof landscape fabric will constrain mint roots.

Harvesting & drying

Plants that resist the nibbling of goats on Mediterranean hillsides have no problem with frequent harvesting. In fact, the more you cut herbs the healthier the plants will be, as long as you don't cut into older, woody stems.

For the best flavor, gather 2–4in. stems, ideally on warm, sunny days and just before flowering begins. Cut with scissors or pruners and aim to leave the plant with a pleasing, balanced shape. Always keep different harvested herbs apart to avoid flavors and scents mingling. Some herbs, such as fennel and dill, are best used fresh and do not store; basil is best stored in oil.

You should dry herbs in the dark in a warm, airy place such as a darkened basement. Store dried herbs in airtight jars in the dark and check for mold from time to time. Herbs can also be chopped and frozen in plastic bags ready to be added, straight from the freezer, to dishes. This is often a better alternative for the softer herbs, such as coriander, parsley, or chervil, and preserves green color.

Home-grown herbs that have been subject to natural stresses often have a better flavor than commercial crops that are grown with perfect watering regimes and rich soil.

Popular herbs

Basil (*Ocimum basilicum*): Annual, 12–24in. tall. Sow with heat in early spring, plant in all-purpose mix or soil when the risk of frost has passed. Cut to prevent flowering. Bring plants in before the first frosts.

Bay (*Laurus nobilis*): Evergreen tree, usually pruned to shrub size. Grow from cuttings in a sheltered site and bring indoors in harsh winters. Cut as needed all year. Z8

Borage (*Borago officinalis*): Annual, 24in. tall. Sow in poor, well-drained soil or pots in spring and summer. Cut flowers and leaves as needed. Self seeds.

Chives (*Allium schoenoprasum*): Perennial, 12–18in. tall. Divide in spring and water well in first year. Cut leaves near ground level as needed. Cut flowers to encourage fresh foliage. Fertilize if foliage yellows. Z3

Cilantro (*Coriandrum sativum*): Annual, 24in. tall. Sow *in situ* from midspring to late summer. Water if dry. Pick leaves in summer, seeds in late summer.

Dill (*Anethum graveolens*): Annual, 24in. tall. Sow from midspring, away from fennel. Water if dry. Pick leaves in summer, seeds in late summer.

Fennel (*Foeniculum vulgare*): Perennial, 3–5ft. tall, spreads to 24in. Grow from seeds, away from dill to keep a clear flavor. Gather leaves in summer. Z4

Lemon grass (*Cymbopogon citratus*): Perennial, 3ft. tall. Sow in spring with heat. Grow in pots and bring in when frost threatens. Cut as needed or freeze. Z9

Marjoram (*Origanum majorana*): Perennial, 12in. tall. Can be grown as an annual in poor, well-drained soil. Z9

Mint (*Mentha* species): Spreading perennial, 18–24in. tall. Grow in fertile, moist soil in a bottomless container to prevent spreading. Pick leaves as needed. Cut back in summer to encourage fresh foliage. Z3

Parsley (*Petroselinum crispum*): Biennial, 18in. tall. Sow in midspring and late summer. Grow in pots or rich soil. Use fresh, dried, or frozen. Z6

Rosemary (*Rosmarinus officinalis*): Evergreen shrub, 5ft. tall. Grow from cuttings in poor soil and a sheltered site. Cut as needed all year. Prune lightly in spring. Z8

Sage (*Salvia officinalis*): Evergreen shrub, 24in. tall. Grow from seeds or cuttings in poor soil and a sheltered site. Cut as needed, and protect in winter. Z5

Tarragon (*Artemisia dracunculus*): Perennial 30in. tall, spreads to 20in. Grow from divisions in spring. Remove flowers during summer. French tarragon has the best flavor. Z5

Thyme (*Thymus vulgaris*): Evergreen perennial, 12in. tall. Grow from seeds or cuttings, in pots or poor, well-drained soil in a sheltered site. Cut as needed. Z4

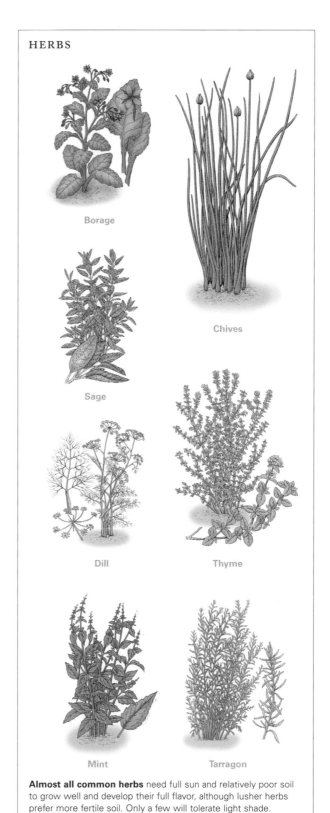

HERBS

Borage

Chives

Sage

Dill

Thyme

Mint

Tarragon

Almost all common herbs need full sun and relatively poor soil to grow well and develop their full flavor, although lusher herbs prefer more fertile soil. Only a few will tolerate light shade.

COMMON PROBLEMS

It can seem at first that vegetables are vulnerable to a host of pests and diseases, and that growing them will be an unrelenting and unwinnable struggle. It is true that there are many creatures poised to enjoy your harvest before you do, and each year some plants will be lost or damaged by disease, but the problems are not really so great. With good cultivation techniques and some defensive measures, losses will be minimal. The key is to watch plants carefully, spot potential problems early, and act promptly, ideally before any damage is done. In the vegetable garden, as everywhere else, prevention is better than cure.

Pests

Some pests, such as slugs, will attack almost any plant in the garden and are familiar to every gardener; these are discussed in Chapter One. Other pests are specific to certain crops, or even a single crop.

Cucumber beetle

Adult beetles are about ¼in. long with yellow wing covers, each with three black stripes or eleven black spots. The adults lay eggs in the soil and the slender, whitish larvae, with black or brown heads, burrow into the soil and feed on the roots of cucumber, squash, melon, and potato plants. The larvae pupate in the soil, the adults emerging in spring to lay their eggs. Predators such as praying mantis and ladybeetles are effective, as are some insecticides.

Squash bugs

Flat-backed, grayish or black bugs, ½–1in. long, suck sap from cucumbers, melons, pumpkins, and squashes. Their activities can be recognized by the plants being marked with brown or yellow dots; in the worst cases, plants become stunted, and the leaves turn black and die. The

Makeshift bird scarers like old compact discs are often used to keep birds away from crops. Sadly, most are not that effective. Vulnerable crops need to be netted, with the net suspended well above the crop.

Brassicas are a favorite food of caterpillars, which can cause extensive defoliation if left uncontrolled. Insect-proof netting or mesh is an effective and environmentally-friendly control.

IDENTIFYING VEGETABLE PESTS

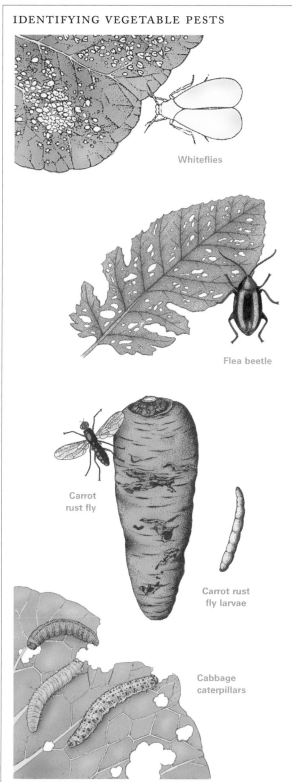

Whiteflies

Flea beetle

Carrot rust fly

Carrot rust fly larvae

Cabbage caterpillars

Tell-tale signs of some pests are obvious, while you may never see others at all because they are very small or hide well. Learn to recognize the typical damage they leave behind.

best protections are using floating row covers until flowering begins, good sanitation, and crop rotation.

Whiteflies
These small insects cluster under brassica leaves and suck sap. Direct damage is minor, but their sugary excrement, called honeydew, encourages sooty molds. Whiteflies are difficult to control; remove all old plants in spring before planting anew to limit reinfection. Spraying with an appropriate treatment will reduce infestations, but the effect may be short lived. Damage is mainly confined to outer leaves, so this pest can often be tolerated.

Flea beetles
Brassicas and allied plants, such as radish, turnip, and arugula, as well as eggplants are prone to attack from these tiny beetles. They are black, sometimes with yellow stripes, and jump from plants when disturbed. They eat small holes in leaves in spring and late summer. Seedlings can be killed or retarded; keep them watered so they quickly grow through the vulnerable stage. If necessary, spray with an appropriate treatment.

Carrot rust fly
This pest attacks carrots and, to a lesser extent, parsnip, celery, and parsley. The maggots, up to $\frac{1}{2}$in. long, leave brown tunnels in roots. Most damage occurs in late summer. Grow under row covers or in a 30in. tall enclosure (*see page 196*) to prevent the low-flying females from laying eggs, or try less susceptible varieties.

Cabbage caterpillars
Brassicas are host plants for several caterpillars, worms, and loopers. They can be a serious problem on young plants, retarding establishment and reducing vigor, as well as damaging maturing plants and reducing their appeal by their damage and their droppings. Remove them by hand on frequent regular patrols, or grow plants under floating row covers or insect-proof net to prevent eggs being laid. Organic control with *Bacillus thuringiensis* (Bt) is also effective.

Pea & bean weevil
Grayish brown adults, $\frac{1}{5}$in long, eat U-shaped notches in leaf edges of peas and fava beans in early summer and feed on pollen. The larvae burrow into the pods and feed on the developing seeds inside, ruining the crop. The holes where the larvae enter often close up, disguising their entry. Sprays and predators can deal with the adults, but once the larvae are inside the pods there is no control.

Mexican bean beetle

Sometimes confused with similar-sized (but beneficial) ladybeetles, Mexican bean beetles are copper colored with symmetrical, black spots. The adults feed on beans and bean foliage; the larvae on beans. Organic and biological controls are effective.

Corn earworm

Earworms, 1in long, vary in color from sandy yellow to brown or green, but always have dark stripes along their sides. On corn, the worms eat the silks and then the ear as it develops. Corn earworm also attacks potatoes and tomatoes, peppers, peas, and beans. Spray with an organic insecticide or introduce predators.

Colorado potato beetle

Both adult beetles and larvae can devastate the plants, sometimes eating all the foliage. Beetles overwinter in the soil so rotating your potato crop is vital. Traps are effective and row covers prevent adults colonizing the crop initially. Consult experts on control methods.

Cabbage root maggot

The white maggots of this pest, up to ³⁄₈in. long, attack the same plants as flea beetles. In late spring to early summer, the root systems of seedlings or transplants can be destroyed. Established plants can tolerate the root damage. Grow young plants under row covers or place collars of roofing felt, carpet underlay, or board, about 6in. wide, around the bases of the stems to prevent female flies laying eggs in the soil near the plants.

Asparagus beetle

The beetles and their creamy gray grubs feed on asparagus foliage and bark. The adults are ³⁄₈in. long and have black wing cases with yellow squares. They emerge in late spring to lay grayish black eggs on stems and leaves. Heavy infestations cause defoliation, with stems turning yellowish brown and drying up. Hand pick the beetles or spray with a hard stream of water.

Potato cyst nematodes

Heavy infestations kill plants and produce marble-sized tubers. Leaves yellow and dry up, starting at the bases of the stems. Young nematodes feed within the roots; mature females burst through the root walls to form tiny, white cysts. Cysts of golden cyst eelworms turn pale yellow, then brown, while those of white cyst eelworms turn directly brown. Eggs can remain viable in the soil for up to ten years. Some potato varieties are resistant.

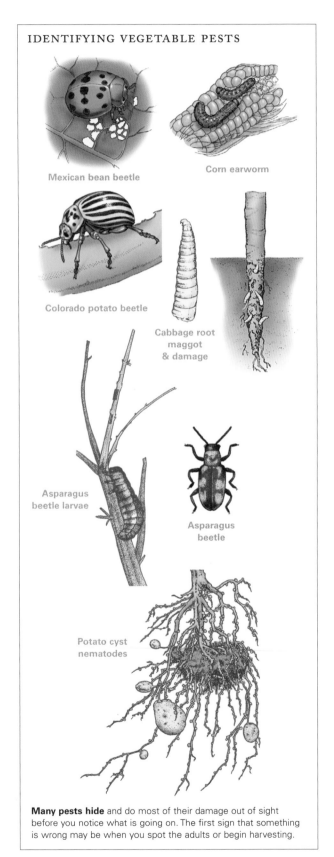

IDENTIFYING VEGETABLE PESTS

Mexican bean beetle

Corn earworm

Colorado potato beetle

Cabbage root maggot & damage

Asparagus beetle larvae

Asparagus beetle

Potato cyst nematodes

Many pests hide and do most of their damage out of sight before you notice what is going on. The first sign that something is wrong may be when you spot the adults or begin harvesting.

DISEASES

Pests, diseases, & other problems *see page 40* | **Taking action** *see page 46* | **Common diseases** *see page 51*

Diseases

Most plant diseases affecting crops are fungal or viral. Airborne fungal infections are spread by spores, so good spacing and airflow help to reduce incidence, but some are spread in the soil and are harder to combat. Viruses are mainly spread by handling, or by sap-sucking insects.

White rust
This fungus is common on many brassicas. White, chalky pustules develop on the undersides of leaves, and the upper surfaces are sometimes distorted and discolored. It is unsightly, but not serious. Remove affected leaves, and reduce incidence by spacing plants well and using rotation.

Onion white rot
Roots and basal tissues develop white, fluffy growth and rot, sometimes causing plants to fall over, and leaves to yellow and die. Dig up and destroy affected plants. The fungus produces black spores that can survive in soil for 15 years. Grow onions elsewhere or replace the soil: do not spread it.

Onion downy mildew
Onion leaves wither and collapse. If humid, an off-white mold develops. The bulbs do not store well. Destroy affected plants and avoid growing onions on the site for five years. Control weeds to encourage good airflow.

Leaf spots
Several fungi and bacteria cause brown spots, particularly on older leaves and in wet seasons. Diseased tissue may fall out to leave shot holes. Destroy affected leaves and if necessary remove alternate plants to improve airflow.

Clubroot
This can affect all the brassica family. Plants are stunted and leaves may wilt on hot days, recovering overnight. On lifting, the roots are thickened and distorted. This is a slime mold, usually introduced on brought-in seedlings, and possibly manure from cattle fed on diseased plants. It can survive in soil for 20 years, and is worst on acid, wet soils. Liming and improving drainage will help, as will raising seedlings in pots and planting out when larger. No chemicals are available, but there are resistant varieties.

Leek rust
This fungus forms elongated pustules of orange spores on leeks, onions, garlic, and shallots. Severe infections can cause dying of leaves and small bulbs. Late season foliage is normally healthy. Applying sulfate of potassium is claimed to help, as will clearing infected material and crop debris, good drainage, wide spacing, and using a long rotation. Resistant varieties are available.

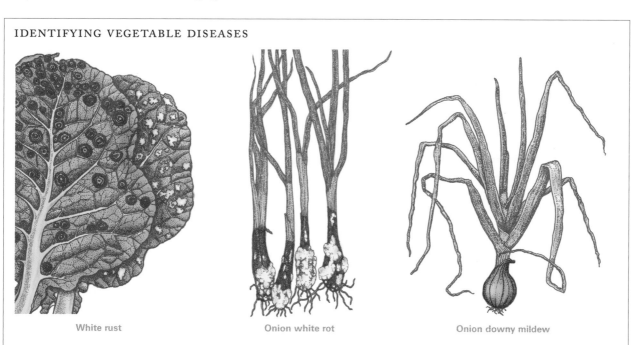

IDENTIFYING VEGETABLE DISEASES

White rust   Onion white rot   Onion downy mildew

Fungal infections are usually highly visible. They commonly cause pustules, from which spores are released to infect other plants.

Another, perhaps more familiar, form of growth is fluffy or dusty-looking mold growing on any part of the plant.

223

Bean rust

Dark brown pustules appear on leaves, stems, and pods of pole and bush beans. The white, cluster-cup stage of the fungus may develop later in the season. Destroy affected tissue when seen.

Sclerotinia

This disease (*see page 52*) affects many vegetables including beans, potato, tomato, and celery. Space plants to encourage air circulation and avoid wetting foliage. Late planting of potatoes sometimes helps limit infection.

Potato scabs

Common scab: This is caused by a bacterium and scabby spots with irregular edges develop on the skin. Although unsightly, the damage is not very serious. Scab occurs on light soils lacking organic matter and is worst in dry years. Dig in compost or other organic matter and ensure a regular supply of water when the tubers are forming, from two to three weeks after emergence, continuing for at least four weeks. Liming can encourage common scab, so avoid growing potatoes on ground limed for a previous brassica crop. Resistant varieties are available.

Powdery scab: This fungal disease causes irregular, brown depressions with raised edges, containing dusty masses of spores. Badly affected tubers are swollen and worthless. It is worst on wet soils and in wet years. Plant tubers that have as low a level of infection as possible. Some varieties are more resistant than others.

Foot & stem rots

Several fungi can cause these rots, and some vegetables such as tomatoes and those of the cucumber family are prone to infections. The roots or stem base rot, and the plant collapses. Irregular watering or a poor root system exacerbate the problem. If caught early, foliar feeding may encourage new root production. Destroy severely affected plants and replace the soil around the roots.

Late blight

Late blight of potatoes and tomatoes is caused by *Phytophthora infestans*. Brown dead patches appear at the leaf tips and enlarge to kill the leaf. In dry weather the infection may slow, but in wet weather it spreads rapidly.

Potato blight: Spores can be washed onto the ground where they infect the tubers. The rot is a hard, reddish brown patch that extends into the tuber. Secondary bacteria often infect these wounds to cause a slimy soft rot. Affected tubers will not store.

The airborne spores can infect plants over wide ranges. Foliage must be sprayed with a protectant fungicide before blight appears. If blight arrives late in the season, it is best to remove the stems and leaves so that the tubers do not get infected.

Powdery mildews

Some vegetables, such as the cucumber family and peas, are particularly susceptible to powdery mildew infection (*see also page 52*), which can spread quickly under dry conditions but causes significant damage when humidity is high and air circulation is poor. Use resistant varieties when available.

Mint rust

This common disease of mint and related plants turns stems and leaves pale and distorted before erupting as masses of orange pustules, which turn black. Leaf tissue dies and plants are defoliated. The fungus is perennial in garden mint, but spores also overwinter in the soil. Apply an appropriate fungicide.

Viruses on tomatoes

Typically, viruses cause mottling and distortion of leaves, stunting, and poor fruit yield, but some symptoms are very similar to those caused by herbicide exposure or cold damage. Tobacco mosaic virus (T.M.V.) is highly contagious and serious. Fruit may not set and young fruit are 'bronzed' or streaked. Destroy affected plants immediately; extensive spread may have occurred but not yet be obvious. Clean tools and hands well, and control pests. Some varieties are marketed as resistant to T.M.V.

Curly top

This virus disease causes foliage to become thick and leathery and the leaves to curl upward. It attacks a wide range of crops including beans, brassicas, and squashes as well as beets, chard and spinach, carrots, and celery. It is especially prevalent west of the Rockies. Curly top is spread by leafhoppers, so use row covers to prevent the leafhoppers attacking the plants.

Smut on corn

This disease is common in warmer regions, and seen in hotter summers elsewhere. Plants may be stunted. Cobs, flower tassels, stems, and occasionally leaves develop dramatic ashen malformations, from which a dark spore mass later erupts to cause new infections or survive in crop debris or soil. Destroy all infected material and grow no corn on the site for five years.

Pests, diseases, & other problems *see page 40* | Taking action *see page 46* | Common diseases *see page 51*

IDENTIFYING DISEASES OF VEGETABLE CROPS

Bean rust

Sclerotinia

Potato scab

Foot & stem rot

Potato blight

Powdery scab

Powdery mildew

Mint rust

Tobacco mosaic virus

The number of diseases that can affect crops may look disheartening, but the overall vigor of a plant can go a long way toward preventing serious damage. Healthy plants may fight off infections that devastate plants suffering from stress. Good growing practices and frequent checks on crops, so that any problems are dealt with promptly, are important to reduce the incidence of disease.

CHAPTER FIVE

GROWING FRUIT

227

PICKING YOUR OWN FRESH FRUIT STRAIGHT FROM A PLANT IN the garden, whether a juicy strawberry or a crisp apple, is one of life's great pleasures. Not only do you get the satisfaction of eating the fruit of your labor (quite literally), but the taste of home-grown fruit will be far superior to anything you can buy from the supermarket. Store-bought fruit can be very expensive, too, and growing your own is certainly cost-effective, especially if you choose a variety that fruits over a long period of time—you can expect an apple tree, for instance, to give you a decent yield for many years.

Concern for the environment makes many people feel uneasy about the distance fruit has to travel around the world—its so-called food miles— before it reaches our plates. In a perfect world, all our fruit would be picked a few steps outside the kitchen door, and you can achieve this to a limited extent by growing your own. This will help, too, to put you back in touch with the seasons, and can also encourage children to think about where the fruit they eat comes from and when they should expect to see it on their plates. Add to this the year-round pleasures that growing your own fruit provides—blossom in spring, luscious and nutritious fruit in summer, colorful fall foliage, and the structural shapes of fruit trees over winter—and the rewards are plain to see.

Where & what to grow

Fruit can be grown in any garden, whether you have a small balcony or the space to plant an orchard. If you have a tiny garden, the trick is to choose your varieties carefully and use training techniques to maximize the space. Many fruit plants can also be grown in containers: you can find more information in the Container Gardening chapter.

There are many plants to choose from, ranging from apples and other tree fruit to soft fruit such as strawberries and raspberries. Grow fruit that you like to eat, although you will also need to consider your local climate, growing conditions, and available space—most fruit prefer a sunny site if the crop is to ripen well. When buying, it pays to visit a specialty nursery, which can supply quality plants that are certified free from pests and diseases—many such nurseries ship plants by mail order.

How to grow fruit

Once you have decided what to grow, this chapter will help you to get the best from your plants, with details on how to plant, prune, train, harvest, and care for many traditional fruit, along with others that you may not have considered, such as currants, grapes, and citrus.

Climate is the determining factor when choosing what to grow. Site selection and protective measures against pests, diseases, and cultural problems are also important. If you live in a cold or exposed area, you may need to wait two or three weeks longer than the times recommended here to carry out some tasks. Growing fruit under protection, in a hoop house, greenhouse, or cold frame, or under floating row cover, can extend the growing season.

Insecticides and herbicides should be used sparingly, if at all, on edible plants. Aim for prevention of pests and diseases rather than control. Buy varieties with natural resistance; protect fruit from pests using barriers, and maintain healthy soil to keep plants tough enough to resist infestations. If you do find a problem, identify the culprit so that you can decide on the most effective and safest remedy.

PREPARING TO GROW

Growing fruit is very enjoyable, but rather than purchasing plants on impulse, take your time to choose, basing your decision on conditions within your yard. This ensures that whatever you decide to grow will thrive and reward you with an excellent crop. It is essential to consider your local climate, which will play a large part in determining what you can grow. The most important aspects of climate are rain, wind, and temperature. The amount of rain and exposure to wind may be tempered by cultivation techniques or protective structures. However, crops may fail or even die in unfavorable temperatures.

Choice of site

Most fruit plants do best in a sunny, sheltered position, where heat and light encourage formation of fruit buds and allow the crop to ripen. Although it may affect the yield, many types of fruit still do well in slight shade, but only if they can bask in sun for at least half the day.

Also consider your garden's altitude. Generally, the higher the altitude, the cooler the climate, and the shorter the growing season. Microclimates within your yard, such as a warm, southfacing slope, may temper these elements and still allow fruit to grow.

Generally, the 'growing season' is considered to be the number of frost-free days between spring and fall. Some crops, such as grapes, need a long growing season, while others, such as strawberries, require only a short season to fruit well. Many tree fruit such as apples, pears, peaches, and cherries require a certain amount of winter cold to satisfy their dormancy requirements.

Rainfall

Moisture is vital for the healthy growth of fruit plants, but very wet conditions and high humidity provide the perfect environment for fungal diseases, and waterlogged soil can cause the roots to rot. Good drainage is crucial in such conditions. Too little rainfall or drought in summer can affect the yield or quality of fruit. Apply a mulch to seal in moisture and water if necessary.

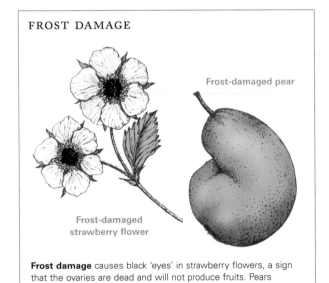

FROST DAMAGE

Frost-damaged pear

Frost-damaged strawberry flower

Frost damage causes black 'eyes' in strawberry flowers, a sign that the ovaries are dead and will not produce fruits. Pears become distorted by frost, but they are still edible.

A sheltered, sunny spot is the best site for a fruit garden. In any yard, you can improve conditions for fruit, ensuring that the plants thrive and produce a good crop every year.

Climate & your garden *see page 10* | **Looking after your soil** *see page 32* | **Pests, diseases, & other problems** *see page 40*

WIND TURBULENCE & WINDBREAKS

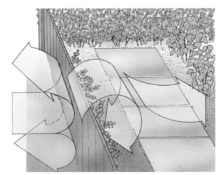 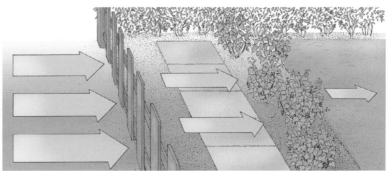

Wind turbulence is very strong on both sides of a solid barrier, such as a fence or evergreen hedge, and can severely damage fruit plants.

Open windbreaks on exposed sites filter wind and slow it down without causing turbulence. A deciduous hedge is attractive, but competes with the fruit for shade, water, and nutrients. Effective artificial barriers include a picket fence, trellis, or robust netting on posts.

Wind

Strong winds can blow blossom or fruit off a tree and scorch leaves, snap branches, and prevent pollinating insects reaching the plants. If needed, erect a windbreak (*see box, above*) or consider a barrier of fast-growing deciduous trees, such as poplar, alder, or willow.

Frost

Spring frosts can damage buds, flowers, fruit, and shoots, so select varieties suited to your growing season. You can build structures around fruit trained against walls or fences. Use floating row covers over smaller plants in the ground and over compact forms of tree fruits in containers or small groups outdoors; you can even buy row cover or burlap sacks that can be slipped over plants (*see page 366*).

Alternatively, try growing late-flowering fruit, such as hardy varieties of black currant, raspberry, and blackberry, or fruit that is known for its blossom hardiness, including many varieties of apple.

Soil

It is possible to grow fruit on most reasonable soils, although a fertile, well-drained soil that is slightly acidic (about pH 6.5) is ideal. Very damp soil can cause roots to rot, so if your soil is heavy and has pools of standing water after rain improve it by digging in plenty of well-rotted manure before planting. If the soil is waterlogged, do not plant until you have installed a drainage system. Improve a lighter soil that dries out fast by adding plenty of organic matter to help retain moisture, and apply regular mulches.

IDENTIFYING FROST POCKETS

Frost pockets are small patches of cold air, often trapped on a slope or at a bottom corner (*shown far left*). Avoid such areas when planting. If there is no choice, improve air flow in the area to help cold air to escape, by using a porous barrier for example (*shown left*). Alternatively, grow only larger trees at the lower end of the pocket, so that the blossom is above the level of the coldest air, or grow smaller plants higher up the slope.

Planning

The lifespan of a fruit tree may be 20–50 years and many soft fruit plants have a life of 10–15 years, so planting a fruit garden, or even a single tree, is a long-term venture. The first decision that you must make is the choice of fruit to cultivate. It is really important to select fruits that you enjoy and have time to harvest when they ripen. Do you have space for a dedicated orchard with a mixture of soft, cane, bush, and tree fruit, or for just a single fruit tree? Do you have easy access to irrigation water? Also note the exposure of your yard—most fruit thrives in full sun or light shade; cold, shaded sites result in slow growth and very poor yields.

Where to place plants

Take note of the ultimate size for your chosen fruit, to avoid buying too many plants and allow each one room to develop to its maximum cropping potential. Often two fruit trees are needed for pollination.

In a small yard, or even a patio, take advantage of any fences, walls, trellis, or other vertical structures to provide a sunny and sheltered spot as support for fruit plants. Fix training wires to the vertical supports and use them to raise grape vines, blackberries, raspberries, and trained forms of apples, pears, and peaches. Vertical supports also make it easy to cover plants with frost or pest protection or to add netting in spring to protect fruit from birds.

When planning a fruit garden, consider whether you want to include some permanent structures, such as fruit cages to prevent birds from stealing or damaging the crop, or supports, such as fencing or trellis, on which to train fruiting canes or restricted tree forms (*see box, right*).

FRUIT TREE FORMS

Oblique cordon

Espalier

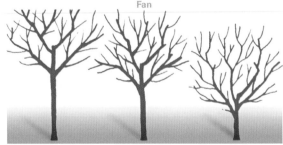

Fan

Standard tree   Semidwarf   Dwarf

Restricted trees include fans, espaliers, and cordons and are ideal for limited space. Free-standing trees are called standard, semidwarf, or dwarf, depending on their overall height and spread, and the length of the main stem, or trunk.

SOFT FRUIT

'Soft fruit' is the general term used to describe a diverse group of perennials or low-growing shrubs that bear soft, juicy fruit. It includes strawberries, blueberries, raspberries, currants, gooseberries, grapes, and melons. Unlike tree fruit, which can need a lot of room to grow happily, soft fruits are ideal for a sunny or slightly shaded position in a small yard because most do not need too much space to thrive. Some can even be grown in containers, making them perfect for patio gardens. Another advantage of soft fruits is that they bear crops soon after planting, in some cases within the same year.

Strawberries

The common, June-bearing strawberry usually has a single, heavy flush of fruit anytime from late spring to late summer, depending on the variety. Everbearing types fruit sporadically from late summer until midfall. Alpine strawberries (*Fragaria vesca*) produce tiny, but intensely flavored berries for months. Select varieties that are

PLANTING & PROTECTING A STRAWBERRY PLANT

1 Fertilize the soil just before planting by forking in a slow-release, all-purpose fertilizer. Plant the strawberries 18in. apart with 36in. between rows. Spread out the roots, keeping the crowns level with the surface. Firm the soil.

2 Water regularly for the first few weeks after planting and in dry spells in the growing season. To avoid risk of fungal diseases, such as botrytis, do not wet ripening berries. A drip irrigation system with a programmable timer, set to water several times a day, is helpful.

3 Trap and destroy slugs and snails to prevent them from feeding on the berries. Cover the ground beneath the berries and between rows with weed-free straw to keep the ripening fruit clean and to prevent weeds growing.

4 Protect the fruit from birds with some antibird netting stretched over frames. Alternatively, make low cages by supporting the nets on posts that are at least 18in. tall—cover the post ends to protect your eyes when bending down to harvest the fruit.

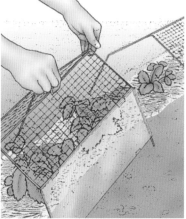

Water crops in pots regularly, especially during sunny, dry weather. Once flowers appear, fertilize weekly with a fertilizer that is high in potassium until the fruit starts to turn red.

suitable for your area. Strawberries are ideally watered by drip irrigation to minimize fungal diseases, and they need at least six hours of sunshine per day.

June-bearing strawberries

Give these strawberries slightly acidic, well-drained soil in a frost-free, sunny place (they tolerate light shade). You can grow them as annuals, planting new runners each year (*see facing page*), but mature plants have larger harvests and a productive life of up to four years. A month before planting, remove perennial weeds and dig in well-rotted manure or compost.

Plant bare-rooted strawberries from midsummer to early fall for cropping the following year. You can plant rooted runners in early spring, but they may crop poorly in their first year—remove blossoms as they appear so that the plant can put its energy into getting established. Plant pot-grown plants at any time; they will fruit the same year if planted in spring.

Everbearing strawberries

Everbearing strawberries produce fewer runners than June-bearing types, and they can be grown in containers or be planted as an edging or ground cover. Plant in spring; in the mildest areas you can also plant in fall. Treat as annuals (*see page 80*) in coldest regions. These strawberries typically produce three flushes of blooms and fruit, in spring, summer, and fall. As these fruit later in the year, you may need to use row covers to protect crops in cold areas to extend the season.

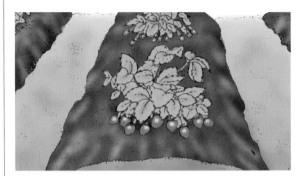

ALTERNATIVES TO STRAW MULCH

Lay black landscape fabric over 3in. ridges of moist soil, 6in. apart. Plant through slits at 15–18in. intervals.

Place strawberry mats around single plants like collars, so that the swelling fruit rest on the mats and are protected.

Alpine strawberries

Sometimes called *fraises du bois*, alpine strawberries bear small crops of tiny, sweet berries in summer and are best grown as edging plants or in containers and hanging baskets. They are best started from seed sown in spring or bought as young plants. Their soil requirement is the same as for June-bearing strawberries (*see above*).

Aftercare & harvesting

To promote flower formation, fertilize plants in early spring with high-potassium fertilizer alongside each row. Pinch off the earliest flowers to promote vigorous growth. Keep all types well watered during dry weather and protect the fruit with straw (*see page 233*), plastic, or matting (*see box, above*).

If you can, harvest the fruit in the morning, when it is fresh and cool, removing each fruit with its stalk and handling carefully to give it a longer shelf life. Once you have picked all the fruit, dispose of the straw and clear up the bed by shearing the leaves off the plants and weeding (*see facing page*). In late winter, tidy up by removing any leaves damaged during winter.

PROPAGATING STRAWBERRIES FROM RUNNERS

1 **Select 4 or 5 runners** from vigorous and disease-free cropping strawberries, from early to late summer.

2 **Secure each runner** with a U-shaped wire firmly in a 3in. pot of potting mix sunk into the soil or into open ground.

3 **Sever from the parent plant**, close to the runner, after the runner has rooted, which should take 4–6 weeks.

4 **Lift out each potted runner** or knock it out of its pot, plant into a new bed, and water. Transplant runners rooted in open ground.

Growing crops in pots

You can grow single strawberry plants in 8in. pots of potting soil, or six plants in a half-barrel. Or you can use a strawberry pot, which has an opening at the top as well as pockets on the sides to accommodate plants. You will get a better, trouble-free crop by raising containers off the ground, where they are less likely to be discovered by slugs and snails. Place them on a board supported by crates or bricks at each end to improve drainage and air flow around the plants. Fruit can trail down the sides without touching the ground. Water containers regularly as they dry out quickly in hot weather.

Growing in the greenhouse

You can grow strawberries for early spring in a cool greenhouse (*see page 385*). Start with rooted runners and transplant into 6in. pots. Keep the soil damp and fertilize the plants every week until early fall. At the end of fall, move them into a cold frame to protect them from frost, and in early winter bring them into the greenhouse, giving them plenty of space to allow air to circulate.

Propagation

Most strawberries produce masses of runners. You can propagate from these after harvesting to start new beds or replace worn-out plants (*see above*). Keep runners well watered until they root, and cut back and discard any surplus. Most alpine and some everbearing strawberries do not form runners, but you can propagate these by division (*see page 422*).

CLEARING UP THE BED

After cropping, cut off old leaves along with surplus runners, using shears. Fork up compacted soil between the rows.

Blueberries

Blueberries are a popular summer fruit, largely because they are regarded as a 'super food' with a high content of vitamins C and E in the berries. They are also a great source of antioxidants. Several types of blueberries are grown in North America. Highbush blueberries are hardy from zones 4 to 10, depending on variety; they grow to 6ft. tall and produce large berries. 'Lowbush' types grow less than 3ft. tall and often mature to only 18in. They produce smaller berries and are hardy in zones 3 to 6. Some hybrid varieties boast the larger fruit size of highbush blueberries along with the hardiness of lowbush types and are between the two types in height. Rabbiteye blueberries may grow to 10ft., and are suitable for the hottest areas of the South.

Where to grow blueberries

Moist, well-drained acid soils, with a pH of 4–5.5, are perfect for blueberries, although acidic, clay or sandy soil can be improved by digging in plenty of acidic soil amendments such as peat moss or leafmold before planting. The plants will not tolerate alkaline soil or even soil that is only mildly acid.

Choose a sunny or slightly shaded spot, avoiding frost pockets, since a frost-free season of about five months is necessary for a good crop. You can also grow smaller blueberries in large containers filled with acidic potting soil. Although blueberries are considered self fertile, it is best to grow at least two different varieties to ensure good pollination and therefore a good crop.

Blueberries, with their delicate, white spring flowers, summer fruit, and attractive, blue-green leaves that turn red in fall are easy to incorporate into ornamental borders. Plant them with other acid-loving shrubs.

Plant highbush blueberries 5–6ft. apart and space lowbush varieties 2–3ft. apart. Rabbiteye blueberries require at least 8ft. between plants.

Aftercare

Blueberries need plenty of moisture in summer to develop a good crop of large berries. In dry weather, water them copiously, preferably with collected rainwater, which has the right pH. Mulch your blueberries with a 3–4in. layer of an organic mulch such as wood chips, leafmold, or pine needles to help keep the soil moist and prevent weeds.

Depending on the variety, blueberries mature in mid- to late summer. For an extended harvest, select several varieties that mature at different times. Harvest berries when they are fully ripe.

Blueberry flowers appear in spring. It is advisable to remove them from first-year plants so that they establish a strong root system. Allow fruit to develop from the second year onward.

Refresh this layer each year to cover and protect roots that grow into the mulch.

For first-year plantings, remove the flowers in spring so that the plants put their energy into establishing a healthy root system. Crops can be harvested the second year after planting.

Although blueberries are not heavy feeders, they will benefit from an annual application of well-rotted manure or compost, spread around each plant in spring.

Regular pruning is not needed, but old bushes become dense. Thin them by removing the oldest, least-productive stems back to ground level or to a strong bud.

Harvesting

Berries range in flavor from very sweet to tart when mature, depending on the variety. Pick the berries when they are blue-black with a whitish bloom and starting to soften. Do not harvest unripe berries because they will not continue to ripen once picked. Eat them fresh and can or freeze the rest.

Highbush blueberries make attractive additions to ornamental beds with their spring flowers, summer fruit, and colorful fall foliage.

PLANTING & PRUNING A HIGHBUSH BLUEBERRY

1 **Dig out** a 12in. square hole before planting. Fill it with a mixture of composted wood chips or leafmold and soil. Mound it slightly and then leave for a few weeks to allow the soil to settle.

2 **Plant bushes** from container-grown stock 5ft. apart, in rows 6ft. apart in fall or spring. With a trowel, make a hole large enough to accommodate the rootball. Fill the hole around the roots and firm the soil.

3 **Apply a fertilizer** high in nitrogen in spring, and repeat for subsequent years. At the same time, mulch with a substance suitable for acid-loving plants, such as leafmold, pine needles, sawdust, or wood chips.

4 **Cut back** fruited branches that have become thin and twiggy to more vigorous shoots, between late fall and late winter. Cut out any damaged or dead branches close to their bases.

Raspberries

These tasty berries grow on canes in all except warmest zones. Raspberries are best in cooler climates and do well in most soils, although they prefer moisture-retentive, well-drained soil that is slightly acidic. If your soil does not drain well, plant in raised beds to discourage root rot.

Except for everbearing types, raspberry canes are vegetative in their first year, bear flowers and fruit in their second year, then die back. New stems grow as suckering shoots (*see page 105*) from ground level.

Raspberries require a strong trellis system with wires. Stretch single or parallel wires between two posts at heights of 30in., 3ft., and 5ft. Use heavy, galavanized wire. Everbearing raspberries (*see box, facing page*) can be grown between two sets of parallel wires strung between either ends of T-supports. To construct the supports, drive 5½ft. posts at least 18in. into the ground and fix two crossbars to the posts at 3ft. and 5ft. from the ground. Stretch wire between the crossbars.

Raspberry varieties belong to the same group of plants as blackberries and other brambles. More unusual types include this fall-fruiting raspberry 'Fallgold', with golden fruit.

PLANTING RASPBERRY CANES

1 **Dig out a trench** in early fall in prepared ground that is 3 spade blades wide by 1 spade blade deep. Cover the base with a 3–4in. layer of well-rotted manure or compost and fork it in thoroughly.

2 **Return the soil** to the trench and roughly level it. Then fork in a slow-release, all-purpose fertilizer at the rate recommended on the package. Leave the soil to settle for a few weeks before planting.

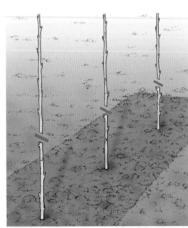

3 **Plant bare-root raspberry canes** between late fall and early spring, at 1½–2½ft. intervals. Spread out the roots of each cane, then fill the hole with the prepared soil. Cut every planted cane to a bud about 10in. above the soil.

4 **Dress the soil** around the canes in early spring with a high-nitrogen fertilizer at least a few weeks after planting. Mulch with a 2in. layer of compost; take care to keep the mulch clear of the canes.

Looking after your soil *see page 32* | **Preparing to grow** *see page 230* | **Common problems** *see page 274*

MAINTAINING RASPBERRY CANES

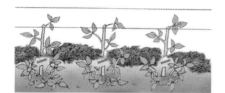

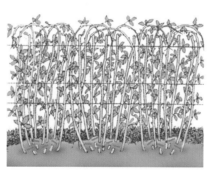

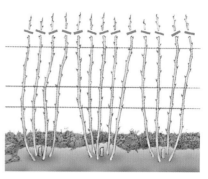

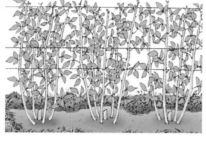

FIRST YEAR

1 **Cut down** the stumps to ground level in spring, when the new canes appear; do not remove the new growth.

2 **In summer, tie in** the new canes to the support wires as they develop. Keep the canes spaced about 4in. apart.

SECOND & SUBSEQUENT YEARS

3 **Cut each cane** back to a bud about 5½ft. high, above the top support wire in late winter. Mulch around the bases of the plants.

4 **In midsummer, pull out** shoots growing away from the row and thin out the weakest new growth to leave canes 4in. apart.

5 **Cut down** fruited canes to the ground after fruiting in summer. Tie in new canes, 4in. apart. Loop vigorous canes over the top wire.

6 **Fertilize plants** with well-rotted manure or a balanced, all-purpose fertilizer, at the rate recommended on the package, in winter.

EVERBEARING RASPBERRIES

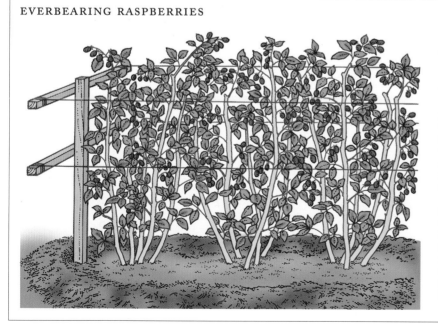

Unlike June-bearing varieties, some raspberries give two crops in a single year. The first one is in late summer and fall, produced on the tops of canes that came up that spring. Once the berries have finished, prune off the tops of those canes, leaving the bottom third or so that did not produce any fruit. The next year, in spring, those canes will grow and produce a new crop in early summer. When they have finished fruiting, you should cut the fruited canes to the ground. Meanwhile, new canes will have grown up to produce the current year's late summer to fall crop.

Some gardeners simplify their pruning regime for everbearing raspberries by cutting all canes to the ground in winter, which means sacrificing the early summer crop. They do this because such a pruning regime may be helpful in controlling overwintering disease spores and may eliminate the need for a trellis system as the single-crop canes do not grow as tall.

Blackberries

These very vigorous, often thorny canes are hardy and do best in well-drained, fertile soil in a sunny spot. Types found in the West, such as the boysenberry, tayberry, and loganberry, are grown in a similar way, but generally are less rampant. Thornless blackberry varieties provide the same delicious fruit, but they lack thorns so are much easier to harvest.

Planting & spacing
Plant blackberries between late fall and early spring. Space thorny types 3–4ft. apart. Plant thornless varieties 4–6 ft. apart. Allow 7–8ft. between rows.

Pruning & training
Blackberries may be trailing or upright types. Trailing types make long canes that need support. Make a support by driving 8ft. posts 30in. into the ground every 12ft. Stretch two wires between the posts, the first fixed 32in. from the ground and the other near the top of the posts. A single top wire may be sufficient for less vigorous types.

First-year canes can be allowed to sprawl over the ground, but tie second-year (fruiting) canes to the wires (*see box, below*) to keep fruit off the ground and make harvesting easier.

Aftercare & harvesting
In late winter, apply a slow-release, all-purpose fertilizer at the rate recommended on the package, followed by a thick mulch, keeping it off the canes. Water during dry spells; avoid wetting the canes to minimize fungal diseases.

Pick the fruit when it is fully colored and soft in summer. At this time, the crop may need protecting from birds with a cover of strong netting.

Thornless blackberries are not only easy to grow but also a breeze to harvest because they lack thorns. For best flavor, wait to pick until the berries are fully colored and detach easily from the stem.

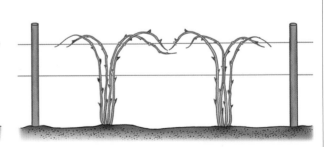

PLANTING & TRAINING BLACKBERRY CANES

Trailing and semitrailing blackberries need to be trained to a trellis, either a single wire (*above*), or more commonly a double wire (*above right*). In spring, select the strongest, second-year (fruiting) shoots and tie them to the wires. Allow first-year (nonfruiting) canes to sprawl on the ground; these will become the fruiting canes the following year. Remove the old fruiting canes after harvest.

Black currants

These currants are very easy to grow and reward you with lots of tangy fruit in the second summer after planting. They are best planted from bare-root stock; look for plants that have three or more shoots. Some bushes reach 6ft. so need plenty of space, but they may provide you with high yields for up to 15 years.

Black currants are tolerant of many soils, but they prefer their roots to be in slightly acidic, fertile, moisture-retentive yet well-drained soil. They tolerate partial shade but prefer a sunny, sheltered position.

The flowers of black currants appear in early spring, so they are vulnerable to hard frosts. Protect from frosts at such times, remembering to remove covers during the day to allow pollinating bees access to the flowers, or buy a hardier or later-flowering variety.

Once established, black currants have a simple pruning regime, but they do need plenty of fertilizer to thrive. Plants also require watering regularly in dry weather, and as the roots are shallow keep the area free of weeds using a hoe rather than a fork, which can disturb the roots.

Red currants, white currants, & gooseberries

Currants and gooseberries—members of the *Ribes* genus— have been grown in America since colonial times, but they fell out of favor in the 20th century due to their status as alternate hosts for the fungal disease white pine blister rust. As a result, cultivation of these berry-producing shrubs was prohibited for many years, and is still restricted in some areas. Still, they are worth growing, as they are undemanding, self-fruitful shrubs.

Planting & spacing

Plant bare-root currants and gooseberries between late fall and early spring, and container-grown plants any time soil can be worked and temperatures are not too high. If planting more than one bush, allow 5ft. between bushes and 5ft. between rows.

Pruning & training

Red and white currants and gooseberries give good yields when trained with open centers (*see below*), with well-spaced branches above a short main stem, 4–6in. tall.

Aftercare

Spread an all-purpose fertilizer around plants in late winter or early spring. Water well in dry weather and keep the soil weed free. The plants' shallow roots make them ideal for drip irrigation. Protect from hard frosts and birds.

Harvesting & storing

Red and white currants and gooseberries are ready to eat in early to midsummer. They often crop heavily, and excess fruit can be canned or frozen.

PRUNING CURRANTS AND GOOSEBERRIES

FIRST YEAR

1 **Maintain a clear stem** on a newly planted bush. The first branches should start about 4–6in. above ground level. In winter, use sharp pruners to remove any growth that has formed below this point.

2 **Cut back**, in late winter, each branch that will form the framework by a half, to a bud that faces the center of the bush and points upward. This formative pruning helps to develop an upright, vase-shaped bush.

SECOND & THIRD YEAR

3 **Shorten leading shoots** by a half to one third in late fall to inward- and upwardfacing buds. Cut well-placed side branches back by one third. Remove any low stems. In the 3rd year, cut again leading shoots, and remove crowded, central stems.

SUBSEQUENT YEARS

4 **Prune out** one third of the bush every winter, cutting older stems first back to the point of origin or to a strong shoot. Also remove badly placed or damaged stems. Remember to fertilize and mulch black currants each year.

241

Grapes

Grapes produce heavily for many years with care and attention. Although images of sun-kissed southern vineyards spring to mind when we think of grape vines, there are grape varieties suitable for almost any home gardens in northern zones, all of them derived from European and American species of *Vitis*. Table grapes usually tend to be sweeter and are either seedless or have fewer seeds than those suitable for wine making.

It is not extreme winter temperatures that thwart grape growers, but rather short summers that prevent fruit from ripening and wet weather that causes fungal diseases. So in cooler, wetter climates it is especially important to choose a suitable variety. In the humid South, native muscadine grapes are a useful option. Your local cooperative extension service can recommend the best varieties grafted onto suitable rootstocks for your climate and soil type.

GROWING GRAPES OUTDOORS

Choose a sheltered, sunny site, either against a sunny fence or wall, in cooler areas, or in the open with a sunny exposure. Grapes thrive in deep, slightly acid, well-drained soil. If the soil is soggy or very alkaline, it will require amendment because these conditions can result in chlorosis caused by nutrient deficiency. Before planting, you will need to prepare the soil and erect a system of supports. Start by removing perennial weeds from the site and dig over the soil in the planting area two to three weeks before you plan to plant. Finish by applying a slow-release, all-purpose fertilizer and rake into the surface.

Planting & training

There are many methods for training grape vines, not only to rein in the growth of these vigorous plants but also to allow for good air circulation and to expose the maximum amount of foliage to sunlight. Some commercial training practices are suitable for the home garden—typically a trellis system with a number of single or double wires to which the growing branches are tied. The method you choose will depend on the amount of space you have and how much construction you are willing to do, but above all the trellis must be sturdy, with strong, galvanized wires and additional bracing for the end posts. In all training systems, the objective is to produce a permanent trunk as a framework and a support for the annual growth of new fruit-bearing canes.

Grape vines trained against a sunny wall should be placed at least 10in. away from the wall. Either build a trellis against the wall, or insert heavy-duty eye bolts into the wall and stretch strong wire through them.

You can also grow grape vines very satisfactorily up and over an arbor or trellis. Grape vines are long-lived

PLANTING & CANE PRUNING A GRAPE VINE

 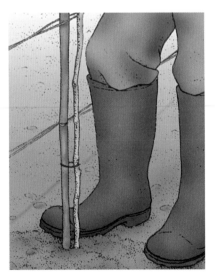 

FIRST YEAR

1 **Erect a trellis** from midfall to early spring. Insert a cane for each plant.

2 **Plant each vine**, then firm, water, and tie in to the support. Cut the main stem back to 2 good buds above soil level.

3 **Fertilize in winter** with a slow-release fertilizer and mulch well.

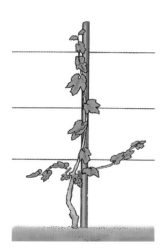

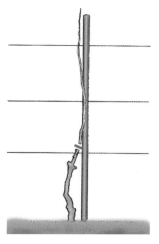

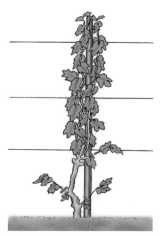

SECOND YEAR

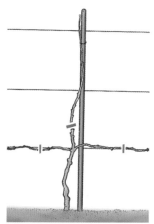

4 **Select the strongest** shoot in the first growing season. Train it vertically up the cane to form the trunk. Pinch back any other branches to just 1 leaf.

5 **Cut down** the trunk of each plant to within 16in. of ground level in late fall. Make sure that you leave 3 good buds.

6 **Train the 3 new canes** vertically from midspring to late summer. Pinch back to 1 leaf any branches that develop.

7 **Tie 2 of the new canes** to the lowest wire in opposite directions. Prune both back to 24–30in. Prune the renewal spur to 3 good buds.

THIRD & SUBSEQUENT YEARS

8 **Train the 3 new canes** that will grow up the central support, in summer. Allow several well-spaced, fruit-bearing shoots to grow vertically from last year's branches. Cut back unwanted sideshoots to 1in. and fruiting shoots to 3 leaves above the top wire.

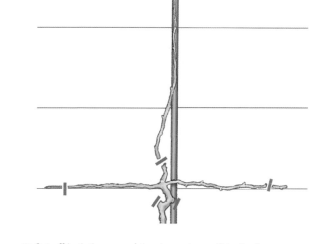

9 **Cut off** both the arms of the vine each year. Take the 3 new canes and tie 2 of them horizontally and cut back to 24–30in. Prune the remaining renewal spur to 2–3 good buds.

and provide a beautiful and reliable shade cover for a sunny patio or deck. The leaves of many grape vines display rich fall colors before dropping for winter. The ripening fruit will, however, attract birds and wasps, so if you live in an area where either pest is a problem you may prefer to plant your grape vine away from the ornamental garden and cover it with netting as the grapes ripen.

One-year-old vines are best planted between midfall and early spring (*see facing page*), as long as the ground is not frozen. If planting a bare-root plant, dig a hole that is wide enough for the roots to spread out fully and deep enough for it to be planted at the same level as before it was lifted. If the variety is grafted onto a rootstock, ensure the graft union is well above the surface of the soil.

Pruning

Grape vines fruit on one-year old canes and spurs and need to be pruned back very hard each year during the dormant season—usually late winter through midspring. Do not prune too early or new growth will be subject to frost. The two most common methods for pruning grapes are cane pruning and spur pruning, depending on the variety. Wine grapes and muscadines usually need spur pruning, where canes are cut back to several buds in the dormant season. New fruit-producing shoots grow on each spur. In cane pruning, each year canes are selected and pruned to 8–14 buds. Fruit-bearing shoots will grow from each bud. In addition to the main fruiting canes, you select an additional strong cane and cut it off, leaving a spur with two or three buds. These are called 'renewal' spurs and they will produce the fruiting canes for the following year.

When you purchase your grape vine, find out which type of pruning it requires (your local cooperative extension service may also offer grape-pruning clinics). Be sure to buy grape vines from a reliable local supplier or mail-order nursery; grape vines have been subject to some serious root-borne pests in the past. The stock should be of highest quality and grown on a rootstock suitable for your area.

Aftercare & harvesting

Every late winter, dress the soil with 2oz. slow-release, all-purpose fertilizer per plant. Then mulch with well-rotted manure or compost. In spring, remove shoots that arise from the roots or base of the trunk.

Once a week during the growing season, fertilize table grapes with an all-purpose liquid fertilizer until the fruits ripen. Plants grown against walls need extra watering since the soil tends to dry out quickly.

Remove some leaves around bunches in late summer to allow air to circulate and light to penetrate the fruit. If any grapes are wizened, moldy, or damaged, cut out carefully with clean pruners.

Grapes should be harvested when they obtain their mature color and maximum sweetness. In most types, all the grapes in a single cluster will ripen at about the same time. When harvesting clusters, cut the branch above the bunch to avoid damaging the fruit or marking the white bloom on some varieties.

GROWING GRAPES INDOORS

In cool climates, a greater choice of grape varieties can be grown in a cool or heated greenhouse. The vines can be planted either in garden soil in the greenhouse, or outside the greenhouse directly into garden soil with the main stem threaded inside the structure through a low hole. Planting outdoors allows the vine to be partly irrigated by rainfall, but indoors the soil warms up quickly in spring, helping to produce earlier growth.

Grape vines are vigorous and will take over the structure if not restrained. There are as many ways to train a grape vine indoors as out in the vineyard, but the objective once again is to establish a permanent framework from which the fruiting canes grow each year. One option is to plant vines in an upright cordon against a series of strong horizontal wires and spur-prune them each year. Place the wires at least 16in. from the greenhouse wall glazing, about 10in. apart, with the highest one approximately 18in. below the roof ridge. Do not secure the wires to your greenhouse framing, instead insert posts in the ground or, if you have a poured foundation, anchor them to the concrete.

Train the young vine with a main stem and side branches running on alternate side wires. Each year, remove the growing tip of the main stem and cut back all side branches. Fruiting canes will emerge from each side branch annually. In spring, tie in these canes as they develop and cut all fruiting canes back to two leaves beyond the flower cluster. Pinch back any subsideshoots to one leaf in summer.

In a smaller space, you can plant a vine near a corner and train a single shoot horizontally along a wire at gutter height. Then train the permanent branches vertically on wires running up to the roof ridge. From these shoots, fruiting canes will emerge each year; spur-prune them as described above.

PESTS & DISEASES OF GRAPE VINES

Botrytis on the cane and grapes

Good air circulation is important for grape vines, so be sure to give plants the proper spacing and prune to keep them open. Botrytis—also called gray mold—often occurs on vines that are not provided with adequate circulation; improve circulation by removing a few leaves around each developing cluster. Other practices that help prevent this and other diseases include selecting resistant varieties, sanitation (removal of infected berries and old leaves), and avoiding excessive use of nitrogen fertilizer.

Melons

These tropical vines require a long period of reliably hot weather. Muskmelons (also called cantaloupes) have thick green or orange, rough skins that are often ribbed. Late melons, such as honeydews, have smooth skins and yellow or green flesh; they typically require an even longer growing season than cantaloupes.

Melons prefer a light, well-drained soil, so incorporate plenty of compost in fall. Sow seeds outdoors two weeks after the last frost date for your area, or start them indoors then plant outdoors after all danger of frost has passed. Your local nursery may also sell seedling melons for your region. Black plastic landscape fabric and row covers can warm the soil and hasten growth. Melons can be planted on hills 3–4ft. apart or spaced the same distance apart in rows. Do not overwater and apply a slow-release balanced fertilizer once a month in the growing season.

Types of melons

Although cantaloupes, honeydews, and watermelons are the most popular types of melon grown in American gardens, there are several others that can be grown where summers are long. All are grown in a similar manner.

Ananas melons: Also called pineapple melons, these produce oval-shaped, medium-sized fruit (4lb.) with pale green to orange, netted rinds. This heirloom variety has a sweet, pale green flesh and a pineapplelike aroma.

Canary melons: Oblong or rounded in shape with a bright orange-yellow rind and mild-flavored, cream-colored flesh.

Casaba melons: Large (4–7lb.) and oval in shape with a wrinkled, yellow skin and very sweet, pale yellow, almost white flesh. The fruit has little or no fragrance.

Charentais melons: Relatively small (2lb.) with smooth, gray-blue skins and bright orange, sweet and juicy flesh.

Christmas melons: Also called Santa Claus melons, these are shaped like footballs and usually weigh 5–8lb. Their mottled rinds are yellow-green, and their flesh is light green and is less sweet than most other types.

Crenshaw (or Cranshaw) melons: A cross between Casaba and Persian melons. Their rinds range from pale green to yellow and their peach-colored flesh is fragrant, sweet, and spicy.

Galia melons: These hail from Israel. They look similar to cantaloupes externally, but their flesh is pale green to white, very firm, and sweet, with a bananalike fragrance.

Persian melons: Similar to cantaloupes, although they are larger and their rinds have finer netting. Their delicately flavored flesh is pinkish orange.

There are many melon varieties to select from; ones that are mildew resistant are a good choice. You can train them over archways, on fences, or let them trail from raised beds.

WATERMELONS

Most watermelons grow best in the South, where they enjoy the long, hot summers needed to ripen them. With good site choice and preparation, northern gardeners may also grow these fruits. Many varieties are available, including early-ripening types for colder areas. Check with your local cooperative extension service for varieties likely to ripen in your area.

Watermelons like rich soil, so dig in plenty of organic material in fall. Start watermelon seeds indoors a month before planting time, or wait until the soil warms up, then sow seeds outdoors. Plant watermelon on small mounds, or hills, 6–8ft. apart. Sow 6–8 seeds per hill, then thin to three plants per hill. Black plastic landscape fabric will help warm the soil and keep down weeds. Floating row covers over young seedlings will also supply warmth to encourage early growth. Supply regular irrigation throughout summer and apply a slow-release, all-purpose fertilizer every four weeks.

Pick watermelons only when ripe, as they do not continue to ripen after harvest. Check for ripeness by tapping; this should produce a dull 'thunking' sound. (A hollow sound means the fruit is overripe.) The stem attachment, or tendril, will also dry and grow darker when the melon is ripe. When harvesting, cut the stem rather than pulling it off.

TREE FRUIT

Tree fruit encompass some of the most popular fruit cultivated by gardeners. Also referred to as top fruit in the horticultural industry, this large group includes plants that, if left to their own devices, grow into trees or very large shrubs. Apples, pears, plums, cherries, figs, peaches, nectarines, citrus, and apricots, are all tree fruit. Although full-sized fruit trees require a good bit of space, particularly if several different types or varieties are desired, a great many dwarf and compact varieties of tree fruits are bred specifically for growing in large pots and other containers, making growing fruit possible for nearly everyone.

Fruit trees in the yard

If you have space, you can establish an orchard of full-size trees, but it is more likely that your choice will be restricted to a few trees. In small yards, grow fruit trees as fans, cordons, or espaliers and train on horizontal wires fixed to a fence or a wall. In a cool climate, the shelter of a wall can be beneficial to some tree fruit, and it helps the fruit to ripen before the end of the growing season.

All fruit trees require pruning for three reasons: to restrict growth, to remain productive, and to keep an attractive shape. Free-standing trees are pruned to an open center (*see page 249*) or with a central leader. Thinning of fruit also ensures that the best possible fruit is obtained.

Most fruit trees do best in a sunny site free from severe frosts, especially when in blossom. They all prefer well-prepared, well-drained, moisture-retentive soil. Tender trees such as citrus may need winter and frost protection.

Climate is a major determining factor when choosing fruit trees to grow in your yard. It is not just a question of cold hardiness. Many trees set fruit during the fluctuating

Fruit trees in the open garden can be very ornamental as well as productive. They do not require a great deal of space if you choose a suitable variety and appropriate rootstock.

Restricted forms of fruit trees, such as fans, cordons, or espaliers, make good use of vacant spaces on walls and fences, and they can also be used to create decorative screens or barriers in the yard.

temperatures of spring and can be damaged by frost, resulting in poor fruit set or misshapen fruit. Other trees, such as apples, have a 'chilling requirement', which means that plants require a certain number of winter days with temperatures below 45°F for proper fruit formation. And others need long, hot summers to set and fully ripen fruit—citrus and pomegranate are examples.

Tender fruits such as citrus, pomegranate, and fig can be grown in some areas with winter protection, such as wrapping with burlap or covering with plastic or blankets. Smaller trees and dwarf varieties can also be grown in containers that are overwintered in a sheltered spot such as a greenhouse, garage, or basement.

Pollination

For fruit to be produced, flowers need to be pollinated. This is the process in which pollen is transferred from the male part of a flower (anther) to the female part (stigma) in order to fertilize the ovule.

More often than not, pollination is carried out by bees or other insects, although pollen can also be transported by the wind. In some circumstances, it may be necessary to carry this out yourself to ensure that fertilization has taken place in as many flowers as possible (*see right*).

Fertilization

Peaches, nectarines, and some plums and apricots are self fertile and can be pollinated by their own flowers. Apples, pears, and most sweet cherries will not set fruit without being pollinated by a different variety of the same fruit. The other variety should flower at the same time and be planted nearby—no more than 50ft. away. Your local cooperative extension service to recommend appropriate pollinating varieties for your chosen fruit.

Bees are essential to pollination. Avoid spraying pesticides that could kill bees along with problem pests. If your native bee population is dwindling, encourage bee colonies by building or buying native bee boxes (*see page 61*).

Some plants have their male and female flowers on different plants; kiwi is an example of this (*see page 267*). You must have both a male and a female kiwi in your yard in order for the female plant to fruit.

Rootstocks

Fruit trees are usually grafted onto rootstocks. The rootstock determines the ultimate size of the plant and the scion (the fruit-bearing part of the plant) determines the variety. Some rootstocks keep the tree dwarf; these are often the best choice for small yards. Other rootstocks provide resistance to diseases.

STRUCTURE OF BLOSSOM

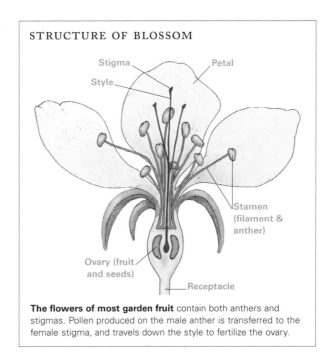

The flowers of most garden fruit contain both anthers and stigmas. Pollen produced on the male anther is transferred to the female stigma, and travels down the style to fertilize the ovary.

HAND POLLINATION

1 **Test if pollen** is being shed by drawing a fingertip over the anthers; they should deposit yellow grains. When it has been warm and dry for 2–3 days, pollinate at midday. Transfer pollen gently from the anthers to the stigmas with a soft camel-hair brush or cotton swab.

2 **If compatible flowers** are on separate plants, strip the petals from a ripe flower, then press its center against the center of another flower to pollinate it. Hand pollinate every day, if possible, until flowering is over.

Planting fruit trees

Plant dormant bare-root fruit trees—available from good garden centers and specialty fruit nurseries—from late fall to early spring depending on your climate. If the trees cannot be planted right away, heel them into the ground (*see box, right*) until you are ready. Container-grown trees are available, and can be planted, year-round as long as the ground is not frozen. One-year-old, bare-root trees are unbranched and referred to as 'whips'.

How to plant

First weed and dig the soil, preferably four weeks before planting. Dig a square yard area for each tree rather than the entire site, unless planting trees very closely. Add plenty of compost if the soil is heavy or sandy. Just before planting, rake in a slow-release, all-purpose fertilizer.

You can use angled or upright stakes to support fruit trees. Angled stakes are ideal for dwarf trees or those bought container-grown, but bare-root fruit trees should have vertical stakes (*see page 99*) to support them. Both types should be hammered into the ground before planting—at least 24in. deep on light soils. For vertical stakes, standard trees need them 8ft. long; semidwarfs 6ft. long; and dwarf trees 3–4ft. long.

HEELING IN FRUIT TREES

Plant bare-root trees as soon as possible, but if a delay is unavoidable dig a shallow trench and lay the tree in the trench at an angle. Cover the roots with moist soil.

Use soft ties to avoid damaging bark. Put a single tie, 1in. from the stake top, for dwarfs; two ties, at the top and halfway down, for standards and semidwarfs; and three ties for pyramidal forms.

PLANTING A FRUIT TREE

1 **Trim off** broken or long taproots, using pruners. If the roots are dry, soak them for an hour before planting.

2 **Stake appropriately** for the type of tree (*see above*)—here, a container-grown plant. Do not plant too deeply.

3 **Replace the soil** and firm gently. Water well and mulch.

Apples & pears

Apples are among the most widely adapted of fruit trees. Most pears are European types, which include favorites such as 'Bartlett' and 'Anjou'. Asian pears, sometimes called apple pears, are also grown in the West and South as they have a lower chill requirement.

Where to grow apples & pears

Both fruit prefer a well-drained, slightly acidic soil, but tolerate a wide range of soils. The soil should be deep, not limited by a high water table or hardpan. Improve light, sandy soils with organic matter. The trees thrive in a sunny, sheltered, frost-free location. If necessary, use windbreaks, or train plants against a wall.

Choosing trees & rootstocks

Apples and pear varieties are grafted onto rootstocks that control the tree's growth rate and its eventual size. Those on dwarfing rootstocks are typically 5–8ft. tall and high. They tend to be more shallow rooted (requiring staking or trellising), produce fruit sooner than larger trees, and are suitable for training into espaliers or cordons. Semidwarf apple trees are typically 50–80 percent of the height of a standard and are 8–12ft. tall. These trees are often very productive and can be planted in a home orchard or trained like dwarf trees in a small garden. Standard apple trees can grow to 25ft. tall and are often hardier than dwarf and semidwarf types.

Pears are typically grafted onto quince rootstocks. Standard pear trees can grow 25ft. or taller, whereas dwarf types reach about 15ft. Dwarf pears are easily trained like apples as cordons, hedges, or espaliers.

When buying bare-root trees, look for healthy, two- to three-year-old specimens with balanced root systems that have not dried out. Plant them as soon as possible

FORMATIVE TRAINING OF AN OPEN-CENTERED APPLE OR PEAR TREE

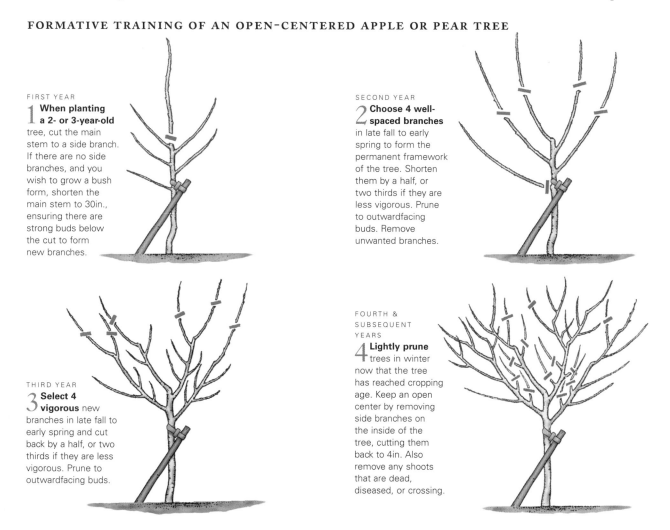

FIRST YEAR

1 When planting a 2- or 3-year-old tree, cut the main stem to a side branch. If there are no side branches, and you wish to grow a bush form, shorten the main stem to 30in., ensuring there are strong buds below the cut to form new branches.

SECOND YEAR

2 Choose 4 well-spaced branches in late fall to early spring to form the permanent framework of the tree. Shorten them by a half, or two thirds if they are less vigorous. Prune to outwardfacing buds. Remove unwanted branches.

THIRD YEAR

3 Select 4 vigorous new branches in late fall to early spring and cut back by a half, or two thirds if they are less vigorous. Prune to outwardfacing buds.

FOURTH & SUBSEQUENT YEARS

4 Lightly prune trees in winter now that the tree has reached cropping age. Keep an open center by removing side branches on the inside of the tree, cutting them back to 4in. Also remove any shoots that are dead, diseased, or crossing.

after purchase; otherwise heel them in (*see page 248*) if they cannot be planted right away.

Free-standing trees

Most free-standing trees need to be trained as open-centered plants (*see page 249*). Dwarf pyramid trees (*see page 252*) are an alternative—they are free standing but grown as a restricted form. The spacing of free-standing apples and pears varies according to tree form, assuming that an appropriate rootstock is chosen for the form of tree. Restricted tree forms are discussed later in the chapter (*see pages 255–258*).

Space dwarf forms 8–10ft. apart. For standard trees, space plants at least 20ft. apart.

Pruning for fruit

Once the formative training stage is over, it should not be necessary to prune the branch framework. On a cropping tree, the only pruning required is the careful management of fruit buds and the branches they grow on.

Most apples and pears fruit on short, stubby spurs found on two-year-old wood. You therefore need to maintain a mixture of side branches at different stages of growth to be cut back after fruiting. This is achieved by spur and renewal pruning (*see boxes, below*). Renewal pruning is best reserved for the tree's outer branches where there is space for extra growth, while spur pruning is most useful for restricted forms. Branches will also need to be removed if they are dead, diseased, or crossing.

SPUR PRUNING

FIRST YEAR

1 **From late fall to late winter**, select a proportion of new side branches that have insufficient space to extend into branches. Cut them back to 4 buds to encourage fruit buds.

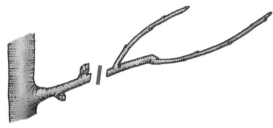

SECOND YEAR

2 **From late fall to late winter**, cut back each side branch to just above the topmost fat flower bud. If there is room for a bigger side branch, cut to 4 wood buds on last year's growth.

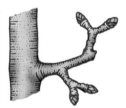

THIRD & SUBSEQUENT YEARS

3 **A spur system forms**, producing flowers and fruit. After some years, the spur will eventually become overcrowded and need to be thinned in winter (*see page 257*).

RENEWAL PRUNING

FIRST YEAR

1 **In late fall to winter**, select a strong, well-placed side branch and leave it unpruned.

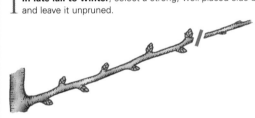

SECOND YEAR

2 **Extension growth will develop** the following summer and fruit buds will form on the older wood. Let it grow and, in winter, cut it back to the joint between the old and new wood.

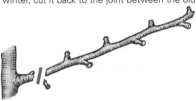

THIRD YEAR

3 **Cut back the fruited stem** in late fall to winter to leave a short stub, about 1in. long, to encourage a replacement side branch to develop.

FOURTH & SUBSEQUENT YEARS

4 **In midfall**, at the end of the growing season, a new, vigorous lateral should have been produced. Leave this unpruned until the following winter, as in step 1.

APPLE & PEAR DWARF PYRAMIDS

The dwarf pyramid was developed by commercial fruit growers as an easier method of producing apples and pears intensively. This method is suitable for dwarf and some semidwarf trees. The aim is to produce a tree about 7ft. tall with a branch spread of about 4ft. at the base of the canopy, which tapers to the top to form a pyramidal shape.

It is vital to keep such a closely planted and compact tree form under control—by summer pruning, early cropping, complete removal of vigorous, upright shoots, and by growing on the right rootstock.

Planting, spacing, & supporting dwarf pyramids

Use single stakes if planting one or two trees. Support a row of trees by running two horizontal wires between two posts, one at a height of 18in. and the other at 36in. Tie the trees to the wires with soft string or tree ties. Place dwarf trees 4–5ft. apart and semidwarf trees 5–6ft. apart.

FORMATIVE PRUNING OF A DWARF PYRAMID

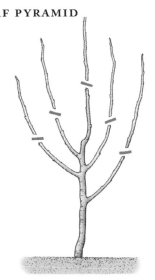

FIRST YEAR

1 **Cut back** one-year-old trees to a bud within 20in. of soil level at planting.

SECOND YEAR

2 **Cut the central stem** to 9in. of its new growth, to a bud. Prune the main branches to 8in. of their new growth.

3 **Cut side branches** not required for the tree framework to 3 leaves in late summer. Cut sideshoots to 1 leaf after the basal cluster.

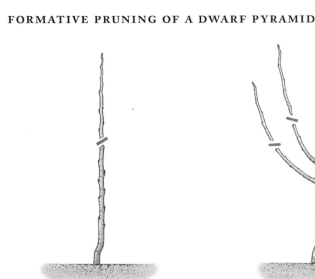

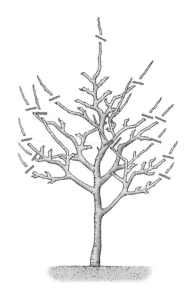

THIRD & SUBSEQUENT YEARS

4 **Cut the central stem** in winter to a bud on the opposite side to the previous pruning. Otherwise repeat as for step 2.

5 **Prune side branches and sideshoots** in late summer, as in step 3. Cut back the tips of the main branches to 6 leaves.

6 **Prune the central stem** in winter, as in step 4. Shorten main branches as needed to downwardfacing buds to keep them horizontal.

THE MATURE DWARF PYRAMID TREE

When the tree has reached a height of about 7ft., cut back the central stem to its origin each year in late spring. Maintain the central stem and retain the pyramid shape by pruning and removal of vigorous shoots. Thin spurs as necessary (*see page 257*).

Dwarf pyramid forms of apple and pear trees make a very ornamental feature and are especially suited to smaller spaces if grown singly. The pyramid or conical shape makes it very easy to pick the ripe fruit.

Pruning & training

At planting, prune to encourage four or five vigorous shoots to grow (*see facing page*). Cut them back in the second winter to begin forming a pyramid shape; when pruning the central leader, cut to a bud that points in the opposite direction of the first pruning. Summer prune side branches to encourage the formation of fruiting spurs. Winter prune in subsequent years to maintain a dwarf pyramid shape by cutting the branches to downwardfacing buds. Thin sideshoots to stop the tree being crowded with branches. Every summer, shorten sideshoots back to three leaves.

CARE OF APPLES & PEARS

Besides pruning, apples and pears need year-round attention to keep them healthy and productive (*see following page*). If your garden suffers from severe late frosts, protect flowers and emerging fruits in spring with floating row covers, where practical.

Harvesting

There is no exact time for picking apples and pears, since this is dependent on variety, the season, and the location of your yard. Generally, you can tell when a fruit is ready to pick by holding it in the palm of your hand, lifting upward, and twisting it away gently. If the fruit comes off the spur easily, without leaving behind any damaged wood, then it should be ready to pick. Test this further on apples by cutting a fruit open to see whether the seeds have turned from white to brown.

Fruit that falls naturally from the tree, known as windfalls, is another indicator that fruit is ready, as is a change in color. Generally, pears turn from a dark to lighter green, while apples tend to become brighter.

As a rule of thumb, fruit is best picked when under-ripe—just after midsummer for early-season pears, late summer for midseason pears, and early fall for late-season pears. Early apples may be ready as soon as midsummer, while later varieties are on the tree in midfall. To avoid

MAINTAINING AN APPLE OR PEAR TREE

1 **In early spring,** apply a slow-release, all-purpose fertilizer, at the rate suggested on the package, over the root area and rake in. Lack of nutrients may hamper the formation of fruit buds, leading to a poor crop.

2 **In midspring,** mulch newly planted and young trees with a 2in. deep layer of well-rotted manure or garden compost. Spread it over the root area to a radius of about 18in., keeping it clear of the stem to prevent it from rotting.

3 **In summer,** water young and newly planted trees copiously every 10 days in dry weather. Lack of moisture can affect yields and formation of next year's fruit. Carry out any summer pruning as necessary.

4 **In summer,** thin overcrowded fruit clusters to avoid small fruit. Trees shed some fruit naturally in early summer, but you may have to thin later in midsummer. First remove small or misshapen fruit. Less thinning is necessary on pear trees.

5 **Support branches** when you have a bumper crop of fruit on a small tree, to stop the branches bowing and possibly breaking. Support each branch with a rope attached to a central, stout post. On larger trees, use Y-shaped supports anchored in the ground to prop up individual branches.

6 **In winter,** maintain a weed- and grass-free circle, 24in. in diameter, around the base of each tree. Carry out any winter pruning as necessary. The maintenance cycle then begins again in early spring with fertilizing around the roots.

bruising, handle the fruit gently and collect it in a container lined with soft material.

Pears that are harvested before they are ripe will continue to ripen off the tree. Keep them in a well-ventilated room, or place them on a windowsill, checking them for ripeness every 1–2 days.

Avoid storing ripe or early fruit, which are best eaten fresh. Keep fruit in a cool (37–45°F), dark place where air flows freely, such as a garage, basement, or shed. Wrap apples in newspaper, but leave pears unwrapped, and place them in old plastic or wooden bins or a purpose-built storage unit (like a chest of drawers with

slatted trays). Check the fruit regularly and remove any that are damaged or rotting.

Biennial bearing

Poor yields often follow the year after a heavy crop, and trees can get into a pattern of biennial bearing. This tendency is more pronounced in some varieties than others. To prevent this, try removing half of the fruit buds in the spring after a poor crop. This causes the tree to produce a more modest crop, leaving enough energy to form sufficient fruiting buds for the following year. Removing water sprouts may also reduce biennial bearing.

APPLE & PEAR CORDONS

Usually planted at an angle, cordons consist of one or more stems with many spurs (*see page 256*). Several cordons, usually dwarf and semidwarf varieties, can be squeezed into a tiny yard, making it easy to overcome problems of cross-pollination. Cordons must be kept to a manageable size and require heavy pruning to keep them in check.

Choosing rootstocks & plants

If your soil is poor, select an apple or pear variety that has been grafted onto a vigorous rootstock. Partially trained one- or two-year-old trees are sold by nurseries, which can reduce the time taken to establish a cropping tree. They also make a more instant screen if the cordons are to be grown along a boundary.

Spacing apple & pear cordons

Cordons need to be spaced about 2½–3ft. apart. Use the wider spacing on poor soils. The plants receive the best light if planted in a row that runs north–south.

Planting & supporting cordons

If you are using a fence or wall, secure three horizontal, heavy-duty, 12-gauge wires 24in. apart between posts or attached to eye hooks in the wall.

On planting, leave 6in. between the wire support and the tree, and ensure the graft union is above soil level when you plant with the stem at the required angle. Lean each tree into the vertical support and tie to a 6ft. bamboo cane, which should be secured at the required angle to the wire support.

Pruning & training

In their first few years, pruning concentrates on forming the cordon framework (*see below*). You should remove all flowers in spring from a cordon in its first two years so that the tree can put its energy instead into growing new branches and filling the framework.

Once the framework is in place, prune cordons through the growing season to encourage fruiting buds and to keep the trees within limits (*see page 256*). If there is too much

FORMATIVE PRUNING OF A CORDON

FIRST YEAR

1 Plant the tree from late fall to early spring against a bamboo cane secured at 45 degrees to wire supports. Cut back any side branches to 4 strong buds. Do not prune the central stem.

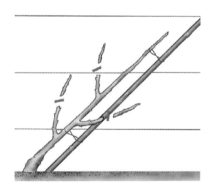

3 Cut back side branches longer than 9in. arising from the central stem to 3 good leaves in late summer, ignoring the basal cluster of leaves. Prune sideshoots arising from existing spur systems to 1 leaf beyond the basal cluster.

SECOND & SUBSEQUENT YEARS

2 Remove flowers in spring to stop the tree fruiting in its second year. Stubby shoots called spurs should have formed on the previously pruned side branches. In subsequent years, do not remove the flowers.

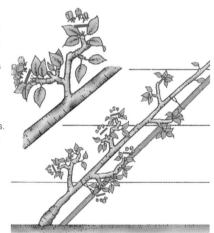

4 Just before leaf fall, if any new growth develops from the pruned shoots, cut it back to the old wood.

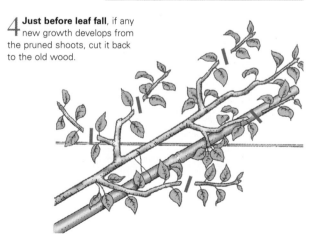

CORDON FORMS

Cordons may be single or multiple, with 2, 3, or more arms, trained vertically or at an angle. Train a multiple cordon initially in the same way as the first horizontal arms of an espalier (*see page 258*). Then treat each arm as a single cordon. Vertically trained cordons are usually more vigorous and less fruitful than those trained at 45 degrees. The angle can be lowered further to increase fruit-bud formation or to check vigor.

secondary growth after late summer pruning, delay to late fall instead. This secondary growth will be damaged by frost if not removed in fall, but if too much is removed it will weaken the tree.

Winter prune to renovate cordons if they have made poor growth. The central stem can be pruned back by one third to promote the development of extra side branches. This time of year is also best for thinning out overcrowded spur systems (*see facing page*).

Cordons are ideally suited to smaller yards because they can be grown against a wall or fence, or planted against a wire fence in the open to create a fruiting barrier or divider in the vegetable garden.

MAINTAINING A FRUITING CORDON

1 **In late spring**, cut back new extension growth on the main stem to its origin when it passes beyond the top wire and reaches the required height of about 7ft.

2 **In late summer**, remove the new leading shoot that has grown in its place at the tip of the central stem, cutting it back to 1in. Prune back to 3 leaves all mature side branches longer than 9in. growing directly from the main stem. Cut back sideshoots from existing spurs to 1 leaf beyond the basal cluster.

APPLE & PEAR ESPALIERS

These restricted tree forms consist of a central stem with tiers of horizontal, fruiting arms trained from either side. Grown against a fence or wall, or on wires stretched between stout, vertical posts, they make an attractive garden feature, providing flowers in the spring, and attractive, delicious fruit in fall. The good looks of the espalier make it more ornamental than the cordon, but it does require more space and maintenance.

Choosing rootstocks & plants

If you have good soil, a semidwarf rootstock is fine. For larger walls, use a standard-size rootstock. Pear rootstocks can be chosen as for cordons (*see page 255*).

You can start espaliers off from one-year-old trees or save time and buy partially trained trees. Some specialty fruit nurseries supply older trees, often with two tiers and a main stem, ready for the gardener to train further arms. You will have less choice of varieties, but it reduces the time taken to establish a cropping tree and it also creates a more instant feature or screen.

Spacing apple & pear espaliers

Space dwarf apples 10–12ft. apart; semidwarf and standard apple trees require up to 18ft. between plants. Dwarf pear trees can be planted 10–15ft. apart.

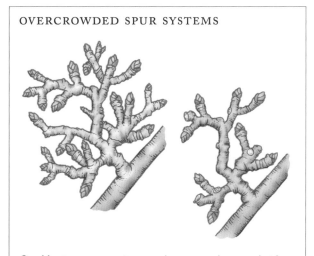

OVERCROWDED SPUR SYSTEMS

On older trees, spur systems can become overlong, overlapping, or congested. Thin out the weaker buds first, and cut back some spur systems to 2 or 3 fruit buds, from late fall to late winter.

Planting & supporting espaliers

Before planting the trees, first construct a support system using galvanized wires stretched between posts or eye hooks. If you are buying partially trained trees, use the arms of the trees to guide the placing of the horizontal wires; usually these should be 15–18in. apart.

To allow room for the trunk to grow, make sure that each tree is planted 6in. away from the supports, leaning slightly toward the support. Also check that the graft union remains above ground.

Pruning & training

To form espaliers, prune your trees in winter to encourage shoots that can form new tiers. On planting, a one-year-old tree should be cut back, leaving three buds that are well placed to form a central, vertical leader and two arms extending in opposite directions.

In the first growing season, train the first two 'arms' temporarily on canes at an angle to encourage extension growth; laid horizontally, branches fruit well but are less vigorous. If the arms are weak, you can angle them slightly more upright to prompt more extension growth. Continue formative pruning and training until the desired number of arms, usually between four and five tiers, have been produced on each espalier. In a good year, if growth is strong, you could leave the central stem unpruned so that more tiers are formed next season.

Once the espalier has reached its mature shape, the new terminal growths on the horizontal and vertical arms should be cut back to their origins, where they join the old wood; this should be done every year in late spring.

Espalier fruit trees, such as these apples growing at the American Horticultural Society's headquarters in Alexandria, Virginia, provide both an ornamental landscape feature, forming an attractive barrier between the parking area and garden, and a source of delicious fruit.

FORMATIVE PRUNING OF AN ESPALIER

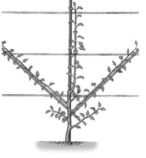 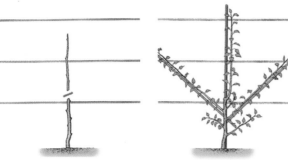 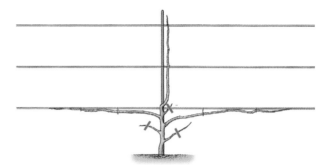

FIRST YEAR

1 **Cut down** to 15in. after planting in late fall to early spring. Keep 3 good buds.

2 **Train** the top bud shoot up a vertical cane and the 2 lower shoots at 45 degrees in summer.

3 **Lower the 2 side branches** to the first horizontal wire in late fall, and tie them carefully with soft twine. Cut back surplus side branches on the main stem to 3 buds.

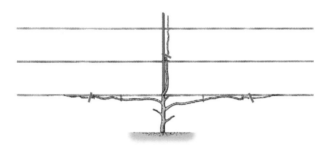 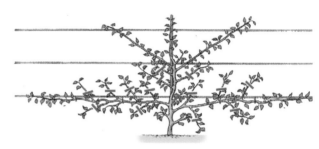 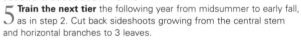

4 **Cut back the central stem** in winter to within 18in. of the lower branches and at a wire, keeping 3 good buds. If growth is weak, prune back the 2 branches by up to one third, cutting to downward-pointing buds.

SECOND & SUBSEQUENT YEARS

5 **Train the next tier** the following year from midsummer to early fall, as in step 2. Cut back sideshoots growing from the central stem and horizontal branches to 3 leaves.

6 **Cut back the central stem** in winter, as in step 4. Tie down the new horizontal branches, as in step 3. Prune back the branches by up to one third, cutting to downward-pointing buds.

7 **Cut back new tip growths** to old wood in late spring, when the espalier has filled its allotted space. Maintain thereafter as for cordons (*see page 256*).

New shoots often develop from these cuts; when the tree is dormant in winter, remove these shoots to maintain a clean framework. From then on, carry out summer pruning of the side branches in the same way as for mature cordons (*see page 256*). Prune in winter to renovate espaliers, if necessary.

After a few years of fruiting, the spur systems can become complicated and should be simplified by thinning weak buds, or by removing those on the shaded side of the system (*see page 257*).

Avoid overfertilizing; a single topdressing of a slow-release fertilizer applied while the trees are dormant is usually sufficient.

Properly maintained, espaliered trees can produce more fruit per foot than standard trees. For best results, select varieties that are well suited to your region.

Plums

Nurseries stock a wide variety of plums, from European and Japanese types to gages, sand plums, and cherry plums. In smaller gardens, plums can be grown in a restricted form, such as a fan against a wall or fence (*see page 261*), or as a pyramid (*see page 260*). They are not suitable for growing as cordons or espaliers.

Where to grow plums

Plums prefer a moisture-retentive, well-drained soil with a pH of 6.5–7.2 in a sunny, sheltered site. They bloom in spring and are sometimes subject to early frosts, so find a sheltered spot in the yard and be sure to choose a type that is not only hardy enough for your zone but that will also bloom after your last hard frost.

The pollination needs of plums vary greatly; some are self fertile, and others require a pollinator. Be sure you know the pollination needs of your plums before you head home from the nursery. Hand pollinate to improve the chances of a good crop (*see page 247*), as plums flower at a time of year when pollinating insects are scarce.

As many plum varieties flower early in the growing season, choose a sheltered, frost-free site. In frosty areas, grow the tree against a vertical structure, such as a wall, which makes it easy to cover the frost-prone flowers and developing fruit.

Choosing trees

Even though many plums are considered self fertile, you will almost always get heavier crops if you plant two or more compatible varieties in your yard. Planting multiple varieties can also extend your harvest season.

Like apple and pear trees, plums are grafted onto rootstocks (*see page 249*) and you should select a variety and rootstock that is suitable for your local climate, the soil conditions in your fruit garden, the available space, and how you intend to grow the tree.

PLANTING & THINNING A PLUM TREE

1 Prepare the soil in fall, clearing away any perennial weeds. Lightly fork in a slow-release, all-purpose fertilizer and a handful of bonemeal per yard.

2 Drive in a stake if the tree is to grow in the open. Use an upright stake for bare-root trees, or a stake at 45 degrees for container-grown trees or those with a rootball. For fan-trained plums, construct a system of wires on the wall. Plant the tree between late fall and early spring and tie it to the stake or wire support.

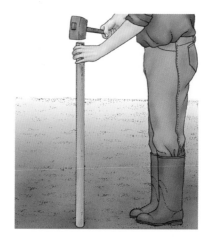

3 Mulch around the tree with a 1–2in. layer of well-rotted garden compost or manure after planting and apply a slow-release, all-purpose fertilizer. Repeat application of mulch and fertilizer annually.

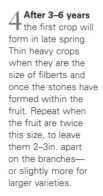

4 After 3–6 years the first crop will form in late spring. Thin heavy crops when they are the size of filberts and once the stones have formed within the fruit. Repeat when the fruit are twice this size, to leave them 2–3in. apart on the branches— or slightly more for larger varieties.

FORMATIVE PRUNING OF A PYRAMID PLUM TREE

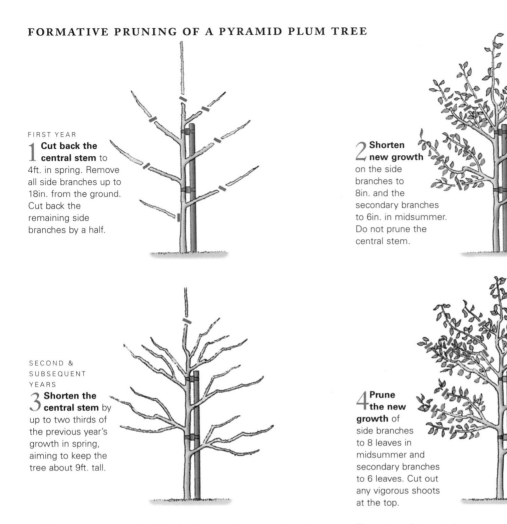

FIRST YEAR

1 Cut back the central stem to 4ft. in spring. Remove all side branches up to 18in. from the ground. Cut back the remaining side branches by a half.

2 Shorten new growth on the side branches to 8in. and the secondary branches to 6in. in midsummer. Do not prune the central stem.

SECOND & SUBSEQUENT YEARS

3 Shorten the central stem by up to two thirds of the previous year's growth in spring, aiming to keep the tree about 9ft. tall.

4 Prune the new growth of side branches to 8 leaves in midsummer and secondary branches to 6 leaves. Cut out any vigorous shoots at the top.

Most plums are 15–20ft. in height; those on dwarfing rootstocks may be only slightly smaller. Few are smaller than 10ft. in height. European plums typically grow better in cool climates, while Japanese plums are more widely grown in warmer areas. Hardy hybrids are available for the coldest winter areas. Consult a specialty fruit nursery or your local cooperative extension service for the best plums for your area.

Plums can be grown as free-standing trees or, in smaller gardens, trained as fans. Instructions are given for each type above and on the facing page.

Planting & spacing

If planting a fan-trained plum, first install a series of horizontal training wires to the wall or fence, spacing them 6in. apart.

Standard plums on vigorous rootstocks should be spaced 18–20ft. apart, while semidwarfs and fan-trained plums can be planted every 11–14ft. Allow 10–11ft. between plums grafted onto a dwarf rootstock.

Pruning & training

Japanese plums, which produce their fruit on one-year-old wood as well as on spurs, require heavier pruning than European types.

The process for pruning and training a pyramid plum is shown above. If growing a free-standing plum, cut back the central stem of a one-year-old tree to a bud—at a height of 36in. for a dwarf, 5ft. for a pyramid, 4½ft. for a semidwarf, and 6ft. for a standard. To thicken up the stem, cut all side branches back to 3in., and in midsummer select four or five of these and cut the rest back to four or five leaves. When pruning side branches for a pyramid plum, always cut to downwardfacing buds to keep growth of new branches horizontal.

In late winter or early spring of the following year, prune the selected branches left unpruned from last year, cutting back each by a half to an outwardfacing bud. Cut back all other side branches to the main stem.

In summer, pull up any suckering shoots that appear from ground level (*see page 105*) and snip out any shoots

FORMATIVE PRUNING OF A PLUM FAN

FIRST THREE YEARS

1 Prune as for a cherry fan (*see page 268*), extending the framework to fill the space. Prune only when the tree is in growth.

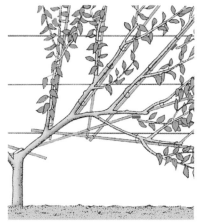

FOURTH & SUBSEQUENT YEARS

2 As growth begins in spring, pinch out shoots growing directly toward or away from the wall between your thumb and forefinger, leaving only those that grow in the direction of the fan, parallel to the wall.

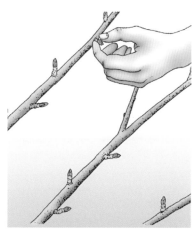

3 Pinch out the growing points of shoots not wanted for the framework when they have made 6 or 7 leaves, from early to midsummer, as new shoots appear. This begins to form the fruit-bearing spur system.

4 Cut back the pinched-out shoots to 3 leaves between late summer and early fall. This encourages fruit buds to form at the bases of the pinched-out shoots in the following year.

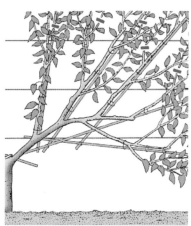

on the trunk below the first set of main branches. In subsequent years, repeat this process, but allow more secondary branches to develop to fill the space. You should eventually aim for about eight, well-spaced branches growing from the main trunk.

The formative pruning of a fan-trained plum is the same as for a cherry fan (*see page 268*), but changes as the tree matures (*see above*). The aim is to encourage fruit bud formation and, in later years, to replace worn-out branches by cutting out a proportion of the old wood back to young replacement branches in spring.

Aftercare

In late winter, spread an all-purpose fertilizer over the root area at the rate specified on the package and rake in, then spread a 2in. layer of mulch in early spring, leaving it clear of the stems. Water during dry periods to avoid a check in growth; irregular, heavy watering causes fruit to split.

Plums can be vulnerable to frost because they flower early in the year when frosts are harsher and more

prevalent. The flowers and young fruit are most at risk. Protect trees growing against walls or fences with floating row covers. Fruit buds and developing leaf buds are irresistible to birds; if possible, protect trees with netting.

To avoid the risk of biennial bearing (*see page 254*) and to preserve the flavor, thin fruit to ensure that they have enough room to develop (*see page 259*). Do this first when they are about the size of filberts and again when they are about twice this size. Tugging off the fruit may tear away next year's fruit buds, so cut them off with scissors or pruners, leaving a single plum every 2–3in.

Support heavily laden branches (*see page 254*) on young trees so they are not damaged by the weight of fruit.

Harvesting & storing

Depending on the weather, local climate, and variety of plum, fruit should be ready for picking any time from midsummer to late fall. Pick ripe fruit with their stalks. Plums do not store, but those picked when slightly under-ripe will keep for a few weeks in a cool place.

Peaches, nectarines, & apricots

Peaches and nectarines do require winter chill (the number of hours below 45°F), yet they cannot tolerate extremely cold winters, so choose varieties suitable for your climate. Nectarines have smooth skin and are more susceptible than peaches to brown rot; otherwise culture is similar. You can plant a single tree if desired, since these tree fruit are self compatible, which means that another tree is not needed for pollination (*see page 247*). Apricots grow in a similar way to peaches and nectarines, however most varieties bloom even earlier in spring. Avoid planting them in low areas where frost tends to collect.

Where to grow peaches & nectarines

Ideally, peaches and nectarines like a slightly acidic or neutral, well-drained soil. Standard peaches can grow to 25ft, but can be kept smaller with regular pruning. Dwarf types are suitable for containers.

Planting & spacing peaches & nectarines

Plant trees in a sunny, protected spot. Remove all perennial weeds and incorporate well-rotted compost or manure into the planting hole about two weeks prior to planting. Cut back newly planted trees to about 30in., just above a lateral bud. Allow three or four lateral branches to develop for the permanent framework.

Pruning & training peaches & nectarines

Prune young plants as for an open-centered apple or pear tree (*see page 249*). Peaches and nectarines call for heavy pruning to control growth. Prune in late winter, cutting back tallest limbs to encourage fruit on lower branches. Keep the center of the tree open.

Peaches and nectarines can be trained on a sunny wall. The warmth captured and reflected by the wall often helps protect buds and flowers from frost damage. For greater protection use floating row covers.

Growing apricots

Like peaches and nectarines, apricots cannot be grown in regions with late frosts as they bloom early and may fail to fruit if subject to frost during flowering. In cool, humid areas, fruit may suffer from brown rot and blight. Apricots also require sufficient winter chill and dry summers. It is important to choose a suitable variety for your region; a reliable fruit nursery or your local cooperative extension service can guide you.

THINNING

Peaches and nectarines set heavy crops. Thin fruits when they are about the size of large peas. Remove poorly placed, small, or misshapen fruit to leave 1 young fruit every 6in. or so. This should encourage good-sized fruit to form.

HARVESTING

Pick the fruit from late summer onward, when the flesh feels soft at the stalk ends. Hold each fruit in the palm of the hand, lift, and twist it slightly. A ripe fruit should come away easily; do not try to tug off the fruit— you will tear the bark.

Apricots are pretty trees with very showy, pinkish white blossoms, and they make good shade trees. Many apricots are self fertile, but a second pollinator may increase the size of the crop. Standard apricot trees reach 15–20ft. tall and wide. Those on dwarfing rootstocks are more typically 8–10ft. Dwarf varieties can be grown in containers and moved into an unheated garage for winter. Hardy Manchurian bush apricots grow 10–12ft. tall and are self pollinating. They are popular choices in small yards and colder areas.

For regions subject to late frosts, consider choosing a late-flowering variety that may escape frost damage. By planting your apricots where they have a northern exposure you will encourage plants to remain dormant longer, which may delay flowering for a week or two. Providing a heavy winter mulch will also delay the break of dormancy by keeping the soil cooler as spring approaches.

Planting apricots

Plant in fall or spring, while the trees are still dormant. Standard sizes need about 30ft. between trees; dwarf types may be spaced 10–15ft. apart. Early pruning should

THINNING FRUIT

For best quality, thin apricots so that remaining fruit is spaced 3–4in apart in warm climates. Elsewhere, thin to 1½–2in. apart.

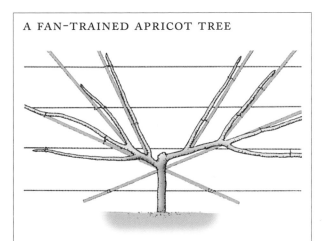

A FAN-TRAINED APRICOT TREE

A 3-year-old, fan-trained tree with secondary branches tied to canes, fixed at angles to the horizontal support wires.

This is a popular way to grow apricots against a warm, sunny wall or fence. Start with a partially trained, 3-year-old tree. Before planting, erect a support of horizontal training wires strung between posts or attached to the wall with eye hooks. Place the wires 9in. apart, starting about 1ft. above soil level. Plant the young tree 6in. out from the support.

Train the young apricot as for a fan-trained cherry (*see page 268*), thinning the fruit as they appear. Remove poorly placed, small, or misshapen fruit when they are each about the width of a little fingernail to leave one fruit approximately every 1½–2in. Protect the young tree from frost by draping with row cover.

aim to develop an open-centered tree, as for apples and pears (*see page 249*). Do not give additional fertilizer to young trees.

Young apricot trees tend to produce vigorous growth for their first three to five years. Excessive growth is subject to winter damage. As the trees mature, their susceptibility to winter injury is reduced.

Because apricots bloom before many pollinating insects are active, you may need to assist with hand pollination (*see page 247*). In warm climates, apricots may fruit heavily; thin crops to 3–4in. between fruits. Apricots are subject to various pests and diseases that may require preventive spraying; your local cooperative extension service can advise you about such a program.

Pruning & care of apricots

Apricots, like plums, bear on spurs that produce for a few years and then need to be pruned out and replaced with younger wood. Do not expect a heavy crop until the tree is three or four years old. Once established, apricots do not require hard pruning, but thin new, long shoots back by one half and remove the oldest wood, along with any branches that are diseased or damaged. If die-back is a problem in your area, prune in summer after harvest. Water apricots deeply and infrequently.

Harvesting apricots

Pick apricots when they are soft to the touch and the fruit pulls away easily from its stalk. Apricots do not store well; can or dry them if you do not plan to eat immediately after harvest.

FORMATIVE PRUNING OF A FAN-TRAINED PEACH, NECTARINE, OR APRICOT TREE

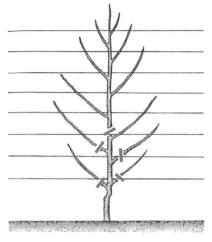

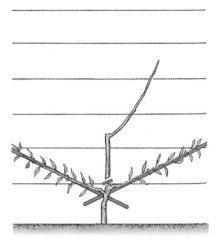

FIRST YEAR

1 **Cut back the main stem** of a 1-year-old tree to a side branch at about 24in. from the ground, in late winter. Cut other side branches back to 1 bud.

2 **Select 3 side branches** in early summer. Tie to the wires the topmost branch and the lower branches to the left and to the right. Remove all other branches from the main stem.

3 **Tie the lower side branches** to canes, set at an angle of 45 degrees, in early or midsummer. Late in summer, cut out the central stem.

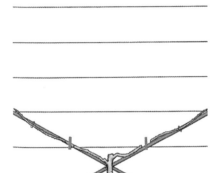

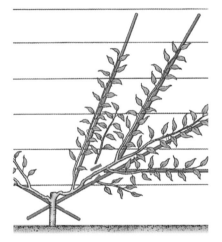

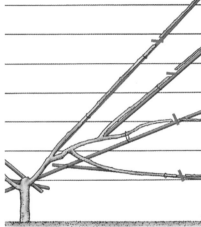

SECOND YEAR

4 **Cut back the 2 side branches** in late winter to a wood or triple bud (*see below*) at 12–18in. from the main stem.

5 **Remove all but 4** secondary branches on each side branch in summer to form the ribs. Tie them to canes attached to the wires.

THIRD YEAR

6 **Shorten the tip** of each rib by one third in late winter, cutting to a downward-facing wood bud.

For a fan-trained peach, nectarine, or apricot, start with a one-year-old tree with 5–12 evenly arranged side branches (*see above*), or use a partially trained tree with several well-trained, evenly spaced side branches (or ribs).

On one-year-old trees, if there are no suitable side branches to prune back to, cut back to a wood bud, which is slender and pointed. If in doubt, cut to a triple bud, which consists of two round flower buds and one pointed wood bud. Once the buds have grown, select three branches and remove the rest, cutting them back to the main stem (*see above, step 2*), then continue as shown.

In the second year, aim to develop eight ribs on the fan, keeping the center clear. In the third year, allow the ribs to extend and increase the spread. To fill in the framework, train three shoots on each rib: remove those that grow into or away from the wall; let others grow on every 4in.

From the fourth year, allow the tree to cover the allotted space. Fruit is borne on one-year-old wood, so you will need to remove fruited stems and encourage new ones to replace them. In late spring, prune the side branches of every rib so they have three shoots: one at the base (a replacement shoot), one in the middle (in

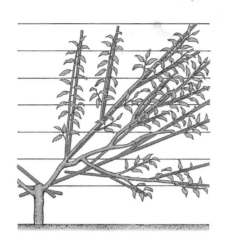

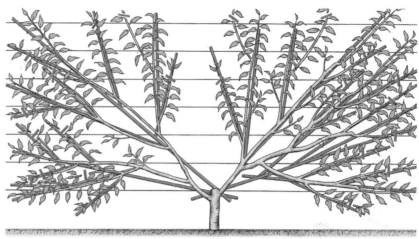

7 **Train 3 shoots** outward on canes from each of the ribs. Leave other shoots every 4in.; remove the rest.

8 **Remove the growing points** of each shoot once they have made 18in. of growth, unless they are needed to extend

the framework. This encourages the formation of fruit buds. In late summer, tie in the cut-back shoots to canes on the wires.

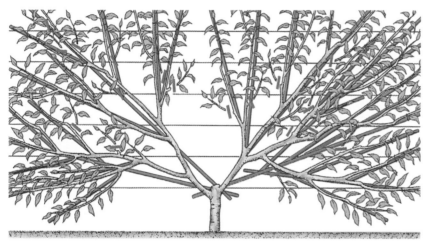

FOURTH & SUBSEQUENT YEARS

9 **Prune each year** in late spring to renew fruiting wood and maintain the framework. First remove shoots growing directly toward or

away from the wall or fence (*above*); if any have rounded flower buds at their base, cut them back to 1–2 leaves. Prepare for renewal by

pruning the side branch of each rib to 3 shoots (*top*) in late spring. Cut back after fruiting (*bottom*) to the replacement shoot.

reserve, in case the base shoot fails), and one at the tip (for extension growth); cut other shoots back to two leaves. When the base and middle shoots are 18in. long and the leader extension has six leaves, cut off the tips. After fruiting, cut each side branch back to the basal shoot.

Aftercare

You may need to protect the early flowers from frost by draping each tree with floating row cover or burlap at night. As there are few pollinating insects around when the trees flower, you may also need to hand pollinate the

flowers. As they develop, thin young fruits and protect them from birds and squirrels. Fertilize over the root area with an all-purpose fertilizer, at the rate on the package, in late winter, and from late spring with a high-potassium fertilizer. Water well, particularly in dry periods, but not while the fruit is ripening to avoid skins splitting.

Harvesting & storing

The summer fruit is ripe when it develops full color for that variety and you can pull it off easily with a gentle twist of the hand. They are best eaten fresh.

Citrus

Citrus are tender, sun-loving plants. For lucky gardeners in zones 10 and 11, it is common to have an orange or lemon tree in the yard. In cooler zones, you can still enjoy citrus but will have to provide winter protection, put plants in containers and bring them indoors for the winter, or grow them in a heated greenhouse year-round. In addition to bearing fruit, citrus are attractive, evergreen trees with fragrant flowers and make a good addition to the ornamental garden.

Oranges, lemons, and limes are the citrus most widely grown by home gardeners, but there are other types. In areas where citrus are grown, nurseries stock varieties of mandarin, tangelo, tangerine, and tangor. Kumquats are shrubby plants with small fruit that can be eaten rind and all. Generally, the sweeter the fruit, the greater the plant's heat requirements. Lemons and limes need the least summer heat; grapefruits the most. A knowledgeable nursery and your local cooperative extension service can provide more information on suitable citrus in your area.

Rootstocks

Most citrus are grafted or budded onto rootstocks that determine the ultimate size of the plant and are adapted to particular soil conditions. Standard trees can reach 30ft. in height and width; dwarf citrus, which grow 6–12ft. high, are grafted on a trifoliate orange rootstock. Prune off any suckers that arise from the rootstock.

Planting citrus trees

Citrus are planted from container-grown plants and can be set out anytime, but the tree's root system will develop best if planted in fall or winter to take advantage of winter rains. Choose a sunny spot that is sheltered from winds. Citrus must have good drainage, so dig in organic material such as compost to the planting hole. Hose as much potting soil as possible off the roots before planting.

Planting depth for citrus is important as the trees can suffer from crown rot: The top of the rootball should be positioned just at soil level. Wrap citrus bark with trunk bands or paint with diluted white latex paint to protect it from sunburn.

Caring for citrus trees

Water newly planted citrus thoroughly for the first weeks, depending on soil type, rainfall, and time of year. Thereafter, water consistently when the soil dries out to a depth of an inch or two. An organic or gravel mulch can help retain moisture for these shallow-rooted trees.

PRUNING CITRUS

Citrus trees generally require very little pruning other than removal of dead or damaged wood, eliminating crossing branches, or controlling the tree's size. To reduce a tree's size, cut back branches to just above a leaf.

REMOVING SUCKERS

Look for suckers developing from the base of the tree or anywhere below the graft union and remove them as soon as they are noticed.

PROTECTING FROM FROST

To protect trees from damage by frost, water them well because bare, moist soils radiate more heat than dry soils. A protective covering can be placed over a frame constructed around the plant.

PAINTING THE TRUNK

Citrus bark is thin, and can be damaged by too much sun. Protect it by painting the trunk and lower branches with a diluted solution of white interior latex paint.

Trees & shrubs *see page 96* | **Preparing to grow** *see page 230* | **Greenhouse gardening** *see page 368*

When the tree begins new growth after planting, start to apply fertilizer once a month through the growing season with a slow-release, high-nitrogen fertilizer. In addition to nitrogen, citrus need iron, manganese, and zinc; without these micronutrients, plants commonly develop chlorosis. Symptoms of chlorosis include leaves that are yellow, mottled, or blotchy. Foliar sprays can correct the immediate deficiency, but regular applications of a citrus fertilizer may be necessary to prevent the problem from recurring.

Citrus trees are pruned primarily to control tree size and to remove dead, diseased, or damaged wood. Excessive pruning will destroy the natural shape of the plant and lead to twiggy, unproductive growth.

Growing in containers

The smaller citrus types are best suited to container culture, but all will grow in containers for a limited time. Plant citrus in a light, well-drained potting soil. Fertilize monthly with a high-nitrogen citrus fertilizer that includes zinc, iron, and manganese. Water regularly, but allow the soil surface to dry slightly before watering again. The soil should never become soggy.

Frost protection

Citrus are damaged when the temperature drops below freezing. In areas where occasional hard freezes strike, you can prepare the tree in advance. Thoroughly irrigate the ground around the tree. Drape blankets, burlap, or plastic over the tree for further protection. Remove plastic coverings during sunny days to avoid scorching the trees. Permeable covers can be left in place until the freeze danger has ended.

Some gardeners erect a tented, wooden frame around their citrus trees and place small lights (such as Christmas lights or workshop lights) or small electric heaters at the base of the tree.

Despite these efforts, citrus plants are occasionally damaged by frosts, but they can often recover. Wait until spring to prune off cold-damaged branches, a few weeks after new growth has emerged and once you can determine which branches are healthy. Plants frozen to the ground may appear to regrow, but the growth may be from the rootstock only.

Harvesting citrus

Most citrus fruit is ripe in fall and winter, but the fruit can stay on the tree for months without spoiling. Citrus must be ripe when you pick it, as it will not ripen further once off the tree.

Kiwi

There are two species of edible kiwi. Hardy kiwi (*Actinidia arguta*) produces fruit eaten with its smooth skin. The more familiar, fuzzy-skinned kiwi (*A. deliciosa*) is less hardy but can grow nearly 30ft. in one year. Check the hardiness rating before purchasing. Kiwi vines have male and female flowers on separate plants, so for fruit production you need at least one male and one female plant. Kiwi are not ideal for small yards.

Planting, training, & pruning

Place kiwi vines in a sunny, sheltered spot where they will be protected from wind. The plants need deep, well-drained soil and cannot stand waterlogged roots; plant in a raised bed if necessary. Kiwi vines are vigorous, large, and long-lived, and can produce a heavy crop, so they need a strong, permanent support structure that is 6ft. tall. Like citrus, newly planted kiwi bark can suffer from sunscald; wrap the trunk or paint it with a diluted, white latex paint.

Prune young plants to establish a framework. The aim is to develop a single, straight trunk from the top of which permanent cordons are trained across the support. Kiwis fruit on shoots that grow from one-year-old canes (last year's growth). Head back all fruited canes in the dormant season. Always remove suckers from the base of the vine.

Care & harvesting

If frost is expected, cover fuzzy kiwi vines with floating row covers to protect the flowers. Vines need regular water throughout the growing season, and an all-purpose fertilizer monthly in spring and early summer.

Kiwi fruits ripen in fall. If picked while still hard, fuzzy-skinned kiwi fruits can be stored for months in a refrigerator; hardy kiwi fruits store for a shorter period.

KIWI

Kiwis are vigorous vines that need a substantial support. Grow them on a sturdy trellis, fence, or arbor. They can also be trained to grow on a wall. For fruit to develop, both male and female plants are required.

Cherries

There are three main types of cherry: sweet cherries generally fruit from early to midsummer; sour cherries, such as morello, are harvested in late summer and early fall, are more widely adapted except in hottest zones, and are suitable for cooking and canning. Duke cherries taste like a cross between sweet and sour types.

Where & how to grow cherries

Cherries will grow on light soil if you improve it before planting and then fertilize, mulch, and water regularly, but they fare best in well-drained, deep soil. Give them a sunny, sheltered site away from frost pockets; they flower early in the year and are vulnerable to cold snaps. Hardier, sour cherries can be grown on cold, shady walls.

Sweet cherries require many hours of chilly winter temperatures. They do not do well in areas with extreme summer heat or extremely low winter temperatures. Most types need pollinators to produce fruit. They can be very large trees, to 25ft., but some varieties are grown on a dwarfing rootstock. Your local cooperative extension service can recommend varieties appropriate for your area as well as suitable pollinators.

Sour cherries are typically self fruitful. They come in standard, dwarf, and semidwarf varieties. Semidwarf and dwarf cherries can be grown as fans against a wall or fence (*see below and facing page*).

Birds love cherries and can strip a tree clean before you have a chance to pick them. A restricted or dwarf form, shown here, is much easier to protect from birds, so you can gather a good crop.

Planting & spacing

If training cherries as a fan, you will need to construct supports with horizontal, 14-gauge wires spaced 6in. apart. Even on a dwarfing rootstock, each fan needs plenty of wall space—about 11ft. wide by 6ft. high—to grow. Free-standing bushes and trees on the same rootstock need to be

FORMATIVE PRUNING OF A FAN-TRAINED CHERRY TREE

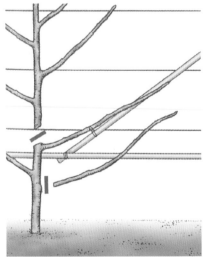

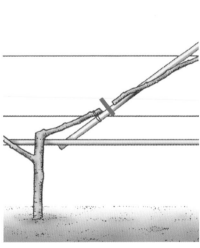

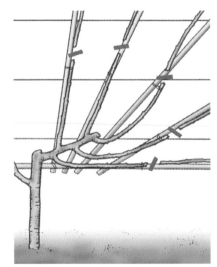

FIRST YEAR

1 **Tie 2 strong side branches** to canes on wires at a 35-degree angle in spring. Cut the central stem back to the uppermost of the selected branches. Remove all other branches.

SECOND YEAR

2 **Shorten each branch** to about 12in. in spring. Cut to a bud that points in the direction of the fan. This encourages shoots to develop that will be used as the ribs of the fan.

THIRD YEAR

3 **Cut back all the new** secondary branches to suitable buds in spring, leaving 18–21in. of new growth.

Looking after your soil *see page 32* | Trees & shrubs *see page 96* | Common problems *see page 274*

8–10ft. apart. Cherries on other, more vigorous rootstocks can only be grown in large gardens as they need at least 15ft. between free-standing bushes, trees, or fans.

Pruning & training

Sweet and duke cherries fruit on two-year-old and older wood and can be trained as fans from one-year-old trees (*see below*) against a wall or fence. Prune sour cherry fans hard to obtain lots of new shoots; training is similar to that of peaches, nectarines, and apricots (*see page 264*). In the first year, remove any flowers.

To grow a cherry as a free-standing tree, prune the upper branches to three or four buds in spring to develop a head of branches (*see page 249*). Prune in spring to avoid disease, and, instead of removing the lower branches to form a clear trunk, pinch them off to four leaves; then in the summer of the second year pinch out their growing points. Do not remove these lower branches until the fourth year, because they help stiffen the main stem. Cut out dead, diseased, dying, or badly placed branches each year in midsummer.

Aftercare

Soil around fan-trained trees can dry out quickly, so water often, especially once the fruit have started to form; a sudden deluge after drought can split the fruit.

In late winter, spread an all-purpose fertilizer over the soil and rake in. In early spring, spread a 3in. mulch of well-rotted garden compost or manure over the root area.

A mature, fan-trained cherry makes an attractive tree and takes up little space in the garden. It boasts pretty spring blossoms, followed by bright and tasty, marble-sized fruit, which are commonly red, although varieties in different colors are available.

If frost is predicted, protect the flowers with floating row covers. You may also need to protect the winter buds and summer fruit from birds by netting the tree.

Harvesting & storing

When the fruit is ripe, pick your cherries with their stalks intact to discourage brown rot (*see page 278*). Eat, can, or freeze them when fresh as they do not store well.

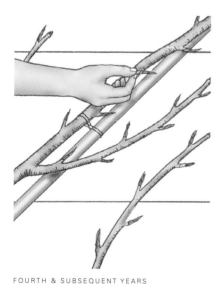

FOURTH & SUBSEQUENT YEARS

4 **Remove any new shoots** that grow directly toward or away from the wall. Do this in spring, when most of the wall space has been filled.

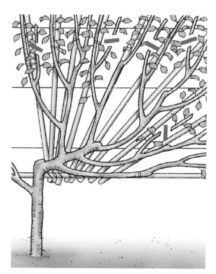

5 **Cut to 6 leaves** any secondary branches not needed for the framework, in midsummer. Cut stems that reach the top of the wall to a weak branch just below, or bend and tie it down.

6 **Cut back to 3 leaves** the branches that were pinched out in midsummer, in early fall. This encourages fruit buds to form at the bases of the shoots for the next year.

Figs

Common in Mediterranean regions, figs are a gourmet fruit that can be grown successfully in cooler climates as long as temperatures do not drop below 10°F in winter. As well as tasty fruit, many fig trees have showy foliage, some with long and extended, lobed leaves. Many varieties, with much variation in the shape, color, and taste of the fruit, are readily available. Figs are parthenocarpic, which means that the fruit develop without needing to be pollinated.

How figs fruit

Figs produce up to three crops a year, depending on where they are grown. In tropical regions, they bear three flushes of fruit, in subtropical areas they crop twice, while in cool-temperate regions they produce two crops, but only one will ripen successfully.

Outdoors in cool climates, the first crop appears in early summer, but as there is not enough time for the fruit to ripen, they are still green by fall and so should be removed before winter. The second crop appears in late summer; these are carried over the winter as pea-sized embryo fruit. Provided these are not destroyed by cold, they develop the following spring and summer to ripen in late summer and early fall.

Where to grow figs

As a native of warm-temperate climates, the fig prefers a warm, sunny wall or fence for a fan, or a warm, light, protected corner for a free-standing specimen. They are happy in most well-drained soils. If space is restricted, rather than plant straight into the soil, dig a specially

Figs are attractive plants to include in an edible landscape, with their large, lobed leaves and their delectable fruit. They are bothered by few pests, although birds often eat their fruit.

prepared, concrete-lined pit to restrict the roots or plant in a large container such as a half-oak barrel.

Supports & planting

To train a fig as a fan against a wall or fence, you will need to construct a series of horizontal support wires, spaced

FORMATIVE PRUNING OF A FAN-TRAINED FIG TREE

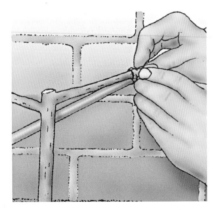

1 **Prune the tree** after planting to stimulate 2 strong side branches to develop. In summer, tie new side branches onto angled canes.

2 **Cut back the new side branches** by one third in late winter to early spring, so more will grow to form the framework.

3 **Tie in shoots** that radiate from the center. Remove shoots growing toward or away from the wall.

PRUNING A MATURE FAN-TRAINED TREE

1 Remove the growing points in early summer of one half of the young shoots carried by the main framework branches. This encourages new shoots and embryo fruit. As the shoots develop, tie them to the wires.

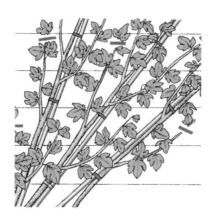

2 Prune half the fruited shoots in late fall to 1in., to encourage new shoots from the base. Tie in remaining shoots parallel with the wall and 9–12in. apart. Remove any crossing shoots or those growing into or away from the wall.

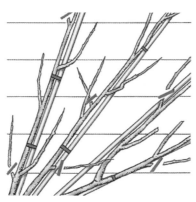

12in. apart, using heavy galvanized wire. To obtain a fan 6ft. tall by 11ft. wide, excavate a planting hole 4 square feet in size.

The size of the planting hole determines the eventual size of the fig tree; to restrict growth plant in a lined pit. Partially trained trees are available to buy, lessening the time you have to wait for the first crop.

Pruning & training

Formative training of a fig fan (*see facing page*) follows the same principle as for a cherry fan (*see page 268*), aiming to fill the wall space with a strong framework of branches. This should take three to four years; thereafter, prune it as for a mature, cropping fan (*see above*) to encourage a plentiful supply of young shoots and—in cool climates—a mixture of ripe and embryonic fruit each fall.

Free-standing fig trees need little pruning after the first year (*see right*), except to remove dead, damaged, diseased, or badly placed branches. On old figs, where branches have become gaunt and bare, cut out a portion of old wood in late winter to a young shoot or, if there are none, to a 1in. stub, to encourage fresh young growth.

If you inherit a fig that has not been planted to restrict the roots, the growth may be extremely leggy, resulting in poor fruit. Rejuvenate overgrown plants by pruning out a number of branches every late winter until the tree achieves a satisfactory shape.

Aftercare

Figs are capable of dealing with dry conditions, but in drought are unlikely to produce a decent crop of fruit. Plants can sometimes shed their entire crops of fruit if they become too stressed through lack of water. Start to water when the fig comes into growth in early spring, daily from midsummer for figs in pots. When the figs are ripening, do not water too much to avoid causing the fruit to split.

PRUNING A FREE-STANDING TREE

FIRST YEAR

1 Cut back each side branch of a 2- or 3-year-old tree in late winter, by about a half to an outwardfacing bud.

SUBSEQUENT YEARS

2 Remove badly placed branches in late winter. If needed, cut out some older wood back to young shoots to fill out the tree.

Persimmons

Two kinds of persimmons are grown for their edible fruit. Japanese, or Oriental, persimmons (*Diospyros kaki*) grow in warm climates only (zones 7 to 11). The tree is multi- or single-stemmed, grows to 25ft. high, and bears large fruit that vary in shape and astringency depending on the variety. 'Izu' is a smaller variety. Native North American persimmons (*D. virginiana*) may grow to 60ft. high and usually produces smaller fruit than the Japanese type. American persimmons are hardier and have a greater chilling requirement than Japanese types.

Some persimmons have both male and female flowers on the same tree; others require a pollinator. Both are attractive ornamental trees, with striking fall foliage, and are tolerant of many soils.

Planting & care

Persimmons require pruning when young to create a framework, while mature trees need pruning only to remove dead or broken branches. Do not overfertilize; a single application of all-purpose fertilizer in spring or fall should be sufficient. Provide consistent water and mulch young trees to conserve soil moisture, as persimmons can drop fruit when drought-stressed.

Harvesting

Persimmons hang on the tree long after leaves have dropped in fall, making an attractive ornament for the winter garden. The fruit may be very sour and astringent until the fruit has softened—either on the tree or in storage. The degree of astringency differs depending on variety. Catalog or nursery listings should include information on fruit flavor and whether the fruit is astringent or nonastringent.

HARVESTING PERSIMMONS

Pick Japanese persimmons when they are still firm but have developed their mature color. Harvest American persimmons after their flesh has softened and is almost mushy and their skin has become somewhat translucent, otherwise they will be too astringent.

Pomegranates

Pomegranates are considered something of a super-food for their high nutrient content. For those in hottest climates, though, pomegranates are undemanding and attractive plants for the edible garden. These small trees or shrubs grow no larger than 15ft., with a dense, twiggy growth habit; they may be evergreen in warmest climates. The trees sport large. tubular. crimson flowers that attract hummingbirds. The flowers turn into large, seedy fruit—although temperatures must be high for the plant to fruit. Most pomegranates are self pollinating. Dwarf types are available and can be grown in containers.

PLANTING A POMEGRANATE

Pomegranates are not fussy about soil, but if your soil is heavy, incorporate some well-rotted compost into the planting hole. To assure good drainage, set the tree on a small rise of soil in the planting hole before filling it in and watering thoroughly.

Planting & care

Plant bare-root trees in winter. Container-grown plants can be planted from spring onwards. Water regularly until established.

Plants fruit on new wood, so can be pruned back heavily, although it is not necessary to prune except to shape the tree and remove damaged branches. Remove suckers as they appear.

These plants are very drought-tolerant but watering should be consistent. Feed with a high-nitrogen fertilizer for the first few seasons.

Harvesting

Pomegranates ripen in fall, reaching a full-deep color when fully ripe. Eat them fresh or extract the juice for drinking or cooking in jellies or jams.

Mulberries are very easy to grow, and a mature tree can produce several bushels of fruit each year. Avoid planting trees near walkways or parking areas where the ripened fruit can be a nuisance when it falls.

Quince fruit matures from green to golden-yellow and is very aromatic. Its fresh flavor is somewhat sharp and its texture a bit gritty, but the sweetened fruit is great for making delicious jams and jellies.

Mulberries

Edible mulberries include the red mulberry (*Morus rubra*) and the black mulberry (*M. nigra*). Red mulberries are native to the eastern United States and west as far as Nebraska and can reach 50ft. in height. Black mulberrries hail from Asia and grow as a shrub or a tree of 15–30ft., depending on the variety. They are less hardy than the red mulberry. They thrive in rich, moisture-retentive yet well-drained, slightly acid soil.

Since these deciduous trees can take up to ten years to produce fruit, it is easier to save time by buying a three- to five-year-old plant from the nursery.

Prune free-standing plants in winter, aiming to create an attractive shape by reducing any side branches that are not needed for the main framework to four or five buds. Once a good framework is developed, little additional pruning is necessary.

Make sure that the trees are watered thoroughly in warm, dry weather. In late winter, apply a slow-release, all-purpose fertilizer to the soil. Mulch with well-rotted manure or compost in spring.

Mulberries are ready for picking in late summer. When they are ripe, they fall off trees, so you may want to place a cloth on the ground to collect them.

Quinces

Requiring very little attention when established, the quince is an attractive and compact tree with spreading branches. In fall, it is festooned with highly perfumed, large, pear- or apple-shaped fruit.

Quince trees prefer a warm, sunny, and sheltered site in most soils as long as they are deep, light, fertile, and moisture-retentive. When you buy, look for a goblet-shaped tree or a partly trained, three- or four-year-old standard. Before planting, drive a stake into the ground to provide support, ensuring that the top will be just beneath the lowest branches. Water in dry, sunny weather and apply a slow-release, all-purpose fertilizer over the soil in fall. Mulch well in spring.

Quinces are usually pruned with a central leader. For the first few years, prune back the main framework. After four years very little trimming is required, apart from removing suckering shoots that emerge from the base (*see page 105*) and cutting out overcrowded branches. The fruit grows on spurs or on the tips of the previous summer's growth and are usually ready for harvest from midfall— leave them on the tree as long as possible.

COMMON PROBLEMS

Perhaps you have a well-loved fruit tree that has been healthy, vigorous, and high-yielding for many years but has suddenly succumbed to a pest infestation or an outbreak of disease. Or maybe you have acquired a new yard with a badly neglected tree that is in dire need of remedial action. It is inevitable that you will encounter problems from time to time as a fruit gardener, and it is worth keeping an eye out for early signs of infection or infestation, so that you can control them swiftly before you are overwhelmed.

Stunted, overvigorous, & neglected trees

Apart from looking awful, trees that have been pruned poorly or have not had any tender loving care for some time will probably furnish you with misshapen, small, or unpleasant-tasting fruit. They may also have outgrown their allotted space, become stunted, or have diseased growth. Assess the tree and decide if it can be rescued; it makes sense to remove a tree that is badly diseased, but others can be restored to their former glory over two to three years by undertaking remedial action.

Stunted trees

A tree can become stunted for a variety of reasons: the ground around it may have become overgrown with weeds, resulting in competition from the weed roots for soil moisture and nutrients; the tree may have been planted badly and failed to anchor itself effectively in the soil; there may be insufficient light reaching the foliage because of other trees nearby; or the tree may have been damaged by pests or diseases.

Aim to restore a stunted tree's vigor by removing competing weeds, applying an all-purpose fertilizer, and mulching around the root area with an 3in. layer of well-rotted manure or garden compost, leaving a gap between the trunk and the mulch. If any pests and diseases are present, treat them as necessary.

If the tree has not been staked, drive one or two strong stakes into the ground—avoiding damage to the roots—and secure with a tree tie. This will prevent the roots of the tree from being rocked in heavy winds.

Use pruners, loppers, or a pruning saw to remove any dead, diseased, or dying branches. If the head of the tree is a congested mass of spurs, thin these out, while

RENOVATING A STUNTED TREE

1 **Remove weeds** and grass all around the tree to a distance of 4ft., then mulch. Drive in a stake and tie in with a tree tie.

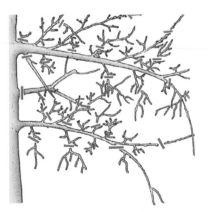

2 **Thin out overcrowded spurs**, if needed, in winter. Prune hard any young wood. This admits light and air and prompts new shoots.

3 **Remove most or all** of the young fruit in spring, for 1 or 2 years. Fertilize and mulch well each year and control pests and diseases.

Looking after your soil *see page 32* | **Weed control** *see page 53* | **Apples & pears** *see page 249*

RESTORATIVE PRUNING OF AN OLD, BADLY PRUNED APPLE TREE

1 Inspect the tree in winter, when the branches are bare, to determine the work that needs to be carried out. This apple has areas of congested growth, particularly around pruning cuts made 2–3 years ago.

2 Thin out strong shoots around congested wounds where major branches were once removed. Cut them out at the base, taking care to leave the collar intact so that the wound can heal cleanly (*see page 104*). Do not prune out more than one third of such growth in a single year. Remove crossing branches.

3 Aim to leave a healthy, evenly balanced, open framework of branches that are 24–36in. apart. Continue the pruning over 2–3 years, starting each winter by removing any dead, diseased, or damaged branches to keep the tree healthy.

4 In summer, a more graceful and balanced open crown will develop with productive, new growth. Fertilize, water, and mulch, then resume normal pruning and maintenance once renovation is complete.

shortening any young wood to allow air and light into the tree. For the next couple of years, remove any fruit as it forms to allow the tree to regain its vigor. After this, carry out a normal pruning and maintenance program.

Overvigorous trees

Excessive fertilizing, very fertile soil, or being grafted onto a vigorous rootstock could result in a tree having rampant topgrowth and very poor yields of fruit. Incorrect pruning, such as 'topping' trees, can cause excessive growth of unproductive shoots.

Plums and other stone fruit can be root pruned. To do this, dig out a circular trench around the trunk of the tree during late fall or early winter. Cut the trench 5ft. away from the tree, or farther out if it is particularly large. Use a pruning saw to cut back any thick roots, then refill the trench with soil and firm down.

Neglected trees

An unpruned tree may produce plenty of blossom, but have small, pest-ridden, or diseased fruit. Prune dead, diseased, or dying branches, and any that are badly placed, crossing, or that spoil the shape. Reduce the number of side branches on main stems. Then fertilize, water, and mulch.

Renovating apple & pear trees

Masses of vegetative growth on apple and pear trees is usually the result of overenthusiastic pruning. Any further trimming aimed at stemming this vigorous growth often exacerbates the problem because hard pruning prompts more nonfruiting extension growth.

To curtail the vigor of such a tree, the first step is to mulch over the root area and fertilize moderately until the tree is fruiting well. Then carry out restorative pruning from late fall to early spring, while the tree is dormant (*see above*). It is important to spread this renovation work over a two- to three- year period to lessen the shock to the tree. Winter pruning stimulates extension growth, whereas summer pruning checks it, so only a proportion of the overgrown stems should be removed each winter and the resulting new shoots then pruned again in summer to encourage formation of fruit buds.

If possible, steer clear of cutting back horizontal shoots because these usually produce more fruiting spurs. Young vertical shoots, which tend not to fruit, can also be bent over and tied down, to encourage production of fruit-bearing spurs. After three years or so, the tree should begin to produce better fruit and you can resume a normal maintenance regime.

Fruit pests

Correct cultivation and good weed control will help to keep the plants healthy, but the best protection against fruit pests is vigilance—inspect the plants regularly to spot signs of infestation early on so that you can take prompt action to control any pests. Consult with your cooperative extension service for appropriate controls.

Gooseberry sawflies
The caterpillarlike larvae of several species can defoliate gooseberries and red and white currants. The larvae are up to ¾in. long and pale green, sometimes with many black spots. Another pest called sawfly is the larvae of a wasplike insect. These attack pear and cherry trees and resemble tiny, black slugs. Hand pick to remove pests.

Plum curculios
This weevil causes damage both at the larval and adult stage. The adults overwinter in garden debris, then the females lay their eggs in developing fruit. The larvae feed in the fruit, then crawl out to pupate in the soil.

Clear fallen leaves and dropped fruit. Shake the tree to dislodge the adults onto a tarp, then dispose of them.

Stink bugs & tarnished bugs
Stink bugs are colorful, winged insects about ½in. long. Tarnished bugs (sometimes called lygus bugs) are smaller (about ¼in. long), light brown with a distinctive V-marking. They attack many fruit plants, including berries, pears, and plums, sawing into leaves and sucking out plant juices. Floating row covers can protect berries; some beneficial insects, including parasitoid wasps or tachinid flies, may help control the pests.

Codling moth
Maggoty apples are caused by codling moth caterpillars. The female moths lay eggs on or near the developing fruit in early summer. A single caterpillar then bores into a fruit and feeds in the core before tunneling out of the fruit in late summer. Clean up fallen leaves and dropped fruit. Wrap trunks with sticky barriers.

Woolly aphid
Apples, including ornamental crabapples, are the main host plant for woolly aphid. The brownish black aphids are covered in fluffy, white, waxy fibers secreted from their bodies, which help to protect them from contact sprays. Resistant rootstocks are the only defense against underground infestations. You can sometimes control woolly aphid on small trees by scrubbing colonies with a stiff-bristled brush in spring.

Leaf rollers
These caterpillarlike larvae feed on tender, young leaves, then curl the leaves around themselves with silken threads. Serious infestations can defoliate fruit trees. Several biological controls are available.

Pear midge
When blossom is at the white bud stage, the pear midge, a tiny fly, lays its eggs on the buds. The orange-white, tiny maggots feed inside the young fruits, which become abnormally enlarged but soon blacken and drop from the tree in late spring or early summer. Pick and destroy any blackening young fruits before the larvae go into the soil to pupate.

Raspberry fruitworm
Whitish brown larvae, up to ⅜in. long, feed on raspberry, blackberry, loganberry, and other cane fruit. They start at the stalk end, causing it to dry up, then move inside to feed on the core. The pale brown adult beetles lay eggs in late spring to midsummer, so everbearing raspberries are less affected.

Weevils
These chewing insects have long snouts and feed on many edible plants, including strawberries, blueberries, and grape vines. The adults chew leaves, blossoms, and bark at night and hide during the day. The females lay their eggs in the soil, the emerging larvae feed on roots. You can encourage natural predators (such as birds, beneficial nematodes, and ground beetles) to eat the larvae and adults. Hand pick adults at night. Rotate strawberry plantings if infestations persist. Check with your local cooperative extension service for biological or chemical controls for edible plants.

Bird damage
Birds can devour an entire fruit crop before you have a chance to harvest it. Protect the ripening fruit by covering plants with plastic netting.

Other pests
Other pests that may affect fruit include aphids, deer, rabbits, and squirrels (*see page 49*), as well as scales (*see page 117*), caterpillars, cutworms, and beetles.

Pests, diseases, & other problems *see page 40* | **Weed control** *see page 53* | **Preparing to grow** *see page 230*

COMMON FRUIT PESTS

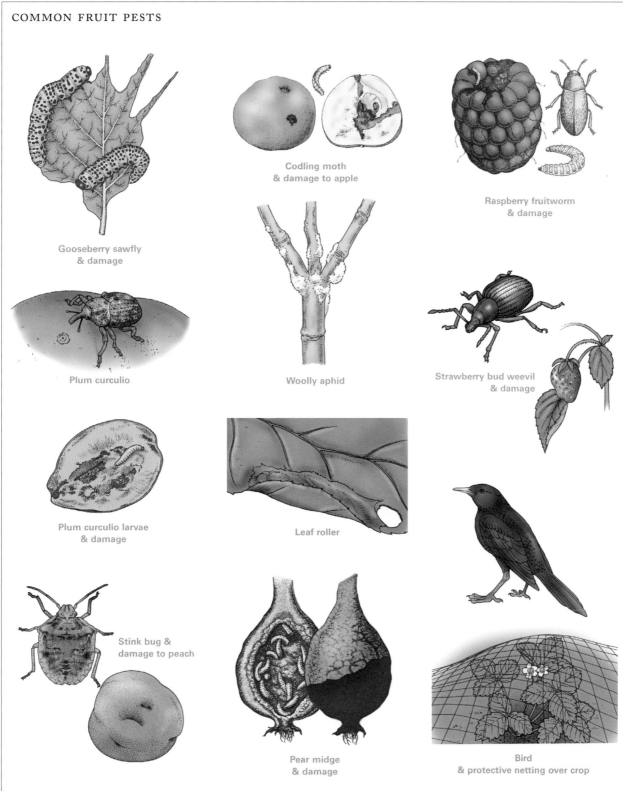

Gooseberry sawfly
& damage

Codling moth
& damage to apple

Raspberry fruitworm
& damage

Plum curculio

Woolly aphid

Strawberry bud weevil
& damage

Plum curculio larvae
& damage

Leaf roller

Stink bug &
damage to peach

Pear midge
& damage

Bird
& protective netting over crop

Pests may not harm the fruit crop if caught early—pick them off and destroy them and burn affected plant material. If allowed to get a hold, they can cause more serious problems. Often, the first signs of infestation may be blemishes or distortions on fruit, caused by the larval stages of the pest. Other pests may appear at first glance to be a disease.

Fruit diseases

Many fruit diseases are caused by fungal infections; contact fungicides only check or prevent attacks so should be applied before the disease appears. Systemic fungicides, absorbed by the plant tissues, have short-lived effects and may cause resistant strains to occur if used too often. Be sure to consult with your local cooperative extension service for control recommendations.

Apple & pear scab

Brown, scabby blotches form on the skins of young fruit. If the skin cracks, rot can occur. Felty, brown blotches appear on leaves, which drop; shoots may also be affected. Remove diseased tissue, thin overcrowded branches, and rake up fallen leaves. Plant resistant varieties. Apply an appropriate fungicide just as the leaf tips appear.

Cedar apple rust

Bright yellow blotches appear on apple or crabapple leaves in summer, turning orange with black dots. The fungus also lives on juniper. Removing affected cedars and junipers helps, but spores can still be blown some distance. Trees treated for scab infection are rarely affected by rust. Plant resistant varieties. Practice good sanitation and remove infected galls and fruits.

Leaf spot

Irregular, brown spots blacken leaves of fruit trees, grape vines, strawberries, and other berries. Shoots or fruit may also be affected. Remove and discard all infected tissue and fallen leaves.

Powdery mildews

Powdery, white patches cause leaves to die and stunt shoots. Prune out infected tissue; grow resistant varieties. Avoid overuse of nitrogen-rich fertilizers and prune plants to improve airflow. Keep well watered and mulched during periods of dry weather.

Cane fungal diseases

Anthracnose: Small, elliptical purple spots appear on raspberry and other berry canes in early summer, and sometimes on leaves and fruit, causing tip die-back. Remove affected tissue and use an appropriate fungicide just as the bud tips emerge.

Cane blight: In summer, raspberry canes suddenly die back; brown lesions appear at stem bases and the bark ruptures. Cut back diseased wood to healthy tissue. Prune carefully to avoid infection through wounds, avoid waterlogging, and improve airflow between canes. Spray with an appropriate fungicide in spring.

Spur blight: In late summer, purple patches appear around buds of new raspberry or loganberry canes and kill many buds. The blight thrives on overfertilized or overcrowded plants. Remove affected canes and spray with an appropriate fungicide. Some varieties show resistance.

Peach leaf curl

On peaches, nectarines, and close relatives, red or pale green blisters form on new leaves. These become swollen, curled, and later covered in white spores. Some spores overwinter on dormant shoots. Remove diseased tissue promptly. Control with an appropriate fungicide.

Brown rot

Many stone fruit trees can be affected. Spots of soft brown rot develop on fruit and rapidly enlarge; rings of buff spores appear on this tissue and initiate more infections. The fungus can invade the spur, so it is vital to prune out diseased spurs and remove all rotten fruit. Brown rot can affect stored fruit, so plant resistant varieties. Control with an appropriate fungicide.

Crown gall

A large gall at soil level or on the roots indicates infection by crown gall. Soil-borne bacteria parasitize injured or diseased roots or the stem, causing the gall to grow. Remove and destroy infected plants.

Bacterial canker

In this serious disease of stone fruits, long lesions occur on branches, often on one side, and tissue dies above those points. Large amounts of gum may seep from the canker. In late spring, small brown spots may form on leaves and fall out to leave 'shot holes'. In late fall, rain splashes bacteria from the leaves onto the bark to form new cankers. Prune during active growth to reduce infection. Some plum and cherry varieties are resistant.

Fireblight

Leaves of affected branches wilt and brown, as if scorched. Bacteria spread from old infections or by insects travel down the inner bark to form sunken cankers, with reddening of the growth tissue. It can occur in warm, sunny but wet conditions. Swiftly prune out affected branches and sterilize your tools. Apples and pears are affected, but not cherries. Plant resistant varieties.

Pests, diseases, & other problems *see page 40* | Weed control *see page 53* | Preparing to grow *see page 230*

COMMON FRUIT DISEASES

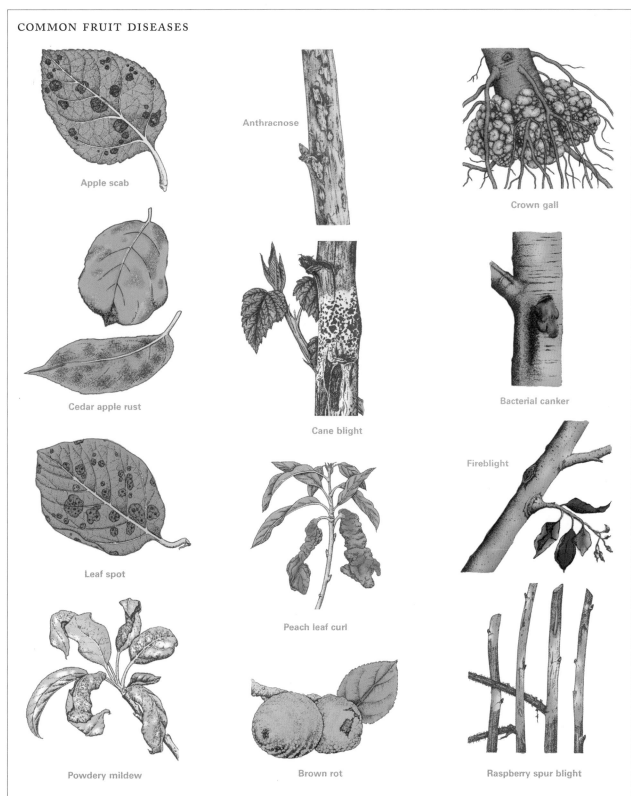

Apple scab

Anthracnose

Crown gall

Cedar apple rust

Cane blight

Bacterial canker

Leaf spot

Fireblight

Peach leaf curl

Powdery mildew

Brown rot

Raspberry spur blight

Fungal diseases such as canker, scab, rust, and mildew are caused by spores carried in the air, so it is important to prune at the right time and to watch for early signs of infection. Many of these diseases spread by overwintering in plant debris or through wounds. To prevent their spread, disinfect pruning tools between use on different plants and gather up and destroy all plant debris from infected plants.

CHAPTER SIX
LAWNS

EVERYBODY LOVES THE SMELL OF FRESHLY MOWN GRASS. A lush, green carpet of lawn is a traditional part of many American and Canadian gardens.

Lawns & their place in the garden

Grass is a cheaper means of surfacing a garden than using hardscaping materials such as pavers or decking. Its soft texture makes it ideal for children to play on or for adults to relax and sit on and its flexibility makes it easy to lay following contours and slopes.

For enthusiasts, a lawn can be a feature in its own right. For others, areas of turf may be used to define specific areas in a garden or to bind together all the disparate elements of the garden. A lawn may soften the contours of hardscaping or act as a neutral backdrop for borders and other features.

Lawns may be incorporated to suit many styles of garden—from the sharply defined, structured symmetry of formal gardens to the sweeping, informal contours of wildflower meadows. Long grass also increases local biodiversity by creating a home for a huge range of wildlife, as well as providing food and nesting material for other creatures, such as birds. With a little imagination, you can cut a lawn into any shape or pattern you wish.

Lawns & alternatives

However, lawns are not suitable for every climate. In summer-drought areas, such as the Northwest, they will not stay green without additional irrigation. In desert climates, a lawn is not going to survive without enormous inputs of water. Forcing a lawn to stay green can mean large applications of fertilizer and water that may run off into nearby waterways, causing damage to the aquatic ecosystem. A lawn does require maintenance if it is to look good year-round. Frequent mowing—sometimes twice a week—during the growing season is essential; other maintenance tasks such as reseeding bare patches, clearing leaves and annual fertilizing, aeration, watering, and weeding are needed to keep a lawn at its peak. Other disadvantages of lawns are that they can become slippery and muddy in winter and wear rapidly in high-traffic areas.

You can sidestep some of these challenges by choosing a lawn alternative for all or part of your yard. One option is a wildflower meadow (*see page 66*), which may be a mix of annual and perennial grasses and flowering plants. Another is to install hardscaping, such as a deck or patio, to provide an outdoor resting or dining area. A third option is to plant some kind of ground-cover plant. Ground cover has the advantage of being low maintenance and of providing a solution for difficult areas such as shaded parts of the yard, steep slopes, or poor soil conditions.

Choosing the type of lawn

Nearly all lawns are composed of a selection of different grasses and it is important to select the best combination. Garden centers offer a huge range of grass seed mixtures for different styles of lawns, including customized mixes for individual clients. Mixtures are also available to suit particular environmental conditions, such as slow-growing grasses for sunny sites, or varieties that are suitable for shaded, damp, or dry soils. By starting with the best grass type or blend for your particular site, you will cut down on maintenance and reduce problems that might arise in the future.

PLANNING & PREPARATION

A smooth stretch of lawn in both the front yard and backyard is a mainstay of many north American gardens, and makes a great surface for recreation or relaxation, from throwing a football to hosting a barbecue. If you have purchased an older home, you will probably inherit an older lawn along with it. If you are starting a lawn from scratch, it takes a lot of preparation—leveling, removing weeds and debris, and improving the soil, even before planting the grass. Choosing the right grass and planning a lawn that is no bigger than you are able to care for will make the ongoing maintenance easier.

Types of grass

Turfgrasses are categorized as warm-season or cool-season, depending on their growth habit.

Generally, warm-season grasses thrive in the South, where they grow vigorously during the hot summer months, then stay dormant through winter. They tend to be fairly drought-tolerant. Turfgrasses in this category include bahia grass, Bermuda grass, carpetgrass, centipede grass, St. Augustine grass, and zoysia. Because these grasses turn brown in winter, they are sometimes overseeded with grasses such as annual ryegrass for a green lawn year-round.

Cool-season grasses prefer the cool temperatures and wetter conditions in the North, where they thrive in spring and fall, becoming dormant when temperatures are high in summer. In mild-winter regions, cool-season grasses can remain green from fall through into spring until hot summer temperatures and drought arrive. Common cool-season turfgrasses include bent grass,

Circular lawns work well in a small garden because they distract the eye from the straight lines of the boundaries. If it mirrors circular features, such as a seat back (*above*), the lawn unifies the space.

Use curves to accommodate changes in grade, and undulate the edges of the lawn to avoid shady spots, which are anathema to the cultivation of a successful lawn.

Creating a wildflower meadow *see page 66* | **Seed or sod?** *see page 287* | **Lawn maintenance** *see page 290*

Kentucky bluegrass, chewing fescue, red fescue, tall fescue, and perennial ryegrass.

In addition to the broad categories of North and South, there is a transition zone that runs from southern California to the District of Columbia. Gardeners in this area may need a warm- or cool-season grass, depending on the region and microclimate.

Different lawn grasses vary not just in growth habit but also in appearance, irrigation needs, and disease- and pest-resistance. Some are very fine-textured and delicate and cannot survive a lot of foot traffic or ball-playing. Others are stronger, and coarser in texture, with larger blades. Many seed mixes and turf contain several different types of turfgrass. Your local cooperative extension service will advise on the right type of lawn grass for your area and the best time of year for establishing it.

Practical considerations

Because a lawn does require a significant amount of maintenance and irrigation, plant one that is only as large as your needs.

Although some lawns can survive in shadier spots, none thrives in deepest shade, especially under trees, where the roots also compete with lawn grasses for water and nutrients. Likewise, some drought-tolerant trees will not thrive if they receive the amount of irrigation required by a lawn. So if you have mature trees in the landscape—

or young trees that are likely to grow quickly—plan the lawn so it curves around them, or leave a large area around the trunk grass free and cover it with mulch instead.

Irrigation

The job of caring for your lawn will be made much easier with the help of an automatic sprinkler system. Such a system should be installed before you prepare for planting, as the main feeder lines are run about 18in. under the ground. Pop-up sprinkler heads deliver water evenly to the entire lawn surface, and an automatic timer can be set to water the lawn on a schedule, at a time of day when water is less likely to be lost to evaporation.

Turfgrass alternatives

In addition to the traditional turfgrass lawn, many homeowners are choosing to plant alternatives in order to reduce water, fertilizer, and pesticide use. These may not provide a velvety expanse of green, but can be just as serviceable as a typical lawn and have their own charms as more naturalistic, meadow-style planting.

Suitable plants may be native prairie grasses such as blue grama, buffalo grass, or crested wheatgrass, or grass alternatives such as low-growing sedges and fescues, which are planted as plugs (*see page 287*) and quickly spread to create a natural-looking lawn that can tolerate foot traffic and requires only occasional mowing.

Large lawns can be made more interesting by planting around the edge. This approach is most suitable for informal gardens. A well-defined edge to the lawn will help prevent lawn grasses from creeping into your borders. Whatever the shape, it will be easier to keep the lawn neat if its edges are bordered with some kind of hardscaping material—bricks, pavers, or stones.

Preparing the site

Preparation for creating a lawn should begin at least eight weeks before planting. The best time to plant depends on the type of grass. Cool-season grasses establish best if sown from late summer to early fall, while warm-season types are best sown or planted as plugs (*see page 287*) from late spring through early summer.

    You can lay sod any time as long as the ground is not frozen or there is not a drought or extremely hot temperatures. Any lawn requires consistent watering to get established, so try to plant when the grass will receive as much natural rainfall as possible.

Clearing the site

The first stage is to clear the site of any debris (*see right*) before leveling can begin. This includes removing any construction debris and any stones and bricks. You will also need to dig out tree stumps, removing as much of the root system as possible. Leaving them in the soil will encourage fungi and other diseases. Small tree stumps can generally be dug up using a pickaxe and spade, but for really large ones it might be necessary for you to hire a tree removal service.

Preparing the soil

You can now deeply rototill the soil, as this reduces the compaction and allows air into the soil. Grass prefers a well-drained soil to a depth of at least 8in. Add builder's sand to poorly drained soil. Most soils, whether heavy and poorly drained or sandy and very well drained, will be improved by incorporating well-rotted organic matter. Most soils should be within the pH limits of 5.5–7; a soil test will tell you if you need to amend the soil's pH.

    Lawns require good drainage for optimum growth and to deter moss and fungal diseases. If the soil is severely waterlogged, seek professional advice about installing drainage, or consider more hardscaping, such as a deck or patio, instead of a lawn.

Grading & leveling the site

The term grading means the elimination of surface irregularities. Leveling is the process whereby a sloping site is made level (*see box, right*). Both jobs can be expensive, and on larger properties they may not be necessary as gentle slopes or undulations can form an attractive feature in the landscape. Minor irregularities can be corrected by adding more topsoil. Do not take this from higher points on the site, as this can leave it very thin in places, causing bare patches.

LEVELING THE SITE

It is not essential to have a perfectly level site; a gentle slope is quite acceptable and has the advantage of assisting surface drainage as long as the slope runs away from the house. To level the surface, you will need to create a level grid of wooden stakes, each one with a mark 4in. from the top. Select one of these as the main stake, from which all the other stakes will take their guide. You will need to add or remove soil to the level on each stake, only discarding the stakes once all the soil is evenly firmed throughout the site.

1 **Hammer the stakes** into the soil in a grid system 6ft. apart. If the garden has an existing path or patio, then make sure that the mark on the main stake is level with it.

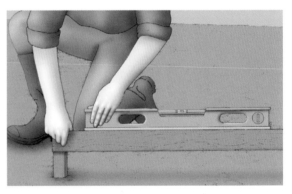

2 **Use a straight board** and level to ensure that the stakes are all at the same level, working away from the main stake. Adjust the height of the secondary stakes until all are even.

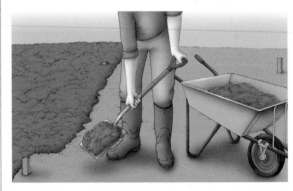

3 **Add or remove topsoil**, firming it down so that the surface is level with the mark on each stake. Fill in any dips or bumps.

Looking after your soil *see page 32* | Types of grass *see page 284* | Alternatives to lawns *see page 302*

Final site preparation

The soil should ultimately be broken down into a fine tilth. Use a metal rake or garden fork to break up clods of soil and to level out any bumps or dips. Work the soil to a fine crumbly texture. It will need to be fairly dry to do this as wet soil sticks to tools. A heavy, clay soil may require the addition of more organic matter over a period of several months. Firm the soil evenly to remove any air pockets, then rake it over. This can be repeated a number of times, but be careful not to compact the soil too much. After this is done, check the levels and make the appropriate adjustments if necessary.

At this point wait a few weeks, during which time weed seedlings can be killed periodically by light hoeing. About a week before seeding (*see page 288*) or laying sod (*see page 289*), a base dressing of a handful of slow-release, all-purpose fertilizer per square yard can be raked into the soil bed.

Seed or sod?

There are advantages to starting your lawn with both seed or sod, depending on your budget, time frame, and the amount of work you are able to take on. For gardeners in the west and south, there is a third alternative: planting from plugs (small, circular or square sections of turf with a plug of soil) or sprigs (small, rooted tufts of grass). Bermuda grass, St. Augustine, and zoysia are often planted from sprigs. Native grasses and clumping sedges are available as slightly larger plugs. Plugs and sprigs can be purchased from local sod suppliers, or ordered by mail.

Advantages of seed

Seeds are far cheaper than sod, easier to store, and lighter to work with. They have a longer shelf life, allowing the gardener to wait for suitable weather conditions. Different seed mixes allow the lawn to be tailored to the function, climate, and conditions of the yard.

Disadvantages of seed

It can take months before a seed-sown lawn is ready for use; even then it might still be patchy and need more work. After sowing, you will need to prevent birds eating the seeds. Weed seeds may blow onto the site and compete with the seedling grass for nutrients and water.

Advantages of sod

Sod is a better choice for an instant lawn that can be used fairly soon—six weeks for light wear—after it has been laid. Sod can be laid in winter when there are fewer other jobs to be done in the garden.

Disadvantages of sod

Sod is far more expensive than raising a lawn from seed. Also, be wary about the quality of the sod.

Advance notice will be needed if the sod is delivered. Once delivered or purchased, the sod must be laid within a few days. If the weather turns wet or cold, it will be very difficult to lay the sod properly, resulting in a loss of sod—and money.

Laying sod is hard work. It involves carrying and handling heavy rolls of sod, often from the front yard around to the backyard. If it does not rain, the lawn will need constant irrigation after laying to help it root down into the soil—not an environmentally friendly option.

Grass seedlings are very delicate and should not be walked on at all for at least 10 weeks and not much more than that for the first growing season, to allow it to establish a good root system.

Recently laid sod, if it is kept well watered, will root together and into the soil quickly and can be used much sooner than seed-sown lawns. It is still wise to avoid heavy wear in the first 6 months.

Sowing a lawn

Choose a seed mixture that suits your region, soil type, and exposure. Also consider whether you want a fine-textured lawn or a more coarse-textured and tougher surface.

Grass seed needs a slightly moist soil to germinate successfully. If the soil is dry, lightly water it a couple of days before sowing, then rake the soil over again.

Choose a calm day for sowing—any wind will blow the seeds about and result in uneven distribution. Do not sow in wet conditions because the wet soil and seeds will stick to your boots and also to the wheels of the seed spreader. Rake over the site just before sowing to break up any surface crusting of the soil and ensure that the seeds settle well.

Check the sowing rate for the seed mix to avoid any problems. The usual rate is 3–5lb. per 1,600 square feet, but this will be listed on the package. Sowing too much seed increases the surface humidity, which encourages damping off disease. Sowing too thinly leaves bare patches of lawn, which allow weeds to establish.

Sowing grass seed by hand

Divide the area up and calculate how much seed is needed to fill each grid section. Use a measuring cup to portion out the seeds. Sow in two directions for an even distribution (*see above, right*). To get a clean edge to the lawn, cover the perimeter of the site with plastic or tarps to stop any seeds falling outside the area. Alternatively, an edge could be cut with a half-moon edger once the grass has established.

Sowing grass seed with a seed spreader

A mechanical spreader sows seeds evenly at the required rate. As with hand sowing, the edges may be covered to obtain a straight edge. Push the machine onto the sheeting at the end of each row to stop seeds falling out as you turn.

Aftercare

A light topdressing of mulch can aid germination. It is important to keep the soil moist, so if the weather remains dry, water frequently using a sprinkler system with a fine spray. Avoid dragging a hose over the site as this will disturb the seeds. You may need to deter birds with netting or other devices. Remove weeds by hand.

Seedlings should start to appear 7–21 days after sowing. When they reach about 2½–3in. tall, lightly cut the grass, taking care not to rip out seedlings. Continue mowing at the same height throughout the growing season.

SOWING GRASS SEED

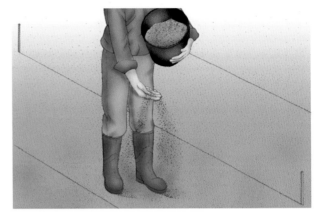

To hand sow, spread seeds within a grid of stakes and strings. For each area, scatter half the amount needed in one direction over the soil. Sow the other half of the seeds at right angles to the first spreading.

To use a mechanical spreader, fill the machine with half the required amount of seeds and push it up and down the area in one direction. Refill the machine and repeat, in the other direction.

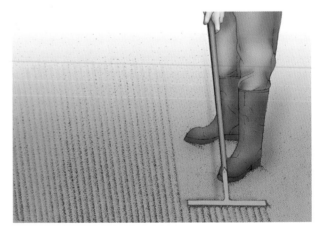

After sowing the seeds, lightly rake over the seedbed to bed the seeds gently into the soil. Work backwards to avoid treading on the raked soil and do not bury the seeds too deeply since this inhibits germination.

Types of grass *see page 284* | **Lawn maintenance** *see page 290* | **Lawn weeds** *see page 296*

Laying sod

Lightly water the prepared site a couple of days before laying the sod if there has been no rain, but do not saturate the soil because this will make it too sticky and unworkable. Sod is relatively expensive to purchase and it's best to inspect it before purchasing to ensure that the grass is of a good quality. Sod should be laid as soon after delivery as possible, as it can quickly deteriorate even if stored in optimum conditions.

When laying the sod, avoid walking on the prepared soil or the newly laid sod. Use wooden boards to stand on, to distribute the weight and avoid compaction and indentations. Make sure that each row is tightly butted up against the previous one. Never plant right up to a tree to avoid damaging the tree with a mower or string trimmer. It is best not to cover steep banks as they are hard to mow.

Aftercare

Water frequently if the weather remains dry. Wait for the grass to start growing before you mow, then cut with the mower on a high setting. You can walk on the new lawn right away, but full use should be postponed until the roots have knitted into the soil.

LAYING SOD

1 **Apply a starter fertilizer** to the prepared soil unless it is already very fertile. Fertilizer can be purchased from most garden centers. Follow the manufacturer's instructions for the rate of application.

2 **Rake the soil** before laying the sod. Start by positioning the sod at the edge of the site, ideally along a long, straight edge such as a path or against a patio.

3 **Mark out the first line** with wooden stakes and string if there is no straight edge. Work facing the prepared site and avoid compacting it, by standing on a wide board or piece of plywood.

4 **Lay the first row** of sod out along the line, butting the edges of each piece right up to the next. Start the second row by cutting a strip in half and use one half as the first piece before continuing with full-sized pieces.

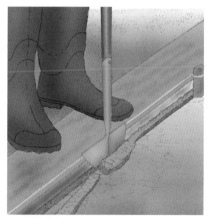

5 **Trim the edges** once all sod pieces are laid, using a half-moon edger. Stand on a wooden board and use it as a guide to make sure that the cut is straight. Use a hose as a guideline to create curving edges.

6 **Firm the new lawn** with a light roller to eradicate any remaining air pockets. Do not roll the turf if it is wet; instead, wait until the sod has grown together. Water thoroughly.

LAWN MAINTENANCE

Planting the right grass for your region, along with regular upkeep, helps keep the lawn healthy. Frequent maintenance is the key to achieving a lawn that resists pests and diseases. On the other hand, neglect results in the lawn becoming weedy or even dying off in parts. As well as mowing, you will need to fertilize and irrigate the grass, and carry out an annual overhaul of dethatching, aerating, and topdressing the lawn. This promotes healthy, strong growth, giving the grass a greater capacity to combat attacks from pests, diseases, mosses, and weeds.

Fertilizing lawns

The three main plant nutrients are nitrogen, phosphorus, and potassium, frequently seen expressed as a ratio N:P:K on fertilizer packets. Iron (Fe) is also a key ingredient; it helps to 'green up' the grass without stimulating growth, making it useful in fall fertilizers. Other essential minerals are required for healthy lawn growth, but in far lower quantities. Overfertilizing grass results in runoff and weak growth.

USING A MECHANICAL SPREADER

Lawn fertilizer may be applied using a mechanical spreader. Push it up and down the lawn as if it were a mower. Take care to distribute the fertilizer evenly; apply half a batch in one direction and the other half at right angles to it.

When to fertilize

Fertilizing twice a year is sufficient for most lawns. Excess fertilizer does not improve the health of the lawn. In fact, it can cause overdevelopment of thatch and topgrowth at the expense of healthy root formation. In addition, fertilizer runoff from lawns is a major cause of excess nutrients in waterways, where it can cause algal overgrowth and disrupt ecosystems. Remember that a soil test can tell you if your soil is deficient in nutrients.

Most cool-season lawns will benefit from a fall application of fertilizer; if the lawn does not seem to be growing well by midspring, consider another application. Warm-season grasses should be fertilized in summer, typically at the beginning and toward the middle of their growing season. Choose a slow-release fertilizer that is formulated for lawns and apply it at the rate specified by the manufacturer.

The organic approach

Natural phosphorus may be added by sprinkling bonemeal over the lawn in fall. If you leave grass cuttings on the lawn after mowing, they take nitrogen into the soil as they break down. You can also topdress with well-rotted, friable compost to add nitrogen and potassium.

Application methods

Overapplication of fertilizer can damage the lawn, so read the instructions carefully. Fertilizers should be applied in dry weather when rain is predicted in the next couple of days. If no rain appears, gently water in the fertilizer, using a sprinkler. Apply fertilizers by hand or using a mechanical spreader. Always wear gloves when handling chemicals.

Aerating & topdressing *see page 292* | **Lawn weeds** *see page 296* | **Lawn pests & diseases** *see page 298*

Dethatching & raking

In spring, lightly rake the lawn to remove winter debris before mowing. In late spring and summer, rake the lawn occasionally to ensure even mowing by lifting the grass blades. In the fall when the growth of the lawn starts to slow, you may need to remove a heavy buildup of thatch. Chances are you will be giving the lawn a thorough raking at this time anyway, when clearing fallen leaves.

Dethatching involves slightly aerating the soil surface and removes excess thatch (*see right*) from the lawn. A small amount of thatch is fine, but heavy thatch impedes the development of new blades of grass, shades out sunlight, and encourages the growth of moss. It can also stop fertilizers reaching the grass roots, and thatch absorbs moisture during damp periods, harboring fungal diseases, as well as preventing water from penetrating the soil in drought.

To dethatch, vigorously scrape a rake over the lawn surface, keeping the tool well pressed down so that the tines penetrate the soil. Work across the grass from one edge, scraping toward yourself. Once you have raked all the lawn, rake it again, working at right angles to the original direction. Mow the lawn afterwards to remove any loose pieces of thatch. Add all the thatch to the compost pile. Dethatching should also remove any

Thatch is the springy remains of dead grass and other fibrous material that accumulates among the blades of grass; a small amount retains moisture during drought and protects the lawn from wear.

blackened, dead pieces of moss. You may need to reseed any bare patches.

Dethatching with a rake is tiring work, so you may prefer to rent a dethatching machine. Dethatching attachments for some mowers can also be effective.

DETHATCHING & RAKING TOOLS

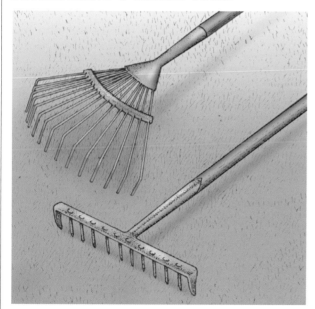

A spring-tined rake (*top*) is preferable to a standard garden rake (*bottom*) because the flexible wire tines penetrate and aerate the soil without lifting it up or dragging out the grass roots.

A dethatching machine is useful for larger areas of lawn. These lift the thatch as they travel across the lawn. Rake up and remove the thatch, and mow afterwards to leave the lawn looking neat.

Aeration & topdressing

Over time, lawns become compacted by children's play, garden furniture, or even frequent mowing. Compaction can result in major problems for the health of the lawn by impeding the flow of air and water into the soil.

Grass roots, as in all other plants, rely on air to assist with the uptake of water and nutrients. In compacted soils their growth is physically restricted. Water drains poorly, causing surface waterlogging, and in drought, irrigation water cannot penetrate. Compacted lawns soon weaken and become infested with tougher weeds.

Regular aeration reduces compaction and encourages strong root growth. In the aeration process, channels are created in the lawn to allow the air and water to penetrate deeply into the soil.

Methods of aeration

Dethatching forms part of the aeration process by removing thatch (*see page 291*). True aeration, however, needs to penetrate deeper into the soil, making holes to a depth of at least 3in., but ideally 4–6in.

A hollow-tined fork can be used to aerate small areas of lawn. A power lawn aerator, with hollow tines, is best for larger areas.

Aerate the lawn in early spring or fall. The ground should be neither bone dry nor soggy, but the soil should be moist so the plugs are easily extracted; water the lawn thoroughly the day before if needed. Flag any irrigation sprinklers to avoid damaging them with the tines. Begin in one corner of the lawn and work in a criss-cross pattern. Fill the holes with compost or a sandy topdressing and avoid excessive foot traffic for a few days.

Methods of topdressing

A lawn can be improved by a layer of specially prepared fine soil. This encourages new basal growth from the grass, creating a much denser lawn. Topdressing is also used to fill any hollows that may have developed over the year in your lawn.

When to topdress

Topdress lawns every one to three years, as needed. Aerating the soil prior to topdressing is recommended, particularly on heavy soils, because this will make it easier for the topdressing to penetrate the soil.

Topdressing should be carried out in early fall, while the grass is still growing, after dethatching (*see page 291*) and aerating (*see below*). After completion, new shoots will appear through the topdressing.

Making topdressing mixes

Ready-made mixes are available from garden centers, but it is easy to make up your own mix. Lawn topdressing has three ingredients: good garden soil, sand, and organic matter. Do not use sea sand as it may be very alkaline. The organic matter is often peat moss but may be leafmold or garden compost. A typical mix contains 3:3:1 parts of sand, soil, and organic matter, but the blend may be modified to suit individual soil types.

The amount of topdressing required will vary depending on the state of the lawn and the type of soil. For example, more may be used if the lawn has been hollow-tined, as there will be holes to fill. An average lawn requires 3–4lb. per square yard.

METHODS FOR AERATING LAWNS

A lawn aerator cuts through the thatch on the surface of the lawn and creates parallel holes that sink up to 3–4in. into the soil. This allows air and water to penetrate.

Hold a fork with the tines curving towards you and drive it into the ground. Move the fork back and forth slightly to enlarge the holes, and remove it without lifting the turf. Repeat across the lawn.

Drive an aerator into the ground to remove small plugs or cores from the lawn. Each time you sink the fork into the soil, the previous plugs will fall out. When you have finished, remove the plugs.

Lawn tools & mowers

There are two basic types of mower: rotary and reel. Rotary mowers are most popular: they have horizontal blades that spin beneath a motor and are ideal for less formal grass areas, uneven ground, and longer grass. Although rotary mowers do not provide as clean a cut as a reel mower, they are generally easier to use on uneven ground. A riding mower is a time- and labor-saver if your property is more than half an acre and does not have too many obstacles while mowing.

Traditional reel mowers give the best cut. The blades are mounted around a cylinder that revolves as the mower moves forward, slicing the grass between the blades and a stationary bar that lies parallel to the ground. With hand-driven reel mowers, the pushing action spins the cylinder; they are light, easy to use, and the most environmentally friendly option. These are best suited to smaller lawns that are relatively level. Mowers may have a grass catcher designed to catch clippings. 'Mulching' mowers have blades that shred the clippings and drop them on the ground.

Gas or electric mower?

Mowers that run on gas are more powerful, more expensive, and heavier than electric mowers and may be rotary or reel, self propelling, or require pushing. They are suitable for larger gardens because their range is not restricted by a power cord, but some may find them too heavy to maneuver. They last longer than electric mowers, but need regular maintenance.

Electric mowers are light, easy to maneuver, and good for small spaces. They are also quieter than gas models. Some are battery powered or cordless, so you do not need to worry about cutting the wire, which is a potential hazard of some electric mowers.

The waterwise lawn

Conserving water supplies is a concern in many areas of the U.S. and Canada. In desert areas, where rainfall can be as low as 10in. per year, a lawn can be maintained only with enormous and ecologically unsound inputs of water. In many communities, municipal water restrictions have become common, especially during annual summer droughts. This does not mean you have to give up your lawn. But it does mean that you should be as waterwise as possible. You should always choose a grass type suitable for the amount of rainfall in your area. For an even more

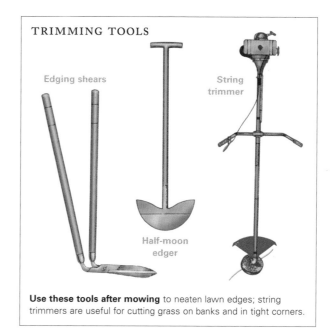

TRIMMING TOOLS

Edging shears

String trimmer

Half-moon edger

Use these tools after mowing to neaten lawn edges; string trimmers are useful for cutting grass on banks and in tight corners.

drought-tolerant option, consider planting a ground cover or lawn alternative. There are native grasses available for a variety of conditions in different regions (*see page 284*). Most are well suited to poor soils, where normal turfgrass will struggle, and will do well even in high altitudes in the mountain states, or in seaside gardens with salt-laden winds. Native grasses may be low growing or taller, and many can be mown for a neater appearance in the garden.

Or you can choose a meadow planting with a blend of drought-tolerant grasses, sedges, and wildflowers (*see page 66*). The appearance will not be that of a formal garden, but it may be more in keeping with your local landscape. Your local cooperative extension service or native plant nursery can provide advice for your region.

Also consider if you need a green lawn year-round. In summer-drought areas on the West Coast, brown lawns during mid- and late summer are seen as evidence of responsible gardening. In desert areas, the lawn must not only be watered in summer but must also be overseeded with annual grasses and watered in winter when the turfgrass goes dormant. Desert plantings may be more appropriate in such locations.

Finally, fertilize your lawn only as needed (*see page 290*). Mow high rather than 'scalping' the lawn. Be sure to water in the early morning, and make sure you have the most efficient spray pattern for your lawn.

293

Irrigation

Thorough watering helps grass to develop deep roots that can assist it through periods of drought. As a general rule, most turfgrasses need 1–2in. of water, from irrigation or rainfall, per week, but this varies depending on your soil type and the temperature. Warm-season grasses such as Bermuda grass can be very drought tolerant and require less watering unless they show signs of drought.

The best time of day to water is early morning; you will lose less water to evaporation and the lawn has time to dry during the day. Water penetrates different soil types at different rates; 1in. of water can penetrate sandy soil to a depth of 12in. but far less in clay soil, which retains the water for a longer period and so may require less watering. After watering, wait until the top inch or two of soil has dried out before watering again (check the soil by digging into it with a screwdriver or trowel).

How to water

The most efficient and hassle-free way to keep your lawn irrigated is by installing an automatic sprinkler system. Without such an automatic system, your challenge is to provide consistent water for the lawn, and the best way to do this is with hose-end sprinklers. You can find many different kinds, including oscillating sprinklers, pulsating types, revolving-arm sprinklers, and even 'walking' models that move along a hose laid on the ground. The delivery pattern will vary depending on the model; try to

Symptoms of drought in a lawn include dulling of color and slowing growth. The leaves then turn yellow and brown. Eventually, the grass shrivels up and begins to die back, allowing weeds to invade.

find one that concentrates most of the water on the lawn and not on adjacent hardscaping. Rotary types often give better and more flexible coverage than oscillating types.

To evaluate a sprinkler's coverage, place a series of equal-size containers at a regular distance from the sprinkler head. Run the sprinkler and note how long it takes to fill a container with 1in. of water.

WATERING EQUIPMENT

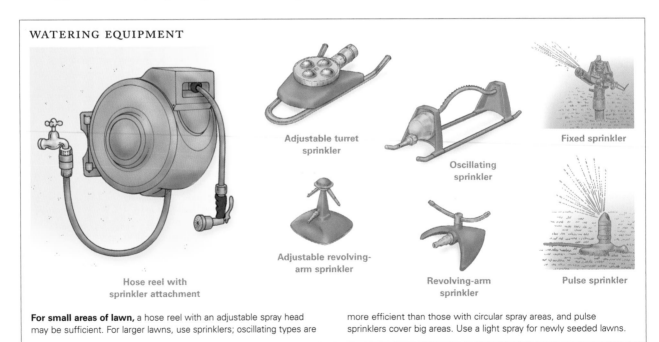

Adjustable turret sprinkler

Oscillating sprinkler

Fixed sprinkler

Hose reel with sprinkler attachment

Adjustable revolving-arm sprinkler

Revolving-arm sprinkler

Pulse sprinkler

For small areas of lawn, a hose reel with an adjustable spray head may be sufficient. For larger lawns, use sprinklers; oscillating types are more efficient than those with circular spray areas, and pulse sprinklers cover big areas. Use a light spray for newly seeded lawns.

Mowing lawns

Regular mowing, using a good technique, encourages healthy new grass growth and a strong root system. Mowing also helps prevent a buildup of pests and diseases and keeps down weeds and removes their seedheads.

Different types of grass are mown to different heights (*see box, below*). Generally you should remove no more than one third of the grass height at a time. Cutting grass so short that it scalps the lawn will leave unsightly bare patches of soil as well as blunt the blades.

When to cut

Typically, most lawns require mowing once a week in the growing season. Factors such as the season, weather conditions, the health of the grass, irrigation, and weeds all influence the rate at which grass grows, and a good gardener will adapt the mowing methods accordingly. Never mow when it is wet because the grass sticks to the blades, giving a poor cut. Avoid mowing early in the morning if dew is on the ground. Leave the grass to grow slightly longer in prolonged dry periods as this will help it to survive and reduce the need for watering.

The lawn may be mown in winter during mild spells, to tidy the garden and remove fallen leaves; raise the cutting blade to a high setting. Never mow in frosty conditions or when cold winds are blowing as this will scorch the leaf tips.

Removing grass clippings

If the lawn has become very weedy, rake up clippings and remove both clippings and weeds after mowing. There are benefits, however, to leaving grass clippings on the lawn: it makes mowing easier—you needn't rake or bag the clippings and carry them away as they break down—and the clippings return nitrogen to the soil, increasing the fertility of the grass. In dry periods, the clippings act as a mulch by helping to retain moisture and slow the rate of evaporation from the lawn. Some mowers have a built-in mulcher, which chops the cuttings into tiny pieces before dropping them back onto the grass.

You can compost clippings by adding them in layers to a compost pile. Dried clippings can also be used as a mulch around the garden, but they may contain weed seeds. Never mulch with clippings that have been treated with an herbicide.

Mower safety

Before mowing, remove all debris; stones and twigs can fly out from under the mower and harm the operator as well as the mower blades. Keep pets and children away while you are mowing. Wear heavy shoes or boots, and always keep your hands and feet away from the mower's blades. Thoroughly clean and dry your mower after use, and service it once per year.

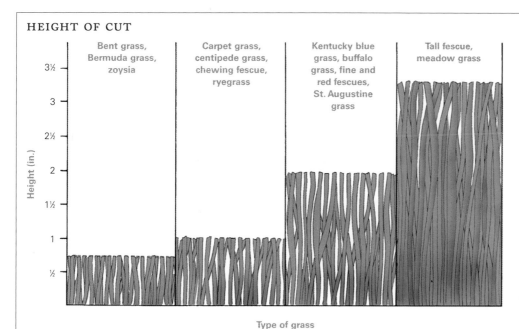

HEIGHT OF CUT

Bent grass, Bermuda grass, zoysia

Carpet grass, centipede grass, chewing fescue, ryegrass

Kentucky blue grass, buffalo grass, fine and red fescues, St. Augustine grass

Tall fescue, meadow grass

Height (in.)

Type of grass

This chart indicates the heights to which different lawns should be cut during the main growing season. Set the blade on your mower to the correct height.

When the grass starts to grow in spring, the first few cuts should be made slightly higher than the optimum height for the lawn type, and gradually reduced down to the correct height for the rest of the growing season.

Meadow grass and natural lawns require mowing only once or twice per year.

COMMON PROBLEMS

Lawns may be invaded by a wide range of weeds. However, the degree to which you need to control them depends on the effect required. A fine display lawn has no place for weeds and moss, but a practical family lawn may be less pristine; some lawn weeds may form part of a meadow garden. Pests and diseases are much easier to control if dealt with at an early stage, but before you do so make sure you have the correct diagnosis—the most common problem in lawns is discolored grass, which could be caused by pests or diseases but is often a sign of problems such as poor mowing, pet damage, or drought.

Lawn weeds

The best way to keep weeds out is to encourage lawn grasses to thrive, producing a dense, healthy turf in which weeds cannot establish. Light, well-cultivated soil, good drainage, reasonable fertility, and an open, sunny position are ideal, together with regular mowing.

Weeds exploit poor conditions such as compacted ground, poor drainage, shade, lack of water or nutrients, and grass that has been mowed too short. Trees, especially if they have overhanging branches and are shallow rooted or evergreen, provide such conditions as they deprive grass of water and nutrients. A solution for smaller specimen trees is to cut a circular or square bed around them, which can be planted with shade-tolerant plants.

Main types of lawn weed

Rosette-forming weeds: These form a flattened whorl of leaves, smothering the grass beneath and escaping mower blades. Dandelions are an example.

Creeping weeds: These colonize gaps in turf, outgrowing grass in poor conditions. The stems lie lower than mower blades. White clover (*Trifolium repens*) is an example.

Weed grasses: These include coarse species like Bermuda grass, quack grass, and crabgrass. They cause uneven color and texture.

Mosses, algae, and lichens: These are most often a problem in lawns where the soil is compacted, poorly drained, or very shaded. Moss is almost always present, in

COMMON PERENNIAL LAWN WEEDS

Yarrow (*Achillea millefolium*) is able to survive drought and mowing. It has spreading roots and forms mats on well-drained soils. The flowers appear from early summer to late fall.

Hawkweed (*Hieracium* species) has a basal rosette. It prefers dry, sunny places, spreading by rooting stem tips (stolons) and flowering from late spring to midfall.

Broad-leaved plantain (*Plantago major*) has a large rosette and long, straight roots from a short rhizome. It survives in high-traffic areas and flowers from early summer to midfall.

Speedwell (*Veronica* species) is a low, creeping weed that forms dense mats and can root from stem fragments. It thrives in grassy terrain, flowering from midspring to early summer.

Creating a wildflower meadow *see page 66* | **Lawn maintenance** *see page 290* | **Repairing neglected lawns** *see page 301*

SPOT TREATMENT

Use a spot weeder if you have only a few weeds in the lawn, especially weeds that form basal rosettes or small patches of creeping weeds. Some are available in the form of a ready-to-use spray.

Spot weeders are also available as a solid, waxy stick or as a liquid applied by roller ball. Some weeds, such as plantains, will succumb after 1–2 applications of herbicide; other weeds may require several treatments over 4–6 weeks.

BROAD APPLICATIONS OF HERBICIDE

Lawn herbicides may be applied in a variety of ways. Concentrated liquids require dilution before use and should be applied using a watering can, or a hose-end sprayer on a coarse setting to reduce the risk of spray drift.

Granular products are applied dry and are more economical over large areas. Scatter the granules by hand or with a hand-held spreader. A mechanical spreader is useful. Usually, you need to water in the granules if it does not rain within a few days of application—check the instructions for details.

wetter climates, but too much can smother fine grasses and weaken the turf's resilience to wear. Algae and lichens make the soil slippery.

Selective herbicides

These target broad-leaved weeds but do not harm grass if used correctly. Some weeds are resistant to particular herbicides, so most products contain a blend of active ingredients. You may need to repeat the application; if some weeds persist, use a product with different active ingredients. A few weeds resist all lawn herbicides. Dig them out, or use a non-selective herbicide—which will also kill the grass—and reseed or resod the affected area. Preemergent herbicides help control germinating annual weed seeds on established lawns.

Removing grass weeds manually

Selective herbicides do not affect all weeds; some you will need to remove by hand. For large areas, the only option may be to resod or reseed the affected lawn. You can remove moss by dethatching in spring. Lichens and algae may be raked or scraped off the soil.

HAND WEEDING

Ease out rosette-forming weeds with a small tool called a dandelion weeder, getting out as much of the taproot as possible. Tackle creeping weeds when they first invade as they are much easier, and cheaper, to control at this early stage.

Lawn pests & diseases

As with any problem, prompt action at the correct time will be the most effective.

PESTS

It is important to distinguish pest problems from cultural problems and to identify pests correctly.

White grubs

The curved grubs of Japanese beetles, June bugs, and chafers destroy grass roots, making it easy for armadillos, raccoons, and skunks to dig up the turf as they feed on the grubs. Larvae start feeding in early summer; treat with biological controls such as nematodes or milky spore at this time. Dethatch the lawn (*see page 291*) and apply an appropriate control.

Crane fly larvae

Also called leatherjackets, these tubular larvae eat grass roots and can kill areas of lawn during late winter to summer. The adults, known as crane flies, emerge and lay eggs in early fall. Control the larvae with a biological control or an appropriate insecticide.

Chinch bugs

These widespread pests suck the sap from the crown and stems of turfgrasses, leaving brown, sunken, irregular patches of dead turf. To detect the pests, sink a bottomless can into the turf and fill it with water; chinch bugs will float to the surface. Chinch bugs thrive in hot, dry weather; good watering practices may help the lawn to avoid severe damage. Control thatch and do not overfertilize. Some turfgrass types are resistant to damage. If cultural practices do not control the pest, use an appropriate insecticide, applying it in early evening.

Billbugs

These weevils lay their eggs in grass stems; the grubs hatch and feed on the plants' crown and roots. Infested plants are easily detached by tugging on them. Parasitic nematodes or *Bacillus thuringiensis kurstaki* (Btk) may control the grubs. An appropriate insecticide may kill the adults in early summer.

Armyworms

Fall armyworms are large caterpillars up to 2in. long, the larvae of moths that migrate northward starting in early spring. Fall armyworm infestations usually occur late in summer and early fall, but several generations of the pest may occur in a year, especially in the South. The caterpillars chew on lawn grasses, usually in early morning or late evening, leaving the lawn ragged and covered with brown patches. They can be controlled with natural predators, including trichogramma wasps, assassin bugs, and tachinid flies. *Bacillus thuringiensis kurstaki* (Btk) may be effective against smaller caterpillars; alternatively, use an appropriate insecticide.

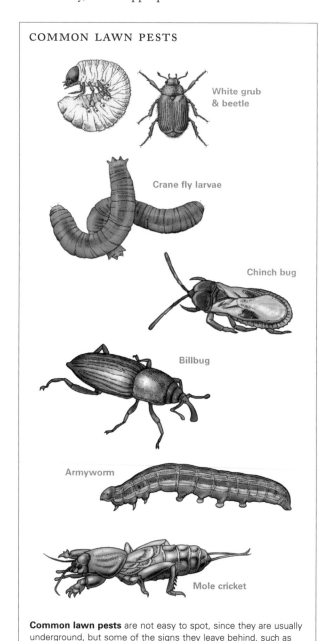

COMMON LAWN PESTS

White grub & beetle

Crane fly larvae

Chinch bug

Billbug

Armyworm

Mole cricket

Common lawn pests are not easy to spot, since they are usually underground, but some of the signs they leave behind, such as tunnels and poor growth, are very obvious.

Rabbits and other animals, such as opossums, squirrels, and foxes, can cause damage by burrowing or digging for grubs or nuts.

Molehills look unsightly, kill off grass, and interfere with mowing. All the molehills on a lawn may be caused by one solitary mole.

Dead patches can be caused by drought, poor aeration, dog urine, buried debris, and fertilizer scorch, as well as various pests and diseases.

Mole crickets

These are serious pests of southern lawns, using their clawlike forelegs to dig through the turf, leaving bare patches. Some types feed on roots, stems, and leaves of turfgrasses, leaving visible tunnels. If you suspect mole crickets, pour soapy water on a patch of turf; the large insects will be forced to the surface. Dethatch the lawn regularly (*see page 291*). Treat with the beneficial nematode *Steinernema scapterisci*, or an appropriate insecticide in early summer.

DISEASES

There are several turf diseases that can kill, weaken, or disfigure large areas of turf, most of them caused by fungi and some encouraged by humid conditions.

Fairy rings

Several soil-borne fungi disfigure lawns by forming fairy rings—one or more rings of lush green grass, sometimes with mushrooms at the periphery in appropriate weather conditions. The most serious form of fairy ring is also accompanied by an area of dead grass. There is no chemical control. Remove mushrooms and dispose of them, keeping them out of the compost and away from healthy areas of grass. You may need to dig up affected turf to a depth of at least 12in. and the same distance beyond the edge of the ring. Fill with fresh soil and reseed or lay new sod. Alternatively, call for the services of a lawn-care professional.

Other fungi may appear in lawns that do not stimulate grass growth. They may be feeding on decaying woody matter in the soil; to treat the problem, find the food source and remove it.

Take-all patch

This disease appears in summer. Circular, bronze-colored depressions a few inches across appear and increase in size each year. Grass dies off in the center. The disease is fostered by wet conditions, high soil pH, and heavy liming. Avoid it by ensuring good drainage and aeration, and feeding with sulfer to lower pH if necessary. Lay new sod in small affected areas.

FAIRY RINGS & TAKE-ALL PATCH

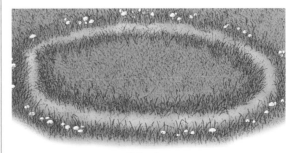

Fairy ring

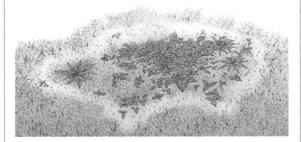

Take-all patch

Fungal diseases can cause fairy rings and disfiguring patches. Laying new sod or reseeding are often the only remedies.

MORE LAWN DISEASES

Snow mold

Slime molds

Red thread

Pythium blight

Molds and fungi are the causes of most of the common lawn diseases. Some are not treatable by fungicides, so good cultural practices are the best way of preventing them.

Snow mold

This serious disease, which is sometimes called gray or pink snow mold, may be associated with areas of grass that were walked on when covered in snow. Usually it becomes evident during mild, moist weather in early spring when small patches of yellow, dying grass appear. These turn brown and increase in size. In humid conditions, white or pink fungal growth may mat the blades of grass.

The disease is worsened by poor air movement and late applications of nitrogenous fertilizer. Dethatch the lawn (*see page 291*). Consult with your local cooperative extension service and apply a recommended fungicide, according to the directions on the label.

Slime molds

These harmless organisms often coat blades of grass in late spring or early fall. They vary in color but are commonly white or yellow; they develop into gray, round, spore-bearing structures.

Slime molds are superficial and short-lived, so no control measures are necessary. They can be easily washed away if desired.

Red thread

This fungal disease is most troublesome in late summer and fall. Infection is most apparent after heavy rain. Reddish patches of grass appear and pink, gelatinous fungal structures grow among the blades. When dry, these can be easily spread by foot to cause new infections. Many grasses are susceptible, but fescues and some ryegrasses are worst affected. Although it is unsightly, the grass usually recovers.

Improve the aeration of the turf to help affected grass to recover and apply fertilizers if needed. Plant resistant varieties. Control with an appropriate fungicide.

Pythium blight

This serious turf disease causes dead patches. Often, as new grass attempts to recolonize the dead areas, the young seedlings rot at their bases and topple over. The organisms responsible for this blight thrive in waterlogged conditions, so improve the drainage to reduce the problem.

Moss

Beautiful in forests, moss can invade shady lawns, especially if the soil is compacted or has high acidity. It is a common problem in high-rainfall areas. Add lime to raise the pH and aerate the lawn (*see page 292*). Improve the drainage as necessary.

Repairing neglected lawns

Without regular care and attention, lawns can rapidly fall into disrepair. Surfaces can become uneven and weeds take hold where the grass has struggled to establish itself. General wear and tear from children playing, pests, collapsing mole tunnels, and severe weather conditions are all causes of lawn deterioration.

Most neglected lawns can be reinstated to their former glory in a relatively short period of time. First, examine the lawn. Are the dominant plants weeds, mosses, and coarse grasses? Does much of the original turfgrass remain? If the problems are not too widespread, the lawn can probably be renovated. Spring is a good time to start a renovation program (*see below*), as there are several months of active growth ahead. In regions where cool-season grasses are grown, lawn renovations may be best accomplished in the fall.

On neglected lawns where coarse grasses and weeds dominate, it is probably worth stripping off the turf and starting again; this means leveling the whole area and then reseeding or resodding.

RENOVATING A LAWN

1 **Mow the lawn** with a rotary mower set at a cutting height of 2in., or with a string trimmer, to remove the dead grass as well as weed stalks and seedheads. Mowing too closely at this stage will weaken the grass.

2 **Rake off the mowings**. After a week, cut the grass again, if possible with a reel mower, set at the highest cut. Repeat over the next 2–3 weeks, reducing the cut height to a level appropriate to the type of lawn.

3 **Fertilize the grass** with an all-purpose fertilizer, and follow it with a treatment of selective herbicide 10–14 days later. Take care to avoid any recently seeded areas—the new grass may get scorched.

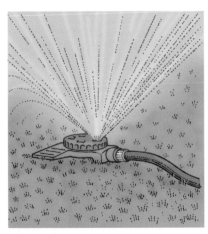

4 **Water the lawn** in dry periods. Reseed any bare patches and keep well watered. If a soil test indicates that pH is too high or too low, apply sulfur or lime as needed.

5 **Examine the lawn** for weeds and poor growth; fork out areas of coarse grasses and reseed ready for next year. Aerate the turf where required in the usual way to keep it healthy.

6 **Apply a topdressing** of soil and sand or garden compost. Add a slow-release fertilizer to the topdressing. The following spring, it should be possible to return to a standard lawn-maintenance routine.

ALTERNATIVES TO LAWNS

A well-maintained expanse of lawn is beautiful, but it comes with a high environmental cost. Given current concerns over water use, toxic emissions, and energy consumption, large lawns may no longer be practical. Fortunately there are good options for replacing lawns; each offers advantages for the home gardener. A hillside planting of ornamental grasses or daylilies, for example, can eliminate mowing while protecting the soil from erosion. A dense carpet of sweet woodruff can remove the struggle to grow grass in low light conditions. Select the best alternatives for your yard by first determining your outdoor needs.

Reducing your lawn area

One of the best ways to reduce your lawn is to consider it as a means of connecting spaces—your gardens, patios, and play areas. A well-cared-for ribbon of lawn sets off each area while unifying the entire landscape.

In areas that are difficult to mow, such as steep slopes or next to walls or under fences, eliminating the lawn will save you lots of mowing and trimming time and you will have more time to enjoy your garden. Slopes that can be dangerous and time-consuming to mow can be planted with shrubs, ground covers, grasses, or perennials. Replace turf growing against a wall with gravel mulch or pavers, and mulch or plant ground covers beneath fences to avoid the need for trimming in tight spaces.

If you want to retain an area of turf as a feature or play area, consider converting its edges to beds. Island beds can also be planted within the lawn area. Construct the beds with wide curves that are easy to mow around. If you have lawn trees, consider removing the turf beneath their branches and installing a mulch or ground cover. This makes mowing easier and eliminates the thin grass that often struggles in shaded areas.

Ground-covered beds are an attractive alternative to turf. Broadly curved edges make mowing the adjacent lawn easier.

A bed of bulbs and perennials replaces a uniform green lawn with a seasonally changing display of color and texture.

Gardening with the environment *see page 17* | **Creating a wildflower meadow** *see page 66* | **Creating a perennial garden** *see page 83*

Ground covers for sunny sites

Ground covers stabilize soil and protect it from erosion, define areas and help direct traffic through the yard, and contribute a variety of textures to a garden. Those that bear colorful flowers or fruit, or foliage that changes color in fall provide interest at ground level that changes with the seasons and often complements nearby trees and shrubs. Additionally, ground covers provide shelter and sometimes food for ground-nesting birds and other wildlife. As an alternative to lawns, they reduce the need for regular mowing and they generally require significantly less water and fertilizer. Although they take a bit of time and effort to get started, once established they are usually easy to maintain.

Selecting sun-loving ground covers

Sun-loving ground-cover plants may be herbaceous or woody, deciduous or evergreen. They are typically low growing and have a spreading habit, although some large shrubs, such as chokeberry, forsythia, and sumac, make spectacular, tall ground covers, especially on sunny slopes. Ground covers are spaced so that as they grow they create a solid carpet of vegetation.

Choose a ground cover that is well suited to your growing conditions. If you are planting in an open area that is a considerable distance from a water spigot, for example, choose a ground cover such as sedum or St. John's wort (*see below*) that tolerates dry conditions. If you live near the seashore, consider ground covers such as bearberry (*see below*) or beach wormwood (*Artemisia stelleriana*), which tolerate salt spray and wind. Many perennial herbs such as oregano, santolina, creeping thyme (*see below*), and lavender provide fragrance as well as beauty, and they thrive in poor soil.

Establishing and maintaining ground covers

To plant a ground cover, prepare the soil as you would for an herbaceous border (*see page 83*). Be sure the soil surface is free of weeds and turf. Unless you are planting herbs or other plants that prefer a lean soil, add a generous amount of well-rotted compost or manure. If you are planting a shrublike ground cover, dig individual planting holes as you would for any shrub (*see page 97*). If you are planting on a slope, build up a ring of soil around each plant to help retain water.

Space plants according to their mature size, although closer spacing will achieve a finished look more quickly. Water well after planting to settle the roots and continue to water regularly until plants are established. Apply a liquid fertilizer, such as fish emulsion or compost tea, to get plants off to a good start, and mulch with an organic material such as hardwood bark or pine needles to help retain soil moisture, prevent weeds, and improve the look of the bed until the ground-cover plants knit together. Lightly fertilize your planting each spring to encourage new growth. Some ground covers, such as winter jasmine and cotoneaster, will develop roots where their stems touch the ground, making new plants. These can be allowed to grow *in situ* or carefully transplanted after a season or two to extend the bed.

The most time-consuming task in establishing a ground-cover planting is weeding. Hand weeding is generally required since the plants are close together. Remove weeds as soon as you notice them; do not let them go to seed. Use a dandelion weeder to remove deep roots of perennial weeds. The amount of weeding needed lessens as the plants fill in. Mature ground-cover plantings will suppress weed growth.

GROUND COVERS FOR SUNNY SITES

Bearberry performs best on infertile, sandy soils, forming a dense evergreen mat, 4–12in. tall.

St. John's wort is deciduous and grows 1–4ft. tall. Its bright yellow, summer flowers show off well against its blue-green foliage.

Sempervivum, also known as hens-and-chicks, is very drought tolerant. It forms tufted rosettes of leaves up to 6in. tall.

Creeping thyme is intensely fragrant with a low, spreading habit. Plant it near a walkway where you will enjoy its scent.

Ground covers for shady sites

Shady sites are notoriously difficult for growing a thick, healthy lawn, so shade-loving ground covers provide a welcome alternative. Low-growing plants that are tolerant to shade act as a living mulch for woodland gardens and shady beds, helping to keep the soil moist and cool and contributing organic matter as they drop their leaves and flowers. Unlike turf, however, most shady ground covers cannot take much foot traffic, so provide paths or stepping stones for access through the garden.

Selecting & planting shady ground covers

Like the choices for sunny sites, shade-tolerant ground covers range in habit and size. Wintergreens (*Gaultheria procumbens*), pachysandras, and periwinkles (*Vinca minor*, *see below*) provide a year-round presence with their evergreen leaves. Although ajugas, sweet woodruff, and lamiums (*see below*) are deciduous, they spread quickly, adding seasonal interest to shady beds.

Some shade-tolerant ground covers have a grasslike appearance, but they only need mowing once a year, usually in early spring before new growth begins. Liriopes, mondo grass (*Ophiopogon*), and variegated Japanese sedge (*Carex morrowii* 'Variegata') can be massed to grow beneath trees or along paved walkways.

In an informal woodland garden combining low-growing perennials can create an exciting tapestry of ground-covering plants. Good choices include hostas, ferns, Canadian wild ginger (*Asarum canadense*), bleeding hearts (*Dicentra*), coral bells (*Heuchera*), and foam flowers (*Tiarella*). If you are planting a ground cover in a bed beneath taller plants, or mixing ground covers in a single bed, be sure that they are compatible. Most ground covers are shallow rooted, and may absorb available water at the expense of neighboring shrubs. In addition to water requirements, check their preferred pH range and fertility requirements. Epimediums (*see below*), brunnera,s and hellebores are good choices for dry shade.

Surface roots are often a problem for planting beneath trees. You cannot work such soil as you would in an open bed; instead, develop planting pockets, working small areas of soil between roots. Add a bit of well-rotted compost to each hole as you plant your ground cover and water well to settle the roots. Take particular care of watering; frequent applications of water may be necessary as the ground cover becomes established because it will be competing with surrounding trees and shrubs. Mulch to maintain even soil moisture and prevent weeds. If weeds do appear, remove them immediately.

A mixture of shade-loving perennials, including Japanese painted ferns and hostas, provide a textured carpet of foliage near a brick walkway.

GROUND COVERS FOR SHADY SITES

Epimedium is a tough, deciduous ground cover. In spring, its stems of heart-shaped leaflets often sport a copper blush.

Lamium spreads by underground stems in shady beds, where its variegated leaves and summer flowers add seasonal color.

Periwinkle produces trailing stems of evergreen leaves topped with blue, purple, or white flowers in spring.

The fragrant, arching flowers of lily-of-the-valley show off well against its broadly lance-shaped leaves, which form a dense mat.

Gardening with the environment *see page 17* | Creating a wildflower meadow *see page 66* | Creating a perennial garden *see page 83*

More lawn alternatives

Minimizing repetitive maintenance chores such as mowing and raking up grass clippings is one of the best reasons to reduce or eliminate a traditional lawn. Meadow plantings that include native grasses and wildflowers are a good option for an informal setting (*see page 66*).

For the ultimate low-maintenance lawn replacement, construct areas for entertaining or relaxing in the yard using permanent materials such as brick, flagstone, or interlocking pavers. These hardscaping products can be expensive to purchase and require skill to install properly, but once your patio or seating area is finished it is almost maintenance free. With proper furnishings, including containers filled with assorted plants, this area will become an integral part of your landscape.

Minimal-mow lawns

Another replacement option for traditional lawns is grasses or grasslike plants that do not require regular mowing. Texas sedge (*Carex texensis*) and California meadow sedge (*C. pansa*) grow only 3–4in. tall and form a pleasing, natural-looking lawn in full sun or part shade. Once established, they even tolerate foot traffic.

Although taller ornamental grasses are not suited to being walked on, they provide a landscape with seasonal

Comfortable seating arrangements provide a relaxing spot for dining or simply siting and enjoying the garden.

interest and graceful movement and require very little maintenance. Fountain grass (*Pennisetum*), muhly grass (*Muhlenbergia*), moor grass (*Molinia*), and blue oat grass (*Helictotrichon sempervirens*) are just a few of the many ornamental grasses available that can be individually massed or mixed for dramatic plantings.

This meadow garden at the American Horticultural Society headquarters in Alexandria, Virginia, replaced a huge expanse of lawn. It requires mowing only once a year, and provides a seasonally changing display of wildflowers that attracts birds and butterflies.

CHAPTER SEVEN

WATER GARDENING

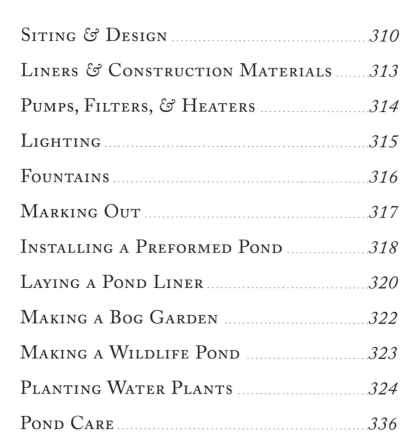

PERHAPS YOU HAVE PLANS FOR A WILDLIFE POND, OR you might only have space for a simple barrel water feature in your yard. Maybe you have an awkward, naturally damp piece of land that could take on new life if transformed into a pond with a bog garden at the edge. Whatever the choices available, there is no doubt that water can become an important part of your property.

The benefits of water in the yard

Moving water can add life to a static space. The gentle trickle of a stream or the gurgle of a bubble fountain can help you to unwind and mask unwanted noise, while plunging cascades or waterfalls add drama. Features such as rills can lead the eye from one area to another, connecting different areas of the yard. Still water can be exploited for striking visual effects. Specimen plants, statues, or buildings near the edge will be reflected, and a large body of water can also create the illusion of greater space by reflecting the sky.

A pond provides the opportunity to grow a wider range of plants, from floating waterlilies to marginal plants, and a bog garden allows an even greater variety. A water feature in your yard will also encourage wildlife. Birds will visit a simple bubble fountain to drink or bathe, while a well-planted pond can become a magnet to frogs, toads, turtles, birds, and insects such as dragonflies, or even an important watering hole for foxes and other animals.

The secrets of success

The success of a pond depends on the interaction of the water, air, nutrients, plants, temperature, and wildlife that make up its complex ecosystem. The right balance means clear water and thriving fish and plants, while imbalance leads to algal growth, suffering fish, poor plant growth, and weeds.

For a pond to work well, it needs plenty of oxygen. Plants in a pond produce this, while animals in the water consume oxygen and turn it into carbon dioxide. You can promote a healthy level of oxygen in your pond by incorporating both running water and submerged oxygenating plants. Plants are also essential to prevent the growth of algae, which pollutes and colors the water. Since algae spreads rapidly in sunlight and in water with high nutrient levels, surface-covering plants help to limit its development by providing shade and taking up the nutrients.

A healthy community of microorganisms is also essential for clean water and a food chain that supports many creatures. Fungi, snails, and bacteria that feed on decaying plants will be eaten by dragonfly larvae and water beetles, which in turn will become food for frogs, toads, and fish.

Creating a healthy pond

The design of your pond will have an impact on its ecosystem. Areas of deep water will remain frost free in winter and cool in summer, keeping microorganisms alive through extremes of temperature. Shallow water, however, can heat up quickly, providing the perfect environment for algae, and, in cold-winter zones, freeze solid, killing most wildlife in winter.

How you look after your pond can also have a huge effect on the life it sustains. You should prevent pesticides or fertilizers from entering the water, and avoid cleaning too often, as this disrupts the delicate natural balance. Try to keep your pond at a neutral pH and avoid sudden changes or extremes of pH, which can happen when fresh water is added to the pond.

SITING & DESIGN

When building a pond or water feature, you are aiming to create a healthy underwater world, where creatures and plants thrive. To ensure that a pond develops to its full potential, think carefully about its size and shape, along with where it is constructed in relation to the house and other major features, such as trees. Also consider whether you are able to take on the entire job of construction yourself, or if you require the services of a professional, such as an expert with a backhoe to do the initial excavation of the pond, a mason to build stonework, or a qualified professional to fit pipes or run electrical connections.

Pond designs

A formal pond or canal with a few key plants is a classic feature for a restrained or minimalist space. It may be circular, square, or another regular shape, perhaps echoing features such as neatly clipped topiary. Use materials that match other hardscaping features, such as paths or walls. This is particularly important for raised ponds, which are usually formal and make perfect focal points.

An informal pond should look like part of the natural landscape and not a construction. Its outline should be sweeping curves, rather than straight lines, and it should be well planted, allowing for the introduction of fish.

An informal pond will attract many creatures, but you can maximize its potential by turning it into a wildlife pond. Fill it with many native species of plants, and ensure that the edges provide access and plenty of cover so that visiting creatures feel protected. If you have the space, a modern alternative is the swimming pond, planted to be a magnet to wildlife, but big enough to allow swimming.

Many water features need a large yard, but even a small space can accommodate a bubble fountain or a wall-mounted fountain with a small pond below. Small aquatic plants such as pygmy waterlilies fit barrels and tubs.

Informal cascades are one of the more difficult features to design and build, but when successful they look stunning.

Even the smallest feature can add variety and life to a yard. This fountain will attract birds even without a large, accessible pond.

Formal symmetry does not have to limit your creativity, as demonstrated here by the use of mixed materials and a topiary peacock.

Gardening with the environment *see page 17* | **Methods & materials** *see page 313* | **Planting water plants** *see page 324*

Siting practicalities

Aquatic plants thrive in sunlight, so you should avoid siting a pond in an area of the yard that is heavily shaded throughout summer. A spot that receives partial shade is ideal, as too much sun can promote the growth of algae, while too much shade will result in low oxygen levels.

If possible, plan your water feature in summer when deciduous trees are in full leaf, so you can avoid densely shaded sites, but remember to take into account buildings, which will cast more shade in winter because the sun is lower in the sky. Unfortunately, some small yards remain shady year-round. A pond will not thrive under such conditions, but fortunately there are several bog-garden plants that do well in lower light levels. A simple fountain can make a great alternative to a pond.

As well as casting shade, trees can cause other problems. Tree roots can damage the pond liner; it will leak and you will need to rebuild it. Falling leaves will clog the pond and rot. Ideally, you should site your pond at least 15ft. from any trees. Windy sites are not attractive to wildlife, so ensure that your site has some shelter and is not in a frost pocket.

Before you dig, locate any water, sewer, gas, or other utility lines on your property. Also avoid any area with a high water table, which could lift a preformed pond or alter the shape of a liner. There is also a risk that water from the soil, which may contain fertilizers or pesticides, could enter the pond.

Should you be uncertain about the height of your water table, dig a hole in the proposed site in late winter when the ground is saturated. If the water table is within 24in. of the planned level of the pond floor, choose a different site if possible. Alternatively, you could drain the site; seek professional advice in such cases.

If your property contains an existing natural body of water, do not attempt to alter it without consulting with your local authorities. Natural wetlands, ponds, and streams may be protected by law and subject to restrictions.

SAFEGUARDING CHILDREN

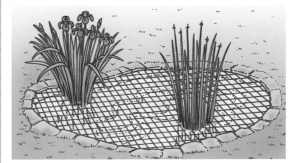

Water is a hazard, so site the pond close to the house where children can be supervised. It can also be made safer with a fence or grille. Secure grilles placed over the pond or just beneath water level are one of the least obstructive methods; they should be able to support the weight of an adult.

RAISED PONDS & FLAT PONDS

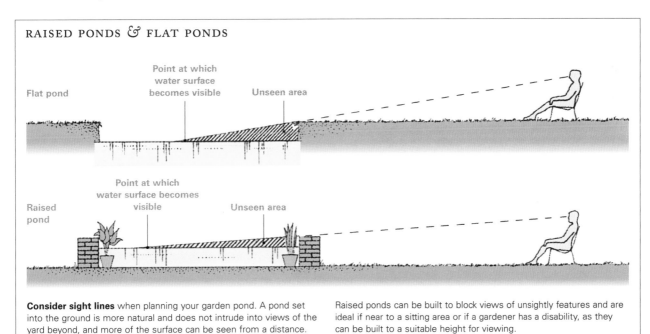

Flat pond

Point at which water surface becomes visible

Unseen area

Point at which water surface becomes visible

Raised pond

Unseen area

Consider sight lines when planning your garden pond. A pond set into the ground is more natural and does not intrude into views of the yard beyond, and more of the surface can be seen from a distance.

Raised ponds can be built to block views of unsightly features and are ideal if near to a sitting area or if a gardener has a disability, as they can be built to a suitable height for viewing.

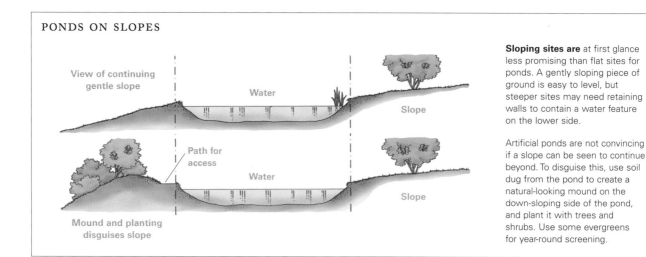

PONDS ON SLOPES

View of continuing gentle slope

Water

Slope

Path for access

Water

Slope

Mound and planting disguises slope

Sloping sites are at first glance less promising than flat sites for ponds. A gently sloping piece of ground is easy to level, but steeper sites may need retaining walls to contain a water feature on the lower side.

Artificial ponds are not convincing if a slope can be seen to continue beyond. To disguise this, use soil dug from the pond to create a natural-looking mound on the down-sloping side of the pond, and plant it with trees and shrubs. Use some evergreens for year-round screening.

Suiting the site

When designing a pond think carefully about how the area of water will be viewed from the main seating area of the yard or from the house—it will look different when you are sitting or standing, as well as from different distances. Also consider how to make the pond appear an integral part of the yard, rather than an afterthought.

From plan to perspective

After deciding where you want to site the pond, trickle sand onto the ground to outline its shape, then go to the area of the yard where you spend most time, or step inside the house to gaze from a window. Look at the shape on the ground and it will give you a good idea of what the finished pond will look like.

Also try to imagine what the pond will look like with plants, because these will conceal some of the water from your view; enlarging photos of the site and drawing in plants may help you visualize the effect. If you think the shape you have laid out on the ground will not enable you to see as much water as you would like, try altering it by making it longer from front to back.

Linking features

To help marry the pond to the rest of the yard, you could create a bog garden to accompany it (*see page 322*). These are planted with species that like moist soil, but not standing water. They can be made in any shape, but tend to look best with bold, sinuous lines.

On a larger property, you could link several separate water features together with moving water. A geometric rill is perfect in a formal garden, while a meandering stream would suit a more naturalistic setting.

THE EFFECTS OF PERSPECTIVE

Island

Planting

1

Planting

Position of viewer

Plan view

Unseen

2

View as seen from standing

3

View as seen from sitting

Seen as a plan ❶ your pond may look like a large expanse of water, but it will not be viewed from this perspective once built. When you are standing ❷, the surface appears much smaller, and areas beyond the pond are obscured by planting. Viewed from a seating area ❸, the surface becomes smaller still and much of the pond itself can be hidden by foreground planting.

Installing a preformed pond *see page 318* | **Laying a pond liner** *see page 320* | **Pond care** *see page 336*

METHODS & MATERIALS

Once you have planned the look and position of your pond, there are decisions to be made about its construction. You can choose from a variety of different, flexible or rigid liners, depending on the shape and size of pond you want. Unless you live in a very mild region, heaters may be necessary in cold weather and, if you plan to incorporate moving water, you will need to equip your pond with a pump and filter. Last but not least, carefully placed lighting can really enhance your pond and ensure that it remains an attractive feature until long after darkness has fallen.

Liners & construction materials

Ponds can be constructed from a variety of flexible and rigid materials, each with advantages and disadvantages in durability, ease of laying, and cost.

E.P.D.M.: A synthetic rubber that is long-lasting, easy to work with, highly flexible, heat- and cold-tolerant, and resistant to ultraviolet.

P.V.C.: Less durable than E.P.D.M., but also less expensive; it is tough, and easy to lay.

Reinforced polyethylene: A high-density, laminated material that is especially tear-resistant. Usually supplied to your precise specifications to suit your site.

Underlay: Placed under a flexible liner to protect it from damage by stones, insects and animals, soil chemicals, and other hazards.

Blended polymers: Rigid preformed ponds made of polyethylene, polypropylene, or fiberglass.

Concrete: Once a commonly used material but not now recommended, especially in cold climates. Can make a tough base for a simple shape, but may need to be constructed by a professional. If properly prepared, concrete needs little or no repair work for many years; if badly prepared, it cracks and flakes.

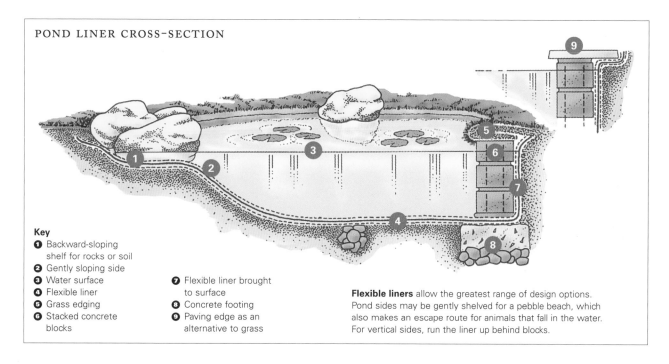

POND LINER CROSS-SECTION

Key
1. Backward-sloping shelf for rocks or soil
2. Gently sloping side
3. Water surface
4. Flexible liner
5. Grass edging
6. Stacked concrete blocks
7. Flexible liner brought to surface
8. Concrete footing
9. Paving edge as an alternative to grass

Flexible liners allow the greatest range of design options. Pond sides may be gently shelved for a pebble beach, which also makes an escape route for animals that fall in the water. For vertical sides, run the liner up behind blocks.

Pumps, filters, & heaters

All small artificial ponds need a pump to keep the water moving and a filter to keep the water clean. Larger ponds and small lakes often settle down to a natural balance, but if they are shallow they may benefit from constant aeration to add oxygen to the water. This benefits fish and other wildlife.

Pumps & filters

Pumps are either submersible (*see right*) or placed on the surface. Surface pumps are more powerful, used for high jets or faster flows over larger-scale features. They must be kept in a dry chamber just below the water level of the pond.

Filters remove impurities, such as algae, from the water, but they are not a substitute for a properly maintained and planted pond. They are mechanical or biological. Mechanical filters are the simplest (*see right*). You might not need a filter if you have a naturally balanced pond, but if you keep fish a biological filter, sited outside the pond, is often a necessity, as it contains bacteria that neutralize fish waste and clean the water.

Pond heaters

In some areas a simple floating heater will help to keep a small area free of ice (*see page 337*). Koi owners sometimes use specialized heaters for temperature control of water, but these are not necessary for most other fish.

SUBMERSIBLE PUMP

Easy to install, quiet, and with enough power to operate most small-scale, gently moving water features, these pumps are popular and competitively priced. You simply place them on the bottom of the pond.

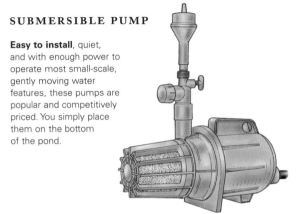

MECHANICAL FILTER

A simple structure consisting of a foam filter covered in charcoal or gravel and housed in a plastic box, these filters are sited on the pond floor and connected to the pump.

WATER FLOW USING A WATERFALL PUMP

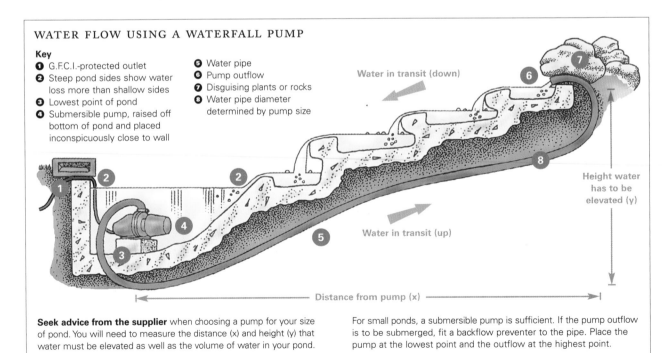

Key
❶ G.F.C.I.-protected outlet
❷ Steep pond sides show water loss more than shallow sides
❸ Lowest point of pond
❹ Submersible pump, raised off bottom of pond and placed inconspicuously close to wall
❺ Water pipe
❻ Pump outflow
❼ Disguising plants or rocks
❽ Water pipe diameter determined by pump size

Water in transit (down)

Water in transit (up)

Height water has to be elevated (y)

Distance from pump (x)

Seek advice from the supplier when choosing a pump for your size of pond. You will need to measure the distance (x) and height (y) that water must be elevated as well as the volume of water in your pond.

For small ponds, a submersible pump is sufficient. If the pump outflow is to be submerged, fit a backflow preventer to the pipe. Place the pump at the lowest point and the outflow at the highest point.

Lighting

You can create many effects with both submerged and above-water lights, but for the best and least intrusive show use them sparingly and avoid your pond resembling an airport landing strip at night.

Above-water lights can be bought individually or in packs of three or more. Placed around the edge of your pond, spotlights can pick out a sculpture, waterfall, or specimen plant. Placed behind a feature, floodlights will silhouette it and illuminate the marginal plants and area around it, leaving the water a sheet of black.

Underwater lights give a ghostly glow to the pond or, placed on the surface of the pond, glance upward toward a plant. Traditional white lights are popular, but colored filters can create lively or festive effects.

Another option is simply to light the water itself. Floating or permanently submerged lights, which sit just beneath the surface of the water, provide a mysterious look and are perfect in a contemporary garden. An illuminated fountain can look magical—these are available as kits, with a spotlight that sits beneath the fountain head and illuminates the jet of water. White, single-colored, and multicolored lights, as well as color-changing filters, are all widely available.

A simple alternative to electric lights is to create a mood by using floating candles. There are even some that are molded, to resemble waterlilies for example.

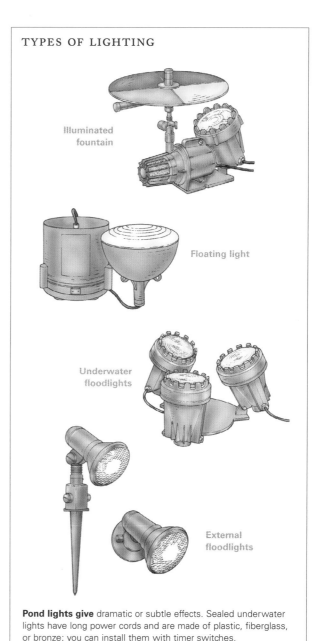

TYPES OF LIGHTING

Illuminated fountain

Floating light

Underwater floodlights

External floodlights

Pond lights give dramatic or subtle effects. Sealed underwater lights have long power cords and are made of plastic, fiberglass, or bronze; you can install them with timer switches.

Lighting is most effective when the source of the light is concealed. Here the water and the wall glow, but the bulbs are hidden behind the wall and below the bridge, or obscured by the falling water.

SAFETY

Pond lighting kits are designed to be safe and easy to install. They contain lights attached to a length of cable, a low-voltage transformer, and a plug that can be used in a protected outdoor socket or routed through a wall to a socket inside; make sure that there is always a G.F.C.I. Low-voltage cables can be clipped along a wall or buried in a shallow trench (fed through a length of tubing for protection). Any electrical work beyond the simple installation of such a kit should be undertaken by a qualified contractor.

Fountains

Water fountains can transform your pond or pool into a spectacular focal point, or simply add sound and movement to the yard. All fountains work in the same way: a fountain head is attached to a pump that drives water up and through the head. The fountain head controls how the water is released (*see box, bottom right*), and some are adjustable, so you can vary the effect.

Choosing & installing fountains

Before adding a fountain, think carefully about whether it will suit your yard and fit within the constraints of your pond. Your pond should be large enough to contain the spray of water and capture drift, which could be considerable on a windy day. As a rule of thumb, the pond should be twice as wide as the spray is high.

Choose a spray effect that suits your style of yard. A natural-looking bubble fountain suits modern and smaller yards, while a plume is best in a grand garden with a large pond to capture the spray. A bell fountain suits a classical space and again needs a large pond, as do high jets or columns of water and fountains with several tiers.

ORNAMENTAL FOUNTAINS

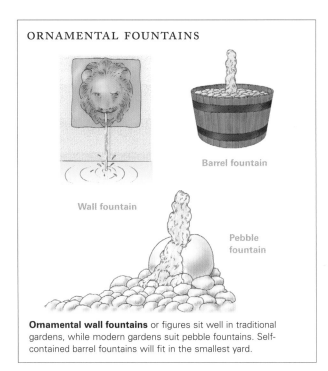

Wall fountain

Barrel fountain

Pebble fountain

Ornamental wall fountains or figures sit well in traditional gardens, while modern gardens suit pebble fountains. Self-contained barrel fountains will fit in the smallest yard.

POSITIONING THE FOUNTAIN PUMP

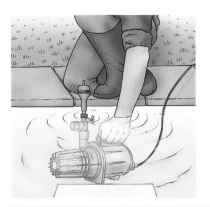

If the fountain head is directly attached to the pump, set it 3in. above the water level. Raise the pump on a brick if necessary, and place a piece of pond liner or geotextile beneath the brick to prevent damage to the liner.

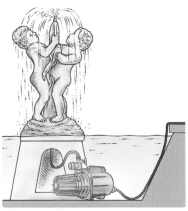

A separate fountain head on a length of pipe can be threaded through an ornamental figure or sculpture to produce a spray above the pond. The pump can sit on the bottom of the pond if it makes it less visible.

FOUNTAIN SPRAYS

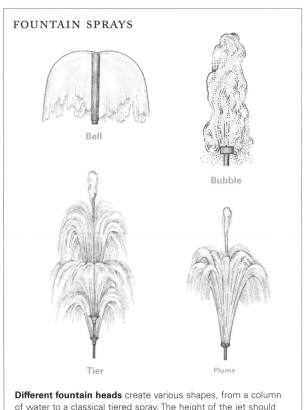

Bell

Bubble

Tier

Plume

Different fountain heads create various shapes, from a column of water to a classical tiered spray. The height of the jet should be adjustable; remember that spray drifts farther than solid water.

Wildlife ponds *see page 64* | **Siting & design** *see page 310* | **Planting water plants** *see page 324*

Marking out

Marking out level ground before installing a preformed pond or laying a liner is quite easy. All you need are some 12in. stakes, a sharp pointed stick, string or hose, some bricks, a mallet, a wooden board, and a level.

Marking out irregular shapes

Place your preformed pond on the ground and raise it up on bricks by 3in., keeping it horizontal (*see below, top left*). To mark out its perimeter, place a level vertically against the rim of the pond with its lower end on the ground. Mark the position on the ground by hammering a stake in to a depth of 4in. Repeat this at 12in. intervals around the pond.

If installing a liner pond, first draw your design on paper so you have a plan to work from. Then mark the desired shape on the ground by hammering in stakes 4in. deep, every 12in. When you are happy with the outline,

join up the stakes using sprinkled sand or a length of string or hose (*see below, top right*), then score the ground with a sharp, pointed stick.

Leveling & excavating

Once the shape has been planned on the ground, remove the string or hose. Next, use a level and mallet to ensure that the tops of the stakes are all level, by choosing a main stake and placing a wooden board between it and an adjacent stake.

Check with the level and knock the adjacent stake in or move the other out slightly if necessary. Continue to measure around the outline. Once all the stakes are level, make any adjustments needed to the ground level so that the same length of stake is visible all round. This ensures the pond edge sits level and the liner will not be exposed. Now you can start to excavate (*see below, bottom*).

MARKING OUT A PREFORMED POND

For preformed ponds, support the unit on bricks, making sure that it is level when you start. If it is not, the shape you mark on the ground will be distorted. Take vertical readings from the perimeter down to the ground and mark their positions all around the pond. Alternatively, mark a rectangular area that will fit your pond (*see following page*).

MARKING OUT A LINER POND

For pond liners or concrete ponds, mark the outline with stakes. Use a hose, string, or sand to show the outline clearly. Take into account both the width or length and the depth of the pond when buying a liner. If you dig before buying, you will have accurate measurements, but check the sizes and costs of liners before you start.

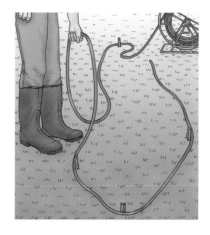

EXCAVATING THE POND

1 **Use a level** on a wooden board to check that the tops of the stakes, and the surface of the surrounding ground, are level. Measure from stake to stake around the edge, and straight across for added certainty. You may have to build up one side of the edge or excavate the other to achieve a level rim.

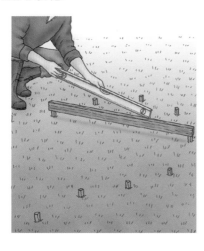

2 **Start by digging** a trench inside the stakes. Excavating by hand is far more accurate than using a digger. For lined ponds, make sure any sloping sides are no steeper than 20 degrees to avoid instability. If you decide to include a marginal shelf make it at least 9in. deep and wide.

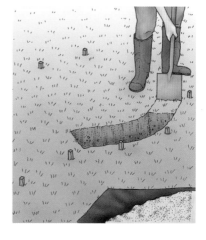

Installing a preformed pond

Preformed ponds can be easier to install than lined ponds as they are already molded into shape. The installation is a job for two people, however, as the shell can be awkward to handle. Fiberglass ponds tend to be more rigid than plastic shells, which can distort as they fill with water.

Underlay

After excavating the hole (*see previous page*), prepare the base of the hole and any marginal shelves so that they will cushion the shell when it is full of water. Even though the preformed ponds are quite rigid, they can still be damaged if not properly supported or if they come into contact with sharp objects as the pond is filled.

Remove any large stones, twigs, or debris and roughly level the base with a rake. Use your feet to tamp down the soil, then spread a 1in. layer of damp sand over the base. To get an even layer across all surfaces, use a rake and then a polishing trowel.

Installing the pond

With assistance, place the liner centrally in the hole. Make sure it is firmly embedded in the sand, and if any shallow areas of the base are not well supported, shore them up with flat stones or bricks so that it is held firmly.

Check that the pond is level by placing a level on a wooden board laid across the rim from side to side, and from end to end (*see facing page, step 5*). Add or remove supporting material as necessary, then add 4in. of water to the base of the shell and check the levels again.

Slowly start to backfill the excavation with a gardener's trowel (*see facing page, step 7*). If the excavated soil is too stony or lumpy to flow in around the pond easily and provide good support all around, it may be worth buying gravel or sand instead. Firm in the soil with your hands as you go to prevent the pond from moving later and changing the water level. Keep checking the levels and fill up to the lip of the pond.

INSTALLING A PREFORMED POND

1 Mark a rectangle or contoured shape that completely encloses the outline of your pond (*see previous page*), with space to spare around the edges for backfilling. Remove the soil, digging the hole 1in. deeper than the pond.

2 Remove sharp objects, such as roots or stones, from the floor of the hole. Rigid ponds are stronger than flexible liners, but they can still be damaged. Tread down the base of the hole until it is flat and level.

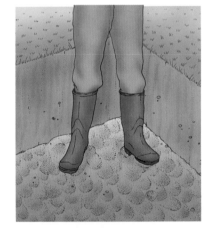

3 Lay damp sand on the floor of the excavation in a 1in. layer. The sand will support and cushion the pond when it is installed.

4 Position the pond in the hole. Build up bricks or flat stones under areas that are not touching the ground and so are not supported, such as the planting shelves.

INSTALLING A PREFORMED POND

Siting & design *see page 310* | **Liners & construction materials** *see page 313* | **Planting water plants** *see page 324*

EDGING WITH PAVING

1 Lay a bed of mortar around the edge of the unit after making any necessary adjustments to the ground around the pond so that it meets the level rim of the pond. The mortar should be about 1in. deep.

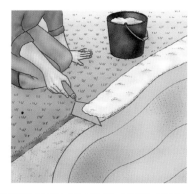

2 Lay each paving edge so that it is firmly supported on the mortar but overhangs the edge of the pond slightly. Point the joints between the paving and leave to set completely before carrying out any further work.

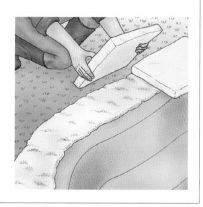

Laying the edging

Stone, paving, plants, or sod (*see page 321*) are ideal for masking the edges of a preformed pond. If you are planning on using stone or slabs (*see box, above*), start by laying a 1in. thick bed of mortar. You can buy ready-mix mortar with waterproofing compound from a home-supply center. Bed the slabs into position, ¼in. apart. They should overhang the pond by at least 2in. to conceal the rim; overhang by at least 3in. if cats or raccoons are a problem.

If you are planting up the area around the edge of the pond instead, use garden plants rather than aquatics, to help your pond to marry with the rest of the yard.

5 Check that the pond is absolutely level in the excavation, using a level laid on a wooden board across the rim. Remember to check in both directions. Adjust the sand beneath the pond if necessary; any slope will be obvious once the pond is filled.

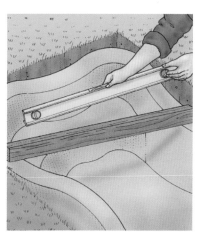

6 Fill the pond with water to approximately 4in. before starting to backfill around the preformed pond. This weight gives the unit stability while the soil is filled in around the sides, helping to ensure that it stays level.

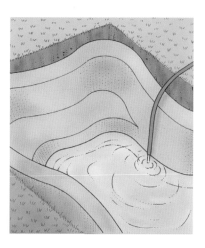

7 Backfill with soil around the pond with a gardener's trowel. Start by laying a 6in. layer, firming it in as you go. Build up the layers, making sure that you work the soil well into the contours of the pond.

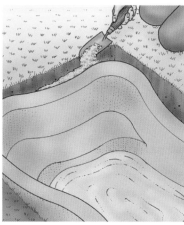

8 Keep checking that the pond is level. Backfill in layers, ensuring good contact with all parts of the pond unit. Work all the way around the pond and check that it is still level before starting the next layer.

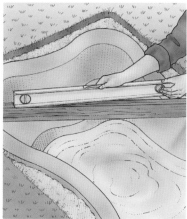

Laying a pond liner

Building a pond with a flexible liner is a popular option. Flexible liners are ideal if you want a custom-built pond and do not want to be confined by the range of shapes and sizes that are available with preformed ponds. Although more preparation work is required than when installing a preformed pond, it is a straightforward job as long as you have prepared the ground well and correctly calculated the amount of liner needed.

Although liners are versatile, some pond shapes are simpler than others. It is easier to lay a liner when the shape is full of sweeping curves and not intricate, geometric lines and angles, which will cause you problems when trying to smooth out folds and wrinkles in the liner. To prevent soil slippage, make the marginal shelves fairly wide.

Calculating the liner size

There is a simple formula for calculating the amount of liner you need for a square, rectangular, or irregularly shaped pond. The same technique can also be used to calculate the amount of liner needed for a stream.

First double the maximum depth of the pond. Add this figure to the length of the pond to find the total length of liner needed. Then add double the maximum depth to the width to give the total width of liner needed. Multiply your two figures together to find the total area of liner. This will allow you to estimate the cost. Liners are widely sold in precut sizes, but for an unusual shape there are suppliers who will cut to order; individual sheets can also be welded together.

INSTALLING A LINER

1 **Mark out the shape** of the pond and excavate the hole. Incorporate a marginal shelf to maximize planting, and make sloping sides no steeper than 20 degrees for stability.

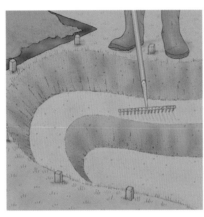

2 **Remove any sharp** sticks, roots, or stones from the walls and floor of the hole. If left, they could puncture the liner. Rake over the floor and shelf to smooth the surface.

3 **Fit an underlayment** in the hole. This nonwoven fabric will protect the liner. It can be cut to fit awkward areas—as long as all the surfaces are covered.

Alternatively, spread sand 1in. deep to protect the liner. It may be hard to make it stick to all but the shallowest slopes.

4 **Center the liner** over the pond. Spread it out and weigh down the edges. Try to arrange any excess liner into neat folds.

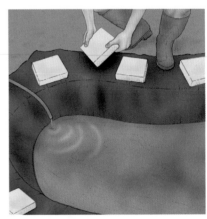

5 **Slowly fill the pond** and remove the weights as the water pulls the liner taut. It is now ready to be edged (see facing page).

LAYING A POND LINER

Siting & design *see page 310* | **Liners & construction materials** *see page 313* | **Planting water plants** *see page 324*

EDGING WITH PAVING & STONES

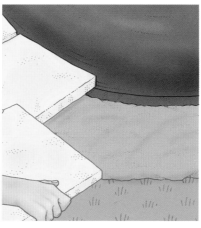

1 **Trim the excess** liner away using scissors, leaving at least 6in. all around. Dig out the soil around the pond to at least 3in. and bury the edge of the liner.

2 **Lay a bed** of mortar 1in. deep for slabs. Lay the paving edges on it and add more mortar between them. Natural stone may need a deeper bed of mortar than paving to accommodate its irregular contours.

EDGING WITH SOD

Grass gives a natural look to a pond edge. Bury the liner edge, ensure that the soil is level and compact, then lay closely butted sods. Do not use fertilizers or herbicides on the lawn, as these can disrupt the pond ecosystem, and clear away grass clippings, which can discolor water and add unwanted nutrients.

Excavating & underlayment

After excavating your pond, remove any large stones, sticks, or other debris that could puncture the liner from the sides and floor. Although the liner may seem tough, it can become vulnerable with the weight of water pushing down on it and out against the sides. Rake the base of the hole level, then add an underlayment as extra protection. Taking this precaution now may save having to patch the liner later. Calculate how much underlayment you need, employing the same formula used for working out the area of liner required, as the sides as well as the bottom of the pond need cushioning.

Place the underlayment in the hole and push it in so it fits the contours. Alternatively, for a smooth underlayment you could spread a 1in. layer of damp sand over the base of the hole, but you may still need to use underlayment at the sides, where sand is unlikely to stick.

Installing the liner

If at all possible, spread the liner out in the sun for a while before laying it in the pond, because the warmth will make it more flexible. Once you are ready to install it, fold or roll the sides of the liner into the middle so that it is easier to handle.

Unroll or unfold the liner over the excavation, keeping it placed as centrally as possible—it will make life easier if you have at least one other person to help you. It may take considerable adjustment to position the liner correctly for an irregularly shaped pond. When you have found the right position, hold the edges of the liner in place by weighing them down with bricks or paving, and try to smooth wrinkles together into a few larger folds or pleats. Slowly fill the liner with water from a hose.

Allow the weight of the water to pull the liner down into the hole, removing the weights as necessary, while at the same time trying to ease out any creases. At the end of filling, the liner will be pressed into the outline of your excavation perfectly, and should have the minimum of wrinkles showing at the edge.

Finishing the edge

After the pond has been filled with water, work out how much liner to leave for edging and cut away the excess. If you are planning on using sod, stones, or paving, leave 6–15in., or double this if you want to fill the area around the edge of the pond with plants.

For stones, paving, or sod, you will need to cover the edge of the liner with soil at least 3in. deep (*see above*). Stones and paving give a pond a formal look and should be set in a 1in. bed of mortar, placed so that they overhang the pond by at least 2in.

If you intend to plant around the edge of the pond, dig around it to a depth of about 6in. and bury the liner, keeping it in place with bricks. You could use this opportunity to enrich the excavated soil. Plant with normal garden plants rather than water or bog plants, because the soil will only be as moist as the rest of your yard. Choose plants that are in keeping with your style of yard but complement the pond planting to provide a visual 'bridge' between the two.

Making a bog garden

A naturally soggy area of ground makes the ideal site for a bog garden—where wet but not completely water-logged soil is host to a range of plants that thrive on ample moisture. A bog garden at the edge of a pond creates a visual transition from the water feature to the rest of the garden.

Preparing the bog garden

Make a bog garden no bigger than the surface area of any pond, so that it is kept in scale with the rest of the water garden, and dig it to a minimum depth of 12–15in. to prevent it from drying out too quickly. An integrated bog garden should be no more than 4in. away from the pond, with an interconnecting wall 3in. lower than the edge of the pond. Excavate the hole, remove any sharp stones or debris, and add an underlayment. Then cover with a liner (you might need two), weigh down the edge with bricks, and fill the pond.

EXCAVATING WATER FEATURES

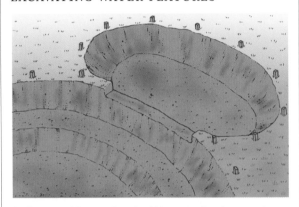

An integrated bog garden should be created at the same time as the pond and will initially draw most of its water from it. Dig out both features to the required depth and make the wall where they join lower than the edge of the pond. This will allow water to flow into the bog garden from the pond.

MAKING A BOG GARDEN

1 **Dig and line** your bog garden in the same way as for a pond with a liner (*see page 320*). If it joins a pond, aim to lay a single, large liner over both areas if possible. A wall must separate the pond from the bog garden (*see box, above*). Fill the pond to just below the level of the wall between it and the bog garden.

2 **Lay gravel** 1¼in. deep in the bog garden, top with soil, and soak well. Then place large, heavy stones along the wall. Remember to place a strip of underlayment beneath the stones, to avoid them puncturing the liner. The gravel provides drainage, and the heavy stones will keep the wall stable.

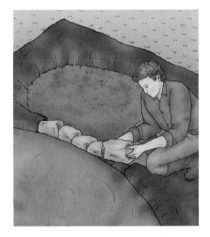

3 **Top up the soil** until it is level with the surrounding ground and place a strip of fine-mesh plastic netting along the stone barrier, on the bog garden side. This will prevent any soil or debris from the bog garden entering the pond. Firm the soil into place behind the wall.

4 **Fill the pond** with water and allow it to seep through the stone barrier into the bog garden. Once the soil in the bog area is damp, it can be planted up with your chosen plants. Remember to check the soil regularly and top up with water when necessary.

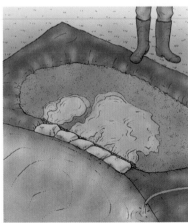

Making a wildlife pond

A well-designed and richly planted wildlife pond will act as a magnet to all sorts of creatures. The design will need to be slightly different to that of an ornamental pond to ensure that the pond appeals to wildlife.

Design tips

The best wildlife ponds will have a simple shape that includes a peninsula or inlet to provide a secluded spot for wildlife, and are about 36in. deep in the center.

Make approximately one third of the edge a beach with gently sloping sides at about 20 degrees, to allow easy access to the pond by wildlife for drinking or bathing. The remaining perimeter should be steep, about 75 degrees, with wide marginal shelves.

If your pond is larger than 65 square feet, you can add an island to act as a refuge for wildlife. This should be built at the same time as the pond.

Filling the pond

Cover the floor and marginal shelves with a layer of soil and arrange pebbles on the beach (*see below*). Then trickle water into the pond slowly to prevent it from disturbing the soil too much. Plants can still be grown in baskets (*see page 325*) in a wildlife pond, but a layer of soil in the bottom gives a more natural look, allows native plants to establish themselves, and acts as a habitat for wildlife.

FISH IN THE POND

There is a place for fish in all but the smallest or shallowest ponds, as long as there is a sufficient volume of water to avoid extreme temperature fluctuations and the pond does not freeze solid in winter. Fish are beneficial in areas where mosquitoes are a problem, as they eat the larvae. To begin with, stock your pond carefully, as a pond overcrowded with fish will soon develop high levels of nitrogen and become depleted of oxygen. The key is to find the right balance of plants and fish and, if needed, to use a biological filter to help convert fish waste to byproducts that can be absorbed by the pond plants. Protect your waterlilies from rooting koi by putting the plants in a container at least twice as deep as the soil and adding large rocks up to the container rim.

CONSTRUCTING A WILDLIFE POND

1 **Fit an underlayment** after excavating the site and removing any stones or debris. Place a liner on top and smooth out any wrinkles until it fits the contours of the pond. Bury the edges in 3in. of soil.

2 **Add a layer of soil** 4in. deep to the base of the liner and any marginal shelves. Spread the soil part of the way up the gently sloping part of the sides.

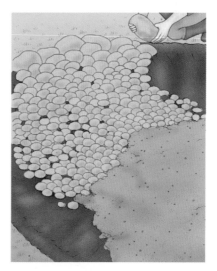

3 **Make a pebble beach** on gently sloping areas. Use larger stones around the edge and smaller pebbles and gravel as you work down the slope. Aim to build a ramp from the edge to the floor of the pond.

PLANTING WATER PLANTS

Generous planting not only looks attractive but also helps to keep the water free of algae, which prospers in light. Aim to cover a least one third of the surface of the pond with foliage. Submerged oxygenating plants will also keep the pond ecosystem balanced. Once you have equipped the pond with functional plants, you can choose more decorative ones to plant around the edges. When the planting becomes established, you can expect the pond to become a magnet to visiting wildlife.

Planting basics

There are six different groups of aquatic plants: deep-water plants that root at the floor of the pond and send their flowers and some of their leaves to the surface; submerged plants, which are useful oxygenators; floating plants; marginal plants; waterlilies; and bog plants.

For a long season of interest, choose a mixture of plants with assorted flowering times. For a wildlife pond, choose plants that provide food and nectar, and a few taller marginals for visiting birds and insects. If you are planning to keep fish, introduce them a few weeks after planting.

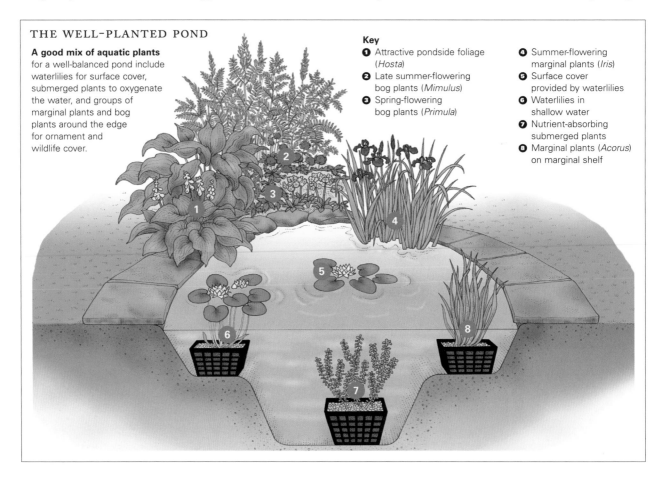

THE WELL-PLANTED POND

A good mix of aquatic plants for a well-balanced pond include waterlilies for surface cover, submerged plants to oxygenate the water, and groups of marginal plants and bog plants around the edge for ornament and wildlife cover.

Key
❶ Attractive pondside foliage (*Hosta*)
❷ Late summer-flowering bog plants (*Mimulus*)
❸ Spring-flowering bog plants (*Primula*)
❹ Summer-flowering marginal plants (*Iris*)
❺ Surface cover provided by waterlilies
❻ Waterlilies in shallow water
❼ Nutrient-absorbing submerged plants
❽ Marginal plants (*Acorus*) on marginal shelf

SOIL STRUCTURE TEST

Aquatic plant soil is widely available, but you can make your own. Take soil from an area where healthy plants grow, but no fertilizers or pesticides have been used recently. Sieve it to remove any large stones and debris, then test the soil structure. Dry a small amount of the soil and crumble it into a jar half filled with water. Put the lid on and shake to mix. Leave until the water is clear—about five days. There will be layers of sand, clay, water, and floating organic material. If the clay layer is twice as deep as the sand layer, with very little organic material, then it is ideal.

Growing in baskets

In most small ponds, aquatic plants should be grown individually in mesh basket containers. There are several reasons for this: water can flow freely in and out through the mesh sides, allowing the plant to take up nutrients from the water; the confinement of the container prevents the plant roots from spreading too far and invading the territory of other plants; and growing in baskets also makes it easy to move individual plants around to change the display or to lift them out of the pond when they need tidying up or dividing.

Square, round, and elongated baskets are available in many different sizes. Choose one that is large enough to accommodate the eventual size of the plant and to keep it stable as it grows. Curved baskets can fit the contours of marginal shelves or a preformed shell. More recently, flexible planting bags have become widely available. These are flexible enough to mold to the shape of uneven shelves, but should not be used where there might be sharp stones on the floor. Always plant in aquatic soil, and topdress around the plant with pea gravel.

PREPARING A BASKET

1 Place the basket on a piece of lining material and cut out a square twice the size of the basket so that the fabric will come right the way up the sides. You can also buy precut lining squares, but cutting your own is more economical.

2 Line the basket with the fabric, folding excess neatly in the corners. If you are planting tall marginals, it is a good idea to weight the basket with a brick for stability, but if you do this you will need to choose a larger basket to make up for the soil volume that will be lost.

3 Fill the basket with aquatic potting soil or suitable garden soil to within 1in. of the rim. Firm the soil lightly with your hands and trim off any excess lining fabric from around the edges of the basket.

4 Soak the soil thoroughly and evenly. To avoid displacing the soil, use a watering can with a very fine rose attached. The water will fill all the spaces in the soil and drive out all the air.

PLANTING A BASKET

1 Make a hole that is large enough to accommodate the roots of your chosen plant, using a trowel. If you are planting a small division, it may be less fiddly to just make the hole by hand. Place the plant in the hole.

2 Cover the roots and firm the soil around them. If you are planting container-grown plants, it may be easier only to half fill the basket at first. Sit the plant rootball on the soil and then fill in more soil around it. Water in after firming the soil.

3 Cover the surface of the soil with a layer of gravel ½in. deep. This is essential to keep the soil in the basket, preventing the surface from being washed away whenever the water of the pond is disturbed.

4 Water the basket thoroughly before lowering it into the pond to drive out any pockets of air in the planting medium. If they are left in, they will rise to the surface to escape when the basket is submerged, and this will disturb the plant roots.

To prevent soil from being washed through the sides of baskets and clouding the water, most baskets will need to be lined before planting (*see page 325*). Squares of burlap or plastic mesh are both suitable and sometimes sold cut to the appropriate size. Lining is unnecessary for micro-mesh containers with fine perforations or planting bags.

Placing the plants

Once you have planted up your baskets (*see above*), you can place the plants. Aim for a natural look when siting marginal plants. This is best achieved by positioning plants slightly closer than their optimum spread, which will allow the foliage to knit together quickly.

Baskets need to be at the correct depth to ensure that the plants will thrive. In some circumstances they may need to be raised up on bricks to reach the desired position. If this is necessary, remember to fit a piece of underlayment or other cushioning under the bricks to protect their rough edges.

In shallow ponds, baskets can easily be lowered in by hand, but if the water is deep you may need to thread string through the basket (*see above, step 5*). If the basket

5 Lower the basket into position. If the level it is being planted at is beyond easy reach, use lengths of heavy duty string to lower it in. Make sure that you thread string through each side or corner and hold them all, or the basket will tilt and spill soil.

is heavy, enlist a second pair of hands to help out. To place a container in the center of the pond, it may be necessary to lay a wooden board over the pond to work from.

To remove baskets from a shallow pond, you can simply reach in and retrieve them with ease, aiming to keep the container upright at all times. In deeper ponds, you may need to wear chest-high waders to take them out by hand. As this will disturb the water, plant life, and any wildlife, aim to do it as infrequently as possible.

Small ponds & containers

Even if you have only a small pond or a container water feature, you can still include plants. The range will inevitably be more limited than in a large pond, and you may not be able to vary the planting levels much.

If the container is large enough to accommodate small mesh baskets, a selection of different aquatics can be planted in these and then added to a container just as they would be to a large pond. For example, many barrels are large enough to accommodate several plants arranged on the base of the container. If necessary, secure a waterproof liner inside the container with rustproof fasteners, leaving a gap of about ¾in. between the top of the liner and the rim, so the liner will remain hidden as much as possible. Then add your plants, using bricks if necessary to provide different planting heights. Once your plants are arranged, put a hose over the side and fill slowly to avoiding disturbing the plants and soil. The surface of the water should be just below the top of the liner.

If the container is too small for baskets, plant with the rootballs wrapped in burlap tied loosely around the neck. You can also plant directly (*see below*), a method usually avoided with vigorous plants in a large pond, because they might spread aggressively and become tangled if their roots are not kept in check. The more restrained plants suitable for small water features should not present a problem.

When planting small ponds, use exuberant planting around the pond to compensate for a restrained choice within it. Avoid vigorous plants, or you will have to remove them more often than is good for the pond.

PLANTING A SMALL POND OR CONTAINER

1 Spread a layer of aquatic potting soil or suitable soil about 4–6in. deep on the floor of the container. Soak it gently but thoroughly, using a watering can fitted with a fine rose or fine spray from a hose-end sprayer.

2 Plant your chosen aquatic plants directly into the soil. Once they are all in place, cover the surface with a layer of gravel ½in. deep to keep the soil in place.

3 Lay a plastic bag flat on top of the plants and soil and lay the end of your hose on the bag. Turn the water on at a very low pressure so that it flows gently from the hose across the plastic bag.

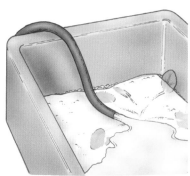

4 The bag spreads the water out and protects the plants and soil from any disturbance. It will float up as the container slowly fills. Once the water is at the required level, the bag can be removed.

Waterlilies

Waterlilies are the most elegant and dramatic of all aquatic plants, and their flowers are the showpiece of any pond. The coverage provided by their floating foliage also contributes to the overall health of the pond, shielding wildlife from predators and shading out algae. Many kinds of waterlily are available from suppliers, from small-leaved diminutive types suitable for an oak-barrel water feature to vigorous, fast-growing plants to fill for a large pond. Most waterlilies need about five hours of direct sun each day, but a few varieties are more shade tolerant.

Types of waterlily

Hardy waterlilies can overwinter in ponds in even the coldest climate zones, going dormant in winter and then blooming throughout spring and summer. The blossoms are held close to the surface of the water and come in a wide range of colors and sizes, ranging from pygmy types to those that spread up to 8ft. or more.

Tropical waterlilies bloom later in summer than hardy types, often with large, fragrant blossoms that are held several inches above the surface of the water. Some types are night-bloomers, offering a wonderful addition to the scented night garden. Best planted when daytime temperatures rise above 70°F, tropical waterlilies cannot survive freezing winter temperatures. In zone 8 and colder, you will need to treat them as annuals or lift their planting baskets or bags in fall and store them in a tub of water in a frost-free place.

NUPHAR & NYMPHAEA

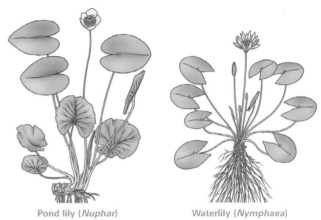

Pond lily (*Nuphar*)   Waterlily (*Nymphaea*)

Although they look similar, waterlilies (*Nymphaea*) and pond lilies (*Nuphar*) grow differently. Many waterlilies are ideal in small ponds, but vigorous pond lilies (*see page 330*) require large areas of water.

Planting waterlilies

To prepare waterlily tubers for planting, remove any long-stalked leaves and flowers, and trim the roots (*see box, below*). Place the tuber of a hardy waterlily almost horizontally in the container, with the growing tip angling up to the center; tropical waterlilies have a more vertical tuber and can be planted in the center of the pot. The crown should be just above the soil line. Insert a few tablets of slow-release fertilizer and then topdress with a layer of pea gravel.

WATERLILY PLANTING DEPTHS

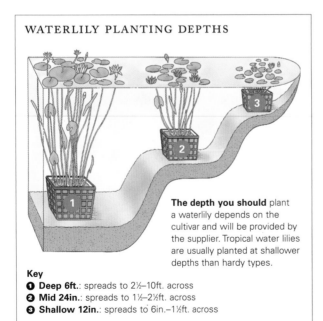

The depth you should plant a waterlily depends on the cultivar and will be provided by the supplier. Tropical water lilies are usually planted at shallower depths than hardy types.

Key
❶ **Deep 6ft.**: spreads to 2½–10ft. across
❷ **Mid 24in.**: spreads to 1½–2½ft. across
❸ **Shallow 12in.**: spreads to 6in.–1½ft. across

PREPARING WATERLILIES FOR PLANTING

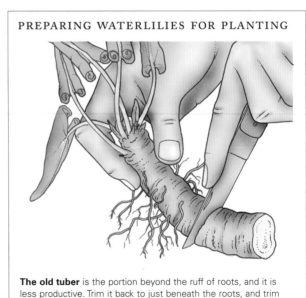

The old tuber is the portion beyond the ruff of roots, and it is less productive. Trim it back to just beneath the roots, and trim the roots themselves back to 1in.

Deep-water plants

Plants that have their roots at the base of the pond and their flowers and some of their leaves above the surface are known as deep-water, or floating-leaf, plants. Most love to grow in sun, although the pond lilies (*Nuphar* species) will tolerate a certain amount of shade.

This is a useful group of plants, especially if you are planting a stream, because some tolerate moving water. Their leaves provide shelter for wildlife, and their shade helps to inhibit algal growth.

All of these plants need a minimum depth of 12in. of water to thrive, and the spread of their foliage is roughly one to one-and-a-half times the depth at which the plant grows, although this is also influenced by the size of the planting basket.

What to grow
Cape pondweed (*Aponogeton distachyos*): This plant will provide your pond with a reliable show of white flowers from early spring until fall. The highly scented, forked blooms float on the water among green leaves that are often splashed purple. It needs a depth of 12–36in. For warm climates only. Z9
Golden club (*Orontium aquaticum*): Thriving in moving water, this plant produces pencillike spikes of yellow flowers in late spring, which stand proud of the water between slender leaves. Although it is sometimes grown as a marginal, it is much more successful if planted at a depth of around 18in. Z6
Lotus (*Nelumbo*) are favorites for large ponds in warm climates but some, including the American lotus (*N. lutea*), are hardy to zone 4. The large blooms open early in the day and eventually become woody seedpods that can be used in dried arrangements.

Lotus need 5–6 hours of sunlight and will not bloom without several weeks of temperatures above 80°F. Grow lotus in large containers and fertilize regularly; they are heavy feeders. As the plants grow, gradually lower the depth of the container to 2ft. for largest types; smaller cultivars can stay at 6–9in. Z4
Pond lily (*Nuphar lutea* subsp. *advena*): Most pond lilies are not as attractive as waterlilies, but this is a worthy rival. It has large, yellow flowers with purple or green tints in summer, held above oval, floating leaves. Although it will tolerate growing in the shallows, it prefers water that is at least 18in. deep. This vigorous species will grow at depths of 5ft. and will spread to fill as much space as it is allowed unless it is constrained by planting in a mesh basket. Z3

DEEP-WATER AQUATICS

Cape pondweed

Golden club

Pond lily

These seasonal performers are all deciduous, dying back beneath the surface in winter. Their leaves, however, provide invaluable shade and shelter through summer.

Lotus (*Nelumbo*) are large plants whose foliage and flowers rise dramatically above the surface of the water.

Submerged plants

Submerged plants, also called oxygenating plants, help to keep ponds clear of algae, oxygenate the water, and provide shelter for pond life. Plant them no more than 36in. deep in sun or light shade, adding a bunch for every square yard of surface area. Push them into a mesh basket of soil, firming in well to prevent them from floating free. They can spread widely, so be ready to remove excess plants.

What to grow

Curled pondweed (*Potamogeton crispus*): Translucent foliage and tiny purple and white flowers in summer. Z7
Eelgrass (*Vallisneria americana*): Native to eastern U.S.; has long, ribbonlike leaves and tiny flowers. Z4

Hair grass (*Eleocharis acicularis*): Good in formal ponds as it remains under the surface at all times. Z3
Hornwort (*Ceratophyllum demersum*): Ideal for shady, deep ponds, it has brittle stems and bristly leaves. Z6
Whorled milfoil (*Myriophyllum verticillatum*): Fernlike foliage and small, yellow flowers in summer. Z3

Plants to avoid

Some submerged plants outcompete native plants if they escape, and so deprive some wildlife of food. Never plant parrot's feather (*Myriophyllum aquaticum*), Canadian pondweed (*Elodea canadensis*), or curly waterweed (*Lagarosiphon major*, sometimes sold as *Elodea crispa*).

Curled pondweed has submerged leaves but carries purple and white flowers just above the surface of the water.

Hair grass is a diminutive plant that gives the appearance of an underwater lawn if its roots spread through a soil-bottomed pond.

Hornwort floats to the surface during summer. Buds break off in fall and sink to the bottom, where they take root.

Eelgrass has long, graceful leaves that may be a food source for pond wildlife. Small, pale flowers grow to the surface in summer.

Marginal plants

Grown around the pond edge on purpose-built marginal shelves, these plants soften the transition from water to land and are essential for an attractive pond. They also provide cover, food, and a place to perch for wildlife. Growing 6–24in. in height, they like to have their roots in wet mud or several inches of water, and most will tolerate up to around 6in. of water.

Planting marginals

Set marginal plants in containers or baskets placed in the pond on bricks or stones, or on low shelves at the edge of the pond. Use large containers for upright marginal plants, as they can become topheavy and topple over if the container is too small. Adding ballast to the plant's container, in the form of stones or bricks, and setting them on wide, stable planting shelves will also help keep the plants vertical in windy conditions. Planting in solid containers (not baskets) will keep in check the more vigorous marginals such as cattails (*Typha*), umbrella grass (*Cyperus alternifolius*), and horsetail (*Equisetum hyemale*), which can all become weeds if planted directly in the soil.

Marginals purchased in nursery containers will need to be trimmed back before planting (*see box, below*). Plant in aquatic soil, not regular garden dirt, and spread a layer of gravel on the surface of the soil.

Pickerel weed (*Pontederia cordata*) has spikes of soft blue flowers in late summer, but the less common *P. c.* f. *albiflora* is white-flowered.

Arrowhead is the name given to several species of *Sagittaria*, due to their leaf shapes. They have white flowers in summer.

PREPARING MARGINALS FOR PLANTING

Trim back roots to within 1in. of the crown. If planting mature plants from midsummer onward, trim back the topgrowth by two thirds, using a sharp pocket knife or pair of pruners.

Water irises, such as the glorious *Iris laevigata* and its striped variety 'Variegata', are hard to beat in summer.

This deep koi pond is surrounded with natural boulders and densely planted, moisture-loving marginals and bog plants, including giant rhubarb (*Gunnera*) and grasslike, variegated sweet flag.

What to grow

There is a rich selection of marginals to choose from.

Blue flag (*Iris versicolor*): The flowers are violet-blue and gold; those of the variety 'Kermesina' are plum purple. Z3

Bog arum (*Calla palustris*): Produces white flowers in summer. Z4

Bowles' golden grass (*Carex elata* 'Aurea'): Clumping, grasslike plant to 2½ft. tall; bright yellow, straplike leaves are striking against darker foliage. Z5

Cardinal flower (*Lobelia cardinalis*): Tall, slender perennial with dark foliage and crimson flowering spikes in midsummer. Z4

Corkscrew rush (*Juncus effusus* f. *spiralis*): Grown for its curiously curled leaves. Z6

Indian shot (*Canna* species): Large, often striped or variegated leaves and brightly colored flower panicles. Z8

Obedient plant (*Physostegia virginiana*): Free-flowering perennial with light purple, pink, or white blooms. Z4

Sensitive fern (*Onoclea sensibilis*): A deciduous fern with coarsely divided, pale green fronds to 18in. Z4

Sweet flag (*Acorus calamus*): This has similar foliage to irises, but less showy, yellow flowers. Z4

Water forget-me-not (*Myosotis scorpioides*): Bright blue flowers bloom in early summer. Z5

Zebra rush (*Schoenoplectus*): Leafless, gray-green stems, 3 ft. tall and banded creamy white. Ideal for sculptural effects and minimalist water feature. Z4

FLOATING PLANTS

Unlike other aquatic plants, you simply float these plants on the surface of the water. Floating plants can be highly decorative, and they play an important role in ponds by reducing the risk of algae. They absorb mineral salts that are necessary for its growth and provide surface cover, reducing the amount of sunlight that falls into the water.

All floating plants have the potential to be invasive. Be a responsible water gardener and dispose of them carefully by composting—never put them into drains or local ponds or creeks. Do not buy any of the 'plants to avoid' listed below, and only buy properly labeled plants that give both botanical and English names from a reputable supplier. Even some of these recommended plants, while safe to grow in colder areas, may prove invasive in warmer zones.

What to grow

To find out more about plants that may be invasive in your region, consult your local cooperative extension service or the United States Department of Agriculture (U.S.D.A.). Most aquatic nurseries will have a good choice of noninvasive floating plants that are ideal for garden ponds.

Fairy moss (*Azolla caroliniana*): This small, floating fern spreads across the surface of the pond; its green leaves turn purplish red in fall. Avoid the very similar *A. filiculoides*, an invasive weed; if you doubt the identification of the plant, do not buy it. Z7

Water soldier (*Stratiotes aloides*): This forms a rosette of upright leaves that resembles the top of a pineapple, and produces small, white or pinkish flowers in summer. Z5

Plants to avoid

Conservationists advise against growing the following plants, due to their ability to colonize natural waterways with great speed if they escape from the garden.

Floating pennywort (*Hydrocotyle ranunculoides*): This plant may be mislabeled as the noninvasive marsh pennywort (*H. vulgaris*).

New Zealand pygmy weed (*Crassula helmsii*): Sometimes this is sold as Australian stonecrop (*Tillaea helmsii*) or *T. recurva* (*see page 335*).

Water fern (*Azolla filiculoides*): This may be hard to distinguish from *A. caroliniana* (*see above*).

Water hyacinth (*Eichhornia crassipes*): A problem in areas with mild winters; hardier strains are starting to appear.

Water lettuce (*Pistia stratiotes*): Invasive in frost-free areas.

Water soldier   Fairy moss

These plants are hardy in all but the coldest regions, dying back under water during winter. Control them by simply removing any excess growth with a net.

Bog plants

Acting as a bridge between your water feature and the rest of the garden, bog plants provide color and interest from early spring until fall. They range in height from creeping ground cover to towering specimens, so choose plants that will fit your yard. Bog plants thrive in damp soil, but they will not survive long in standing water.

Preparing & planting

Bog plants are planted directly into the soil like any other perennial. If planting from midsummer onward, remove any fading flowers and reduce the height of vigorous, clump-forming plants by about one third before planting. Water well while still in their pots, an hour before planting if possible. Dig a hole wider than the pot but at the same depth, remove the pot, and place the plant in the hole. Backfill with soil, firm, and water, ensuring that the crown is just above or at the same level as the soil.

What to grow

Astilbe (*Astilbe*): Attractive foliage topped by plumes of flowers up to 4ft. in summer. Z4 or Z5

Daylily (*Hemerocallis*): These statuesque plants have showy, yellow flowers in summer, like the scented blooms of *H. lilioasphodelus*. Z3

Giant rhubarb (*Gunnera manicata*): If space is not an issue, nothing is more dramatic than this foliage plant. The huge, deciduous leaves grow swiftly and it easily makes a 10ft. clump in one season. Z7

Broad swathes of bog plants visually extend a pond and anchor it in its surroundings. They are essential to creating an informal, natural look.

Monkey flower (*Mimulus*): Compact forms, such as yellow *M. luteus* and *M. guttatus*, are ideal. Their bright flowers liven up late summer. Z6 or Z7

Primrose (*Primula*): These give essential color in spring and summer, and many types suit bog gardens: *P. rosea* has red flowers in early spring, and *P. bulleyana* is a candelabra type with orange-yellow flowers in summer. Z2–Z4

Swamp rose (*Rosa palustris*): Long-lasting, red fruits. Z3

Royal fern (*Osmunda regalis*) is a stately, architectural plant with an upright habit and large, leathery fronds up to 6ft. long.

Drumstick primula (*Primula denticulata*) flowers from midspring to summer. Reddish and white-flowered varieties are also available.

Ferns and grasses and the large, heart-shaped, blue-green leaves of a hosta such as *H. sieboldiana* provide a lively mix of textures.

Aquatic weeds

Ponds can provide ideal growing conditions for vigorous plants, which may outgrow their welcome. Planting in baskets helps to control them by restricting the roots, and makes it much easier to lift and divide plants. Keep in mind that plants that are invasive in some states may be well behaved in others. Your first choice should usually be plants that are native to your area. Your local cooperative extension service or the United States Department of Agriculture (U.S.D.A.) can provide good advice.

Many gardeners are concerned about introduced aquatic and marginal plants, some of which are highly invasive. These include common reed (*Phragmites australis*), purple loosestrife (*Lythrum salicaria*), giant reed (*Arundo donax*), and water hyacinth (*Eichhornia crassipes*). They can become a nuisance in a pond, but cause far more serious problems if they escape. They can choke waterways, crowd out native vegetation, and displace the wildlife that depends on it.

Controlling native plants

Remove large, vigorous plants rooted in the sides or base of the pond and replace with less vigorous species. Fall is the ideal time for this work, and it is easier if you can lower the water level of the pond before you start.

Limit regrowth by reducing the nutrient levels in the pond, and make sure that fertilizers introduced on other parts of the yard cannot seep in from surrounding areas. Keep out falling leaves, avoid overfeeding fish, and top up the pond with rainwater, rather than municipal water.

REMOVING DUCKWEED

The plants of duckweed are tiny, but they are simple to remove if you use a fishing net. If the pond is too large to reach the middle, use a hose to drive the weed to the sides first.

Controlling introduced plants

Prevention is better than cure, so avoid buying plants known to be invasive. Always check newly acquired pond plants for unwanted 'hitchhikers'—these problem plants can develop rapidly from small fragments. If you already have them in your pond, pull up, rake out, or scoop off excess plants. Never take the debris out of the yard; compost the plants or bury them.

New Zealand pygmy weed or Australian stonecrop looks harmless, with its dainty, white flowers, but it is very difficult to control.

Purple loosetrife (*Lythrum virgatum*) has naturalized in many areas, clogging streams and crowding out native plants.

Cattail, with its reedlike flower spikes, is a classic pond plant, but for large, natural ponds only. Elsewhere, treat it with caution.

POND CARE

The changing seasons bring alternating temperatures, greater or lesser amounts of rainfall, variable plant growth, and falling leaves, leading to the natural balance of a pond becoming disrupted. The result may be overgrown plants, murky water, and a buildup of algae or pond weeds. To keep a pond or water feature in good shape, treat it like any other part of the garden and carry out seasonal tasks and maintenance so that all its elements—water, plants, and wildlife—continue to function as a balanced ecosystem, with no one element dominating and so causing problems.

Seasonal care

Like every other part of your garden, a pond has its own annual cycle of maintenance. These tasks range from weed control and plant division to water replenishment in summer and frost protection in winter. Take advice for the seasonal care of your pond from local water garden specialists or your local cooperative extension service. In zones 9 and above, maintenance is less seasonal than in colder areas; you should maintain equipment and remove weeds and leaves regularly throughout the year.

Spring
Take filters, pumps, and lights out of storage, check that they are working and place them back in the pond. Every few years it may be necessary to empty and clean a pond

As winter approaches, clear the pond and surrounding area of all debris. It may be possible to keep a small patch free of ice (*see facing page*).

KEEPING A POND CLEAR OF FALL LEAVES

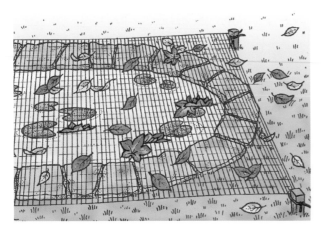

A net stretched over the surface of a pond and secured to the ground with stakes is essential if deciduous trees overhang the water, but clearing leaves from the center can be tricky on large ponds.

A net fence around a pond can be put in place in less vulnerable sites, where leaves are likely to be blown in from the ground. Secure with wire to stout canes, spaced 24in. apart around the perimeter.

(*see page 338*), but avoid frequent cleaning as it will upset the pond's ecosystem. Feed your pond plants as they are coming into growth with an aquatic fertilizer (*see page 340*).

Summer

Perhaps the biggest problem in a long, hot summer is the water level dropping through evaporation. Top it up once a week or more in hot weather. If possible, use rainwater or well water, but if none is available use municipal water. Whatever the water source, top up little and often to prevent the shock of colder water disturbing fish.

To keep the water clean over summer, regularly deadhead flowers and remove dying foliage to prevent it from rotting in the pond. Twirl out blanket-weed with a stick and leave it on the side before disposing of it so that any creatures within it can find their way back to the water.

Fall

Leaves drop for many weeks over fall, and many will find their way into your pond, where they will look unsightly and discolor the water. If there are trees directly over the pond, stretch a net over it (*see facing page*). If the trees are farther away, you could construct a low fence around the perimeter instead. The netting can be left in place over winter or until all the trees are bare. Fall is also the time to remove dead, dying, and tattered foliage from waterside plants and to divide overcrowded clumps.

Winter

The treatment of your pond in winter depends on where you live. In any areas where the pond freezes over and the yard is used much less in winter, remove lights, filters, and

CONCRETE PONDS

Expanding ice can cause concrete pond liners to crack, so it is very important they are not allowed to freeze over completely. Reduce the risk by floating a rubber ball or a piece of wood on the surface—as the water freezes the softer ball or wood will absorb the pressure and prevent fractures.

pumps. Clean them well and store them inside. In zones 7 and 8, where ponds may freeze but very thick ice rarely develops, it helps the general health of the pond, its plants, and its wildlife if an opening can be maintained in the ice (*see below*). This allows oxygen to penetrate and toxic gases to escape. The easiest way is to add an electric pond heater to the pond.

Plants like waterlilies are usually safe if any frozen area remains above their roots. Frost penetration in a small pond can be reduced by covering the pond with wooden boards after cutting back marginal plants and removing equipment. Pile conifer branches, dry leaves, or even sealed bags of synthetic insulation over the boards and secure them well. A deep, early snowfall may add to the insulating effect.

CREATING A VENTILATION HOLE IN WINTER

Fill a saucepan with boiling water, put the lid on, and sit it on the ice. Several refills may be needed to melt a hole in thick ice.

A floating ring will freeze in place. Treat it as a well: the ring will hold boiling water in one place, so the ice there can be melted.

Electric pond heaters will keep a small area free of ice, and may be the best solution if you are unable to check on your pond regularly.

Cleaning ponds

Unless overcome with invasive aquatic weeds, lakes and very large ponds are usually self-balancing ecosystems. But occasionally you need to clean out most garden ponds to remove sediment and reduce the tangle of plants.

The best time to give your pond an overhaul is in spring, because this gives the pond plants plenty of opportunity to reestablish themselves before summer. Although it is hard work, it is not something that needs doing often—every five years or so if the pond is small and every ten years with larger ponds.

Removing water

Before you can clean the pond you need to empty it. You should direct the water onto your garden plantings; never empty it into a drain or creek as this can cause potentially invasive water plants to escape into the wild.

If part of the surrounding land is lower than the pond, you can try siphoning out the water using a piece of hose. The pull of gravity should help most of the water drain from the pond and any that is left in the bottom can be removed with a bucket. If siphoning is not possible, you will have to pump or bail out the water.

Removing plants & pond life

Be careful not to throw away fish when you are draining a pond. Most will remain in the wet soil on the pond floor. Use a net or mug to remove them to bowls of clean pond water and add a few pieces of submerged aquatic plant to provide shelter and food. Remember to feed fish with their usual dried food if they remain in the buckets for a few days. Try not to disturb other beneficial pond wildlife, such as snails, amphibians, or dragonfly larvae.

Put marginal plants in a shady place and keep all other aquatics in buckets, bowls, or tanks of pond water. Ensure that submerged plants are completely covered with water. If any plants have outgrown their containers, now is a good to time to repot and divide them.

Cleaning the pond

Remove any mud, taking care not to damage a flexible liner. You can use a spade with care, but scraping with an empty pot is safer. When dry, the mud can be mixed into your garden soil. Scrub the sides and floor of the pond with a stiff brush and clean water, and finish by removing all traces of water added to the pond while cleaning.

CLEANING A POND

1 Empty your pond by siphoning off the water with a hose, bailing out with a bucket, or pumping out. Take care where you empty the water; some plants become invasive, and aggressive weeds can, if they are allowed to, enter ditches or creeks.

2 Bail out the last of the water with a bucket. Remove plants as you go, and scoop out any fish or other livestock as you see them. Be careful not to bail out small fish or snails with the mud accidentally.

3 Keep plants and fish in a shady place. The bowls for fish should be at least 4–6in. deep, with a large surface area for oxygen exchange, and free of any trace of detergent. Keep snails separately, or the fish may attack them.

4 Empty the mud from the floor, being very careful if your pond has a liner. Remove dirt and algae by scrubbing the pond vigorously with a brush and fresh water, then bail this out. Never use detergent, because any trace left behind will cause problems.

Pond repairs

While a pond is empty you can make good any damage to the liner. Make sure that any repair work is dry before water, fish, and plants are returned to the pond.

Many liners can be repaired with a special kit (*see below, top*), while a concrete pond will need more dextrous treatment to mend cracks or areas that have deteriorated

(*see below, bottom*). Preformed fiberglass ponds can be mended with a car body repair kit, but the whole liner is best removed and patched from underneath. If you have a rigid pond of any kind that cannot be repaired, the best alternative may be to treat the pond as an excavated hole, lay an E.P.D.M. liner in it, and make a new edge.

REPAIRING A FLEXIBLE LINER

1 **Clean any dirt** or traces of algae from the damaged area to ensure the repair patch will stick.

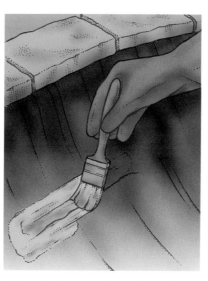

2 **Roughen the area** with sandpaper. Use a paintbrush to spread adhesive over a wide area around the damage.

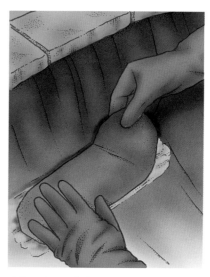

3 **Lay the patch** down on the damaged area once the adhesive becomes sticky. Press firmly, and leave for at least 12 hours to dry.

REPAIRING A CONCRETE POND

1 **Hammer a V-shaped groove** with a brick-set chisel along the crack, at least 1in. deeper than the depth of the crack.

2 **Mix the concrete** and waterproofing compound. Fill the channel and smooth it level, using a polishing trowel.

3 **Treat with sealant** once the concrete has dried, mixing and applying it according to the manufacturer's instructions.

Fertilizing plants

Aquatic plants are essentially the same as any other plants in the garden, and they will do best if they are supplied with nutrients. Waterlilies, especially, are very hungry plants and require plentiful nutrients to perform well.

Testing your water

Extremes of acidity or alkalinity can affect the growth of water plants. Iron, an essential trace element, cannot be absorbed by plants in alkaline water, while plants in very acid conditions do not respond to fertilizers, and the foliage of waterlilies can even turn brown. The only option in such conditions is to empty the pond, clean it, refill with fresh water, and stock with new plants.

Use a test kit to check the pH value of your pond water. Simply take a sample from the pond and pour it into a tube, mixing it together with the solution that is supplied with the kit. Checking the color against the supplied chart will tell you its pH value (*see page 33*).

Adding aquatic fertilizers

Feed aquatic plants when they are just coming into growth, in spring. Some marginal plants will need to be divided and replanted in fresh soil. Generally, aquatic fertilizers arrive in perforated packets or as tablets that are pushed into the growing medium among the plant roots. You can also make your own fertilizer balls (*see below*). Never use fertilizer with added herbicide; nor should you sprinkle regular garden fertilizer or use liquid fertilizer in your pond as this will upset the natural balance and be harmful to fish and other wildlife.

Looking after the nutrient balance

Inevitably, some nutrients will leach into the water. These will be taken up by floating aquatics, because aquatic plants absorb nutrients through their leaves as well as their roots. Too much fertilizer in the water, however, will encourage algal growth.

ADDING AQUATIC FERTILIZER

1 Push fertilizer packets into a planting basket, after peeling off the protective tape. Place it close to the crown of the plant so the maximum amount of fertilizer reaches the plant instead of leaching out into the water.

2 Cover the packet over with a handful of gravel. This makes doubly sure that the nutrients go where they are supposed to and are not leached out. The gravel also covers the disturbed soil so that it stays in place when the basket is returned to the water.

HOME-MADE FERTILIZERS

1 Take a handful of moist clay or heavy soil; it should hold together in a ball fairly well when rolled and squeezed. Crumble the soil and add approximately 1tsp of organic fertilizer to each handful of soil.

2 Roll the mixture into pellets the size of golf balls between the palms of your hands. Insert these into the soil in the planting basket, next to the crown of the plant, just as you would a brand-name fertilizer packet or tablet (*see left, step 1*).

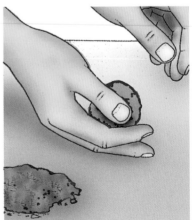

Overcoming problems

Ponds are generally trouble free, but there may occasionally be problems. If you inherit a neglected pond with too many problems, give it a complete overhaul. Drain and clean it and make repairs if necessary. You may need to restock it with plants, but save any in good condition.

Problems in the water

Algae is a common problem, although a well-balanced pond discourages it. Twirl out mats of algae on a stick, leaving it at the sides so that pond life can crawl back into the water. A filter with an ultraviolet clarifier causes cloudy algae to clump together so it can be sifted out. Top up the pond with rainwater or well water, rather than municipal water, as it is less likely to upset the pH balance of the pond, which can take a long time to put right. Algacides are a quick fix if used carefully, but do not cure the causes.

Muddy water is usually a result of fish disturbing planting baskets in search of insect larvae to eat. Soil builds up on the pond floor and swirls up when a fish passes. Always topdress containers with gravel to minimize this; clean out the pond in severe cases.

Pond defenses

Plastic herons around the pond, together with netting close to the water's surface or a low fence, will deter herons. To keep cats and raccoons away, grow strong marginals and ensure that any paved edge has an overhang for fish to hide underneath (*see box, right*).

PROTECTING THE POND

Key

❶ Bird bath to draw birds away from the pond
❷ Thick marginal planting to discourage herons and to keep cats from the water
❸ Fence of fishing line or wire on 6in. stakes to deter herons and raccoons
❹ Planting baskets covered with ½in. of gravel to minimize soil disturbance by fish
❺ Overhang of 3in. to prevent cats from fishing
❻ Fish need hiding places, like dense plant growth, deep water, or sunken pipes

Perhaps the greatest predators of ponds are herons, which will quickly pick off your fish until you are left with an empty pond. Local cats and raccoons also pose a problem.

SEASONAL CHANGES

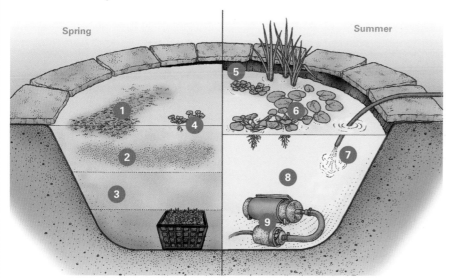

Algal growth may be rife in spring when aquatics are starting into growth and the filter has not been put back into the pond after winter. The condition of the pond is likely to improve in summer when the plants flourish and the filter is reinstalled.

Key

❶ Blanket-weed
❷ Filamentous floating weed
❸ Suspended free-floating algae
❹ Overwintered floating and submerged aquatics
❺ Reduced water level due to evaporation
❻ Surface cover provided by waterlilies
❼ Collected rainwater to top up pond
❽ Clear water free from algae
❾ Filter and pump

341

CHAPTER EIGHT

CONTAINER GARDENING

PLANTING CONTAINERS FOR SEASONAL OR PERMANENT displays can be great fun, and it provides an excellent opportunity to experiment with planting combinations. You can create some truly eye-catching displays, with the knowledge that replacing them is easy if they don't work out as planned or when their performance begins to fade.

Container displays make great garden props, not dissimilar to scenery or stage sets inside theaters; they are an intrinsic element of the overall beauty of our yards and open spaces. Containers filled with attractive combinations of plants can enhance the plainest of environments, brightening up patios and balconies. They can also help to soften paved surfaces.

We often think of planted containers as a small oasis for plants, but they also provide habitats for beneficial insects in environments where there is very little natural habitat. This can be seen in urban areas where large-scale planters, rather than plants in the ground, are prevalent. In dry climates and when watering is restricted, containers may provide the opportunity to grow lush and luxuriant plants.

Planting trends

Recently the availability of a range of plants and of different and unusual styles of container has increased dramatically, providing ever-greater opportunities for gardeners to experiment creatively and imaginatively. The trend has been to move away from traditional, seed-raised annuals to plants that either extend the growing season or provide a more permanent display that can be used, perhaps with variations, over a number of years.

Plants that have become more popular include herbaceous perennials, tender tropical perennials, grasses, bulbs, shrubs, and trees. One advantage of these plants is that they provide an opportunity for more sustainable gardening. For example, herbaceous perennials can be planted in container displays for two or three seasons and then removed from the container, divided, and reused either in the container or planted out in a permanent site in the garden. Alternatively, tender tropicals planted in containers can be propagated in late summer to produce plants for future displays.

Seed-raised annuals are always popular and still produce dazzling displays. They are often used to enhance permanently planted container displays containing trees, shrubs, grasses, or herbaceous perennials, where their vibrant colors provide a welcome addition. Although they are short-lived, these annuals provide an opportunity to make small-scale seasonal planting changes to rejuvenate displays when they start to fade.

Types of container

There are many different styles of container on the market, designed to suit all tastes and budgets. The types of container available are boundless, ranging from traditional terra-cotta or rustic wood to modern, contemporary designs constructed out of glazed ceramic, metal, plastic, and recycled materials. Your vision need not be limited to the designs available specifically for plant use: with a little imagination, almost any vessel can be adopted as a versatile planter.

Keep an open mind as you select the plants and containers for your garden displays. Enjoy the experience, be imaginative, and most importantly have some fun. If you keep this in mind, whatever planter you create will be a unique expression of your personality.

CHOOSING CONTAINERS

Always buy the best containers you can afford. It is better to buy one or two large containers rather than three or four small ones, because the more space you have for the plant roots the more choice you will have when it comes to selecting suitable plants, and the easier it is to keep plants adequately watered and fertilized. Remember that small containers look insignificant in front of large homes, classical styles do not suit contemporary settings, while sleek, modern styles look out of place against cedar shingles.

Types of container

In addition to style and size, an important consideration for your container selection is the material from which it is constructed. Each has its advantages and disadvantages: heavy concrete may be needed for stability in a windy position, while lighter fiberglass or metal can be moved around as displays fade or for winter protection.

Terra-cotta & clay

Terra-cotta pots are used in many container gardens. They are aesthetically pleasing, come in a variety of shapes and sizes, and age and weather gracefully. Their porous nature allows for the evaporation of water, which helps to reduce overheating when weather conditions are

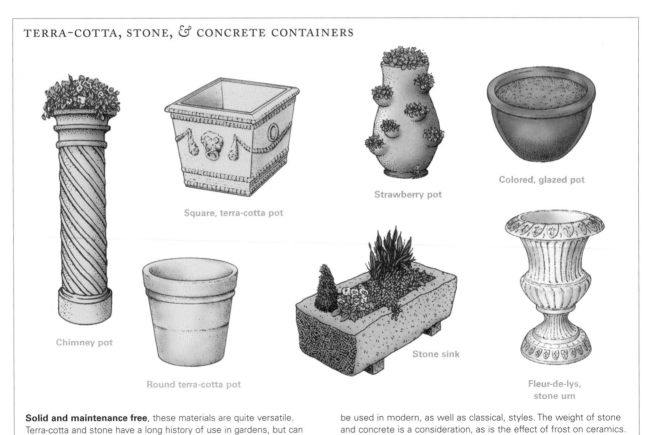

TERRA-COTTA, STONE, & CONCRETE CONTAINERS

Chimney pot

Square, terra-cotta pot

Strawberry pot

Colored, glazed pot

Round terra-cotta pot

Stone sink

Fleur-de-lys, stone urn

Solid and maintenance free, these materials are quite versatile. Terra-cotta and stone have a long history of use in gardens, but can be used in modern, as well as classical, styles. The weight of stone and concrete is a consideration, as is the effect of frost on ceramics.

WOODEN, METAL, & PLASTIC CONTAINERS

Box planter

Metal pedestal basket

Wall-mounted, metal window box

Plastic pot

Oak half-barrel

These materials provide containers for all situations. A pair of box planters flanking a path is a classic combination for a formal space, while half-barrels may suit a more rural garden. Lightweight metal baskets are inexpensive, and have many uses.

hot but also makes them less water retentive. Not all are frostproof. Other ceramics have colored glazes, which both improve their water-retaining and frost-resistance qualities and provide an opportunity to design creative color combinations with a variety of plants.

Plastic & fiberglass

Gardeners today are looking for containers that offer ease of use and value for money, without compromising on appearance. As a result there is a wide range of plastic and fiberglass containers on the market. The advantages of these materials are that they are lightweight, durable, and also relatively inexpensive. The best of them can also be attractive in their own right or make remarkably realistic replicas of more expensive materials, such as terra-cotta, glazed ceramics, stone, lead, and wood.

Concrete

The advantage of concrete containers is their durability. On the downside, they are heavy and can be difficult to move, especially when planted.

Concrete is versatile, with various finishes available, so you will be able to find something that is in keeping with your garden's style. Very large containers made out of concrete are often used in urban areas, while on a smaller scale relatively inexpensive concrete garden containers are sometimes clad with other materials to enhance their appearance.

It is also possible to make natural-looking concrete containers at home by adding peat to a concrete mix and using plastic boxes to form a mold.

Metal containers

Another modern trend is the increased use of metals, such as galvanized steel, copper, and zinc. These containers provide a contemporary twist on planting design and are surprisingly lightweight, due to their thin-skinned, often double-walled, construction.

The main disadvantage of metal containers is that they rapidly absorb heat from the sun, which in turn accelerates the drying out of the potting soil. The only solution is to water regularly and attentively and maybe restrict their use to shady areas.

Recycled materials

It is becoming easier now to purchase containers made from a variety of recycled materials, including wood, plastic, and premolded synthetics. These make fine alternatives to buying more familiar materials. It is also often rewarding to see what you can recycle yourself or adapt with a little bit of effort (*see page 350*).

Wooden containers

Wooden containers are very versatile and can range in style from rustic half-barrels to square boxes. Unlike some of the other materials described here, they provide a cool environment for the roots of plants to thrive in, and they retain moisture exceptionally well.

When planting, it is advisable to use a waterproof liner inside the wooden planter to help protect its interior from rot. When buying wooden containers, make sure that the timber is properly certified as being harvested from a renewable source.

Baskets & window boxes

Hanging baskets and window boxes make great additions to any container-garden display, as they make it possible to suspend colorful plants and decorative foliage in doorways, porches, and sunrooms. A well-planted basket or window box is a living, cascading flower arrangement, constantly changing as it grows.

With careful plant selection and maintenance you can achieve stunning results. A good lesson to learn when first caring for any container display (but particularly baskets and boxes) is the need to water frequently: long-handled watering wands provide a longer reach to make this easier. Another tip is to check on the quality of the chain that is supplied for suspending a hanging basket. Consider the weight of the potting soil, plants, and water once it is planted, to avoid a potential calamity.

Wire baskets

Wire baskets are one of the more popular and traditional types of hanging basket available. They are usually made out of plastic-coated wire. Large steel baskets can be used beneath windows, but tend to be heavier. Both need liners to contain the soil (*see facing page*).

Always consider the shape and the size of the spaces in the wire frame, as you may want to plant through the sides. There is nothing more frustrating, or damaging, than trying to squeeze a plant through a very small hole when planting up a hanging basket. The best baskets overcome this problem by having large gaps in the sides so plants can be positioned easily.

Wood & terra-cotta

Wooden baskets or window boxes are good alternatives to wire ones, and in themselves can be decorative. It is also possible to construct your own by recycling scrap lumber, the obvious benefit of this being that you can tailor the size and shape to suit your needs.

Terra-cotta bowls or half-bowls tend to be displayed fixed to walls or fences. They make attractive planters, and are a natural-looking alternative to wire or plastic.

Plastic baskets

Over recent years there has been an increase in the variety and quality of plastic hanging baskets. These may be solid with built-in saucers, which provide a water reservoir and help to catch any drips, or have removable sides and slots to allow for easier planting. It is helpful to have a built-in reservoir, but they cannot be relied upon to give sufficient watering for more than a short time.

A window box with summer and winter displays can provide an oasis of color to look out on and enjoy from the comfort of your home.

Woven & fiber baskets

Woven baskets are attractive and relatively inexpensive, and have become a very popular choice. Often conical in shape, they have a basic wire frame interwoven with a natural wicker weave. They are usually planted only at the top, so plant selection is important and needs to include

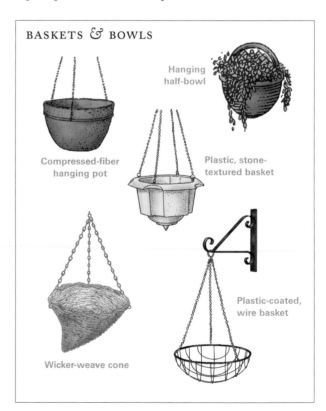

BASKETS & BOWLS

Hanging half-bowl

Compressed-fiber hanging pot

Plastic, stone-textured basket

Wicker-weave cone

Plastic-coated, wire basket

When choosing a basket, remember that it will look different once planted. Some designs look attractive in themselves, but plainer structures will need to be concealed by lots of foliage and flowers.

Growing ornamentals *see page 70* | **Planting** *see page 353* | **Aftercare & maintenance** *see page 364*

a combination of upright and trailing plants. Expect wicker to last for only two seasons: it tends to degrade quickly with constant watering and drying out.

Fiber hanging baskets are made from compressed fiber shaped into a bowl. These are strong enough to last a season, or can be used as liners.

Basket liners

Moss is a traditional liner, but there are other materials that are just as effective and easier to find (*see box, right*). Biodegradable liners include those made from cardboard and coconut fiber. Foam- or plastic-sheet liners are generally concealed by straw or home-harvested moss, sandwiched between them and the basket mesh.

Hanging & fixing

Baskets come with a chain or rope, but you can buy spring-loaded suspension devices, which enable you to raise and lower the basket for maintenance. Always make sure you have a strong metal bracket, securely screwed into a solid structure. Window boxes need to be fixed securely; placing a batten behind them to maintain an air gap between them and the wall is also a good idea.

BASKET LINERS

Foam-plastic liner

Cardboard disk liner

Compressed-fiber liner

Holes for planting through the liner can be made with an apple corer or knife. Coconut fiber can be hard to cut, while foam is easier and cardboard liners often have precut holes.

MAKING A WOODEN HANGING BASKET

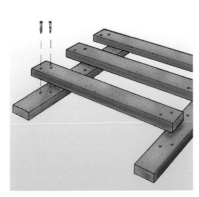

1 **Make the base** by screwing several slats to 2 outer ones, using pieces of at least ¾in. width and depth. Use 2 screws at each end for rigidity. Brass or decking screws will last longest. Drill pilot holes to prevent splitting.

2 **Drill a hole** in each end of the 2 outer slats. This should be large enough to fit a galvanized wire about ½in. thick (14 gauge), which will run through the basket corners.

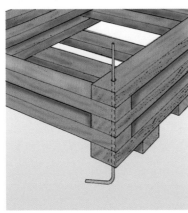

3 **Thread a wire** through each corner, bending it over the bottom end, and build up the basket with slats in alternating directions, each drilled to fit over the wire. Too shallow a basket will dry out quickly, but too deep a basket is heavy.

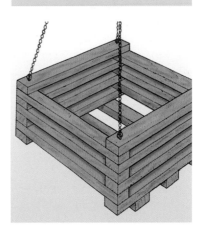

4 **Bend the wires** into loops at the top of the basket with pliers. Hang the basket on chains attached to the loops at each corner. This basket will need some kind of liner inside it; you can make holes for plants to grow out between the slats.

Improvised containers

When designing container displays, you can often come up with exciting and imaginative plant combinations. However, many good planting schemes are compromised by the style and shape of their containers, particularly if these are of inferior quality or design.

If you want to design your container displays with imagination and flair, there is nothing better than recycling a potential container that has the merits of being a little bit out of the ordinary. Aim to raise a smile with your ingenuity and imagination, and you can achieve some stunning displays.

If you open your eyes to new possibilities, practically anything can be used as a container. The important considerations are that there must be adequate drainage, and the container must provide sufficient space for the roots of plants to grow and develop in a healthy manner. You can also tailor your plant selection to suit your improvised container's shape and color.

Recycling smaller containers

There are many ceramic objects that can be used as containers, including construction materials of various kinds. Terra-cotta plant pots can even be stacked on top of

each other to make a strawberry planter (*see page 363*). Secure the pots together, using rebar or heavy-gauge wire through the drainage holes.

Wooden wine boxes, wicker baskets, or galvanized watering cans all present planting possibilities. Chicken wire can be shaped into a variety of sculptural forms for the yard; this technique can be adapted to make versatile containers.

An old wheelbarrow, the leakier the better, can make an attractive feature on the lawn if planted with trailing annuals. Look out for one at yard sales and, if it is not leaky enough, drill some extra drainage holes!

Creating larger containers

Old sinks have long been used as alpine troughs, sometimes with a coating to simulate stone, but defunct household goods can provide more modern styles as well. Garden centers today sell a variety of metal containers, but these are often expensive; consider using the stainless steel drum out of an old washing machine as a suitable container instead. With a little care and patience, the drum can be removed from the frame, and it has several advantages: plenty of holes mean there is always adequate

Many household food containers can be recycled for use in the garden, making colorful and unique planters for growing salad greens and herbs. Ensure good drainage by punching or drilling plenty of holes in the base of every container.

drainage, it has a good depth and width for planting, and being stainless steel it will not rust.

Recently, planting bags of strong, woven plastic have become popular, particularly for crops. Similar in construction but more generous in size are the disposable bags used by builder's suppliers to deliver materials such as sand. They are incredibly tough and durable and can be recycled into large containers that look good and are simple to construct (*see below*).

The important thing with all improvised containers is only to pursue ideas that will fit well into your garden setting, so use those that match the materials already in your house or landscape. Containers that suit a neighbor's yard might look out of place in yours.

CONSTRUCTING A FRAME FOR A PLANTING BAG

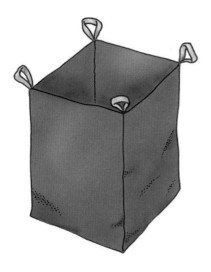

1 **Measure your bag** to work out the dimensions. You can fold in the tops and sides to smaller dimensions if you prefer. With a knife, make slits for drainage at the bottom.

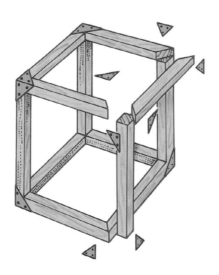

2 **Make a simple crate** to the dimensions of your bag, perhaps from scrap lumber such as wooden pallets. Triangular metal plates provide strength and stability at the corners.

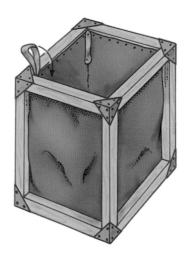

3 **Position the bag** inside the crate and attach it with nails or staples around the top. Remove or fold down the handles.

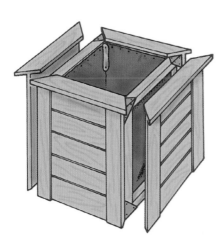

4 **Design facing panels** to your own taste. You can use wood, metal sheets, woven willow, or plastic. Interchangeable panels can give your planter a versatile appearance.

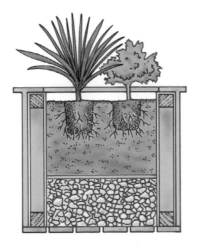

5 **Fill your planter** to one third of its depth with lightweight drainage material, such as expanded polystyrene. Lay landscape fabric over this, top up with potting soil, and plant.

AN ALTERNATIVE FRAME

The flexibility of planting-bag fabric means it can be used to line structures of almost any shape, such as this one.

Raised beds

Versatile raised planters in keeping with the style of your home and yard can be built from wood or brick, and are ideal for growing crops. You can adapt the size of the beds, to fit your yard and growing needs, and the height, to allow easy access. They are easy to protect with row covers and cold frames, and are a good way to encourage children to grow vegetables on a small scale. Always use a good-quality soil to fill the bed, and if your planter is on paving you will need to provide drainage holes.

Wooden beds

Always use rot-resistant lumber or lumber treated with a safe preservative, to prevent deterioration and insect damage. Colored stains can be used to improve the look of the lumber. Railroad ties not only ooze tar in hot weather but can also harbor ants after a few years.

Brick planters

As these require more preparation, they must be carefully sized and sited. It is important to get the height of the bed right to allow for easy maintenance; about 3ft. is adequate in most gardens. For drainage, make a number of weep holes in the bottom course of bricks, about 3ft. apart, and add rubble to the base (*see box, top right*).

Raised bed kits

There are a number of flexible and versatile kits for building beds to size. Some consist of plastic units, often recycled, others of precut and treated wooden blocks; they are either slotted together or secured with stakes.

Prominently placed beds form part of the garden landscape, and they need to be thoughtfully integrated so they don't look out of place.

A BRICK RAISED BED

Key
❶ Copestone on walls to protect brickwork
❷ Soil-based mix or good garden topsoil
❸ Old grass sods laid upside down, or permeable membrane
❹ Stones for drainage

When planning the height of a brick raised bed, keep in mind that it is well worth part-filling it with broken bricks or stones to aid drainage, so you should allow for some extra depth.

JOINING BOARDS OR RAILROAD TIES

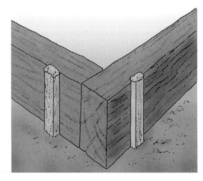

Heavy-duty stakes driven into the ground at the corners of a bed can hold the wooden boards together. Short tree stakes are ideal for this purpose.

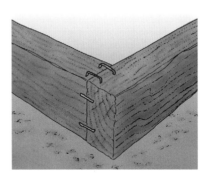

Large staples can be hammered into the corners, instead of using stakes. Alternatively, you can use large screws. Beds will be most durable if built from wooden boards at least 2in. thick.

Growing ornamentals *see page 70* | **Growing vegetables & herbs** *see page 148* | **Aftercare & maintenance** *see page 364*

PLANTING

Always buy the best plants you can afford: it is better to have a few well-grown plants than an array of sad-looking specimens. When making your selection, be aware of not only the color but also the texture and height of the plants, choosing those that will contrast or complement each other and the container you have in mind. Once you have bought your plants, give them the best possible chance of creating a successful and long-lasting display. Plant them in a suitable soil or mix, incorporating any additional ingredients necessary to improve either drainage or water retention.

Preparing for planting

When selecting plants for container displays, visit your local garden center or nursery to see what is on sale. Take a basket or cart and see what captures your eye. Start with an open mind, and if you favor a particular color scheme assemble a group of plants based on this. Select your favorite plants from the group and return the rest to their stands. Beware of plants that are discounted, as there may be something wrong with them.

When choosing plants, be aware of texture and height, and if they are to share a pot consider whether they have compatible needs. Check that they look healthy, with no signs of disease or damage. It is always worth carefully lifting a plant out of its pot or growing flat and checking that the plant is not rootbound and the root system is healthy. You are looking for strong, white roots that have penetrated through the potting soil and hold it together.

Schemes with bulbs need to be planned well in advance, using the pages of a catalog as a guide rather than the plants themselves. Many suppliers now sell combinations of bulbs to make planning easy.

Color comes first in almost any display because it is the first thing we notice. But do not neglect the shapes and textures of plants, because these are what draw the eye back a second or third time.

Potting soils

You can purchase premixed potting soil or make your own. If you plan to use soil from your garden, it will need to be pasteurized by heating it to 180°F and maintaining that temperature for 30 minutes. This will kill most diseases, insects, and weeds that may be present. Other components you might include in your home-made mix are compost, leaf mold, perlite, vermiculite, and coconut coir.

There are many named brands of premixed potting soil; some are available all over the country, and some are seen only regionally or locally. Unless you are planning to use great quantities of soil, it is usually most economical and convenient to purchase a good-quality bagged mix.

Many brands are now respecting the environment by reducing the peat moss content, adding coconut fiber or other materials in its place. Another invaluable innovation is the addition of water-retaining crystals, to reduce the need for watering, and a wetting agent to allow water to soak in quickly if the soil is allowed to dry out.

There are also potting soils specially formulated for individual groups of plants. These include acid-lovers, citrus, cacti and succulents, palms, and orchids.

Useful additives

Water is vital for flourishing containers. Water-retaining crystals that expand to hold water and slowly return it to the potting soil can be incorporated into your mix, if they are not already included in it.

You can reduce the weight of a container by half filling it with perlite. These lightweight crystals are pH neutral, well drained, and used in the nursery industry as a lighter alternative to grit for blending well-drained soils.

MOVING CONTAINERS

Moving large pots can be risky, for both the pots and the toes or back of the person moving them. If you have pots you move regularly, invest in either a cart or a platform on casters to make the job easier and safer.

Moving heavy pots is a job for 2 people. A hand truck makes the chore much easier. It is particularly useful in fall if you need to move several large containers of tender, tropical plants indoors for the winter.

PROVIDING DRAINAGE IN CONTAINERS

Drill drainage holes in the base of any container that lacks them. Turn the container over and drill 2–3 holes—each with a minimum diameter of ½in.—in the base.

Fill the base of the container with broken pot pieces or large chunks of packing foam. This prevents water-logging because water collects in the drainage material instead of the potting soil if the flow out of the holes is slow.

PLANTING CONTAINERS

Growing ornamentals *see page 70* | **Growing vegetables & herbs** *see page 148* | **Aftercare & maintenance** *see page 364*

Planting containers

Containers are like stage sets for plants—with careful planning and planting, you can create spectacle, drama, and intrigue. Group your plants together on the floor, still in their individual pots, before you go ahead and plant them. This gives you the chance to move them around and decide which arrangement works the best.

You often see containers planted with a mix of plant types, and this is an excellent way of extending the season and display. However, in too many cases you will see a large plant, perhaps a shrub or a tree, planted in the center of the container with smaller plants grouped around it. This is a safe and reliable arrangement, but can become dull, and there are more dynamic approaches for those willing to experiment.

In a successful stage set, painting, or photograph, the main feature is often offset, so try placing the largest plant in your display away from the center of your container. Then mix plants with varying heights around the largest plant, rather than following a simple gradation from the tallest down to the shortest around the container edge.

By using this approach, you will achieve a better visual result, particularly when you are grouping a number of containers together informally.

How to plant

Before planting, water the plants and leave them to drain. Ease them out of their pots or boxes and carefully tease away some of the soil from around the neck of each plant. This is useful because the area around the neck may contain weed seeds or surplus soil that is best removed at this stage. If you have limited space in your container, you may want to tease away some of the soil from around the roots of each plant as well, and gently compress the rootballs to allow easier planting.

Once the plant is in the soil, make sure you fill in any gaps remaining around the plants and firm in gently. If the container is relatively light, you can tap it firmly on a hard surface, which will help settle the soil down. A good soak from a watering can fitted with a waterbreaker will also help to eliminate any air pockets.

PLANTING FROM POTS OR BOXES

1 **Water the plant well** then remove it from its pot by turning it upside down with your fingers spread to either side of the plant stem, and tapping the base of the pot firmly. Small plants in cell packs can be pushed out from below with a pencil.

2 **Dig a hole** in the soil large enough for the rootball, and place the plant in it. For ease of working, start with the plants at the center of the container and work outward to the edge.

3 **Firm the soil** around the plant to eliminate air pockets. You can do this with the end of the trowel handle, or you may prefer using your fingers. It is important not to overcompact the soil.

4 **Plant the rest** of the container in the same way, finishing with the plants at the edge. Level the surface of the soil and then give the container a thorough soaking.

Planting hanging baskets

Hanging baskets can be bought planted and in flower, but for a display that fits best into its surroundings and matches your own tastes it pays to choose the plants and plant the basket yourself.

Good basket displays tend to be the ones where you cannot see the basket's wire or plastic structure, so with that in mind allow for plenty of plant material. Select young plants based on color, texture, and trailing habit. Most baskets are hung at or above eye level, so plants that have a tendency to trail are ideal. Choose a basket that suits your location and the plants you are intending to grow, and allow for good-sized planting holes that will help to minimize damage to plants when potting up.

How to plant

Most baskets have rounded bottoms, so use a large pot to stand the basket in while filling it. This will provide a supportive base from which to work.

Line your basket with your preferred liner (*see page 349*) and part-fill with soil (*see page 354*). A mix specially formulated for hanging baskets is ideal. At this stage you may want to add some water-retaining crystals to the soil; these are particularly useful for hanging baskets, which contain many plants in a small amount of soil.

Insert your young plants through the slots of the basket, remembering to handle them carefully. Cup the stems or foliage with your fingers or wrap them in paper to avoid damage. Gradually work your way around the the basket, placing young plants in the planting slots at intervals, then firming in additional soil. If using loose lining material, infill with more between each plant's collar and the inside of the basket.

Once you have reached the top of the basket, add a little more soil if necessary and finish planting the top. Dust off any soil that has fallen on the plants and give the basket a thorough watering.

PLANTING A HANGING BASKET USING A MOSS LINING

1 Line the basket to one third of the way up with damp moss or a synthetic liner. Over the liner, it is worth placing a piece of plastic sheet or a shallow dish in the base of the basket, to help retain water, before filling it with soil.

2 Insert the plants that are to trail from the basket. It may be easier to put each rootball through the hole from the outside, or the foliage through from the inside. If the latter, it is often worth wrapping the leaves in paper to protect them. Continue around the basket sides.

3 Fill the basket with soil to about 1in. below the rim. This small gap will prevent the basket from overflowing when it is watered. Plant the top of the basket, using your fingers to make holes without damaging the roots of the plants below. If necessary, pack the rim with more lining material.

4 Water in well, using a watering can with a fine rose to avoid disturbing the potting soil. Some liners will absorb water, so allow for this by leaving the basket to stand and then watering it again, to ensure that the soil is thoroughly moist throughout.

Growing ornamentals *see page 70* | **Aftercare & maintenance** *see page 364* | **Propagating plants** *see page 392*

Annuals

Garden centers often begin to offer annuals early in the growing season. It is rarely wise to buy these plants when they first appear in the stores, and it always pays to check carefully for frost damage to the shoot tips and the edges of the leaves before purchasing. If you are fortunate enough to have a sunroom, however, you can buy early, plant your containers, and keep them safe from late frosts. They can then be moved into their final position, after the last frost in your area. In areas with frost-free winters, of course, annuals may flower for an extended period.

Annuals grown from seed provide vibrant displays of color, mainly for summer display. There are a number of seed companies that supply a wide range of varieties of the plants listed below, and new varieties are constantly being introduced. It is worth checking through seed catalogs or suppliers' websites to see what varieties are being offered. Once you've selected, you can order the seed or plants online or look for them at local suppliers.

Petunias provide season-long color in a variety of shades. Trailing types are particularly well suited to hanging baskets.

Some types of begonia are grown as annuals, although they are actually perennials. They cost a little more, but make showy plants.

ANNUALS SUITABLE FOR CONTAINERS

- Ageratum
- Alyssum
- Amaranthus
- Angelonia
- Antirrhinum
- Argyranthemum
- Basil (ornamental)
- Begonia (shown)
- Bidens
- Brachyscome
- Briza maxima
- Calendula
- Calibrachoa
- Celosia
- Chrysanthemum
- Cineraria
- Cleome
- Cobaea scandens (vine)
- Coleus (shown)
- Colocasia
- Coreopsis
- Cosmos
- Dahlia
- Dianthus
- Diascia
- Eccremocarpus (vine)
- Evolvulus
- Fuchsia
- Heliotropium
- Impatiens
- Isotoma
- Kale (ornamental)
- Lantana
- Lathyrus (vine)
- Lobelia
- Marigold *(Tagetes)*
- Mimulus
- Morning glory (vine)
- Musa
- Nasturtium (trailer/vine)
- Nemesia
- Nicotiana
- Ornamental sweet potato
- Pansy *(Viola)*
- Pelargonium
- Pennisetum
- Petunia (shown)
- Portulaca
- Rudbeckia
- Salvia
- Sanvitalia
- Scaevola
- Thunbergia (vine)
- Tithonia
- Torenia
- Verbena

The foliage of coleus can adds lots of color to a container planting. Many varieties can be grown in either full sun or part shade.

357

Bulbs & corms

Bulbs are a fabulous addition to any container for spring display, providing exuberant color at a time of year when it is most welcome in the garden. Perennials are limited during winter, so in many areas bulbs make an excellent alternative. Once a display is past, lift the bulbs and plant them in the yard for next year.

Containers can be planted in layers to provide flowers in succession. By using different types of bulbs you can have flowers from midwinter (in some areas) through late spring from the same container. For example, plant a layer of lilies at the bottom followed by tulips and finally a top layer of anemones and crocuses; they should be layered according to the depth they need to be planted (*see box, below*), rather than the order in which they flower.

Buying & keeping bulbs

Always buy from a reputable source: most garden centers carry a good range of bulbs from early fall. Check for firm bulbs with no signs of rot. Most bulbs remain in the soil year after year where they gradually increase.

Lilies are ideal bulbs for containers. When in flower, they can be placed on show, then moved away once they fade until next year.

BULBS SUITABLE FOR CONTAINERS

Spring displays
- *Anemone*
- *Crocus*
- *Cyclamen coum*
- Daffodil (*Narcissus*)
- *Erythronium*
- Grape hyacinth (*Muscari*)
- Hyacinth (*Hyacinthus*)
- *Leucojum*
- *Ornithogalum*
- *Puschkinia*
- *Scilla*
- Snowdrop (*Galanthus*)
- Tulip (*Tulipa*)
- Winter aconite (*Eranthis hyemalis*)

Summer displays
- *Achimenes*
- *Allium*
- *Begonia*
- *Caladium*
- *Crocosmia*
- *Dahlia*
- *Fritillaria*
- *Gladiolus*
- Lily (*Lilium*)
- *Polianthes*

Fall displays
- Autumn crocus (*Colchicum*)
- *Cyclamen hederifolium*
- *Sternbergia*

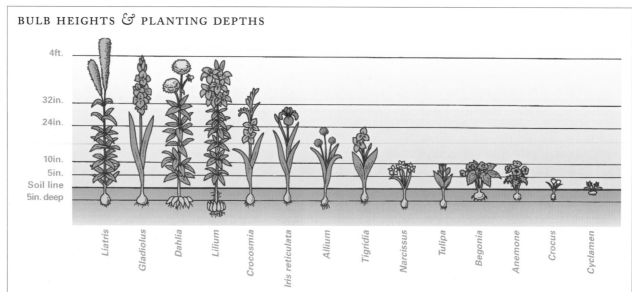

BULB HEIGHTS & PLANTING DEPTHS

4ft.
32in.
24in.
10in.
5in.
Soil line
5in. deep

Liatris — *Gladiolus* — *Dahlia* — *Lilium* — *Crocosmia* — *Iris reticulata* — *Allium* — *Tigridia* — *Narcissus* — *Tulipa* — *Begonia* — *Anemone* — *Crocus* — *Cyclamen*

As a rule of thumb, plant bulbs 3 times their own depth, so smaller bulbs are planted shallowly, while larger bulbs with greater reserves of energy are planted more deeply. You need not be too precise, however; bulbs can use their roots to 'fine tune' their position by pushing the bulb up or pulling it down if it is planted at roughly the correct depth. Position the bulbs close to each other but make sure that they do not touch each other or the sides of the container, because this contact could encourage rotting.

PERENNIAL PLANTS

Herbaceous perennials & ornamental grasses *see page 83* | **Bulbous plants** *see page 91* | **Aftercare & maintenance** *see page 364*

Perennial plants

Perennials work particularly well in both containers and raised beds, either mixed with other types of plants, such as trees or shrubs, or as a perennial-only display. Once they outgrow their space, many are easily refreshed by division (*see page 87*). Buy small plants in pots; they bulk up quickly, especially if they receive plenty of fertilizer and water. New or slightly tender plants may need some cover early in the year (*see page 382*).

Tender perennials thrive in summer but are killed in winter in cold climates. On the other hand, some perennials happy in areas with cool summers may not tolerate hot and humid summers elsewhere. For advice, consult your local cooperative extension service.

Grasses

In recent years, grasses have become a popular choice for containers. They are exceptionally versatile, combining well with all types of plants, and add an air of naturalistic beauty to a display. Grasses provide both movement and a transparent quality that enhances companion plants.

Geraniums can give long-lasting color in summer, and their low, spreading habit means that they can be planted among taller plants.

Easy to grow coreopsis perform well in a sunny site. Their brightly colored flowers appear from late spring through summer in most areas.

PERENNIALS SUITABLE FOR CONTAINERS

- Achillea
- Acanthus
- Agapanthus
- Alchemilla mollis
- Alocasia
- Aster
- Astrantia
- Bleeding heart (*Dicentra*)
- Cacti and succulents
- Caladium
- Campanula
- Canna
- Catmint (*Nepeta*)
- Colocasia
- Coreopsis
- Cosmos atrosanguineus
- Daylily (*Hemerocallis*)
- Echinacea
- Echinops
- Eryngium
- Euphorbia polychroma
- Gaura lindheimeri
- Geranium (shown)
- Geum
- Hedychium
- Hellebore (*Helleborus*)
- Helenium
- Heuchera
- Hosta
- Knautia macedonica
- Kniphofia
- Melianthus major
- Musa
- Orchids

- Persicaria
- Phlox
- Pink (*Dianthus*)
- Primula
- Rudbeckia fulgida var. fulgida
- Salvia
- Sedum
- Sisyrinchium striatum
- Strelitzia
- Zantedeschia

Grasses & grassy plants
- Acorus
- Calamagrostis brachytricha
- Carex
- Chionochloa rubra
- Deschampsia
- Elymus magellanicus
- Eragrostis airoides
- Festuca
- Hakonechloa macra
- Hordeum jubatum
- Juncus 'Curly-wurly'
- Luzula nivea
- Miscanthus
- Molinia
- Muhly grass (*Muhlenbergia*)
- Ophiopogon planiscapus 'Nigrescens'
- Panicum
- Pennisetum
- Phormium
- Stipa
- Uncinia uncinata

Trees, shrubs, & vines

Small trees, shrubs, and vines can be planted to give height and structure to a container display. When purchasing trees and shrubs for containers, keep in mind where their final planting position will be, because trees and shrubs will inevitably outgrow the largest pot over time and need moving to the open ground.

Planting

Container-grown trees and shrubs can be planted at most times of the year, but early fall or late winter is generally best. Select a large pot with a suitable diameter to accommodate the rootball of the plant and allow a 3–4in. gap between the plant and the pot.

Place a good layer of drainage material in the base of the pot and fill with potting soil. Ensure that the rootball of the plant is thoroughly soaked by immersing it in a bucket of water for half an hour. Plant and firm soil well. Once planted, give the container a good watering to settle the plant and the soil.

Until the plant develops roots, some support may be required. Use a sturdy stake with an attractive finish because it will be very visible in a container. A short stake encourages the tree to develop a stronger stem and root system by allowing the upper part to move with the prevailing wind.

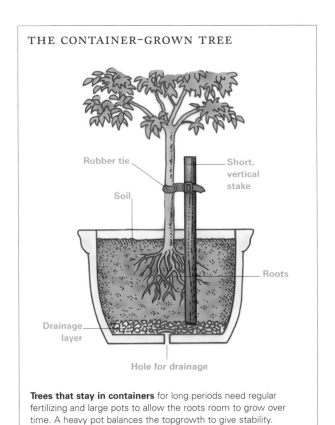

THE CONTAINER-GROWN TREE

Rubber tie

Short, vertical stake

Soil

Roots

Drainage layer

Hole for drainage

Trees that stay in containers for long periods need regular fertilizing and large pots to allow the roots room to grow over time. A heavy pot balances the topgrowth to give stability.

Some container displays rely solely on foliage effects to make an impression. Potted boxwood topiary is a popular element of formal gardens, often repeated regularly along a path or around a space.

The exuberant display of a rhododendron in flower will last only a few weeks. The advantage of growing in containers is that when the flowers fade, the shrub can be moved out of a prime position.

TREES, SHRUBS, *&* VINES
SUITABLE FOR CONTAINERS

- *Aucuba*
- Bay (*Laurus*)
- *Bougainvillea*
- Boxwood (*Buxus*, shown)
- *Brugmansia*
- *Camellia*
- *Caryopteris*
- *Ceratostigma*
- *Chaenomeles*
- *Chamaecyparis*
- *Chamaerops humilis* (palm)
- *Choisya*
- *Cistus*
- *Clematis* (vine, shown)
- *Clerodendron*
- *Cordyline*
- *Cotoneaster*
- *Cycas*
- Dogwood (*Cornus*)
- *Elaeagnus*
- *Erica*
- *Euonymus*
- *Fatsia*
- x *Fatshedera lizei*
- *Fothergilla gardenii*
- *Hibiscus*
- Holly (*Ilex*)
- *Hydrangea macrophylla*
- *Hypericum*
- Jasmine (*Jasminum*, vine)
- Juniper (*Juniperus*)
- Ivy (*Hedera*, vine)
- *Lagerstroemia*
- *Lantana*
- Lavender (*Lavandula*, shown)
- *Loropetalum*
- *Magnolia stellata*
- Maple (*Acer*)
- Myrtle (*Myrtus*)
- *Nandina*
- Oleander (*Nerium oleander*)
- Olive (*Olea*, shown)
- *Osmanthus*
- *Photinia*
- *Pittosporum*
- *Potentilla fruticosa*
- *Rhododendron* (shown)
- Rose (*Rosa*)
- *Santolina*
- *Sarcococca*
- *Skimmia*
- *Trachycarpus* (palm)
- *Trachelospermum* (vine)
- *Vaccinium*
- Willow (*Salix*)
- Yew (*Taxus*)
- *Yucca*

Some Mediterranean trees are particularly suitable for growing in containers. Olives do well in a well-drained soil mix, and can be moved or protected if heavy frosts threaten.

Many lavenders are hardy, but some of the most fragrant types will not survive a cold winter in the ground. These Mediterranean shrubs take well to pots, and can be moved indoors for winter.

Patio areas often leave no planting space. The solution here is to grow bold plants in large pots, for example trees or shrubs, or vines on tall, strong supports, such as this clematis on an obelisk.

Vegetables & herbs

Vegetables and herbs both make ideal container plants, particularly if they are planted in pots near a door, where they can be picked fresh, ready for immediate use. You can plant a pot with a selection of salad crops or three or four herbs that you use on a regular basis. This type of container gardening is a great way of encouraging children to grow and eat fresh produce.

Vegetables and herbs can be bought as young plants or they can be raised from seed by sowing them directly into pots. This provides an ideal opportunity to grow successional crops for harvesting as you need them.

Planting

Select a large container with a good depth, ideally no less than 18in. Fill with a potting soil that has been mixed with well-rotted organic matter or bagged garden soil to help retain moisture. Most herbs prefer shallower containers with less rich but good drainage (*see page 216*).

VEGETABLES & HERBS SUITABLE FOR CONTAINERS

Vegetables	Herbs
• Beans	• Basil
• Cucumbers	• Chamomile
• Eggplant	• Chives
• Kohlrabi (shown)	• Cilantro
• Lettuce	• Fennel
• Onions and shallots	• Marjoram
• Peppers	• Mint
• Radish	• Parsley
• Swiss chard	• Rosemary
• Squash	• Sage
• Tomatoes (shown)	• Tarragon
• Zucchini (shown)	• Thyme

The swollen stem of kohlrabi grows above the soil and is harvested when young and tender. Purple varieties are particularly ornamental, and all types grow well in raised beds.

Tomatoes are well suited to growing in containers, raised from seed or young plants every year. An underplanting of basil makes a perfect aromatic and culinary combination.

Highly productive zucchini grow quickly and need to be checked and harvested daily to be enjoyed at their peak. Containers in a sunny spot near the kitchen are therefore an ideal place to grow them.

FRUIT

Growing vegetables & herbs *see page 148* | **Growing fruit** *see page 226* | **Choosing containers** *see page 346*

Fruit

Fruit plants can be included in any ornamental container display; they tend to be long-lived so require more care and attention from one year to another. Consider what types of containers will best suit what you want to grow. Trees need large containers that hold enough soil to act as a buffer in dry conditions—particularly important when fruit is swelling and ripening. Strawberry pots look decorative and are space-saving; hanging baskets planted with three strawberry plants per basket are also a possibility. You will need to turn the pots and baskets from time to time to ensure even ripening.

You can create a Mediterranean look in your garden by planting figs and citrus trees in pots. Figs prefer to have their roots constricted, so they can be planted in relatively small containers. This helps to reduce vigorous foliage and promote fruiting.

Apples in tubs are a popular choice. Choose a large container, and select two-year-old trees that have been grafted onto dwarfing rootstocks such as M27 or M9 (*see page 249*). To ensure good pollination (*see page 247*), grow several compatible varieties and in separate pots, or grow a family tree where three or four compatible varieties are grafted onto the same rootstock. In cold areas, the roots of fruit trees in containers may need protection from severe winter frost; move them into the garage or porch.

Strawberries in pots are easy to care for as the delicate fruit are raised off the ground. There are several container stacking systems on the market, but terra-cotta pots stacked in decreasing sizes work well.

Blueberries need acid soil (*see page 33*), so in many gardens growing them in containers filled with acidic-soil mix is the only option. Grow a few varieties for the best pollination and fruiting.

FRUIT SUITABLE FOR CONTAINERS

- Apples
- Blueberries (shown)
- Cherries
- Citrus (shown)
- Figs
- Peaches
- Pomegranates
- Strawberries (shown)

All citrus fruit prefer their soil warm, moist, and well drained, making terra-cotta the perfect container material for them. Constriction keeps the plants compact—essential if you need to overwinter them indoors.

AFTERCARE
& MAINTENANCE

Unlike plants in the open ground, plants in containers are entirely dependent on you to fulfill their needs. No water can seep from surrounding soil to refresh them or bring additional supplies of nutrients, and little rain will fall on the small surface area of their soil. Their roots are far more constricted than those of plants in the ground, so their needs are even more urgent. Above the ground, they may have no neighboring plants to shelter and support their growth. There are various types of equipment available that can help with maintenance, but regular attention is the most important aspect of plant care.

Watering & fertilizing

An established basket or container may need to be watered at least twice a day during hot weather. Drip irrigation systems allow water to be trickled to each container without waste. It is worth investing in a timer device to automate your watering system, particularly during periods of absence for vacations.

Hanging baskets are particularly vulnerable to drying out, because they are usually packed with plants, and water can evaporate from the sides as well as the top. A long-handled wand with a curved tip allows easy watering, as will a rise-and-fall device (*see box, facing page*).

While it is important to ensure that pots and tubs stay damp, it is also vital to ensure that they do not become waterlogged. Containers should never be stood directly on the ground—always raise them up slightly using 'pot feet' (attractive, purpose-made, ceramic blocks) or small blocks of wood. This allows water to drain away through the drainage holes and not become trapped in the pot.

As always with irrigation, avoid watering during the hottest part of the day, when much of the water will simply evaporate. Instead, water in early morning or evening when conditions are cooler.

WATERING HANGING BASKETS

Use a hose on a low flow rate for baskets you can reach; high flows will displace soil.

An extension or wand is almost essential for high baskets unless you use a ladder.

A watering can with a long spout is an option, but it is heavy and time-consuming.

Fertilizing

The nutrients in most potting mixes will last only a limited time after initial planting. After this the plants need fertilizing regularly, depending on their needs. Fertilizer products for container plants range from slow-release pellets, which you push into the mix, to liquid fertilizers that are applied when you water and come in a variety of formulations to suit the plants that you are growing. Liquid fertilizers can be applied through a diluter connected to a hose or faucet, which dilutes granular or liquid fertilizer at a set ratio; alternatively, use a watering can and mix according to instructions.

As a general rule, if a fertilizer contains a higher proportion of nitrogen it will be beneficial for plant foliage growth, and if it has a high-phosphorus content it will be beneficial to flower production (*see page 35*).

RISE-&-FALL BASKET FIXING

A special pulley mechanism allows a basket to be pulled from a high position to a low one for watering or maintenance. A gentle push on the base of the basket returns it to the high position.

Staking & supports

Many plants grown in containers require some form of staking to help provide them with support. There are a number of products on the market, many of which make handsome additions to your container display in their own right. These include woven willow tepees, wooden or metal obelisks, or modern spiral stakes (*see below*). If you want to make your own supports, you can use bamboo canes, plastic-covered wire stakes, galvanized mesh, plastic netting, twiggy sticks, or heavy stakes for trees.

All supports need to be installed at planting time or while the plants are young as this allows the plants to grow over and through the support, disguising it. By

summer, this will lead to the impression that no staking is in place. If you are using twiggy sticks, they are best collected from deciduous trees like birch in late winter when they are without leaves, and so are ready to use when you plant your containers in spring.

Vines that are to be grown in containers for many years can be placed against a wall or fence and supported on training wires, as can wall shrubs and restricted fruit trees (such as cordons and espaliers). Woody plants will need a robust support. Consider the growth habit and pruning needs when choosing plants as this will affect the type of support you choose.

METHODS OF SUPPORT

Cane tripods are simple, but beware of sharp cane ends.

Twiggy sticks blend in quickly. Push them in and trim neatly.

Netting cylinders held by canes provide sturdy support.

Modern supports include spiral stakes made of metal.

Wind & frost protection

Container displays can be prone to wind and frost damage because they often lack the shelter of surrounding trees and shrubs. In late fall, move containers on exposed patios to a sheltered spot next to a wall or hedge, positioned so that the container will benefit from winter sunshine. Alternatively if you have a porch, sunroom, greenhouse, or even just a shed or garage with windows, move containers under cover.

Protect your plants

Heavy and cumbersome containers, and plants in raised beds, cannot be moved, so it will be necessary to protect them from frost individually where they are growing. This can be done by wrapping plants with row cover material, straw, or burlap sacking (*see page 16 and below*).

Tree ferns need to have their crowns protected from both wind and frost, but their trunks can remain exposed. Wrap the top section of the plant with row cover material, covering the fronds and protecting the crown; row cover bags make this easy work as they simply need to be slipped over the top of the plant.

Soil in smaller containers may freeze entirely if they are left outdoors over winter, killing the plant roots and ultimately the entire plant. If such plants cannot be moved under cover, keep them away from frost pockets and wrap the containers with burlap or bubble wrap.

Protect your pots

It is easy to forget the containers themselves, but if you have unglazed terra-cotta pots or other containers that are not frostproof lift them off the floor and support them on pot feet or something similar. Wrap containers in burlap, bubble wrap, or row cover material. If they are empty, move them into a shed to keep them dry—moving them into a protected place is always the best option. You can save yourself a lot of expense by siting pots carefully.

Overwintering container gardens indoors

If you live in a cool climate and you want to keep your tender perennials, trees, or shrubs for the following year, you will probably need to bring them indoors for winter. This should be done when night temperatures begin to drop to 50°F. A greenhouse or sunroom are ideal, but a room that receives abundant natural light is often satisfactory. Plan ahead so that you have adequate space in a location that will suit your plants, and clean your windows to maximize light.

Before you bring your plants indoors, inspect them carefully for pests. Soak pots in warm water for about 15 minutes to dislodge soil pests. If a pesticide is necessary, apply it while the plant is still outdoors. Often, a good spray of water from the hose can dislodge insect pests. Prune plants if necessary.

Large containers often require two people and are easiest to move with a hand truck (*see page 354*). Once indoors, your plants will probably go through an adjustment period while they adapt to their new environment. They may drop leaves, but new ones will usually replace them.

Since the plants are likely to receive less light than when outdoors, cut back on the frequency of watering. Plants grown indoors commonly suffer from low humidity; grouping several containers together often helps increase the humidity in their immediate vicinity.

WIND & FROST PROTECTION

Wrap row cover fabric or burlap around free-standing plants. Push four canes into the edge of the container and secure the wrapping around these. Plastic sheeting gives less protection and can cause condensation and encourage mold.

Form a cage of plastic mesh or galvanized wire netting around the plant and stuff it with straw. This method can be used quite easily to protect plants that are growing against a wall, making them difficult to wrap.

Transplanting & replanting

Fall is a good time to make changes to long-term displays and start thinking about the following year. Many plants benefit from being removed from their containers and transplanted into something larger (*see below*). By spring they will be healthy and ready to be planted into the garden for new or existing displays.

Refreshing displays

Once a container display has passed its peak, it is tempting to pull out the plants and replant into the same soil to save money, but the old soil will be spent and may also be harboring pests and diseases that could be harmful to a new planting. It is far wiser to remove the old soil from the container and start afresh, to give the new plants the best possible start.

After a time, you may have to repot existing trees and shrubs in order to reinvigorate the display. This is not always the easiest of tasks due to the weight and size of such container-grown plants. The best technique is to roll the container onto its side and get some help. Once the plant is out of its pot, use a garden fork to tease away the old soil and free up the root system. If you are potting into the same container, or one of a similar size, remove some of the outer roots with pruners to provide space for the new soil. Place the plant back in the pot and firm in fresh soil around the sides. Finish off by giving the plant a thorough watering.

KEEPING PLANTS TIDY

Cut back overlong stems that spoil the shape of a plant or threaten to get out of control. This also encourages sturdy, bushy growth. Use a pocket knife, sharp scissors, or pruners.

Remove dead flowers or dying leaves as soon as seen. This not only improves the general appearance of the plant but is also good hygiene, and the practice—known as 'deadheading'—often stimulates production of fresh flowers.

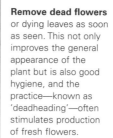

If you have a large container with long-term planting that is difficult to move and replant, it may be worth topdressing it with fresh soil to add nutrients. To do this, remove the top layer of existing soil from the pot, using a hand fork to loosen it. Then apply a fresh layer of new potting soil.

TRANSPLANTING

1 **Water the plant** thoroughly and leave it to drain before removing it from the container.

2 **Choose a container** 2 sizes larger than the one the plant is currently in. Turn the plant upside down and tap it from its container.

3 **Place the rootball** in the new container. Trickle fresh soil into the space around the sides. Firm with your fingers and water in.

CHAPTER NINE

GREENHOUSE GARDENING

THE PROTECTION OFFERED BY A GREENHOUSE, even one that is unheated, allows you to extend the cropping season for many vegetables, whether you grow them to maturity under glass or whether you start plants from seed, then transplant them into the kitchen garden when outdoor temperatures allow it. A greenhouse also offers a place to raise plants from cuttings or by other propagation methods, for the ornamental or edible garden. Growing under glass allows you to cultivate a wide range of tender plants that would not normally thrive in the open in cooler zones, such as late-summer and winter bulbs, tender shrubby perennials such as fuchsias, and shrubs such as acacias or angel's trumpet (*Brugmansia*). You can also use a greenhouse to cultivate your passion for specialty plants with exacting cultural needs, such as orchids, cacti, bromeliads, or alpines. Finally, as you bring your tender potted citrus or bougainvillea into the greenhouse for overwintering, you will see how quickly you have come to rely on it; for each month of the year, a greenhouse has its uses.

Building your greenhouse

Investing in a greenhouse can be a rewarding and profitable addition to any garden, large or small. There is an enormous range of greenhouses, hoop houses, and potting sheds to suit the type of plants you wish to grow—from simple wooden structures to climate-controlled sunrooms that extend the living space of your home. If you are a beginning gardener, a comfortable, sturdy structure that provides room for storage, propagation, and perhaps some hanging plants is usually sufficient.

Your first decision will be whether to choose an unheated or heated greenhouse. Both have their uses: even an unheated greenhouse will provide warmer temperatures year-round and may be all you need, if you wish only to get an early start on the growing season. The addition of a heating system will further expand the range of possibilities for plant cultivation. With a bit of thoughtful preparation and some basic understanding of plant needs, you can quickly learn the necessary techniques to propagate and grow plants.

Meeting plant needs in the greenhouse

Plants growing under protection depend on you to manage their environment. Consider both the kind of plants you wish to grow and the local climate conditions when selecting equipment such as irrigation, lighting, and humidification or dehumidification systems for the greenhouse.

Your approach to growing plants inside the greenhouse will be influenced by the outdoor environment: your local climate, weather conditions, and seasonal changes—all of these variations are greatly magnified indoors. Spring and fall often bring variable weather conditions; the greenhouse will require careful attention to ventilation so that plants are not stressed during unseasonably warm days or early and late frosts. Summer can be more predictable, but in very hot regions plants will require shading from the intensity of the sun, and the greenhouse may need additional humidity so that plants do not dry out. In the South, the opposite may be the case, calling for dehumidification and increased ventilation. Finally, when winter temperatures drop below expectations, you may need the assistance of extra heating or insulation.

Many of the climate-control functions in the greenhouse can be automated, including ventilation, shading, irrigation, heating, and humidification. Electronic control units that monitor temperatures and humidity can save you much labor and guesswork.

GREENHOUSES & EQUIPMENT

Many factors influence the size and style of greenhouse you should buy, as well as the type of equipment you are going to need. The primary consideration must be the needs of the plants, but affordability comes a close second, as well as the amount of space you have in your garden for a greenhouse. It is best to purchase the largest structure that will fit comfortably into your garden. You must also consider where it is going to be placed in order to make the most of the sun. Furthermore, you must think about your neighbors, any setback requirements, and access to power and water supplies.

Basic requirements

The key features to look out for are a well-built structure that is easily secured to a foundation, a glazing system that makes the structure as efficient as possible, and a sufficient number of vents and fans to control the flow of air through the structure (*see page 375*).

Headroom, shelving, and doorway space are also important. If you want to grow plants in the ground, the greenhouse should be fully glazed. Alternatives to a fully glazed greenhouse include a structure with wooden knee walls or even a potting shed with a glazed wall.

Greenhouse framing & glazing

A wooden-framed greenhouse needs to be quite bulky in order to provide structural strength, and it may require regular painting in order to preserve the wood. Rigid P.V.C. pipes work well for small greenhouses; flexible P.V.C. pipes can be used for simple hoop houses. Light-gauge aluminum or steel tube-framed greenhouses are widely available as kits that you can assemble yourself.

The traditional glazing material is glass, but rigid, transparent plastic or polycarbonate are common greenhouse materials. Polyethylene sheeting is suitable for covering P.V.C. greenhouses and hoop houses. Greenhouse suppliers sell U.V.-treated sheeting that resists sun degradation. It can also be used as a temporary glazing if a glass or polycarbonate panel is broken. Ask to compare the R value, or insulation factor, of any glazing material; a larger number represents greater insulation and therefore more efficient heating and cooling in the greenhouse.

TYPES OF GREENHOUSE

Aluminum, circular greenhouse

Small lean-to

Wooden-framed lean-to

Styles of greenhouse are diverse: free-standing types are the most common. Against sunny walls, lean-to structures benefit from residual heat stored in the wall during the day.

TYPES OF GREENHOUSE

Growing under glass *see page 379* | **Using cold frames & cloches** *see page 382* | **Propagating plants** *see page 392*

Types of greenhouse

The size and complexity of your greenhouse will depend on your needs, your budget, and the amount of space you have available. Hoop houses and cold frames make good alternatives to a full-sized greenhouse.

Kit greenhouses

Greenhouses built from kits are easy to erect and can be found to suit almost any budget, from simple P.V.C.-framed models to elaborate ones that resemble conservatories. You may order them through the mail or purchase one at a garden center or building supply store. Home and garden shows are good places to view options from different manufacturers.

Putting together a kit usually consists of preparing the site and foundation (*see page 374*), then bolting together the framing and fitting the glazing into channels in the framing. Most greenhouse kits can be assembled in a weekend or two and call for just a few basic tools. Construction options include building the structure yourself or hiring someone with a little construction savvy to lend a hand. Some building supply stores offer delivery and construction for a reasonable fee.

In general, get the largest greenhouse you can afford. Choose a model that offers not only sufficient floor space but also enough head room for whoever will be using the greenhouse. A kit should always include vents and a door; shelves and heating and cooling equipment are extras.

Hoop houses & cold frames

Hoop houses and cold frames can perform many of the functions of a greenhouse on a smaller scale, from housing cuttings that are rooting to overwintering tender ornamental plants. Hoop houses are functional structures consisting of a P.V.C. frame (or a row of flexible P.V.C. hoops) covered with heavy-duty polyethylene.

A cold frame is a simple, bottomless structure. The low, insulating walls may be framed with a material such as lumber, aluminum, concrete block, or brick. A lid, sloped at an angle, is typically glazed with glass, acrylic, polycarbonate, or polyethylene. Cold frames no larger than 3ft. wide are easy to reach inside and are light enough to pick up and move around the garden as needed. Cold frames heated with electric cables—known as 'hot beds'—are even more versatile.

COLD FRAME & HOOP HOUSE

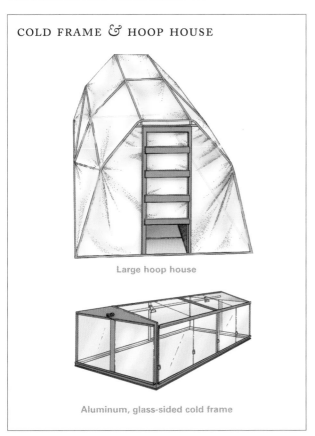

Large hoop house

Aluminum, glass-sided cold frame

When buying a greenhouse kit, make sure it comes with complete instructions and check that you have all the materials and tools on hand before you begin to put it together.

Site & situation

An ideal situation for a greenhouse is one that receives good light levels all year round, is sheltered from the wind, and is close to water and electrical outlets. A freestanding structure receives sunlight from all sides, but a lean-to requires a south- or eastfacing wall for the greatest light exposure.

Consider the microclimate of your garden. An exposed site increases air movement and therefore greater heat loss; even a modest breeze of 15mph will double the amount of heat drawn from the greenhouse. Use a windbreak, such as a hedge, to mitigate this problem. Also assess your site for shade cast from buildings, walls, fences, and trees. If your greenhouse is in shadow for long periods, plant growth will be poor. Most greenhouses need a minimum of six hours of sunlight per day.

Base, foundation, & construction

Build your greenhouse on a level, well-drained site. Whether you build your greenhouse from scratch or assemble it from a kit, it should be securely anchored to the ground. Small or temporary models may be held down with simple anchor stakes; any structure over about 240 square feet calls for a more secure, skid foundation. This may be a single tier of pressure-treated or rot-resistant wooden members, or a small, wooden platform.

A well-sited greenhouse should not only be in an accessible position, but also in a sheltered site that receives adequate light. In summer, some shade may be welcome, but not in late winter and early spring.

Wooden corner posts can be sunk into concrete-filled post holes or, in frost-free areas, driven into the ground with metal post spikes. Another alternative is to set a wooden foundation on precast concrete piers.

Larger or heavier structures may require a permanent foundation, especially in colder areas, to avoid frost heave.

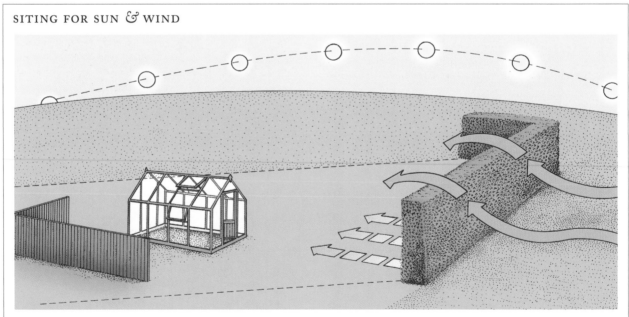

SITING FOR SUN & WIND

You can reduce the effect of wind by using semipermeable walls, fences, or hedges. Site windbreaks carefully sited so they do not shade the greenhouse. Also evaluate the sun's angle to determine the orientation of the greenhouse. In general, an east–west orientation provides maximum exposure for a greenhouse. In a very hot, sunny region, a north–south orientation may be a better choice.

Climate & your garden *see page 10* | **Growing under glass** *see page 379* | **Controlling the environment** *see page 398*

Shading & ventilation

When the sun shines on a greenhouse, the air inside heats up rapidly, and you will need to control the temperature by using a combination of ventilation and shading. Ventilation also brings in fresh air and controls humidity.

Ventilating the greenhouse

Generally, the more ventilation a greenhouse has the better, but as a minimum the area covered by vents in your greenhouse roof should be the equivalent of at least 20 percent of the total floor area. Additional side vents, covering an area equal to the roof vents, speed up air changes and create a chimney effect (*see box, right*).

In spring and fall, you must take care when opening and closing vents, as increased sunlight causes indoors temperatures to rise, but the outdoor temperatures remain very low. At such times, open roof vents partially to regulate the temperature, but keep side vents closed so that tender plants do not receive blasts of cold air. Likewise, you can close vents on the windward side when cold winds are blowing.

Keep vents in good working order and make sure they close tightly. If pests such as mice are entering the greenhouse through the floor vents, cover the vents with window screening material or hardware cloth.

Automated vents & exhaust fans

Roof and side vents can be opened and closed by automatic mechanisms that respond to changes in temperature. Individual vents may be controlled by a thermostatically-controlled electric motor, or a mechanical opener that senses heat buildup and activates a lever to open the vent. You can also use a central controller to operate automatically not just vents but also heaters, fans, and lighting.

Exhaust fans provide an alternative to the passive movement of air through vents. The size of the fan and inlet area should be proportional to the volume of the greenhouse. The fan works in conjunction with low intake vents at the opposite end of the greenhouse.

Swamp coolers

In warm or very dry areas, evaporative or 'swamp' coolers help to cool the air inside the greenhouse by drawing air from a reservoir and through a wet pad.

THE CHIMNEY EFFECT

Ventilation expels hot air from roof vents and introduces cooler, fresh air from side vents. Good air circulation allows plants to 'breathe' and is vital for a healthy growing environment.

METHODS OF VENTILATION

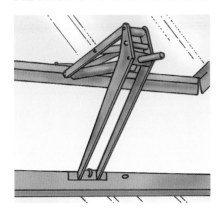

Automatic vents may be solar powered or thermostatically controlled.

Exhaust fans circulate fresh air and should be placed above the door in small greenhouses.

Louvered vents are often seen on side panels, located at the bases of the walls.

Shading

In summer, ventilation alone will not be enough to maintain the interior temperature of your greenhouse at a comfortable level for your plants. The strong summer sunshine through glass can also overheat and scorch your plants, and only those adapted to such harsh conditions, such as cacti and succulents, will escape damage.

To prevent this from happening, you will need to provide the necessary degree of shading for the type of plants you are growing and their stage of development. Specialty plants like orchids require plenty of shade for many months of the year. Seedlings and young plants growing in spring can be shaded from the short periods of strong sunshine in the middle of the day by draping them with shade cloth.

Into summer, mature plants need longer periods of shade, as well as protection from extreme temperatures. You can provide this effectively by applying a shade paint or by introducing external covers or screens (*see below*). Internal blinds provide adequate shade, but they are less effective at reducing temperatures, and can be hard to open and close.

METHODS OF SHADING

Shade paint should be thinly applied onto the outside of the glass in spring.

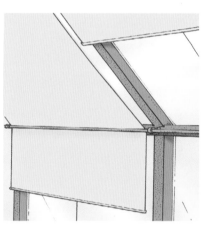

Interior blinds tend to be less effective than exterior shading at protecting plants.

Use greenhouse shade cloth for improvised shading. It must not exclude light.

Electricity & heating

When electrical power is required for a greenhouse, be it for lighting, propagating units, heaters, or fans, it must be installed by a qualified professional. Power can be run to the greenhouse from the house service panel, as long as the circuit is grounded and the cables are buried underground according to local electric codes. All greenhouse outlets and switches should be G.F.C.I. (Ground Fault Circuit Interrupter) protected.

Before you add supplementary heating, consider ways to improve the efficiency of your greenhouse. Eliminate any air leaks by regularly inspecting glazing to ensure it fits snugly into the framing and by sealing any gaps with a silicone sealant.

In cold regions, insulate the greenhouse in winter by fixing a temporary material such as bubble wrap or polyethylene sheeting (*see box, facing page*). Select a heater with sufficient capacity to maintain the required temperature in your size of greenhouse.

Sources of heating

The minimum temperature in your greenhouse will depend on the plants you grow; in an area with warm winters, solar heating may be sufficient if you are just using the greenhouse for spring propagation. In most cases, however, some kind of additional heating is required. The temperature in a cool greenhouse should not drop below 40–45°F, whereas a warm greenhouse for heat-loving plants such as orchids may call for temperatures that never drop below 60°F or 70°F.

When deciding on a heating source, keep safety in mind. Heaters can easily melt plastic or crack glass, so position them carefully. Determine venting needs for any gas- or oil-burning models. All heaters should have an automatic safety shut-off mechanism.

For most gardeners, electrical heaters are the easiest and most versatile method of heating. You can choose between free-standing or wall-mounted models that run

ELECTRICITY & HEATING

Climate & your garden *see page 10* | **Growing under glass** *see page 379* | **Controlling the environment** *see page 398*

TYPES OF GREENHOUSE HEATER

Small and portable, electric fan heaters can be positioned in the greenhouse where needed. A safety switch will cut power should the heater be knocked over.

Portable greenhouse heaters can be used to protect container-grown ornamental plants when outdoor temperatures dip below freezing. Always set heaters on a level, stable surface such as a bench or table.

on 120 or 240 volts. Features typically include a fan, built-in thermostat, and safety shut-off mechanism. A separate heater thermostat can control the heater in response to changing temperatures in the greenhouse. A heating/cooling thermostat can regulate both a heater and an exhaust fan. Some heaters can draw and recycle warmer air from the roof section of the greenhouse.

If you have no power supply to the greenhouse, or you live in an area prone to power outages, a heater

fueled with propane or natural gas may be a better choice. Gas-burning heaters produce waste gases (including carbon dioxide, which can be beneficial to plants) and they are usually vented to the outdoors. Some gas heaters are sold as 'nonventing' models, but local building codes may prohibit their use, especially if your greenhouse is attached to the house or garage.

Alternative forms of energy such as wind turbines and solar panels are becoming more viable as technology advances. Sunrooms and lean-to structures can be heated directly or indirectly by the house heating systems.

Greenhouse heaters are rated in British Thermal Units (Btu). To determine the size of heater you need, you will need to perform a calculation (*see box, below*) based on the lowest average temperature for your area (you can get this information from your local cooperative extension service) and the minimum temperature you wish to maintain in the greenhouse in winter. If you are purchasing a greenhouse kit, the supplier can usually save you the trouble of making this calculation and advise you on an appropriately sized heater for your needs.

INSULATING A GREENHOUSE

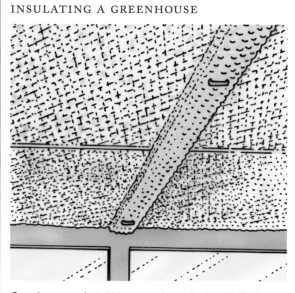

Greenhouse-grade bubble wrap makes a simple and effective insulating material in winter. You can attach the material with spray adhesive or double-sided tape.

HOW MUCH HEAT DO YOU NEED?

To work out the appropriate Btu rating for the heaters in your greenhouse, you must first calculate the total surface area of the greenhouse sides and roof in square feet ('A'). Then determine the difference between the coldest outdoor winter temperature and the lowest temperature you require in your greenhouse, in degrees F° ('T'). Multiply A x T x 1.1 to get the required Btu rating for your heaters. If you have double glazing or insulation, subtract 30 percent from this number; if your greenhouse is a lean-to on a heated wall, subtract a further 30 percent.

Irrigation

In a small greenhouse, you can water by hand. During the growing season, many greenhouse plants require daily watering; it is best to do this in the morning. Overwatering may kill your plants, while underwatering will result in stunted growth and poor yields.

For an automatic watering system, you can run lines to the greenhouse from the house plumbing system, or attach irrigation tubing to a nearby outdoor faucet. Whichever water outlet you use, you can fit the greenhouse with automatic drip or spray irrigation, misting systems, or automatic capillary watering systems. A timer to automate the system is helpful for plants that require consistent moisture. A misting system will cool the greenhouse, although the additional dampness can encourage fungal diseases. A humidistat can activate the system when the greenhouse air becomes too dry.

Some plant problems can be traced to water that is either too hard or too soft (pH too high or too low); symptoms can include mineral deposits on the soil surface or on leaves. A reverse osmosis system can remove excess minerals from the water.

Raising humidity

Hot, dry conditions are stressful for most plants. You can raise the humidity in the greenhouse with a humidifier, a misting system, or by hosing down the greenhouse floor and shelves several times a day.

METHODS OF WATERING

Capillary matting suits pot plants of all sizes. Keep the absorbent mat moist, and use containers with a substantial number of drainage holes.

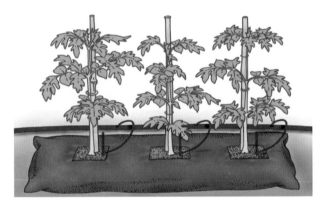

Drip irrigation is good for watering pots and grow bags. Water may come from plumbing lines on a nearby faucet.

WATER HARVESTING METHODS

Gutters can lead to a water tank inside the greenhouse, or rain barrels on the outside. Such a system will help reduce your dependency on the house water system and is useful during times of drought and water restrictions. Rainwater is beneficial for watering acid-loving plants and orchids.

Rain barrels should have tight fitting lids and a strainer to trap organic matter. Place the barrels on a level surface and connect a standard hose to an overflow valve. Barrels should be sized to meet the water needs of the greenhouse or garden. You may need more than one.

Misters range from simple kits with P.V.C. pipes to plumbed-in systems with heavy-duty nozzles, like these.

Container gardening *see page 342* | **Hygiene & maintenance** *see page 387* | **Propagating plants** *see page 392*

GROWING UNDER GLASS

Of all the disciplines of gardening, growing under glass is the most specialized. Not only are greenhouse plants dependent on you to provide a comfortable environment in which they can flourish, but you also need to give them something in which to grow. Plants under glass have access to lower levels of soil nutrients than do plants in the open garden, so soil in beds needs to be enriched, and special potting mixes or soil blends are needed for containers. If you follow good growing practises, your greenhouse will be visited less regularly by pests and diseases, as this is the most important means of controlling them.

How to grow

You should use as much of the greenhouse space as possible for cultivating plants. Set container plants on benches and shelves, attach additional shelves to the sidewalls, and use the space under benches for holding or overwintering dormant plants in large pots or tubs.

Greenhouse growing systems are based either on open beds or some form of container. The size, type, and site of the greenhouse, and the choice of plants to be grown, will determine which kind of growing system you should use. If you intend to use your greenhouse for propagating plants, you'll need benches and shelves at a comfortable working height, typically 30–36in.

Growing in containers

Containers offer the best growing system if a large number of different plants are to be grown in a greenhouse, as they can be moved as the plants grow.

Grow bags are useful for crops such as tomatoes and peppers. They usually contain up to three cubic feet of peat, perlite, vermiculite, or a blend of these three. The blend is sterile and may include water-retaining crystals. After cutting out planting holes, moisten the potting soil and allow it to soak overnight so that the soil is uniformly moist. The volume of growing medium in the bag will appear to double.

THREE DIFFERENT WAYS TO GROW PLANTS IN THE GREENHOUSE

Grow bags are a convenient way to grow a range of greenhouse plants, particularly short-term crops such as tomatoes, cucumbers, peppers, salad crops, and strawberries.

Large containers can hold tender plants during the winter months. Small batches of plants can also be started off under protection and moved outdoors as weather conditions improve.

Garden soil is ideal where the greenhouse is fully glazed (glass to ground) and is suitable for both short-season crops or permanent plants, such as fruiting and ornamental trees or vines.

Utilize your greenhouse space efficiently by making use of different growing systems. Here, young plants and seedlings grow on shelved benches, with larger ornamental plants growing in the garden dirt.

Because of the limited rooting volume in containers, you must take great care when watering to ensure that roots do not become saturated or dry out. Give small amounts of water frequently, to match the weather conditions and stage of plant growth. Seedlings and young plants are especially prone to drought stress and need consistent irrigation. For drought-tolerant plants, such as cacti and succulents, allow the soil to dry out between waterings.

All containers need drainage holes; in grow bags, cut horizontal slits just above the bases to allow excess water to escape and to avoid oversaturating the soil, which can lead to fungal diseases and root rots.

Growing in the soil

Where plants are to be grown directly in the greenhouse garden dirt, a deep, well-cultivated soil is required to produce healthy plants and good yields. It is important, therefore, to keep the soil in good condition by digging in deeply plenty of well-rotted organic matter to improve the structure, drainage, and water-holding capacity.

A soil pH of 6.5–7 is best for vegetables and salad crops. If you are going to be using the beds intensively, measure the soil nutrient level and pH status each year, as additional amendments will be required to replace the nutrients taken up by the crops. A simple soil test can help you to do this (*see page 33*).

Before planting and sowing, ensure the ground has been well watered, thoroughly incorporate plenty of well-rotted organic matter, and produce a firm, level finish.

If plants are to be grown in the greenhouse garden dirt for a number of years, consider building small raised beds. This will contain the soil and allow you to add soil amendments, such as compost, on top of the soil without them spilling over. This helps provide a well-aerated rooting zone for long-term plants.

You can grow plants in bottomless pots set on top of garden dirt. In the early stages, the pot provides a warmer rooting zone than the garden dirt. As the roots grow into the garden dirt, the plant is buffered from changes in moisture levels that might occur in a container.

PLANT SUPPORTS

Looking after your soil *see page 32* | **Vines & wall plants** *see page 138* | **Sowing & growing** *see page 156*

Plant supports

For climbing vines and tall plants, you will need to provide a range of support and training systems in your greenhouse. These range from simple canes and string systems, for short-term crops such as tomatoes and cucumbers, to netting and wires permanently fixed to the inside of the greenhouse, to support perennial vines and woody plants such as trained fruit trees.

There are many plant-support aids available for greenhouse plants, most of which do a tidy and reliable job. They include molded plastic hooks, clips and spacers, special metal bolts and eyes that fix into the framing, and a range of adjustable, soft plant ties. Hoops and adjustable plant rings can also be used to support bushy or tall plants.

Temporary plant supports

A stake or bamboo cane driven into the soil provides a very quick and easy rigid support for tomato vines. Tie the plants in at regular intervals, preferably just below a leaf junction, using plant ties or one of the several types of molded plastic clips.

You can use strong twine as a support for vines to twist around. Loosely tie the twine around the base of the plant stem and run a length up to the greenhouse roof. Fix it there, allowing considerable slack so that as the plant grows the string is gently twisted around the head of the plant. Make sure that the twist is under a leaf junction to prevent the stem slipping down the string as its length and weight increase. There is always a chance that branches may be snapped off in this operation, so use a light touch and check regularly that the twine is not overtight.

Permanent plant supports

Long-term plantings of trees, shrubs, and vines need a robust and permanent plant support system. One option is to secure a framework of wooden supports to the greenhouse wall or frame, onto which netting, wire, plastic mesh, or other materials can be attached.

Tie climbing plants, fan-trained shrubs, and fruit bushes onto plastic mesh or netting, using soft twine or plastic clips and allowing some slack for the stems to expand. Tall plants or those with branches will need a strong support covering a large area.

Galvanized wires set out horizontally at regular intervals can be used for plants such as grape vines or kiwi. Selected side branches should be tied in at regular intervals along the horizontal wire. Wires can also be used for other vines.

TYPES OF PLANT SUPPORT

Canes and stakes are pushed into the soil. Tie or clip the plant to the support, under the leaf junctions.

String and twine fixed to the roof makes a good support for tomatoes to climb up.

Mesh or netting is a versatile support and can be adapted for most greenhouse plants.

Tall plants need a comparably tall support. For heavy crops, make the support strong.

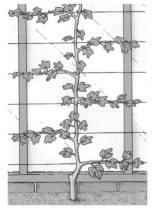

Cordon grape vines need to be trained along horizontal wires to support their side branches.

Walls in lean-to greenhouses can be covered in supports for the cultivation of vines.

Using cold frames & cloches

Beyond the greenhouse, cold frames, mini greenhouses, and hoop houses (*see page 373*) can be used to great advantage in producing edible crops, raising plants for the garden, and for overwintering plants in cold regions of the U.S.

Cold frames

In cold-winter regions, these provide enough protection during early spring to start early crops of radish, lettuce, spinach, carrots, and spring onions. At this time of year, late frosts and spring storms can strike unexpectedly, so you must manage the environment in the frame to protect the young plants.

When outdoor temperatures are forecast to fall below freezing, drape old blankets or bubble wrap over cold frames at night. Row covers are useful as an insulating blanket, if folded over the plants inside the frame, and can remain in place if frost persists during the daytime.

Another option is to turn the cold frame into a hot bed by laying heating cables in a bed of sand at the base of the frame. Partly open up the frame each morning for ventilation. When the daytime weather conditions are dry and temperatures rising, you can ventilate the frame fully for an hour or two in the middle of the day.

Cold frames are also used to wean, or harden off, greenhouse plants from warm to cool, outdoor conditions (*see below*). Slightly tender plants, or those that require protection from high winter rainfall, can also be overwintered in these structures.

Cloches & hoop houses

Low hoop houses and plastic or glass cloches are versatile growing aids, easily moved from crop to crop, providing protection and creating a microclimate that can induce speedy growth. Plants under cloches require careful watering, as well as ventilation.

HARDENING OFF IN AN UNHEATED FRAME

1 Place flats or pots of greenhouse-reared young plants into the cold frame in spring. The purpose is to gradually acclimatize these plants to the outdoor environment. Sudden exposure can kill plants. Hardy plants can be introduced to the outdoors much faster than those that are tender to frost.

2 Open up cold frames for part of the day for ventilation during the first week, but only during mild spells of weather. Close the window each night as cold, frosty air may harm the young plants.

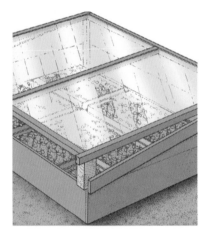

3 Leave cold frames open all day as the weather warms up, from midspring. They can also be opened a little at night. Remove the cover completely toward the end of spring, except in windy weather.

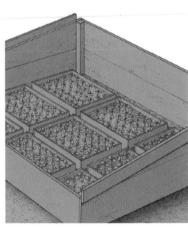

4 Remove plants from the cold frame and plant in their permanent positions outdoors once the risk of frost has passed. By this time, the young plants should have doubled in size and will thrive in the ground.

Bulbous plants *see page 91* | **Types of greenhouse** *see page 373* | **Sowing seeds** *see page 405*

The unheated greenhouse

Unheated greenhouses and walk-in hoop houses are used to extend the growing season, particularly in spring when the garden soil temperature is low and cold winds can chill and dry out young plants. Such greenhouses are, in effect, no more than a protective covering against extremes of cold, wet, and wind.

Growing vegetables

The range of vegetables and salad crops that you can grow under protection is extensive: salad leaves, lettuce, carrots, green onions, radish, and spinach are all reliable early vegetables, and there are great opportunities to experiment with others.

You can start young plants in the greenhouse for later transplanting into the garden, or you can grow them directly in the greenhouse beds to maturity. Keep some polyethylene sheeting or floating row covers at hand to protect young plants if temperatures drop. Continue to sow seeds for transplanting into the garden as weather conditions improve.

In areas with short summers, tomatoes, peppers, cucumbers, eggplants, and heat-loving herbs can be grown in unheated greenhouses. All are easy to raise from seed, or you can buy them as young plants from a garden center. As these crops are sensitive to low temperatures, delay planting until midspring when night temperatures do not fall below 46°F during the daytime. Close vents early in the afternoon during these early stages to keep the greenhouse warm in the evening and hasten growth.

Forcing bulbs

Spring bulbs such as daffodils and hyacinths (*see below*), potted in early fall and brought into a greenhouse, will provide color and interest long before the bulbs bloom in the garden. Early bulbs make excellent gifts for indoor display if grown in ornamental pots. You can buy pre-chilled bulbs, such as hyacinths, for this purpose. The bulbs have been treated so that the period of cold needed to bloom is shortened by several weeks, but they still need to spend 9–10 weeks at temperatures below 45°F.

FORCING HYACINTH BULBS FOR EARLY FLOWERING

1 **Plant bulbs** in containers in early fall. Choose bulbs that are of equal size and plant them in potting mix so that the top half of each bulb is left exposed. You can sow more than one bulb per container in large pots.

2 **Plunge the containers** up to their rims into the garden dirt once they are all potted. This can be done either in a greenhouse or a cold frame. Cover the bulbs with more potting mix or lightweight mulch. Keep the soil around the bulbs moist.

3 **Remove the containers** from the bed 8–12 weeks later when shoots begin to appear. Stand the containers in a cool and shady, frost-free place, such as beneath the greenhouse shelving.

4 **Move the bulbs** into full light when the buds begin to color. Flowering will take place in early spring, at which time the plants can be moved for indoor display. After flowering, keep the bulbs cool and slightly shaded while the foliage dies away and store for next year or plant in the garden in fall.

Starting annuals

Annual bedding plants can be started in the greenhouse for later transplanting. Sow warm-season annuals so you'll have seedlings to plant out soon after the last frost date in your area. The seed packet will list the time seedlings require to grow to transplanting stage. For cool-season plants in warm areas, count backward from the time that cooler fall temperatures typically arrive.

Growing ornamentals

An unheated greenhouse can be a good place to store tender plants in winter or when there is a threat of sudden frosts in marginal areas. In zone 8, shrubs such as flowering maples (*Abutilon*), angel's trumpets (*Brugmansia*), banksias, many fuchsias, plumerias, bananas, birds of paradise, princess flowers (*Tibouchina*), and tender vines such as bougainvilleas can be brought into the greenhouse and kept warm with portable heaters when temperatures drop. In colder zones, container-grown shrubs such as camellias and azaleas may require such shelter.

If the outdoor temperature drops below 32–37°F, it is likely that there will be several degrees of frost inside the greenhouse; in such instances, wrap frost-sensitive plants or switch on portable heaters.

GROWING ANNUALS FOR SPRING FLOWERING

1 **Sow seeds** in sterilized seed starter mix, following the instructions on the seed packet for handling.

2 **When the seedlings appear**, place the container on the greenhouse bench, or a well-lit windowsill or shelf. Keep the mix just moist and ventilate carefully.

3 **When large enough to handle**, transfer the individual seedlings into small pots of well-drained potting mix.

4 **Pot the seedlings on** into larger containers as they increase in maturity and size. Hold them by the leaves, not stems.

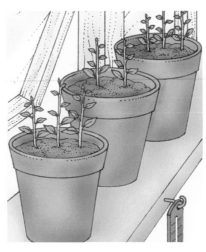

5 **Ventilate young plants** if the greenhouse becomes humid and to accustom the plants gradually to outdoor conditions.

6 **Seedlings should be** several inches tall, with well-developed root systems, when ready to plant out in spring or fall.

The cool greenhouse

By providing some artificial warmth to a greenhouse—with a minimum temperature of 40°F, even on the coldest night of the year—you can ensure that it will be full of interesting plants year-round. Nearly all of the plants from the world's temperate zones will grow under such warm conditions.

Raising plants

Sow annuals for greenhouse display, such as primulas, schizanthus, and cinerarias, in pots in late summer for flowering in early spring. Transplant to larger containers as they grow to obtain large specimen plants of good quality at flowering time.

The cool greenhouse is an ideal place to raise summer annuals and vegetables. Their rates of growth and your first and last expected frost dates determine when you should sow them; devise a monthly sowing plan, starting in late winter for the slowest-growing types. Specific cultivation instructions will be given on the seed packets. Even in a cool greenhouse, development will be slow at first because of low light levels in winter.

In late spring, when the young plants are big enough and there is no chance of frost, you should gradually introduce them to the outdoor environment by placing them in a cold frame to harden off (*see page 382*) or by turning off the greenhouse heating system. Gradually increase the ventilation, by day and then also by night, before moving them outdoors permanently.

Growing ornamentals

In cooler regions, summer-dormant bulbs are satisfying to cultivate in a cool greenhouse, as they provide a welcome splash of color from late fall to early spring. *Nerine sarniensis* hybrids flower in fall, veltheimias in late winter, and lachenalias from midwinter into early spring, according to the species. You need to fertilize and water these bulbs from the time they start into growth in late summer until the foliage begins to die back after flowering. You should then allow the dormant bulbs to rest in their pots throughout summer, keeping the potting soil just moist. Repot the bulbs only when they have outgrown the space in their containers. Other bulbs to try indoors include freesias, gladioli, ixias, and sparaxis.

Plumbago and mandevilla are two examples of free-flowering vines that are easily contained in a tub and grown up a greenhouse frame or wall, but there are many others to choose from, including wax flowers (*Hoya*), passion flowers, and scented jasmines.

Cacti and succulents enjoy a frost-free greenhouse, and many cacti produce hugely flamboyant flowers in the late spring. Agaves, aloes, echinopsis, and euphorbias are good plants to start with. To grow unblemished specimens, you will have to keep the atmosphere of your greenhouse dry, allowing the soil to dry out between waterings, when you

Even in spring and early summer, a cool greenhouse is a refuge for frost-tender or specialty plants that are not yet ready for full-time residence in the garden.

385

should add a diluted liquid fertilizer. Almost no water at all is needed in winter.

You can also grow specialty plants for cutting and display such as florists' chrysanthemums or dahlias. Keep the pots outdoors in summer and bring into the greenhouse for late fall and winter flowering.

Trees & shrubs for the cool greenhouse

Container-grown trees and shrubs can significantly enhance the internal landscape of both cool greenhouses and sunrooms. Many acacias, for example, are almost-hardy trees that make great late-flowering container plants, if grown as small standard trees or shrubs; prune them after flowering to control their size. Check before purchasing any tree or shrub for the cool greenhouse—many can grow to enormous sizes and are not so easy to control by regular pruning.

Bougainvilleas are happy to grow in a cool greenhouse, if trained on a wall trellis or metal frame. Water them sparingly in winter and prune back overlong stems in early spring as growth commences. They may be deciduous in a cool greenhouse.

Citrus make very pretty, evergreen trees and shrubs with the additional benefit of fragrant blossom and edible fruits. They respond well to quite heavy watering and fertilizing with long intervals in between, so that the potting mix is almost dry before being watered again.

Growing fruit & vegetables

As well as growing popular crops, such as tomatoes, cucumbers, and peppers, you can use a cool greenhouse to cultivate more tender and exotic vegetables, such as okra, and tropical fruit like kiwis or guavas—if space allows. Strawberries, salad crops, and herbs are also good plants for the cool greenhouse, as the extra warmth means that you can have crops ready for harvesting in early spring and during fall.

Widening the range

Even though there are very many plants that you can grow easily in a cool greenhouse, it is worth experimenting to test your limits. Some plants thought to need a higher temperature than a cool greenhouse can provide may in fact be acclimatized to such conditions—as long as the temperature does not fall below 40°F, at which point plant cells can be physically damaged. A lot depends on avoiding extremes and sudden changes in the heat, humidity, and ventilation of the greenhouse.

The warm greenhouse

The variety of plants that can be grown in a warm greenhouse is staggering; tropical plants, including flowering trees, shrubs, and vines, can be grown year-round. The cost of heating a greenhouse to a minimum night temperature of 55°F, however, can be very high, which is an important consideration.

The atmosphere of a warm greenhouse is different from a cool or unheated house, as you are not just enhancing the outdoor environment, but creating an entirely artificial one. Although the way a warm greenhouse is used varies from gardener to gardener, the overall look and feel will generally be lush and tropical, with many of the plants grown purely for ornament. Foliage plants, such as ferns and palms, create the backdrop for exotic flowering plants like orchids, African violets, and Cape primroses.

Many orchids have special requirements and so need very exacting conditions. There are still many types, however, that are fairly easy to grow in a warm greenhouse. These include cymbidiums, some odontoglossums, and dendrobiums, although it is best to consult a specialty nursery for advice on growing requirements before you buy.

Many orchids are epiphytic, meaning they grow on tree bark and must be attached to cork or some other tree bark. Their root systems have evolved to absorb moisture and nutrients from the air, and therefore you need to keep the atmosphere around the plant humid. You should also fertilize them at a very diluted strength. Although many orchids come from warm parts of the world, they still need shading and cooling, through ventilation, in summer.

Vines suitable for a warm greenhouse or sunroom include *Allamanda cathartica*, which makes a stunning flowering vine, if given the support of a trellis or back wall of a sunroom, producing buttercup-yellow flowers continuously throughout the year. *Brunsfelsia paucifolia*, a medium-sized flowering shrub for a large pot or tub, produces an abundance of simple, blue flowers and is rarely out of flower.

Foliage plants suitable for a warm greenhouse include zebra plants (*Aphelandra*), colorful-leaved begonias, codiaeum, marantas, peperomias, and many other plants that are popular as houseplants.

Sowing & growing *see page 156* | **Growing under glass** *see page 379* | **Propagating plants** *see page 392*

HYGIENE & MAINTENANCE

To maintain the best environment for plants to grow, you must ensure that your structure is kept in good, clean condition. Keep wood free from mildew, heaters and fans serviced, and roof gutters clear, and make sure doors and vents are well lubricated to prevent them seizing up. It is worth making an annual checklist, but deal with structural defects, like broken glazing, immediately. Keep some polyethylene film available for temporary repairs. Cleaning is important as it keeps pests and diseases at bay; despite your best efforts, however, you are still likely to encounter problems from time to time.

Keeping clean

Tidiness is part of the greenhouse routine, helping to reduce the conditions that might promote diseases and harbor pests. Each year, thoroughly wash down your greenhouse both inside and out (*see below*) with warm, soapy water. Do the same with your containers and tools; pruners and pruning knives need to be sterilized.

You will notice that through the year the transparency of a greenhouse is reduced by a buildup of dust and other pollutants, and the more dirty the glazing becomes, the less light can penetrate. In such conditions, plant growth will be poor, particularly in the early months of the year.

Remove unhealthy plants as soon as they are spotted, as they may be infected, and take all plant debris and used soil mixes to the compost pile for prompt disposal. Used pots and containers are best put outside the greenhouse ready to be cleaned. Potting mixes deteriorate quite quickly if allowed to become too wet or dry, so keep them in their original bag inside a sealed container, and remember to buy fresh mix every year. Some products, like rooting hormones, pesticides, and packets of seeds, will quickly deteriorate in a warm greenhouse, so must be stored safely in a cool building away from direct sunlight.

CLEANING THE GREENHOUSE IN FALL

Scrub down the framework to remove pests and diseases that may overwinter there.

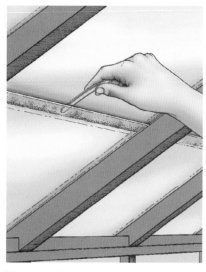

Wash the glazing as recommended by the manufacturer, especially where panes overlap.

Scrub all surfaces, including the floor and walls, to remove algae or any other deposits.

Greenhouse pests

Good greenhouse hygiene is an essential starting point in the avoidance of pests. Listed below are the most common pests you are likely to encounter, with recommended controls. Other common greenhouse pests are vine weevil, aphids, slugs, and snails (*see page 49*).

Whitefly

These small, white-winged insects and their whitish green nymphs suck sap from the undersides of leaves of many indoor ornamental plants and vegetables. Honeydew is excreted, making the foliage sticky and coated with sooty mold. Adult whitefly readily fly up from plants when disturbed. They breed throughout the year.

From spring to early fall, control whitefly biologically with parasitic wasps and lacewings, which kill the nymphs. Hang yellow sticky traps. Horticultural oils and insecticidal soaps can also be used, but need frequent application to be effective.

Caterpillars

Caterpillars are the larval form of many different species of moths and butterfly. Some caterpillars eat leaves, petals, and fruit. Others bind leaves together or curl over the leaf margin with silk threads. Hand pick caterpillars and dispose of them. Squeeze bound-up leaves to crush any caterpillars that are concealed within. Treat with the biological control *Bacillus thuringiensis* (Bt) or, for severe infestations, an appropriate insecticide.

Scale insects

Several species of these soft-bodied, sap-feeding insects occur: soft scale is common on citrus, ficus, scheffleras, and bay trees; brown scale attacks peaches and grapes; oleander scale infests many ornamental plants. The insects are covered by scales that may be hard, waxy, or fluffy, and are immobile for most of the time, attached to the stems and leaves. Some species excrete honeydew and make the foliage sticky and covered in a sooty mold. Dab at scales with a cotton swab soaked in alcohol or scrape them off with a small file. Horticultural oil and insecticidal soap give some control of newly hatched scale nymphs.

Leafhoppers

Both the adult leafhopper and their creamy nymphs suck sap from the lower leaf surfaces of many plants. This causes a coarse, pale mottling of the upper leaf surfaces. Leafhoppers are active year-round in greenhouses. Control with insecticidal soap.

Fungus gnats

These small, grayish black flies cause no damage but are a nuisance; put up yellow sticky traps to capture them. Their larvae live in the soil where they feed mainly on dead plant material, but they also damage seedlings and soft cuttings. The predatory mite *Hypoaspis miles* is a useful biological control. Help seedlings and cuttings through the vulnerable period by providing good growing conditions. Keep soil moist but not waterlogged, don't leave standing water in the greenhouse, and clean up decaying plant matter from soil surfaces.

Mealybugs

Mealybugs are small, sap-feeding insects that are often hidden under fluffy, white, waxy fibers. Cacti and succulents are commonly attacked, but many other indoor ornamental plants and grape vines are susceptible. Heavily infested plants lack vigor and may be soiled with a sugary excrement (honeydew) and sooty mold.

Use the mealybug destroyer *Cryptolaemus montrouzieri*, parasitic wasps, and lacewings. Spray with insecticidal soap or horticultural oil. Blasts of water from a hose can remove mealybugs, or you can dab at the pests with a cotton swab dipped in alcohol.

Leaf miners

These tiny flies lay eggs on the leaves of many plants. The maggots bore into the leaves, creating wiggly tunnels. Several generations can occur each year. For light infestations, remove affected leaves or squeeze the tunnels to kill the larvae. There is no effective chemical control.

Red spider mites

Barely visible to the naked eye, this pest may be orange-red or yellowish green. The mites suck sap from the lower leaf surfaces, causing the upper surfaces to develop a fine, pale mottling. Leaves become increasingly discolored as the infestation builds up, causing premature leaf fall. A fine silk webbing may be seen on heavily infested plants. Many indoor plants are susceptible, as well as some outdoor plants during the second half of summer.

Biological control with *Phytoseilus persimilis* is effective when introduced from spring to early fall. Infestations of red spider mites can increase when humidity is low; misting or wetting down the greenhouse shelving and floor may help. Otherwise, spray affected plants with horticultural oil or insecticidal soap. Thorough application is required, especially under the leaves.

GREENHOUSE PESTS

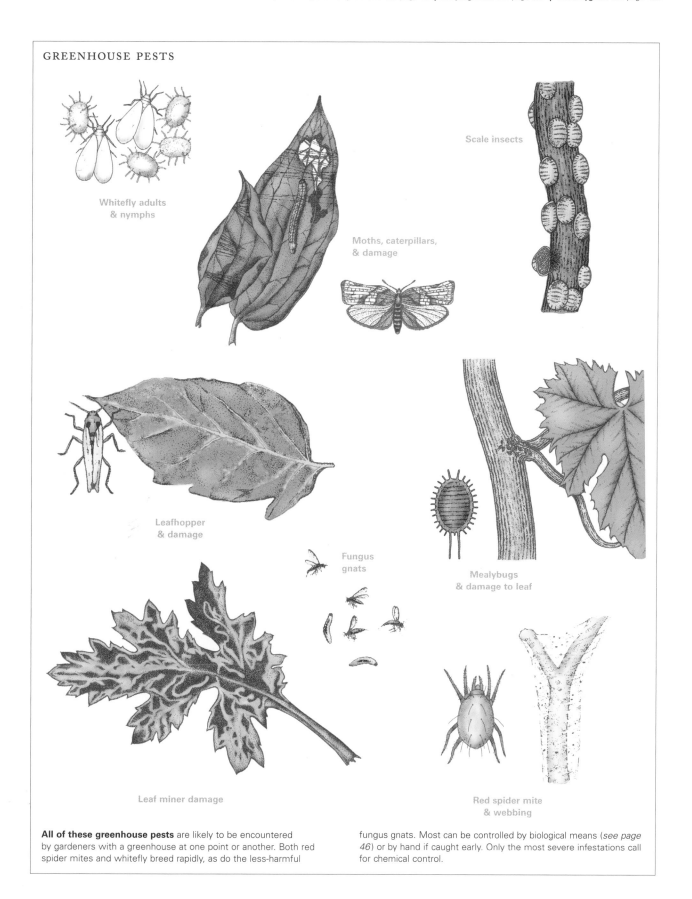

Whitefly adults & nymphs

Moths, caterpillars, & damage

Scale insects

Leafhopper & damage

Mealybugs & damage to leaf

Fungus gnats

Leaf miner damage

Red spider mite & webbing

All of these greenhouse pests are likely to be encountered by gardeners with a greenhouse at one point or another. Both red spider mites and whitefly breed rapidly, as do the less-harmful fungus gnats. Most can be controlled by biological means (*see page 46*) or by hand if caught early. Only the most severe infestations call for chemical control.

Greenhouse diseases

You can avoid most diseases in the greenhouse by growing things well. Lapses in transplanting, ventilation, fertilizing, watering, temperature control, and other routine tasks will expose your plants to infection.

Damping off

This disease causes seedlings to collapse at soil level, often all at once, and the roots may be decayed. To reduce incidence of this disease, use sterile growing medium and equipment, sow seeds thinly, and water with municipal water. Provide good light and air circulation with adequate ventilation; avoid excessive heat. Discard affected seedlings and growing medium.

Viruses

Plants exhibit a range of symptoms when infected by viruses, with yellowing patches on leaves the most commonly seen. These patches often take the form of mosaic, ringspot, or mottled patterns. Dead patches can also result, and an infected plant may appear stunted when placed next to a healthy one. Viruses are most often seen in plants that are propagated by division or cuttings, such as dahlias and cannas. Insects usually transfer viruses, but some viruses are highly contagious and can spread by contact between a plant and a surface on which virus particles are present. Some common viruses include:

Cucumber mosaic virus (C.M.V.): Common on peppers, tomatoes, cucumbers, and other edible and ornamental plants, it causes leaves to be spotted and distorted.

Impatiens necrotic spot virus: This can affect a huge range of plants, causing diverse symptoms.

Tobacco mosaic virus (T.M.V.): Affects many plants, including tomato, pepper, and tobacco-family plants.

Viruses cannot be cured and affected plants must be destroyed. To help prevent infection, keep pests under control and sterilize cutting tools when propagating. Plant varieties listed as resistant.

Wirestem

This disease affects brassica seedlings, especially cauliflowers. Stems shrink at ground level and then topple. Prevent it by sowing thinly in sterilized potting mix and avoid overwatering. There is no treatment.

Leafy gall

This bacterial disease causes soil-level tissue to proliferate, forming a mass of stunted and distorted shoots. Sweet peas, dahlias, chrysanthemums, and pelargoniums are

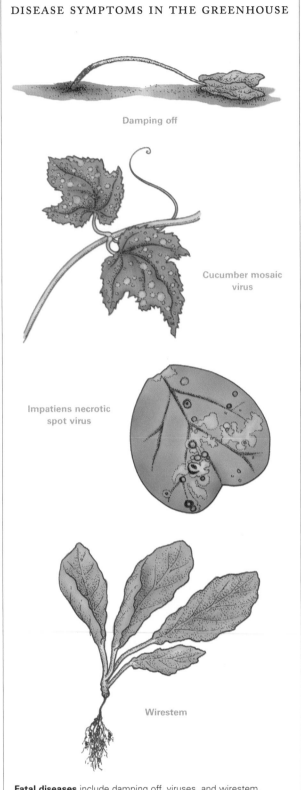

DISEASE SYMPTOMS IN THE GREENHOUSE

Damping off

Cucumber mosaic virus

Impatiens necrotic spot virus

Wirestem

Fatal diseases include damping off, viruses, and wirestem. By the time symptoms are evident, it is often too late. Other greenhouse diseases can also prove fatal if not treated promptly.

GREENHOUSE DISEASES

Pests, diseases, & other problems *see page 40* | **Keeping clean** *see page 387* | **Good hygiene** *see page 403*

particularly prone to leafy gall. Destroy affected plants and their soil. Always sterilize hands, tools, and, if necessary, work surfaces.

Botrytis (gray mold)

Affected plant tissue rots and becomes covered in gray, fluffy mold, and the flowers may develop small, brown spots on the petals. As gray mold can spread very rapidly by contact between diseased and healthy tissue, ensure that dead plant material is promptly removed. Keep your greenhouse well ventilated and water in the morning to reduce humid conditions, which encourage the fungus. Gray mold can sometimes infect plants in the greenhouse through wounds caused by pests or pruning.

Downy mildew

These mildews affect many plants, indoors and out. In a greenhouse, they are most likely to infect young brassicas, melons, lettuces, cucumbers, and tomatoes. An off-white mold forms on the leaf undersides, which may be outlined by the veins, with corresponding yellow blotches on the upper leaves. Downy mildew spreads rapidly through seedlings. Remove diseased plants on sight and improve ventilation. Avoid overhead watering, as moisture on leaves encourages the disease. Resting spores can persist for years, so change soil in beds where the disease is established.

Corm and bulb rot

Rots can develop rapidly on bulbs and corms, causing plants to collapse. Investigation reveals brown areas on the corms with rotting roots. The tissue can be very soft and smelly. If a small area is affected, cut it out. Otherwise destroy badly affected plants and replace the soil in which they were growing. Inspect bulbs and corms before planting or storing.

Rust

Many plants, edible and ornamental, are susceptible to rust. Symptoms include pustules on the undersides of leaves; these fungal spores may be yellow, white, or reddish brown. Yellow or pale green spots may appear on upper leaf surfaces. Severe infection causes defoliation and a reduction in flowering. Destroy affected plants immediately. Plant rust-resistant varieties.

As a precaution, strip lower leaves from cuttings when they are taken and when transplanted, and avoid wetting leaves when watering. Provide good air circulation. Remove and destroy affected plant tissue. Contact your local cooperative extension service for advice before choosing a fungicide to treat rust.

MORE DISEASE SYMPTOMS

Downy mildew

Fluffy molds are typical of downy mildew and gray mold. Both spread rapidly through host plants, and both can be discouraged by providing adequate ventilation in the greenhouse.

CULTURAL PROBLEMS

Cultural problems in the greenhouse are often caused by inadequate or excessive nutrition, ventilation, or irrigation. Many cultural problems can mimic viruses or other plant diseases; if you are in doubt about the cause of a particular problem, consult your local cooperative extension service for a definitive diagnosis. Some common cultural problems include:

Algae and moss growth: Visible moss and algae on the soil surface indicates overwatering or excess humidity. Improve air circulation and allow soil to dry out slightly between waterings.

Drought stress: Symptoms occur from the top of the plant downward. Seedlings wilt and leaves may turn brown from the outside edges inward. Flowers and fruit drop. Red spider mites may attack drought-stressed plants. Try to water consistently.

Fertilizer burn: Leaves wilt and may become dull and brown. Roots are damaged and the entire plant can die. Always apply fertilizer according to the package directions.

Fluoride injury: Some groundwater is naturally high in fluoride, and the chemical is added to many municipal water systems to help prevent tooth decay. If your plants are suffering leaf-tip burning, contact your municipal water supplier and ask whether your residential water is fluoridated. Use rainwater for irrigation.

Iron deficiency: Foliage develops chlorosis and loses color, starting at outside edges inward, with leaf veins remaining green. Soil may be too alkaline (high pH), which inhibits iron absorption in plants. Test soil to measure pH levels and amend if necessary. Give plants chelated trace elements and iron.

Low humidity: Leaf tips and edges may turn brown. Install a humidifier, or hose down the greenhouse floor and shelving several times a day to raise humidity.

Nitrogen deficiency: Older leaves may turn yellow and drop; plants grow weakly and slowly. Improve soil fertility and apply a fertilizer containing nitrogen.

Poor pollination: Plants flower but fail to develop fruits. Pollinate by hand, or buy self-pollinating varieties.

Sunscald: Plants too close to unshaded glazing may develop pale brown or bleached spots on leaves, and fruit such as tomatoes can get light, hard patches. Improve greenhouse shading or move susceptible plants out of direct sunlight.

CHAPTER TEN

PROPAGATING PLANTS

GENERATING NEW PLANTS, WHETHER BY RAISING THEM from seed, creating divisions, or taking cuttings from an existing plant, is one of the most challenging but rewarding aspects of gardening. It is also extremely economical—you can get plants essentially for free. You must choose the best technique for the plant you want to propagate, carry it out at the optimum time of year, and follow the procedure with care.

Methods of propagation

Some methods of propagation apply to many plants, others to only a few. You can raise almost any plant from seed, but it may not be the best method for slow-growing plants. Also, seed-raised plants may turn out to be very different from their parents. Seeds from highly bred plants, such as varieties of roses and fruit, and F1 hybrids of flowers and vegetables, are likely to produce inferior offspring. To avoid this genetic variability and produce mature plants more quickly, you can use vegetative propagation—growing on new plants from parts of an existing, or parent, plant. Some of these techniques, like division, mirror natural processes; others, such as cuttings, are more artificial, but they can yield large numbers of new plants.

Propagation basics

Propagation begins with choosing suitable parent plants, which may need special treatment to encourage them to produce good propagating material. The material then needs suitable conditions in which to regenerate and to grow on into a self-supporting plant. Often, the optimum conditions for regeneration are not the best for growing on, so the switch from one stage to the next must be carefully timed.

❧ Selecting suitable plant material

When collecting seeds or vegetative material, it makes sense to do so from healthy plants with the characteristics you want, such as the largest, brightest blooms or good crop yields. The capacity of a plant to regenerate vegetatively is affected by the age of the parent plant and the growth from which it is taken. Material from the current year's growth regenerates more easily than older tissue, and the best response is gained from juvenile plants that have not yet flowered or fruited. Old plants regenerate much less readily.

Plants of the same variety that have been increased vegetatively over many years will all be genetically identical clones, and physiologically the same age, so even a young plant of an old variety may be difficult to propagate.

For some propagation techniques, it is worth stimulating the parent plant in advance to produce suitable propagation material, for example by pruning it to encourage new shoots or forcing it into growth earlier in the season by providing additional heat and light.

❧ Providing suitable conditions for regeneration

Once you have collected and sown your seeds, and prepared your cuttings or divisions, they will need the optimum conditions in which to thrive and grow into healthy new plants. You can create the most favorable environment by choosing an appropriate growing medium, providing appropriate levels of warmth and moisture, and controlling pests and diseases. Once the new plant has established and started to grow, you will need to gradually acclimatize it to outdoor conditions so it can be planted in the yard.

PROPAGATION BASICS

You can start propagating plants without any special equipment at all—a few basic garden items will enable you to tackle many propagation techniques. Just as important to success are observing good hygiene and providing appropriate conditions for the plant material. So it is worth choosing the most appropriate container and growing mix, paying attention to watering, and doing what you can to create a favorable environment for fragile new plants, such as seedlings and cuttings. A heated propagating unit will make many tasks easier and extend the range of plants from which you can propagate.

Tools & equipment

For many propagation tasks, you do not need any special equipment at all—a few flats and plant pots, some potting mix, some plastic bags, a decent garden knife or your pruners will do. If you want to try some of the more advanced techniques, or take material from plants that are more difficult to propagate, then you may want to invest in a few extra tools or try out some specialist containers and mixes.

A heated propagating unit is a very useful tool as it will make it easier for you to control the environment of the plant material and encourage germination of seeds or rooting of the various types of cuttings.

If you are lucky enough to have a dedicated area such as a garden shed where you can propagate plants, then it is worth setting up a workbench at the proper height (*see box, below left*) and allocating shelf space to keep all your propagating kit together. This will help you to work quickly and efficiently, which in turn will reduce the stress on the plant material and increase your chances of success.

Otherwise, you can use a greenhouse bench or an area in the basement. Wherever you work, it is helpful to first get all your equipment ready and to make sure that the area is clean and brightly lit. After using propagation tools and equipment, clean and, if needed, service them.

ADJUSTING THE WORKBENCH

To prevent backache, it is well worth adjusting your workbench to the correct height. To establish this, stand up straight in front of the bench, drop your arms to your sides, then lift your forearms at right angles to your body and drop your wrists. Your fingertips should just touch the bench top.

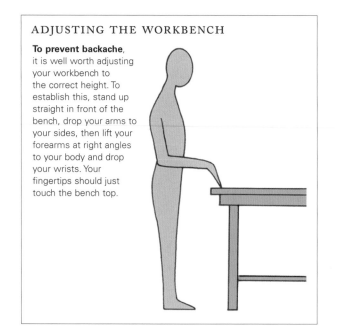

CUTTING HARD WOOD

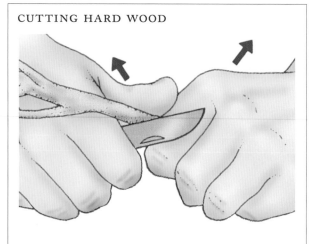

To cut wood safely, first hold the stem in your left hand, with the knife blade below and the right thumb above it. Make a shallow-angled cut from beneath by drawing the right forearm backward and maintaining a gap between the right thumb and the blade. Avoid cutting up toward your thumb.

Choosing & using a knife

A well-made knife with a sharp blade and comfortable handle is a pleasure to use and will cut plant material cleanly with the minimum of damage to the plant tissue. If plant material is bruised it is more likely to die, as this provides an opportunity for diseases like rot, which will infect your cuttings and spoil your efforts.

Gardeners' knives are available in a range of designs. You should choose one that has a stainless steel blade, is well balanced, and sits in your hand nicely. Check that it is easy to open and that the shoulder of the blade is set back into the handle when in use (*see box, below*). This reduces play from side to side and prevents the blade from working loose; this is especially important when using knives on tough material such as woody cuttings.

Knife blades may be ground to a cutting edge on one or both sides (*see right*). Both types of blade are equally effective, but while one-sided blades are either left handed or right handed, two-sided blades can be used by either hand. Blades may also be flat ground or hollow ground: a flat-ground blade is more concave and needs to be sharpened at a steeper angle.

It is best to keep one knife for propagation and not use it for other garden tasks. Use the knife to prepare and trim plant material, cutting soft wood against a clean pane of glass laid flat on the workbench. Cut hard wood carefully while holding it securely (*see box, facing page*).

The easiest way to keep a good edge on your knife is with a broad, flat sharpening stone. In time, the knife blade will inevitably become clogged with plant sap or resin, which reduces cutting efficiency. Clean the blade with a rag dipped in a solvent, such as alcohol, or with a fine grade of sandpaper.

A craft knife with disposable blades or a safety razor blade in a solid metal holder can be very useful for cutting very soft material, such as dahlia or chrysanthemum cuttings. The blades must be very sharp.

SHARPENING A FLAT-GROUND BLADE

1 **Lay the blade** on the stone at the end nearest you. While applying a slight, even pressure on the edge, draw the blade along the stone toward the opposite end. Repeat the movement several times. If necessary, turn the blade over and sharpen the other side of the edge.

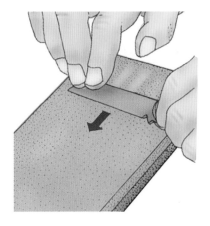

SHARPENING A HOLLOW-GROUND BLADE

1 **Lubricate the coarse side** of the stone with oil or water, according to the manufacturer's recommendation. Hold the blade at one end of the stone so it faces forward at an acute angle to the surface of the stone.

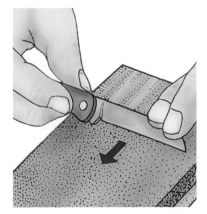

2 **Push gently along** the whole length of the stone, while maintaining the angle between the blade and the stone. Lift it off and repeat several times. Give a final rub to the blade along the fine side of the stone. Repeat with the other side of the blade if it has also been ground.

CHOOSING A KNIFE

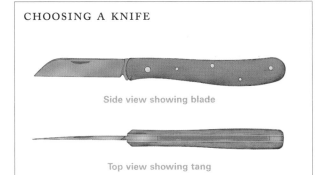

Side view showing blade

Top view showing tang

The most important quality of a good gardening knife is that it should be sharp, so choose one with a blade that has a straight cutting edge. This should be easier to sharpen. Another point to look for in a good knife is a full-length tang; that is, where the steel extends the full length of the handle to give the knife better strength and stability when being handled. The back end of the blade, or shoulder, should also be set well back into the handle when opened. An all-purpose gardening knife has a rounded blade (*see above*), and a budding knife has a spatula at one end.

Choosing & using pruners

Pruners can be used to collect tough material for cuttings more quickly and easily than a knife and, if sharp enough, they can be used to prepare the cuttings.

There are two basic designs of pruners (*see box, right*): anvil and bypass. Anvil types have one sharp, thin, straight-edged blade at the top. Its cutting edge is usually hollow ground on both sides and cuts against a broad, flat surface—the anvil—at the bottom, crushing the tissue. Bypass, or scissor, pruners also have just one sharp blade, but it is heavy, curved, and flat ground only on the inside edge. It cuts with a shearing action, like scissors, by sweeping past the lower, unsharpened anvil blade, so it makes a cleaner cut than anvil pruners and causes less bruising.

When choosing a pair of pruners, ensure that the size and handles are comfortable in your hand. Get a spring-loaded pair, which reopens after each cut automatically. When collecting propagating material from a shrub, follow the same rules as when pruning to make a clean cut and avoid leaving snags (*see page 102*).

Maintaining pruners

Pruners are much more effective when they are regularly maintained, especially when they are used for precision work like propagation. Ensure the blades are always clean

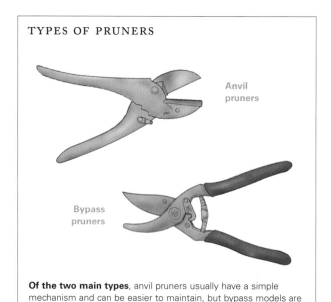

TYPES OF PRUNERS

Anvil pruners

Bypass pruners

Of the two main types, anvil pruners usually have a simple mechanism and can be easier to maintain, but bypass models are generally preferred for propagation as they make a cleaner cut.

of sap and other residues, and keep the moving parts lightly oiled. Sharpen the blades as required to keep them cutting cleanly. Some models can be sent back to the manufacturers for maintenance; with other models, follow the manufacturer's instructions.

Controlling the environment

The main challenge in propagation is to ensure the survival of propagated material, be it a seed, cutting, or piece of root, until it becomes an independent, young plant. This requires controlling the environment—above and below ground—to create optimum conditions for plant growth while reducing risk of drying out or rotting.

A favorable aerial environment produces minimum water loss from plant material, has cool air temperatures, enough light for photosynthesis, and adequate ventilation. Below ground, the ideal is warm, moist but well-drained soil, with an open, aerated structure, neutral pH, and low nutrient levels. The softer or less hardy the material, the more environmental control is needed. While most propagation methods happen under cover, sowing hardy seeds, taking hardwood cuttings, or dividing herbaceous perennials can take place entirely outdoors.

Home-made plastic covers

If you propagate indoors, you can better control the environment and keep a close eye on developing plants. Maintaining humidity is still important, but cheap and

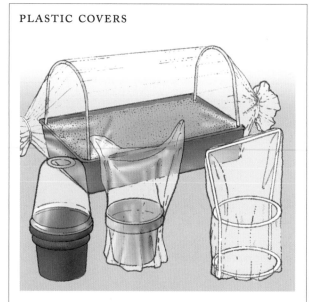

PLASTIC COVERS

There are various covers that will create a closed environment, from plastic bags or sheeting supported on wire hoops or frames to specially designed, individual pot cloches.

CONTROLLING THE ENVIRONMENT

Pruning & training *see page 102* | **Types of greenhouse** *see page 373* | **Using cold frames & cloches** *see page 382*

WINDOWSILL PROPAGATING UNIT

This type of propagating unit, with individual, miniature seed flats and covers on a heated base, may be all you need to raise a few tender seedlings and take small numbers of cuttings.

simple arrangements are sufficient for easily propagated plants (*see facing page*). Place a clean, clear plastic bag over a pot of seeds or cuttings, support it with one or two canes, then seal with a rubber band around the pot.

Cloches

Cloches protect individual plants or small groups of seedlings from pests, and they warm the air and soil. Traditional glass or plastic cloches are available from greenhouse or garden suppliers, or you can make your own. Secure plastic sheeting or row cover material on wire hoops, securing the edges and closing up the ends.

Cold frames

Essentially, these are boxes with glass or clear plastic lids and sides, with a wood, metal, or plastic frame, or with solid wood or brick sides. You can make a serviceable cold frame from second-hand materials like old bricks and windows, or you can buy a ready-made frame. Choose one that is large enough to hold all the plants you want to grow and heavy enough to withstand strong winds. It should be easy to access and to fix the lid open, closed, or ajar for ventilation. Plastic is usually lighter and safer than glass, but glass conserves heat more effectively, so is a better choice for use from late fall through to early spring (*see pages 373 and 382*).

Windowsill propagating unit

If you need additional warmth for your seeds or cuttings, a heated propagating unit is the most straightforward

THERMOSTAT-CONTROLLED UNIT

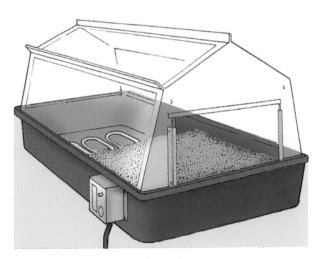

Larger propagating units have heated bases, sometimes covered with sand to spread the warmth and hold moisture, and tall, transparent covers, which may be divided into 2 or more units.

solution (*see above*). It also creates a closed environment to maintain humidity. Locate it on a well-lit windowsill, out of direct sunlight to avoid overheating.

Use a propagating unit with a heating unit and thermostat to maintain the temperature. This is normally preset to 64–70°F, which is the preferred germination temperature of many tender garden plants. Most propagating units require a background temperature of at least 41°F and preferably 50°F in order to maintain a soil temperature of 64–70°F. Larger propagating units can be used in the house if there is sufficient light, but they are better in a greenhouse or sunroom.

Grow lights are useful for gardeners who lack a greenhouse or available windowsill, or to supplement low light levels. Special incandescent lights emit wavelengths that are optimal for plant growth.

Containers

Most gardeners accumulate a motley collection of plastic pots and flats when buying plants. If they are clean and about the right size (pots smaller than 3in. across dry out too quickly), they are fine for propagation, as are plastic food containers with added drainage holes. If you buy containers, you will need a mixture of pots and flats.

Choosing containers

You only require a few different types for most purposes. Wide, shallow pots are useful for seeds and small cuttings that do not need very deep potting mix, and long pots are good for deep-rooted plants. Pots with almost vertical sides have greater stability and hold more mix. Seed flats should be 2–2½in. deep; shallower ones dry out too quickly and deeper ones use too much mix. Cell packs (*see right*) are useful for large numbers of seeds, but they may be rather flimsy and can be awkward to fill with potting mix and difficult to clean.

Cell packs and growing cells keep the rootballs of the young plants separate and are easier to move than lots of individual pots.

SEED CONTAINERS

Most seed containers, whether flats (*shown top*), cell packs (*center*), or shallow or deep pots (*bottom*), are made of plastic, and are cheap, lightweight, durable, and easily washed and stored. They retain moisture better than clay or wood containers.

PEAT POTS

Peat pots are made of sphagnum peat moss and pulp. They allow plant roots to penetrate into the pot materials, so you can plant the pot and its contents with little disturbance to the roots. The pot eventually rots away.

Growing mixes

Some types of propagation, including layering and division, take place outdoors, directly into the soil. In most cases, however, garden soil is not a suitable growing medium; you need to use a good, sterile growing mix.

Starting mixes

Some mixes are all-purpose, suitable for seed raising, taking cuttings, and other forms of propagation, as well as growing plants. This inevitably makes makes them a bit of a compromise, but for most jobs they are perfectly adequate. Cuttings need a rooting medium that is permanently moist to prevent them from drying out and that has an open structure so that air can circulate. If you are using an all-purpose potting mix, add a handful of vermiculite or grit to every four handfuls of mix to improve drainage and reduce the risk of rot.

Seeds require similar conditions but may be more sensitive to the nutrient and chemical content of the mix. An all-purpose mix may be too coarse, or contain too much fertilizer, for some finicky or fine seeds. For these, a mix formulated especially for seed-starting (called a starter or germination mix) may give better results.

Soilless mixes

Soilless mixes are lightweight, porous, and free from soil-borne diseases. They usually contain either vermiculite or perlite blended with an organic component—typically peat moss, a material harvested from sphagnum peat bogs.

Alternatives to peat moss, such as coconut fiber, are increasingly found in mixes as concerns about the sustainability of peat bogs increases. Soilless potting mixes often include additional ingredients, such as bark to assist drainage, wetting agents for water retention, and nutrients.

Soil-based potting mixes

Most mixes contain soil and some combination of ingredients which can include sand, peat moss, vermiculite, perlite, and fertilizer. Garden centers and nurseries stock a wide range for different plant types.

You can also experiment with making your own mix (*see box, below*). Make sure all ingredients are sterile. For large quantities, blend the ingredients on a clean, solid floor with a clean shovel.

MAKING YOUR OWN POTTING MIX

- **2 parts pasteurized soil**
- **1 part peat moss**
- **1 part coarse sand, perlite, vermiculite, leaf mold, or well-rotted compost**

to each 2 gallon bucket of mix, add:

- **1 tsp ground chalk**

Mix all the ingredients thoroughly and store, covered, in a cool, dry place. To pasteurize soil, put it in a broad, flat, heatproof container, such as a baking sheet, cover with aluminum foil, and put in the oven at 180°F for 30 minutes. For starter mix, sift the peat moss through a sieve.

USING HORMONE ROOTING POWDER

Plant growth is controlled, in part, by naturally occurring hormones. You can encourage a shoot to produce roots by applying hormone rooting powder to the cut surface. If it is dry, dip the end of the cutting in water first. Avoid getting powder on the outside of the stem; it is wasteful and may even inhibit root development.

Hormone rooting powder does not keep well. Buy it fresh each season and store in a cool, dry place. When using it, tip a little into a small dish, then discard any surplus to avoid contaminating the main stock. Hormone rooting powder is effective only on cut stems; it does not aid rooting of root or leaf cuttings. Rooting hormone is also available in gel form.

Watering

Watering is much easier if you start with potting mix that is already moist—dry mix can be hard to rewet. Check the mix by taking a handful and squeezing it. When you open your hand, the ball should crack open in just one or two places. If it remains in one lump it is too wet, and if it all falls apart it is too dry.

It is possible to water from above, but if the water drops are too large you may displace seeds or cuttings. For very small seedlings, a sprayer is the best watering device. Watering from below takes longer, but does not disturb seeds or plants. Standing containers in water works well and is the best way to rewet containers that have dried out. If you overwater the potting mix, stand the containers on newspaper to draw out excess moisture.

Capillary systems

An alternative way to water from below is with a capillary system. Stand the containers on a permanently damp base so that the potting mix can absorb moisture by capillary action continually, but without becoming so wet that the mix becomes waterlogged. The great advantage of this system is that you are unlikely to overwater and only need to top up water in the base material, rather than to one container at a time. Plants may dry out if there is poor capillary contact, especially if they are moved around a lot. You can set up a system with capillary matting, or use sand as a base material (*see right*).

MAKING A SAND BED

Water via a sand bed to reduce the risk of the potting mix drying out. Choose a flat with raised sides and good drainage, and line it with plastic sheeting. Pierce holes in the sheeting about ½in. below the required surface level, then fill the flat with fine sand. Level the surface, then water well and allow to drain. Set the containers firmly on the sand bed so that there is no air between the sand and the potting mix to impede the uptake of moisture from the sand into the pot. Keep the sand moist by adding water from time to time.

WATERING FROM ABOVE

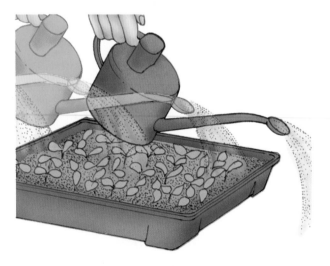

This is a quick way of watering, but it needs a steady hand and a fine, upturned waterbreaker that does not drip. Start pouring the water away from the container; once you get an even flow, direct it over the mix. Move the spout away from the container before stopping the flow.

WATERING FROM BELOW

A shallow bath of water—a cat-litter tray is ideal—provides the simplest way of watering containers from below. Stand them in the water bath and, as soon as moisture appears on the surface, remove the containers and leave them to drain.

GOOD HYGIENE, PESTS, & DISEASES

Pests, diseases, & other problems *see page 40* | Watering & fertilizing *see page 364* | Hygiene & maintenance *see page 387*

Good hygiene, pests, & diseases

Recently propagated plants are especially vulnerable to pests and diseases, so extra care must be taken to protect them. Good hygiene is the first line of defence. All pots, flats, tools, and work surfaces used for propagation should be scrupulously clean. Garden disinfectants are useful allies. If you use a greenhouse, give it a good clean in early winter. Bag up unused potting mixes for reuse on established container plants or put it on the compost pile, rather than leaving it lying around. Also, it is important to check your plants frequently—daily if possible—and remove dead or dying leaves. Take action quickly if you spot any pests or diseases.

Common pests

Whiteflies: Small, white, mothlike adults and greenish white, scalelike larvae suck the sap and excrete a sugary substance (honeydew), which makes foliage sticky and feeds growth of sooty mold (*see page 388*).

Fungus gnats: The small, grayish-white larvae of these tiny, black flies eat roots of young plants. They like wet soil, so do not overwater. Catch the flies on yellow sticky traps or use a predatory mite, *Hypoaspis miles*, which is a biological control.

Slugs and snails: These wreak havoc among seedlings and soft cuttings. Check hiding places regularly, such as under pots and between plastic flats (*see page 49*).

Spider mites: You can detect these by their wispy webs and the yellow mottling of affected leaves. Control is difficult, but high humidity discourages them. Discard badly affected plants (*see page 388*).

Vine weevils: The adults lay their eggs in soil or potting mix; the grubs are C-shaped, cream with dark heads, and feed voraciously on roots and stem bases. Such plants may be killed during fall to spring (*see page 50*).

Common diseases

Botrytis (gray mold): This thrives in cold, damp conditions. A brown area of rot anywhere on a seedling or cutting, in time, develops a covering of grayish mold. Promptly remove infected material, ventilate where possible, and provide warm conditions. There is no chemical treatment.

Damping off: Soil- and water-borne fungi kill tissues near soil level, so seedlings keel over and die. Always use fresh mix and clean flats, do not sow densely, give seedlings plenty of light, air, and warmth, and do not overwater.

Foot and root rots: These rots are caused by soil- and water-borne fungi. Practice good hygiene and growing practices to promote strong root growth.

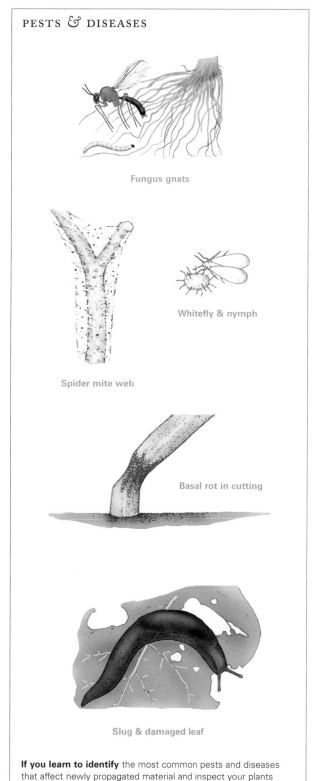

PESTS & DISEASES

Fungus gnats

Whitefly & nymph

Spider mite web

Basal rot in cutting

Slug & damaged leaf

If you learn to identify the most common pests and diseases that affect newly propagated material and inspect your plants regularly, you can nip any attack in the bud.

Methods of propagation

Some plants increase readily, others may be propagated in several ways, and some are much more difficult than others. You will increase your chances of success if you choose an appropriate method for the plant. The chart below gives an indication of the best methods of raising some common garden and houseplants; other examples are discussed in the following pages. Many can also be raised from seed. Most plants may be increased by means of one or more of the methods described here, and you will discover which you prefer.

PLANT	METHOD OF PROPAGATION	PLANT	METHOD OF PROPAGATION
Acanthus	root cuttings	*Hydrangea petiolaris*	layering, softwood cuttings
Acer japonicum, A. palmatum	air layering	*Hypericum calycinum*	division
African violet (*Saintpaulia*)	leaf cuttings	*Incarvillea*	division
Agave	offsets	Ivy (*Hedera*)	leaf-bud cuttings, layering
Anemone x hybrida	root cuttings, division	Juniper (low-growing types)	conifer cuttings
Aster	division	*Kalmia*	layering
Aubrieta	division	*Kerria japonica*	suckers, hardwood cuttings
Bamboo	division	Lady's mantle (*Alchemilla*)	division
Bellflower (*Campanula*)	division	*Lavatera*	semihard cuttings
Berberis	heel/mallet cuttings	Lavender (*Lavandula*)	softwood cuttings
Bergenia	division	Lemon (*Citrus limon*)	air layering
Black currant	greenwood/hardwood cuttings	Lilac (*Syringa*)	air layering, root cuttings
Bottlebrush (*Callistemon*)	softwood cuttings	*Magnolia*	layering, air layering
Boxwood (*Buxus*)	hardwood cuttings	*Mahonia*	leaf bud cuttings
Canna	rhizomes	*Miscanthus*	division
Cape primrose (*Streptocarpus*)	lateral vein/midrib cuttings	New Zealand flax (*Phormium*)	division, offsets
Cardiocrinum	bulblets	Pampas grass (*Cortaderia*)	division
Catmint (*Nepeta*)	rhizomes	Passion flower (*Passiflora*)	semihard cuttings
Ceanothus	greenwood/evergreen cuttings	*Pelargonium*	greenwood cuttings
Choisya ternata	semihard/evergreen cuttings	Peony (herbaceous)	division
Clematis	layering, leaf-bud cuttings	*Peperomia*	leaf cuttings
Coleus (*Solenostemon*)	softwood cuttings	*Philadelphus*	greenwood/semihard cuttings
Convallaria majalis	rhizomes	*Phlox*	root cuttings, division
Cotoneaster (large hybrids)	hardwood cuttings	*Pieris*	layering
Crassula	offsets	*Pileostegia*	softwood cuttings
Cypress (*Cupressus*)	conifer cuttings	Poppy (*Papaver*)	root cuttings, division
Daphne	evergreen cuttings	*Potentilla* (herbaceous species)	runners
Daylily (*Hemerocallis*)	division	*Primula*	division
Delphinium	division, greenwood cuttings	*Pyracantha*	evergreen cuttings
Dogwood (*Cornus*)	layering, semihard/ hardwood cuttings	Red and white currant	hardwood cuttings
		Rhubarb	division
Echeveria	offsets	Rock rose (*Cistus*)	semihard cuttings
Elaeagnus	evergreen cuttings	Rose (species and hybrids)	hardwood cuttings
Escallonia	evergreen/semihard cuttings	*Rudbeckia*	division
False acacia (*Robinia*)	suckers, root cuttings	*Saxifraga*	offsets
False cypress (*Chamaecyparis*)	conifer cuttings	Sea holly (*Eryngium*)	root cuttings
Fleabane (*Erigeron*)	division	Sea lavender (*Limonium*)	root cuttings, division
Flowering currant (*Ribes*)	semihard/hardwood cuttings	Sedge (*Carex*)	division
Flowering quince (*Chaenomeles*)	softwood cuttings, suckers	Smoke bush (*Cotinus coggygria*)	layering, suckers
Forsythia	greenwood/semihard cuttings	Solomon's seal (*Polygonatum*)	rhizomes
Fuchsia	softwood cuttings	Spider plant (*Chlorophytum*)	runners
Geranium	division	*Spiraea*	hardwood cuttings
Gesneria	leaf cuttings	Spotted laurel (*Aucuba*)	evergreen cuttings
Gladiolus	cormlets, scoring	Sumac (*Rhus*)	root cuttings, suckers
Gloxinia	tubers, leaf cuttings	Sweet box (*Sarcococca*)	division
Gooseberry	greenwood/hardwood cuttings	Trumpet vine (*Campsis radicans*)	layering, root cuttings
Hebe	evergreen cuttings	Virginia creeper (*Parthenocissus*)	layering
Helenium	division	Waterlily (*Nymphaea*)	tubers, leaf bud cuttings
Hens-and-chicks (*Sempervivum*)	offsets	Wax flower (*Hoya*)	leaf-bud/softwood cuttings
Hibiscus	softwood cuttings	Willow (*Salix*)	hardwood cuttings
Honeysuckle (*Lonicera*)	leaf bud/hardwood cuttings	Witch hazel (*Hamamelis*)	layering, air layering
Hydrangea macrophylla	division, semihard cuttings	Yew (*Taxus*)	conifer cuttings

SOWING SEEDS

A seed consists of a miniature plant or embryo, a food supply, and a protective seed coat. Outside this may be other layers, such as a fleshy fruit (as on a plum) or a tough skin. The embryo consists of an undeveloped root, an undeveloped shoot, and short section of stem between them. Attached to this embryo stem are seed leaves (cotyledons). These may remain in the soil or emerge above ground when a seedling germinates. They are usually simply shaped and may be quite unlike the plant's true leaves. The seed's food reserves come from the cotyledons or from a separate food store.

Collecting & storing seeds

You can grow many annual and perennial flowering plants, and many vegetables, successfully from seeds that you collect yourself. Avoid collecting from highly bred hybrids, especially those labeled F1 in seed catalogs; these seedlings will not grow true to type and are likely to give disappointing results.

Seed needs to be collected as it becomes ripe but before it is dispersed (*see below*). This means keeping a careful eye on the plants and, as soon as the dead flowers start to break up or the seedheads start to dry out, collect what you need. Do your collecting on a mild, dry day. Snip off small seedheads, pods, or capsules from plants when they are nearly dry; they often fade to brown and become papery when ripe. Place the seedheads in an open paper bag or in a flat and leave them to dry further. Alternatively, you can collect the entire flower stem. Break up dried seed capsules, and clean the seeds by sifting or just picking out the debris.

Provided you dry the seeds properly and then keep them cool and dry, you can store most flower and vegetable seeds for two or three years. A good way to do this is to place the seed packets in a sealed plastic container, with a sachet of silica gel to absorb any moisture, and store it in the refrigerator or in a cool, dry place.

COLLECTING & STORING FLOWER SEED

  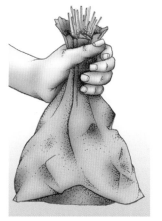 

Spread fleshy seed capsules on tissue or paper towel in a flat or shallow box. Leave to dry in the sun or a warm place.

Bunch together stems of whole flowerheads, then enclose the heads in a paper bag—avoid plastic bags because they trap moisture that can lead to rotting.

Tie the neck of the bag and hang up in a dry, well-ventilated place. Shake the bag occasionally to help release the seeds into the bag.

Label bags or envelopes with the plant name and date, and place the seeds inside once they are properly dried and cleaned of any chaff. Store in a cool, dry place.

Sowing in flats

Before choosing a container, consider the needs of the seeds. How many seeds are you sowing, and how large will the seedlings grow before they are transplanted? Seed flats or wide, shallow pots are best for small seeds, but you can improvise with food-packaging trays if they have plenty of drainage holes. Larger seeds often germinate more successfully since they have large food reserves. You can sow them evenly spaced in flats, but it is better to sow them singly into small pots or cell packs.

Preparing containers

Make sure that any container is scrupulously clean before you start. Always use fresh potting mix, ideally that is newly bought; older or second-hand mix can be used safely on more mature plants. Multipurpose mix should be adequate for the great majority of seeds. Specialty seed mixes contain less fertilizer and may be better for some seeds that are sensitive to high nutrient levels. Seed of acid-loving plants is best sown in a specialty mix.

SOWING SEEDS IN CONTAINERS

1 **Soak large seeds** in water for 12–24 hours before sowing so that they can absorb the necessary moisture more easily.

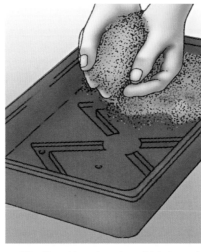

2 **Fill a flat** with potting mix until it is heaped above the rim, then tap it on the work surface to settle the contents.

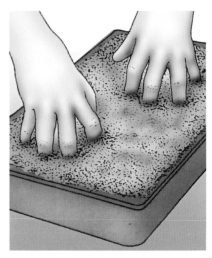

3 **Firm the mix** gently into the corners and base, using the tips of your fingers to eliminate air pockets.

4 **Level off excess** mix with a sawing action, using a piece of wood, so that the surface is level with the container rim.

5 **Firm the potting mix** lightly to ¼–½in. below the rim, using a piece of wood that just fits inside the container. This creates space for watering.

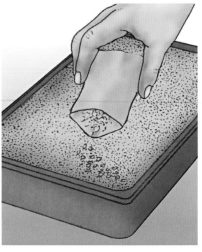

6 **Sow half the seed** as evenly as possible right across the surface, keeping your hand low to prevent the seeds from bouncing.

Before sowing your seed, it is important to ensure that the potting mix surface is smooth and level. If the surface is uneven, seeds can drop into gaps and end up buried too deeply. In addition, moisture tends to become unevenly distributed. Sift very coarse mix, or pick out large fibrous pieces, before use.

A presser board—a flat piece of wood with a handle—that fits the inside of the container makes it a great deal easier to firm the mix evenly. A useful alternative is an empty, flat-based seed flat or pot of the same size. Take care not to compact the mix when firming it.

Sowing seed

Scatter the seed in two directions across the mix to get an even spread over the surface. If the seeds are very fine, it is easier to distribute them evenly, and see where they are sown, if you mix them thoroughly with some dry, fine sand first. Cover the seeds with a uniform thickness of sifted mix. Some seeds, often fine seeds, require light to germinate so should be left uncovered; check the recommendation on the seed packet. Once sown, cover the container (*see below*) and leave it in a warm place to germinate, or put uncovered in a dark, warm place.

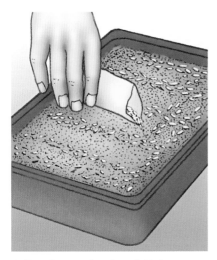

7 **Turn the container** through 90 degrees and sow the remaining seed evenly across the surface.

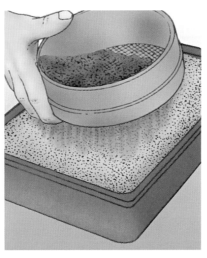

8 **Cover the seeds** to no more than their own depth by sifting potting mix over them.

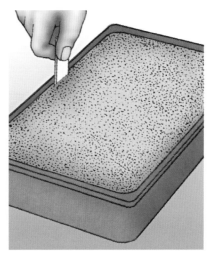

9 **Label the seeds** with the full name of the variety and the date of sowing. Use an indelible marker for this.

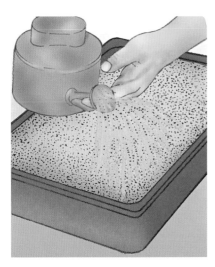

10 **Water the seeds** using a watering can with a fine waterbreaker (*see page 402*). Alternatively, stand the container in a tray of water for 15 minutes, then allow it to drain.

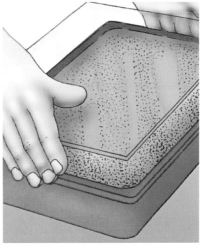

11 **Cover the container** with a pane of glass or a sheet of plastic wrap to keep the seeds moist. Normally, this can be left in place until the seeds germinate.

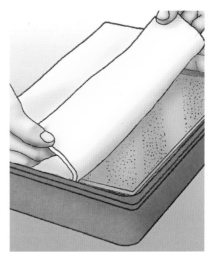

12 **Place a sheet** of paper over the glass or wrap to minimize temperature fluctuations. Stand the container in a warm place—around 70°F suits most plants.

The developing seed

Once sufficient water has penetrated the seed coat, the warm, moist environment sets off a series of chemical reactions in the seed. These release nutrients from the seed's food store, giving the embryo the energy to start developing and to emerge through the seed coat to become a seedling. This is the process known as germination.

In broad terms, the higher the soil temperature, the more quickly germination will occur. However, forcing the seed to develop rapidly can lead to weak seedlings if light levels are low—as they often are in spring. In this situation, it is better to maintain a lower soil temperature to encourage slower, sturdier growth. Seed packets will generally give you a good idea of the best temperature range for any particular seed.

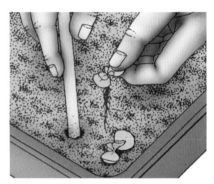

THE GERMINATING SEED

As a seed germinates, the embryo develops an initial root system below ground and a shoot system above. The seed leaves, or cotyledons, may stay under, or emerge above, the soil surface. They are usually simply shaped and rarely bear any resemblance to the plant's true leaves.

CARING FOR SEEDLINGS

1 **Uncover the container** as soon as the seedlings appear and place it in a well-lit area. Spray the seedlings with water as necessary, but do not get them waterlogged.

2 **Transplant the seedlings**, once they are large enough to handle, to move them on and give them more room. Using a dibble or similar small tool, loosen a group of seedlings, then gently lift one free. Handle seedlings by their leaves; never touch the fragile stems.

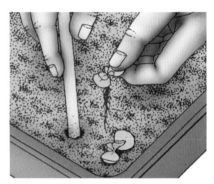

3 **Hold each seedling** in one hand and make a hole with the dibble in fresh potting mix in a prepared container. This may be another flat, an individual pot, or cell packs, depending on the plant's requirements.

4 **Lower the seedling roots** into the hole and firm the potting mix gently with the dibble. If the stem is a bit long, insert it a little deeper than it was before. Aim for 24–40 seedlings per flat.

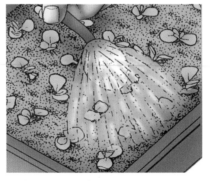

5 **Water the seedlings** once the container is filled, to settle the soil and allow to drain. Place the container in a warm, well-lit area to reestablish—a temperature of around 70°F suits most plants.

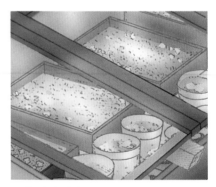

6 **Harden off the seedlings** once they start to grow again, to acclimatize them to outdoor conditions. Move them to a cool site, such as a cold frame, unheated greenhouse, or well-lit windowsill in a cool room. Raise the cold frame lid on sunny days, but close and insulate it overnight if severe frost threatens.

Hygiene & maintenance *see page 387* | **Growing mixes** *see page 401* | **Methods of propagation** *see page 404*

Seed-sowing troubleshooter

Raising plants from seeds is one of the easier methods of propagation and should be straightforward, but if things go wrong the cause may not be obvious. This guide to the commonest problems affecting seeds and seedlings will help you to diagnose the problem and avoid it in future. You should maintain good hygiene, use sterile potting mix, and provide suitable conditions, usually warm, moist, and light—but not too hot, wet, or humid.

PROBLEM	CAUSE	SOLUTION
Seeds do not germinate	Seeds not viable (dead)	Buy fresh seeds. Most seeds can be stored for no more than three years in a cool (max 50°F), dry place.
	Potting soil too dry or too wet	Sow in moist soil. Water and drain after sowing. Water with a sprayer only if it is dry below the surface.
	Wrong temperature	Seeds can rot if too cold or cook if too hot. Check the temperature needed for your seeds (for example on the seed packet) and use a max–min thermometer to monitor the ambient temperature.
	Seeds requires special treatment	Unusual seeds may need different treatment; check the seed packet for special requirements.
Seeds germinate but do not emerge (dig some up to check)	Capping—the seedlings are unable to push through a crust of dried mix	Do not overheat the container and check seedlings daily. If the dry surface of the mix is heaving, use a sprayer to rewet it so the seedlings can push through.
	Seeds sown too deep	Use fine vermiculite to cover very fine seeds—they often need light to germinate and vermiculite lets it through. Also it is easier to cover the seeds thinly.
Seedlings emerge in patches	Uneven conditions	Firm and level mix carefully before sowing and water from below.
	Uneven sowing	Mix small seeds with fine vermiculite or sand so that you can see where you have just sown them.
	Seeds naturally variable	Some seed, such as that of wild flowers, germinates erratically. Home-saved seed may also be variable.
Seedlings are etiolated (thin, pale, and drawn)	Too much heat and not enough light	If you cannot provide more light, keep them at a lower temperature.
Seedlings are lopsided	Uneven light	Rotate the container daily so they are evenly exposed or use grow lights
Seedlings wither	Not enough moisture	Check daily and water just enough to keep moist.
	Too much heat, often from direct sun, can wither leaves even if the mix is moist	Maintain a humid atmosphere around newly emerged seedlings and shade them from direct sunlight.
Seedlings collapse	Seedlings affected by damping off (which rots the stems near the base)	This can occur soon after germination, or after transplanting, and is caused by a fungal infection (*see page 390*).
Seedlings fail to grow	Too little warmth	Newly germinated seedlings require similar temperatures to those for germination—harden them off slowly to avoid a check in growth.
	Too few nutrients	Seed mix contains only enough nutrients for germination; transplant seedlings promptly or apply liquid fertilizer.
	Too much water	Do not overwater small seedlings in large pots or newly transplanted seedlings that may have damaged roots.

Raising trees & shrubs from seed

You can grow many trees and shrubs from seed, and surprisingly rapidly in good growing conditions. Sow your own collected seeds as soon as they are ripe; they may germinate immediately or in the next spring. If you let the seeds dry out, they may become dormant and germinate far less readily. This is a survival mechanism to avoid the seeds germinating in unfavorable conditions, but it can be frustrating for the gardener.

There are ways to overcome seed dormancy. Seed of trees and shrubs used to cold winters may need a period of chilling at 34–37°F. With home-saved seed, sowing in fall and placing the pot outdoors is often enough. You can also store and chill seed in the refrigerator over winter for a spring sowing (*see below*). Chill purchased seed for six to eight weeks before sowing.

Hard seed coats

A tough coat may delay germination, perhaps for years. Pea-family seeds, such as laburnum, can be soaked for 24 hours in warm water; rinse the container well after use as some of these seeds are poisonous. The seeds are ready to sow when they sink. You could also abrade the seed coats: line a glass jar with sandpaper, add seeds, replace the lid, and shake for ten minutes or so.

CHILLING SEED

1 **Sift leafmold**, peat moss, composted bark, or vermiculite through a coarse sieve after measuring out by volume about 4 times as much of this medium as you have seeds. On its own, vermiculite does not need sifting.

2 **Add sufficient water** to the mix in a waterproof container, so the mix exudes a little water when it is lightly squeezed in the hand. If it is too wet, the seeds may rot.

3 **Sprinkle the seed** evenly over the surface of the damp growing mix.

4 **Mix in the seeds** well. If the mix looks too dense to hold enough air, add 1 part by volume of sharp sand. Transfer the mix to a plastic bag.

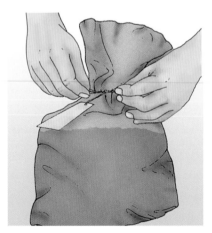

5 **Label the bag** and leave it in a warm place for 2–3 days. After this, chill the seed by placing the bag in the refrigerator for up to 18 weeks, depending on the species.

6 **Check the bag** weekly: remove any germinating seeds and turn and shake the bag to keep the seeds aerated—most will not germinate until sown in warmer conditions.

Bulbous plants *see page 91* | Trees & shrubs *see page 96* | Methods of propagation *see page 404*

ROOTS, BULBS, CORMS, & TUBERS

Most gardeners will be familiar with the idea of propagating plants from sections of shoot, but many are unaware that the same process can also be carried out using roots. Some plants naturally produce buds and shoots from their roots as a way of spreading out and colonizing new ground. Other plants produce buds and shoots from severed sections of root, for example when plants are damaged by burrowing animals or landslides. These natural processes can also be exploited to propagate modified stems that grow underground, including rhizomes, tubers, corms, and bulbs.

Woody shrubs with suckers

Some woody plants produce suckers—shoots arising from the roots at a distance from the main stem (*see page 105*). You can sever these from the parent plant and transplant them. They are used to propagate raspberries and a number of other plants. Suckers generate a new plant quickly and with little effort. The drawback is that you have to wait for them to appear naturally, although many suckering plants can also be propagated by root cuttings.

Plants that sucker freely, such as sumacs, can be a nuisance—the suckers are difficult to control and may emerge far from the parent. Some plants, especially budded or grafted roses, plums, cherries, and lilacs, sucker from grafted rootstocks (*see page 249*). These suckers are often quite vigorous, and because they emerge from the rootstock, and not the topgrowth, they are unlikely to exhibit the same properties if propagated.

PROPAGATING WOODY SHRUBS FROM SUCKERS

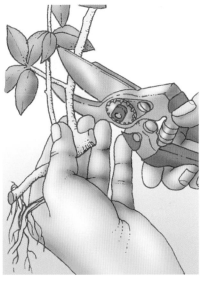

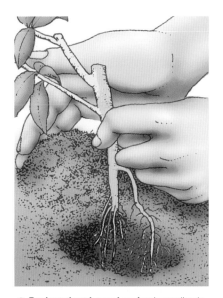

1 **Lift isolated suckers** from woody shrubs during the dormant season.

2 **Trim the roots** and cut back some of the topgrowth to reduce stress on the roots.

3 **Replant the trimmed sucker** immediately, to the same depth, and water in well.

Root cuttings

Relatively few plants propagate by root cuttings; the technique is used most often on a small number of herbaceous perennials, but a number of trees, shrubs, and vines can also be propagated in this way.

Root cuttings can be easier to care for than stem cuttings and less likely to dry out, but they can be relatively slow to develop and the process is more stressful for the parent plant. You can greatly increase your chance of success by preparing the parent plant in the previous year (*see below*) to encourage plenty of new root growth from which you can take cuttings.

When to take root cuttings

Some plants such as phlox, Japanese anemone, trumpet vine (*Campsis*), and flowering quince can produce new plants from root cuttings. Horseradish (*Armoracia rusticana*) is a notorious example, as any piece of root broken off at any time will quickly grow into a new plant, and it can easily become an invasive weed. Many troublesome weeds such as bindweed (*Convolvulus arvensis*) and bishop's weed (*Aegopodium podagraria*) also regrow readily from underground fragments, but these are not roots—they are rhizomes.

PREPARING THE PARENT PLANT FOR ROOT CUTTING MATERIAL

1 **Lift a healthy plant** from the ground during its dormant season.

2 **Cut back** any topgrowth. Shake any excess earth from the roots.

3 **Wash the roots** in a bucket of water, or hose them clean.

4 **Cut off the large roots** close to the crown, using a clean, sharp knife, and leave the fine roots.

5 **Replant the trimmed rootstock**, at the same level as it was before.

6 **Allow the plant** to reestablish during the growing season; it should develop plenty of vigorous, new roots ready for propagation.

ROOT CUTTINGS

Growing under glass *see page 379* | **Propagation basics** *see page 396* | **Methods of propagation** *see page 404*

With most plants, however, the best time to take root cuttings is in the middle of the plants' dormant season. In the case of most herbaceous and woody plants, this will be during winter. Some herbaceous perennials, however, such as pasque flower (*Pulsatilla vulgaris*), start into growth as early as midwinter and are fully dormant in late summer and early fall.

Trimming root cuttings

Root cuttings are sometimes potted up so that they lie horizontally in the rooting medium. Much better results are obtained by inserting the cuttings vertically, but they must be the right way up. To make sure that you never

plant your cutting upside down, always make a straight cut at the upper end, so that the top is flat, and a sloping cut at the lower end, so the bottom is tapered.

Size of the root cuttings

Once separated from the parent plant, the root cutting must have sufficient stored food in its tissues to survive and produce shoots and leaves. The minimum size of cutting needed will depend on the ambient temperature.

At lower temperatures, the cutting develops shoots and leaves more slowly, so it needs more stored food. It must therefore be larger than a cutting that is rooted in warmth. As a rule of thumb, if you are propagating your

OBTAINING CUTTING MATERIAL

1 **Trim off any topgrowth** that remains on the parent plant in the middle of the dormant season. Lift the plant carefully.

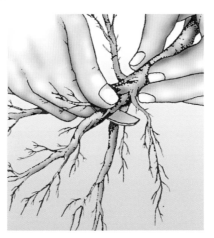

2 **Wash the soil from the roots** and take cuttings (*see below*) from the newly formed roots close to the crown.

3 **Return the parent plant** to its usual position in the garden and leave to grow and develop more new roots for next year.

PREPARING A ROOT CUTTING

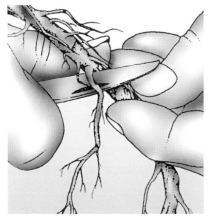

1 **Select roots** that are firm, plump, and undamaged. Cut off any side roots, with straight cuts close to the main root.

2 **Trim each root cutting** by first making a straight cut across and just below the severed top of the root cutting.

3 **Use a sloping cut** to remove the tapering, thin end of the root, to leave a cutting of uniform thickness.

STARTING ROOT CUTTINGS

1 **Fill a pot** with moist rooting medium, and firm to ½in. below the rim. Make a hole with a dibble. Plant the cutting vertically, so that the flat end is uppermost and just flush with the surface. Space the cuttings 1–1½in. apart in the container.

2 **Cover the top** of the mix with grit or vermiculite. This stops the tops of the cuttings drying out, but it is less moist than the rooting medium, which could promote rotting.

3 **Label and date** the pot after leveling off the surface using a ruler or piece of wood. Place the pot in a cold frame or propagating unit out of direct sunlight, or in a sheltered, shaded position outdoors.

4 **Keep watering** to the absolute minimum, but just enough to maintain a humid atmosphere, until the new plants are established and have developed new roots, then apply liquid fertilizer. Move the pot to a well-lit position once shoots appear, and gradually increase watering.

root cuttings outdoors, they will need to survive for up to 16 weeks before establishing and should be no less than 4in. long. In a cold frame, rooting should occur in about eight weeks and so each cutting should be no less than 2in. long. In a warm greenhouse or propagating unit at a temperature of 64–75°, the cuttings should establish in as little as four weeks, so they need be only 1in. long. If there is plentiful propagating material available, however, make them a little longer than necessary to ensure successful reproduction.

Starting root cuttings

Insert the prepared cuttings into 3½in. pots (*see above*). Use a rooting medium that retains a good balance of air and moisture and provides some nutrients once the cuttings start to grow.

Unlike stem cuttings, root cuttings do not respond to hormone rooting powder; in fact, it has an adverse effect and actually inhibits formation of buds. If you space the cuttings evenly, you can fit seven into a 3½in. pot. Cover the cuttings to keep the latent buds at their tops moist and aerated, but do not water them.

Care of the new plants

Often the first new shoots appear from root cuttings before they send out any new roots. Watering at this stage can cause rotting, so do not water the cuttings until you can see signs of rooting, such as the new roots emerging through holes at the base of the pot.

Once the cuttings are established, you can plant them directly in the ground if the soil is reasonably light, or in a cold frame in soil that has been improved by the addition of sand or peat moss. However, unless you are dealing with very large numbers, it is usually more convenient to grow on the cuttings singly in pots. Cuttings that have been rooted in a heated environment will need to be hardened off before they are moved to a cooler area or planted outdoors.

Root cuttings of some plants, such as tree poppy (*Romneya coulteri*), do not like being dug up and having their roots disturbed. In such cases, it is best to place only one or two cuttings from the thickest roots in each pot and treat them as a single plant. When transplanting, handle the rootball carefully and avoid disturbing the roots as much as possible.

TUBEROUS ROOTS

Growing under glass *see page 379* | **Propagation basics** *see page 396* | **Methods of propagation** *see page 404*

Tuberous roots

Some plants store food in swollen areas on their roots. This enables them to survive through dormant periods and provides a ready source of nutrients when growing conditions improve. In temperate climates, the dormant season is in winter, and the plants start to grow in spring, but in other parts of the world the dormant season may be at other times of year, when there is drought for example. Tuberous roots are often loosely called tubers, although true tubers are swollen underground stems, such as potatoes and Jerusalem artichokes (*see following page*). Tuberous roots may be annual or perennial (*see box, right*).

Dividing tuberous roots

Tuberous roots are propagated by division, but it is crucial to make sure that each portion has at least one healthy bud attached. On annual tuberous roots, the buds will be in the crown at the bases of the old stems; the tuberous part of the root alone does not have any buds and cannot reproduce itself. On perennial tuberous roots, there should be a cluster of buds in the center of the crown; divide up the buds between slices of the tuberous root.

After potting up the pieces of root individually, leave them in a frost-free place. Do not water them. Once new shoots appear from the tubers, move the containers to a well-lit place such as a windowsill or potting shed and begin to water the plants normally. Once all risk of frost is passed, you may plant the tubers outdoors.

TYPES OF TUBEROUS ROOT

Begonia
(perennial roots)

Dahlia
(annual roots)

Perennial tuberous roots from plants such as cyclamen and begonias consist of just one, large, central tuber, from which the shoots and fibrous, feeding roots emerge in the growing season. This type of tuberous root persists and grows in size sideways from one year to the next.

Annual tuberous roots from plants such as dahlias grow every year in a cluster around the crown. The energy stored in these tuberous roots is used in the following year to produce new growth; as this happens, the old tuberous roots disintegrate and die.

DIVIDING ANNUAL TUBEROUS ROOTS

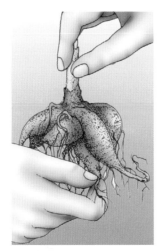

1 **Lift a plant**, here a dahlia, in fall. Clean the crown and roots thoroughly, dusting off any dirt clinging to the roots.

2 **Wrap the crown** in a sheet of newspaper. Store in a cool place at about 37–41°F until the buds swell in spring.

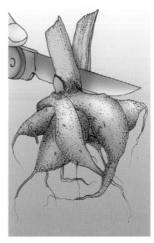

3 **Divide the tubers** into pieces, each with at least 1 crown bud. Leave in a dry, airy place at 68°F for 2 days.

4 **Once the cut surfaces** have developed a corky protective layer, pot up each piece in moist potting mix. Keep in a frost-free area, in light or dark.

Tubers

True tubers develop on modified underground stems, usually annually, to help the plant get through periods of harsh weather, such as drought or cold. Potatoes have large numbers of tubers; most other plants with tubers, for example caladium and waterlilies, produce very few. Several plants, including Jerusalem and Chinese artichokes, have edible tubers. On washed potato tubers you can clearly see the many buds, or eyes, on their skins. These rapidly develop into new shoots when the environmental conditions are right. When dividing potato tubers, dry the cut pieces for a few days to develop a protective coat that will help prevent fungal disease.

Dividing tubers

When growing tubers as a food crop, it is normal to plant the whole tuber and allow each plant to develop a number of shoots. However, if you have only a few tubers, and want more plants, they can be divided.

To divide waterlilies, cut the tuber in several pieces, each with at least one growing bud. Discard the end portion of the tuber (*see page 328*). Trim back the roots and the growing shoots, then repot each piece in a separate planting bag or basket filled with aquatic soil.

Tubercles

A few plants produce miniature tubers (tubercles) above ground, in the leaf joints. If left, they fall off and develop into new plants. You can remove mature tubercles—they should come away easily—and plant them at twice their own depth to develop. Plants that form tubercles include achimenes, *Begonia grandis* subsp. *evansiana*, Chinese artichokes, and yams (*Dioscorea batatas*).

POTATO TUBERS

Tubers are storage organs that develop as roundish, swollen areas on modified underground stems, usually at the tips.

DIVIDING TUBERS

1 **Cut the tuber**, here a potato, into pieces with a clean, sharp knife, just before growth begins in spring. Ensure that each piece has at least 1 good bud or eye. Eyes usually consist of several buds close together.

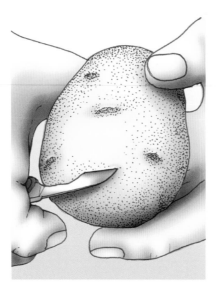

2 **Plant the pieces** in the open ground in a hole that is twice the depth of the tuber. Do this as soon as the cut surfaces form a protective corky layer. If you leave them too long, they will start to dry up.

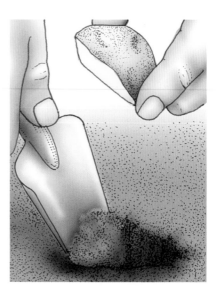

Rhizomes

A rhizome is a modified stem that grows more or less horizontally, on or just below the soil surface. Since it is a modified stem, it readily produces new shoots and leaves, and most rhizomes have roots already or will produce them if separated from the parent plant. They are therefore highly suitable for propagation.

Some rhizomes, such those of bearded irises, are used by the plant mainly as storage organs. They are relatively short and fat, and grow in recognizable sections year by year. The plant tends to spread outward, then die off in the center as the oldest rhizomes deteriorate. To maintain the vigor and appearance of the plants, propagate them regularly from new rhizomes and discard the older ones.

Other plants produce much thinner, longer rhizomes. Although they often have some food-storage function, these rhizomes are mainly used by the plant to help it spread out and colonize new ground.

Many troublesome weeds, such as Bermuda grass and quack grass, and some garden plants such as mints and spreading types of bamboo, are invasive because of their rhizomatous habits. As well as being very efficient colonizers, they use stored nutrients to develop new plants rapidly from broken rhizomes. Luckily, you can also benefit from the regenerative ability of rhizomes to increase such garden plants as arum lilies (*Zantedeschia*), bergenias, cannas, and rodgersias.

DIVIDING RHIZOMES

1 Divide mature rhizomes (here of a bearded iris) after flowering, when old roots die back and new rhizomes start to form.

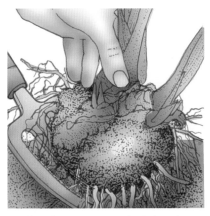

2 Lift a clump using a garden fork, and carefully knock as much soil as possible from the roots.

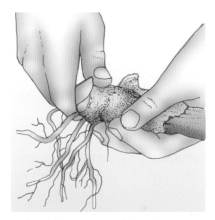

3 Carefully cut away and discard any old rhizomes from the clump, leaving the current season's growth.

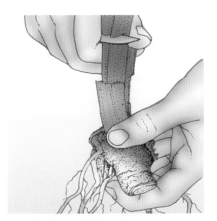

4 Prepare each rhizome by shortening the leaf blades (or stems in other plants) by about half. This will reduce water loss until the new roots are established. Cut back the existing roots to 2–3in.

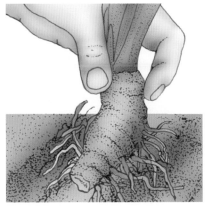

5 Replant each rhizome at the same depth as it was before. For irises, this is at the surface: plant the rhizome on a ridge of soil, and spread out its roots in small trenches on either side.

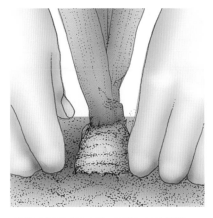

6 Firm back the soil over the roots. With irises, leave the rhizome itself barely covered. Label and water well to settle the soil in place.

Corms

Corms look similar to bulbs and both store food while the plant is dormant. However, they have evolved from different structures. Unlike bulbs, corms are modified underground stems composed of solid tissue and usually flattened in shape. Thin, fibrous modified leaves enclose the corm to protect it from injury and drying out. One or more buds at the top produce leaves and, if the corm is large enough, one or more flowers. Roots develop from the often concave base. Plants that grow from corms include gladioli, crocuses, dieramas, freesias, and liatris. In cool climates, you can dig and divide corms of tender bulbs in fall, storing them indoors over the winter.

When the leaves die down at the end of the season, new corms develop at the base of each shoot. These form on top of the previous year's corm, which gradually withers. In this way, one corm naturally divides into several over time. If it is necessary to increase corms more quickly, they can be propagated by division (*see below*).

Dividing corms

Cut a large, healthy corm into several pieces in fall and replant each section (*see below*). For small corms, or those that have too few buds, remove the main stem by snapping it off or cutting it out with a knife to induce the side buds to produce shoots. At the end of the growing season, you should have several small corms or a large corm with several buds that can be cut up.

PROPAGATING FROM CORMELS

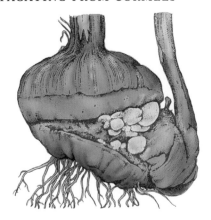

Cormels are miniature corms that sometimes form between the new corm and the old, disintegrating corm. The number produced can vary widely, and will increase the deeper the corm is planted—a gladiolus corm may produce as many as 50 cormels.

To use cormels for propagation, lift the parent corm at the end of the growing season and separate all the cormels. Cormels of hardy crocuses can be immediately replanted. For tender species like gladioli and freesias, allow the cormels to dry in a well-ventilated area at 65°F for a few days. Store them in an environment that is dry, well ventilated, and frost free but cool—below 41°F. Plant out the following spring—soak them first for 24 hours if they have become dried out. Cormels usually produce only grasslike new foliage for the first year, and they are likely to take at least 2 years to reach flowering size.

DIVIDING CORMELS

1 Cut each corm into several pieces, ensuring that each piece has at least 1 bud, just before planting time in fall. Use a clean knife to avoid contamination.

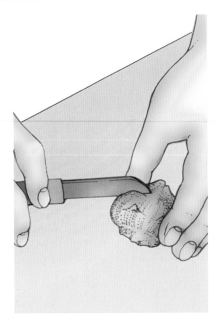

2 Once the pieces have formed a corky protective layer over the cut surfaces, plant each singly in a pot of potting mix, or in open ground. Label and date clearly.

Bulbous plants *see page 91* | Propagation basics *see page 396* | Methods of propagation *see page 404*

Bulbs

Bulbs propagate themselves naturally by division, forming new bulbs either side of the parent bulb at the end of the growing season. The large parent bulb either persists, as in daffodils and amaryllis, or disintegrates after flowering, as with tulips and bulbous irises. The bulbs can be dug up and separated at the end of the growing season, and planted at twice their own depth. For many vigorous garden bulbs, this is the ideal method of propagation, since it is quick and easy.

BULBLETS & BULBILS

A small number of bulbs, particularly lilies, form tiny bulbs called bulblets on their stem underground. All of these have the potential to grow into new plants. Lilies that produce bulblets can be encouraged to produce more from their leaf bases by burying the plant (*see below*).

Bulbils are tiny bulbs that develop in leaf bases of some lilies and in the flowerheads of some alliums. After flowering, pot up the bulbils (*see bottom*).

PROPAGATING FROM BULBLETS

1 Select a suitable lily in flower. Pinch back any buds and flowers. Twist the stem out of the bulb, leaving the bulb in the ground.

2 Dig a sloping trench two thirds as long as the stem, 6in. deep at one end. Lay the stem in the trench, with the top protruding; fill with sand or well-drained soil and label.

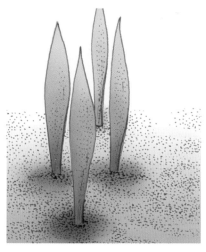

3 Dig up the remains of the stem in fall. Bulblets should have formed in the leaf axils on the lower stem. Detach them and replant at twice their own depth to grow on.

PROPAGATING FROM BULBILS

1 Remove all the flower buds just before they start to open, from a suitable lily species, such as *Lilium bulbiferum*, *L. canadense*, *L. longiflorum*, and *L. pardalinum*.

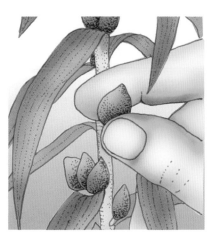

2 Bulbils should develop in the leaf axils. Fully developed bulbils often darken and are pulled away easily. Fill a pot with soil-based potting mix.

3 Set the bulbils about 1in. apart and one third buried. Cover with grit. Place in a cold frame, cold greenhouse, or sheltered site to bulk up. Plant out in fall of the next year.

BULB SCALING

You can bulk up virtually any lily species and other scaly bulbs, such as fritillaries, by scaling. Use bulbs freshly lifted at the end of the growing season for the best plump, healthy bulbs. You can use prepacked bulbs, but they are often not available until spring and are therefore in poorer condition. To reduce disturbance to the parent plant, you can simply dig down carefully next to the parent bulb where it is growing and snap off a few scale leaves. Replace the soil, wash the scales free of soil, then place them in bags to form new bulblets (*see below*).

BULB SCALING

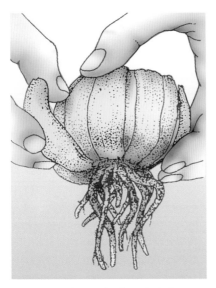

1 **Remove a few scales** from the bulb, one at a time, by pressing them outward until they snap or cutting them off close to the base plate. The remaining bulb can then be planted normally.

2 **Place the bulb scales** in a plastic bag and mix with 4 times their volume of damp vermiculite or 1 part sand and 1 part peat moss.

3 **Blow into the bag**, then tie around the neck. Store in a warm, dark place at 68°F, so that new plantlets can develop.

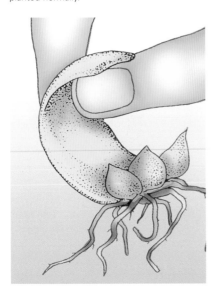

4 **Remove the scales** from the plastic bag as soon as the bulblets appear on the broken basal surface. This is likely to take 6–8 weeks.

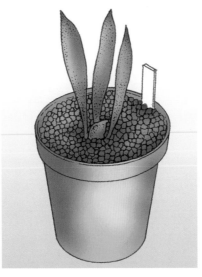

5 **Plant scales** singly into 3–3½in. pots, or line out in a deep tray, of moist potting mix. Make sure the scale tips are visible above the surface, cover with grit, and label. Place in a warm, light area.

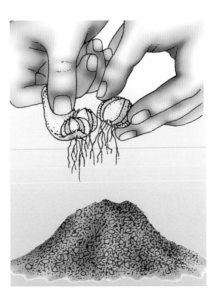

6 **Separate new bulblets** from the remains of the scales in summer or fall, after the bulblets' new leaves have died down. Replant the bulblets and leave to develop.

Bulbous plants *see page 91* | Propagation basics *see page 396* | Methods of propagation *see page 404*

BULB SCOOPING & SCORING

Some bulbs, like hyacinths, develop bulblets very slowly, so you need to induce their formation in order to be able to propagate them. There are two techniques by which you can use to do this: scooping and scoring.

Scooping involves removing the entire base plate with a curved cut. Use a sharpened teaspoon if possible—not only will it make a cleaner cut, cutting straight across with a knife would remove too much tissue from the base of the outer layers of the bulb. The cut surfaces will callus over, then bulblets will form. Move the scooped bulbs

into a cold frame, cold greenhouse, or sheltered site outdoors in spring. The bulblets will produce leaves and the old bulb will slowly disintegrate.

Scoring works in the same way as scooping. It produces fewer bulblets, but as these are likely to be larger, they should flower more quickly. Other bulbs such as grape hyacinths, daffodils, snowdrops, and scillas can be propagated by scooping or scoring, but, unless you are dealing with a variety that is very slow to increase, most of these reproduce quite quickly by natural methods.

SCOOPING BULBS

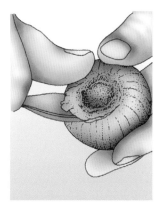

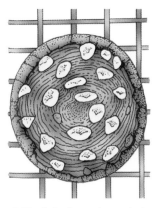

1 **Sharpen the edge** of an old teaspoon. Use it to remove the basal plate cleanly without crushing the rest of the bulb.

2 **Check the base** of every leaf scale is removed. Dust the cut surface with fungicidal powder. Set upside down on a wire rack or a small flat of dry sand.

3 **Leave in a dry**, dark place at 68°F. In 2–3 months, when bulblets appear, plant the bulb upside down, with the bulblets just below the surface.

4 **Separate the bulblets** after lifting the remains of the old bulb at the end of the season. Replant at once. They should flower in 3–4 years' time.

SCORING BULBS

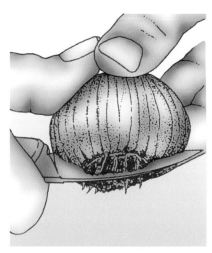

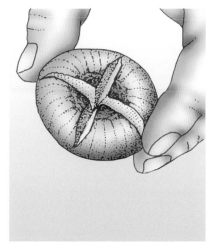

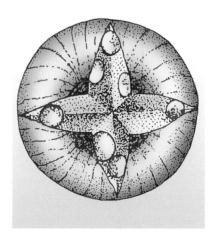

1 **Score 2 cuts** at right angles to each other across the basal plate of the bulb and about ⅜in. deep, with a sharp knife. On large bulbs, make 2 further cuts at 90-degree angles to produce an eight-pointed star.

2 **Leave the bulb** in a warm, dry area for a day or so, until the bulb opens out. Dust the cut surfaces with a fungicide, such as powdered sulfur.

3 **Place the bulb** on a wire tray. Store in a warm place at 68°F until bulblets develop, then treat as for scooped bulbs. Bulblets should reach flowering size in 2–3 years.

DIVISION

Dividing clump-forming plants is such a straightforward process that it barely merits being called a technique at all. However, timing can be important, and it is also worth knowing about ways of making the process easier and more successful. Although it does not yield as many new plants as seeds or cuttings, division is a common way to propagate many herbaceous perennials and ornamental grasses, and is also used periodically to rejuvenate plants, keeping them young, vigorous, and free flowering. Some herbaceous perennials produce offsets or runners that lend themselves to division.

Herbaceous plants

Most division is carried out on herbaceous perennials; many naturally form crowns with numerous, distinct stems that make it easy to separate the crown into sections. Often, the crown extends outward, producing the newest shoots at the edges, and the center becomes woody and less productive over the years. Division is the easiest method of rejuvenating such plants. As well as perennials with fleshy or fibrous crowns, shown here, you can divide those with tuberous roots, tubers, and rhizomes.

Plants with fleshy crowns

Many herbaceous perennials, such as astilbes, hostas, and meadow rues (*Thalictrum*), develop a compact, fleshy crown that is not easy to pull apart. The best time to divide these plants is toward the end of their dormant season, when buds will begin to shoot and you can more easily select the most vigorous sections of the crown. Replant or pot up the divisions quickly to avoid the roots drying out too much (*see below*).

DIVIDING A HERBACEOUS PLANT WITH A FLESHY CROWN

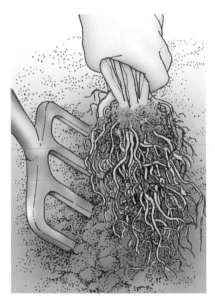

1 **Lift the plant** to be divided toward the end of its dormant season, using a garden fork. Shake off as much soil as possible.

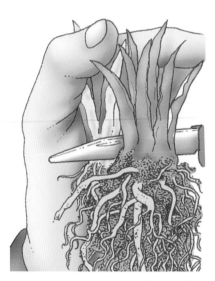

2 **Cut the crown** into pieces with a suitably sized, sharp knife. Hosing off the crown will help you to see the roots. Make sure that each section has at least 1 well-developed bud.

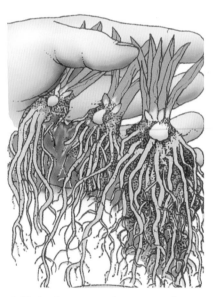

3 **Shake the roots** gently to remove dirt. Replant immediately, either in the ground or in a container filled with potting mix.

Herbaceous perennials & ornamental grasses *see page 83* | Methods of propagation *see page 404* | Roots, bulbs, corms, & tubers *see page 411*

DIVIDING A HERBACEOUS PLANT WITH A FIBROUS CROWN

1 **Dig up the plant** to be divided at a time when new shoots are being produced; this depends on when it flowers.

2 **Shake off** as much soil as possible. Wash the crown and roots in water or hose it clean to make the task easier. Remove any weeds at the same time.

3 **Cut down tall stems** to minimize water loss while the new divisions are being prepared; this is especially important if you are dividing the plant during summer.

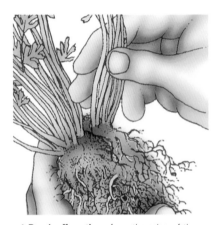

4 **Break off sections** from the edge of the crown, where the young shoots are generally produced, making sure that each has at least 1 good basal bud or shoot.

5 **Replant new divisions** without delay, at the same depth as the plant was before. Discard the woody sections from the center of the old clump.

6 **Water very thoroughly** to settle the soil in around the roots, using a watering can with a waterbreaker. Keep the new plants free of weeds while they become established.

Plants with fibrous crowns

Many herbaceous perennials that have fibrous roots and relatively loose crowns, such as chrysanthemums and New York daisy, need to be divided every two or three years to maintain performance (*see above*). For most species, the best time to do this is immediately after flowering; for very late-flowering plants, it will be the following spring. If the crown is very tough, use an old carving knife or saw to split it up.

Plants that divide naturally

Some plants, such as bellflowers (*Campanula*), are very easy to divide since their crowns separate naturally into individual plantlets each year. After flowering, or in spring if the plant flowers in fall, lift the plant and tease apart the plantlets. Replant as soon as possible and water well. Crowns that are lifted and divided fairly frequently will produce large numbers of divisions; plants left where they are growing for a long period may produce only a few, although the divisions will be larger.

Dividing shrubs

A few shrubs and shrublike perennials such as Cape fuchsias naturally develop as dense clumps of stems: lift each plant in its dormant season and wash off any soil. Divide the clump into suitably sized portions; discard any older parts that have few roots. Cut back the stems fairly hard. Replant the divisions to the same depth as the original plant. You can also divide shrubs that produce suckers (*see page 411*).

Offsets & runners

Offsets and runners are very similar: they are both plantlets that develop on the ends of stems arising from the parent plant. The main differences are that offsets tend to have thicker, shorter stems and may be slower than runners to develop their own roots.

If a plant produces few offsets, remove its growing tip to prompt offsets to form. Most offsets can be removed in their first year, but with some plants, such as yuccas, the offsets grow slowly and should be separated only when they are a few years old.

Offsets

These plantlets develop on the ends of sideshoots growing above or below ground (*see bottom*), on plants such as hen-and-chicks (*Sempervivum*) and New Zealand flax (*Phormium*). Most offsets initially have only minimal roots and are dependent on the parent plant. Roots normally develop toward the end of the growing season; encourage them by severing the connecting stems.

Runners

A runner is a more or less horizontal stem that arises from the plant crown and creeps over the ground (*see below*). It will produce a plantlet at the end, although it may first develop scale leaves and roots at intervals along its length. Once a new plant establishes, the runner often dies away. This is how strawberries, *Geum reptans*, herbaceous potentillas, and some grasses reproduce.

PROPAGATING WITH RUNNERS

1 **Thin out some runners** in early summer to encourage strong growth: if new plants are required, it is best to have a few, larger plants rather than a tangled mat of smaller ones.

2 **Fill a pot** with potting mix and firm to within ½in. of the rim. Dig a hole beneath the plantlet; set the pot in the hole, and pin the plantlet onto the mix.

3 **Pin down as many plantlets** as you need in a star-shaped pattern around the plant. When they are fully established, sever the connecting stems and transplant.

PROPAGATING WITH OFFSETS

1 **Separate a young offset** from the parent plant, here a hens-and-chicks plant, by gently pulling it away, preferably in spring. Trim any broken stems from the parent plant to avoid rot.

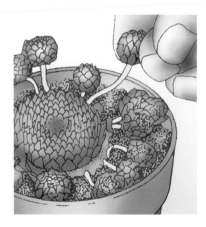

2 **Plant each offset** in a pot filled with potting mix specified for succulents and cacti; it will be well drained and encourage good root development. Once the offset has established, you can plant it outdoors.

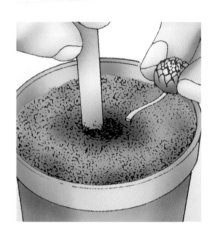

Growing under glass *see page 379* | **Propagation basics** *see page 396* | **Methods of propagation** *see page 404*

STEMS

Growing plants from short sections of stem is the most useful method of vegetative propagation, because it can be used for so many different plants. The various techniques all involve initiating, developing, and establishing a root system on a portion of stem. This may be done by encouraging the stem to produce roots before severing the new plant from the old, a technique known as layering, or you can separate the stem section from the parent plant first, to create a cutting. Layering usually produces only a small number of new plants; cuttings, on the other hand, can yield a large quantity of new plants.

Understanding cuttings

Cuttings may be taken successfully from almost any type of plant, and they are widely used to propagate vines, conifers, herbaceous perennials, herbs, shrubs, and soft fruit, as well as many indoor plants.

Suitable cutting material

The ability of a stem to produce roots, and therefore its suitability for propagation, depends greatly on its age. New shoots from a hard-pruned plant root more easily than old stems. However, if the plant is old, even new shoots root less readily than new stems from a young plant.

Plants that can only be propagated vegetatively, such as named varieties of camellia, are often difficult to propagate. This is because all the plants in cultivation are clones and therefore all the same age. You will find it easier to root cuttings taken from a newly introduced variety than one from a plant bred 50 years ago.

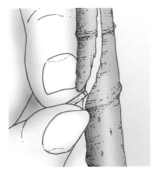

PARTS OF A STEM

Apical, or terminal, bud

Node

Internode

Leaf

Leaf axil

Axillary, or lateral, bud

Different types of cutting may use different sections of stem, so it is useful to recognize the parts of a stem. At the top, or apex, is the apical, or terminal, bud. Below it are the leaves, each joining the stem at an angle at the axil; in each axil is an axillary bud.

The often slightly swollen area of stem that produces the leaf and bud is called the leaf joint, or node. The section of stem between two nodes is called the internode.

WAYS TO GIRDLE A STEM

When layering, you may find it difficult to encourage old stems, or the stems of old plants, to take root. One ancient technique that can be useful in such cases is girdling, where the stem is wounded deliberately—in one of a variety of ways (*see right*)—to either impede or stop the flow of nutrients to the rest of the branch. This extra bit of help should stimulate rooting if it is layered in the normal way (*see page 426*). Girdling is also used in air layering (*see page 428*).

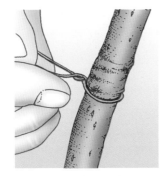

Twist wire tightly around the stem where it will be bent.

Cut at an angle into the bark. Push a wooden shim in the gap.

Remove a ring of bark, ¼in. wide, from around the stem.

Layering

This is one of the oldest techniques used to propagate woody plants, exploiting a process that occurs naturally with some shrubs such as dogwoods. The advantage of layering is that the young, new plant is kept alive by the parent until its own roots are established. For this reason,

layering can be successful with plants that are very difficult to propagate from cuttings. The technique is most often used for shrubs and vines and is the best way to propagate desirable but difficult shrubs, such as magnolias, crimson glory vine (*Vitis coignetiae*), or

SIMPLE LAYERING

1 **Prune back some** low branches on the parent plant during winter. This will encourage the production of young, flexible, vigorous shoots that will root more readily and are more amenable to being layered.

2 **Cultivate the soil** around the plant in late winter or early spring. If needed, add grit and bulky, organic material to open up the soil for good rooting.

3 **Trim the leaves** and sideshoots from a young, vigorous stem, along a 4–12in. length below the growing tip.

4 **Bring the stem** down to ground level and mark its position on the soil, 8–10in. behind its tip.

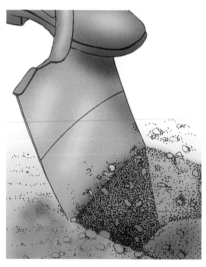

5 **Dig a small trench** from the marked point. Start the end of the trench with a straight side 4–6in. deep and slope it up toward the parent plant.

6 **Bend the stem** at right angles 8–10in. behind the tip. If necessary, girdle the stem to promote rooting (*see page 425*). Peg the shoot down in the trench against the straight side, using a strong wire staple.

parrotias. Simple layering (*see below*) is also good for raising perennial carnations, which will root in just six weeks if pegged down in mid- or late summer.

The main drawback of layering is that it is usually practical to take only one or two layers at a time from the parent plant. Also, it is not always convenient to propagate shoots where the plant is growing.

Bending the shoot during the process induces root formation by restricting the movement of food and hormones through the tissues of the stem. With plants that are reluctant to root, you should also wound the stem by girdling it (*see page 425*). While the stem is buried, keep the soil reasonably moist, especially in dry periods. Rooting usually occurs in summer.

7 **Return the soil** to the trench, burying the stem, but leaving the tip exposed. Firm in well. Excluding light from the stem is vital to encouraging rooting, so the earlier this is done, the earlier roots will start to form.

8 **Water the stem well**, using a watering can with a coarse waterbreaker. Keep the soil moist, especially in dry weather. Rooting should occur during summer.

9 **Sever the layered stem** close to the parent plant in fall, using clean pruners. Leave the stem buried and undisturbed to establish independently.

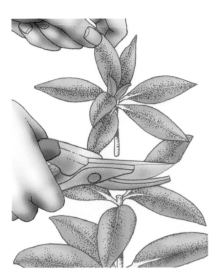

10 **Cut off the growing tip** from the rooted layer 3–4 weeks later, in order to direct the plant's resources to the roots.

11 **Lift the layer** to check whether it is well rooted. If not, replant it and leave in place for another year.

12 **Replant the well-rooted layer**, either in the open ground or in a container filled with potting soil. Label, and leave the young plant to develop further.

AIR LAYERING

This makes it possible to layer a plant without having to bend a stem to soil level or find space for the layer to root. It is useful for plants such as Japanese maples, citrus, ficus, and witch hazel. Damp moss surrounded by polyethylene film keeps a wounded stem sufficiently moist and dark to allow roots to develop. Carry out air layering in spring on mature growth of the previous season, or in late summer on semihard shoots of the current season's growth.

AIR LAYERING

1 **Trim any leaves** and sideshoots from a 6–12in. length below the tip of the stem to be air layered. Girdle the stem (*see page 425*) to encourage food and growth hormones to build up in this region of the stem and help root formation. Treat the stem or cut surfaces with hormone rooting powder.

2 **Soak some sphagnum moss** overnight so that it is thoroughly wet. Knead 2 large handfuls into a ball about 2½in. across. Split the ball in half, using your thumbs, in the same way as you would divide an orange. Place the two halves around the wounded stem and knead the moss together again so that the ball remains firm around the wounded stem.

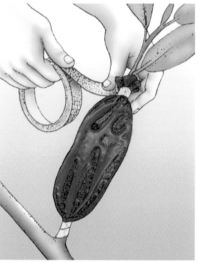

3 **Secure the moss** in place with a square of black plastic. Fix it to the stem with tape. The plastic will retain moisture, maintain a warm environment, and exclude light from the wounded area of the stem.

4 **Prune back** any new growth on the rooted layer toward the end of winter. The layered stem will usually take at least a full growing season to produce adequate roots—remove the plastic to check.

5 **Cut the stem** just below the point of layering, using a pair of pruners, once it has produced a good root system. Remove the plastic wrapping.

6 **Loosen the moss** and roots slightly. Then plant in potting soil and firm in gently. Place in a protected environment until more roots grow and the new plant becomes established.

LAYERING

Growing under glass *see page 379* | **Propagation basics** *see page 396* | **Methods of propagation** *see page 404*

TIP LAYERING

This specialized technique is used for blackberries and other *Rubus* species. Many of these plants tip layer themselves naturally—a process that enables wild blackberries to colonize new ground. You can harness this ability, with a little modification, to increase suitable plants. Cultivate the soil where the layer is to root, to ensure that it is opened up for good rooting. It also minimizes damage to the roots when the layers are lifted.

TIP LAYERING

1 **Select a stem** arising from the plant crown in spring; it should be new and strong. As soon as the stem reaches 16–18in., remove the tip. Continue to remove the tips until midsummer when 6–8 sideshoots should have developed. Cultivate the soil, adding grit and bulky organic matter to the top 6in.

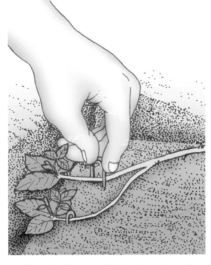

2 **Dig a sloping trench** 4in. deep where the bent stem tip touches the ground. It should be sloped toward the parent plant. Pin down the stem tip in the deepest part of the trench with a strong wire staple.

3 **Firm and water**, using a watering can fitted with a coarse waterbreaker, after you have replaced the soil, completely covering the tips of the shoot. Shoots should appear above ground level in about 3 weeks.

4 **Cut the stem** close to the parent plant in early fall, to encourage the layer to become established as an independent plant.

5 **Cut away the** remainder of the layered stem, on the side of the parent plant, once it has dropped its leaves. Shorten some of the new topgrowth made by the rooted layer.

6 **Lift the layer** carefully to avoid damaging its fine, fibrous roots. Plant it at once in well-cultivated soil. Protect layers that cannot be replanted immediately from drying out by wrapping in damp newspaper in a plastic bag.

Stem cuttings

Taking a cutting is very simple—the difficulty lies in keeping the stem alive and healthy while encouraging it to root and develop into a new plant. Drying out and attack by fungal rots are your main enemies.

Until the cutting forms new roots, it relies on its food reserves to stay alive. Immature (softwood) cuttings have the lowest food reserves and are at greatest risk of dehydration and rot; you must encourage them to root as quickly as possible, by artificially controlling the environment. Hardwood cuttings are less prone to drying out or rotting as they have greater food reserves; they can be left to root more slowly, with less protection.

Environmental control

The rate at which a stem cutting roots depends on the temperature around it. If the entire cutting is warm, the tip grows, diverting nutrients away from new roots, so keep the base warm and the rest of the shoot cool.

Softwood cuttings benefit from bottom heat of 68°F and cool air; keep them enclosed to maintain humidity and stop them wilting. Hardwood cuttings root well outdoors if the soil is warm enough. Protect greenwood, semihardwood, and evergreen cuttings in a cold frame, hoop house, or greenhouse.

WHERE TO CUT A STEM

Nodal cut   Internodal cut

You can take cuttings at several different places on the stem. A nodal cutting is severed just below a bud at a leaf joint, known as a node. Nodal cuttings are used for soft, immature stems because the tissue just below a node is harder and is more resistant to fungal rots. With an internodal cutting, you sever the stem between the nodes; this type of cutting is used mainly for more mature, woodier stems and is more economical since you can obtain more cuttings from a stem.

WHEN TO TAKE CUTTINGS

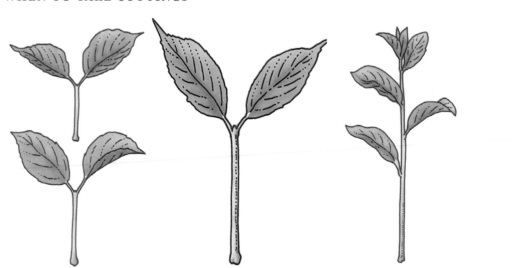

Softwood cuttings (*see page 432*) are taken from the first flush of spring growth. They root very quickly but often need complex environmental controls to minimize water loss and ensure their survival.

Greenwood cuttings (*see page 433*) are taken from the tips of leafy stems from early to midsummer. Their stems are still soft, and they need the protection of a controlled environment.

Semihardwood cuttings (*see page 435*) are taken in late summer from stems that are growing more slowly, although still in active growth, and have started to harden. They are more resilient than softwood cuttings.

Hardwood cuttings (*see page 436*) are taken from the leafless, dormant stems of deciduous plants. They require only minimal environmental control to ensure their survival.

STEM CUTTINGS

Growing under glass *see page 379* | **Propagation basics** *see page 396* | **Methods of propagation** *see page 404*

MAKING A LEAF-BUD CUTTING

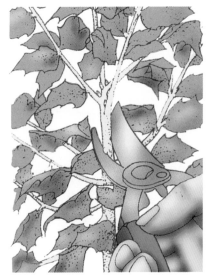

1 **Prune the parent plant** in winter to encourage new, vigorous stems. Select a new, semihardwood stem later in the summer.

2 **Cut the chosen stem**, which should have viable buds in its axils. The leafshown here is divided into leaflets.

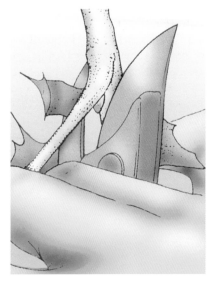

3 **Make an angled cut** just above the leaf axil bud (here, the stem is held upside down).

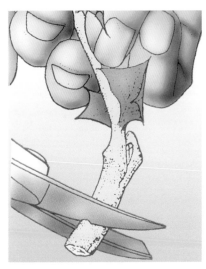

4 **Cut straight across** the stem, 1¼–1½in. below the top cut, to give enough stem to anchor the cutting while it produces roots.

5 **Reduce the size** of the leaf or leaflet if it is large, so that the cutting is easier to handle and takes up less space. It will also reduce water loss from the cutting.

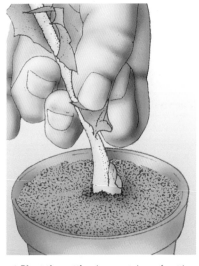

6 **Plant the cutting** in a container of potting mix so that the bud is roughly level with the surface. Firm sufficiently to prevent rocking, and water in.

LEAF-BUD CUTTINGS

This type of cutting is generally taken from semihardwood stems. Each cutting consists of a leaf, a bud in the leaf axil, and a very short piece of stem. The leaf supplies energy to support the cutting and regenerative process, the bud forms the basis of the new stem system, and the section of stem produces the roots. A large number of cuttings can be taken from a small amount of propagation material. As with other types of cutting, young shoots produce the best results so, where possible, prune the parent plant back hard beforehand to encourage new, vigorous growth. Take care to select suitable shoots with healthy, mature leaves when taking the cuttings. An immature leaf may wilt or continue to grow and use up nutrients needed to produce new roots.

After preparing, place cuttings from hardy plants in a cold frame, and less hardy material in a well-lit, protected environment, such as a propagating unit.

SOFTWOOD CUTTINGS

Soft stem growth is produced continuously at the tips of all stems during the growing season. As it matures, this new growth gradually hardens and becomes woody. Softwood cuttings are taken in spring from the fast-growing tips, as soon as they are long enough.

Because they are taken from the youngest part of the stem while it is in active growth, softwood cuttings have the greatest capacity to form new roots relatively quickly. Unfortunately, they are also the most difficult type of cutting to keep alive; their immature leaves dry out very easily, especially in warm conditions, and the soft stems are very vulnerable to attack from fungal rots.

Many houseplants are also propagated from softwood cuttings. They will frequently root more readily in a heated propagating unit, which keeps the bases of the cuttings at a temperature of 70–75°F. Some plants, such as impatiens and fuchsias, root so easily that they can simply be placed in a jar of water.

MAKING A SOFTWOOD CUTTING

1 **Firm the potting mix** to within ½in. of the rim. Do this before taking the cuttings, so they can be potted up as quickly as possible.

2 **Remove a fast-growing tip** of a stem in spring or take shoots less than 4in. long with a heel (*see page 434*).

3 **Put the cuttings** at once into a plastic bag or bucket of water in shade, or store in the refrigerator for use later.

4 **Shorten each cutting** to about 4in. long, cutting ⅛in. below a leaf joint with a sharp knife—or trim the tail if the cutting has a heel (*see inset*).

5 **Remove the leaves** from the lower one third of the stem. Hormone rooting powder may encourage some softwood cuttings to root, but it is not usually needed.

6 **Make a hole** with a dibble in the medium. Plant each cutting up to its leaves, taking care not to damage the stem bases. Space the cuttings so their leaves do not touch.

STEM CUTTINGS

Growing under glass *see page 379* | **Propagation basics** *see page 396* | **Methods of propagation** *see page 404*

PREPARING THE PARENT PLANT

If you have time to plan ahead, in winter you can prune back hard woody plants from which you want to propagate. This encourages the production of fresh, fast-growing stems in spring, providing a good supply of cuttings material with a high capacity to produce new roots.

Tips of plants taken later, in early summer, will be slower growing, more mature, and root less easily than softwood cuttings. They are referred to as greenwood cuttings and are often used to propagate herbaceous plants. The procedure is the same as for softwood cuttings.

Taking a softwood cutting

First prepare the containers so that you can plant the cuttings immediately, as it is vital to avoid any water loss from the cuttings material. Fill the container with moist, well-drained, rooting medium or potting soil.

Early morning is the ideal time to gather cuttings material, because the shoots will be turgid (full of water) after the cool of the night. Take fast-growing tips of stems because they will be full of growth hormones. If you cannot deal with the cuttings immediately, you can store them for approximately 24 hours by putting them in a sealed, plastic box in the refrigerator.

After planting the cuttings, cover them to avoid loss of moisture through transpiration: put the container in a propagating unit or cover with a plastic bag supported on a loop of wire, and seal it around the pot with a rubber band. It is important that the cuttings root quickly, before they succumb to the vagaries of their environment, so use bottom heat if possible to encourage rooting. If the atmosphere is too warm, it will force cuttings to grow upward, diverting energy from root production; too dry an atmosphere will cause the cuttings to wilt. They need a delicate balance of warmth, bright, indirect light, humidity, and adequate ventilation.

7 Water in the cuttings from above, using a watering can with a fine waterbreaker. Label, then place in a propagating unit, or cover with a plastic bag, to maintain humidity.

8 Harden off cuttings gradually when they have rooted, by opening the vents in the propagating unit, or cutting off the corners of the plastic bag.

9 Pot the cuttings individually in potting soil once they are hardened off. When they are at an appropriate size, plant them out in the yard or into a yet larger container.

HEEL & MALLET CUTTINGS

With some plants, it helps the cutting to survive if a small section of older, parent wood is left attached to the cutting, which helps to protect the base of the cutting from fungal rots. The technique is used with material taken from plants that may be particularly susceptible to rot, such as those with hollow stems, and for cuttings that take a long time to root. The two methods of taking such material are heel cuttings and mallet cuttings.

Heel cuttings: These can be taken as greenwood, semihardwood, or hardwood cuttings (*see below, top*). They are often used for some evergreen shrubs such as azaleas and pieris, deciduous shrubs with pithy stems like berberis and elder, and those with greenwood stems, like broom.

Mallet cuttings: These are taken as semihardwood or hardwood cuttings (*see below, bottom*) from shrubs with hollow or pithy stems, like spiraea and deciduous berberis.

MAKING A HEEL CUTTING

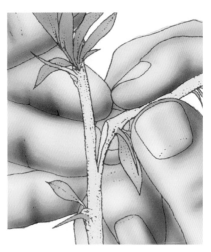

1 **Hold the base of a sideshoot** between your thumb and forefinger. Pull it down sharply so it comes away with a tail, or heel, of bark. If it does not come away easily, use a knife to cut it away with a small heel.

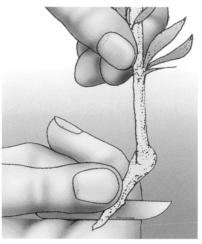

2 **Neaten the long tail** on the heel with a knife and remove any leaves near the base of the shoot. If the cutting is from semihardwood or hardwood, remove the tip of the cutting. Dip the base in hormone rooting powder.

3 **Make a hole** in the soil, insert the cutting, and water in. You can plant hardwood cuttings directly into open ground, semihardwood cuttings in a cold frame, and less hardy cuttings in a propagating unit.

MAKING A MALLET CUTTING

1 **Cut horizontally** with pruners across the parent stem, just above a healthy, semihardwood or hardwood sideshoot. Make this top cut close to the sideshoot to reduce the risk of die-back and rotting.

2 **Make a basal cut** ¾in. below the sideshoot so the cutting has a stump or 'mallet' of old stem attached. Split the mallet with a knife if it is thick. Then dip the basal cut in hormone rooting powder.

3 **Make a hole** that is large enough to bury the mallet and about one third of the sideshoot. Plant semihardwood cuttings in potting mix in a cold frame and hardwood cuttings in the open ground. Water in well.

434

SEMIHARDWOOD CUTTINGS

In late summer, when growth slows and stems harden up, you can take semihardwood cuttings. They are thicker and harder than softwood cuttings, so with a greater store of food they survive more easily and can form roots even when grown on under poor light levels.

Semihardwood cuttings do not need extra heat, but like humidity. Root them in a cold frame or in a pot in an unheated greenhouse or on a bright but cool windowsill.

Put in an unheated propagating unit or cover each with a plastic bag on a wire hoop, sealed with a rubber band.

Before taking cuttings, dig over the soil in the cold frame and add peat moss, to improve its waterholding capacity, and grit to aid drainage. Cover with a ³⁄₄–1¹⁄₄in. layer of fine sand. Semihardwood cuttings root mostly in late winter and spring, but some root in mild falls. Insulate the cold frame over winter until spring.

MAKING A SEMIHARDWOOD CUTTING

1 **Prune the parent plant** at the start of the winter, if possible, to encourage strong stems to grow rapidly.

2 **Cut off the** current season's growth from a main shoot, or sideshoot, in late summer. Remove the soft tip, unless it has stopped growing. Trim the cutting to 4–6in.

3 **Remove the leaves** from the bottom 2in. of the stem. Dip the base in rooting powder. Insert each cutting 1¼–1½in. deep, so its end enters the soil below the sand.

4 **Space the cuttings** 3–4in. apart, with leaves not touching. Close and shade the frame. Water as needed. In fall, remove any fallen leaves. Insulate over winter.

5 **Remove the insulation** during the day once buds develop, but replace it at night if still frosty. Open the frame fully once all risk of frost has passed.

6 **Apply liquid fertilizer** regularly to the cuttings in the frame all summer and water as needed. Lift and transplant the new plants once their leaves drop, in fall.

435

HARDWOOD CUTTINGS

These are taken from dormant shoots of woody plants. They are undemanding, as they have no leaves and plenty of food reserves. The best time to take them is during fall. Run your hand down the stems, as the leaves start to turn. If they come away easily, take your cuttings.

Choose a sheltered site to prepare a trench for your cuttings, and place a layer of builder's sand in the base of the trench to improve drainage if needed. Make cuttings of an exact length. This does not work on plants with hollow or pithy stems, as the stem is prone to rotting; if the leaf nodes are reasonably close together, cut just below a node that is 6in. or more from the stem tip. The stem at a node should be solid and more resilient. However, if the nodes are too far apart to make this practical, cut at 6in. and seal the stem by dipping it into partly molten candle wax.

MAKING A HARDWOOD CUTTING

1 **Prune the parent plant** hard during the dormant season. The following leaf fall, when the shoots are fully mature and buds firmly dormant, remove a new shoot.

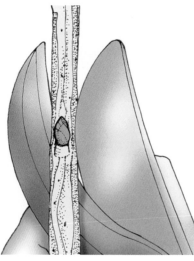

2 **Make a sloping cut,** using pruners, just above the proposed top bud of the cutting.

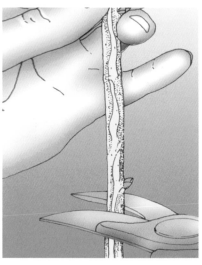

3 **Cut horizontally** across the stem, exactly 6in. below the top cut. Dip the basal cut only in hormone rooting powder.

4 **To plant cuttings,** dig the soil over, then make a trench 5in. deep with 1 vertical and 1 sloping side. Place the cuttings against the vertical edge, 4–6in. apart.

5 **Backfill the soil** and firm, leaving about 1in. of each cutting exposed. Leave in place until the following fall. Water when needed to keep them moist.

6 **Lift the cuttings,** which should have rooted and produced several stems. Transplant to their final positions.

Roses that are grown from cuttings develop roots from the bases of the cutting and are known as own-root roses. You can take hardwood cuttings to grow own-root roses from many roses, but hybrid teas and floribundas often do not root well. Take cuttings, 1ft. long, in late summer or fall from stems of about a pencil's width. Remove the leaves and twigs and dip the bases in rooting hormone. Insert about half of each cutting in a trench (*see facing page*).

EVERGREEN CUTTINGS

Evergreen cuttings are taken from very ripe, almost hard, wood. They are not hardwood cuttings as they have leaves and need protection from water loss. You can wound cuttings from difficult-to-root shrubs such as daphnes, elaeagnus, and *Magnolia grandiflora* to improve the chances of rooting. Take cuttings from softer wood earlier in the season: treat them according to the condition of the stems (softwood, greenwood, or semihardwood wood).

MAKING AN EVERGREEN CUTTING

1 **Prune the parent plant** in winter to encourage strong, young shoots that will root easily. Dig over the soil in the cold frame; add grit and peat moss as needed, to improve drainage and water retention.

2 **Take a heel cutting** (*see page 434*) from a stem of the current season's growth in late summer or early fall. Trim the tail of the heel and pinch back any soft growing tip on the cutting.

3 **Remove any leaves** from the bottom one third to half of the cutting stem. The cuttings will normally be 4–6in. long, although they will be shorter on dwarf and slow-growing shrubs.

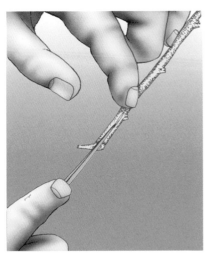

4 **Wound the cut base** with a shallow, ¾in. cut, for slow-growing plants. Dip the basal cut in rooting powder, so it is covered. Cut down large leaves to reduce water loss.

5 **Insert each cutting** up to its leaves in the cold frame. Ensure leaves do not overlap. Water; close the lid. Shade, water, and protect from frost as needed. Harden off in spring.

6 **Transplant the cuttings** in fall, after you have given them all summer to grow. Take care when lifting them—many evergreens produce brittle, fleshy roots.

CONIFER CUTTINGS

Although not all conifers root well from cuttings, you can propagate them from softwood, greenwood, semihardwood, and ripewood cuttings. Spruces, firs, and pines do not grow well from cuttings and are best propagated from seed.

Select cuttings from young, actively growing plants that are clipped regularly and so have many strong, vigorous shoots. Take Japanese yew, cypress, false cypress, Leyland cypress, and *Thuja* cuttings in fall or winter, and English yew, hemlock, and juniper cuttings in late winter, after the parent plants have been subjected to frost.

Conifer cuttings can be rooted under cover (*see below*) or in a cold frame. Lift the cuttings the following fall, and transplant into the yard or another container.

Prepare the soil in a cold frame by building it up to 8in. from the lid. Insert the cuttings in the soil, firm in, and water. In cold weather, you will need to insulate the frame by draping old blankets or plastic over the lid.

MAKING A CONIFER CUTTING

1 **Take cuttings** from actively growing leaders or lateral shoots (sideshoots). Avoid feathered shoots, which lack the vigor to root.

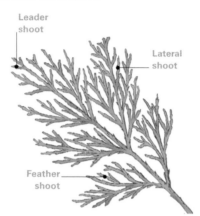

Leader shoot

Lateral shoot

Feather shoot

2 **Cut off** a suitable leader or lateral shoot, then fill a container with potting mix, firmed to within ½in. of the rim. Trim the leaves from the bottom 1–1½in. of the cutting stem.

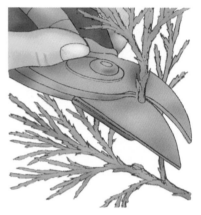

3 **Dip the basal cut** in hormone rooting powder. Apply to the cut surface only; if it is dry, dip the end of the cutting in water first. You can also wound the cutting to encourage rooting (*see page 437, step 4*).

4 **Make a hole** about 1in. deep in the mix, using a dibble or pencil. Insert the cutting and gently firm into place. If placing several cuttings in a single pot, space them 1½–2in. apart. Label and date.

5 **Water in the cuttings** with a fine waterbreaker. Place the pot of cuttings in a propagating unit to stop them from drying out. Alternatively, cover the pot with a plastic bag supported on a hoop of wire; seal the bag around the pot with a rubber band.

6 **Leave the cuttings** in a warm environment to root—this should take 3–4 months. Harden off the cuttings once they have developed a good set of roots, and pot them up or plant them out the following fall.

LEAVES

Of all the propagation techniques, leaf cuttings are perhaps the most magical. You can watch, in a few weeks, how they create one or many miniature plantlets from the cut surface of a mature leaf. A few plant species produce these plantlets naturally, including foamflowers (*Tiarella cordifolia*), echeverias, and airplants. Some others, most of which are houseplants, can be induced to do so under particular conditions. The range of plants that can be propagated from leaf cuttings is relatively small, but many of them are commonly grown and popular species.

Leaf cuttings

Leaf cuttings should be taken from leaves that have recently expanded fully to their mature sizes. If a leaf is less than full sized and immature, all its energy will first go toward developing and maturing. This will delay the production of young plantlets, and allow more time for problems such as drying out or rotting.

A newly expanded leaf will photosynthesize (manufacture energy) efficiently, so there will be food to produce the new plantlets. It will also still have a good life expectancy and will be young enough to have a high capacity to reproduce. The selected leaf should be complete, typical for the plant, and undamaged. It should also be free of pests and diseases.

Making the cuttings

The most common cause of failure in propagation of leaf cuttings is the leaf rotting before it has a chance to produce an independent plant. It is therefore crucial that all the materials—knives and pruners, containers, potting mix, and leaves—are clean.

Conditions required

Most plants propagated by leaf cuttings are normally grown indoors, or in a greenhouse, so you can take leaf cuttings year-round, provided that there is a suitable leaf available. However, with lower temperatures and light levels, propagation is likely to be slower in winter.

Once separated from the parent plant, a leaf loses moisture quickly, so you need to raise the leaf cuttings in a closed environment, such as in a propagating unit, under plastic on the greenhouse bench, or in a pot with a plastic bag over it.

SUITABLE PLANTS FOR LEAF CUTTINGS

Hen-and-chicken fern
(*Asplenium x lucrosum*)

African violet
(*Saintpaulia*)

Foamflower
(*Tiarella cordifolia*)

Mother-in-law's tongue
(*Sansevieria trifasciata*)

Cape primrose
(*Streptocarpus*)

Begonia rex

Many of the plants that are suitable for leaf cuttings are popular houseplants, so you can use this easy and efficient method of propagation to increase and rejuvenate the plants in your home.

439

Leaf-stem cuttings

The simplest and most reliable way to produce new plants from leaf cuttings is to use a complete leaf with its stalk. The disadvantage is that it produces only a few new plants from each leaf. Rotting and disease are the main causes of failure, so always use clean tools and containers and fresh, sterile potting mix. You can take a cutting at any time, if a new, fully expanded leaf is available.

To prepare a container for leaf-stem cuttings, fill it with equal parts of sifted peat moss and perlite or coarse sand. This lessens the risk of rot and holds air. Inserting the cuttings at an angle (*see below*) also allows air to reach the cut surfaces of the stems, where the plantlets develop, and it encourages them to root more quickly. Use this method for African violets and succulents such as haworthias.

MAKING A LEAF STEM CUTTING

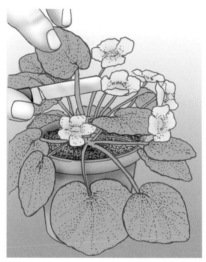

1 **Slice off an undamaged leaf** that has recently matured. Cut the leaf stalk about 2in. below the leaf blade; use a sharp knife or safety razor blade to reduce bruising.

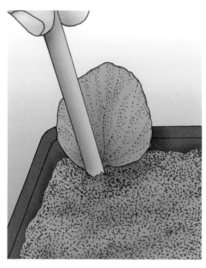

2 **Make a shallow**, sloping hole, with a pencil or dibble, in the potting mix and insert the cutting at a shallow angle, so that the leaf blade almost lies flat.

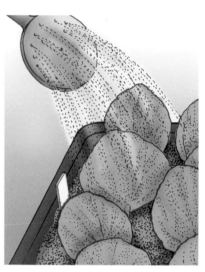

3 **Firm in gently** around the stalk, then insert the rest of the cuttings at the same angle. Label them and water, using a fine waterbreaker to avoid damaging the leaves.

4 **Place the cuttings** in light shade in a propagating unit that is heated from below, ideally at about 68°F. This will create the warm, humid conditions required.

5 **Leave the cuttings** for 5–6 weeks, then apply liquid fertilizer once plantlets appear on each cutting. Leave them to grow until they are large enough to handle.

6 **Pot up the plantlets** individually, once they can be separated without damage, into pots of well-drained potting mix. Once they are established, harden them off.

MIDRIB & LATERAL VEIN CUTTINGS

Growing under glass *see page 379* | **Propagation basics** *see page 396* | **Methods of propagation** *see page 404*

Midrib & lateral vein cuttings

A few species, such as rex begonias and Cape primroses, will produce plantlets from the veins of their leaf blades. Always use leaves that have recently expanded fully. You can cut them across the midrib (*see below*) or across the lateral veins (*see bottom*). Plantlets should appear after five to eight weeks, but they will not be big enough to handle, and transplant, for several more weeks.

The midrib cutting technique can be adapted for leaves with several main veins, such as begonias, by simply making ½in. cuts across several of the main veins with a very sharp knife or safety razor blade. Lay the leaf flat on a flat of moist potting mix and weigh it down so that the cut ends of the veins are in contact with the soil. Then treat the leaf as for a midrib cutting.

MAKING A MIDRIB CUTTING

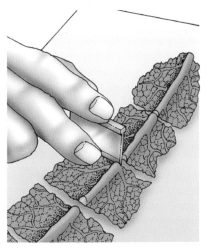

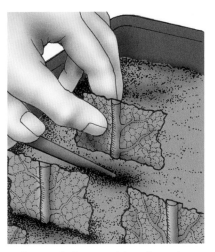

1 **Cut an undamaged leaf** from the parent plant. Lay the leaf upside down on a clean sheet of glass. Cut it into strips no wider than 2in., using a safety razor blade.

2 **Draw a shallow trench** in moist potting mix. Insert each cutting just deep enough to stay upright. Firm gently. Space the cuttings 1in. apart.

3 **Place the cuttings** in humid conditions at 68°F, such as in a heated propagating unit. Rewet as needed: stand the flat in water, then allow it to drain.

MAKING A LATERAL VEIN CUTTING

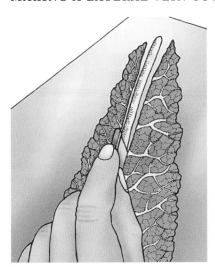

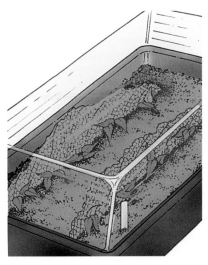

1 **Lay a suitable leaf** upside down on a clean sheet of glass. Remove the midrib with a razor blade, so all lateral veins in the 2 halves have an exposed cut surface.

2 **Draw a shallow trench** in moist potting mix. Insert each cutting, or leaf half, vertically, with the cut surfaces facing downward. Firm and label.

3 **Place the container** in a propagating unit. Plantlets should develop from the cut veins in 5–8 weeks. Separate and transplant once they are large enough to be handled.

Monocot leaf cuttings

Monocotyledonous plants, such as snowdrops and mother-in-law's tongues (*Sansevieria*), have a series of parallel veins running the length of each leaf. Some of these plants have the capacity to produce a plantlet on the cut surface of a leaf vein, so may be propagated from leaf cuttings. The leaves of bulbous plants tend to be very soft and rot easily; when preparing cuttings, make sure that you keep the propagation environment scrupulously clean. It will also help to provide optimum conditions for plantlets to develop as quickly as possible.

Making a monocot leaf cutting

Before taking the cuttings, prepare a container, such as a standard seed flat, by filling it with suitable potting mix. Press it down lightly to within 1/2in. of the rim, water it, and allow it to drain. Prepare the cuttings and insert in the potting mix (*see below*).

Place the container in a warm (68°F), humid environment, so the cuttings do not dry out and wilt. Ensure that the cuttings are in bright but not direct sunlight, which can cause scorching. Plantlets should develop at the bases of the cuttings after four to eight weeks. Repot the young plants once they are large enough to handle easily, allow them to establish indoors, then harden them off if they are for outdoor planting.

HOOPING LEAF CUTTINGS

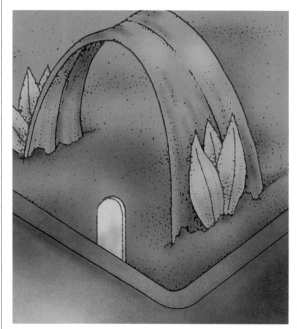

Leaf cuttings of heloniopsis will regenerate from both ends. Reduce a leaf to 1½–2in. by cutting off the top and bottom ends. Plant the cutting in a hoop, with both ends set into the potting mix. Treat the cutting as other monocot leaf cuttings.

MAKING A MONOCOT LEAF CUTTING

1 **Remove a leaf** that is fully expanded and undamaged from the parent plant, here a mother-in-law's tongue.

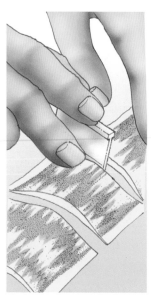

2 **Make a series of cuts** across the leaf, 1in. apart and at right angles to the veins, using a safety razor blade.

3 **Draw shallow trenches** with a dibble and insert the cuttings vertically, in rows 1in. apart. Firm in and label.

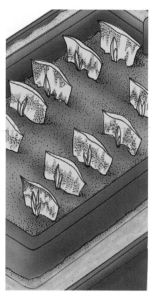

4 **Leave the cuttings** to form plantlets. Rewet the mix when necessary by standing the flat in water.

GLOSSARY

Acid: Soil with little or no lime content, less than 7 on the pH scale.

Aerate: To expose the soil to air, either by digging or, on lawns, by puncturing the turf.

Alkaline: Soil with a high lime content, more than 7 on the pH scale.

Alpine: Plant suitable for rock garden or alpine house.

Annual: Plant that survives for only one season. Germination, growth, flowering, seeding, and death all take place in this time. *See also* Biennial, Perennial.

Apex: Growing tip of a branch or shoot. For example, apical bud refers to the bud at the tip of a branch. *See also* Axil.

Axil: Junction between a branch and a side branch or a leaf stalk that grows from it. For example, axillary bud refers to the bud at the base of a leaf stalk. *See also* Apex.

Bedding plant: Plant used for temporary display.

Biennial: Plant that lives for just two seasons. Germination and growth usually take place in the first season; flowering, seeding, and death in the second season. *See also* Annual, Perennial.

Bog garden: Garden where the soil is kept damp at all times.

Bonemeal: Slow-release fertilizer high in phosphorous and nitrogen, with some calcium. Manufactured from ground animal bones.

Brassica: Plant belonging to the cabbage family.

Bulbous plant: Underground plant organ. The term includes true bulbs, tubers, corms, tuberous roots, and rhizomes.

Chitting: To promote the germination of seed before sowing, or the sprouting of potatoes before planting.

Chlorosis: Yellowing of leaves, often caused by mineral deficiency, or it is the result of damage by sucking insects or mites.

Cloche: Temporary glass cover, which can be placed over plants where they are growing to offer frost protection.

Cold frame: Glass or plastic frame, into which plants are placed for frost protection and hardening off.

Compost: Decayed organic matter used as a mulch, fertilizer, or soil amendment.

Conifer: Cone-bearing tree or shrub, such as a pine or fir.

Controlled-release fertilizer: Type of fertilizer that releases its nutrients slowly over a long period of time.

Coppice: To cut a tree or shrub back to ground level to produce new stems.

Cordon: Plant trained to a single stem, or double stem if a U-cordon.

Crop rotation: System of growing vegetable crops whereby the same crop is not grown in the same place for a number of years.

Cultivar: A combination of the words 'cultivated' and 'variety' to describe a plant variety that is derived from cultivation. *See also* Variety.

Cutting: Part of a plant removed for the purposes of propagating a genetically identical plant to the parent.

Damp down: To spray the floor and benches of a greenhouse to reduce the temperature and increase humidity in hot weather.

Defoliation: To lose or remove leaves from a plant.

Dethatch: To remove an excessive layer of dead leaves and stems that can build up in lawns so that water can more easily reach grass roots.

Division: To split the roots of a plant into two or more pieces for the purposes of propagation or to reinvigorate an old plant.

Dormancy: A period of slowed or stalled growth during unfavorable environmental conditions, usually winter. Also refers to seeds before they germinate.

Dressing: Application of dried fertilizer to the soil. Base dressings are applied before planting; topdressings after planting.

Dwarf: Term used by nurserymen to describe a short tree grown with little or no stem.

Ericaceous: Plants in the heath or heather family, such as azaleas and blueberries, that require an acidic soil to thrive.

Espalier: Tree with a vertical trunk and several vertical branches trained horizontally.

F1 hybrid: Plant with very consistent characteristics, such as size, shape, vigor, and color. They are created by crossing two pure varieties of plant. F2 and F3 hybrids are second and third generations respectively and may show much less consistent characteristics.

Floribunda: Type of bush rose, with flowers that grow in clusters. *See also* Hybrid Tea.

Frost pocket: Area in a garden more prone to frost than other areas.

Germination: First growth stage of a plant, as it emerges from a seed.

Graft: Where a shoot or bud is inserted onto a rootstock to create a new plant. *See also* Rootstock.

Green manure: Fast-maturing crop that is dug into the soil while still green to improve soil fertility.

Grow bag: Plastic bag containing growing media for planting fruit and vegetable crops or ornamental plants.

Harden off: To adjust plants slowly to lower temperatures and other conditions outdoors before planting in the open ground.

Herb: Plant grown for its aromatic, culinary, or medicinal properties.

Herbaceous: Nonwoody plant.

Hilling: To cover the base of plants with a heap or ridge of soil to prevent greening of stems or tubers.

Hoe: Tool for weeding.

Humus: The stable, colloidal substance that results from the thorough decomposition.

Hybrid: Offspring from the cross-fertilization of two different parents.

Hybrid Tea: Type of bush rose, with flowers that grow singly or in clusters of three. *See also* Floribunda.

Larva: Immature stage in the life cycle of an insect.

Lateral: Sideshoot or stem growing from a larger branch.

Layering: Method of propagation where stems are buried or anchored to the ground to induce root formation.

Mulch: Soil covering, often but not always made of organic material.

Neutral: Soil that is neither acid nor alkaline with a pH of 7.

Peat: Water-retentive, low-nutrient constituent of potting soil mixes harvested from bogs.

Perennial: Plant that lives more than two seasons. Many die down over winter. *See also* Annual, Biennial, Herbaceous.

pH: Measure of the acidity or alkalinity of a soil.

Pollination: Transfer of pollen from the male to the female part of a flower, leading to fertilization.

Pot-bound: Container plant where the roots have filled all the available space, circling around the pot.

Potting up: To move a plant from a smaller to a larger container.

Rambler: Type of rose with a rambling habit.

Rootball: Root system and enclosed soil of a contained plant.

Rootstock: Root and trunk system of a woody plant onto which a shoot or bud of another plant is grafted. See also *Graft*.

Semidwarf: Tree with a short, unbranched trunk to 3ft.

Sexual propagation: Reproduction of a plant by seed to create a new, genetically distinct plant. *See also* Vegetative propagation.

Species: Group of plants that share the same characteristics and breed freely with one another.

Specimen plant: Plant set out in a prominent position to create a focal point in a garden.

Standard: Plant grown on a tall, single, upright stem or trunk.

Subsoil: Layer of soil immediately below the topsoil. *See also* Topsoil.

Sucker: Shoot arising from the root or rootstock of a plant.

Tamp: To lightly compact the soil.

Thatch: Layer of dead plant matter that collects at soil level on lawns.

Thinning: To remove seedlings, flower buds, shoots, or branches to reduce overcrowding and improve performance.

Topiary: To create an elaborate shape from a shrub by close clipping and training.

Topsoil: The top layer of soil.

See also Subsoil.

Variety: Group of plants of the same species that form a slight variation on common species characteristics, but are not sufficiently distinct to form a separate species. Varieties may arise naturally or in cultivation. *See also* Cultivar, Species.

Vegetative propagation: To remove tissue from a parent plant and grow it on to form a new plant. The new plant will be a clone of the parent. *See also* Sexual propagation.

Vine: Plant that has a climbing habit.

INDEX

Page numbers in *italics* indicate an illustration; those in **bold** a main section on a topic; and those in ***bold italic*** a topic in a text box.

C

cabbage aphids 173
cabbage flea beetles 172, 173
cabbage loopers 173
cabbage root fly
    mats against *47*
    radishes 198
    rutabaga 201
cabbage root maggot **222**, *222*
cabbage whitefly 172, 175
cabbage worms 172, 173
cabbages **168–76**
    caterpillars *221*, **221**
    transplanting 157
cacti *147*, 359, 385
    propagation *424*
Caladium 358, 359
    division 416
    lifting and storing 93
Calamagrostis
    C. x *acutiflora* 'Karl Foerster' **75**
    C. brachytricha 359
Calendula 357
California poppy *see Eschscholzia*
    californica
Californian meadow sedge *see Carex*
    pansa
calla lily *see Zephyranthes*
Calla palustris (bog arum) 333
Callibrachoa 357
Callistemon (bottlebrush) **75**

propagation ***404***
Calluna vulgaris 29, **75**
Caltha palustris (kingcup) 76
Camellia 28, 76, **77**
    for containers 361
    pruning 115
camellia blight *120*, 120
camouflaging utility areas 26
Campanula (bellflower) 359
    propagation ***404***, 423
Campsis spp. 60
    C. 'Madame Galen' **75**
    C. radicans (trumpet vine),
        propagation ***404***, 412
Canada climate zones 11
Canadian pondweed *see Elodea*
    canadensis
Canadian wild ginger *see Asarum*
    canadense
canary melons 245
cane fungal diseases 278, *279*
canker 44, *44*, 120, *120*
    fruit 278, *279*
    roses 137, *137*
Canna spp. (Indian shot) 333, 359
    lifting and storing 93
    propagation ***404***
canteloupes 245
Cape fuchsia, division 423
cape pondweed *see Aponogeton distachyos*
Cape primrose *see Streptocarpus*
capillary systems 402
    matting *378*

sand bed *402*
capsid, black-kneed *41*
cardinal flower *see Lobela cardinalis*
Cardiocrinum
    C. giganteum 76, **77**
    propagation ***404***
Carex spp. (sedge) 359, ***404***
    C. elata 'Aurea' (Bowles' golden grass)
        333
    C. morrowii 'Variegata' (Japanese
        sedge) 304
    C. palustris (bog arum) 333
    C. pansa (Californian meadow sedge)
        305
    C. texensis (Texas sedge) 305
carrot fly, barrier *47*
carrot rust fly 196, **221**, *221*
    larva *221*
carrots **195–6**
    splitting *45*
    storage 195
    types 195
Caryopteris
    for containers 361
    pruning 110
casaba melons 245
cascades *310*
Catalpa bignonioides (Indian bean tree),
    pruning *111*
catch cropping 153
caterpillars *50*, 50, *61*, 89, *89*
    brassicas 170, 172, *220*, **221**, *221*
    moths 388, *389*

453

E

earwigs 40, *89*, 89

Eccremocarpus 357

Echeveria, propagation ***404***, 439

Echinacea spp. 359

    purpurea 'White Swan' 29

Echinops 359

    E. ritro 29

echinopsis 385

edema *45*

edging shears *293*

eelgrass *see Vallisneria americana*

eggplants **211**

    for containers 362

Eichhornia crassipes (water hyacinth) 333

Elaeagnus 361

    propagation ***404***

elder

    golden-leaved *see Sambucus nigra*
        'Aurea'

electrical appliances

    in greenhouse 376–7

    safety in ponds ***315***

Eleocharis acicularis (hair grass) 331, *331*

elephant's ears *see Colocasia*

Elodea spp.

    E. canadensis (Canadian pondweed)
        331

    E. crispa (curly waterweed) 331

Elymus magellanicus 359

endive **163**

English peas 182

environmentally friendly gardening 17

Epimedium 76, *304*, 304

Equisetum hyemale (horsetail) 332

Eragrostis airoides 359

Eranthis hyemalis (winter aconite) 76, **77**,
    358

    planting 92

Erica (heather) 361

    E. carnea 'Springwood White' 31

    trimming 107, *107*

Erigeron (fleabane), propagation ***404***

Eryngium 359

    E. bourgatii **75**

    cutting back 88

    propagation ***404***

Erythronium 358

    E. 'Pagoda' **77**

Escallonia, propagation ***404***

Eschscholzia californica (California
    poppy) **75**

espaliers *232*, 257–8

Eucomis, planting 92

Euonymus 361

    E. fortunei 'Emerald 'n' Gold' 31

    pruning 112

Euphorbia spp. 385

    E. characias subsp. *wulfenii* **75**

    E. polychroma 359

evergreen cuttings 437

evergreen shrubs, pruning 106–7

Evolvulus 357

exhaust fans for greenhouses 375, *375*

F

fairy moss *see Azolla caroliniana*

fairy rings 299, *299*

fall garden 30

    containers 358

    pond maintenance 337

false acacia *see Robinia*

false cypress *see Chamaecyparis*

family yards *20*, 20

fan heater *377*

fan training *232*

    see also apples; cherries; figs; pears

× *Fatshedera lizei* 361

Fatsia japonica 76, 361

fava beans ***184***, **186–7**

    pinching out tops *187*

fences, against rabbits and deer 47

fennel 362

    Florence 219

fern

    in greenhouse 386

    royal *see Osmunda regalis*

    sensitive *see also Onoclea sensibilis*

    for shady gardens 76, *85*, 304

    water *see Azolla filiculoides*

fertilizer spreader *290*

fertilizers 35

    burn from *391*

    containers 364

    for fruit

        apples and pears *254*

P

467